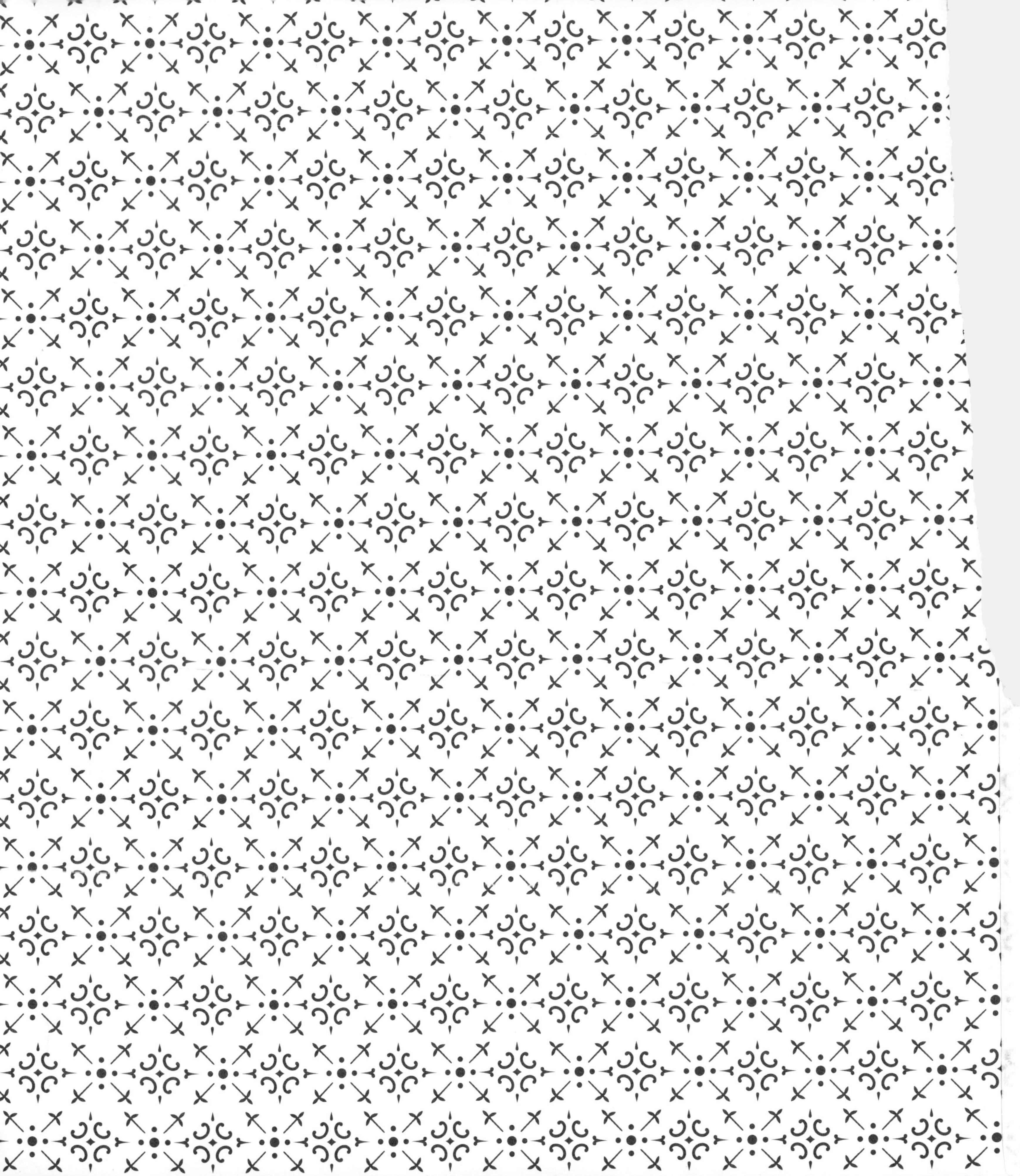

"And even if the whole world should collapse,
he will stand fearless among the falling ruins."

—ARNOLD GENTHE,
QUOTING THE ROMAN POET HORACE (65–8 BC),
ON APRIL 18, 1906

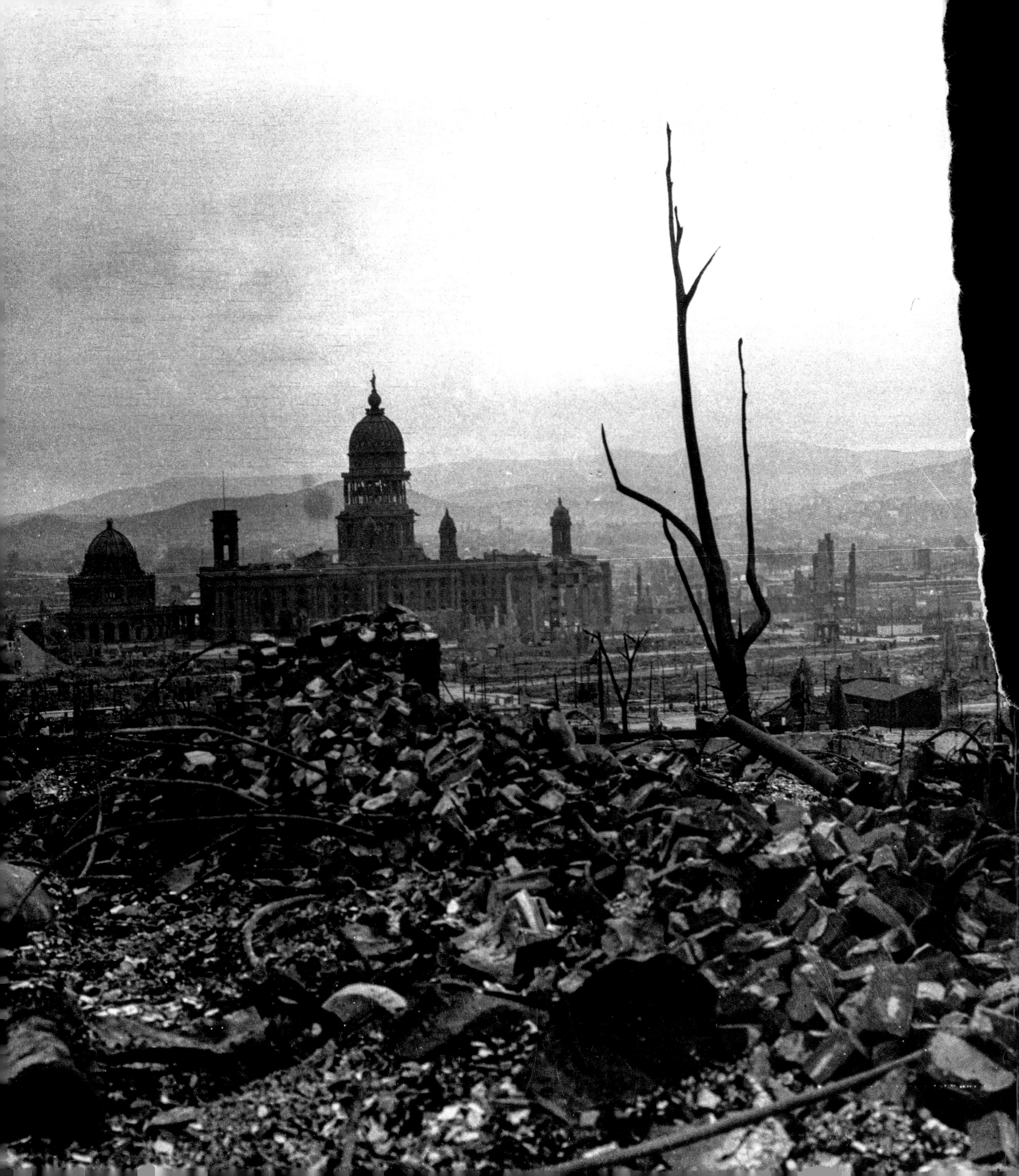

AMONG THE RUINS

ARNOLD GENTHE'S PHOTOGRAPHS

OF THE

1906 SAN FRANCISCO EARTHQUAKE AND FIRESTORM

KARIN BREUER

with VICTORIA BINDER, RODGER C. BIRT, JAMES A. GANZ, CAROLIN GÖRGEN,

RICHARD MISRACH, *and* COLLEEN TERRY

FINE ARTS MUSEUMS OF SAN FRANCISCO   CAMERON+COMPANY

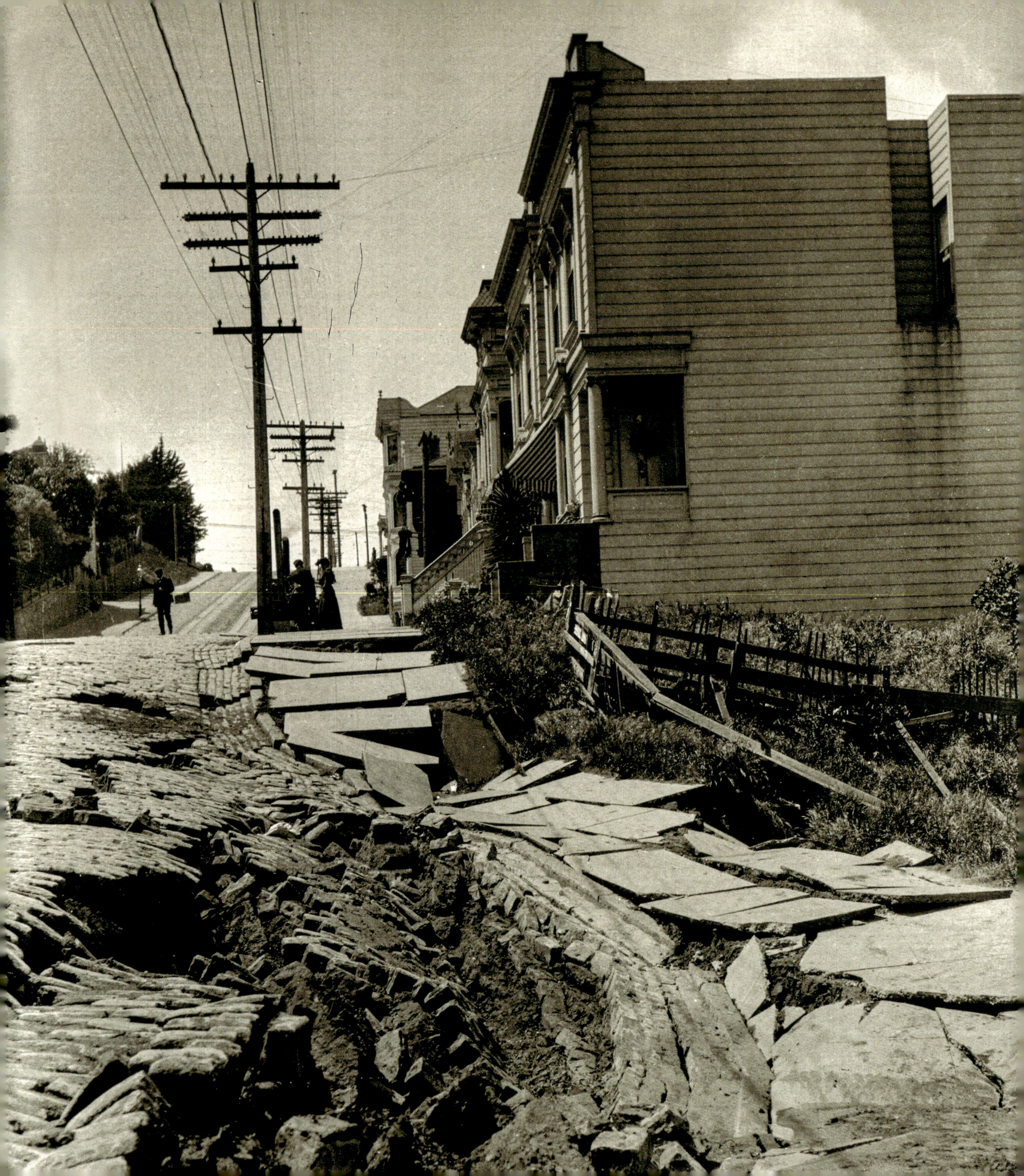

◆ ◆ ◆ ◆

ESSAYS

PLATES

◆ ◆ ◆ ◆

APPENDICES

FOREWORD

"San Francisco found its way straight to my heart.
For here was a city with a flavor all its own."

—Arnold Genthe, *As I Remember* (1936)

When Arnold Genthe arrived in San Francisco in 1895, his imagination had already been captured by America's energy and freedoms that he observed during his brief train trip across the country. The pace of the "American epic was only short of a miracle," the German-born academic later wrote in his memoir, *As I Remember*, in which he described himself as having come from a structured society and a civilization that was centuries in the making.

It's very likely that Genthe was already aware of the unprecedented development of San Francisco; the young city's rapid growth from a Gold Rush–era boomtown to a bustling metropolis was well chronicled in the press in both the US and Europe. Newspaper and magazine stories, replete with photographs, lauded the speed with which the city, in a few decades, grew from a ramshackle collection of wood-frame buildings to an urban development with defined neighborhoods and a densely built downtown. Featuring a mix of architectural styles that any European would find curious, the city's eclectic environs held a strange enchantment for the young Genthe.

San Francisco's dramatic topography of steep hills overlooking the Pacific Ocean was, however, something that many news reports and photographs failed to capture adequately. Consequently, Genthe was not prepared for the stunning natural beauty of the landscape in which the city was situated. On the day of his arrival, from a perch atop Russian Hill, he formed his first impression of the city, writing in *As I Remember* of its "approach through a vestibule of cliff and mountainside; the golden stretch of the dunes; the Bay, misted by the silver fog, or captured by the softly incandescent blue of a clear sky." He later observed that even the fog conferred a "magic patina" that seemed to conceal the city's less attractive features.

And there were many unappealing aspects of the new metropolis, among them class bias and ethnic conflict so obvious that Genthe cannot have been unaware of them. However, despite his stance as an intellectual and a liberal, he remained somewhat aloof to the socioeconomic issues of San Francisco at the turn of the century. While acknowledging that there was "human wreckage" to be observed in some quarters of the city, "there was little of the kind of misery that comes from real want," he recalled in his memoir. He was focused instead on establishing himself as an artist and making a living as a photographer.

Even as he was left homeless by the earthquake and fire, Genthe remained in the city in the hours and days after April 18, 1906, to take photographs. Indeed, several of his photographs in this volume show the destruction of the neighborhoods populated by San Francisco's Chinese and African American residents. Genthe's images also depict the neighborhood ruins and relief camps that housed San Francisco's working class and marginalized populations, in shock at first, then struggling to survive in the days and weeks after the quake while more affluent citizens fled the city to lodge at second homes or estates or with nearby friends and relatives whose homes survived. They are poignant photos, respectful rather than intrusive, although some are seemingly posed and staged with the agreement of the subjects whose cheerful faces belie the real hardships they must have experienced. As a whole, the photographs convey an atmosphere of resilience, perseverance, and resolute coping.

Genthe's photographs also show the activities of the city's reconstruction: men clearing the rubble, brick by brick, with wheelbarrows and horse-drawn carts, and carpenters erecting a wooden framework with new lumber. For him, these were the activities that symbolized healing and a population in recovery.

The similarities between the San Francisco of Genthe's time and the San Francisco of 2021 are irresistible and compelling: today's city, recently fueled by the technology boom that has created incredible wealth and opportunity, has been humbled by a global pandemic and now struggles to rebuild its businesses and communities. Had he been alive today, would Genthe have remained in the city to chronicle this long recovery?

Perhaps the answer lies in his own words, written in his memoir thirty years after he was faced with the choice to stay or leave his beloved city: "The temptation was great, but I was not willing to leave San Francisco then. I wanted to stay, to see the new city which would rise out of the ruins. I felt my place was there. I had something to contribute, even if only in a small measure, to the rebuilding of the city. I felt I belonged in San Francisco. . . . I loved the city not only for its beauty and its spirit but for its generosity and the opportunities it had given me."

Now, 115 years later, we can certainly be inspired not only by Genthe's words but also by the vivid testimonial presented in his photographs of the 1906 San Francisco earthquake and fire. This exceptional catalogue is the first to document Genthe's photographic record of the catastrophe, a lasting legacy of both the city's destruction and his incredible artistry. It has been made possible by the generosity of the many donors to the Genthe Negatives Preservation Fund, which enabled the restoration of Genthe's negatives in the collection of the Fine Arts Museums of San Francisco and the creation of new prints of the work, all of which are reproduced in these pages. Among the donors, we especially acknowledge Dagmar Dolby in honor of Hannah Dolby, Stella Dolby, Julia Dolby-Frist and Violet Dolby-Frist; Lucy Young Hamilton; Anne M. Zucchi; and the San Francisco Auxiliary of the Fine Arts Museums of San Francisco.

This detailed project was expertly led by Karin Breuer, curator in charge of the Achenbach Foundation for Graphic Arts at the Museums, who has served as the book's volume editor. Karin's work was supported by the efforts of Victoria Binder, head of paper conservation, and James A. Ganz, former curator at the Achenbach and now senior curator of photographs at the J. Paul Getty Museum. We are further grateful to the roster of other authors who have so elegantly illuminated this body of work: Rodger C. Birt, Carolin Görgen, the artist Richard Misrach, and Colleen Terry, former associate curator at the Achenbach. The curatorial component of this endeavor has been further bolstered by the members of the advisory groups to the Achenbach: the Achenbach Graphic Arts Council, the San Francisco Auxiliary, and the Belvedere-Tiburon Auxiliary. It is due to the tremendous work on this project that Genthe's fascinating series, like the city of San Francisco, is able to rise from the rubble of history to greet a new generation of admirers.

Thomas P. Campbell
Director and CEO
Fine Arts Museums of San Francisco

MAJOR DONORS

DAGMAR DOLBY IN HONOR OF HANNAH DOLBY,
STELLA DOLBY, JULIA DOLBY-FRIST AND VIOLET DOLBY-FRIST

LUCY YOUNG HAMILTON

ANNE M. ZUCCHI

SAN FRANCISCO AUXILIARY OF
THE FINE ARTS MUSEUMS OF SAN FRANCISCO

MARQUEE DONORS

MICHAEL AND JOYCE AXELROD

KEN BECKER AND NANCY LUTER

RAYNA BERNARD

PEGGY AND TIM BROWN

DANIEL F. DONOVAN

KARLA GIBSON

MARY JO GORDON AND PATRICK DOWD

THE HANDLERY FOUNDATION

PAM MARTORI AND BOB McCASKILL

ANDREW C. McLAUGHLIN III AND CARRICK C. McLAUGHLIN

JEROLD B. ROSENBERG

DONORS TO THE GENTHE NEGATIVES PRESERVATION FUND AND CATALOGUE PROJECT

Lawrence Banka and Judith Gordon; Pat and Penny Barrett; F.S. Bayley III; Edith H. and Erik E. Bergstrom; Sandra and Paul Bessières; Lucia Bogatay; Ellen and Howard Brown; Roger Budge, M.D. and Leslee Jane Budge; Catherine E. Burns; Lisa Dolby Chadwick; Karin and David Chamberlain; William and Polly Clark; A. Crawford and Jess Cooley; Ann M. Dawson; Pamela Anne Dekema and Richard Champe; Claudia M. Dencker; Dan and Boo DeWitt; Irene M. Dobbins; Deborah Doyle and Eric Hall; Jane Elkins; Alan J. Fishleder; Morten Steen Hansen; Cathie Hehman; Eloice and John Helms; Robert C. and Susan L. Hill; Charles D. Himmelblau; Dave Himmelblau; Holly Hitchcock; Jennifer and Gordon Hull; Ann Jennings and Robert Polacchi; Linda Kraft Jesmok; Giacinto A. Jondonovan; Pia D. Jondonovan; Cynthia Kelly; Carla and Robert Kennis; Janet King and Stephen Yeatman; Wesley and Elizabeth Kinnear; Jim and Elaine Kohn; Spring Kraeger; Mary N. Lannin; Judy and Bob Leet; Karen A. Levine and Mark Nigara; Evan and Joan Lewis; Peter Lewis and Emiko Kaji; Mark Liao; Lourdes Livingston; Jane R. Lurie; Leslie and Diane Lynch; Simone Manganelli; Heather Marx and Steve Zavattero; Andrew C. McLaughlin III and Carrick C. McLaughlin; Howard and Ellie Miller; John L. and Susan L. Molinari; Justice John B. Molinari; Elizabeth D. Moyer, PhD and Michael C. Powanda, PhD; Joanne Murray; John A. Musante; John Nerness Family; Ayako Onoda; Charles S. Pyle and Tina Hittenberger; Guillermo Rettally and John Garvin; Justin Roberts; Sylvia G. Ross; Phyllis Brooks Schafer; Schauble Family; Shirley and Farrel Schell; Charles and Norma Schlossman; Alan Selsor; Elena Sheehan; Matthew Silverberg; Wendy Soule; Bob Spivock; Lynda Tunney; Anne Turner; Jack and Margrit Vanderryn; Margaret and Tom Vinson; Sylvia S. Walters; James Wesley and Elizabeth Kinnear; Karen and Malcolm Whyte; Michelle L. Wilson; Daniel Woodhead III; Wummer Family; Constance and Bernard Yu; Joyce and Al Zavattero; Michael Zimmer

This book is dedicated to Toby Gersten Quitslund (1939–2017)

ARNOLD GENTHE AT THE LEGION OF HONOR

Acquiring and Honoring a Historical Document

KARIN BREUER, CURATOR IN CHARGE,
ACHENBACH FOUNDATION FOR GRAPHIC ARTS

ARNOLD GENTHE DIED OF COMPLICATIONS from heart disease on August 9, 1942, while visiting friends in New Milford, Connecticut. By that time he was effectively retired from a successful thirty-year career as a studio photographer in New York, most famous for his portraits of personalities in the arts, politics, and high society. The popularity of his style of soft-focus photography had waned by the late 1930s, and demands for his studio work declined, enabling him to indulge his love of travel with trips to his beloved San Francisco in 1937 and to Italy in 1938. For Genthe, travel was the perfect remedy for his diagnosed illness. "Since I have been breathing San Francisco air I have improved more in a single week than in all the months they worked over me," he said while visiting his former home (see fig. 1).[1]

Although they were therapeutic, the final trips Genthe made at the end of his life may have contributed to the neglect of his extensive photo archive and his business and personal affairs; they were in considerable disarray at the time of his death. A. Jocelyn Magrath, Genthe's attorney and the executor of his will and estate, disregarded the artist's request that all the prints remaining in his 49th Street studio after his death "be burned by fire" and that any photographic plates and films "be immersed in hot acid wash."[2] Such contravention was not surprising given the extent of the studio contents (more than twenty thousand prints and negatives) and a possibly increased aversion to destroying archival artifacts during the war years.

In the months following Genthe's death, the representatives of his estate hastily prepared the contents of his studio for sale. One large transaction was quickly made: transferring the majority of his prints to the Library of Congress. The remainder of his holdings were scheduled for public auction early in 1943. On December 3, 1942, Magrath wrote to Bertram Alanson, a prominent, socially connected San Franciscan and longtime friend of Genthe's, about a group of negatives and a few prints of "the San Francisco fire" that remained available.[3] After a delay of several weeks, Alanson forwarded his letter to Thomas Carr Howe Jr., director of the California Palace of the Legion of Honor, San Francisco, who was immediately interested in the material for the museum's collection. Howe and Nancy Lee of the Genthe estate exchanged telegrams over a period of days, and on December 24 Howe cabled Lee: "Accept your proposition to purchase all Genthe San Francisco fire pictures and negatives plus 20 representative prints of Chinatown for three hundred dollars." Lee responded that although the prints had already been packed for the Library of Congress, she would intercept the shipment and send the work to San Francisco. Nearly one month later, on January 20, 1943, Lee confirmed that two shipments had been made: one with the prints and another with the negatives. Genthe's studio, she wrote, was now closed.

On February 23, 1943, the Legion of Honor's board of trustees met and approved the purchase. The board also instructed the museum director to have prints made for board members.[4] It was likely around this time that additional prints were made for the exhibition *Photographs of the San Francisco Fire*, which opened at the Legion of Honor on April 1, 1943.[5] The thirty-nine prints in that show—all in large format on glossy paper—were developed from the original negatives by then museum staff photographer Hy Hirsh.[6] The exhibition garnered a scant single notice in a local newspaper, which simply extolled its appeal to "old-time San Francisco residents."[7] Nevertheless, the mention brought considerable exposure to the Legion's acquisition.

Requests from a variety of publications for copies of the photographs soon followed and continued well into the 1950s. Among the most notable uses were Barnaby Conrad's *San Francisco: A Profile with Pictures* (1959) and William Bronson's chronicle of the 1906 San Francisco earthquake and fire, *The Earth Shook, The Sky Burned* (1959). Many of these were prints from negatives that had been made for the museum by Henry E. Seutter, a San Francisco–based commercial photographer. A limited number of images were selected for general press distribution.[8]

A brief correspondence in November 1949 between Howe and Paul Vanderbilt, chief of the Prints and Photographs Division at the Library of Congress, resulted in the first recorded inventory of the acquisition. Enclosing a description of the library's album of 164 contact prints, Vanderbilt wrote: "I understand from Ansel Adams that you have the original negatives corresponding to the album on the enclosed card. We would be interested in knowing the particulars concerning any other Genthe material . . . and any holdings which you can conveniently furnish."[9] Howe's description was as follows:

> 147 negatives measuring approximately 3 × 5 inches and bearing the photographer's number in ink
>
> 11 negatives of similar size but unnumbered
>
> 1 glass negative measuring 4 × 3¼ inches
>
> 1 glass negative measuring 5 × 7 inches
>
> 4 negatives measuring approximately 3 × 5 inches which do not appear to pertain to the fire and earthquake
>
> A set of 25 photographs depicting San Francisco's Chinatown before the fire. These prints are signed by Genthe.

Ansel Adams's interest in the negatives is of significant importance in their postwar history. In 1955, as the fiftieth anniversary of the earthquake approached, Peter Pollack, curator of photography at the Art Institute of Chicago, detailed plans for reprinting Genthe's negatives in a letter to Howe:

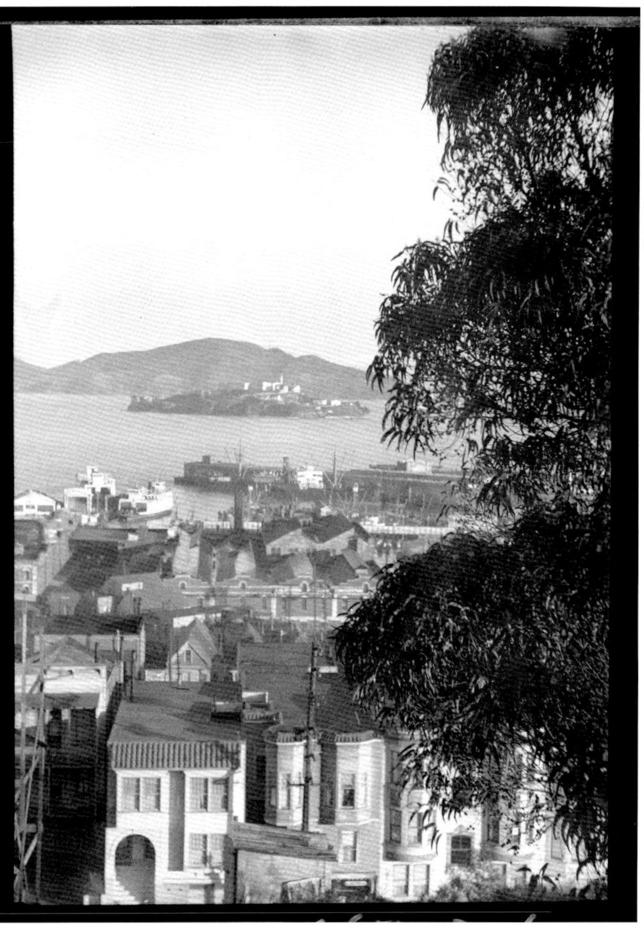

Fig. 1. Arnold Genthe, Untitled (San Francisco view from the residence of Mr. Bertram Alanson), ca. 1937. Interpositive from cellulose nitrate negative, 5 × 4 in. (127 × 102 mm) (approx.). Arnold Genthe Collection, Prints and Photographs Division, Library of Congress, Washington, D.C.

> I gave 20 original negatives by Arnold Genthe dealing with the San Francisco earthquake and fire to Ansel Adams, who will make 11″ × 14″ prints. I shall pay him the sum of $200 for the prints. He is to try to get the same amount of money from Beaumont Newhall at the George Eastman House in Rochester for a similar number of prints, and make one set for you, for which there will be no charge.[10]

Pollack was likely assisting the California photographer with a commercial project rather than an exhibition. The following year, however, the Legion of Honor hosted the exhibition *The San Francisco Fire Photographs by Arnold Genthe*, featuring twenty-two reprints by Adams (see fig. 2). In a statement, Adams described Genthe's work as "remarkable indeed in its sensitive awareness of the scenes of human misery and the scenes of general desolation." He continued:

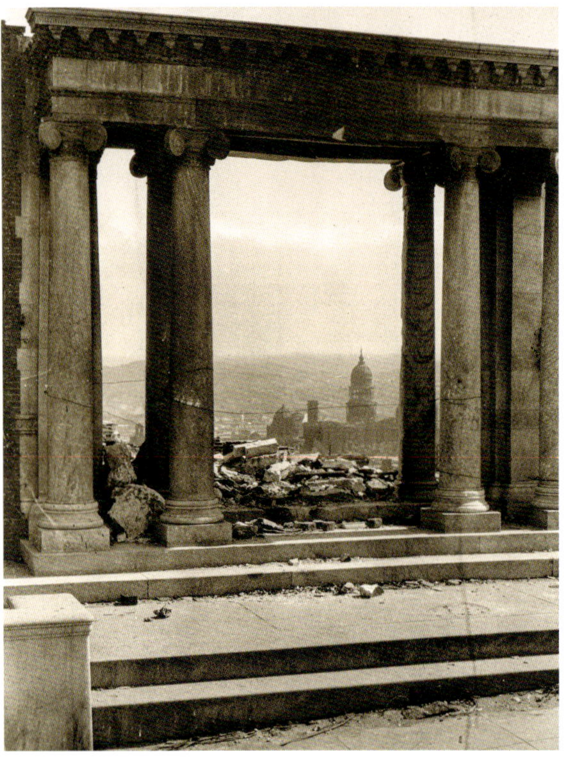

Fig. 2. Ansel Adams (American, 1902–1984) after Arnold Genthe, Untitled (Towne mansion, California and Taylor Streets, San Francisco), 1906 (printed 1956). Gelatin silver print, 13 ¼ × 10 3⁄16 in. (33.7 × 25.9 cm). Fine Arts Museums of San Francisco, Museum purchase, James D. Phelan Bequest Fund, 1943.407.130.2

> I personally know that Dr. Genthe worked with great energy and devotion on this tremendous subject, and that he did not have time to carefully compose his images within the framework of his negatives. He intended to "crop" his pictures to the best possible effect, and I have done the same in these prints—although using my best judgment alone, as I had nothing to refer to in this respect. These prints intend nothing but a presentation of his San Francisco Disaster photography. I have printed them with an objective reality, plus some echo of the mood of the original Genthe photographs. Dr. Genthe printed soft and used papers of rather dull surfaces (consistent with the style of the era). When these images are rendered on harsh, black-and-white glossy prints, the defects are greatly magnified and the moods and reflections of his vision and emotions are entirely lost. Hence my choice of a semi-gloss surface, quiet contrasts, and enriched tonalities.[11]

After 1956 there were no further exhibitions of Genthe's work at the Legion of Honor and, in the absence of a curator of photography, very few exhibitions or acquisitions of photographs. Howe retired as director in 1968, and the focus of the exhibitions shifted as the Legion of Honor merged with the de Young museum in 1972 to form the Fine Arts Museums of San Francisco. The Achenbach Foundation for Graphic Arts, with its emphasis on prints and drawings, represented the works on paper initiatives of the institution. It was not until the late 1980s, under the tenure of Achenbach curator Robert Flynn Johnson, that photography began to be actively collected by the Museums. While they did not immediately seem to conform to Johnson's aim to acquire works in which creativity and art take precedence over historical documentation or technique, the Genthe earthquake negatives and prints (which had been relegated to file and library storage) entered the permanent collection records.

In 2005–2006, on the occasion of the centenary of the earthquake and fire, the exhibition *After the Ruins, 1906 and 2006: Rephotographing the San Francisco Earthquake and Fire* was held at the Legion of Honor.[12] The exhibition featured inkjet prints of fourteen of Genthe's San Francisco photographs paired with images of the same locations taken between 2003 and 2005 by Mark Klett with Michael Lundgren (see fig. 3). Although renowned for his "rephotographs" of historic landscape sites, this was Klett's first urban rephotography project. "Genthe was perhaps the only photographer to make pictures that were both personal and articulate records of the disaster," Klett states in the exhibition catalogue. "I think you can tell when a photographer has a personal stake in the images, when an experience steers the vision. So I'd say they were more than documentary recordings."[13]

The renewed interest in Genthe's negatives generated by the centennial prompted action on their preservation. By then it was becoming increasingly apparent that the cellulose nitrate negatives were deteriorating badly, and in 2006 the Museums' head paper conservator, Debra Evans, implemented new methods of proper housing and controlled freezer storage to slow the rate of their decomposition. Although many of the negatives were already compromised, test prints indicated that they still retained amazing detail. A future project was envisioned that entailed digital capture and printing of the images.

It had been known for some time that the state of the negatives was in decline. Fifty years earlier, upon receiving them, Adams had noted: "The negatives from which these prints were made are in very bad condition; to 'reconstruct' them so as to achieve clean, defect-free images would be a tremendous task. Dr. Genthe's negatives are apparently widely scattered; perhaps some day (I hope before they have disintegrated further) they will be brought together, properly organized, and the best ones 'restored' and eloquently printed."[14]

By the early twenty-first century, with the advent of digital technology, there was a way of preserving the negatives as Adams had imagined: they could be scanned and the information contained in them could be seen as a digital image or photographic print. However, the costs for such a project were beyond what the Museums could accommodate. In 2014 the Achenbach Graphic Arts Council, a museum-support organization, began a fund-raising campaign. In addition to the council's considerable efforts, a front-page story in the *San Francisco Chronicle* on April 17, 2015, resulted in an outpouring of donations from greater Bay Area residents, and the fund-raising goal was achieved.[15] The newly raised monies enabled museum paper conservator (now head of paper conservation) Victoria Binder to immediately arrange for production of high-resolution scans and digital printing of Genthe's negatives at Chicago Albumen Works, a company specializing in digital archiving of photograph collections. The resulting scans revealed imagery on the negatives that had never before been seen.

In 2017 Achenbach curator James A. Ganz determined that it was desirable to have a selection of gelatin silver prints made from the high-resolution scans. This would include all of the photographs that Genthe took on April 18 and 19, as well as other notable images of the fire, ruins, survivors, tent camps, and early rebuilding efforts in the city. Barret Oliver, a Southern California–based photographer and printer with a specialization in nineteenth-century photo processes, was enlisted to print from the scans. He was given helpful direction by Binder, who had carefully reviewed the extant gelatin silver prints made by Genthe. The aesthetic choices demonstrated in the Genthe prints guided the overall tone and tonal variations, surface sheen, and format of the new prints. It was decided to print the negatives in their entirety, without cropping or retouching—unlike what Adams had done in 1956—to reveal Genthe's exact field of vision at the moment he took each photograph. Oliver's deliberate yet sensitive work resulted in eighty-eight gelatin silver photographs, which entered the Museums' permanent collection in 2018 and make up the Plates section of this book. Beyond their historical importance, the prints serve as an enduring testament to the artistic vision of one of America's great photographers.

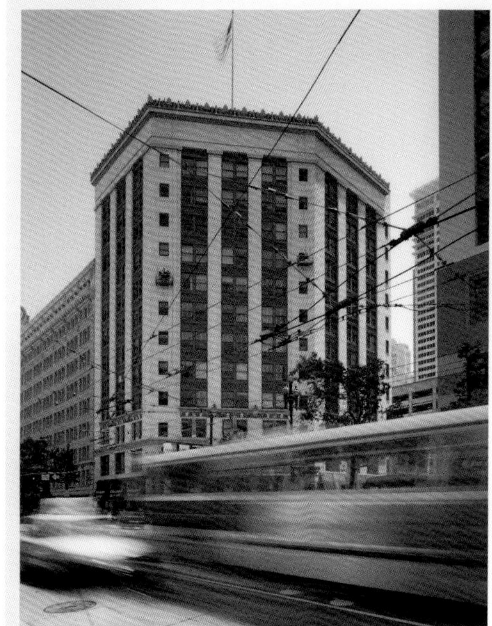

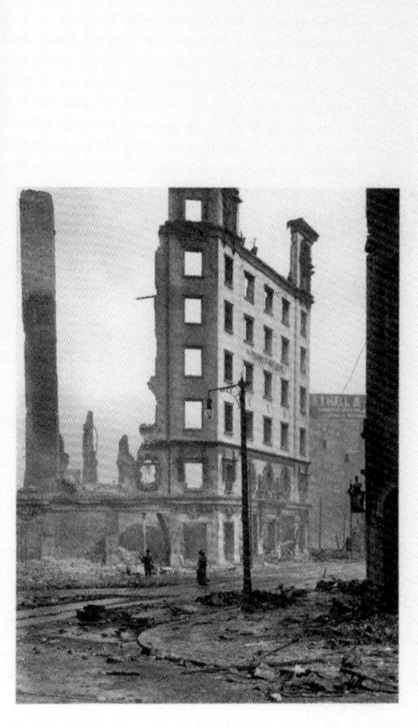

Fig. 3. Mark Klett (American, b. 1952) and Michael Lundgren (American, b. 1974), *Hearst Building, Market Street, 2003 and 1906*, 2005. Inkjet print, 24 × 60 in. (61 × 152.4 cm). Fine Arts Museums of San Francisco, Museum purchase, Dorothy F. Boyesen Bequest Fund and Francesca Deering Howe and Thomas Carr Howe, Jr. Endowment Fund, 2005.97.1

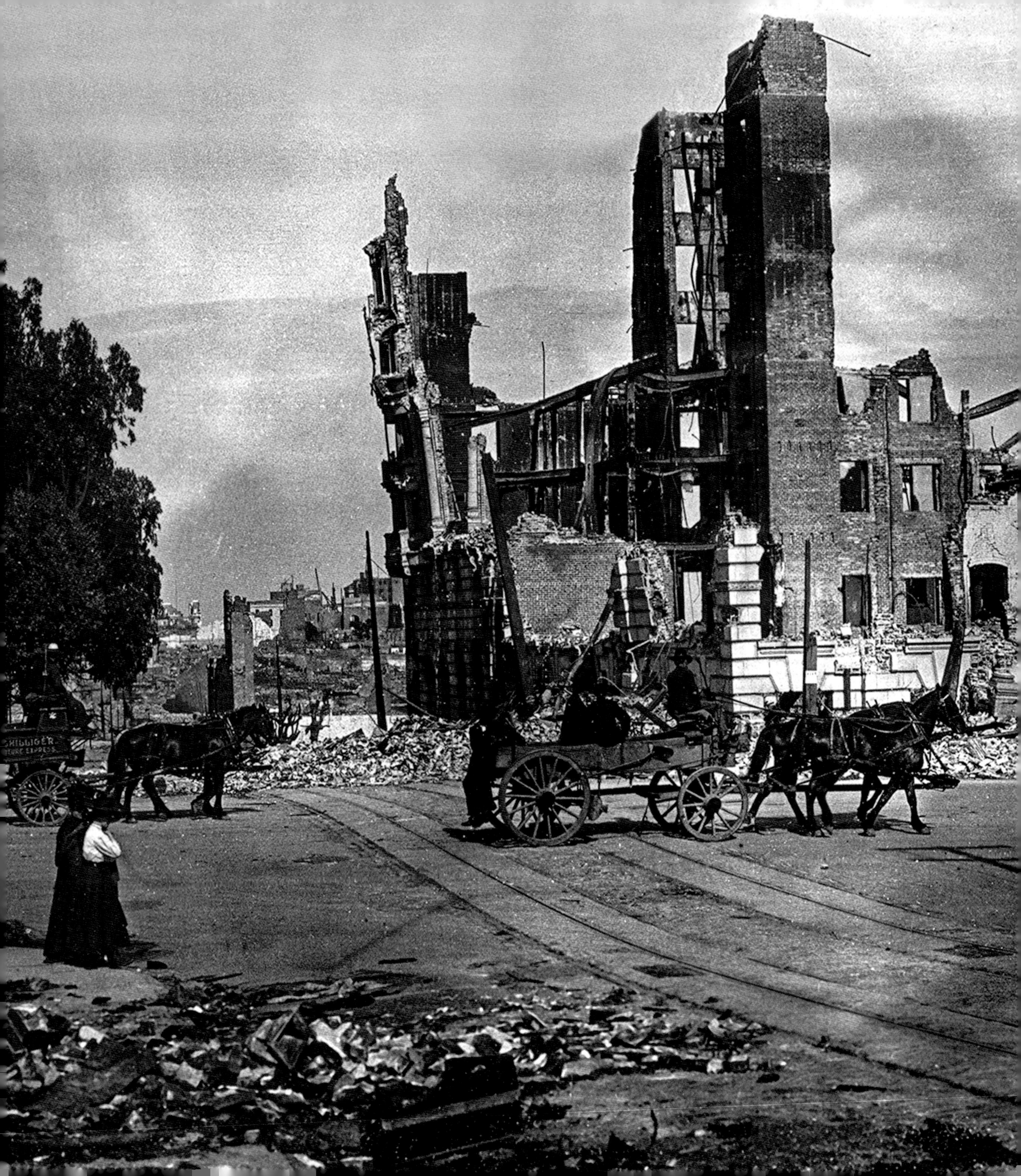

ESSAYS

Arnold Genthe

AND THE CALIFORNIA CAMERA CLUB

Carolin Görgen

BY THE TIME ARNOLD GENTHE FIRST ARRIVED in San Francisco, in 1895, the city's photography scene was steadily growing in professionals, aspiring amateurs, and hobbyists. Only two years earlier, the *San Francisco Chronicle* calculated five thousand "picture-seekers" across California, more than half of whom were local residents.[1] While their interests ranged widely, the city's most active photographers shared an enthusiasm for practicing outdoors, exhibiting prints, and organizing lectures. A considerable number of them were members of the California Camera Club (CCC).

What appears as a marginal organization in Genthe's autobiography was in fact a major venue for photographers in the Bay Area. Established in March 1890, the CCC defined itself as "a social, scientific and art center for photographers." Its aim was to unite the diverse practitioners in the region. As the first article of its bylaws stated: "Any person, eighteen years of age or over, who is interested in photography, shall be eligible to active membership."[2] By 1900 this inclusive policy made it the largest camera club in the United States; its membership of 425 surpassed even that of the Camera Club of New York. And yet, despite the vibrant community it helped build, the CCC, as well as many of its sister organizations, has since faded into oblivion.[3]

In the 1880s, as the photography industry was flourishing and the recently invented gelatin dry process made the medium accessible to beginners, camera clubs started to form across the country. By 1893 ninety clubs with a total of 4,580 members had been established, mostly by an affluent, predominantly male "leisure class."[4] Camera clubs held meetings, exchanged prints, and hosted outdoor excursions. Members displayed their work at exhibitions in Boston, New York, and San Francisco, as well as at international salons. Many of these photographers identified as Pictorialists; their motive was to demonstrate the artistic potential of a mechanical medium.[5]

The history of Pictorialism is largely identified with photographer Alfred Stieglitz and the Photo-Secession movement. In 1902 Stieglitz "seceded" from the flourishing club mainstream to form an exclusive circle with its own magazine, *Camera Work* (1903–1917), and exhibition space in New York City. The group espoused an autonomous, strictly noncommercial idea of photography. This more "avant-garde" objective ran counter to the practices of most American camera clubs, who unequivocally blended artistic endeavors and professional work. Some of the names associated with the Photo-Secession—such as Gertrude Käsebier, Edward Steichen, and Clarence H. White—have become celebrated figures. Over the

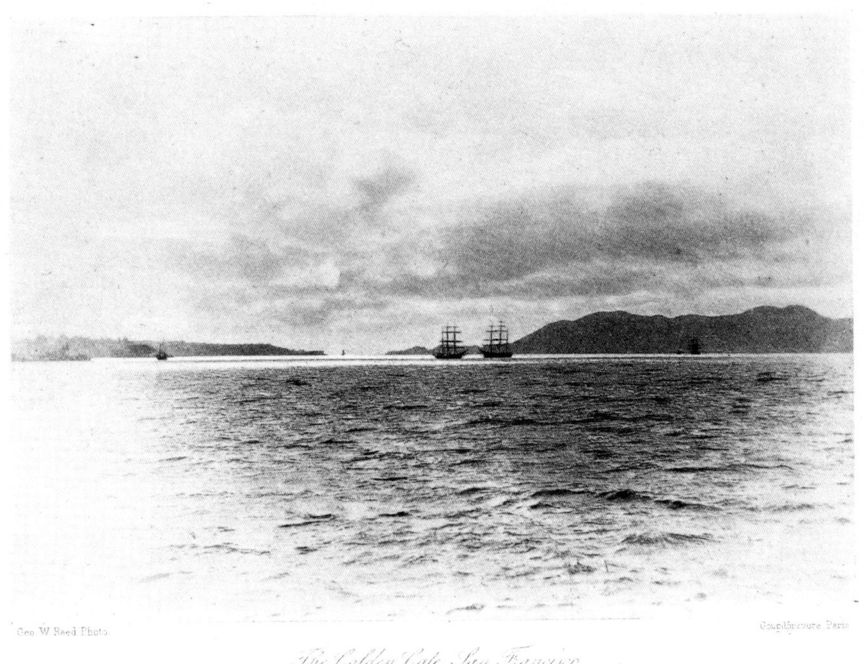

Fig. 4. George W. Reed, *The Golden Gate*, 1887. Dennis Reed Collection

years, this success has relegated the legacy of other clubs to the fringes, including the CCC.[6]

Given his later career in New York—he moved there in 1911—it is tempting to consider Genthe as "San Francisco's Alfred Stieglitz," with a similar proclivity for noncommercial aestheticism.[7] Yet, in the first stages of his career, it is within the CCC that his path unfolded. The club's headquarters, at 819 Market Street, had little in common with the polished Photo-Secession galleries on Fifth Avenue. The CCC kept rooms in the Academy of Sciences, where exhibitions and excursions were planned, retailers displayed products and prints, and painters occasionally joined meetings. Like most camera clubs, the CCC also counted among its members many professionals, who offered advice to amateurs and showcased new equipment.

* * *

The professional membership of the CCC reflected the long-standing ties between photographers and boosters of the American West.[8] Since California's admission to the Union, in 1850, there had been a burgeoning demand from communities and railroad companies for images that promoted settlement in the West. By the 1880s, in Northern California alone, this photography industry employed more than fifteen hundred people whose work contributed to the creation of a distinct regional identity.[9] Thanks to new printing technologies, this production resulted in widely circulated images of Yosemite's majestic landscape, Spanish missions, and orchards that promised an abundant Western soil. Up and down the coast, where cultural institutions were sparse but economic opportunities plentiful, the works of painters, poets, and photographers were mobilized for the enterprise of "selling California."[10]

In this climate San Francisco's first strictly noncommercial camera club, the Pacific Coast Amateur Photographic Association (PCAPA), could survive only a few years. Founded in 1883, the PCAPA included some seventy members, many of whom were attorneys, custom-house brokers, and physicians. Archibald J. Treat, president of the PCAPA, advocated for an outdoor practice that would appreciate

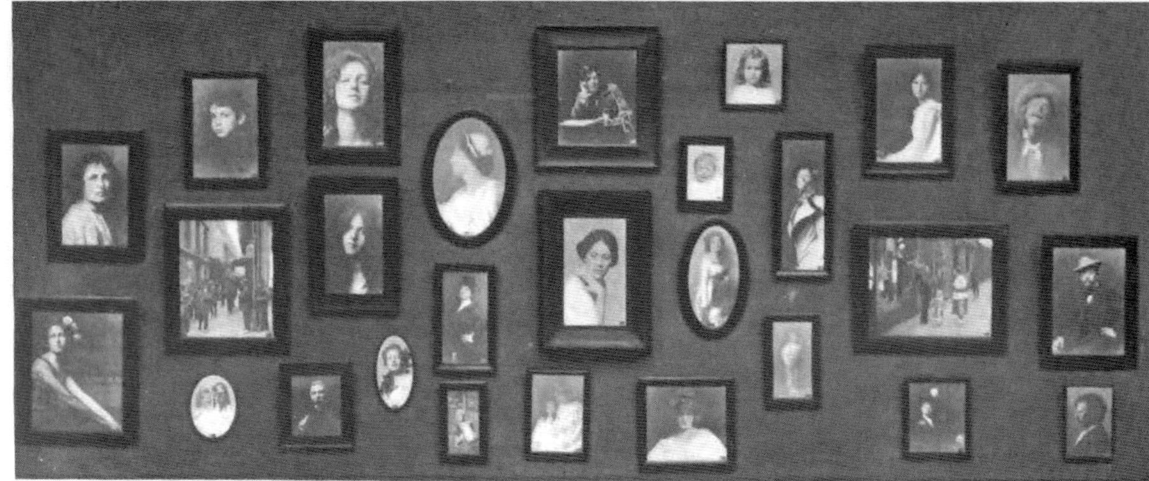

THE GRAND PRIZE COLLECTION.

Fig. 5. Display of Arnold Genthe's work at the First San Francisco Photographic Salon, January 1901

California as "a land of milk and honey, the adopted home of the orange, the olive and the vine . . . [that] should be the home of art."[11] Buttressed by such a clear embrace of boosterism, PCAPA members walked a thin line between amateur and commercial practice. Treat himself was commissioned by Leland Stanford to produce panoramic views of Stanford University's Palo Alto campus.[12] And in 1889 PCAPA vice president George W. Reed overstepped this line entirely when he sold an image of the Golden Gate (fig. 4), leading to his exclusion from the group. Reed proceeded to found the CCC on deliberately inclusive principles, allowing professionals, beginners, and women to join. By late 1891 the club had absorbed most of the PCAPA.[13] Eventual members included notable professionals such as Theodore C. Marceau, who later had studios in Los Angeles and the Midwest; Howard C. Tibbitts, the official photographer of the Southern Pacific Railroad; Thomas P. Andrews, a photography dealer; and renowned Berkeley photographer Oscar V. Lange.[14]

Perhaps the most celebrated feature of the CCC's programming was its lantern slide lectures. Once a month, at San Francisco's Metropolitan Temple, photographic images were projected onto a large screen, accompanied by music and anecdotes that entertained and instructed the local public. The first lecture, in February 1891, took attendants to Yosemite Valley "in a style and on a scale that has never before been attempted," said the *Chronicle*.[15] These lectures worked hand in hand with an excursion program sponsored by the Southern Pacific that provided transportation on special cars. Readers of the club's first magazine, *Pacific Coast Photographer* (1892–1894), were encouraged to join these outings. Upon completion of the first lecture year, Reed, who was in charge of the lantern committee, bragged that more than twenty thousand San Franciscans had seen the results of this outreach.[16]

Attracted by the CCC's facilities, a young Arnold Genthe joined in late 1896 to make enlargements of his photographs of San Francisco's Chinatown.[17] Two years later both his prints and his lantern slides would be regularly shown in club exhibitions, receiving great praise from members and the press.[18] Genthe was inspired by a general enthusiasm for outdoor work. In 1899 he traveled to Arizona and New Mexico with the photographer, explorer, and writer Frederick I. Monsen. His desire to explore the Southwest was sparked by Southern Californian booster Charles F. Lummis. The third edition of Lummis's *Some Strange Corners of Our Country* had just been published when Genthe discovered the romanticized stories of the Painted Desert, the Grand Canyon, Hopi villages, and snake dances—as well as the trains to get there.[19] Genthe's negatives of his trip reveal a fascination with the residents of Taos and Acoma Pueblo, New Mexico, and with the layers of rock and steep valleys of the Grand Canyon—subject matter echoed in his street photography in Chinatown and, later, his dramatic vistas of the earthquake damage.

* * *

In 1900, after experiencing success at the first Chicago photography salon, where Stieglitz sat on the jury, portrait photographer and CCC member Oscar Maurer became an outspoken advocate of having a salon at the nearby Mark Hopkins Institute of Art. For many years the club had considered the institution—affiliated with the University of California, Berkeley, since 1893—to be a desirable exhibition space.[20] In May, with the launch of the monthly publication *Camera Craft* (1900–1942), Maurer seized the occasion to rally further support. Three months later, when the decision was announced to hold a salon in January 1901, *Camera Craft*'s editors declared that "the portals of the highest art institution west of the Mississippi are thrown open for the first time." The Hopkins Institute, perched atop San Francisco's Nob Hill, was indeed an ideal location with its "commanding view of the entire city and the country for miles around."[21] The mansion boasted lavish interiors, which provided an excellent backdrop, and had long been a favorite subject of local photographers. From its tower, in 1878, Eadweard Muybridge had made the first panorama of the city.

The selection committee of the 1901 salon was chaired by CCC members, including Maurer, Treat, and the Paris-trained painter Theodore Wores. To lend further credence to the 475 photographs on display, 123 paintings by members of the San Francisco Art Association were also shown. The club's by then well-known figures William E. Dassonville, Genthe, Lange, and Maurer received unanimous accolades. Maurer wrote an article for *Camera Craft* that includes the only existing interior view of the salon: a display of Genthe's portraits and Chinatown scenes (see fig. 5). That same year, Genthe garnered attention when he published "Rebellion in Photography," a short essay that criticized the "commonplace, lifeless" aspects of commercial portraiture. He encouraged photographers to develop an artistic feeling that would expose "something of the soul, the individuality of the sitter" in a period dominated by easily affordable imagery.[22]

By January 1902 a second successful salon was organized. As the number of photography salons across the country increased, Genthe and Maurer,

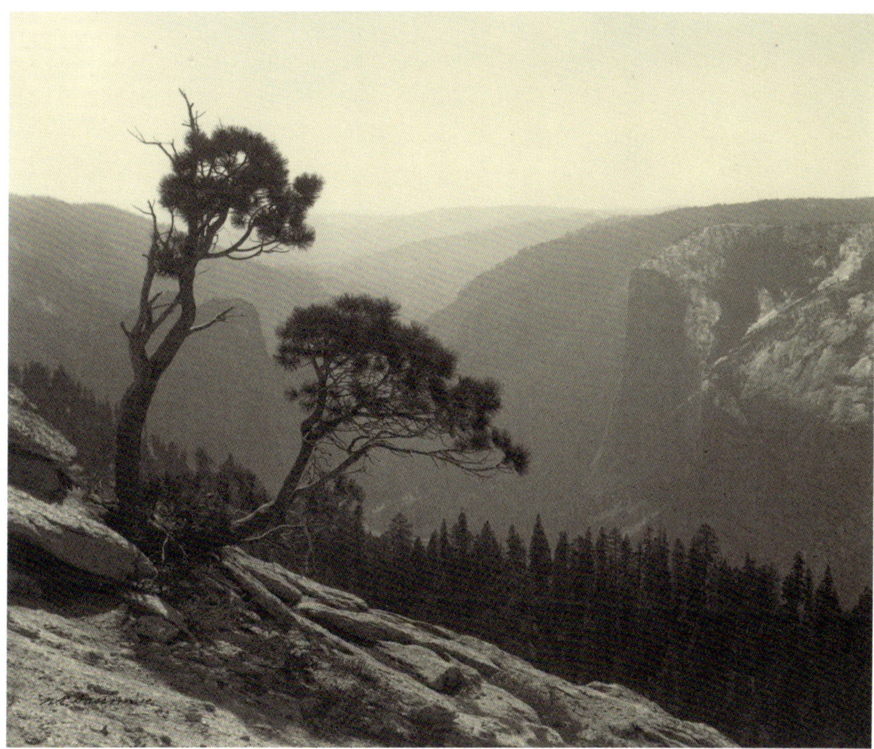

Fig. 6. William E. Dassonville (American, 1879–1957), *View of Yosemite Valley with Pine Trees*, 1906. Platinum print, 16 ¾ × 13 ½ in. (42.5 × 34.3 cm). The J. Paul Getty Museum, Los Angeles, 2005.58.4

as well as club members William J. Street and F.E. Monteverde, also started showing their prints in Chicago and Philadelphia. At the Los Angeles salon in May, twelve members displayed their work and received much praise, including Genthe, who won an award for portraiture.[23] Despite their representation across the country, San Franciscans still felt "so little in touch with the big Eastern cities," as Genthe put it.[24] Indeed, artistic exchanges with New York remained rare. After his success at Chicago, Maurer had been a short-term associate of the Photo-Secession. And in the following years, club contributor Anne Brigman became Stieglitz's only permanent West Coast affiliate. To embolden the connection between the coasts, the CCC requested a loan exhibition from Stieglitz for its third salon. Club official A.L. Coombs wrote to the New York photographer: "We are so far removed from the photographic centers that we have no opportunity to study the work of the best photographers, except through reproductions in the magazines."[25] Stieglitz's response was positive, and the salon, held in October 1903, included a separate exhibition of the Photo-Secession, including prints by Alvin Langdon Coburn, Steichen, and White. For some, the New Yorkers' dominating presence went too far. An unsigned editorial in *Camera Craft* lamented the salon's limited number of prints by and lack of publicity for local photographers, which resulted in the absence of "a strong Western representation."[26]

Other facets of the club's work, however, continued to prominently feature the West. On excursions to the Bay Area, Spanish missions, and Yosemite, Dassonville—who later went on to develop a specially coated bromide paper called Charcoal Black—produced iconic images of California.[27] His photographs of Yosemite Valley masterfully capture the state's unique natural landscape—as seen, for example, in his spare composition of pine trees growing out of steep granite against the Sierra Nevada, receding toward the horizon in a lush range of grays (fig. 6). These works attracted local arts and crafts dealers, and many of them were also published in the pages of *Camera Craft* and *Sunset*. The latter even had a regular column on club activities. In 1905, to further express its local commitment, the CCC redecorated its rooms with Spanish mission–style furniture.[28]

* * *

On the morning of April 18, 1906, after the ground had violently shaken for about one minute, *Camera Craft* editor Fayette J. Clute rushed up the stairs of the Academy of Sciences to his offices on the fifth floor, just below the recently renovated club rooms. Confronted with "a general wreck" and "a strong smell of gas," he had just enough time to secure a small hand camera.[29] That same morning, William J. Street took a photograph down Market Street, one block from the academy, showing the Call Building enveloped in thick smoke. By midday the CCC headquarters were destroyed. Across the city, photographers watched their collections burn. While Genthe was witnessing the dynamiting of his home,[30] photochemistry expert Henry D'Arcy Power faced a similar scene: "Before I left, I saw the house I dwelt in go up in flames, and with it, most of my property, all the results of my labors in photographic art, and over two thousand negatives."[31] On Hyde Street, Archibald J. Treat rushed to save his prints before escaping by ferry to Sausalito, a small city just north of San Francisco.[32] Dassonville, Maurer, and Carleton Watkins also suffered major losses. Probably the most dramatic damage was inflicted on Isaiah W. Taber, whose firm—with its one hundred tons of negatives—was reduced to ashes.[33] In early May the *San Francisco Call* reported that "there remain but a few hundred photographic negatives of the countless thousands taken of persons prominent here in all walks of life for the past half-century."[34] The cover of *Camera Craft*'s May issue (fig. 7), showing the Academy of Sciences in ruins, seemed to embody this report.

In the months following the catastrophe, the magazine was published from Sacramento, and the CCC found provisional offices in the home of club president George Knight, on Pierce Street in San Francisco. Along with Lange, Marceau, and others, Knight managed a relief fund for California photographers that promised swift assistance. The fund consisted of donations from retailers ($1,500 alone from Eastman Kodak) and from clubs across the country whose members gathered money and equipment, and held special lectures for their San Franciscan colleagues. The effort, widely publicized in magazines like *American Amateur Photographer* and *Photo-Era*, raised more than $4,000 by early June.[35]

With sparse equipment and improvised apparatus, local photographers ventured into their destroyed city. Three days after Genthe toured the burning districts with a No. 3A Folding Pocket Kodak, his club colleague Louis J. Stellmann returned to the ruins equipped with a Kodak Premoette Junior No. 1. Using bricks as a tripod, Stellmann captured what he called "the greatest sight that ever invited a photographer." His illustrated account was published the following January in *Camera Craft*.[36] While many professionals sought to make money with spectacular scenes of smoke and flames, others—like Stellmann—were attracted to the ruins for aesthetic reasons. Even as the city was already partly rebuilt, Stellmann remained fascinated with the ruins. In 1910 arts and crafts editor Paul Elder published Stellmann's *Vanished Ruin Era: San Francisco's Classic Artistry of Ruin*. Through twenty-six photographs and poems, the book celebrates "that modern Acropolis" and its "shapes of classic dignity."[37] Like Genthe and many of his contemporaries, Stellmann was particularly drawn to the "Portals of the Past," the marble entrance of Alban N. Towne's mansion on Nob Hill (see pl. 54; cats. 87, 89–90). Although the majority of the structure had been destroyed, the entrance had withstood the fire, and its columns picturesquely framed City Hall's burnt-out dome. It is this image that graces the cover of Stellmann's book.

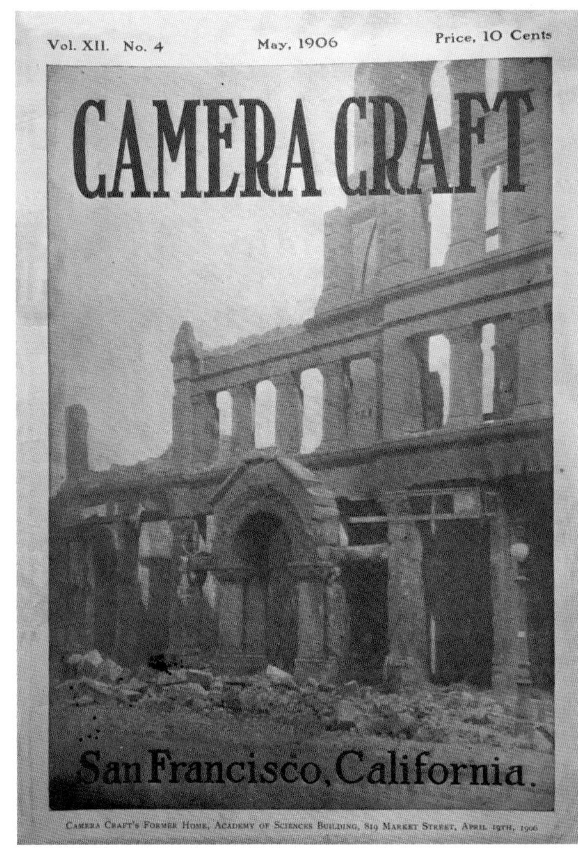
Vol. XII. No. 4 May, 1906 Price, 10 Cents

CAMERA CRAFT

San Francisco, California.

Camera Craft's Former Home, Academy of Sciences Building, 819 Market Street, April 19th, 1906

Fig. 7. *Camera Craft's* San Francisco headquarters at 819 Market Street, April 19, 1906, pictured on the frontispiece of *Camera Craft* 12, no. 4 (1906)

In Genthe's own post-earthquake publication, *Pictures of Old Chinatown* (1908), the photographs that made him famous are reprinted in delicate hues of black and white, tracing his walks through the "romantically mysterious" neighborhood before its destruction. The text was written by the journalist Will Irwin, who only a few years earlier had warned Genthe about frequent fires and advised him to store his negatives in a vault.[38] The book ends with an image of a Chinatown resident standing amid the rubble after the earthquake (fig. 21), facing an uncertain future.[39] Stellmann's and Genthe's accounts are part of a sentimentalized narrative that was quickly fashioned after April 1906. For both artists, the destroyed space became a screen on which to project a nostalgic version of communal life in San Francisco before the earthquake. Each used a soft lens, a technique that seemed to blur the tensions palpable in the city before and after the disaster.

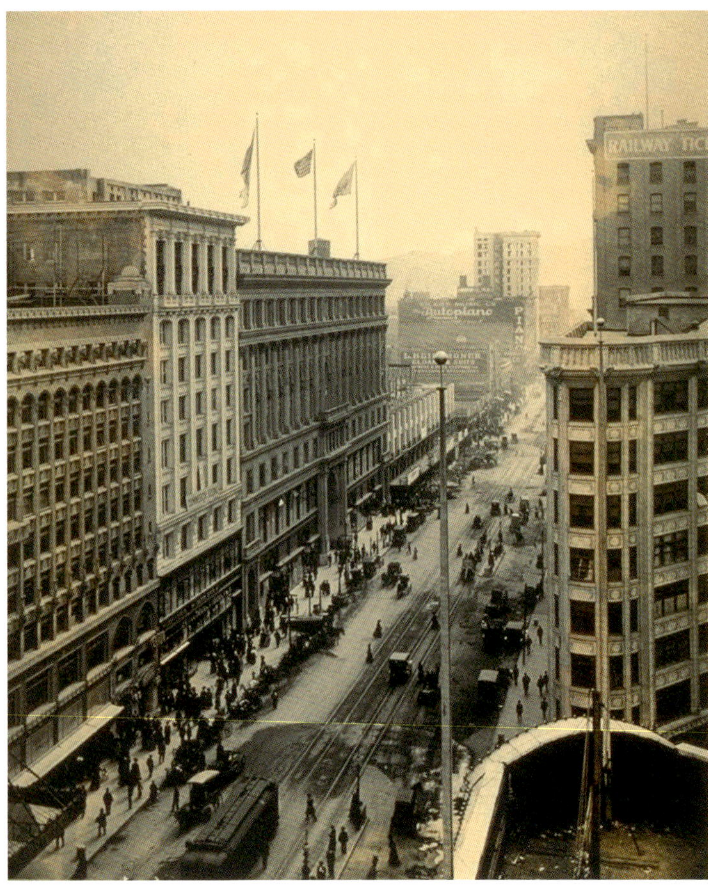

Fig. 8. Edward N. Sewell, Market Street west from Phelan Building, 1909. The building with the white façade on the left is the Commercial Building. The California Camera Club occupied the upper floor.

A similarly distorted vision was shaped by politicians, investors, and insurance companies, who wished to transform the memory of the earthquake into a "great fire." Framing the event as similar to the great fires that had occurred in Chicago in 1871 and Baltimore in 1904 transcribed it into a national experience while also downplaying the unpredicability of earthquakes, which were unfamiliar to most Americans. Professional photographers posted up in the sunny East Bay, producing images of the fire from a safe distance. Some sold before-and-after images that showed a resilient city rising from the ashes. Together these various stakeholders helped sell this "accepted history," as Rodger C. Birt terms it, to the rest of the nation.[40] Numerous CCC members contributed to this narrative. In April 1908 Tibbitts's panoramic views of a metropolis under construction embellished *Sunset* magazine's supplement "San Francisco Two Years After." Club secretary Edward N. Sewell assembled annual albums between 1906 and 1910 that recorded the city's rapid architectural progress. His 1909 album, *New San Francisco*, meticulously documents the rebuilding of banks, department stores, hotels, and offices in the Financial District. These photographs (see fig. 8) offer promising views of neighborhoods teeming with street cars and bustling crowds. The album title was taken from a speech given by Mayor James D. Phelan in 1896 announcing the imperial destiny of the city.

In February 1909 the CCC officially moved into a 2,500-square-foot space in the Commercial Building at 833 Market Street (visible in figure 8), equipped with a daylight studio, several darkrooms, a library, and a reception room.[41] While the aftermath of the earthquake was a tumultuous and transitional time, the club had successfully upheld its program. In 1907 it hosted its first outing to Yosemite as well as an exhibition of Genthe's works. That same year Genthe co-organized the opening of the Hotel Del Monte Art Gallery in Monterey, California, where he showed prints of his earthquake photos alongside works by painters William Keith and Xavier Martinez. Three years later, at the International Exhibition of Pictorial Photography in Buffalo, New York, one of these earthquake photographs was acquired by Stieglitz. When Genthe left for New York City in 1911, great regret was expressed at his departure. One publication lamented the loss of "one more artist whom San Francisco can ill afford to lose."[42] A year later, he was still listed as an active member in the club's annual.

As the Panama-Pacific International Exposition of 1915 approached, the CCC's first generation gradually dispersed. Yet their headquarters remained a key venue for fledgling photographers until the late 1930s. Perhaps Genthe's New York assistant, Dorothea Lange, was following the advice of her mentor when she first arrived in San Francisco in 1919 and visited the club, where she met Consuelo Kanaga and crossed paths with Ansel Adams, Imogen Cunningham, and Edward Weston.[43] As the "social, scientific and art center for photographers" continued its program, much thought was given to aspiring practitioners. It was there that the threads of Northern California's renowned photography scene of the twentieth century were woven together.

Retracing Genthe's Journey

STEP-BY-STEP

James A. Ganz

ARNOLD GENTHE WAS NOT MERELY a chronicler of the 1906 San Francisco earthquake and fire but also a victim who lost his home, his earthly possessions, the tools of his trade, and much of his photographic archive. His financial self-sufficiency enabled him to quickly re-establish his portraiture business and carry on with his life; he was not motivated to sell his images of the disaster and they would remain a lesser-known part of his oeuvre during his lifetime. Along with his friend Jack London, Genthe was the only eyewitness to leave both significant visual and literary accounts of the disaster.[1] "The one thought uppermost in my mind was not to bring some of my possessions to a place of safety," he recalled in his 1936 autobiography, *As I Remember*, "but to make photographs of the scenes I had been witnessing, the effects of the earthquake and the beginning of the conflagration that had started in various parts of the city" (see Genthe, "'Earthquake and Fire,'" this volume).[2] This essay sifts the visual and textual rubble of the San Francisco earthquake and fire to reconstruct Genthe's experience through a detailed investigation of the remarkable body of photographs that he created in its immediate aftermath.

Genthe's narrative opens with his activities on that historic Wednesday morning, from the moment he was jostled awake at 5:12 a.m. to his arrival at George Kahn's camera shop several hours later. Genthe, his home, and his studio at 790 Sutter Street were all shaken but did not incur serious harm in the mainshock, so the photographer pulled himself together to see friends and stroll to breakfast at the St. Francis Hotel on Union Square. Afterward, as he learned of the fires flaring up around the city, he felt compelled to return to his studio for a camera. Finding most of his equipment smashed, Genthe walked six blocks to Kahn's shop at 105 Montgomery Street, which was already uncomfortably close to the flames. Like many business owners, Kahn was there to survey the damage to his store and save his irreplaceable client records. "Take anything you want," he reportedly told Genthe. "This place is going to burn up anyway."[3]

THE FINANCIAL DISTRICT

Armed with a No. 3A Folding Pocket Kodak camera and his pockets bulging with rolls of film, Genthe followed the smoke, walking a half block north on Montgomery to Bush Street. There he turned and paused by Schimmel & Steinkamp's tailor shop in the Eureka Building to snap perhaps his first shot of the day: the burning structures at the corner of Bush and Sansome Streets, including the headquarters of dry goods wholesaler Murphy, Grant & Company (pl. 1). He seems to have struggled with the exposure, resulting in a murky negative that he later retouched to accentuate the figures and flames (fig. 35; see Binder, "Freezing Fire: Arnold Genthe and His Camera," this volume). Continuing

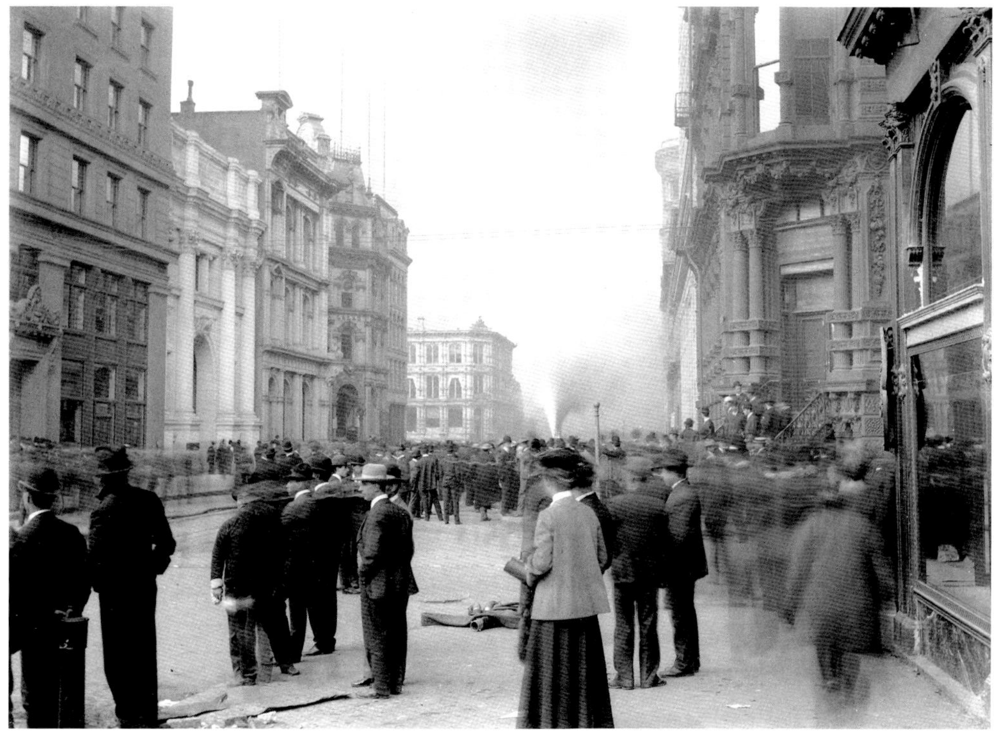

Fig. 9. Edith Irvine (American, 1884–1949), *Montgomery Street at California Street Intersection*, 1906. Scan from gelatin dry plate negative, 5 × 7 in. (127 × 178 mm). Brigham Young University Library, Special Collections, Provo, Utah

two blocks north, Genthe arrived at California Street, where again he turned and braced himself in the doorway of an insurance office to capture the demise of the R.G. Dun & Company Building at the northeast corner of California and Sansome (see pls. 2–3). Known to old-timers as the Friedlander Block, the stately brick-and-iron structure housed financial, mining, and insurance agencies. The sequence of Genthe's photographs, taken just moments apart, is established by the movement from left to right of a group of men tugging a fire hose. A vibration of his camera blurred the second image but, recognizing the historical significance of the scene, he retained both negatives—the first of a number of instances in which he kept two close variants without making any noticeable adjustments to exposure or shutter speed.

It is clear from numerous other photographs taken in this vicinity that most of the major buildings in the Financial District survived the initial earthquake relatively unscathed. Edith Irvine, a professional photographer from Calaveras County who happened to arrive that morning, was among the first photographers drawn to this location during the eight o'clock hour, capturing the nervous businessmen gathering to assess the damage (see fig. 9).[4] She also photographed from an excavated construction site on the northwest corner of California and Sansome, where ledgers and files from nearby businesses had been evacuated to temporary safety (see fig. 10). Reportedly this blaze was sparked in a basement one block south, around Sansome and Pine Streets, and took several hours to spread. According to Lawrence J. Kennedy's report "The Progress of the Fire in San Francisco April 18th–21st, 1906," the Anglo-California Bank on the northeast corner of Sansome and Pine was on fire at eight thirty, as was the Mutual Life Insurance Building on the southeast corner by nine o'clock (the encroaching fire is visible in the adjacent structure to the south of the Mutual Life Insurance Building in Irvine's photographs from the empty lot).[5]

San Francisco photographer Willard E. Worden arrived after Irvine and before Genthe, perhaps during

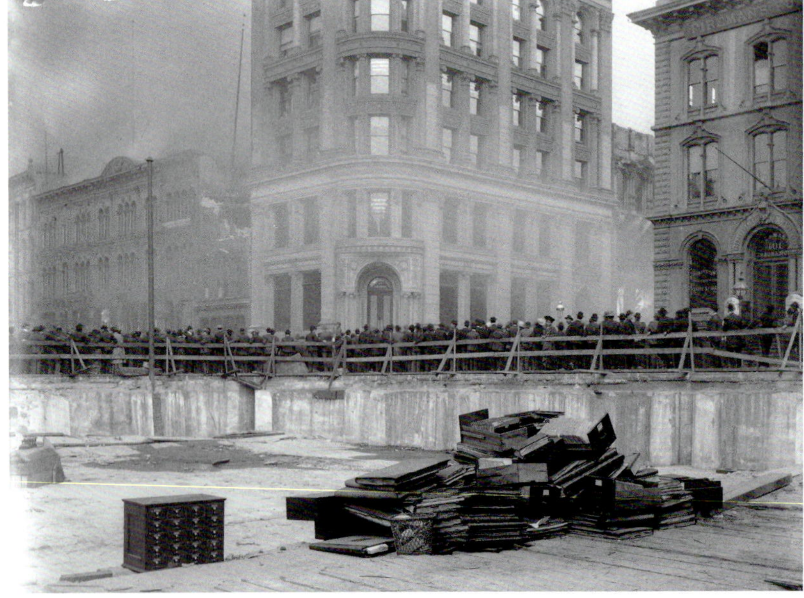

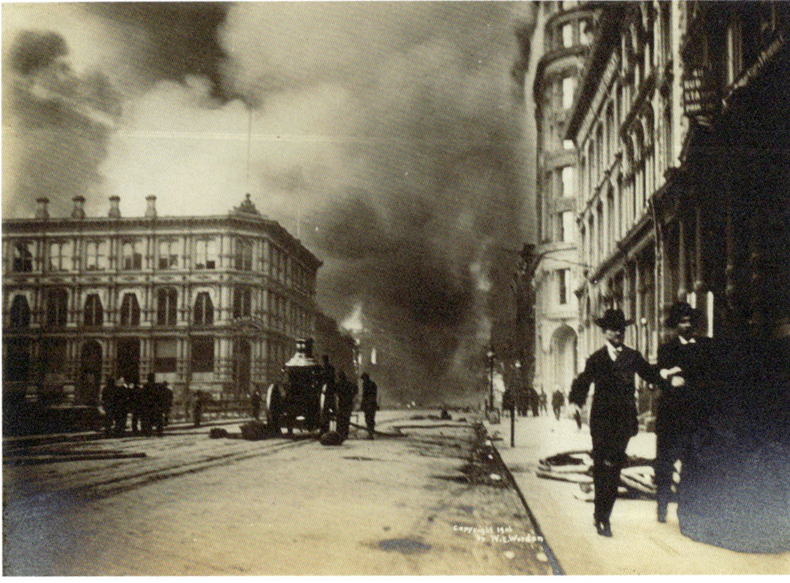

Fig. 10. Edith Irvine (American, 1884–1949), *401 California Street at Right and Sansome Street*, 1906. Scan from gelatin dry plate negative, 5 × 7 in. (127 × 178 mm). Brigham Young University Library, Special Collections, Provo, Utah

Fig. 11. Willard E. Worden (American, 1868–1946), *Fire Scene at California and Sansome*, 1906. Gelatin silver print, 4 5⁄8 × 6 11⁄16 in. (11.8 × 17 cm). Fine Arts Museums of San Francisco, Museum purchase, gift of the Achenbach Graphic Arts Council and Lawrence Banka and Judith Gordon in memory of Edmund A. and Frances Banka, 2017.22.74

the nine o'clock hour, and photographed from the corner of California and Leidesdorff Streets, capturing fleeing businessmen and the crew of Engine Company 31 (see fig. 11). Perhaps he bumped shoulders with insurance executive George W. Brooks, who was standing here negotiating with a competitor for emergency storage space. Brooks "watched the firemen lower a suction pipe through a manhole in the middle of the street and pump sewage on to the old Wells Fargo Building. It had about as much effect as a garden hose and the supply was soon exhausted. The firemen stood perfectly helpless, like soldiers without ammunition, in front of the enemy."[6]

Brooks's narrative of his desperate attempts to retrieve documents from his office at 230 California Street is one of the most harrowing first-person accounts of the fire. Impeded by a rope that stretched across California Street, from the Mutual Life Insurance Building to the Dun Building, Brooks waited until the soldier on guard was distracted to duck the barrier and run to his office:

> I rushed in, threw open my desk and hastily gathered an armful of what I deemed were the more important books and papers. . . . I again received a jolt by noticing that the fire was coming down a light shaft from an adjoining building and through an open window into the rear office. . . . In fact, furniture was already burning in the president's room. This was no place for me. The only avenue of escape was the way I had come, since so rapid was the spread of the conflagration that north, south and east were already in flames.[7]

On his way back to California and Sansome, Brooks was nearly crushed by the collapse of the façade of another insurance building: "Realizing that my safety was measured by a matter of seconds, I was for a moment unnerved. My legs trembled, my heart pounded and my breath came quickly, and only by a great exertion of will induced by the thought that it was time to do and not to hesitate, I made the effort and arrived safely at the rope from which I had started."[8]

Chinatown

During Genthe's early years as an amateur photographer, he was attracted to the culture of Chinatown, roaming its crowded alleys and turning his lens on what he saw as exotic street life around its commercial hub (see fig. 25).[9] On the day of the earthquake, he returned to photograph Clay Street at Dupont Street (now Grant Avenue) in the vicinity of Portsmouth Square (see pl. 4), as well as the residential environs farther uphill between Stockton and Powell Streets. There he directed his camera back toward the waterfront and the heart of Chinatown, capturing onlookers observing the progress of the flames. His image of several Black bystanders congregating near the "Chinese School," a public school designated for Chinese students, reveals a class of victims who are otherwise nearly excluded from the pictorial record of the disaster (see pls. 5–6). The fact that they turn away from the spectacle to face the camera alters the impression of pure reportage, just as the seemingly deliberate placement of a solitary woman in two different views farther up the street suggests a directorial approach (see fig. 12; pl. 7). Genthe's years of experience as a portraitist and a chronicler of street life in Chinatown facilitated his engagement with San Franciscans in this time of crisis, setting his work apart from most commercial photographers, who documented the disaster in a more impersonal and less self-consciously artistic manner.

"Of the pictures I had made during the fire," Genthe wrote in *As I Remember*, "there are several, I believe, that will be of lasting interest. There is particularly the one scene that I recorded the morning of the first day of the fire (on Sacramento Street, looking toward the Bay) which shows, in a pictorially effective composition, the results of the earthquake, the beginning of the fire and the attitude of the people" (see fig. 14; pl. 8).[10] An unknown photographer captured the same vista from a spot slightly higher up the hill at Powell Street perhaps an hour later (see fig. 13). Genthe's claim that he shot this photograph in the

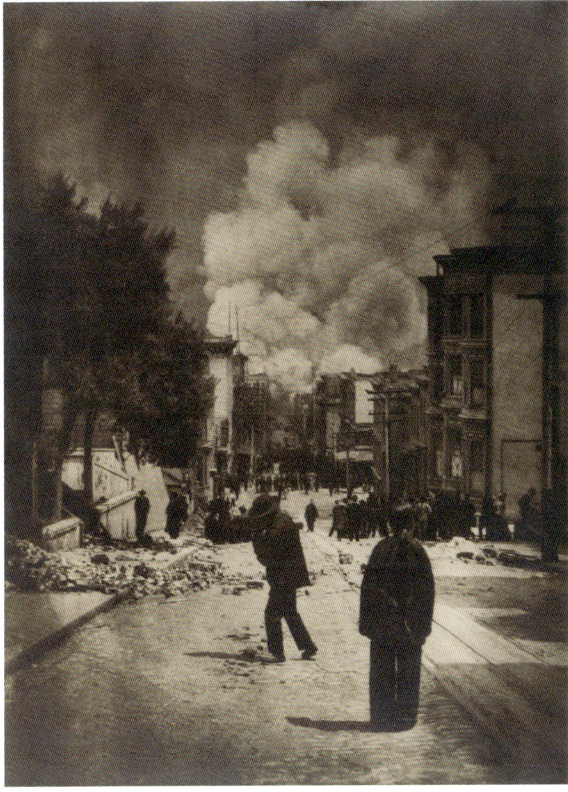

Fig. 12. Arnold Genthe, Untitled (Clay Street), 1906. Gelatin silver print, 10 ¹³⁄₁₆ × 13 ⅝ in. (27.5 × 34.6 cm). Amon Carter Museum of American Art, Fort Worth, Texas, P1980.25.2

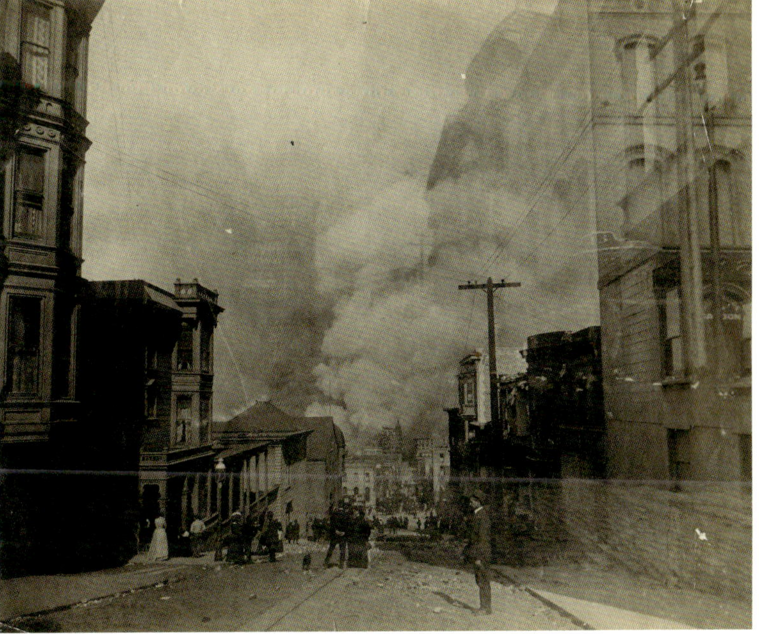

Fig. 13. Anonymous, View eastward from Nob Hill (Powell Street) down Sacramento Street during fire (double exposure), 1906

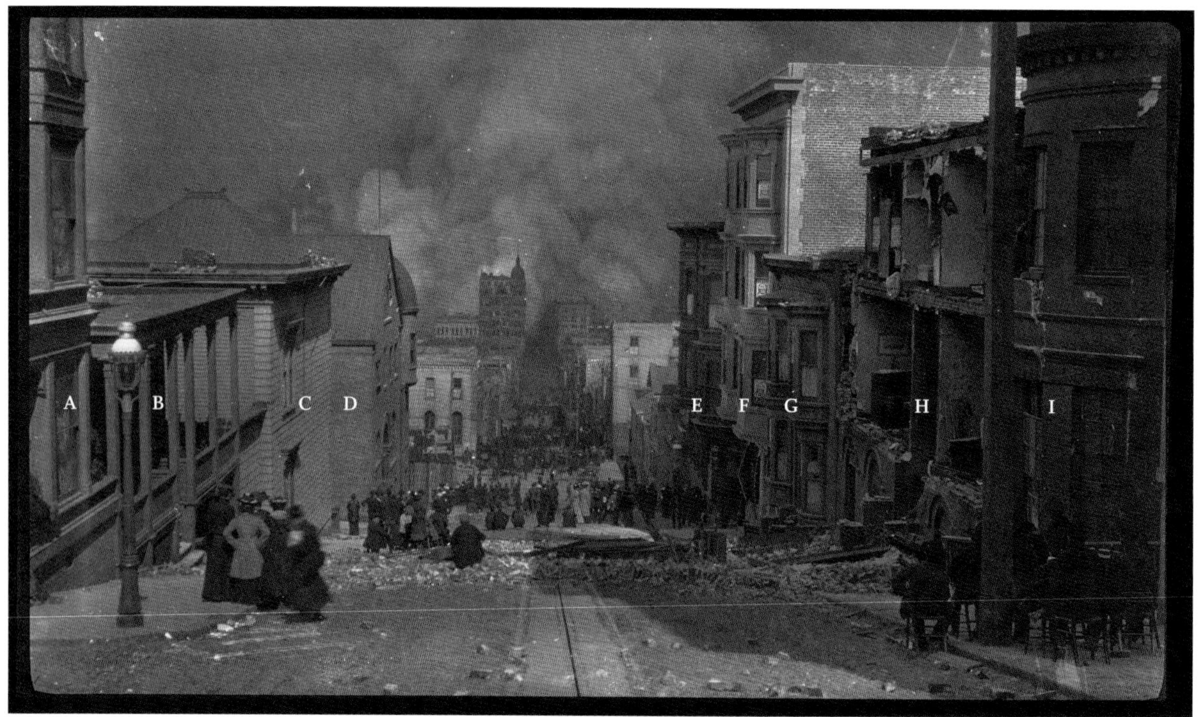

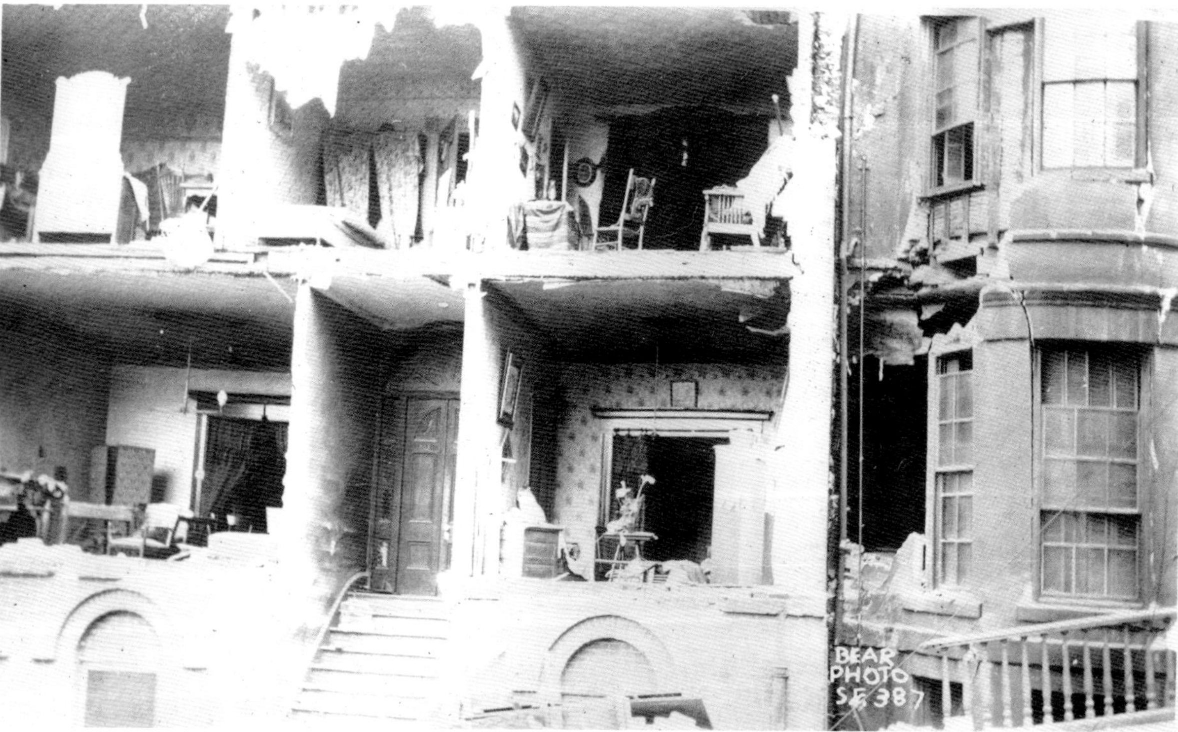

Fig. 14. Arnold Genthe, Downtown from Sacramento just east of Powell, San Francisco, 1906 (pl. 8). Annotated photograph indicating the property owners and residents of the buildings on this portion of Sacramento Street at the time of the photograph.

Fig. 15. Anonymous, 933 Sacramento Street, April 18, 1906

morning—a print he submitted to Ansel Adams's 1940 exhibition *A Pageant of Photography* (Palace of Fine Arts, San Francisco) is inscribed with the specific time of 9:00 a.m.—is refuted by the cast shadows, which indicate his presence at this location between 1:00 and 2:00 p.m., an hour or two after his Clay Street photographs, which he took shortly after noon.[11]

Genthe's extraordinary photographs are among the last visual records of a transitional multiethnic sector where Asian immigrants lived in close proximity to one of the city's most densely populated Black communities as well as to the white denizens of Lower Nob Hill, who cast wary eyes on the encroachment of Chinatown.[12] That the social structure of this neighborhood was deeply fractured well before the earthquake is most clearly illustrated by controversies surrounding the school board's 1894 plan to move the crowded Chinese School from Clay Street up to the former Commercial School building on Powell.[13] To appease residents, the board proposed a forty-five-foot staircase connecting the old and new schools so that the Chinese students could still enter and exit on Clay without setting foot on Powell. But even this concession was not enough for certain residents like John Kelly, an accountant who lived at 928 Sacramento Street and owned several rental homes; a petition circulated by Kelly and signed by 150 neighbors successfully killed the plan.

Although all of the real estate visible in Genthe's Sacramento Street photograph belonged to Caucasians, the block's demographic was relatively diverse (see fig. 14). Even so, the population was effectively segregated from one building to the next. Surveying the street's north side, on the left side of the photo, the first two homes belonged to the Kellys, who lived at number 928 (A) and who rented out rooms to newlyweds Lincoln Carr and Kitty Hackett. They rented the one-story home next door, number 926 (B), to Eugénie Martin, an unmarried dressmaker who had emigrated from France in 1885. The next two buildings, 22 Prospect Place (C) and 920 Sacramento Street (D), served as the Japanese Presbyterian Mission Home for boys, and the Presbyterian Occidental Mission Home for girls.

With permission from the director, Donaldina Cameron, Genthe had photographed the Presbyterian Occidental Mission Home for girls in the 1890s. Cameron recorded her own experience of the earthquake:

> The streets in the neighborhood of the Home were fast filling with refugees from the lower parts of town who sought safety or a better view of the fires from our high hillsides. Chinatown also had begun pouring forth its hordes and even in the midst of the general calamity the ever vigilant highbinder was on the watch for his prey. To have our Chinese girls on the streets among these crowds after nightfall was a danger too great to risk. As hastily, therefore, as we could work amidst the confusion and excitement, we gathered some bedding, a little food, and a few garments together and the last of the girls left the Mission Home.[14]

On the other side of the street were several rooming houses and apartment buildings catering to Japanese lodgers, including numbers 923–925 (E and F), which also housed a grocery store run by German immigrants; number 931 (G); and number 935 (I), previously the site of Yamatoya, the city's first Japanese restaurant.[15]

The most heavily damaged structure on this block was number 933 (H)—owned by the Swedish-born real estate maven Alexander Wilson—which had been the original location of the girls' mission home until 1894. The earthquake caused the brick façade of the second and third floors to collapse. A press photograph (fig. 15) provides a frontal view of the building, exposing its interior furnishings. On the 1905 Sanborn Fire Insurance Company map, number 933 was labeled as "tenements," which at the time implied inexpensive and crowded housing for menial laborers.[16] According to the 1905 *Crocker-Langley San Francisco Directory* and United States Census records, its occupants included laundry workers Howard Congo from Delaware (identified as Black in the 1910 Census) and

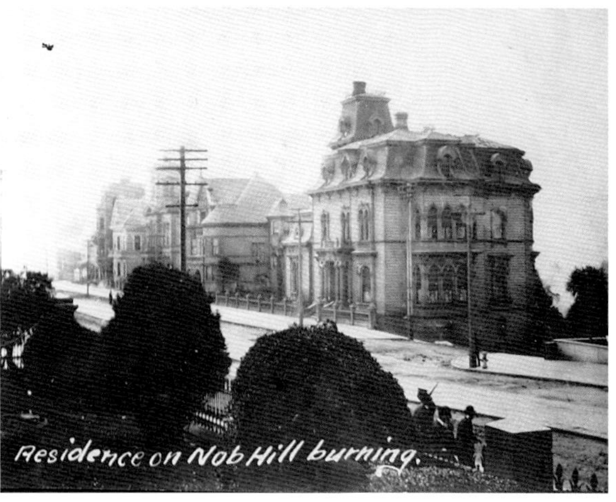

Fig. 16. Anonymous, Residence on Nob Hill burning (Tobin mansion), 1906

John Dean from Louisiana, waiter James Stewart, bellman Richard Woodson from South Carolina, and janitor Thomas Jackson from Georgia. Until the previous autumn, it had also been the home of Reverend Ezekiel Cottman, then pastor of the First African Methodist Episcopal Zion Church on Stockton Street.

Russian Hill

Genthe's return to Russian Hill on April 18 was a homecoming of sorts. At the turn of the twentieth century, he had resided in a boardinghouse at Taylor and Broadway Streets with Edward Swain, supervising architect of the Ferry Building, and playwright Porter Garnett. Perhaps Genthe meant to check on Garnett, who still lived there, and to photograph the sweeping city views that he knew so well. From just above his old street, he looked toward the San Francisco Bay to survey the grid of buildings that had survived the initial quake but which were now in the path of a relentless firestorm sweeping up from the waterfront (see pl. 9). Visible landmarks in this image include the flatiron building at Kearny and Jackson Streets, which was then under construction; the Hall of Justice on Portsmouth Square; the Merchants Exchange Building at California and Montgomery; the Mills Building at Montgomery and Bush; and Old Saint Mary's Cathedral at California and Grant Avenue. Genthe inscribed the verso of an early print "The Burning City / from Russian Hill / April 18th 1906 2 p.m."

Two nearly identical negatives, one marred by technical faults in processing (see cat. 10), also reveal the upper floor of Genthe's former home at 1532 Taylor Street, the fourth house from the left in the middle distance. It is not known whether Genthe encountered his old housemate Garnett, who was injured by a decorative Chinese platter that fell off the wall and sliced open his head but which caused him to jump out of bed and avoid being killed when the wall collapsed into the street.[17]

One block north, Genthe took three photographs on the crest of Russian Hill, where families had gathered to watch the fire (see pls. 10–12). Rising behind them in two of these views is the western spire of Nuestra Señora de Guadalupe Church at the corner of Broadway and Mason Streets, the doomed cornerstone of the neighborhood's large Mexican population.[18] "Evening brought many people to Russian Hill, the most lofty hill within the city proper," reported journalist Henry Lafler in *McClure's Magazine*. "And there those hundreds witnessed the most tremendous of earthly spectacles. The wind veered to the northeast, and lying in the cool, sweet grass on the sloping hill, free from personal danger, we watched the fire burn forty blocks in the city's heart."[19]

Nob Hill

With most of its houses built on bedrock, the tony neighborhood of Nob Hill was among the least shaken by the earthquake.[20] Genthe's walking tour of the wounded metropolis eventually led him here, where, he remarked, "up on the hill the wealthy were taking strangers into their homes."[21] Although he lived just three blocks below them, in an area where upper-middle-class apartment buildings had proliferated in the late nineteenth century, Genthe's rank in the social order was far removed from the lofty atmosphere of California Street. But as a frequent photographer of business leaders and debutantes—both in his portrait studio and at posh gatherings for the gossip columns—he was no stranger to high society. His pre-1906 client register reads like a who's who of prominent families: Crocker, de Young, Flood, Ghirardelli, Hearst, Hopkins, Huntington, and Tobin.[22]

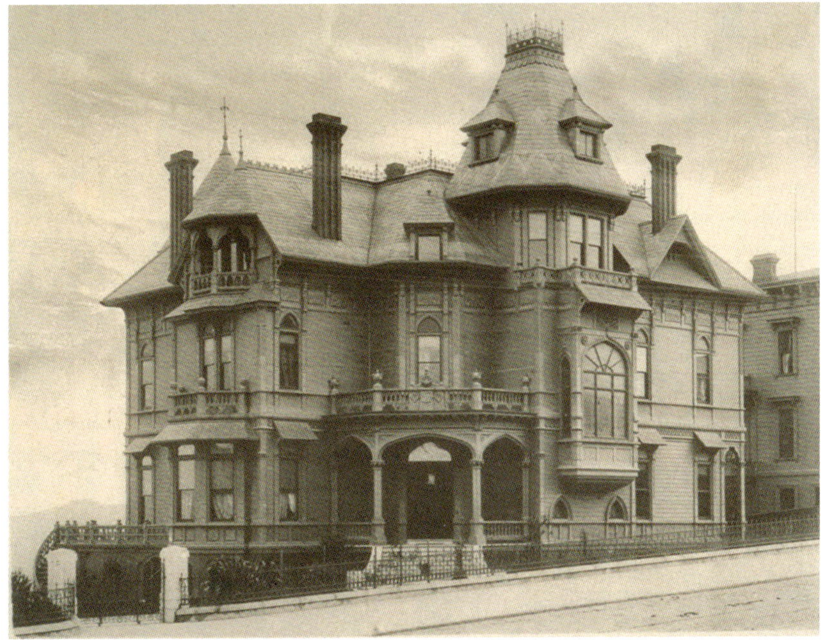

Fig. 17. Anonymous, Residence of Mr. Robert Sherwood, 1123 California Street, San Francisco, 1887

The Second Empire–style Tobin residence at the southeast corner of California and Taylor Streets (see fig. 16) was one of the oldest Nob Hill mansions. Its most striking feature was the five-story observation tower on its east side, which on a clear day offered the hill's most spectacular views of downtown. Genthe gained access to the tower and climbed the staircase to photograph the billowing smoke rising above the traumatized city, including an instant icon of the earthquake: the damaged dome of the recently completed City Hall (see pls. 13–14). One image reveals an ornate dormer window set into the mansard roof. Just beyond it, the large Bella Vista apartment building at the corner of Pine and Taylor Streets—more fully visible in a second unobstructed view—was a popular first-class residence for members of the social elite and a hotbed of Genthe's clientele. The Bella Vista, along with the rest of the surrounding apartment and hotel district, burned on April 19.[23]

Two doors from the Tobin residence, separated by the Towne mansion (see pl. 54; cats. 87, 89–90), stood the grand Victorian home of the Sherwood family (see fig. 17). Like its neighbors the structure seems to have survived the earthquake with limited damage, only to burn on the 19th of April. The back of the house featured a large balcony and semicircular staircase that provided Genthe a view overlooking the flat roofs of homes on Pine Street, framed by the Bella Vista to the east and the Colonial residential hotel to the west; between them, a partially collapsed wall revealed the interior bedroom of an apartment building (see pl. 15). That this balcony was accessible to passersby is suggested by nearly identical viewpoints in photographs by two other Nob Hill visitors on April 18. Clifford Mathewson, the Pacific Coast manager of the Diamond Rubber Company and an amateur shutterbug, photographed from this location with a handheld camera and the same format film as Genthe's (see fig. 18). Irvine also positioned herself on the Sherwood balcony with a 5-by-7-inch camera that she carted around in a baby carriage (see fig. 19). The haziness in Mathewson's view precludes establishing the time, but from the shadows cast in their respective photographs, it is clear that Irvine was here at midday, and Genthe followed within an hour.

Sutter Street

At some point during his afternoon travels, Genthe hastened back to Sutter Street when he realized that his home was in imminent danger of demolition. He had leased the three-story house since 1900 from architect Houghton Sawyer, paying out of pocket

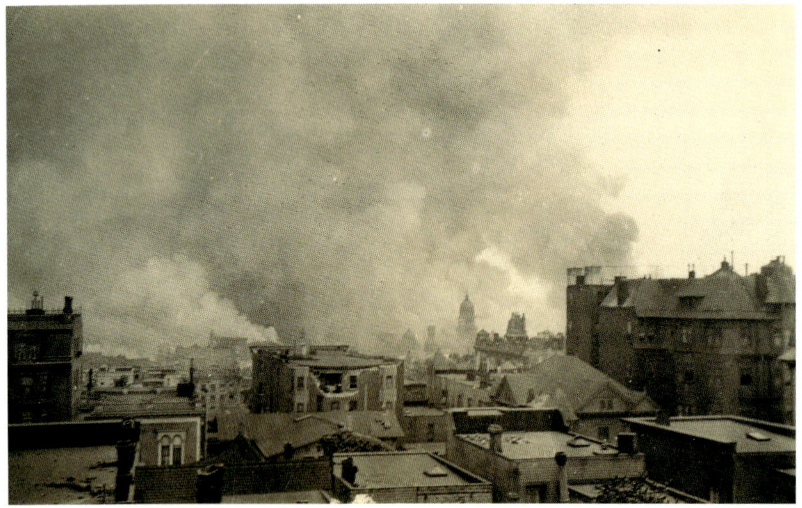

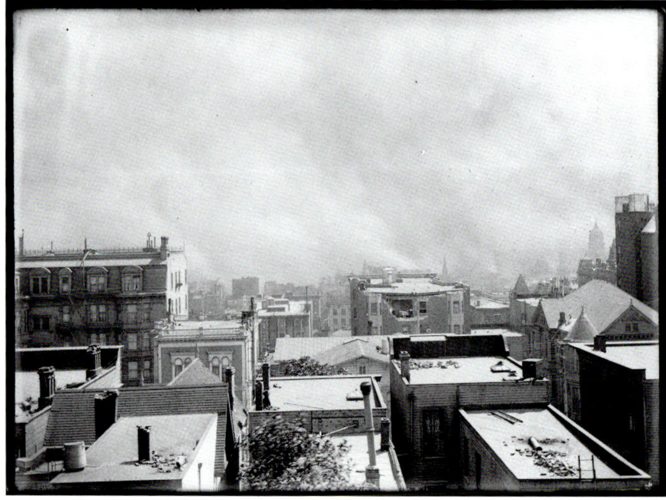

Fig. 18. Clifford Mathewson, View of the fire from the rear of the Sherwood mansion on California Street, 1906. Gelatin silver print, 3 ½ × 5 ⅞ in. (9 × 15 cm). California Historical Society, San Francisco

Fig. 19. Edith Irvine (American, 1884–1949), *Nob Hill Looking South Toward City Hall*, 1906. Scan from gelatin dry plate negative, 5 × 7 in. (127 × 178 mm). Brigham Young University Library, Special Collections, Provo, Utah

to add a fourth-story studio with a skylight, which he later expanded into the top floor of an adjacent house. Back at home he encountered a militiaman who had orders to clear the block. Genthe bribed him with whiskey but, once inside, only had time to pop open a special bottle of 1868 Riesling that had survived the earthquake when he was forced to evacuate at gunpoint. It was presumably at this time that he was able to remove his sitter register, now preserved at the Library of Congress. "From a safe distance," he recalled, "I watched with others the dynamiting of the block of our homes."[24] No photographic record remains of the building.

It was long assumed that Genthe took his two photographs showing the wing of the St. Francis Hotel under construction, the spire of the First Congregational Church, and the burning Palace Hotel from a window of his residence during this brief visit, but the angle of view does not correspond with this location (see pls. 16–17).[25] The most visible building in the foreground of the vertically oriented photograph is the Sutherland Hotel, which stood directly across from Genthe's house, at the southeast corner of Sutter and Jones Streets. The high elevation and oblique perspective overlooking the Sutherland's western side suggests that Genthe shot these photographs from an upper floor of the six-story Hotel Pleasanton, on the northwest corner of Sutter and Jones. Perhaps one of Genthe's clients residing there gave him access; according to his register, they included novelist Charles G. Norris, who later described the Pleasanton as "an old-fashioned comfortable caravansary in the heart of the city where a number of old ladies and old gentlemen, and a few large families, gossiped, thrived and had their being. It was an eminently respectable family hotel, the largest and most pretentious in the city."[26]

Hayes Valley

Five photographs from late in the day on April 18 (pls. 18–20, 23–24) place Genthe on the edge of the fire zone in the working-class Hayes Valley neighborhood of the Western Addition district. The proximity of the flames is suggested by the brisk movement of people in two views of Golden Gate Avenue between Octavia and Gough Streets, opposite Jefferson Square. With sunset at 6:47 p.m., their long shadows indicate an early evening time frame between approximately five and six, when firefighters were working nearby to stop the progress of the destructive "Ham and Eggs Fire," reportedly sparked by a family cooking with a damaged chimney. The earthquake had caused foundation failure in several wooden-frame homes on this block. Number 817, which can be seen at the left in plates 23 and 24, appears to have survived the earthquake in sound condition; its front door is propped open by a chair, and in one view a maid sits on the top step, contemplating the pandemonium. Mary E. Coulter shared the house with commercial tenants Walter Faust and Louis Koesel Jr., whose trunk and valise business, carried on after the disaster, was undoubtedly stimulated by the upsurge of displaced San Franciscans. Next door, at number 819, lived the recently widowed Emily Flood and her two sons Henry and Robert. Their home leans precariously at an eighty-degree angle onto number 821, which included apartments occupied by foundry worker Daniel Dougherty and salesman Homer Mumford. Their house sunk a half story into the ground, detaching it from the front staircase, left in its original position.

"The fire came up to the back doors of the houses on Golden Gate avenue, between Gough and Octavia streets," reported insurance agent Clinton Hutchins. "The great fight was made there."[27] Attorney Frank Hittell lived in the neighborhood and put himself in the middle of the increasingly tense working relationship between the firefighters and soldiers. "I was at the corner of Gough Street and Golden Gate Avenue when a fireman approached a crowd of men who were being kept back by the military, and asked for volunteers. So thoroughly cowed were the citizens by the soldiers that no one responded, although I knew that every man of them was willing to help."[28] Hittell succeeded in corralling a group of men but struggled to convince the soldiers to let them through. Without their assistance, he wrote, "these exhausted firemen could never have stopped the westward advance of the flames from Gough and Golden Gate, and the Western Addition would have been destroyed by fire."[29]

The first of three photographs taken by Genthe one block east, at Golden Gate Avenue and Franklin Street, documents a large crowd being held back by mounted soldiers. He then moved closer to the action. His image captured at Franklin and McAllister Streets (pl. 19) shows him being kept back by a policeman standing in the extreme right foreground. The helmet of the fireman facing the camera with one hand on the engine identifies him as a member of Company 15, which was based on California Street near Lafayette Park. The partially visible pattern of destruction around Franklin and McAllister, including a massive flaming cupola propelled into the center of the intersection, suggests that an explosion has taken place, presumably an intentional detonation to create a firebreak. Captain William Carew of Truck Company 7 reported "considerable dynamiting was done in the vicinity of Franklin and Van Ness" at this time,[30] and Captain Stephen D. Russell of Engine Company 27 left an account of the firefight that took place here:

> Chief Maxwell ordered us to locate a hydrant in the vicinity of Golden Gate Ave. and Van Ness; the fire at this time was burning from Grove St., north, and the nearest hydrant of service was at Eddy and Franklin streets, five blocks distant. The engine was connected at this point, and with the aid of Engine No. 15, we doubled up, using a hose seven hundred feet long reaching to Grove and Franklin streets, we were forced to abandon this position, however, owing to rapid progress of the fire, and the civil authorities who were dynamiting in this district. The final stand was made at Golden Gate Ave., and with the aid of Engine No. 15, we saved the two blocks on the North side of Golden Gate Ave., from Van Ness to Gough.[31]

Ultimately lost to the flames were all of the structures visible in these photographs (pls. 18–20), including the handsome Kronenberg Building, designed in Beaux-Arts style by David Salfield and Hermann Kohlberg, best known for their flatiron Sentinel building in North Beach. Commissioned by Frederick Kronenberg, a German expatriate who owned a successful brewery in the city, the Kronenberg Building housed street-level stores with sixteen apartments above, occupied mainly by skilled laborers and

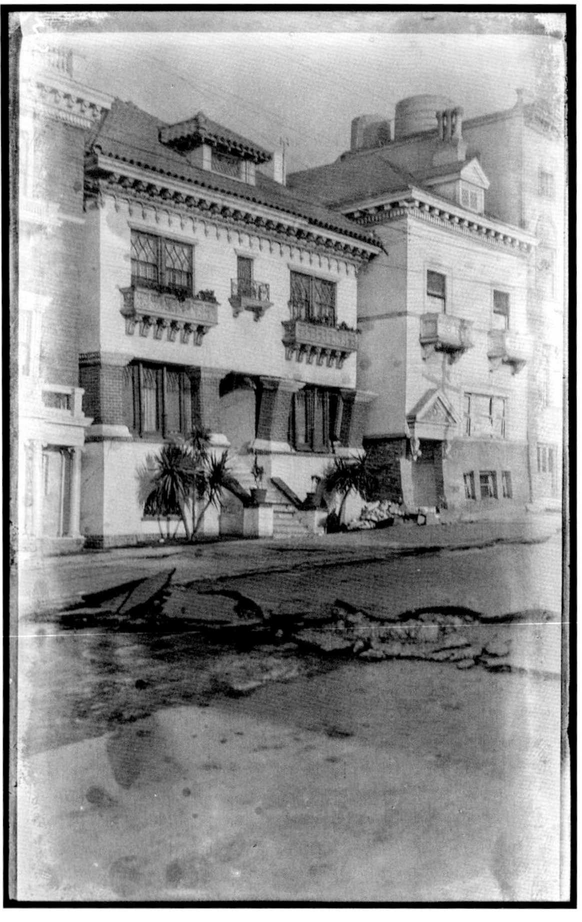

Fig. 20. Arnold Genthe, Musto house, Van Ness Avenue, San Francisco, 1906 (cat. 27)

office workers.[32] The National Horseshoeing Company across the street, at Franklin and Locust Avenue (renamed Redwood Street in 1910–1911), is visible in the left foreground of Genthe's horizontally oriented photograph (pl. 20). Servicing both trotters and roadsters, the company was the site of a different kind of drama little more than two weeks before the earthquake, when protesters attacked the nonunion shop for remaining open during a strike. The shop's manager, brandishing a revolver, kept the mob at bay until the police could dispel them.

After April 18

Genthe continued to photograph around the city during the three days of the fire and for several weeks and perhaps months afterward, but the further out the timeline extends, the more difficult it is to establish a precise chronology. Only a handful of vintage prints bear Genthe's own inscriptions specifying locations and dates, and these have proven unreliable in the face of external evidence. On the afternoon of the 19th, he photographed the damaged residence of Guido and Romilda Musto at 2312 Van Ness Avenue, between Vallejo and Green Streets (see fig. 20). The young, well-to-do couple were patrons of the arts and, like Genthe, in attendance at the opening night of San Francisco's Grand Opera House on April 17. Next to their home, at 2310 Van Ness, was an unoccupied house being advertised for sale, and beyond it stood the headquarters of the Viavi Company at numbers 2304–2306–2308, partially visible at the right edge of Genthe's photograph. A patent medicine firm founded by entrepreneurial brothers Harland and Herbert Law, Viavi sold fraudulent treatments and medications marketed particularly to women. Midday on Friday the 20th, as exhausted firefighters were making significant progress and could envision an end to the conflagration, army officials made the reckless decision to blow up the Viavi Building, failing to consider that flammable chemicals stored inside would ignite a firestorm throughout the neighborhood. The wind drove northward to Russian Hill, ultimately burning another fifty blocks.[33]

Genthe also photographed smoke and ruins very close to this location, at the intersection of Van Ness and Pacific Avenues (see pls. 21–22), inscribing variants with conflicting dates. On the verso of the horizontal print he wrote "Van Ness Avenue near Green Street / April 20th," and on the vertical print, "The last day of the fire," which would have been April 21. These are the darkest of Genthe's early images of the disaster, revealing the apocalyptic horror of the fire's destruction. Darker still is an image of a downtown scene with a charred corpse in the middle of Post Street (fig. 52), dated April 20 and labeled "One of the victims of the fire." This is likely the same man described in police captain Thomas Duke's account: "The first looter was caught while he was making an attempt to burglarize Shreve's jewelry store at Post and Grant Avenue.

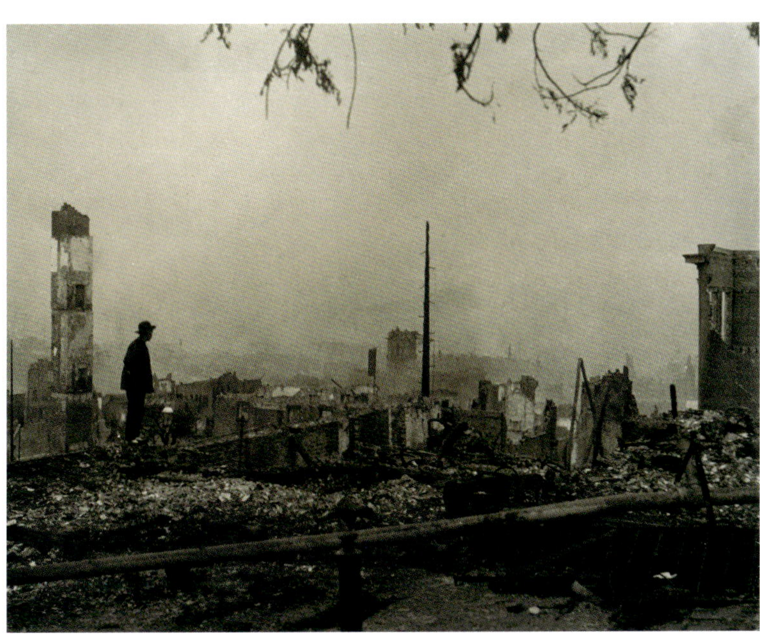

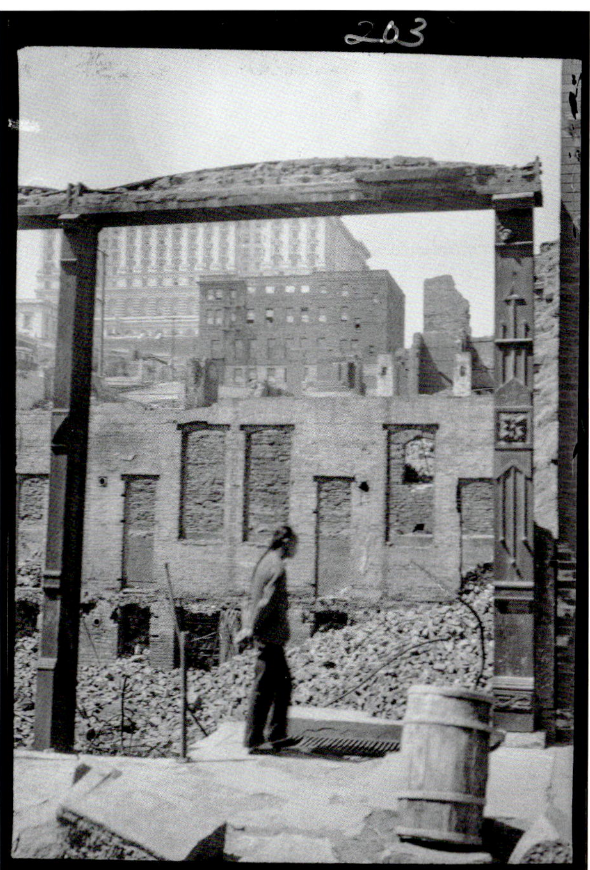

Fig. 21. Arnold Genthe, *The Last of Chinatown*, or *On the Ruins* (Sacramento and Powell Streets), 1906. Gelatin silver print, $7\frac{15}{16} \times 9\frac{15}{16}$ in. (20.2 × 25.2 cm). Fine Arts Museums of San Francisco, Museum collection, Z2003.2

Fig. 22. Arnold Genthe, *After the Fire*, 1906. Interpositive from cellulose nitrate negative, 5 × 4 in. (127 × 101.6 mm) (approx.). Arnold Genthe Collection, Prints and Photographs Division, Library of Congress, Washington, D.C.

He was turned over to a soldier who killed him and left his body to be consumed by the fire."[34] Within the full spectrum of Genthe's earthquake imagery, which spans the romantic pictorialism of *Steps That Lead to Nowhere (After the Fire)* (fig. 51) and the straight reportage of an image of the Linda Vista Apartments reduced to a pile of twisted metal and rubble (pl. 41), this image's unflinching human carnage makes it a shocking outlier.

"The big fire has obliterated Chinatown from San Francisco forever." So began a brief story reported by the Associated Press on the afternoon of April 23. "Mayor Schmitz informed Chief of Police Dinan tonight that all of the Chinese now in the city would be collected and placed in and near Fontana's warehouse, near Fort Mason, and that the new Chinatown would be located at Hunter's Point." The scapegoating of the Chinese for causing the fire had begun, and with it a push to relocate Chinatown to the southern shore of the San Francisco Bay. With these current events in mind, Genthe composed two photographs evoking conventional art-historical prototypes of the figure among classical ruins: *The Last of Chinatown*, or *On the Ruins* (fig. 21), and *After the Fire* (fig. 22). The former, dated April 23 in Genthe's book *Pictures of Old Chinatown* (1908), depicts a Chinese man posing on a foundation diagonally across from the Fairmont Hotel (on the southeast corner of Sacramento and Powell Streets) and mere steps from the site of Genthe's Sacramento Street view taken five days earlier. The streetlamp rising to the right of the figure is the same lamp on the corner of Sacramento and Miles Place in Genthe's April 18 photograph, and the tall ruined structure at the far right is a recently completed apartment building at 100/102 Prospect Place. Similarly, for *After the Fire* Genthe placed a Chinese man among

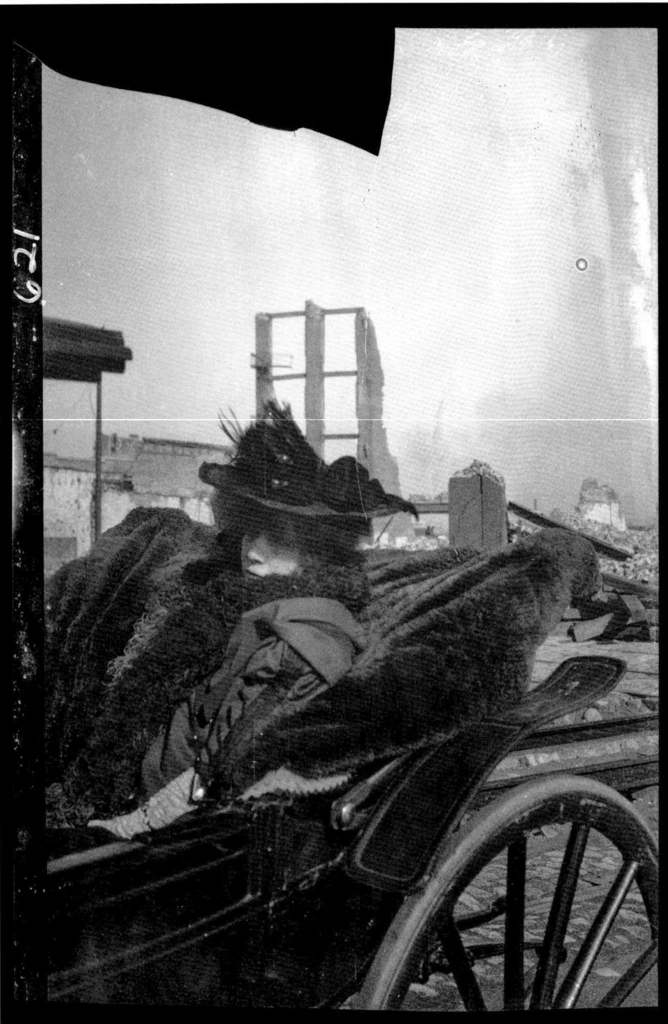

Fig. 23. Arnold Genthe, Untitled (Sarah Bernhardt in carriage in front of the ruins of City Hall), 1906. Interpositive from cellulose nitrate negative, 5 × 4 in. (127 × 101.6 mm) (approx.). Arnold Genthe Collection, Prints and Photographs Division, Library of Congress, Washington, D.C.

ruins in the vicinity of Dupont and Clay Streets with the Fairmont in the distance. At the time he created these photographs, Genthe knew that he was in possession of an important archive of pre-earthquake views of Chinatown and perhaps already had a plan in mind to publish them in book form.

Other images can be securely placed between late April and the middle of May. This includes two photographs of crowds on Fillmore and Bush Streets, around Franklin Hall (pls. 80–81), where a banner announces an April 23 meeting of labor leaders. A photograph of mounted officials near demolition work in the vicinity of the Emporium on Market Street (pl. 66) has been mistaken for an April 18 scene[35] but likely occurred on the 25th, when dynamiting was carried out at this location. Genthe's panorama of the devastated area around his old neighborhood of Pine, Bush, and Sutter (pl. 37), in a print now held at the Bancroft Library at University of California, Berkeley, is inscribed "The City 8 days after the fire. From Nob Hill looking towards the City Hall." This photograph perhaps dates from April 30, the day this item appeared in the *San Francisco Examiner*'s society column:

> Dr. Arnold Genthe has taken some excellent photographs of our poor distracted-looking city. I met him the other day and he, cheerful under the circumstances, said that he had lost all of his plates, his films, his library—in fact, every treasure that he possessed in the world. He, too, like many other splendid men, is prepared to commence all over again.[36]

A photograph of two officials from Wells Fargo Nevada National Bank posing in front of a vault at the bank's burned Pine and Montgomery office (cat. 72) likely dates from May 16, when the red-hot bricks had sufficiently cooled to allow its opening.

Several photographs of Sarah Bernhardt's heavily publicized visit to the city—in order to appear in a benefit performance for earthquake relief at Berkeley's Greek Theatre—can be dated to May 14–17, during the first of her four Farewell American tours (see fig. 23; p. 175). In his autobiography, Genthe records amusement at the diva's melodramatic cablegram to her son, which exaggerated the perils of her excursion: "Have just completed a tour through the ruins of this once so beautiful city. Sights are indescribable. In many sections the fire is still burning, walls collapsing dangerously near us. Thank God I'm safe." "The truth," Genthe noted, "was that at no time were we within a quarter of a mile of the danger zone . . . but such was the power of the divine Sarah's imagination that she projected herself, not as a mere spectator but as a sufferer into the very heart of the disaster."[37] Genthe quotes a letter from Bernhardt sent shortly after her 1906 visit in which she acknowledges his terrible loss while proffering a ray of hope. "You still have your youth and your bravery," she closes. "Life opens before you, fortune takes you by the arm. Go on, have courage, my young friend. I feel, I divine, that everything will go your way."[38]

Bernhardt's prediction came true. While Genthe was in the process of re-establishing his studio on Clay Street near Presidio Avenue, and overseeing the completion of his bungalow in Carmel-by-the-Sea, a small town south of San Francisco, he continued to pour energy into documenting the aftermath of the disaster with his No. 3A Folding Pocket Kodak (see Binder, "Freezing Fire: Arnold Genthe and His Camera," this volume). His images of the shattered remains of the city's architectural splendors emphasized residential hotels and the homes of prominent San Franciscans, including the entrance to the Towne mansion, later dubbed the "Portals of the Past" (see pl. 54). Genthe was also particularly drawn to the monumental wreckage of City Hall (see pls. 47–53) as well as the charred shell of Grace Church (now Grace Cathedral) on Nob Hill (see pls. 38–39), reminiscent of picturesque ruins of medieval churches. At the same time, he captured scenes of survivors cooking in the streets on makeshift stoves (see pls. 61, 79), queueing for relief supplies (see pls. 58, 67–69, 76), and occupying relief camps set up around the city (see pls. 67–79). Unlike the many commercial photographers who rushed to cash in on the demand for earthquake and fire imagery, Genthe chose not to profit from the disaster, printing perhaps two dozen of his approximately 170 negatives in relatively small numbers, and rarely exhibiting or publishing them. Although he went on to earn his fame and fortune in New York in the genres of celebrity portraiture, fashion, and the artistic nude, his extensive photographic records of San Francisco's Chinatown before 1906 and of a modern American metropolis's devastating transformation into a postapocalyptic disaster area endure as his strongest bodies of work.

An African American Presence

REVEALED IN ARNOLD GENTHE'S 1906 EARTHQUAKE AND FIRE PHOTOGRAPHS

Rodger C. Birt

DURING THE YEARS HE WORKED IN SAN FRANCISCO, Arnold Genthe rarely made photographs that included African American subjects. The few extant examples are from negatives he exposed in the aftermath of the April 1906 earthquake (see figs. 24, 27–28; pls. 5, 72). These images are especially significant because they preserve a palpable Black presence in this important body of work. They are also notable for the ways they differ from Genthe's photographs of Chinese San Franciscans—another racialized group—in the city's Chinatown. In these latter images, the photographer employed a Pictorialist and romanticist approach, intentionally erasing visual evidence that reflected the neighborhood's quotidian reality.[1] Instead he rendered Chinatown as if it were an almost foreign place, describing it as a "bit of the orient [*sic*]" and "a city within a city."[2] In contrast, Genthe did not manipulate his photographs of African Americans, imparting to them a blunt photojournalistic character that makes them particularly useful portals into the complicated history of the city's Black community.

In 1906, in San Francisco, there was no Black member of the Board of Supervisors; no Black elected or appointed public official of any kind; no Black medical doctor on a city board or health agency; no Black member on an art or a cultural commission; no Black member of the Bar Association; no Black bank officer; no Black member of any labor union; no Black police officer; no Black firefighter. These absences present one side of a demeaning social equation, the facts of Black exclusion and white supremacy in the city (and throughout the United States) in the early years of the twentieth century. The other side of that equation expresses Black agency, the decades-long effort to live, even prosper, in a race-based social structure. Despite heavy odds against them, Black San Franciscans created a community and successfully maintained their own society, which paralleled—and at times intersected with—the city's white power structures.[3]

The presence of people of African descent in California is as old as the idea of California itself. Listed as *Négro*, *Mulatto*, and *Mestizo*, African people and people of mixed-race backgrounds traveled with European explorers and took part in colony building throughout the Americas. In 1776 they comprised more than a quarter of the members of the Juan Bautista de Anza expedition, which traveled from Mexico to San Francisco Bay to begin the construction of Mission Dolores and the Presidio.[4] Over the following decades, Black individuals of note added their stories to the city's narrative and lore: they include William Alexander Leidesdorff Jr., first hotel operator and US Vice Consul

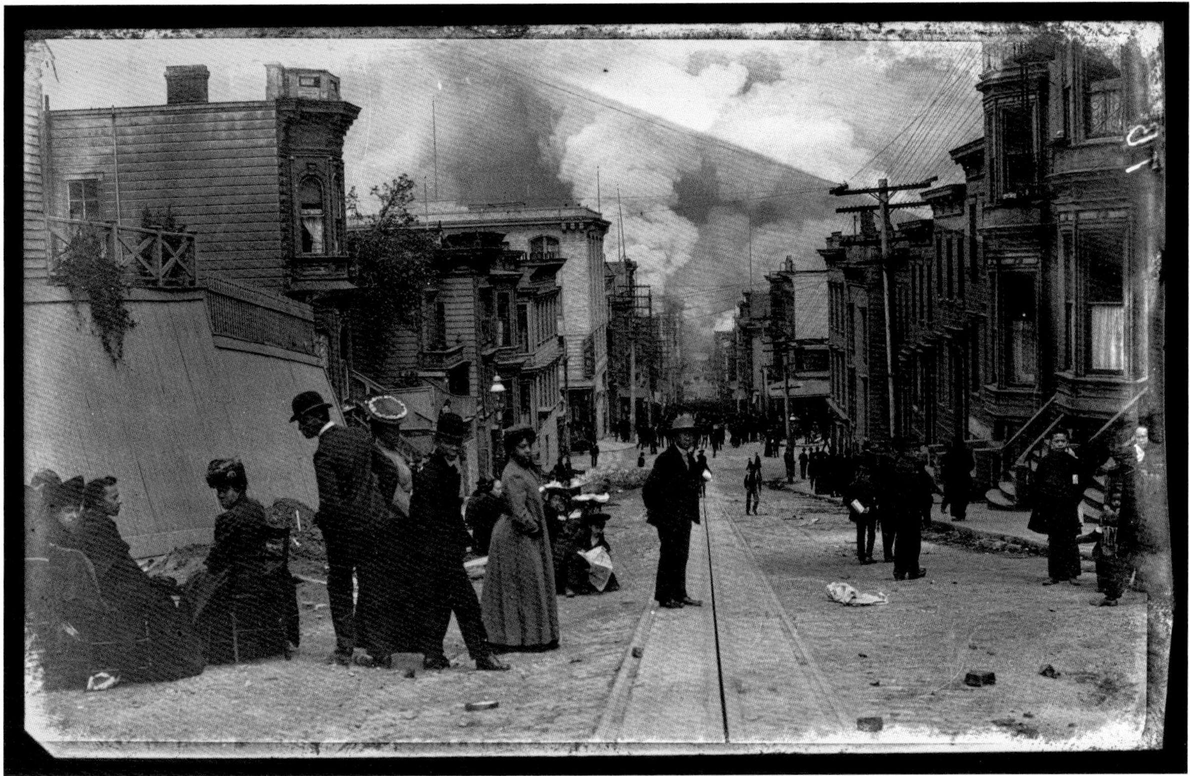

Fig. 24. Arnold Genthe, Clay west of Stockton, San Francisco, 1906 (pl. 6)

to Mexico; Archy Lee, the bondsman who demanded freedom; Mary Ellen Pleasant, contributor to abolitionist causes on the East Coast; Mifflin Wistar Gibbs, wealthy entrepreneur and statesman; and William T. Shorey, Bay Area steamboat captain. Along with these well-known figures were unnamed hundreds who labored unnoticed. They mined in California and Nevada; held conventions where they called for access to the ballot, participated in the judicial system, and demanded other civil rights; built churches; established fraternal organizations and Masonic lodges; created and operated a wide array of businesses; and, in effect, did what all the other migrants to the West Coast sought to do—make new lives for themselves and their families.

By the time the Black San Franciscans in the 1906 photographs found themselves in front of Genthe's camera, they indeed "knew their place." African Americans had studied San Francisco for a long time.[5] Half of all Black migrants to California after the American military conquest in 1848 came from the New England, Middle Atlantic, and Midwestern states. This would continue to be the pattern of migration through the Gold Rush and after. With the end of the Civil War, some Southern freedpeople joined the flow of immigrants along with a trickle of foreign-born Black people. Historian Douglas Henry Daniels said about the latter, "Blacks with Spanish Portuguese, French, British, and other backgrounds imparted a cosmopolitan quality to Afro-San Francisco."[6] Although this international element was an often-commented-on aspect of the city's Black community, Protestant and Northern Black pioneers shaped the community's dominant social and political characteristics. With patriotic fervor, they stressed their American identity. Their ancestors had suffered through three centuries marked as the "other," and they had been declared an absolute contradiction of what a "real American" was or ever could be. Black men disputed their assigned place in a social hierarchy that located them near the bottom and in which only Black females ranked lower. In a social construct that

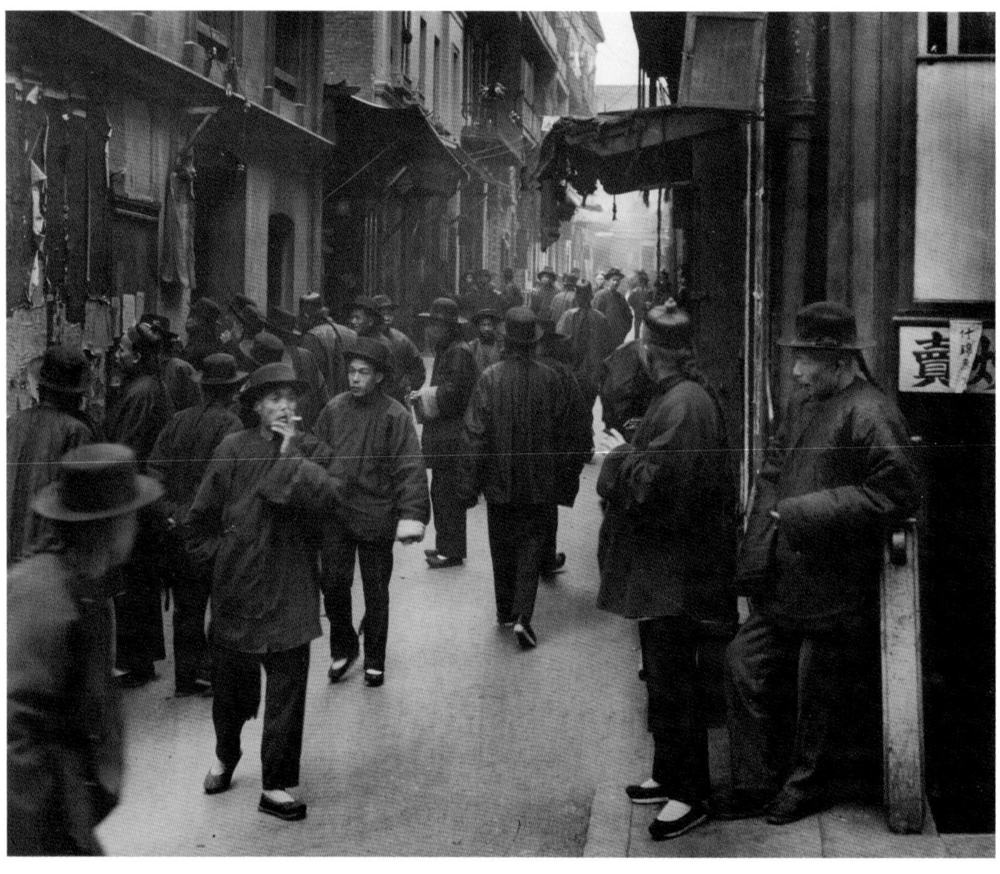

Fig. 25. Arnold Genthe, *Street of the Gamblers* (Ross Alley), 1898. Gelatin silver print, 10 ⅝ × 12 ¹³⁄₁₆ in. (27 × 32.6 cm). Fine Arts Museums of San Francisco, Museum purchase, James D. Phelan Bequest Fund, 1943.408.12. This photograph was printed alongside Ho Yow's essay "The Chinese Question."

positioned native-born white men at the top, American-born Black men asserted that they deserved the same honor as their white male counterparts. Black leaders acknowledged the demand for full equality would have to be fought one battle at a time, but nothing less than full equality was the Black community's shared goal.

Navigating the contested and treacherous currents in American public life was challenging. Black San Franciscans' response to the "Chinese question" illustrates the kind of social dilemma they often confronted. To prove their rigorous "Americanness," Black citizens often joined in the discrimination against the city's Chinese residents. This meant they accepted the anti-Chinese attitudes prevalent among white San Franciscans. The same hate-filled rhetoric found in the white press appeared in African American journals. In an article in a prominent Black newspaper, the writer favorably contrasted Black "American ideas, Christian religion, and family [bonds]" to supposed Chinese "filthy habits, idolatrous worship, and cortezan [*sic*] companions."[7] It should be noted that the readers of contemporary Chinese-language publications encountered the same "Black beast and predator" regularly featured in white popular media.[8] Especially curious is the way that real social conditions contradicted these presumed journalistic facts: Asian American and Black people lived side by side in San Francisco and often spent time together in the more private spaces of the city.[9] Telegraph Hill was an example of this. Until the fire of 1906 destroyed everything there, the neighborhood was the city's most ethnically variegated district, with a population of Asian, Black, Hispanic, Native American, and white San Franciscans.

Genthe knew San Francisco's multiracial districts and immigrant neighborhoods well, and he photographed in them often. Unlike the city's residents of color, Genthe was not conscribed to particular neighborhoods. As a white Euro-American male, he enjoyed a physical latitude that allowed him to move freely among the city's various districts. Genthe embodied the mid-nineteenth-century French cultural construct of the *flâneur*, whom the poet Charles Baudelaire called "a man of the crowd." Of the *flâneur*, he wrote:

> The crowd is his element . . . his passion and his profession are to become one flesh with the crowd. For the perfect *flâneur*, for the passionate spectator, it is an immense joy to set up house in the heart of the multitude . . . in the midst of the fugitive and the infinite. . . . We might liken him to a mirror . . . or to a kaleidoscope gifted with consciousness, responding to each of its movements and reproducing the multiplicity of life and the flickering grace of all the elements of life.[10]

With his cameras in hand, Genthe comfortably wandered the streets and passages of both Chinatown and Telegraph Hill. For most Euro-Americans, these districts appeared as mysterious, almost unknowable zones, a vast terra incognita, a fascinating mixture of the exotic and the sensual. There Black performers like Bert Williams and George Walker were creating a modern, hybrid expression of song and dance, which was beginning to capture the imagination of the American public.[11] And after dusk the whispered calls of young prostitutes issued forth from their "cribs."

Genthe's photographs from these journeys are some of the best any photographer made of these districts at the end of the nineteenth century. In 1901 nine of his Chinatown photographs appeared in the *Overland Monthly*, a popular journal published in San Francisco, as illustrations for an article by Ho Yow, the Chinese government's consul general assigned to San Francisco (see fig. 25). In the essay, Ho Yow makes a case for ending anti-Chinese racism, noting the positive value of having low-paid Chinese workers "[in] manual, unskilled occupations."[12] Here Genthe's descriptively rich photographs are used to illustrate a political and economic argument that called for replacing racial antipathy with sensible market-based policies. However, despite being filled with clever visual notations, his images remain hauntingly mute, appearing agenda free. Given this, as well as the photographer's visual acuity, an editor or writer could easily project their own perspectives onto his work.

This is what happened with John O'Hara Cosgrave, editor of the locally published journal *The Wave*. After seeing Genthe's photographs of Telegraph Hill, Cosgrave hired novelist Frank Norris to develop a human-interest article about life on the hill to accompany the images. Norris found both the photographs and the place itself disturbing, especially the multiracial children he encountered there.[13] Norris and his editor fashioned Genthe's photographs of Telegraph Hill into a composite geography where Norris, a highly esteemed man of letters, could express his xenophobic and racist prejudices (see fig. 26). Missing in these two articles and in other publications where Genthe's photographs appear are articulations of the human actors themselves: they are written about, spoken of, but never truly seen. Without their voices, we have the same deafening incompleteness that bedevils much of the story Euro-Americans tell themselves and broadcast to the wider human community.

Genthe's images illustrate the need for a more comprehensive history of visual culture in America. We have to find the images and visual records that portray nonwhite Americans in full—ones in which Asian, Black, Hispanic, and Native American people appear as more than characters in a fable or shadowy apparitions in a national mythology manufactured by the white majority. Where, in other words, are the images whose subjects are free from the denigration of the white gaze? I suggest that the most likely sources of these images are the popular photographic practices of any era. It is in the mid-nineteenth-century daguerreotypes and ambrotypes or the later, post–Civil War prints on paper, produced in inexpensive, ubiquitous photography studios (there were more than seventy in San Francisco in 1900) that we are likely to discover the faces and traces of fellow Americans who have largely been forgotten or dismissed from the national narrative.[14]

Genthe opened his first photography studio in San Francisco in 1897. By 1906 his clientele included some of San Francisco's wealthiest citizens. However, there is no record of Genthe photographing Chinese or African American sitters. What we have are his photographs from the earthquake's aftermath.

Jolted awake shortly after 5 a.m. on the morning of April 18, Genthe calmly assayed the damage his studio and living quarters had sustained. Then, after selecting what he called "earthquake attire"—a khaki riding outfit—he walked to the St. Francis Hotel, where he enjoyed a free breakfast with friends. After breakfast he determined that he would begin photographing the earthquake-wracked city. Returning home and discovering his camera equipment was too damaged to be of any use, he made his way to Montgomery Street and George Kahn's photography supplies shop. Kahn gave him what Genthe described as a "3A Kodak Special."[15] The Kodak 3A was a highly regarded camera among photojournalists. Its size and relatively fast lens made it ideal for working in ambient light and capturing the kind of images Genthe wanted. Following the initial temblor were severe aftershocks throughout the day. Just before noon, the plumes of flames from scattered fires, especially in areas south of Market Street, were growing in intensity, and about to merge into one vast conflagration.

Genthe's voracious eye benefited from his having a camera better suited for working in a photojournalistic mode than those available to him in the 1890s, before he abandoned the challenges of the streets for the domestic intimacy of his studio. The extant negatives that survive exhibit his speedily regained mastery of a genre he had not worked in for more than five years. In addition to Genthe, dozens of other photographers were also photographing what would ultimately become one of the greatest urban disasters of the twentieth century.[16] However, it is one of Genthe's photographs (pl. 8) that is arguably the most celebrated of all the "fire and smoke" photographs; it is certainly the most often reproduced. About this photograph, he wrote:

> There is particularly the one scene that I recorded the morning of the first day of the fire (on Sacramento Street, looking toward the Bay) which shows, in a pictorially effective composition, the results of the earthquake, the beginning of the fire and the attitude of the people. On the right is a house, the front of which had collapsed into the street. The occupants are sitting on chairs calmly watching the approach of the fire. Groups of people are standing in the street, motionless, gazing at the clouds of smoke. When the fire crept up close, they would just move up a block.[17]

Although Genthe said he took the photograph before noon, "on the morning of the first day," the well-documented timeline of the fire's block-by-block progression suggests that the actual time of the photograph is midafternoon.[18] Further supporting this, within the print there is a relationship between the shadows cast by the few remaining standing buildings on the south side of Sacramento Street and the street's East-West axis. When pieced together, the visual data and the fire's historical reconstructions establish that it would have had to be past midday when Genthe exposed the negative. The resulting print, along with two others (fig. 24; pl. 5), comprise a group of three. The photograph he predicted would "be of lasting interest" is the final exposure in the sequence.

As the downtown fire grew in intensity and jumped Market Street, large crowds of curious onlookers began to gather on the several streets threading their way across Nob Hill, where they were mesmerized by an unobstructed view of the fire. On Clay Street, Genthe initially photographed a crowded streetscape: four African American men and women and a group of seated people wearing identical hats on the north side of the street (pl. 5). Genthe positioned the camera so that the negative would be vertically oriented. The photographer has caught his subjects' attention, but they show no discomfort. In fact, they mirror his gaze. After exposing the film, he moved up the hill several feet and readied the camera to make another exposure. This time he framed the composition horizontally. The resulting view (fig. 24) is more expansive: to the left of the original group of four sit two additional women; the seated group wearing the identical hats seen in the first print, turn out to be young Asian schoolgirls; an adult Asian man now occupies the center of the composition; and there are a number of people, including a young Asian woman, now visible on the street's south side. With only a few exceptions, they all regard Genthe. This second exposure locks them together on the film's emulsified surface. The photographer is also implicated through "taking" the photograph. He has become one with the crowd, wedded to his fellow mortals.

After making that second exposure, Genthe broke away and climbed farther up Clay Street. At the higher elevation on Sacramento Street, he made the third and final exposure. Having gotten what he had hoped for—expressive visual documents of the first fire day's events—Genthe could move on. There was more to see, more for him to photograph. He would photograph for "several weeks," he tells us, before his ardor cooled. Once the fires were brought under control, and even before the last embers were finally put out, a new phase of the earthquake's aftermath began. Municipal authorities, federal military forces, and local community organizations all began to provide the basic necessities to distressed citizens. Throughout the city temporary relief camps sprang up in parks, in empty lots, and anywhere a tent could fit. It is in one of these hastily erected sheltering places that Genthe found two young African American subjects. These photographs (figs. 27–28) very likely date from the end of April or early May. By then the universal benevolence born out of shared calamity had given way to familiar, less charitable patterns of behavior. Chinese citizens were moved into segregated camps, while a growing clamor simultaneously arose in favor of not rebuilding Chinatown. If Chinatown were to be resurrected, then the demand was to build it elsewhere.

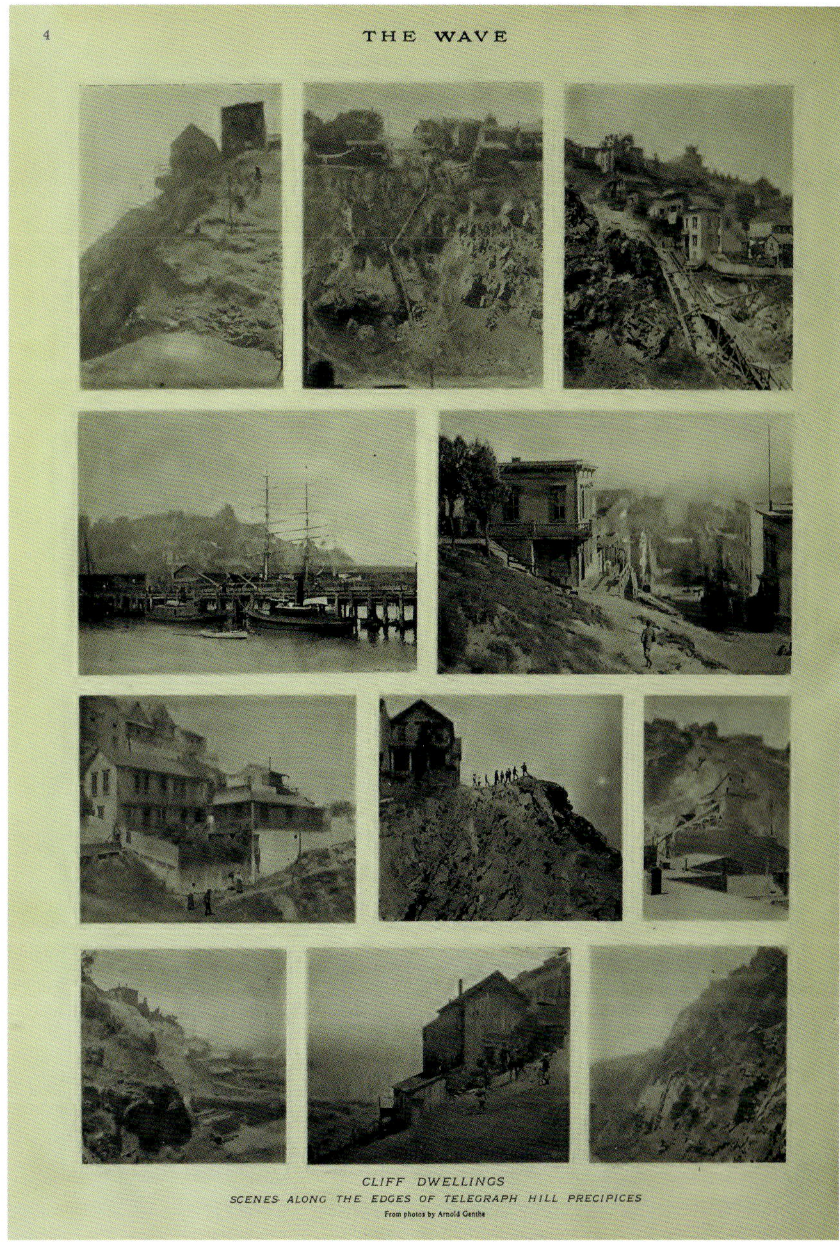
4

THE WAVE

CLIFF DWELLINGS

SCENES ALONG THE EDGES OF TELEGRAPH HILL PRECIPICES

From photos by Arnold Genthe

Fig. 26. "Cliff Dwellers" by Arnold Genthe, published in *The Wave*, May 15, 1897

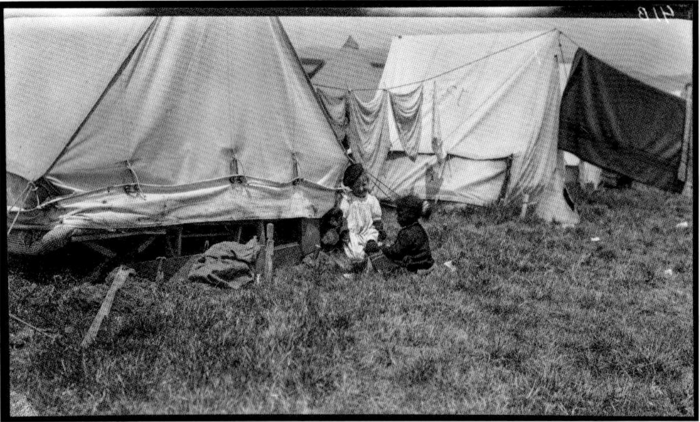

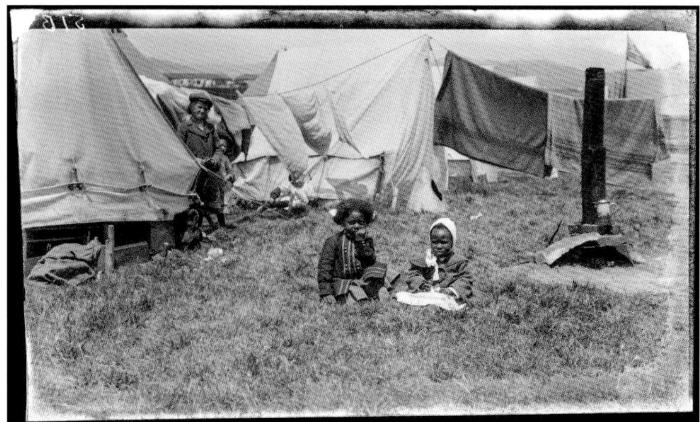

Fig. 27. Arnold Genthe, Two children sit on grass in front of tents in the Presidio in the days following the earthquake and fire, San Francisco, 1906 (cat. 132)

Fig. 28. Arnold Genthe, Two children sit on grass in front of tents in the Presidio in the days following the earthquake and fire, San Francisco, 1906 (cat. 131)

Neither effort succeeded. There was no campaign or practice to bar Black San Franciscans from the camps. However, the historic Black enclave in the heart of the old city never reappeared. The Black population actually decreased in the long aftermath of the earthquake as African Americans moved across the bay to Oakland or to other parts of California. Los Angeles became especially inviting.[19]

In the camp where Genthe photographed the Black children, white San Franciscans were temporarily living there too. In one of the exposed negatives (fig. 27), Genthe recorded cordial play between a Black child and white child. In another exposed negative (fig. 28), Genthe relegates the white children to the edge of the frame, an indication that they were not his primary focus. The print resulting from this negative has affinities with prints he had made a few years earlier in Chinatown; the human subjects (children in both instances) could be foregrounded by cropping every part of the negative that draws attention away from them. When he cropped away visual elements he deemed not essential to his composition, Genthe could then enlarge the remaining details. The result here would have been a plein air portrait of two youngsters seated on a grass floor with an atmospheric, abstract background behind them.

Genthe's portrait doesn't tell us what the future holds for these two young people. The likelihood they ever saw the prints or Genthe again is small. He soon would return to the elite social world he lived in before the earthquake changed everything for a brief while. However, the investigations of several generations of historians offer up a set of their future possibilities: Genthe's young subjects might have enjoyed the Portola Festival, the celebration of the city's substantial rebuilding in October 1909. The Portola Festival also marked the closing of the last relief camps. Then, six years later, they possibly shared Black San Francisco's pride in Virginia Stephens, who submitted the winning entry in the contest to name the world's fairgrounds, which were about to open in February 1915. The judges awarded Virginia first place for her submission, "The Jewel City," without having met her. Black San Franciscans were also aware of the controversy that ensued when contest judges learned Virginia was Black. It was only after months of delay and debate that Virginia received her prize and deserved recognition in the local press.[20] What Black adolescent would ever forget Virginia's story?

If they survived the pandemic of 1918–1919, Genthe's youthful subjects, by then young adults, would have lived to see the Great Depression, bracketed by two World Wars. They would have seen the city's Black population grow in every census after the 1906 earthquake, exploding in 1950 to fifty times what it had been in 1910. And, like their elders, they would have watched another state-sponsored pogrom against an Asian American community—the internment of Japanese Americans. If they were especially long lived, they (and perhaps their children) would see Black workers active in almost every occupation and union. They would know successful Black medical and legal professionals, and even a Black mayor (or two), and throughout their entire lives, they would know the sting of race and caste African Americans before them had experienced. They would understand the profound meaning of "one battle at a time."

As with the people in the Clay Street photographs, Genthe is bonded with the young relief camp residents. Through his photography the "flickering grace" of their lives brightens ours, and they become present among us again.

Freezing Fire

ARNOLD GENTHE AND HIS CAMERA

Victoria Binder

IN HIS AUTOBIOGRAPHY, *As I Remember* (1936), Arnold Genthe provides glimpses of the drama and challenges he endured during the San Francisco earthquake and fires thirty years earlier. But these written accounts are no match for the comprehensive narrative told in the gripping images he left behind. As fires ravaged the city and citizens attended to rubble, Genthe ventured out to capture the harrowing effects of the unfolding disaster. His trusty companion during this endeavor was a small No. 3A Folding Pocket Kodak roll film camera. As an experienced photographer, Genthe was intimately familiar with his equipment and with how to view the world through a lens. Using his camera, he was able to visualize and process the events before him in a way unavailable to the naked eye. Both the advantages and the constraints of the technology available to him at the time played an important role. To understand the relationship between Genthe and his camera is to gain a deeper appreciation for the photographs we see today.

In the years leading up to 1906, photography underwent rapid advancements in technology. In particular, the introduction of hand cameras and roll film offered a portable alternative to cumbersome field cameras and glass plate negatives. Although there were many figures who played an important part in this rapid evolution, it was George Eastman who had the most widespread and lasting impact. Using his inventive mind, business know-how, and masterful promotional skills, Eastman made the practice affordable and accessible, creating a market for amateur photography that dominated the industry for decades to come.[1] With these new advancements, big cities across the nation, including San Francisco, experienced flourishing photography scenes (see Görgen, "Arnold Genthe and the California Camera Club," this volume). By the time the earthquake asserted its first rumbles, legions of professionals and amateurs alike were unknowingly poised to capture its aftermath. Never before had a natural disaster of this magnitude been so widely documented by photographers.[2]

Genthe had arrived for the first time in San Francisco in the summer of 1895, at the age of twenty-six, employed as a tutor for the wealthy and socially established von Schroeder family. Inspired by the city's unique beauty and its diverse neighborhoods, he was almost immediately drawn to photography as a means of perceiving this new world. This inclination would change the course of his life forever. He educated himself in the practice of photography, buying books on the subject, joining the California Camera Club, and developing his first negatives in a small closet converted into a darkroom on the top floor of the von Schroeder family's home. By 1906 he was a seasoned and highly regarded portrait photographer, a dedicated chronicler of urban life (particularly of San Francisco's Chinatown), and a consistent contributor to publications and exhibitions. No doubt this accumulated experience enabled him to deftly navigate and capture the chaos of the earthquake and fires, but it would have never been possible without two understated characters that accompanied him throughout his journey: nitrate roll film and the hand camera.

Roll Film and Cellulose Nitrate

One of the challenges that had long existed with the production of photographic negatives was finding an adequate base to support the thin, light-sensitive emulsion layer. The base had to be compatible with the emulsion, capable of weathering wet and dry processing, and transparent, so light could pass through to expose the print. Sheets of paper and then glass plates served this purpose for many years. Eastman's introduction of nitrate roll film in 1889 was a game changer, offering a new option that was lightweight, transparent, flexible, and capable of holding many exposures.

When most people hear the words *cellulose nitrate*, they think of sensational fires in old cinema houses.[3] Indeed, cellulose nitrate has an explosive past and in its most concentrated configuration was the main ingredient of gunpowder. In less concentrated forms, it found its place as one of the first commercially produced plastics, used for the manufacture of everyday items like billiard balls and men's shirt collars.[4] This variation was still quite flammable. The addition of camphor as a plasticizer produced a more flexible plastic known as celluloid, which was adopted by the photo industry, including Eastman, to create the first plastic film. Despite being manufactured by Eastman Kodak into the 1950s, cellulose nitrate film was eventually discontinued and replaced with newer and less flammable plastic options. It is somewhat ironic that Genthe used cellulose nitrate film, a potentially combustible material, to capture the fires of the 1906 earthquake.

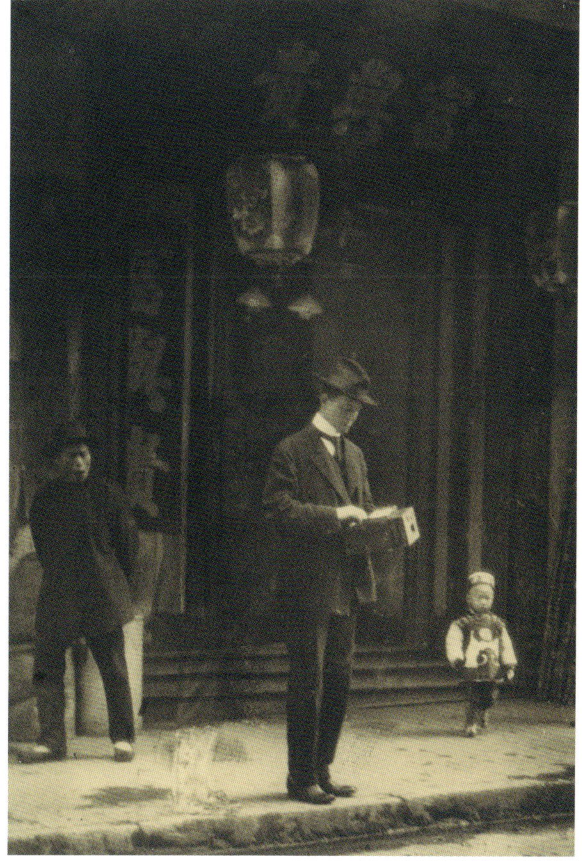

Fig. 29. Portrait of Arnold Genthe in Chinatown, ca. 1896

The Hand Camera

For decades, outdoor photography in the nineteenth century was captured by means of field cameras. These devices were expensive and bulky, typically composed of a wooden shell, large bellows, and a sheet of ground glass at the back onto which the photographer could view and focus the image. Taking pictures with a field camera required a heavy tripod, a cloth hood to block light, and lightproof plate holders for switching out the light-sensitive glass negatives after each exposure. Although field cameras had many advantages, they were impractical for candid, on-the-go photography. The constraints of the field camera long inspired a need for a more portable camera, motivating inventive individuals to come up with a variety of smaller designs. Early forms varied greatly but for the most part resembled their predecessor, the field camera, with wood casings and bellows. In 1888 the Eastman Dry Plate and Film Company revolutionized the camera industry and ignited a snapshot photography craze with the introduction of the Kodak, a small (merely 3¼ by 3¾ by 6½ inches), user-friendly box camera preloaded with one hundred exposures of Eastman's rolled, paper-based American Film. With the Kodak, Eastman also offered a brilliant mail-in photography system, freeing the customer from the complexities of processing. Once owners of a Kodak completely exposed the roll of film, they could send their camera back to Eastman's factory in Rochester, New York. There, the film was processed, prints were made, and the camera was reloaded with new film and sent back to its owner. This ingenious new service gave rise to Kodak's slogan "You press the button, we do the rest." Eastman expanded the Kodak line, increasing the size of the box camera to produce larger photographs, and in 1890 he offered a version with a folding bellows, the No. 4 Folding Kodak.[5] The Kodak line of cameras was so successful that in 1892 George Eastman added it to the company name, creating the Eastman Kodak Company. In 1897 Eastman introduced a compressed camera design with collapsible bellows, the Folding Pocket Kodak, which when closed had a narrower profile than the previous box forms and fit neatly into a coat pocket. In response to the demand for these new cameras, Kodak simultaneously unleashed a slew of accessories and equipment, heralding easy at-home processing and printing in product manuals and advertisements. Versions of the Folding Pocket Kodak would remain on the market for the next fifty years, including the camera used by Genthe to photograph the 1906 earthquake, the No. 3A, manufactured between 1903 and 1915.

Genthe and the Hand Camera

Even though Genthe likely used a large portrait camera and glass plate negatives to capture the sitters in his commercial studio, he probably owned an array of cameras over the course of his career, as did most professional photographers. This would have included a number of different brands of hand cameras, including Kodaks. Recalling the search for his first camera, used to obtain images of Chinatown, he wrote, "It had to be small enough to carry in my pocket."[6]

A wonderful early photograph from around 1896 (fig. 29) shows a young Genthe standing in front of the shadowed façade of a building in Chinatown, intently fiddling with a curious boxy, leather-clad hand camera.[7] It appears that he is loading negatives into the magazine-style design, capable of holding either small glass plates or nitrate roll film. Indeed, many of Genthe's Chinatown negatives—most now held at the Library of Congress—are both glass plate negatives and cellulose nitrate, demonstrating the overlapping of the two technologies and Genthe's affinity for both. Genthe was an avid traveler, and the lightweight and versatile hand camera served as the perfect instrument for capturing his jaunts around the globe. In the cold storage vaults of the Library of Congress, there are thousands of nitrate negatives chronicling his journeys in various film formats, attesting to his familiarity with different hand cameras. Before the earthquake Genthe traveled with cameras to the American Southwest, Europe, and Morocco. During a trip to Mexico in the spring of 1904, his dexterity operating a Kodak hand camera while hunting alligators was detailed in the *San Francisco Call*. The article regaled: "The alligators found the doctor a relentless enemy. Hunted with rifle and camera."[8]

Genthe, the Earthquake, and the No. 3A Folding Pocket Kodak

Perhaps there is no other event where Genthe's experience and skill using the hand camera served him better than capturing the destruction unleashed by the 1906 San Francisco earthquake. On April 18, as the fires began to ignite and the enormity of the situation dawned on him, Genthe felt compelled to do what he knew best: take pictures. As all his hand cameras stored in the fourth-floor skylight studio of his residence at 790 Sutter Street had been badly damaged by falling plaster, he made his way to George Kahn's optics and photo supply shop at 105 Montgomery Street. In better days Kahn's business must have been a fascinating place to visit. Advertisements for his various storefronts over the years touted intriguing merchandise like telescopes, field and opera glasses, barometers, compasses, hearing apparatuses, artificial eyes, and—most relevant to this historical narrative—photographic equipment, including products manufactured by Eastman Kodak. On that day, with fires licking at the heels of his storefront, Kahn urged Genthe: "Take anything you want. This place is going to burn up anyway."[9]

In *As I Remember*, Genthe recalls selecting "the best small camera, a 3A Kodak Special."[10] This is chronologically impossible, as the No. 3A Kodak Special was not available until 1910. It is more likely that Genthe chose the model No. 3A, B2, Folding Pocket Kodak, manufactured between 1904 and 1906 (see fig. 30).

There is exquisite wonderment upon opening a No. 3A Folding Pocket Kodak for the first time. When closed, the unassuming aluminum shell, covered in pebbled leather, roughly resembles the shape and size of a thirty-two-ounce box of sugar. The bed of the camera is released like a drawbridge by a concealed button on the side of the case, uncovering the lens on a metal front board tucked inside the body of the camera (see fig. 31). By squeezing two spring-loaded locks at the bottom of the front board, the entire outfit is pulled out along a rail of metal flanked by decorative polished wood, revealing a deep red, accordion-like leather bellows. It folds back up just as easily and, as advertised by Kodak, fits neatly into a top coat pocket. In this closed state, the silhouette, with its rounded shoulders, seems to uncannily anticipate the design of the modern smartphone. Whereas a hundred years from now, the smartphone in your pocket will likely be nonfunctional, a good Kodak No. 3A (with a little refurbishing) will still elegantly serve its original purpose.

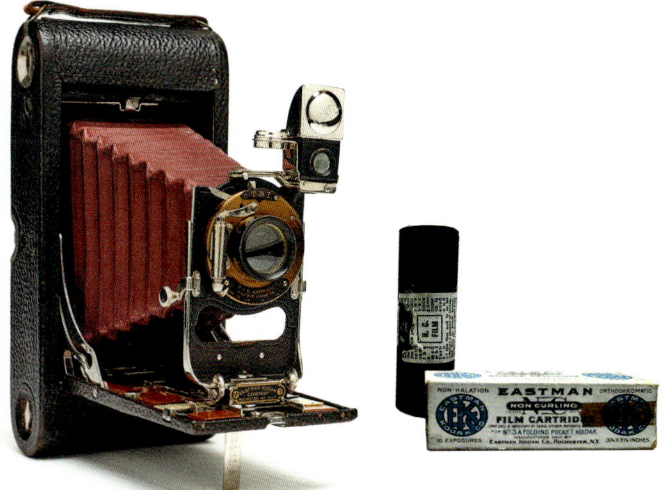

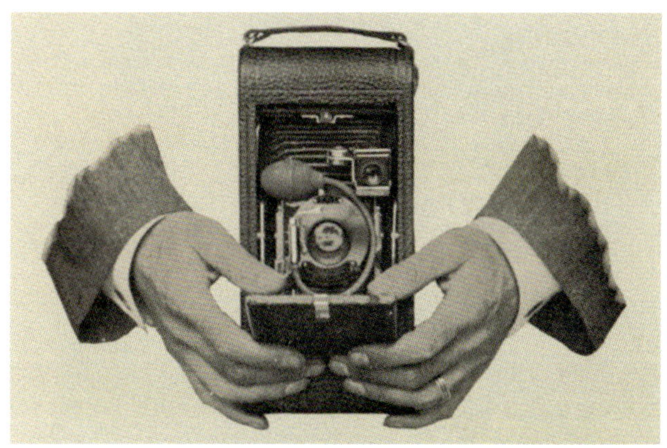

Fig. 30. No. 3A, B2, Folding Pocket Kodak, and Eastman Kodak Company, nitrocellulose (NC), 122 format, roll film

Fig. 31. An illustration from a No. 3A Folding Pocket Kodak manual (1904–1906) demonstrating how to open and close the camera

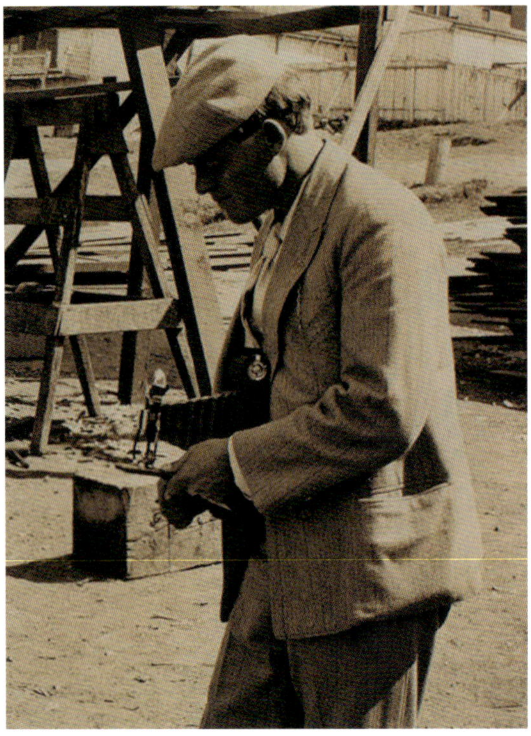

Fig. 32. Jack London peering into the viewfinder of a No. 3A Folding Pocket Kodak

The 1906 Kodak product manual touts the No. 3A Folding Pocket Kodak as a camera worthy of "the most ambitious amateurs," maintaining simplicity while "having all the practical features found in a camera at three times its bulk."[11] Genthe surely knew what he was doing when he chose this particular camera at such a consequential moment. Of the No. 3A's many features, Kodak extols the rapid rectilinear lens, featuring openings ranging from U.S. 4 to 128 (f/8 to f/64) and a pneumatic shutter capable of both instantaneous "snap-shot" exposures and timed exposures, which are controlled by the photographer with a small lever or rubber bulb.[12] Other features include a ninety-degree rotating viewfinder that can be flipped for handling the camera in vertical and horizontal orientations, a spirit level, a focusing scale ranging from six to one hundred feet, and rise and shift capabilities for perspective control. The specifications in this old manual read in a way that any modern camera enthusiast can appreciate.

When you first hold a No. 3A Folding Pocket Kodak, your immediate impulse is to bring the viewfinder directly to your eye, revealing only a blurred circle. In fact the cameras were meant to be held at waist level (see fig. 32). As you peer down into the finder, you see a tiny, faint image of the scene before you, an approximation of what will be recorded on the film. Genthe discouraged the use of the viewfinder as a means of framing the composition. "It is much better to keep your eye on what you are going to photograph than to try to locate your moving subject in the small dinky finder," he wrote in *Camera Craft*.[13] This required an understanding of the angle of view of the camera—that is, visualizing what the lens sees and what will be recorded on the film. Such an approach is easier said than done, and it illustrates Genthe's belief that photographers should endeavor toward an intimate and ingrained understanding of their cameras. No doubt Genthe's years of experience with hand cameras, coupled with his passion for travel and street photography, provided him with the agility to adjust to the uncertain conditions of the earthquake.

When Genthe selected the Kodak No. 3A from Kahn's shop on the first day of the earthquake and fires, he also stuffed his pockets full of film. The camera uses a 122 format, nitrate roll film with either four, six, or ten exposures per roll, each image measuring 3¼ by 5½ inches (see fig. 30). This unusual "postcard" format was first introduced by Kodak together with the No. 3A camera, capitalizing on the popular novelty of printing and sending your own snapshots as postcards. The vertical orientation of the film is notably narrow and somewhat awkward, but in horizontal it offers a composition that is nearly panoramic. Genthe was likely aware of this peculiarity and exploited it. The majority of his earthquake photographs are in horizontal orientation, often offering sweeping views of the desolation. At times he appeared to use the narrow vertical format to his advantage. For example, in his image taken at Ina Coolbrith Park (pl. 11), the eye is drawn immediately to the revelry and repose of the figures in the foreground. However, what makes the image poignantly incongruent is the backdrop of the city on fire, thick smoke billowing upward. If anything, the extended format offered Genthe a certain leeway, as he often drastically cropped his negatives when printing.

Development and Printing of the Earthquake and Fire Negatives

Inevitably questions arise as to where, when, and how Genthe was able to obtain supplies, develop the negatives, and print photographs—possibly amid the chaos of an unfolding disaster. Unfortunately there is no documentation or evidence that provides a concrete answer, although a rough narrative can be pieced together using hypotheses and peripheral facts.

Genthe's Sutter Street studio was completely destroyed by the earthquake. The headquarters of the California Camera Club, whose facilities he had used in the past, were also lost. Still, there were parts of the city that remained untouched by the fires, and there were likely photography shops and studios that survived the quake. Genthe was well connected and cast his social net wide. In the weeks following the earthquake, he stayed with various friends whose homes were preserved. It is not a stretch to speculate that he may have had access to photo studios and equipment as well. The relief effort for the earthquake, both national and local, was almost immediate. In a city teeming with photographers and journalists eager to document the disaster, photography supplies were presumably part of the haul.

Two more possible places where Genthe might have developed and printed the negatives were studios he was in the process of constructing—one begun before the earthquake and one after. In January 1906 Genthe started building a cottage with a darkroom in an artist community in Carmel-by-the-Sea, 122 miles south of San Francisco. Although the cottage was not quite finished, Genthe was known to be in Carmel on May 25, 1906, five weeks after the earthquake.[14] He also began building a new studio in San Francisco after the earthquake. On August 19, 1906, the *San Francisco Call* noted: "[Genthe] has been devoting his time to the rehabilitation of a cottage at 3209 Clay Street, near Presidio Avenue, and which is now converted into a thoroughly attractive and artistic studio."[15]

There are two references that allude to the possible early existence of earthquake prints made by Genthe. The first is in the April 30, 1906, edition of the *San Francisco Examiner*, just twelve days after the earthquake. The writer states, "Dr. Arnold Genthe has taken some excellent photographs of our poor distracted-looking city."[16] The second reference comes from Genthe's autobiography, where he reminisces about his encounters with the actress Sarah Bernhardt during her visit to the Bay Area from May 14 to 17. According to Genthe, he was summoned to Bernhardt's hotel to show her photographic proofs of her tour through the ruins of San Francisco. Genthe notes that the actress later thanked him for his "San Francisco fire pictures" and shares a 1906 letter in which Bernhardt reflects: "Thank you for the beautiful and very painful photographs. You too lost everything in the horrible catastrophe."[17]

From this evidence one can postulate that Genthe made prints as early as April 30 and before May 18, which was the date of Bernhardt's next venue, in Venice, California.[18] Knowing this, we can rule out the possibility that Genthe developed and printed these earliest prints in Carmel or on Clay Street. Rather, it is more likely that he developed and printed them during his nomadic weeks in San Francisco after the earthquake.

The Photographs and Negatives Now

Where are these early prints today? There are roughly several dozen extant photographs of the San Francisco earthquake and fire printed by Genthe. However, it is difficult to differentiate ones that were printed in San Francisco, soon after the earthquake, from ones that were made later in his career, in New York City. There are two existing sets of prints that bear attributes indicating early production: an album of proof prints at the Library of Congress, and a set of twenty-four prints at the Bancroft Library at the University of California, Berkeley.[19]

The album of proofs at the Library of Congress is composed of small contact prints, an intimate format that is made by exposing the negative in direct contact with the paper, creating a mirror image of the same size. Unlike photographs taken with modern digital cameras and smartphones, images shot with a film camera cannot be seen instantly. Printing a quick initial rendition of negatives is a common practice. Genthe's negatives must have been burning a hole in his pocket; the need to see whether or not he had captured these powerful moments would have been irresistible. It is tempting to think that these might have been the very proofs that Genthe presented to Bernhardt.

The select group of prints at the Bancroft, with their subtle tones and careful printing, have a finished look. These early prints not only give a sense of which images Genthe found most compelling but also provide insights into his preferences in composition, cropping, and tone. They were handed down through the decades by a distinguished San Francisco family before being gifted to the Bancroft. With them came a familial oral history and a provenance that leads straight to two of the city's most prominent figures at the turn of the century: the philanthropist Rosalie Meyer Stern and her brother Eugene Meyer. After the earthquake Meyer traveled to San Francisco to help his sister and her family. It is assumed that it was around this time that he acquired the photographs.[20]

The 156 earthquake and fire negatives in the Fine Arts Museums of San Francisco's collection were acquired in 1943 (see Breuer, "Arnold Genthe at the Legion of Honor," introduction to this volume). It is unlikely that these represent a complete set. The practice of photography usually entails amassing numerous images in pursuit of a few good ones. "It is infinitely better," Genthe once wrote, "to waste a lot of films and plates and finally get a simply composed picture."[21] While processing the negatives, Genthe probably also suffered casualties. Furthermore, we cannot account for the life-span of the negatives and what losses occurred as they passed through various hands.

The negatives themselves are thin and fragile and exhibit various amber, black, and milky yellow tones (see fig. 33). Looking at them in their current state, it is easy to assume they were processed in less than ideal circumstances. This is quite possible. We will never definitively know the obstacles that Genthe was up against, including limited access to materials and equipment, the lack of a proper setup, and even compromised water quality. However, it is important to remember that what we see today is the sum of the negatives' experiences and not necessarily the consequence of being part of a disaster. The standards at the turn of the century for the manufacture of photographic materials and chemicals were not as stringent as those of today. Processing of negatives was generally done by inspection and was not the exacting process that would be developed in future decades. And

Fig. 33. Arnold Genthe, Clay west of Stockton, San Francisco, 1906 (cat. 6). Cellulose nitrate negative photographed in normal lighting conditions showing deterioration and processing flaws. The corresponding transmitted-light image (cat. 6) shows the amount of detail captured through the high-resolution scanning of the negatives (see also pl. 6).

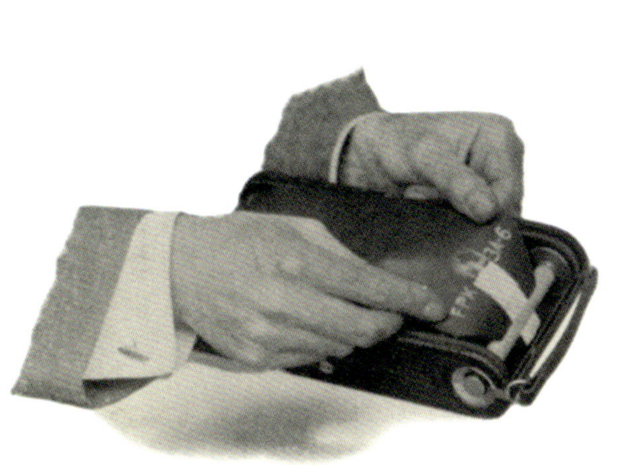

Fig. 34. An illustration from a No. 3A Folding Pocket Kodak manual (1904–1906) demonstrating how to load film into the camera. The roll film is protected by a sheet of black paper allowing the film to be loaded in subdued daylight.

Fig. 35. Detail of a nitrate negative (cat. 1) taken in normal lighting conditions showing retouching in graphite pencil emphasizing the flames in the building and delineating the figures in the foreground (see also pl. 1)

of course, there is the deterioration that occurs with time. All of these factors combine to make a mystery that we may never be able to completely unravel.

Decoding the Negatives

When the curators at the Fine Arts Museums of San Francisco chose to have exhibition-quality gelatin silver prints made from the negatives, they decided to present them in an unaltered state, showing the full image, the edges of the negatives, and every imperfection (see Binder and Oliver, "Arnold Genthe's 1906 Earthquake and Fire Negatives," this volume).[22] Although his surviving prints provide some information, it is impossible to predict Genthe's final vision for all of the images. He was known to significantly alter negatives and prints through cropping, retouching, and, at times, a soft focus. For this reason, these exhibition prints contain a number of curious artifacts that could be the result of materials, process, or deterioration.[23]

Handwritten Numbers

Numbers can be seen in the corners of many of the images. On the prints they appear white and in reverse. On the negatives they are in blue ink. The writing resembles Genthe's hand. This is likely evidence of a numbering system implemented by Genthe that has yet to be decoded.

Light Leaks

Light leaks manifest as white shapes along the edges of the photographs, both diffuse and in wave patterns (note the top edge of pl. 85). They are caused by stray light hitting the film. This might be due to the camera not being sealed properly; however, it is more likely that it occurred while Genthe was loading the film. The film was outfitted with a black sheet of protective paper that enabled loading in subdued daylight (see fig. 34). As the circumstances in which Genthe loaded the film were unpredictable, it is probable that light leaks were a frequent occurrence.

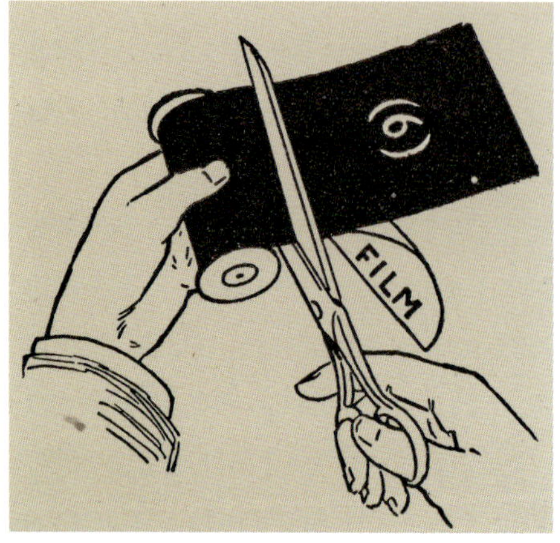

Fig. 36. An illustration from a No. 3A Folding Pocket Kodak manual (1904–1906) demonstrating cutting apart the exposures on the roll film along with the black protective paper before development

SILVER MIRRORING

Silver mirroring appears on the photographs as a soft, white haze along the edges (see pl. 86). It can be distinguished from light leaks by its granular, almost powdery appearance. The effect is due to the deterioration and movement of the tiny silver particles in the negative, resulting in a bluish metallic sheen on the surface.

FINGERPRINTS

Fingerprints can often be seen along the edges, particularly in areas of silver mirroring, where the loose particles are vulnerable (see pl. 64). Though it is possible the fingerprints are from Genthe himself, they could be the result of the handling of the negatives by any number of people over time.

RETOUCHING

Retouch is visible on some of the prints as thin, scribbly lines obscuring unwanted objects like power lines and processing flaws (see pls. 4, 36). Genthe directly retouched the negatives using graphite pencil and scratching. He also used these methods in his Chinatown series, often deleting entire signs and people. Traces of these modifications can frequently be spotted in corresponding prints, such as in figure 29, where a person standing to Genthe's left was erased (for the unretouched version, see p. 171). On the first day of the earthquake, Genthe snapped a deeply underexposed image of a burning building on the corner of Bush and Sansome Streets (pl. 1). On this negative he used graphite pencil to emphasize the flames and delineate the figures in the foreground (see fig. 35).

UNEVEN TRIMMING OF THE EDGES

The edges of the negatives as they appear on the prints are often roughly and unevenly trimmed (see pl. 49). It is possible Genthe developed the negatives in a darkroom aided by a dim red lamp, using a method where he cut each exposure while the black protective paper was attached (see fig. 36).[24] Cutting through two dissimilar materials is not an easy task, especially when each exposure is not clearly marked.[25] This might explain the cuts between each image, but what about the long edges (see pl. 23)? It is possible that the edges curled during wet and dry processing, and Genthe cut the long edges off so that he could make contact prints.[26]

MISSING CORNERS

Many of the images have one or two sharply defined missing corners (see pl. 12). This might have been an early notch-code system, allowing Genthe to keep track of certain aspects, like orientation. However, some of the intact corners show a cinch mark indicating Genthe's possible use of clips for drying the negatives during processing. Breakage of the corners could have occurred as a result of weakening at these junctures.

SOFT IMAGE EDGES

A handful of the exposures show soft, indistinct edges that could be described as vignetting (see pl. 23). This could be an effect of lens limitations. However, this would usually result in a more rounded perimeter, especially at the corners. It is more likely that the soft image edges are a consequence of the film not being taut within the camera. Genthe could have experienced difficulties loading or advancing the film, resulting in the film moving forward without proper tension. In 1906 pressure plates, a device used to secure the film flat in the cameras, had not yet been introduced.

SHORT IMAGES

A few of the images fill only a portion of the full 3¼-by-5½-inch format (see pl. 69). This could suggest that the exposures were made on a different film format and possibly even taken by another camera. However, the images do fit proportionately into the height or width of the 122 film. Alternative possibilities include substantial trimming or simply that Genthe had reached the end of the roll.

SHADOWY BLOCK FORMS

A number of the negatives show shadowy block forms in yellow and black tones (see fig. 33 as well as its corresponding print, pl. 6). The presence of the forms in the prints is subtle. These odd shapes might be a result of extended contact with an acidic material, like old wood pulp paper. Another possibility is that the shapes occurred during processing, either in the developing or fixing bath. If the negatives had been individually cut and placed as batches in a solution and not agitated enough, they could have obstructed thorough access of the liquid, thereby imprinting their silhouette.[27]

Preservation

It is amazing to think how the thousands, if not millions, of tiny silver grains that unite in these negatives to form these beautiful and haunting images. The negatives carry valuable information, but they are also physical artifacts of the earthquake. For this reason, it is important to preserve them.

If kept unchecked, cellulose nitrate can deteriorate at unpredictable and often rapid rates, risking permanent loss of the images contained within the negatives. In 2014, thanks to the generosity of the local community, the Fine Arts Museums of San Francisco raised enough funds to scan the negatives at high resolution. Scanning not only recorded the negatives in their current state but also yielded an astonishing amount of information and allowed for zoomed-in views of details never seen before. The rate of deterioration of the negatives has now been slowed down by placing them in freezer storage protected by vapor-proof packaging. With careful monitoring, these fascinating negatives can be expected to last for years to come.

"Get Out with Your 'Picture-Box'"

PHOTOGRAPHERS AND THE "SAN FRANCISCO HORROR"

Colleen Terry

CHRISTENED THE "SAN FRANCISCO HORROR" by local press, the April 18, 1906, earthquake and fires wreaked devastation across the city, leaving a bleak topography of architectural remains in their wake. The ravaged infrastructure was a direct result of modern building methods, which had been designed to satisfy demands for quick and efficient inhabitancy.[1] Amateur photographer Arthur Inkersley characterized the ruins as "wonderful sights of the modern Herculaneum." Two months after the event, in an account given to the San Francisco–based monthly *Camera Craft*, Inkersley beseeched his fellow photographers to "get out with your 'picture-box,'" urging them to chronicle the period before "the desolated city" and its "tottering walls are being pulled down" to make way for "unsightly wooden and corrugated iron structures of a hideously utilitarian sort." As a photographer, Inkersley couldn't help but view the damage through a lens. "The hammer of the workman," he wrote, "is sounding the knell of the artistic photograph, which, if it is to be made at all, must be made quickly."[2]

Indeed, in the weeks following the earthquake, photographers—both amateur and professional—scoured the city, seeking out picturesque shots of the damage that recalled the landscape traditions of the Romantic era. Some utilized soft-focus techniques and labor-intensive printing processes, resulting in tonally rich views that visibly aligned their photographs with the aesthetics of Pictorialism, a popular movement that prized the artistic rather than the documentary aspects of photography.

Shooting right alongside these photographers, who cast a creative eye on the powerful scenes before them, were commercial photographers. The latter had somewhat contrary aims: their primary objective was to capture images that would sell. This motive resulted in pictures of an altogether different character, most notably manifest in the use of sharp focus, which plainly articulated time and place. Commercial photographs—sold to periodicals across the country—loomed large under sensationalist headlines like "City Totally Destroyed"[3] and "Homeless but Hopeful"[4] (see figs. 37–38). These "documentary" images also served as "evidence" for city officials and engineers hoping to recast the destruction as one caused primarily by fire, which they did with an eye to encourage outside investment in San Francisco's reconstruction. Officials believed that fire—a common threat for cities across the nation that could be mitigated through strict building codes—was more palatable than unpredictable seismic unrest.[5]

Published news sources, literary descriptions, letters, and memoirs offer intimate responses to difficult times, but they can only tell part of the story. Business records and insurance claims also provide data—logistical accounts of profits and loss. Photographs tell their

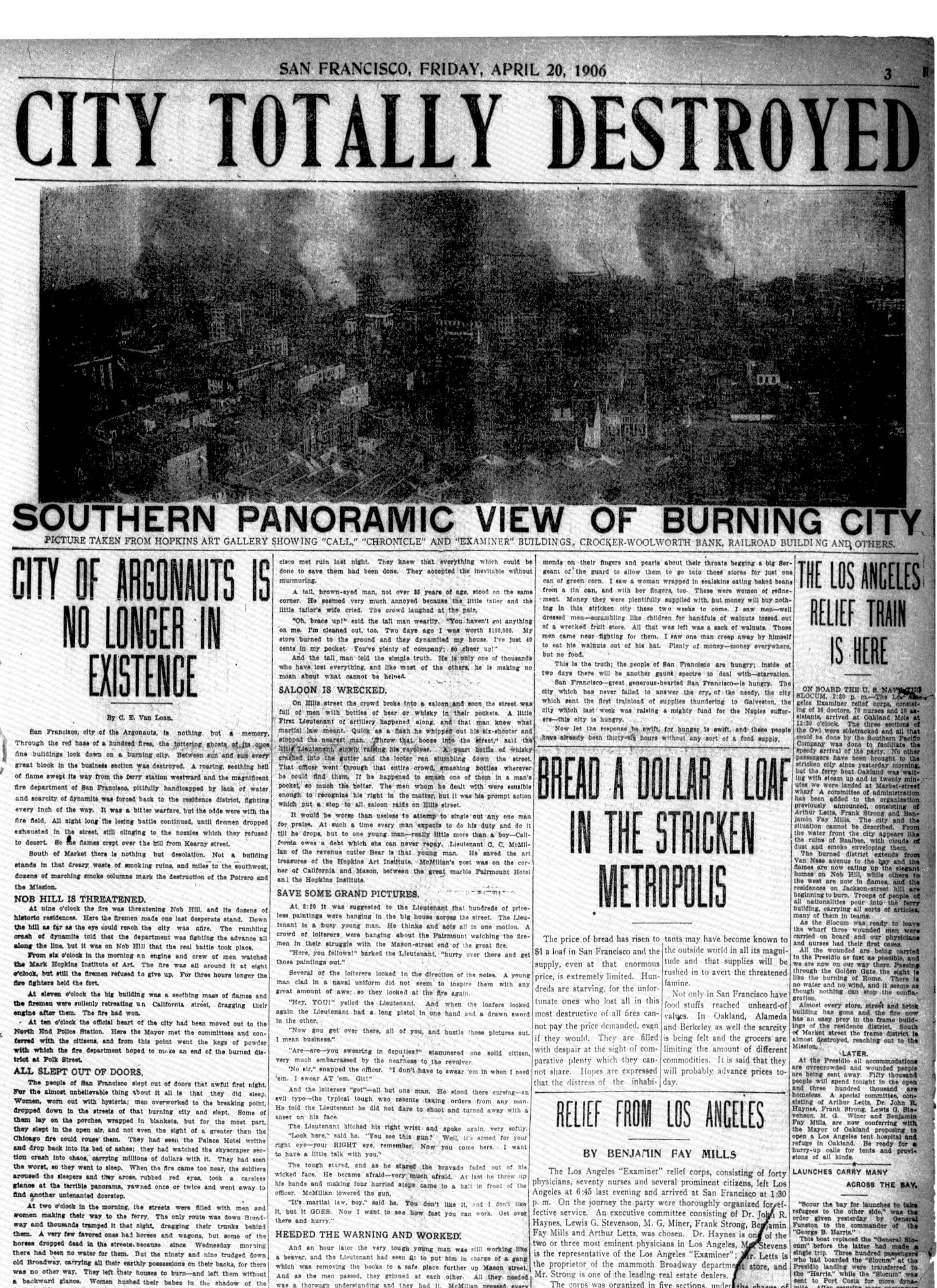

SAN FRANCISCO, FRIDAY, APRIL 20, 1906 3

CITY TOTALLY DESTROYED

SOUTHERN PANORAMIC VIEW OF BURNING CITY

PICTURE TAKEN FROM HOPKINS ART GALLERY SHOWING "CALL," "CHRONICLE" AND "EXAMINER" BUILDINGS, CROCKER-WOOLWORTH BANK, RAILROAD BUILDING AND OTHERS.

CITY OF ARGONAUTS IS NO LONGER IN EXISTENCE

By C. E. Van Loan.

San Francisco, city of the Argonauts, is nothing but a memory. Through the red haze of a hundred fires, the tottering ghosts of its once fine buildings look down on a burning city. Between sun and sun every great block in the business section was destroyed. A roaring, seething hell of flame swept its way from the ferry station westward and the magnificent fire department of San Francisco, pitifully handicapped by lack of water and scarcity of dynamite was forced back to the residence district, fighting every inch of the way. It was a bitter warfare, but the odds were with the fire field. All night long the losing battle continued, until firemen dropped exhausted in the street, still clinging to the nozzles which they refused to desert. So the flames crept over the hill from Kearny street.

South of Market there is nothing but desolation. Not a building stands in that dreary waste of smoking ruins, and miles to the southwest, dozens of marching smoke columns mark the destruction of the Potrero and the Mission.

NOB HILL IS THREATENED.

At nine o'clock the fire was threatening Nob Hill, and its dozens of historic residences. Here the firemen made one last desperate stand. Down the hill as far as the eye could reach the city was afire. The rumbling crash of dynamite told that the department was fighting the advance all along the line, but it was on Nob Hill that the real battle took place.

From six o'clock in the morning an engine and crew of men watched the Mark Hopkins Institute of Art. The fire was all around it at eight o'clock, but still the firemen refused to give up. For three hours longer the fire fighters held the fort.

At eleven o'clock the big building was a seething mass of flames and the firemen were sullenly retreating un California street, dragging their engine after them. The fire had won.

At ten o'clock the official heart of the city had been moved out to the North End Police Station. Here the Mayor met the committees and conferred with the citizens, and from this point went the kegs of powder with which the fire department hoped to make an end of the burned district at Polk Street.

ALL SLEPT OUT OF DOORS.

The people of San Francisco slept out of doors that awful first night. For the almost unbelievable thing about it all is that they did sleep. Women, worn out with hysteria; men overworked to the breaking point, dropped down in the streets of that burning city and slept. Some of them lay on the porches, wrapped in blankets, but for the most part, they slept in the open air, and not even the sight of a greater than the Chicago fire could rouse them. They had seen the Palace Hotel writhe and drop back into its bed of ashes; they had watched the skyscraper section crash into chaos, carrying millions of dollars with it. They had seen the worst, so they went to sleep. When the fire came too near, the soldiers aroused the sleepers and they arose, rubbed red eyes, took a careless glance at the terrible panorama, yawned once or twice and went away to find another untenanted doorstep.

At two o'clock in the morning, the streets were filled with men and women making their way to the ferry. The only route was down Broadway and thousands tramped it that night, dragging their trunks behind them. A very few favored ones had horses and wagons, but some of the horses dropped dead in the streets because since Wednesday morning there had been no water for them. But the ninety and nine trudged down old Broadway, carrying all their earthly possessions on their backs, for there was no other way. They left their houses to burn—and left them without a backward glance. Women hushed their babes in the shadow of the ferry building, and the mere rumor that a boat was about to go out brought cries of thanksgiving. They wanted to get away—anywhere.

WATCH FIGHT OF FIREMEN.

Up in the hills the people waited and hoped against hope. They saw the brave fight that the firemen were making, but while they hoped, they prepared for the worst, and every man and every woman had a little bundle within reach—the things which they dared not leave behind.

One old woman sat on her front porch, her rusty black bonnet tied primly under her chin and her hands busy with a large valise. She was just waiting until the fire patrol should warn her off the block.

"No," said she, "I am not afraid. It is God's will. If the fire comes here—well," and she made the slightest gesture with her black gloved hand. [illegible] That is all. I am ready, but I am not afraid."

[illegible] which those brave people of San Francisco met ruin last night. They knew that everything which could be done to save them had been done. They accepted the inevitable without murmuring.

A tall, brown-eyed man, not over 25 years of age, stood on the same corner. He seemed very much annoyed because the little tailor and the little tailor's wife cried. The crowd laughed at the pair.

"Oh, brace up!" said the tall man wearily. "You haven't got anything on me. I'm cleaned out, too. Two days ago I was worth $100,000. My store burned to the ground and they dynamited my house. I've just 40 cents in my pocket. You've plenty of company; so cheer up!"

And the tall man told the simple truth. He is only one of thousands who have lost everything, and like most of the others, he is making no moan about what cannot be helped.

SALOON IS WRECKED.

On Ellis street the crowd broke into a saloon and soon the street was full of men with bottles of beer or whisky in their pockets. A little First Lieutenant of artillery happened along, and that man knew what martial law meant. Quick as a flash he whipped out his six-shooter and stopped the nearest man. "Throw that booze into the street," said the little Lieutenant, slowly raising his revolver. A quart bottle of whisky crashed into the gutter and the looter ran stumbling down the street. That officer went through that entire crowd, smashing bottles wherever he could find them. If he happened to smash one of them in a man's pocket, so much the better. The men whom he dealt with were sensible enough to recognize his right in the matter, but it was his prompt action which put a stop to all saloon raids on Ellis street.

It would be worse than useless to attempt to single out any one man for praise. At such a time every man expects to do his duty and do it till he drops, but to one young man—really little more than a boy—California owes a debt which she can never repay. Lieutenant C. C. McMillan of the revenue cutter Bear is that young man. He saved the art treasures of the Hopkins Art Institute. McMillan's post was on the corner of California and Mason, between the great marble Fairmount Hotel and the Hopkins Institute.

SAVE SOME GRAND PICTURES.

At 8:20 it was suggested to the Lieutenant that hundreds of priceless paintings were hanging in the big house across the street. The Lieutenant is a busy young man. He thinks and acts all in one motion. A crowd of loiterers were hanging about the Fairmount watching the firemen in their struggle with the Mason-street end of the great fire.

"Here, you fellows!" barked the Lieutenant, "hurry over there and get those paintings out."

Several of the loiterers looked in the direction of the notes. A young man clad in a naval uniform did not seem to inspire them with any great amount of awe; so they looked at the fire again.

"Hey, YOU!" yelled the Lieutenant. And when the loafers looked again the Lieutenant had a long pistol in one hand and a drawn sword in the other.

"Now you get over there, all of you, and hustle those pictures out. I mean business."

"Are—are—you swearing in deputies?" stammered one solid citizen, very much embarrassed by the nearness to the revolver.

"No sir," snapped the officer. "I don't have to swear 'em in when I need 'em. I swear AT 'em. Git!"

And the loiterers "got"—all but one man. He stood there cursing—an evil type—the typical tough who resents taking orders from any man. He told the Lieutenant he did not dare to shoot and turned away with a sneer on his face.

The Lieutenant hitched his right wrist and spoke again, very softly.

"Look here," said he. "You see this gun? Well, it's aimed for your right eye—your RIGHT eye, remember. Now you come here. I want to have a little talk with you."

The tough stared, and as he stared the bravado faded out of his wicked face. He became afraid—very much afraid. At last he threw up his hands and making four hurried steps came to a halt in front of the officer. McMillan lowered the gun.

"It's martial law, boy," said he. "You don't like it, and I don't like it, but it GOES. Now I want to see how fast you can work. Get over there and hurry."

HEEDED THE WARNING AND WORKED.

And an hour later the very tough young man was still working like a beaver, and the Lieutenant had seen fit to put him in charge of a gang which was removing the books to a safe place further up Mason street. And as the men passed, they grinned at each other. All they needed was a thorough understanding and they had it. McMillan pressed every man into service—he stopped reputable citizens and made them climb high fences and carry heavy oil paintings. One fat gentleman had an alibi.

"But I'm a member of the Humane Society. Here's my badge," said he.

"Well, this is a humane job. Jump in and help save those flags and things." And the member of the Humane Society went—after he had seen the muzzle of McMillan's revolver. It was hard work and it was hot work, but in two hours the art institute was empty—thanks to one little Lieutenant and his gun. California should not forget that young man.

Toward noon the patrols began to break into grocery stores in the doomed district.

[illegible]

monds on their fingers and pearls about their throats begging a big Sergeant of the guard to allow them to go into those stores for just one can of green corn. I saw a woman wrapped in sealskins eating baked beans from a tin can, and with her fingers, too. These were women of refinement. Money they were plentifully supplied with, but money will buy nothing in this stricken city these two weeks to come. I saw men—well dressed men—scrambling like children for handfuls of walnuts tossed out of a wrecked fruit store. All that was left was a sack of walnuts. Those men came near fighting for them. I saw one man creep away by himself to eat his walnuts out of his hat. Plenty of money—money everywhere, but no food.

This is the truth; the people of San Francisco are hungry; inside of two days there will be another gaunt spectre to deal with—starvation.

San Francisco—great generous-hearted San Francisco—is hungry. The city which has never failed to answer the cry of the needy, the city which sent the first trainload of supplies thundering to Galveston, the city which last week was raising a mighty fund for the Naples sufferers—this city is hungry.

Now let the response be swift, for hunger is swift, and these people have already been thirty-six hours without any sort of a food supply.

BREAD A DOLLAR A LOAF IN THE STRICKEN METROPOLIS

The price of bread has risen to $1 a loaf in San Francisco and the supply, even at that enormous price, is extremely limited. Hundreds are starving, for the unfortunate ones who lost all in this most destructive of all fires cannot pay the price demanded, even if they would. They are filled with despair at the sight of comparative plenty which they cannot share. Hopes are expressed that the distress of the inhabitants may have become known to the outside world in all its magnitude and that supplies will be rushed in to avert the threatened famine.

Not only in San Francisco have food stuffs reached unheard-of values. In Oakland, Alameda and Berkeley as well the scarcity is being felt and the grocers are limiting the amount of different commodities. It is said that they will probably advance prices today.

RELIEF FROM LOS ANGELES

BY BENJAMIN FAY MILLS

The Los Angeles "Examiner" relief corps, consisting of forty physicians, seventy nurses and several prominent citizens, left Los Angeles at 6:45 last evening and arrived at San Francisco at 1:30 p. m. On the journey the party were thoroughly organized for effective service. An executive committee consisting of Dr. John R. Haynes, Lewis G. Stevenson, M. G. Miner, Frank Strong, Benjamin Fay Mills and Arthur Letts, was chosen. Dr. Haynes is one of the two or three most eminent physicians in Los Angeles, Mr. Stevens is the representative of the Los Angeles "Examiner"; Mr. Letts is the proprietor of the mammoth Broadway department store, and Mr. Strong is one of the leading real estate dealers.

The corps was organized in five sections, under the charge of Drs. Taggart, Shorb, Horgan, Scroggs and Day.

After going to the Presidio on the Government tug Slocum and finding they were not needed, the party returned to Oakland mole to spend the night in the cars. It is now proposed, if necessary, to establish a Los Angeles tent hospital and refuge in Oakland and to have a special train bring provisions from the Southern city.

"RED HOUSE" DAMAGED.

The little red house of Russian Hill which was one of the first adobe residences of this city, was badly damaged by the earthquake. The structure stands on the south side of [illegible] bard street near Jones, and now belongs to the family of James McCloskey. If not destroyed by fire it is likely that it will have to be torn down for safety. The house was put up in the old Spanish days when the Presidio was a gay [illegible] post.

THE LOS ANGELES RELIEF TRAIN IS HERE

ON BOARD THE U. S. NAVY TUG SLOCUM, 2:30 p. m.—The Los Angeles Examiner relief corps, consisting of 26 doctors, 76 nurses and 10 assistants, arrived at Oakland Mole at 12:30 o'clock. The three sections of the Owl were sidetracked and all that could be done by the Southern Pacific Company was done to facilitate the speedy arrival of the party. No other passengers have been brought to the stricken city since yesterday morning, but the ferry boat Oakland was waiting with steam up and in twenty minutes we were landed at Market-street wharf. A committee of administration has been added to the organization previously announced, consisting of Arthur Letts, Frank Strong and Benjamin Fay Mills. The city and the situation cannot be described. From the water front the city appears like the ruins of Baalbec, with clouds of dust and smoke enveloping them.

The burned district extends from Van Ness avenue to the bay and the flames are now eating up the elegant homes on Nob Hill, while others to the west are now in flames, and the residences on Jackson-street hill are beginning to burn. Troops of people of all nationalities pour into the ferry building, carrying all sorts of articles, many of them in teams.

As the Slocum was ready to leave the wharf three wounded men were carried on board and our physicians and nurses had their first cases.

All the wounded are being carried to the Presidio as fast as possible, and we are now on our way there. Passing through the Golden Gate the sight is like the burning of Rome. There is no water and no wind, and it seems as though nothing can stop the conflagration.

Almost every store, street and brick building has gone and the fire now has an easy prey in the frame buildings of the residence district. South of Market street the frame district is almost destroyed, reaching out to the Mission.

LATER.

At the Presidio all accommodations are overcrowded and wounded people are being sent away. Fifty thousand people will spend tonight in the open and three hundred thousand are homeless. A special committee, consisting of Arthur Letts, Dr. John R. Haynes, Frank Strong, Lewis G. Stevenson, M. G. Winer and Benjamin Fay Mills, are now conferring with the Mayor of Oakland proposing to open a Los Angeles tent hospital and refuge in Oakland. Be ready for a hurry-up calls for tents and provisions of all kinds.

LAUNCHES CARRY MANY ACROSS THE BAY.

"Scour the bay for launches to take refugees to the other side," was the order given yesterday by General Funston to the commander of the "George B. Harris."

This boat replaced the "General Slocum" before the latter had made a single trip. Three hundred passengers who had boarded the "Slocum" at the Presidio landing were transferred to the "Harris," while the "Slocum" was sent to Port Costa for more dynamite. After securing more passengers at the foot of Mason street and Van Ness avenue, the "Harris" obeyed orders. As a result many persons were enabled to escape from the city in launches.

SAFE IN VISALIA.

A traveling salesman who arrived this city yesterday afternoon looking for his wife and three small children reports all well in Fresno, Visalia and Stockton. He was in Visalia at the time of the earthquake and says that the shock was so slight that he doubted its reality. There is no damage between [illegible] and Fresno.

Fig. 37. "Southern Panoramic View of Burning City," in the *San Francisco Examiner*, April 20, 1906

Collier's for May 5 1906 21

HOMELESS BUT HOPEFUL

Rich and poor alike never gave way to despair, but made the best of their woful condition. They made themselves as comfortable as possible, maintained perfect order and discipline, and bent all their energies to repairing the damage suffered and to making plans for a future of prosperity

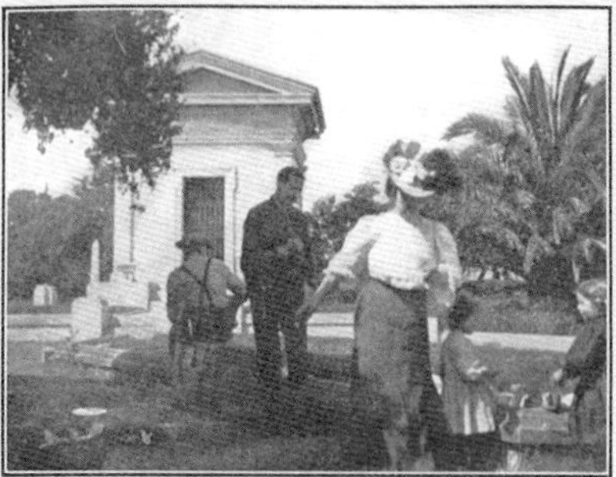

THE LIVING SEEK SHELTER IN THE CITY OF THE DEAD

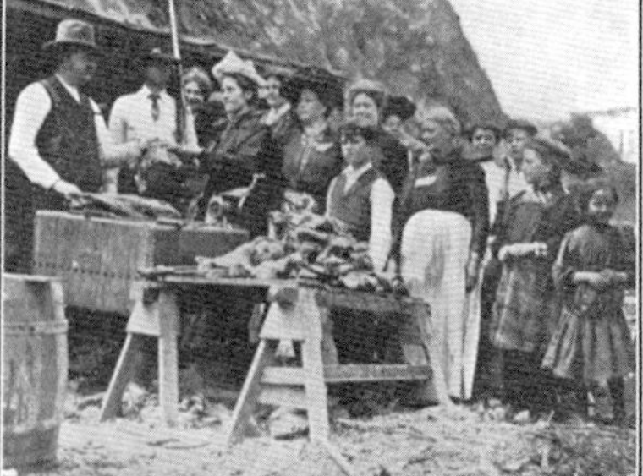

THE FIRST FRESH MEAT TO BE DISTRIBUTED AFTER THE FIRE

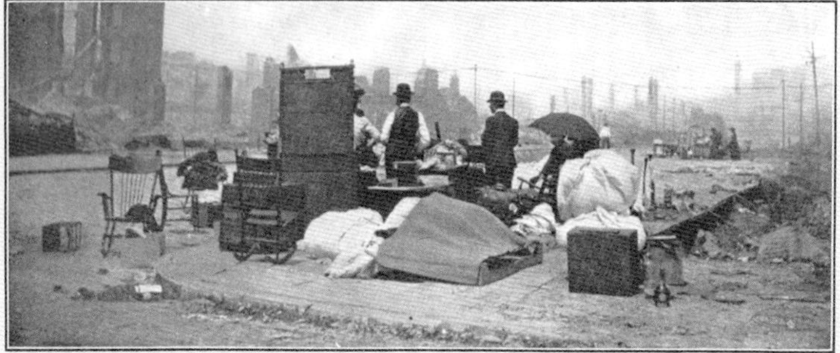

HOMELESS AND ROOFLESS THOUSANDS LIVED FOR DAYS AMID THEIR RESCUED CHATTELS IN THE OPEN STREETS AND PARKS

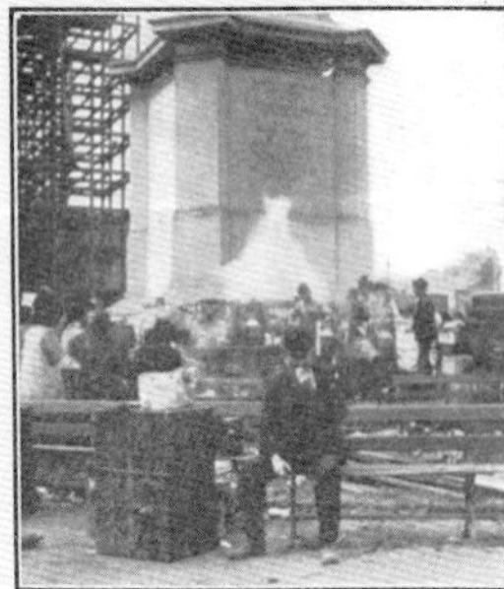

A FOOD STATION AT THE DEWEY MONUMENT

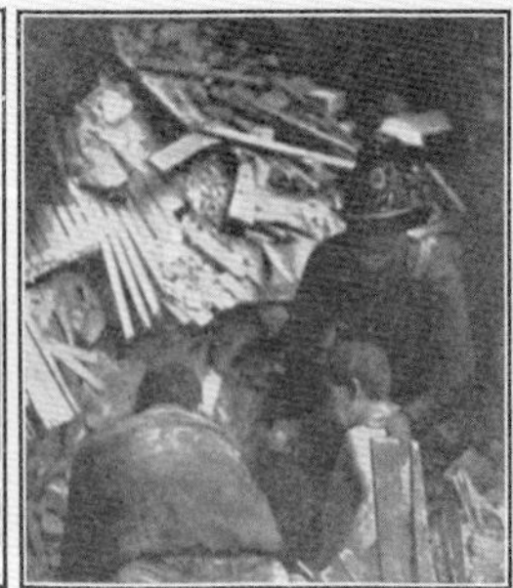

FIREMEN RESCUING A VICTIM

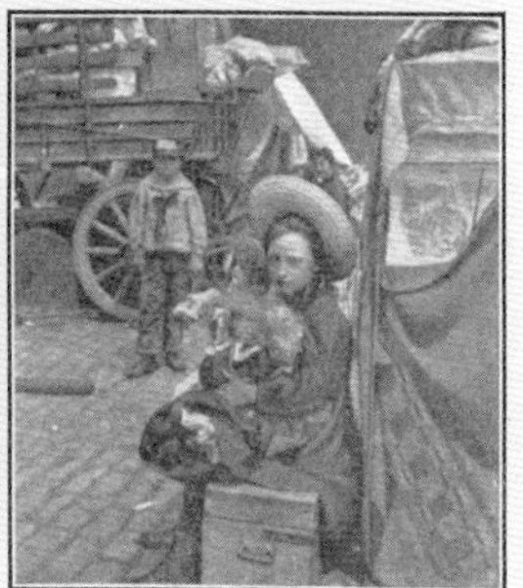

HER FAMILY IS SAVED

Fig 38 "Homeless but Hopeful," in *Collier's*, May 5, 1906

own unique narrative. Although sometimes characterized as impartial "witnesses," photographers create images with distinct and idiosyncratic objectives that present an array of "realities." Photographs, even of the same subject matter, can vary considerably depending on any number of factors, whether controlled by or *for* the photographer. These include which camera and film are used, staging and composition, atmospheric conditions, and sociopolitical circumstances. Work in the field is only part of the equation; photographers can further shape content through manipulation of negatives and decisions made during the printing process, such as cropping, enlarging, dodging and burning, or selection of paper and mounts. These factors play a crucial role in fashioning the visual record, and they affect how the works are read in the future.

◆ ◆ ◆

In the early twentieth century, the low cost of handheld cameras and the recent convenience of roll film endowed a large number of people with the capacity to document defining moments in their lives.[6] At the time of the earthquake, San Francisco was flush with photographers. A local business directory from 1905 lists at least thirty-three businesses directly related to photographic printing, supplies, and maintenance, and more than one hundred residents who self-identified as professional or commercial photographers.[7] Many of these people took to the streets soon after the mainshock to photograph the dramatic changes to their city, covering large stretches of town to record the scene as it evolved.

By 1906 Arnold Genthe had already made a name for himself as a portrait photographer for some of San Francisco's wealthiest and most famous inhabitants and for his images of the city's legendary Chinatown. The earthquake provided him with a strikingly different project, one that captured the essence of a city leveled both physically and socially. In his earthquake and fire photographs, building remnants have a dominant presence, but people also significantly contribute

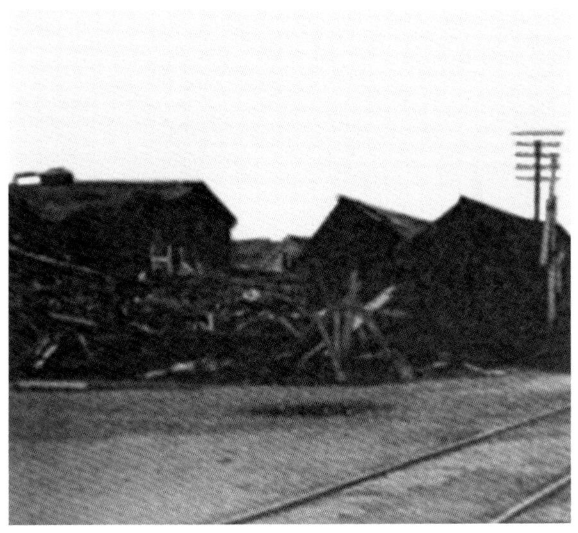

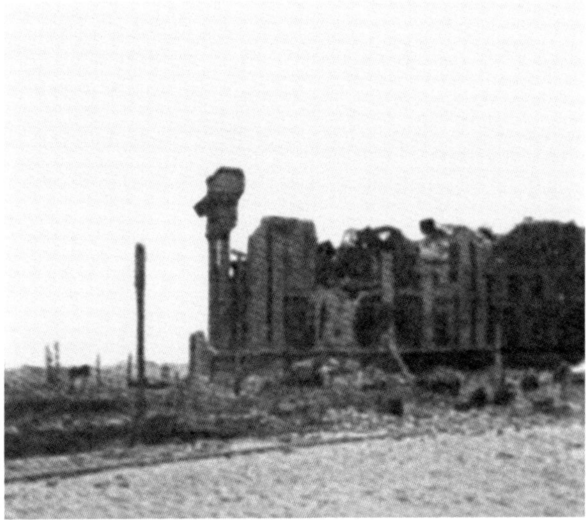

Fig. 39. H. D'Arcy Power, "Wrecked Frame Buildings and West Wing of City Hall," 1906, in *Camera Craft*, May 1906

to the overall composition—as spectators in the midst of chaos (see pls. 4–5, 10, 12, 18); as landscape staffage; and as citizens integral to rebuilding efforts (see pls. 83, 87–88). His skillful employment of the human figure reveals his craft—whereas a painter can create a sense of human interest and scale through the flick of a brush, achieving these effects in photography requires patience as people move in and out of a carefully framed view or are thoughtfully staged. Genthe's artistic education and upbringing surely influenced his aesthetic. His images ascribe to the tenets of Romantic landscape painting—finding beauty both in humankind's ability to control the natural world and in the awe-inspiring power of natural forces—and demonstrate a keen eye for visual reportage. This unique portrait of the city remained largely hidden from the public. Although Genthe shot more than one hundred images of the earthquake and its aftermath, he shared very few of them with the public. He printed a small number, gifting some to the French actress Sarah Bernhardt in commemoration of a tour the two made of the earthquake's damage and exhibiting just a handful in later years.[8]

The San Francisco earthquake was one of the first American disasters to be rigorously recorded by amateur and professional photographers alike.[9] Their diverse interests and skills resulted in a range of representations that today help comprehensively visualize the human and economic devastation as it unfolded in real time. Writing for the June issue of *Camera Craft*, photographer Edgar A. Cohen observed that "everyone who either possessed, could buy, or borrow [a camera], and was then fortunate enough to secure supplies for it, made more or less good use of his knowledge of photography."[10] The results varied. As Cohen warned, the "conditions could hardly have been more adverse and only those equipped with the best lenses had much chance of securing good results."[11] Thick clouds, constantly transforming smoke, and particulates in the air as well as low-quality processing chemicals impacted the legibility of photographs, but there were also other circumstances that set some of the images apart.

One significant factor was that the photographers who ventured out into the city possessed varying levels of experience. Amateurs raced to "snap" a shot while professionals were more likely to carefully stage their compositions, waiting for just the right moment to expose photosensitized emulsion to light. Sociopolitical conditions also affected the outcome. Unless a photographer was in possession of a

Collier's for May 5 1906

THE DESTRUCTION OF THE GOLDEN GATE CITY

Collier's for May 5 1906

THE FIRST SKIRMISH

THE frame buildings on the "Barbary Coast," shown in the two pictures on the right, helped to give the fire its start. Below appears a small section of the huge army of refugees that streamed out of the city for a week after the disaster. It is estimated that in the first five days 225,000 people—more than half the entire population—left San Francisco. Probably a third of these stayed in near-by towns. To carry the rest away free railroad transportation was furnished a distance of five hundred miles

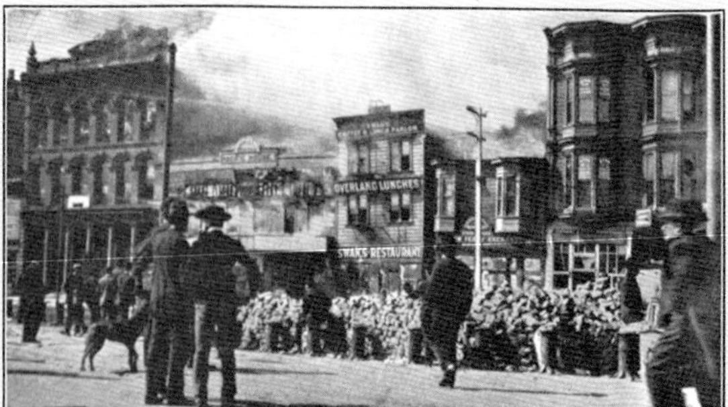

A SECTION OF EAST STREET ON THE WATER FRONT WHEN THE FIRE STARTED

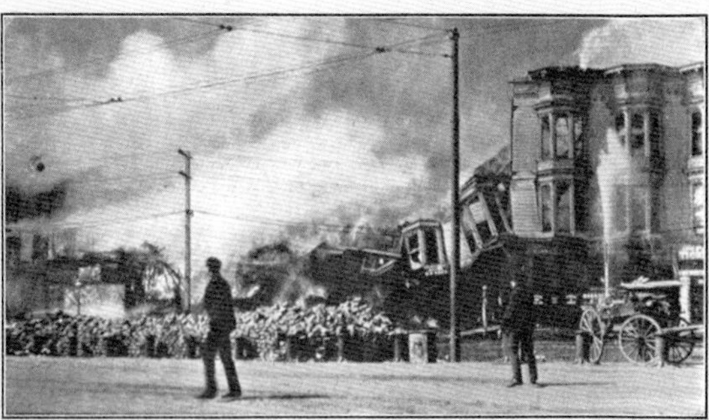

THE SAME HOUSES ON EAST STREET SHOWN ABOVE, FIFTEEN MINUTES LATER

Fugitives picking their way through the ruins about the Native Sons Monument at Mason and Market Streets, not far from the City Hall

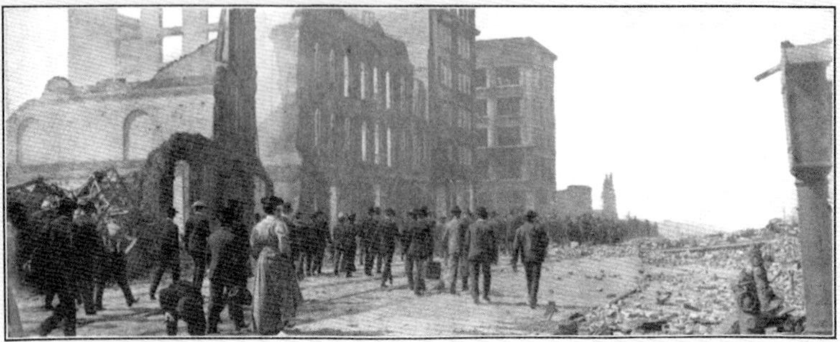

REFUGEES GOING DOWN MARKET STREET TOWARD THE FERRY TO ESCAPE TO OAKLAND, FRIDAY, APRIL 20

24

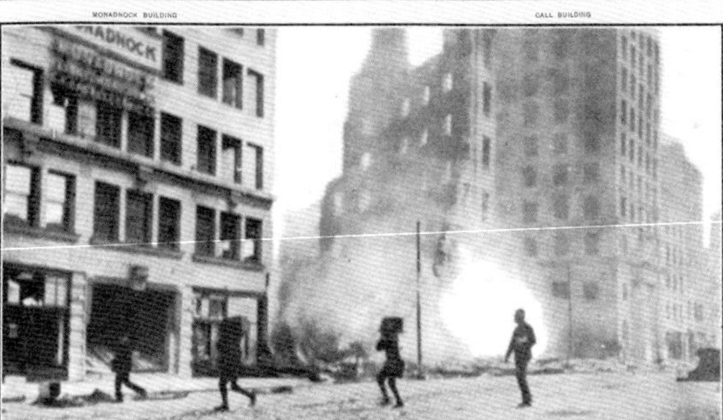

SOLDIERS CARRYING DYNAMITE TO BLOW UP BUILDINGS IN THE PATH OF THE FLAMES

THE LAST STAND

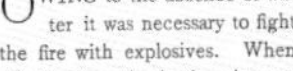

OWING to the absence of water it was necessary to fight the fire with explosives. When all the dynamite in the city was exhausted more was brought from the powder works across the bay. Even that gave out, and barrels of the Government's gunpowder at the Presidio were used. In the last great rally at Van Ness Avenue, a wide street which offered the only remaining line of defense, three-quarters of a mile of sumptuous homes went down under the combined assault of dynamite and artillery

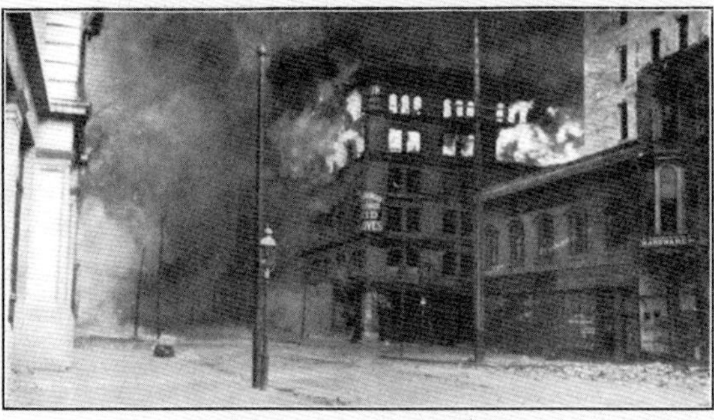

BURNING BUILDINGS IN THE WHOLESALE DISTRICT AT NEW MONTGOMERY AND MISSION STREETS

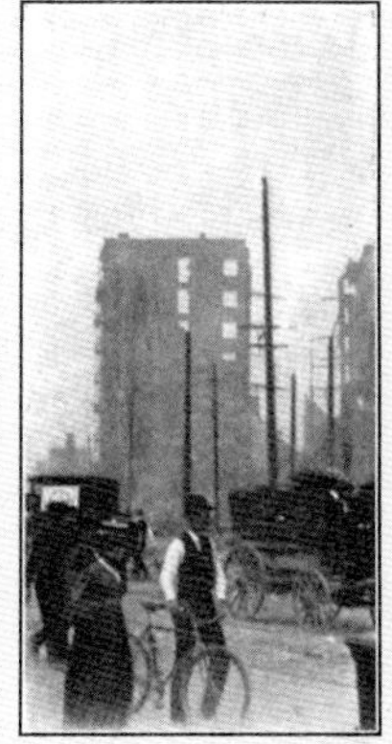

The general exodus from the stricken city, Friday, April 20. Hundreds of people with all they could carry fled by wagon, bicycle, and on foot

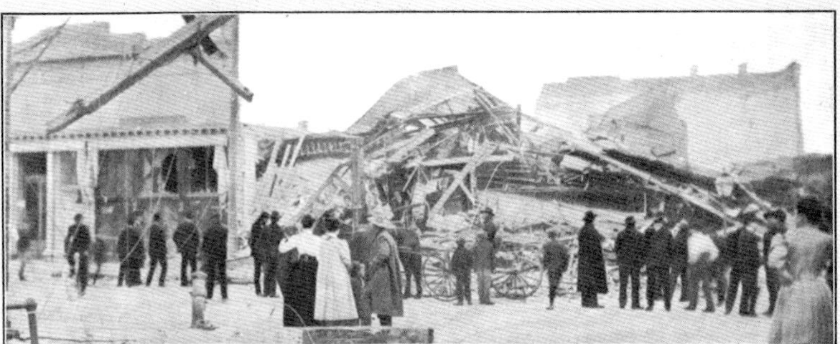

WOODEN HOUSES AND SHOPS ON VALENCIA STREET IN THE MISSION DISTRICT, PART OF WHICH WAS NOT AFFECTED BY THE FIRE

25

Fig. 40. "The Destruction of the Golden Gate City," in *Collier's*, May 5, 1906

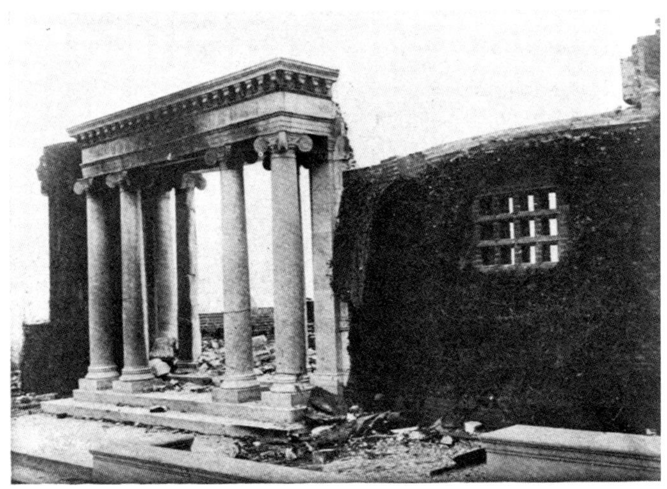

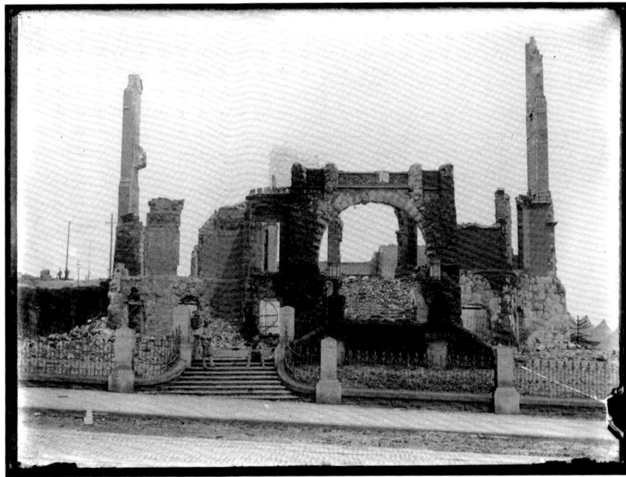

Fig. 41. Edgar A. Cohen, "Doorway, Towne Home," 1906, in *Camera Craft*, June 1906

Fig. 42. Edith Irvine (American, 1884–1949), *Charles Crocker Home on California Street between Jones Street and Taylor Street*, 1906. Scan from gelatin dry plate negative, 5 × 7 in. (127 × 178 mm). Brigham Young University Library, Special Collections, Provo, Utah

press pass, barriers erected by state militias to prevent looting may have presented insurmountable difficulties in gaining access to certain sites. In some cases, an undocumented photographer's encounter with an official could have more serious repercussions, resulting in the confiscation of a camera or exposed film. Some were even compulsorily detained to clear the streets of fallen debris and rubble, as happened to Genthe on more than one occasion.[12] Nonetheless, many took the risk in order to seize what photographer H. D'Arcy Power called "the greatest photographic opportunity of our lives." To illustrate his May 1906 account of the earthquake and fire, Power selected photographs showing the damage done to buildings made with different construction techniques, amassing an "archive" of structural successes and failures. Power observed that frame buildings rarely collapsed unless they were placed atop old, rotting wooden piers, in which case "they broke up into heaps of kindling wood." His image of City Hall (fig. 39, right) revealed it to be decimated, "its skeleton frame . . . an embodiment of the universal ruin!"[13]

As professional and amateur photographers roamed the streets, searching for ideal vantage points from which to capture vivid portraits of the damage, entrepreneurial types keen to make quick cash rapidly set about fulfilling the demands of the country's daily, weekly, and monthly periodicals. "Smoke pictures" taken within the first two days of the disaster were of greatest interest to publishers, one photographer told *Camera Craft*. This same person admitted to putting his own body too close to the fire in an effort to meet their requests.[14] Images of the "havoc wrought by the flames," as described by one headline in the May 5 issue of *Collier's* magazine, filled the pages of local and national publications for weeks after the earthquake. These often took the form of photographic essays, such as "The Destruction of the Golden Gate City," which was printed in *Collier's* alongside a special report written by local novelist Jack London (see fig. 40). Composed primarily of images copyrighted by the San Francisco Ruins Publishing Company, this double-page spread detailed the mayhem as the conflagration intensified: soldiers rushing to demolish buildings along the flames' paths, the displaced escaping rubble-filled streets, and onlookers observing the spectacle of an unharmed wooden house. In these essays, the shells of buildings frequently served as poignant backdrops for resilient survivors, steadfast in their determination to rebuild.

Commercially oriented photographers were not always guided by an eye for quality. The fires' quick-changing conditions whipped some into a frenzy as they combed the streets in search of the next marketable image. As the flames were extinguished and the billowing smoke dissipated, they turned their lenses toward architectural remnants of the famed Victorian city. Haste did not always render a clear or composed image. According to Cohen, one professional admitted to having sold thousands of poor-quality prints east of the Sierras, where obsession with imagery of the ruins was rampant. Cohen wrote: "[H]e said that the lighting of the pictures did not make any difference, that he did not even fill up the pin holes in the negatives; and as for the prints, he did not have to trim, clean, title them or do any spotting; that anything showing ruins, 'went.'"[15]

◆ ◆ ◆

In a city as small as San Francisco—which today covers an area of merely 49 square miles and in 1906 spanned even fewer—it is unsurprising that many photographers gravitated toward the same subjects. Aside from the effect of atmospheric and sociopolitical conditions, certain aesthetic decisions such as perspective, framing, time of day, and including or omitting bystanders also helped shape the overall feel of the final images. A comparison of Cohen's *Doorway, Towne Home* (fig. 41) and Genthe's photograph of the entrance to the Towne mansion, titled *Portals of the Past* (pl. 54), which both show the remains of the Alban N. Towne residence on California Street, reveals how each photographer selected a specific vantage point, thereby framing entirely distinct vistas. With a strong diagonal cutting across the horizon, Cohen positioned the intricate colonnade of the home's doorway so that it ended near his photograph's center. The white marble columns of the entrance, which withstood the earthquake, provide a strong visual counterpoint to a dark, ivy-covered adjacent wall. According to Cohen, a photographer's goal was "to compose his picture in the way it most strongly appeals to his own tastes."[16] Yet, without text to anchor his subject in time and space, Cohen's photograph could have been taken almost anywhere. By contrast, Genthe's photograph, which frames City Hall squarely within the mansion's Ionic columns, endures as an iconic image of the San Francisco earthquake.

Genthe also took another shot of the Towne home from a vantage point similar to Cohen's but to very different effect (see cat. 90). Taking to the streets on a moonlit night, Genthe created a poetic Pictorialist image using soft focus, capturing the ruins in a way that the photographer believed "brought out its classic beauty."[17] A nearby, deeply silhouetted palm contrasts starkly with the crumbling portico; a resolute symbol of nature's resilience even in the face of catastrophe, the tree lends an artistic quality to the work, adding a dynamic visual element to an otherwise decimated middle ground. The palpable differences among these photographs illustrate the effect of artistic intention. "The essential thing," Genthe wrote in his autobiography, "is to perceive a picture in what is before one, to choose an angle that will result in a pictorially interesting composition. The eye behind the camera is far more important than the lens in front of it."[18]

Another curious picture seeker on the streets at that time was Edith Irvine, whose views of the earthquake were occasionally taken from the same locations as Genthe's but at different times of day.[19] A resident of California's Mokelumne Hill, Irvine reached San Francisco on the day of the earthquake, arriving on a Stockton-based packet boat just after the earth ceased shaking. Over the next few days, she took to the streets and composed at least sixty images of the city in disrepair.[20] After each busy day traversing the streets, she returned to Stockton, where she developed her negatives and rested overnight before setting out again.[21] In *Charles Crocker Home on California Street between Jones Street and Taylor Street* (fig. 42), Irvine focused at close range on what little remained standing of the modern, Second Empire–style mansion. Three figures pause on the building's exterior staircase and another two are just visible leaning against a telephone pole in the distance. But it is the architectural ruins, not the people, that are the true focus of this picture. Small details, such as the ornate exterior lanterns, hint at the inhabitants' way of life before the earthquake. The structures, transformed into ruins overnight, lack features typically aestheticized in photographs of older ruins, such as tangled and overgrown foliage. Instead, these elements stand as evocative reminders of a modern civilization wrecked by a natural disaster and of the hubris of humankind.

Despite the overlapping subject matter, works by Cohen, Genthe, and Irvine are today more unanimously regarded as artistic artifacts than are commercial images of the earthquake. This is due not only to stylistic choices but also to processes and materials. Commercial photographs from this era were reproduced using the then relatively new halftone process, printed on the typically poor-quality papers of newspapers and magazines. "Fine art" pictures often survive in the form of scans of negatives or high-quality prints—in Genthe's case, gelatin silver prints, some of which he mounted onto soft gray and tan-colored sheets. The surviving prints illustrate Genthe's careful and deliberate cropping, manifest when compared with contact prints housed at the Library of Congress. His darkroom manipulation of the negatives during printing resulted in images that demonstrate considered composition and tone. This attention to color, composition, and mounting provides his rare vintage prints with a materiality and intention that transforms the photographs into art.

Genthe infrequently exhibited prints from this period, and he never compiled the images into a book-format pictorial meditation, as he did with his Chinatown (1896–1906) and New Orleans (1925) work. Nevertheless, his images—which nimbly straddle both Romantic landscape traditions and the reportage that would come to define photojournalism in the future—are ubiquitous throughout secondary literature on the 1906 earthquake. This prevalence ensures that Genthe's viewpoint, more than any other photographer's, continues to inform and shape the event's narrative.

Bearing Witness

THEN AND NOW

Richard Misrach

The curators asked contemporary photographer Richard Misrach (American, b. 1941) to write a brief essay that compares his and Arnold Genthe's work. Misrach is best known for his large-scale photographs that explore the complex conjunction between humankind and nature. All photographs by Misrach appear here courtesy of the artist; Pace Gallery, New York; Fraenkel Gallery, San Francisco; and Marc Selwyn Fine Art, Los Angeles.

ONE OF THE GREATEST TAKEAWAYS from Arnold Genthe's photographs of the 1906 San Francisco earthquake, and hopefully also from my own images of natural and human-made disasters, is the critical foresight they provide. These sorts of images remind us of the existential threats—earthquakes, fires, floods, wars, pandemics, and climate change—that impact and jeopardize the planet. In this sense, the pictures Genthe made a century ago are as relevant today as if they were made yesterday. They caution us to remain vigilant. History does, in fact, repeat itself.

While we work to preserve the ruins of ancient civilizations (see fig. 43), the remains of recent tragic events, such as the Oakland Hills fire (1991) or Hurricane Katrina (2005), would prefer to be forgotten. Rebuilding and erasure are the primary goals. The physical remains serve only as painful reminders and impediments to the resumption of everyday life. Even commemorative monuments, like the Vietnam Veterans Memorial or the 9/11 Memorial and Museum, somewhat efface memory by distilling and reshaping the narrative. After rebuilding, visual accounts remain to bear witness to civilization's most challenging moments. Think of Alexander Gardner's *Home of a Rebel Sharpshooter, Gettysburg* (1863), Dorothea Lange's *White Angel Breadline, San Francisco* (1933), Pablo Picasso's *Guernica* (1937), or photographs from Auschwitz. These representations permanently embed themselves in our cultural consciousness and become part of the historical record.

One thing I've discovered about photographs over the course of my career is that their meanings change with time. In the wake of any devastating event, photographs can be very difficult to look at, especially for the families and communities who are directly impacted. Over time, however, the immediacy of grief recedes, and other details recorded in the images begin to emerge. Modern viewers of Genthe's earthquake photographs can imagine the thousands of lives lost, a city destroyed, but the acute sorrow has receded with time. Commonplace facets of life in 1906 now inflect the images with fascinating information—horse-drawn fire engines, women's ankle-length dresses and men's formal suits and bowler hats, Victorian architecture.

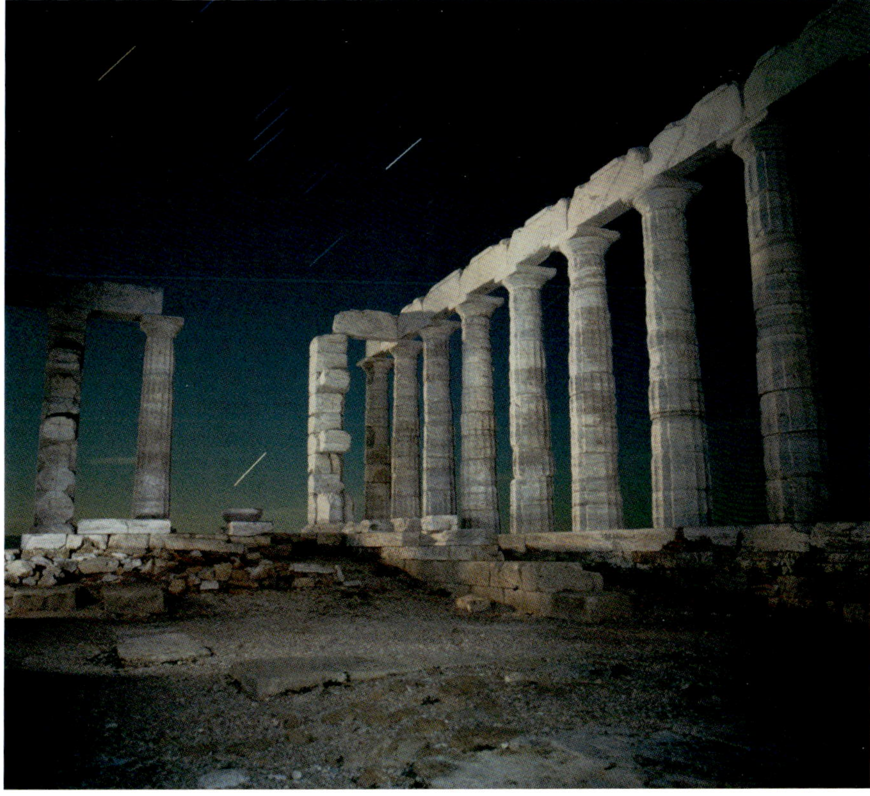

Fig. 43. Richard Misrach, *Sounion (with star trails)*, 1979. Pigment print, 60 × 80 in. (152.4 × 203.2 cm)

The meaning of photographic documents is never fixed. How these artifacts are read is influenced by the social, cultural, and political moment in which they are being looked at. I waited twenty years before exhibiting my pictures of the Oakland Hills fire and am publishing a couple of Hurricane Katrina images (figs. 44, 46) here for the first time, more than fifteen years later. For both of these bodies of work, I was particularly reluctant to contribute to the news spectacle that often accompanies a tragic event. I am more interested in the space where historical as well as aesthetic function displaces the spectacular. In this space, photography's ability to transcribe reality assumes its role in how we remember.

◆ ◆ ◆

Genthe turned from his long-term documentation of San Francisco's Chinatown population to spending weeks photographing the effects of the earthquake. He applied the same formal language to this new project. To paraphrase John Szarkowski, he knew where to stand, where to place his camera in relation to his subject, and how to make the most compelling image. One unique aspect of working in such a dynamic, difficult setting is that photographers must postpone their emotional engagement enough to concentrate on the work at hand. Photographers, like surgeons, need to suspend their own feelings about what they are actually seeing in order to do the job well.

Logistically, it must have been quite tricky for Genthe to get around while obtaining these images. To photograph the devastation along the Mississippi Gulf Coast and New Orleans after Hurricane Katrina, my Volkswagen camper allowed me to move hundreds of miles daily and sleep in the back of my van wherever I was. I had water and food, equipment, and film with me. Similarly, in 1991, I was able to climb the steep hills of Oakland in my VW after the firestorm to get better vantage points (see fig. 48). Genthe did not have that luxury. How did he get around? Mostly by foot, I assume. And because his home and studio were destroyed, he must have been dependent on others for shelter and food.

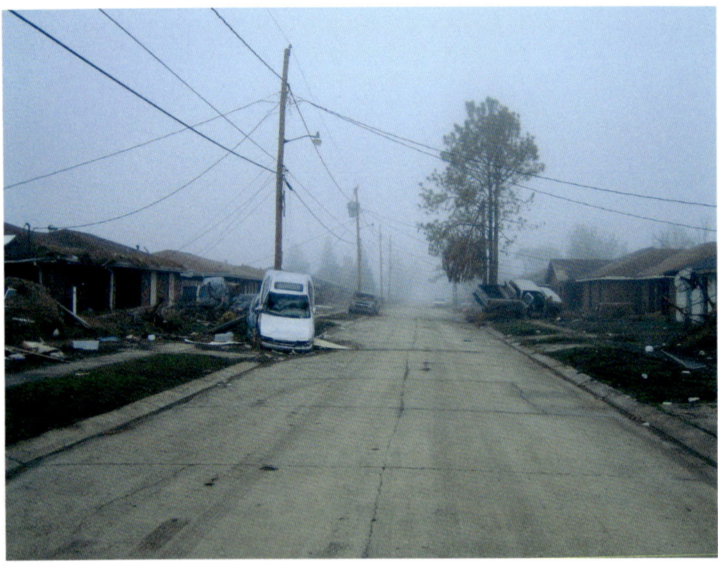

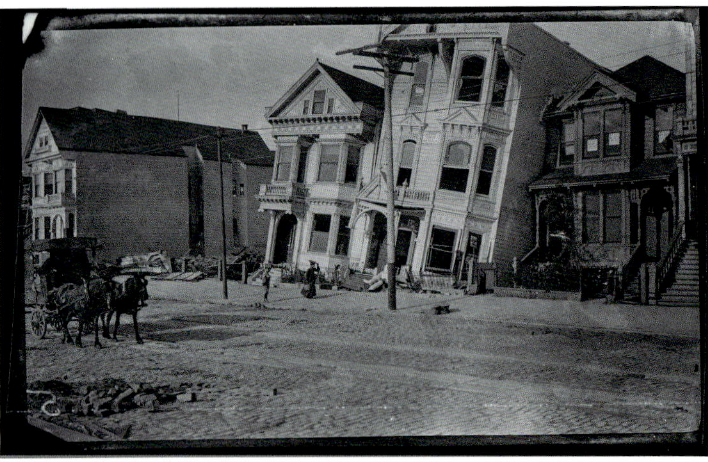

Fig. 44. Richard Misrach, *Hurricane Katrina*, 2005. Pigment print, 16 × 20 in. (40.6 × 50.8 cm)

Fig. 45. Arnold Genthe, Howard [now South Van Ness] near 18th Street, San Francisco, 1906 (pl. 26)

Fig. 46. Richard Misrach, *National Guard, Lower Ninth Ward, New Orleans, Louisiana*, 2005. Pigment print, 8 × 10 ft. (2.4 × 3 m)

Fig. 47. Arnold Genthe, California between Mason and Taylor, San Francisco, 1906 (pl. 65)

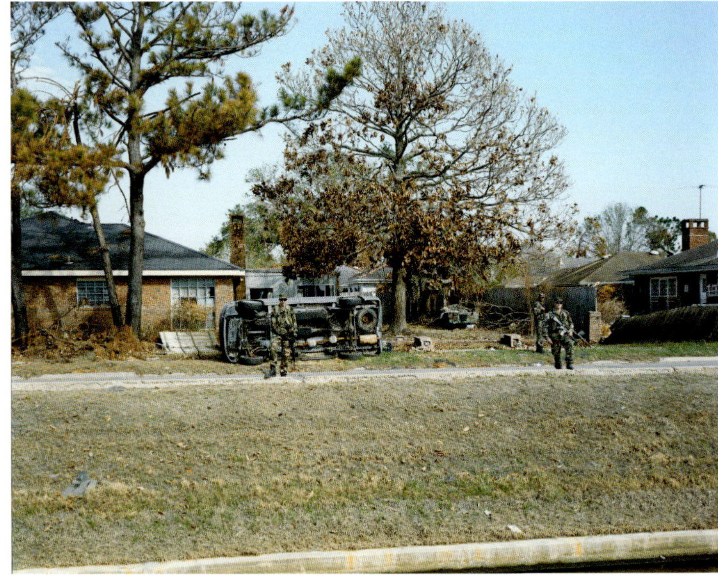

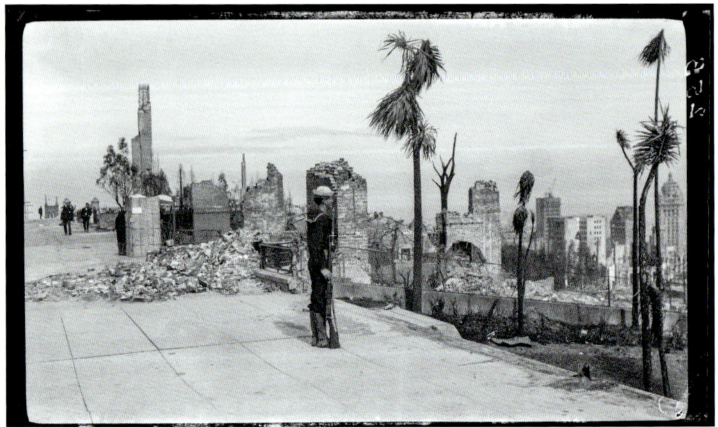

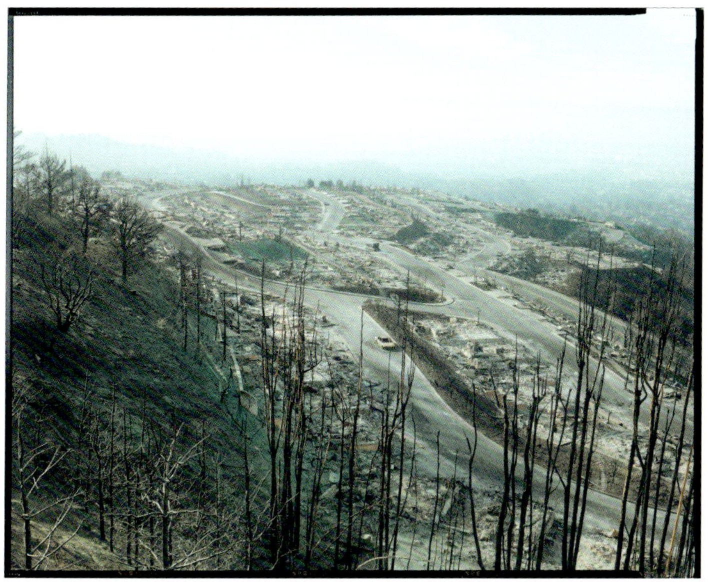

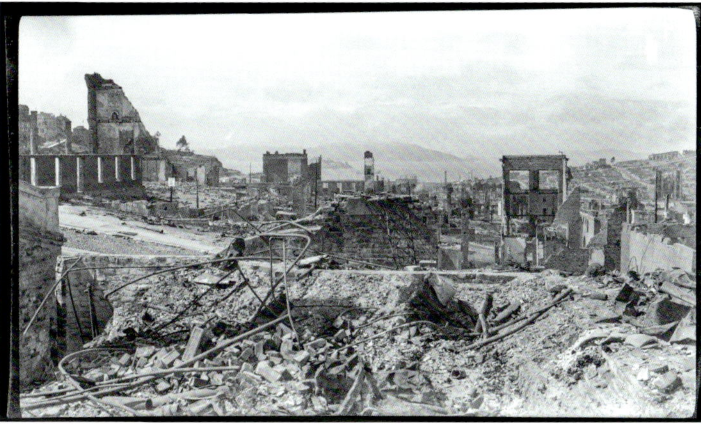

Fig. 48. Richard Misrach, *Oakland Fire #12-91 (Hiller Highlands Overview)*, 1991. Pigment print, 8 × 10 ft. (2.4 × 3 m)

Fig. 49. Arnold Genthe, View north from California between Powell and Stockton, San Francisco, 1906 (cat. 66)

Fig. 50. Richard Misrach, *Oakland Fire #119-91 (Stairway)*, 1991. Pigment print, 60 × 74 in. (152.4 × 188 cm)

Fig. 51. Arnold Genthe, *Steps That Lead to Nowhere (After the Fire)*, 1906 (cat. 91)

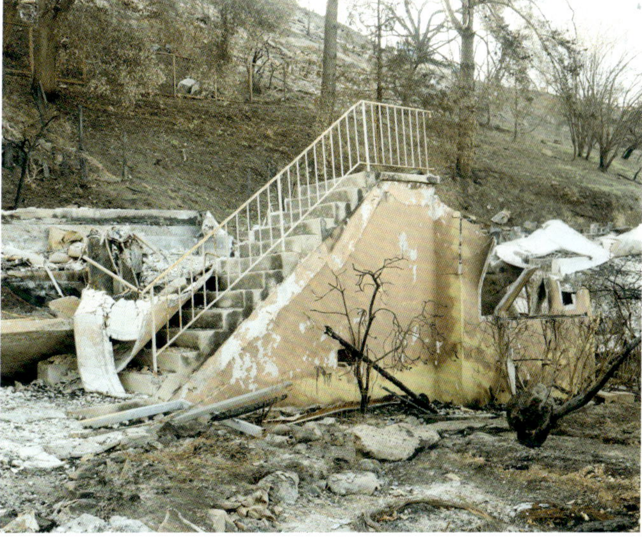

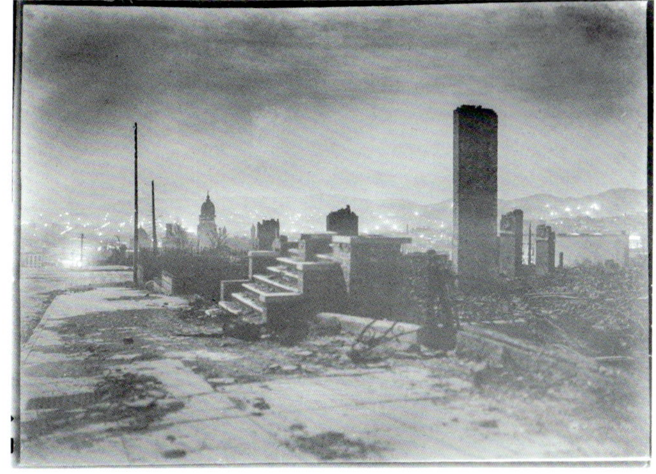

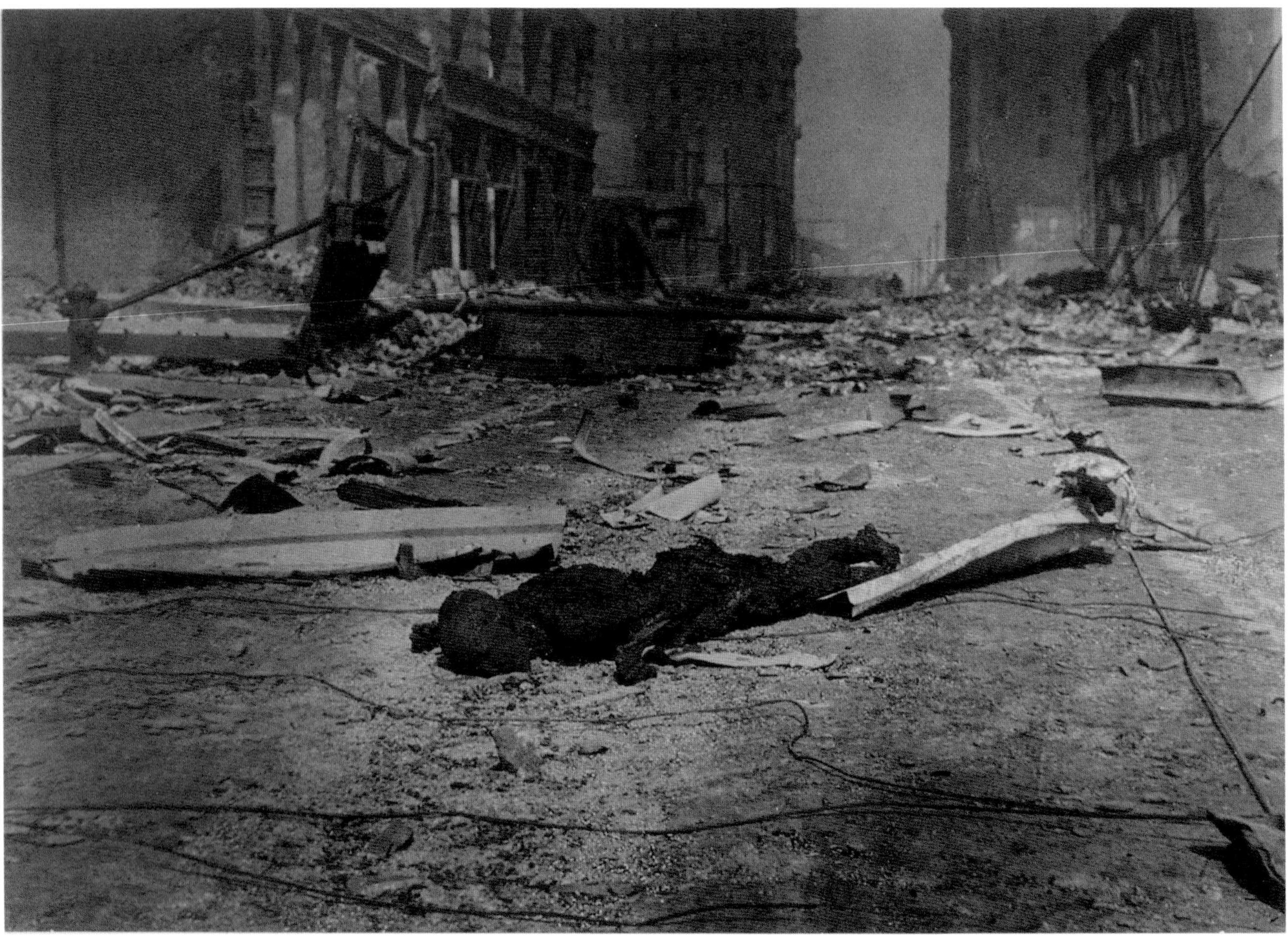

Fig. 52. Arnold Genthe, Untitled (Charred corpse near Post and Dupont Streets near Grant Avenue), 1906. Gelatin silver print, 8 11/16 × 12 5/16 in. (22.1 × 31.3 cm). Fine Arts Museums of San Francisco, Museum collection, Z2003.1

When I compare my photographs to Genthe's, I am struck by how the seemingly incidental details contribute to our distinct vocabularies. The automobile was just becoming part of American life in the 1900s; they are rarely found in Genthe's images. In my Oakland Hills fire and Hurricane Katrina pictures, and also in my images of the Salton Sea flood (1983–1985), destroyed cars are a crucial vernacular component (see figs. 44, 46). The cars represent a way of life that has been violently disrupted, but they also mark a particular moment in cultural history—cars' styles in the 1990s, for example, look significantly different from models made even twenty years earlier. And Genthe's landscapes are heavily populated: firemen and volunteers attend to emergencies; bystanders crowd the streets; onlookers sit on chairs and picnic blankets, even pose for the camera, while San Francisco burns. My images are largely devoid of people. Unlike Genthe, who was working immediately after the earthquake, I began photographing sometimes as much as a month after the actual event, and in areas that had often been evacuated (save for an occasional National Guard team; see fig. 46).

Genthe used a handheld camera and black-and-white film. He made small, beautiful black-and-white prints. As rich and informative as his images were, advances in technology since then allow for an increase in print scale and the use of color, which both provide even more detail. I have shot mostly with an 8-by-10-inch view camera on a tripod with color film and am able to make giant prints that can reach 8 by 10 feet. Details that would have otherwise been invisible are suddenly apparent. The color of clothing, buildings, vegetation, even a smoke-filled sky furnish rich information that black and white simply cannot.

But fundamentally, Genthe and I share identical processes. By necessity photographers work their way through images—positioning themselves, framing, shooting, moving slightly, shooting again, walking to a different angle, repeat. There are lots of misses. Eventually this process can yield a powerful image. All of the formal elements—composition, light, and content, from edge to edge—come together to make a clear narrative statement. Genthe's picture of a charred dead man (fig. 52) is a particularly affecting, if disturbing, example. In this sense, we both possess an impulse common to all photographers: the urgency to communicate a visual moment, knowing it will help define what we will know about our past.

"Verbal representations of such places, or scenes, may or may not have the merit of accuracy," Gardner wrote in *Gardner's Photographic Sketch Book of the Civil War* (1866), "but photographic presentments of them will be accepted by posterity with an undoubting faith." Genthe's photographs effectively communicate the extent of the 1906 earthquake's devastation, and they contain a wealth of period information as well. But it is impossible to guess how these documents will be visually processed a hundred years from now. It makes me wonder about readings of my own work.

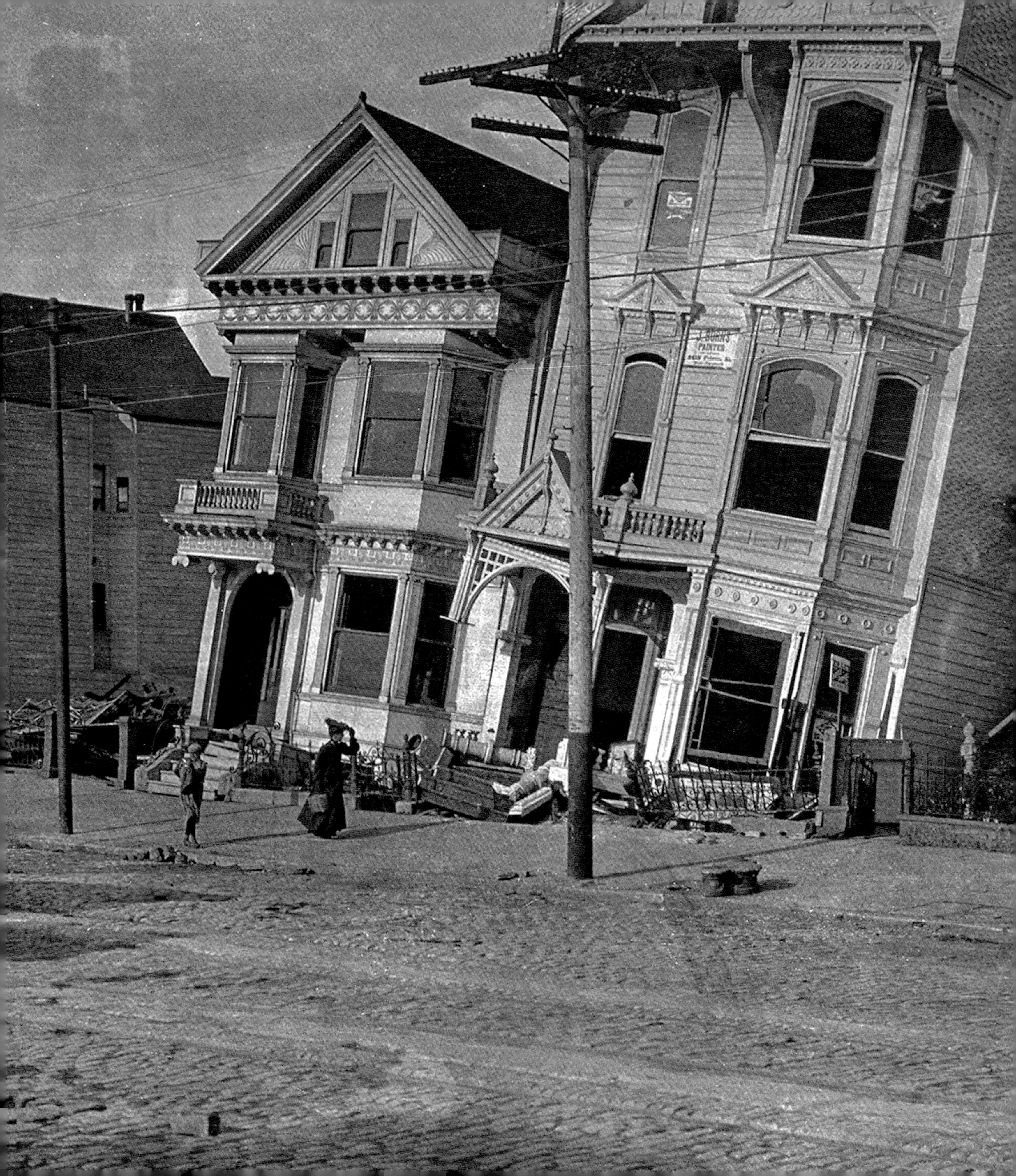
PAINTER

PLATES

FIRE

AND SMOKE

Unless otherwise noted, all works are untitled gelatin silver prints printed by Barret Oliver (American, b. 1973) in 2017 from negatives made by Arnold Genthe (American, b. Germany, 1869–1942) in 1906 and digitally preserved in 2015. Horizontal sheet dimensions are 16 × 20 in. (40.6 × 50.8 cm); vertical sheet dimensions are 20 × 16 in. (50.8 × 40.6 cm). All works are in the collection of the Fine Arts Museums of San Francisco, Museum purchase, Achenbach Graphic Arts Council Genthe Negatives Preservation Fund and gift of the San Francisco Auxiliary of the Fine Arts Museums of San Francisco.
For negative sponsorship information, refer to corresponding catalogue checklist entry.

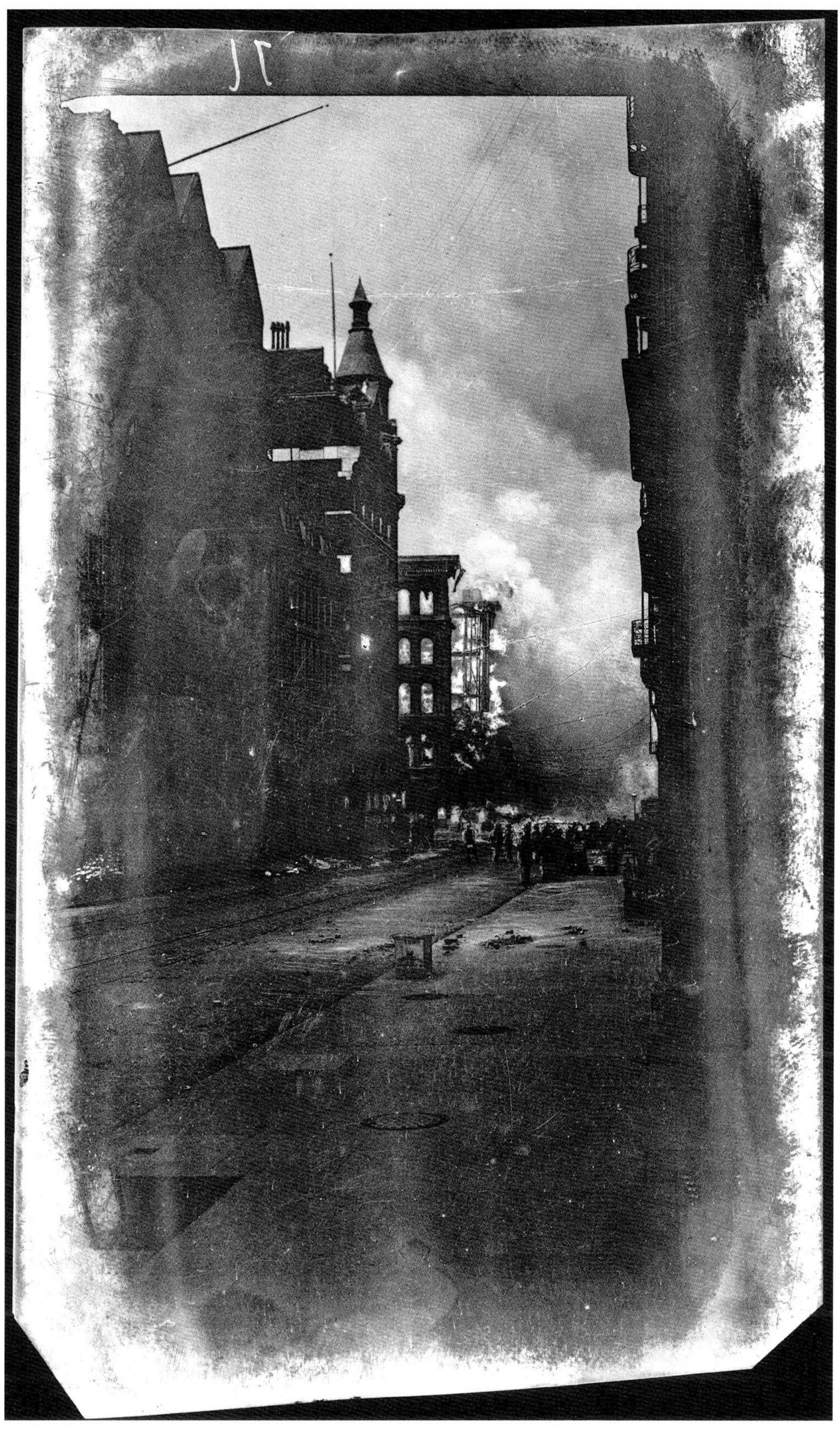

1.

Bush near Montgomery looking east toward Sansome, San Francisco
2018.21.68 (cat. 1)

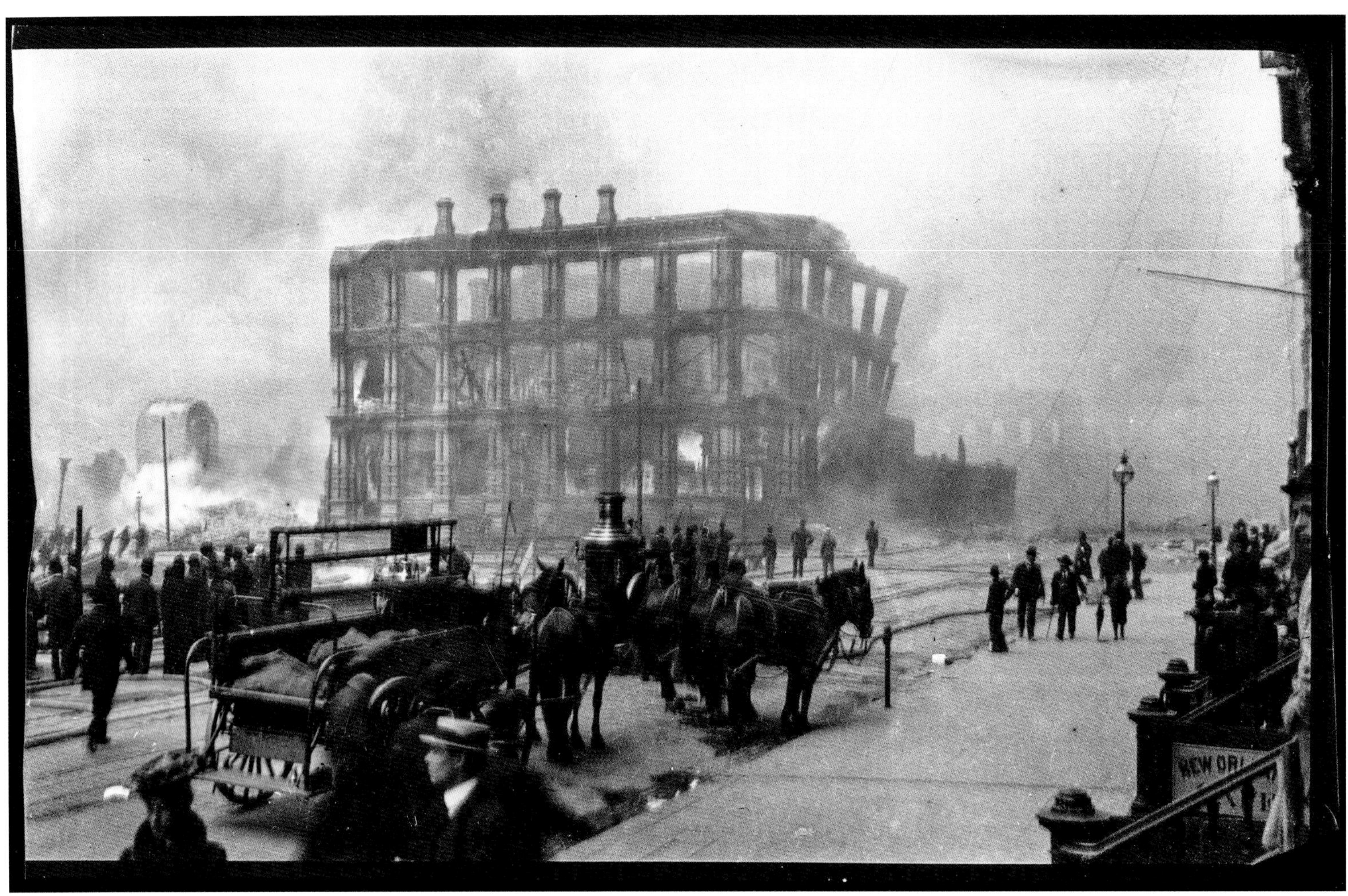

2.

Friedlander Block, northeast corner California and Sansome, San Francisco
2018.21.86 (cat. 2)

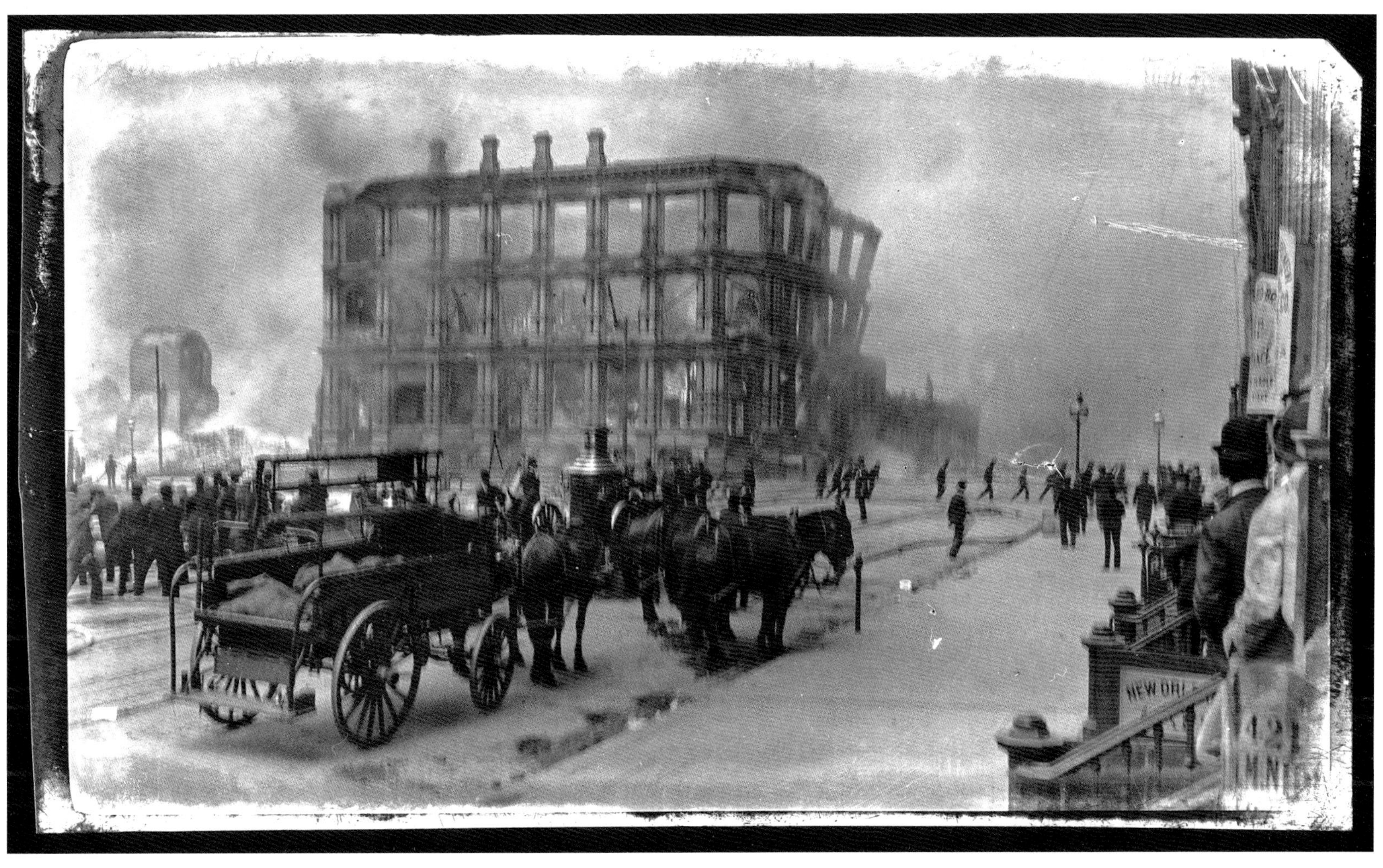

3.
Friedlander Block, northeast corner California and Sansome, San Francisco
2018.21.13 (cat. 3)

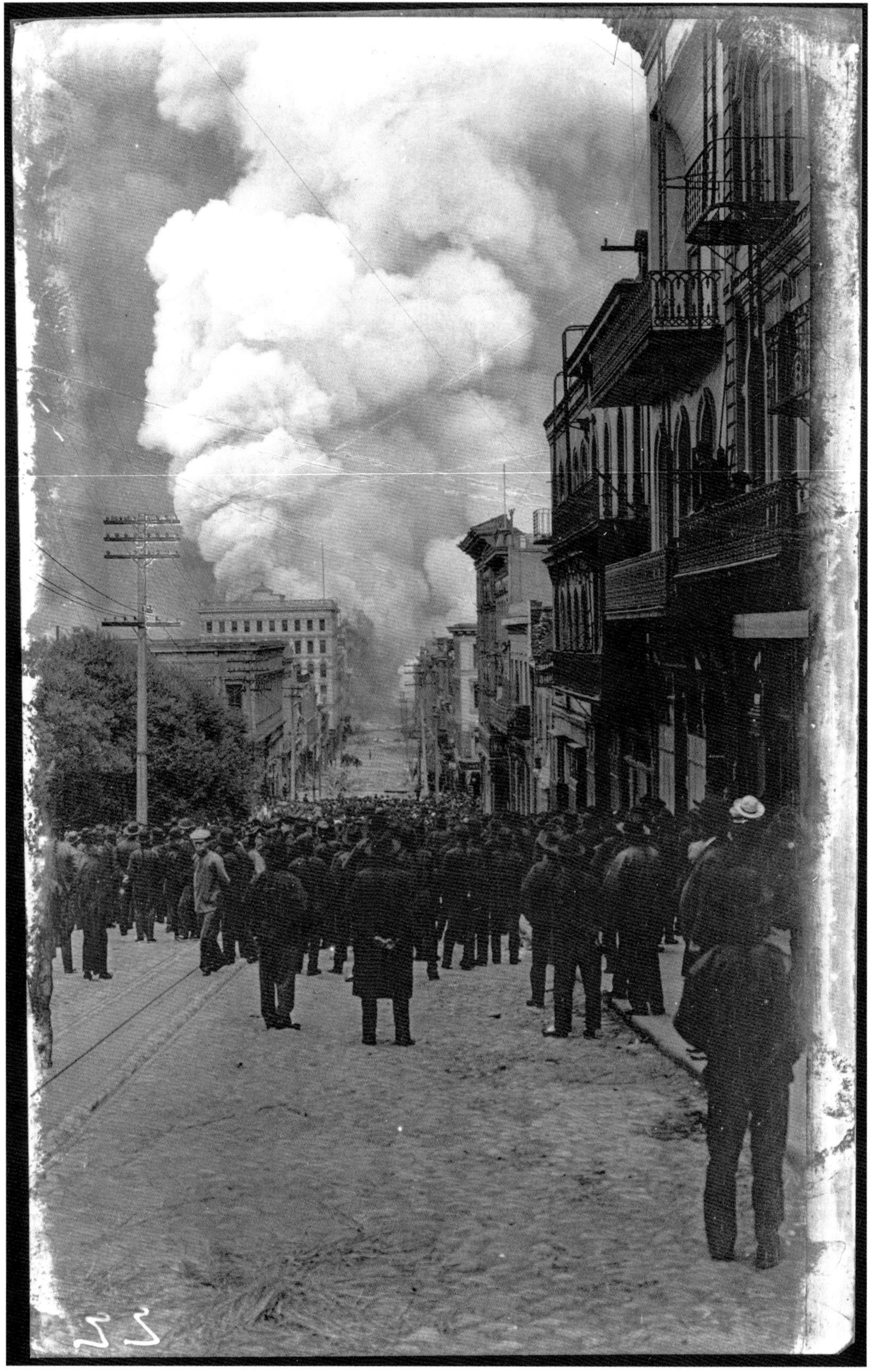

4.

Clay east of Dupont (Grant), San Francisco

2018.21.23 (cat. 4)

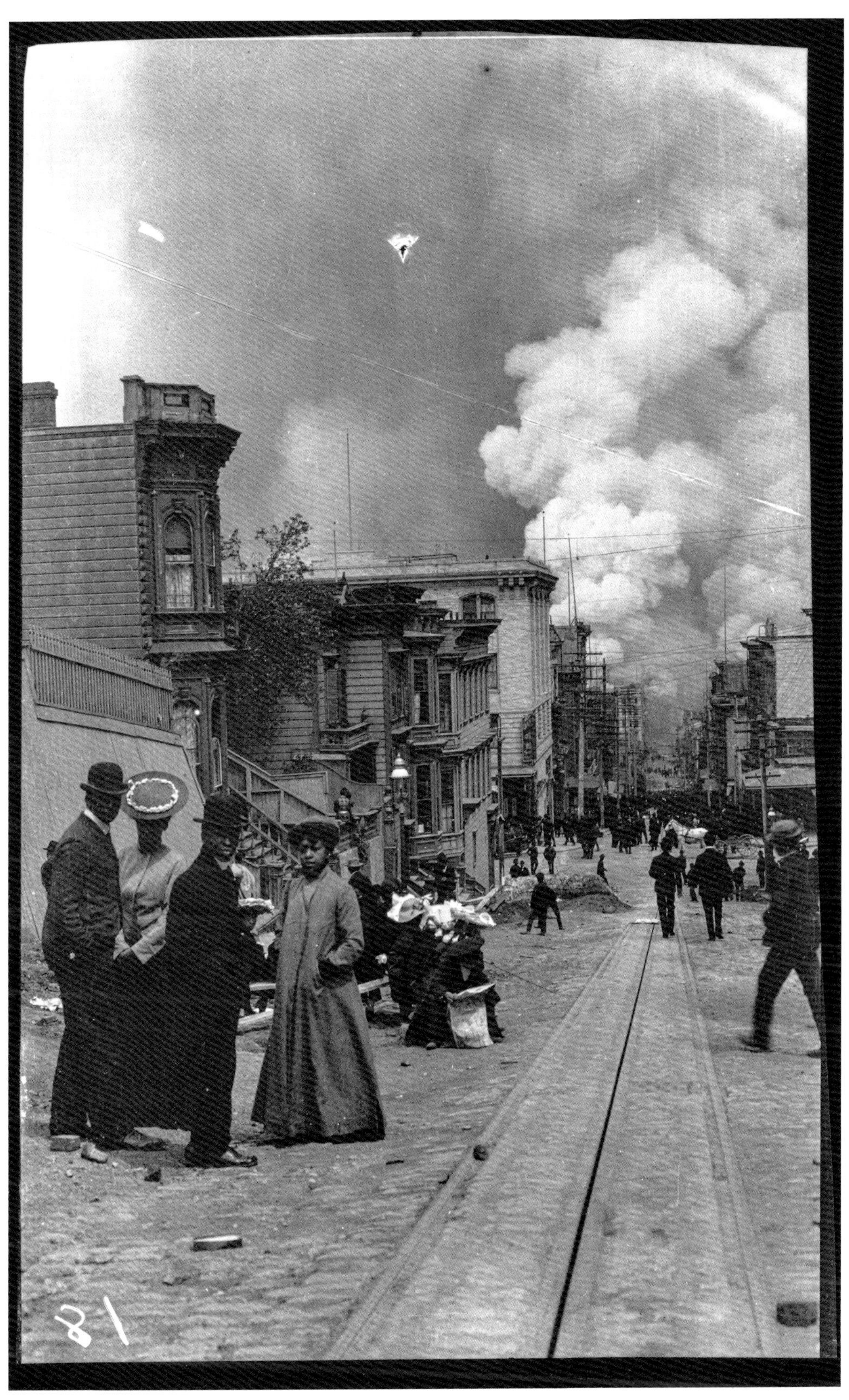

5.
Clay west of Stockton, San Francisco
2018.21.18 (cat. 5)

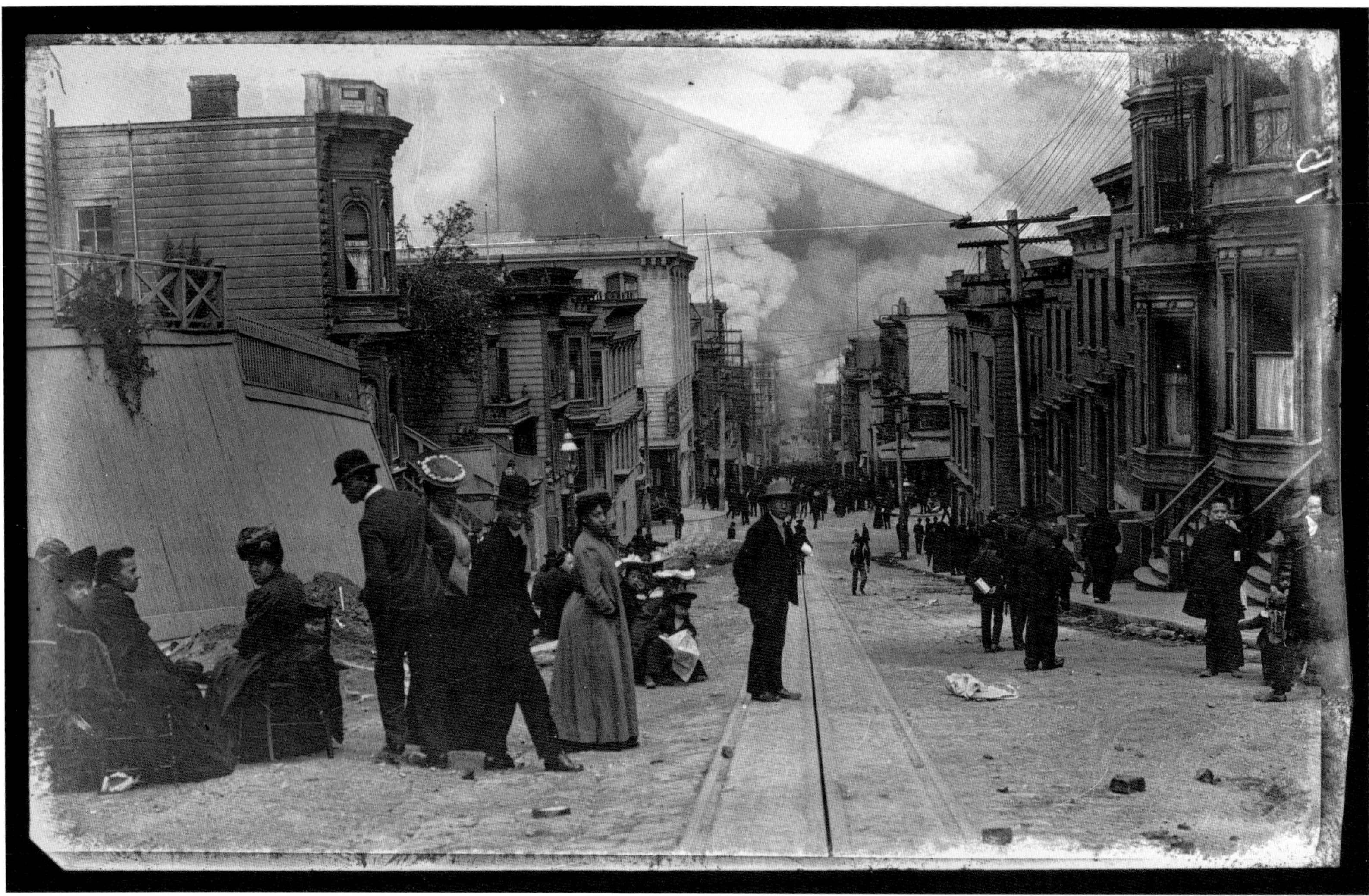

6.

Clay west of Stockton, San Francisco
2018.21.8 (cat. 6)

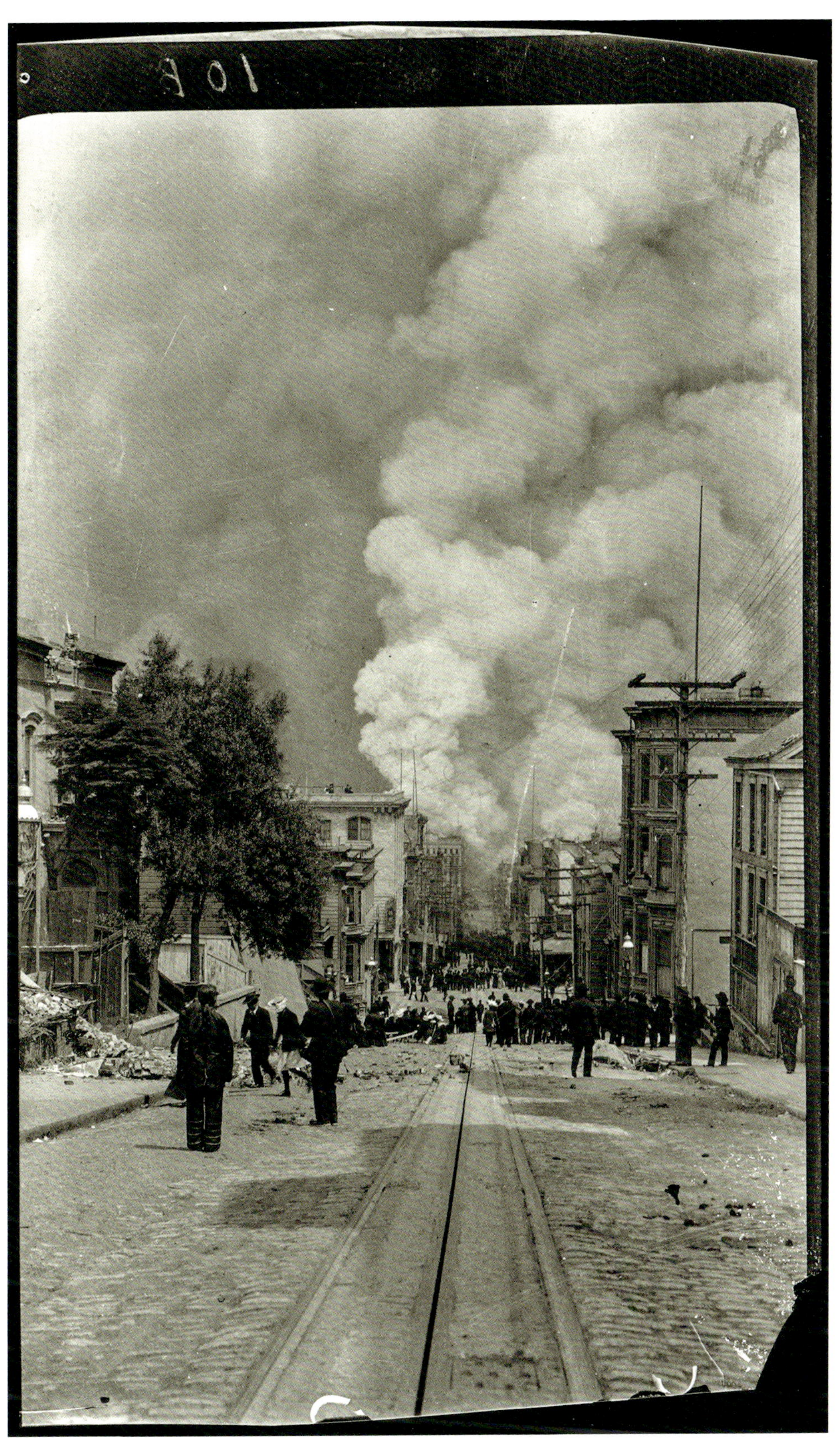

7.

Clay west of Stockton, San Francisco
2018.21.10 (cat. 7)

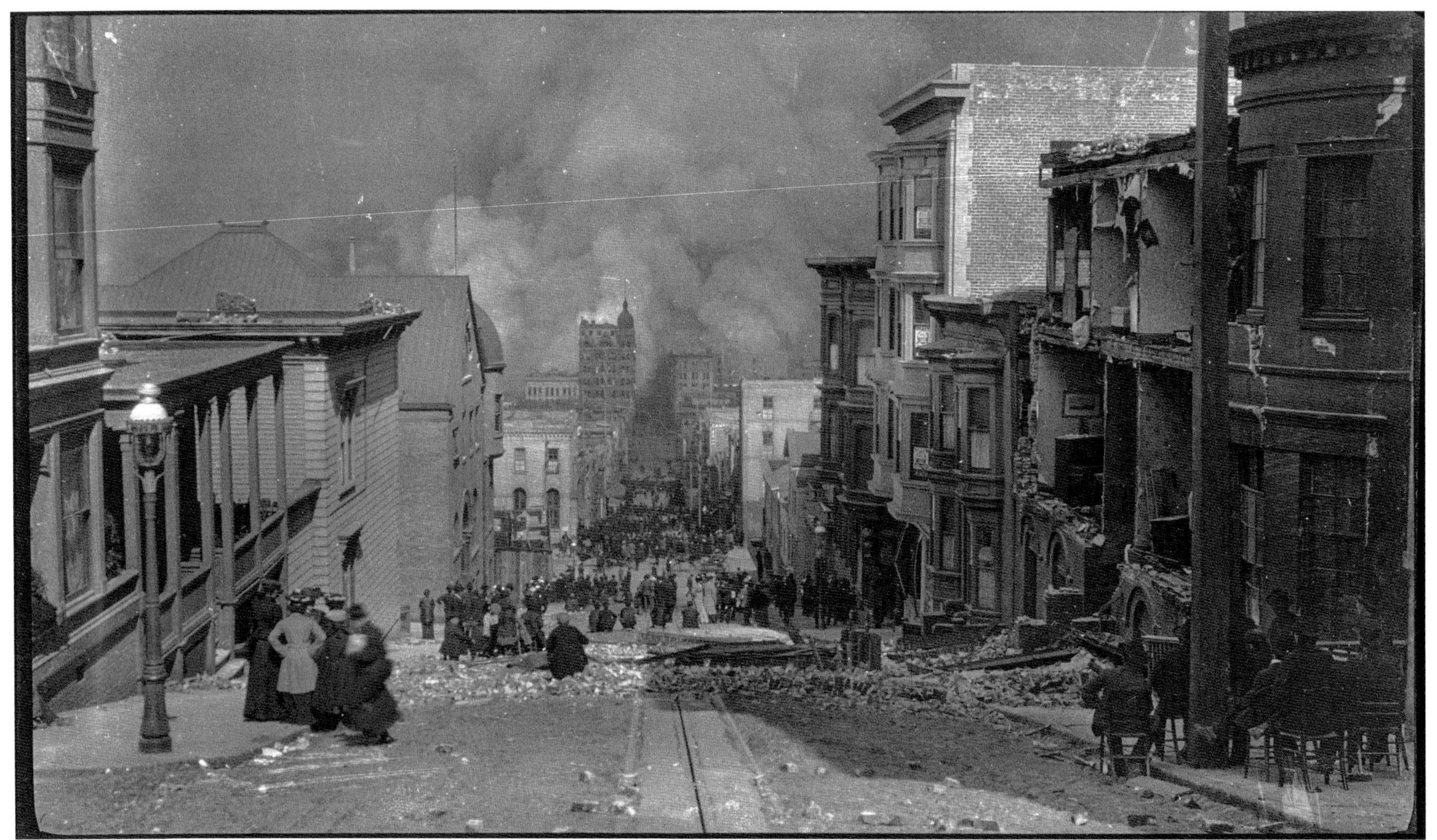

8.

Downtown from Sacramento just east of Powell, San Francisco
2018.21.1 (cat. 8)

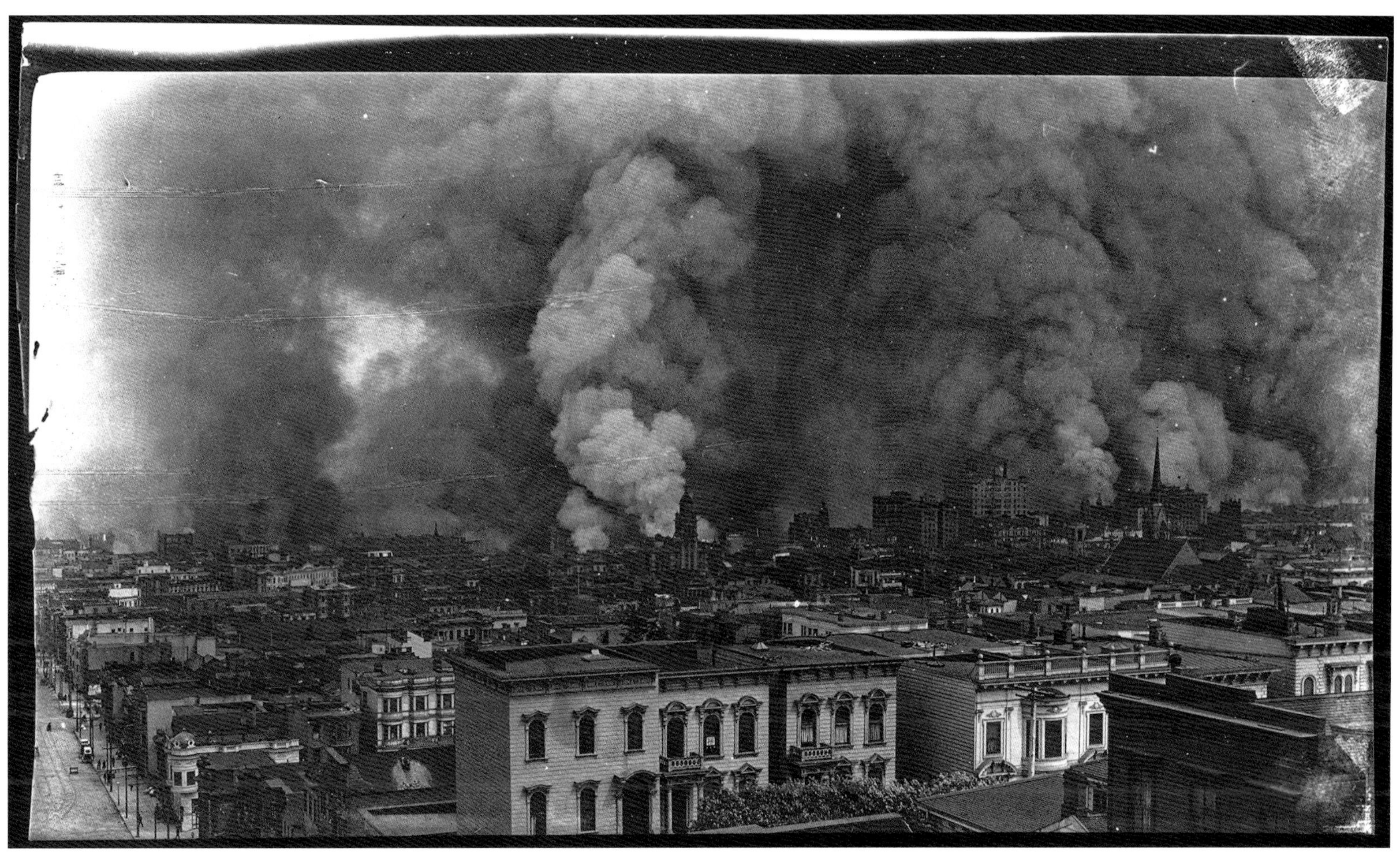

9.
View of the burning city from Broadway west of Taylor, San Francisco
2018.21.22 (cat. 9)

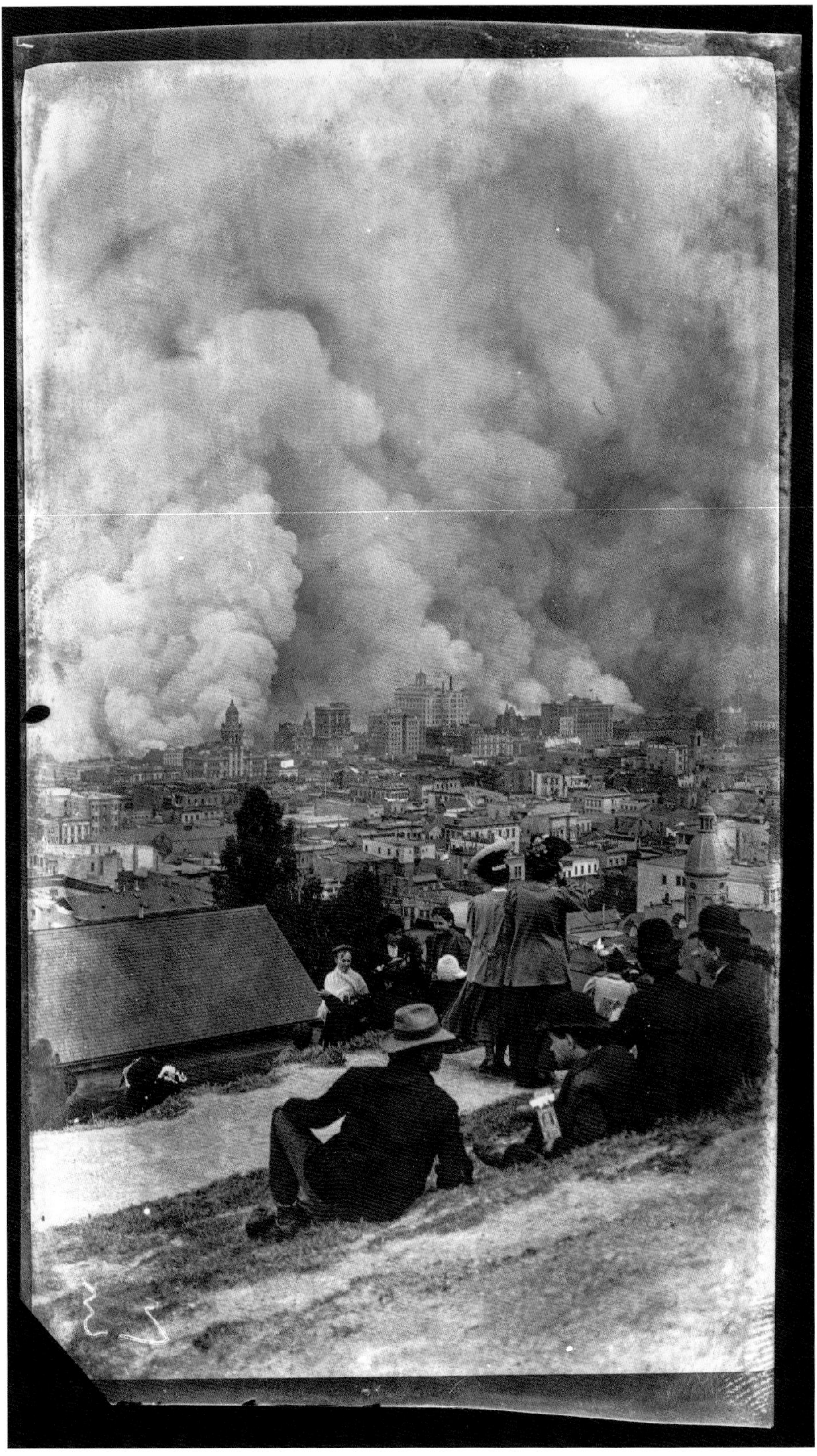

10.

Ina Coolbrith Park, Vallejo and Taylor, San Francisco
2018.21.26 (cat. 11)

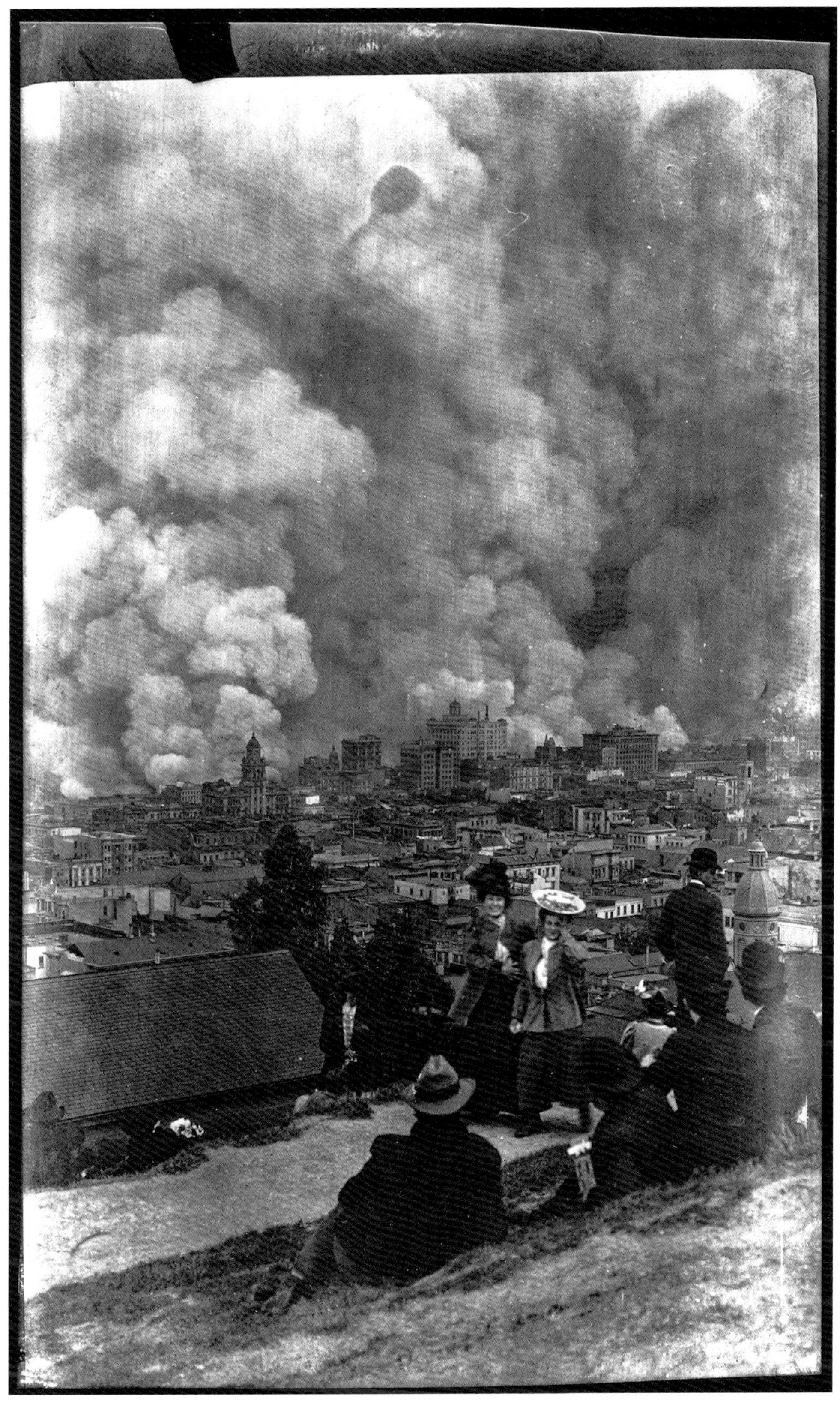

11.

Ina Coolbrith Park, Vallejo and Taylor, San Francisco
2018.21.11 (cat. 12)

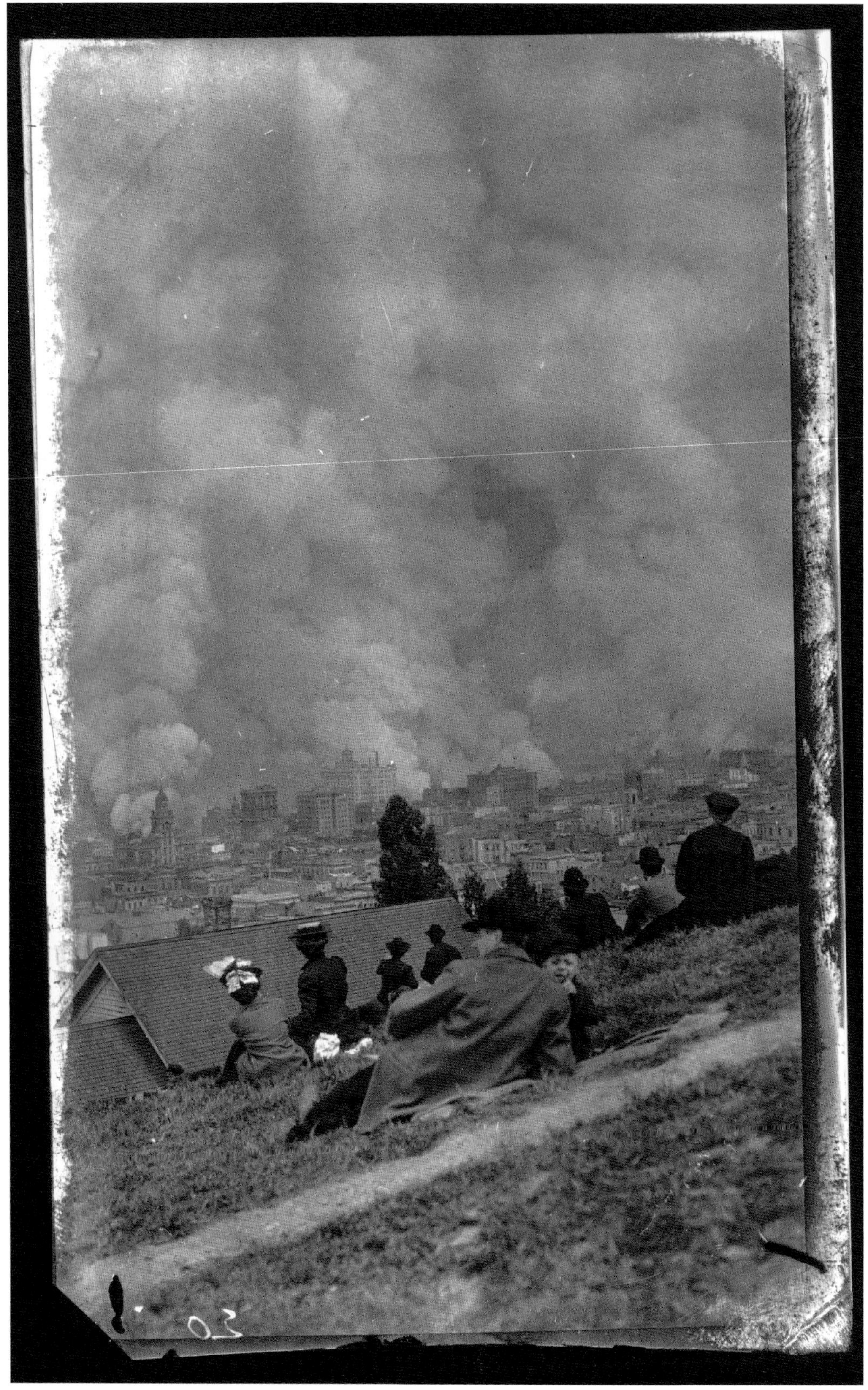

12.

Ina Coolbrith Park, Vallejo and Taylor, San Francisco
2018.21.20 (cat. 13)

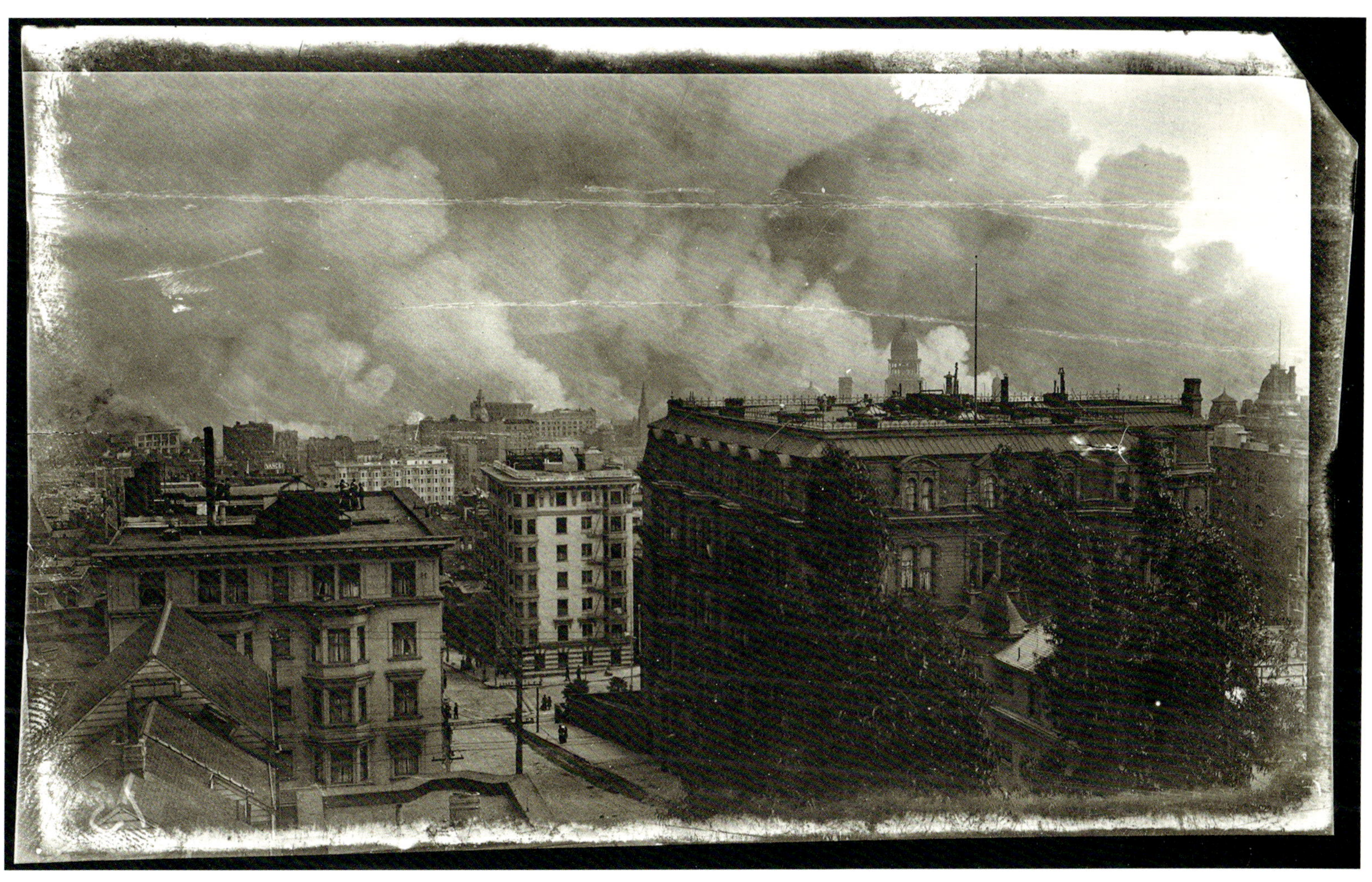

13.

View from the Tobin mansion, California and Taylor, San Francisco
2018.21.12 (cat. 14)

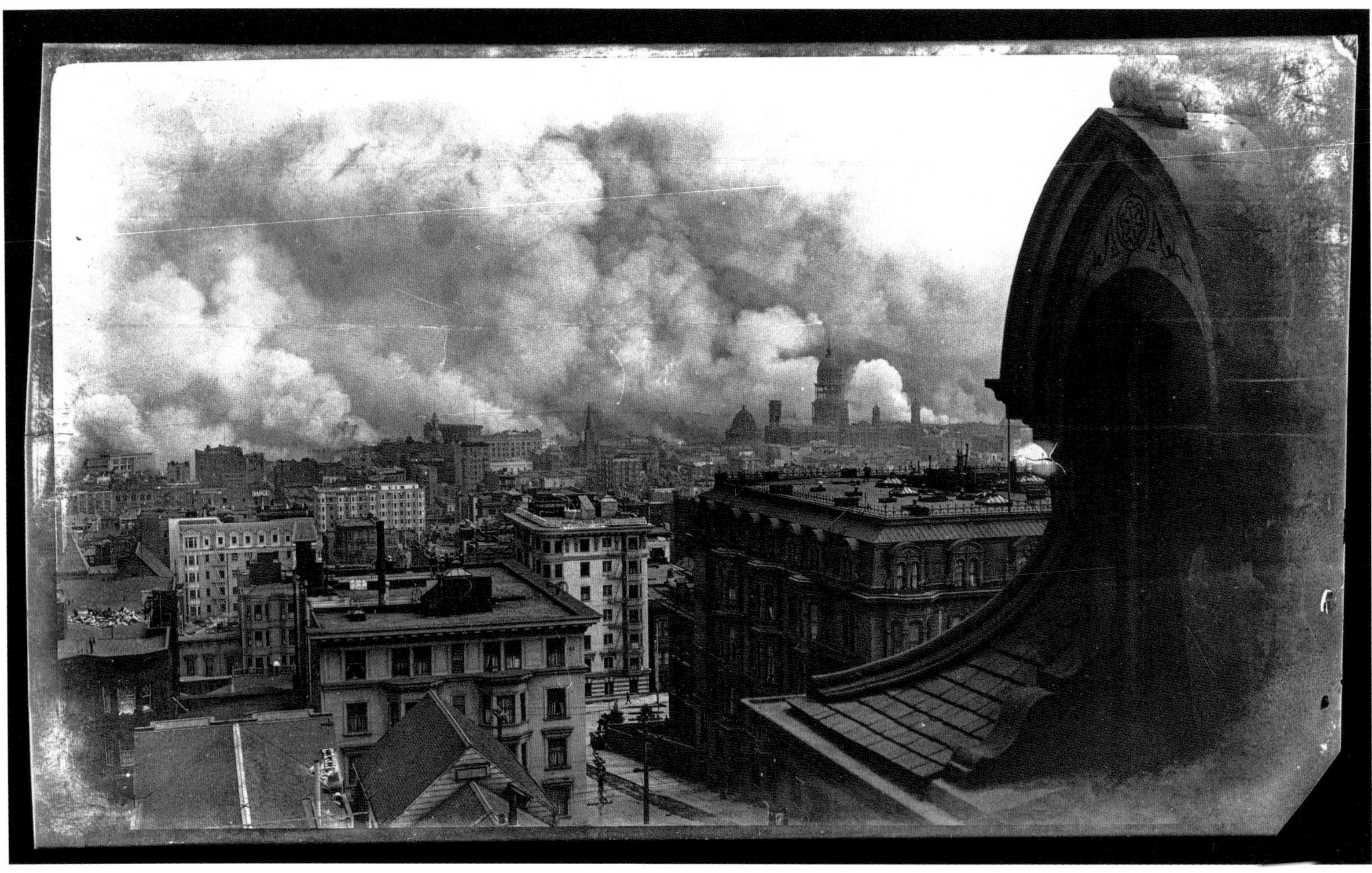

14.
View from the Tobin mansion, California and Taylor, San Francisco
2018.21.15 (cat. 15)

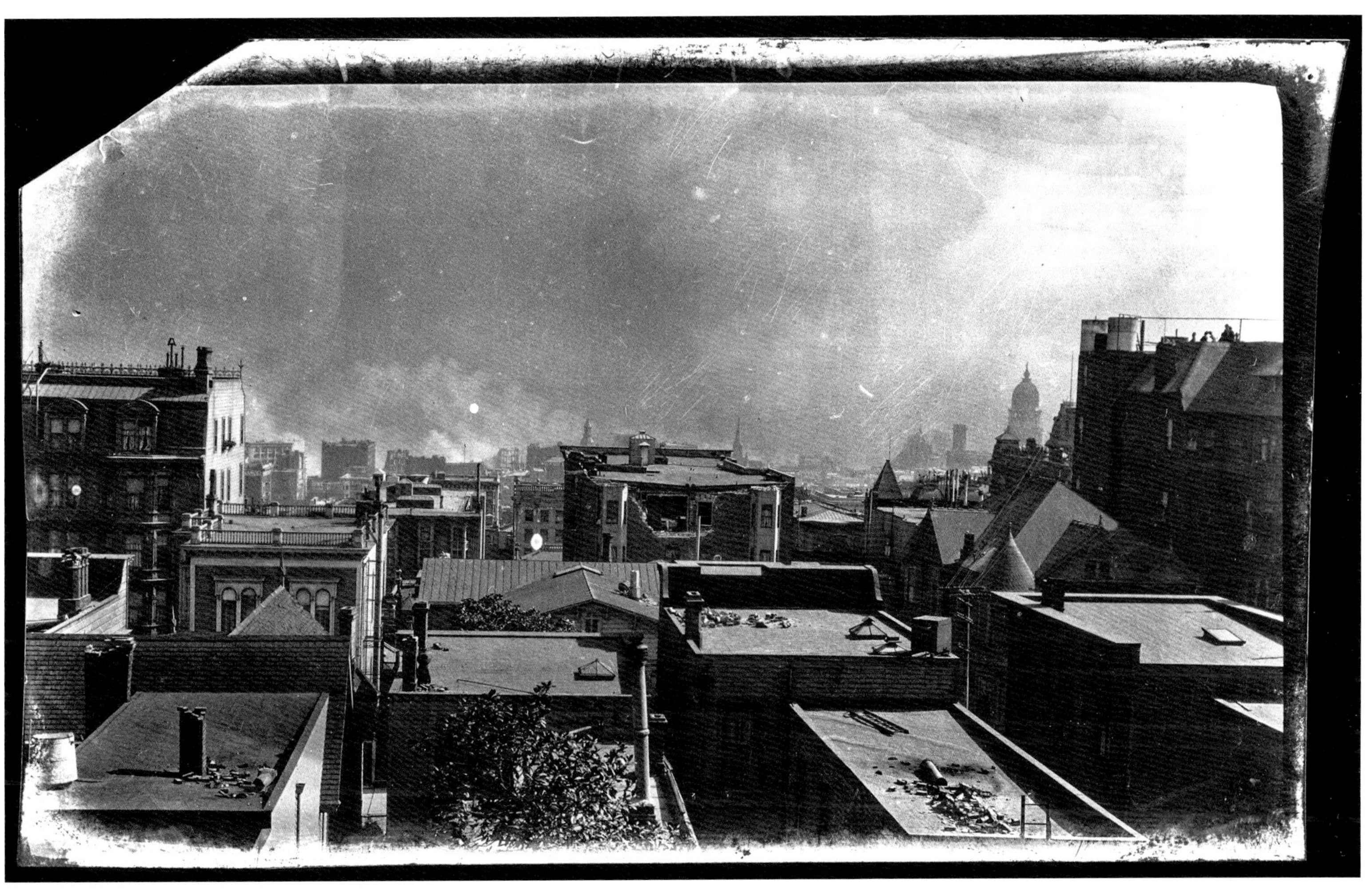

15.

View south from the Sherwood mansion, California between Taylor and Jones, San Francisco
2018.21.78 (cat. 16)

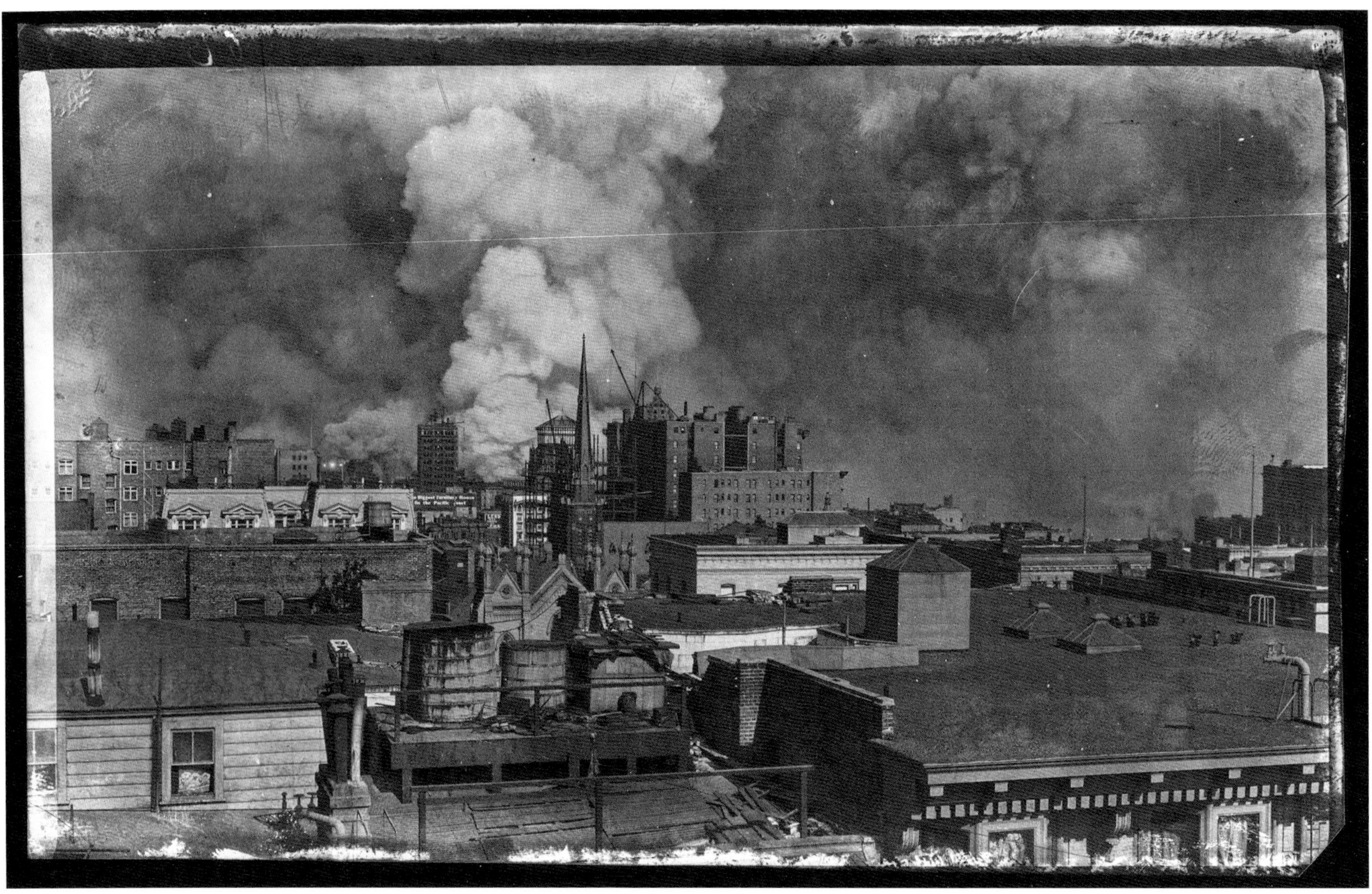

16.

View downtown from Hotel Pleasanton, Sutter and Jones, San Francisco
2018.21.9 (cat. 17)

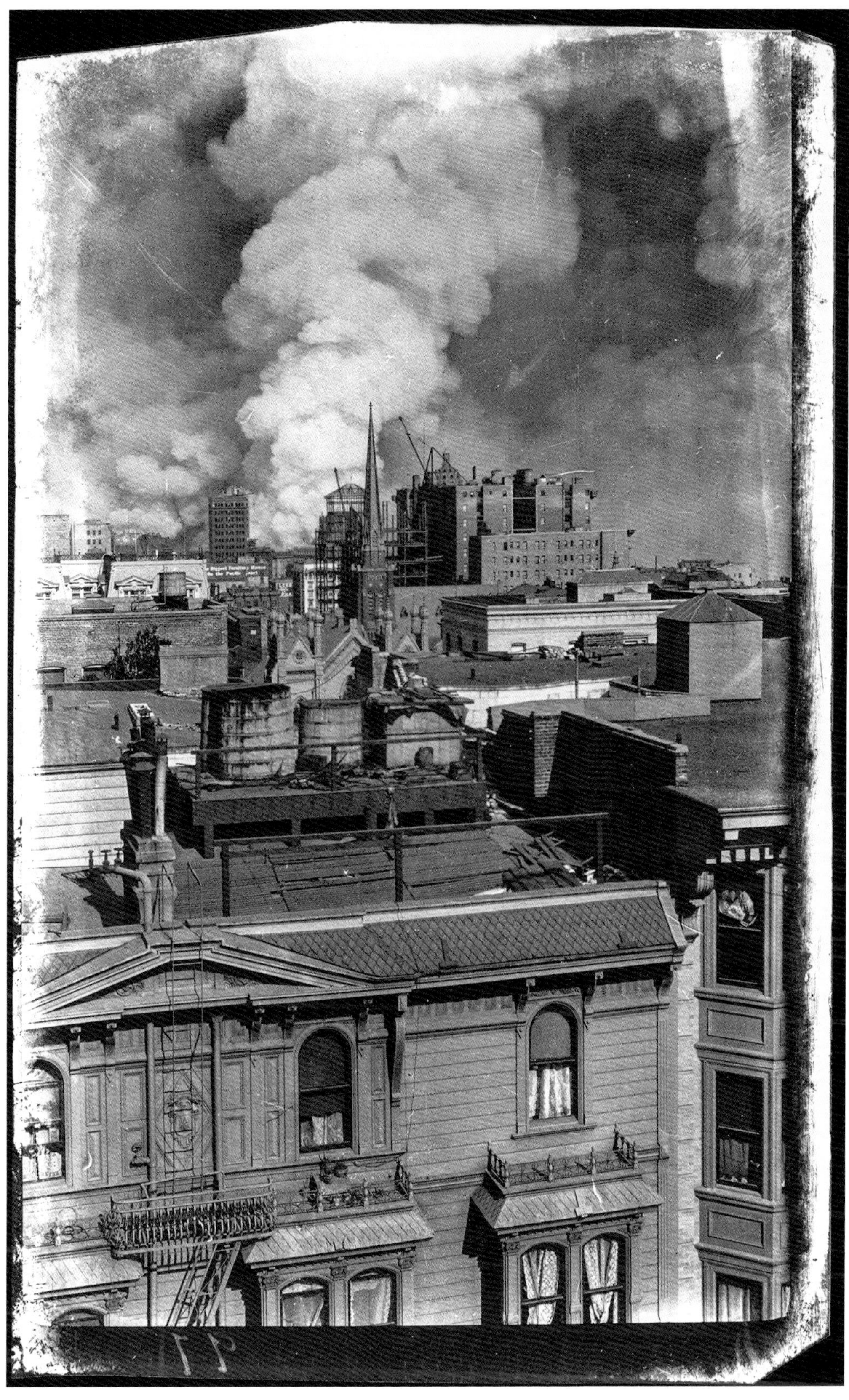

17.

View downtown from Hotel Pleasanton, Sutter and Jones, San Francisco
2018.21.85 (cat. 18)

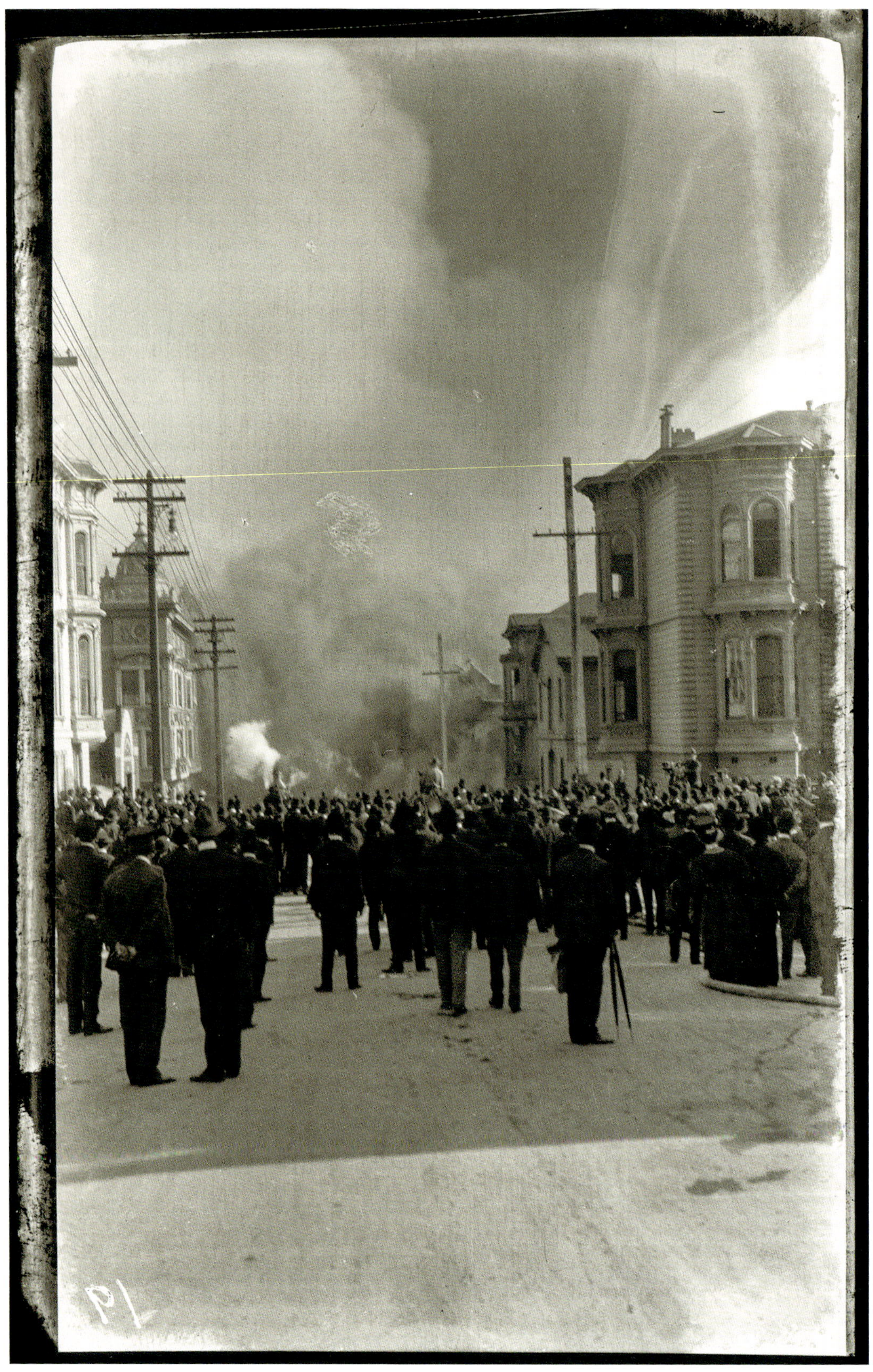

18.

Franklin and McAllister, San Francisco
2018.21.19 (cat. 19)

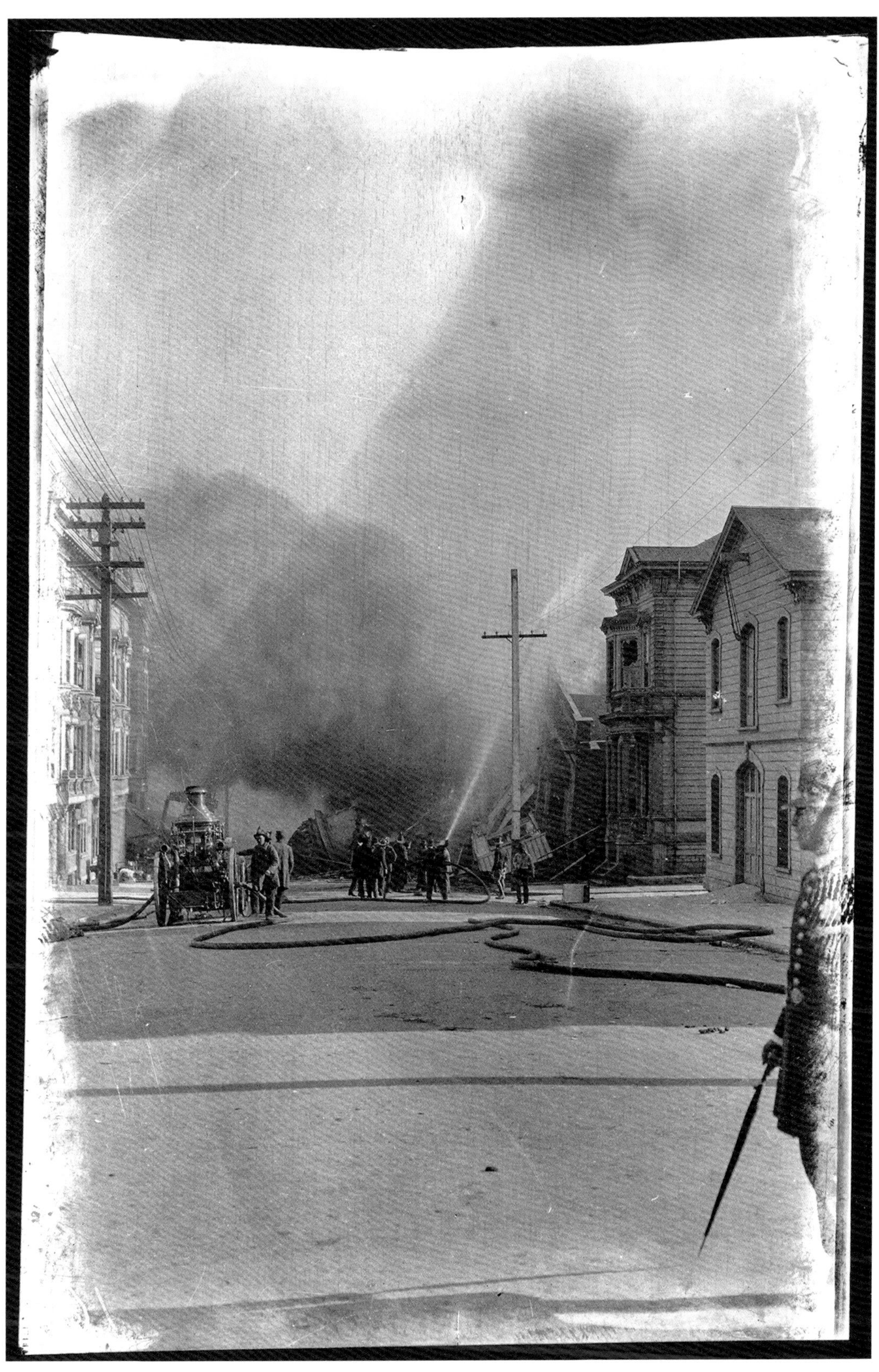

19.

Franklin and McAllister, San Francisco
2018.21.16 (cat. 20)

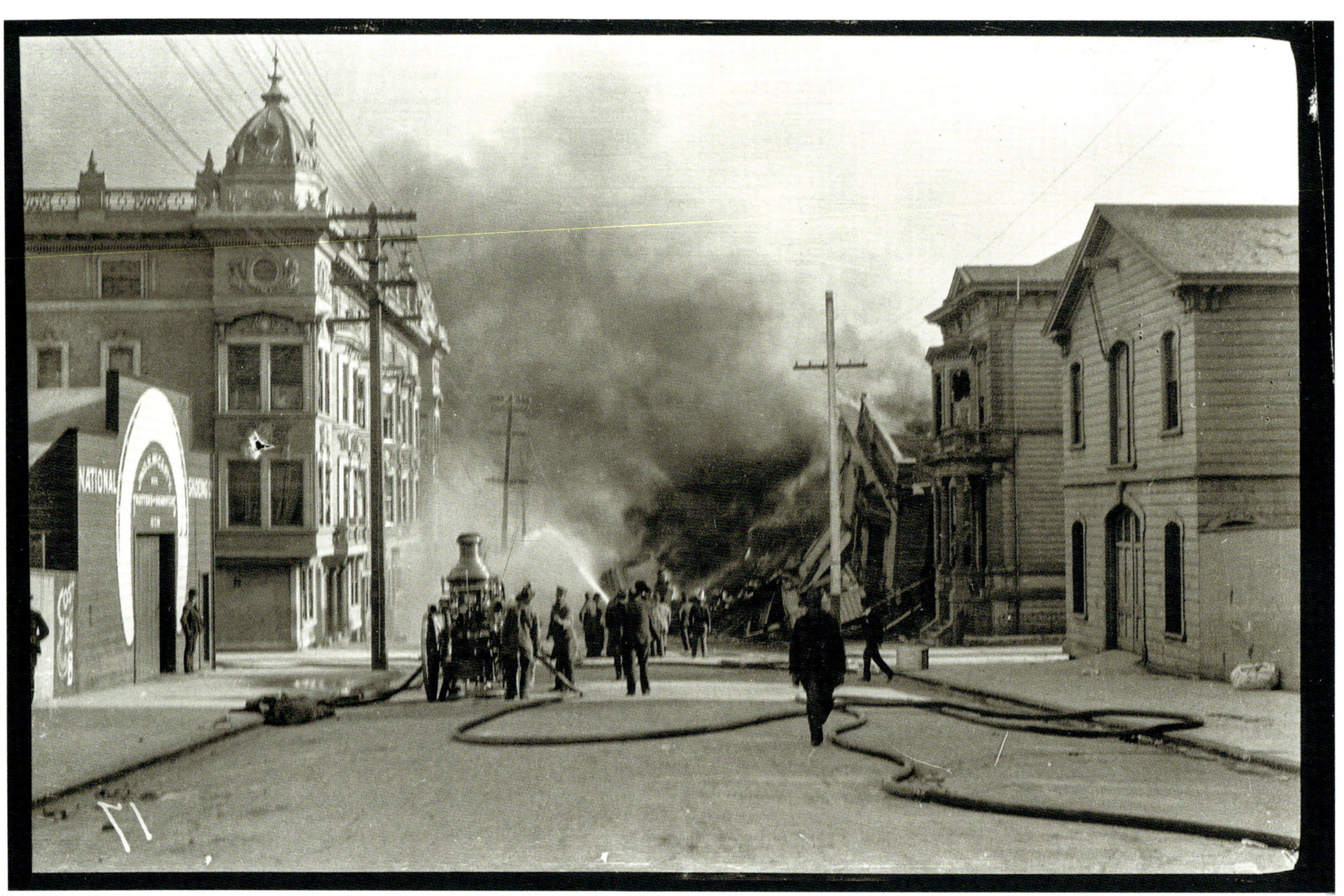

20.

Franklin and McAllister, San Francisco
2018.21.17 (cat. 21)

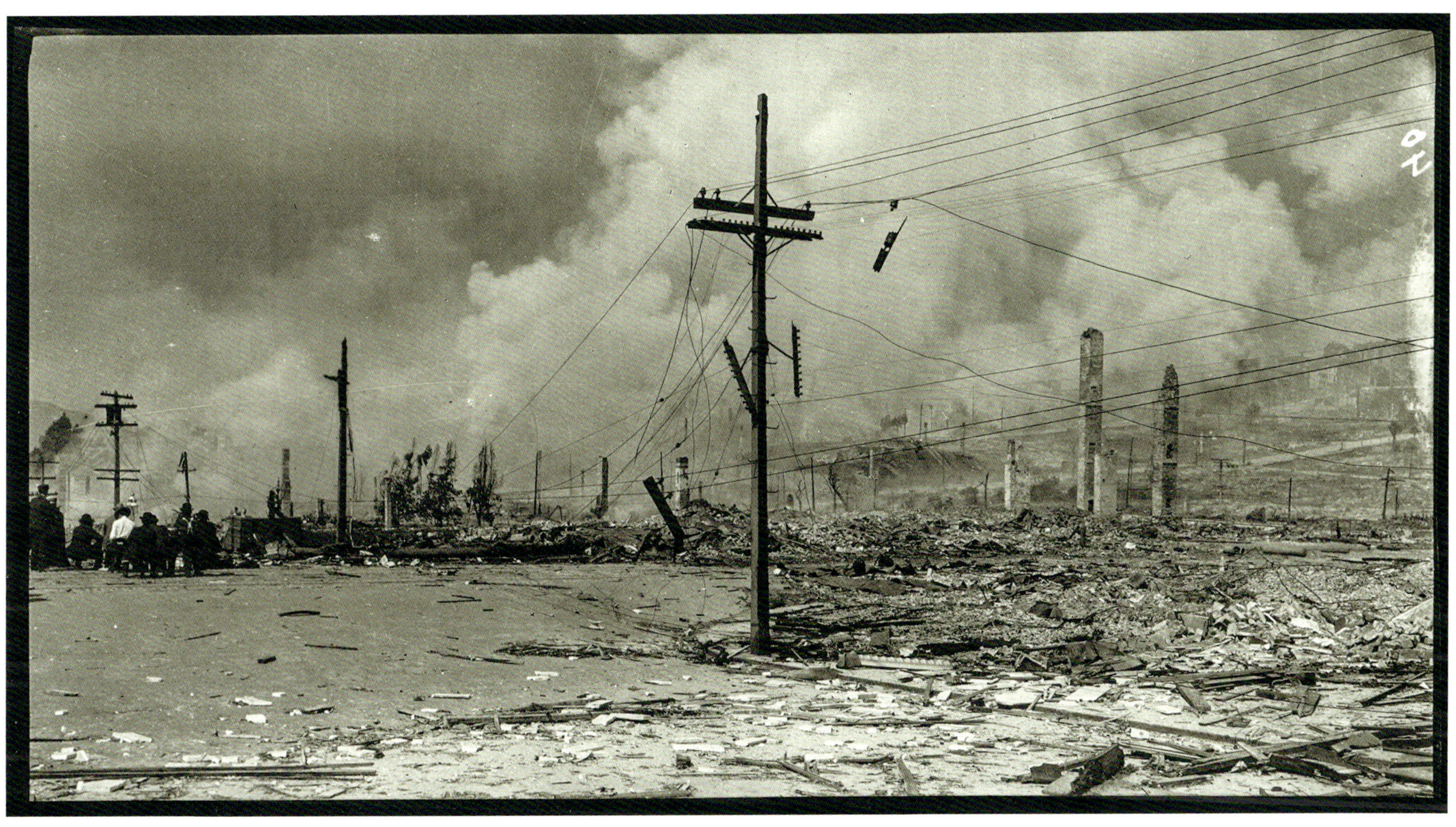

21.

Van Ness and Pacific, San Francisco
2018.21.43 (cat. 22)

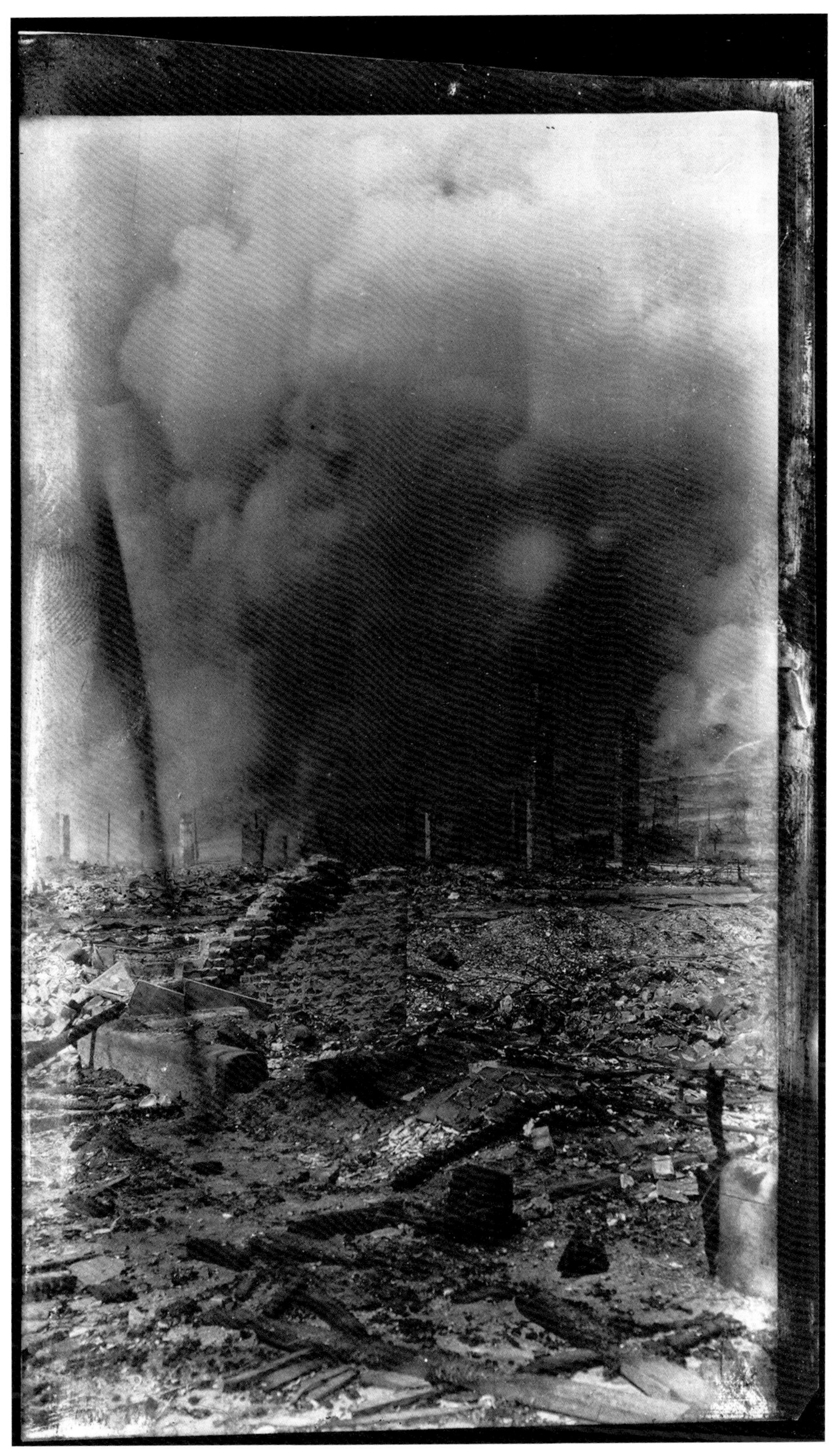

22.

Van Ness and Pacific, San Francisco
2018.21.73 (cat. 23)

EARTHQUAKE

DAMAGE

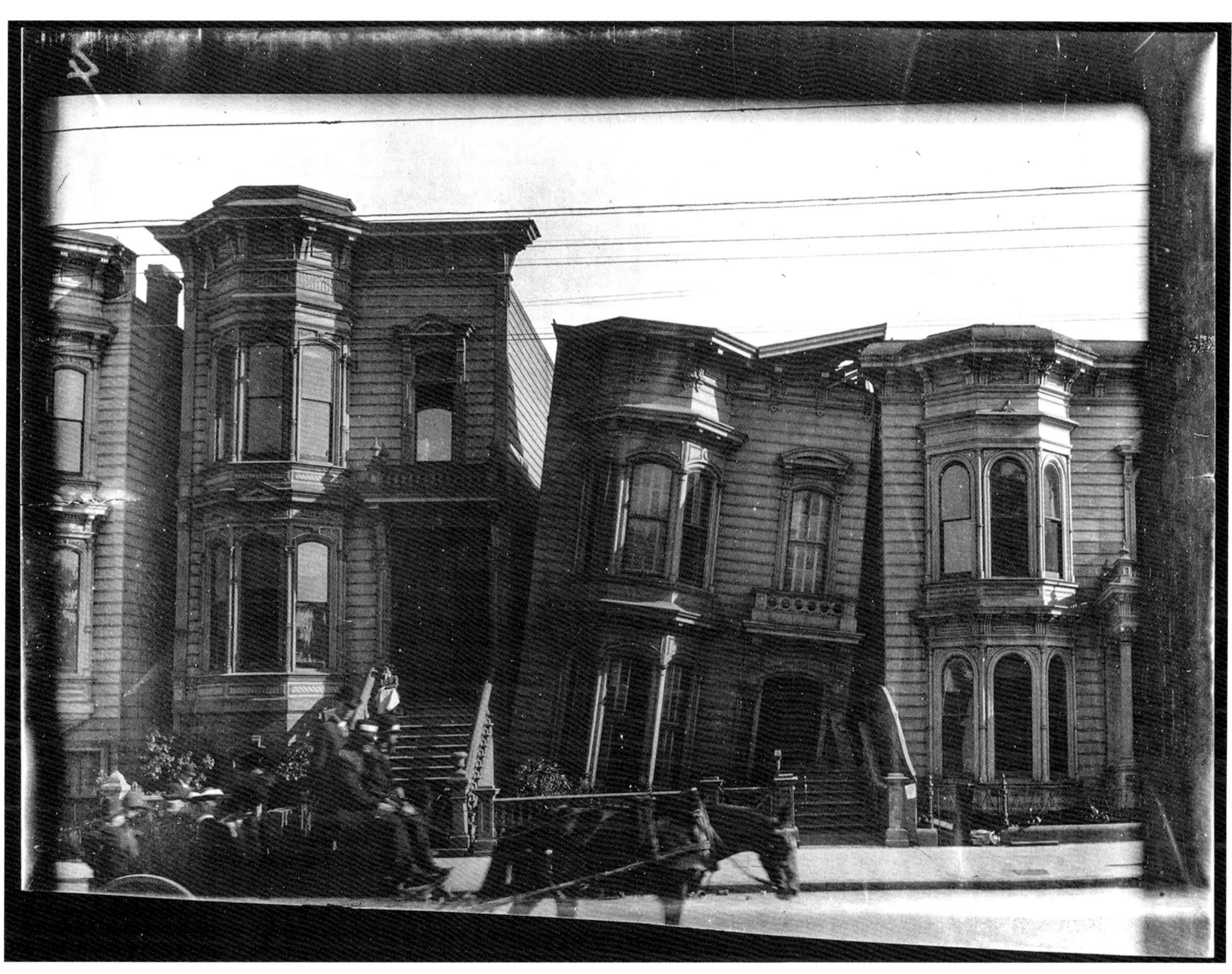

23.

Golden Gate and Gough, San Francisco
2018.21.5 (cat. 24)

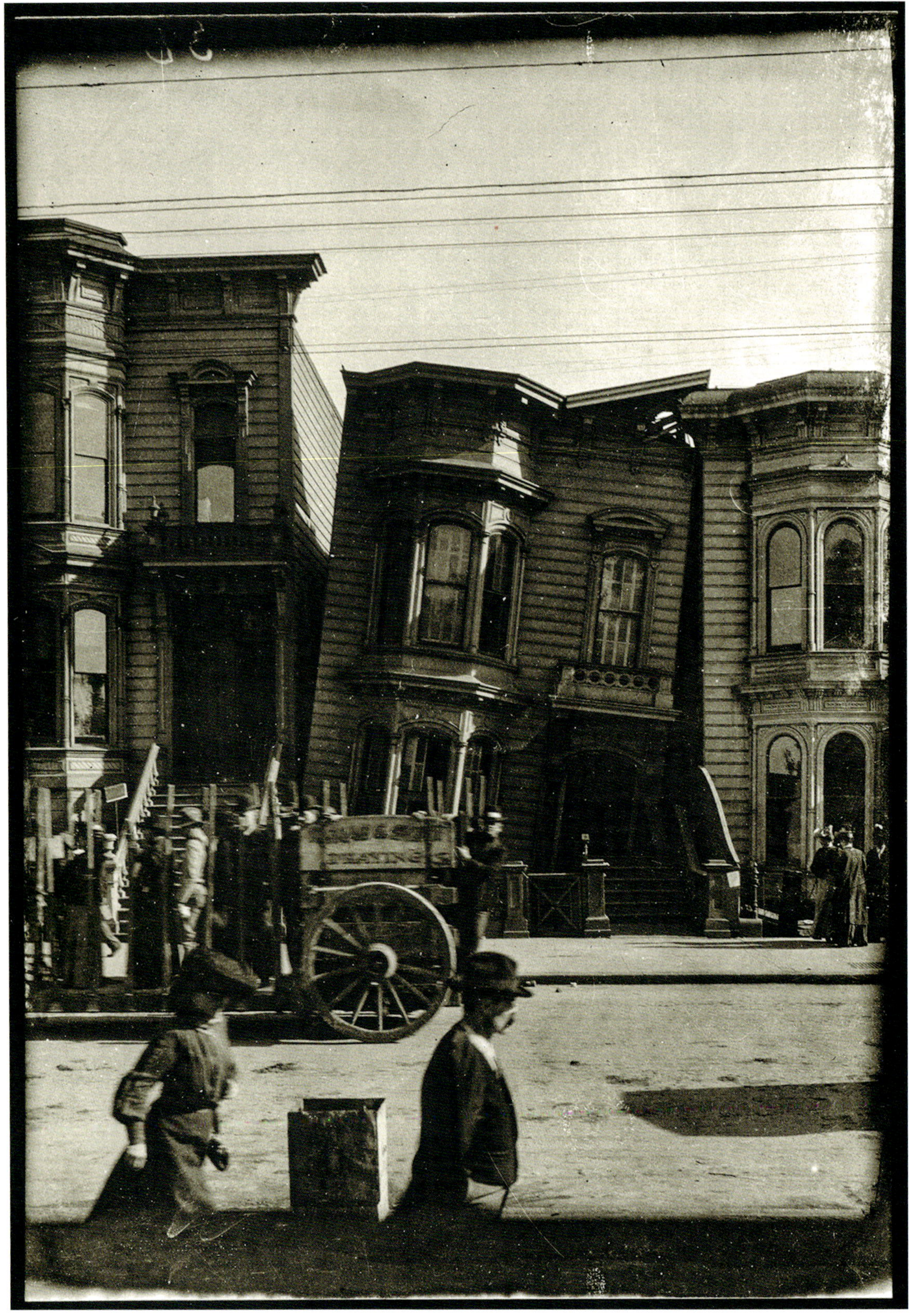

24.

Golden Gate and Gough, San Francisco
2018.21.4 (cat. 25)

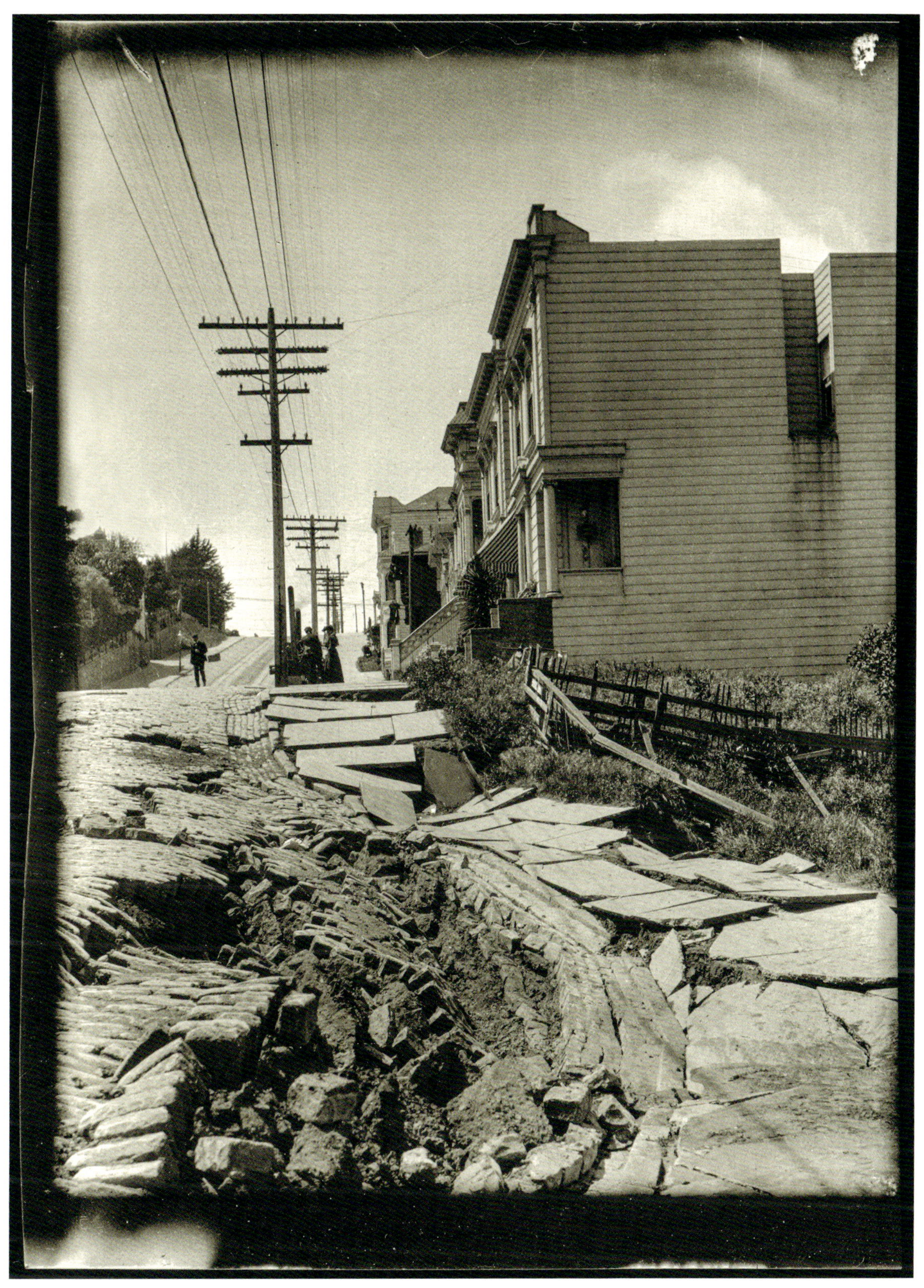

25.

Union west of Steiner, San Francisco
2018.21.3 (cat. 28)

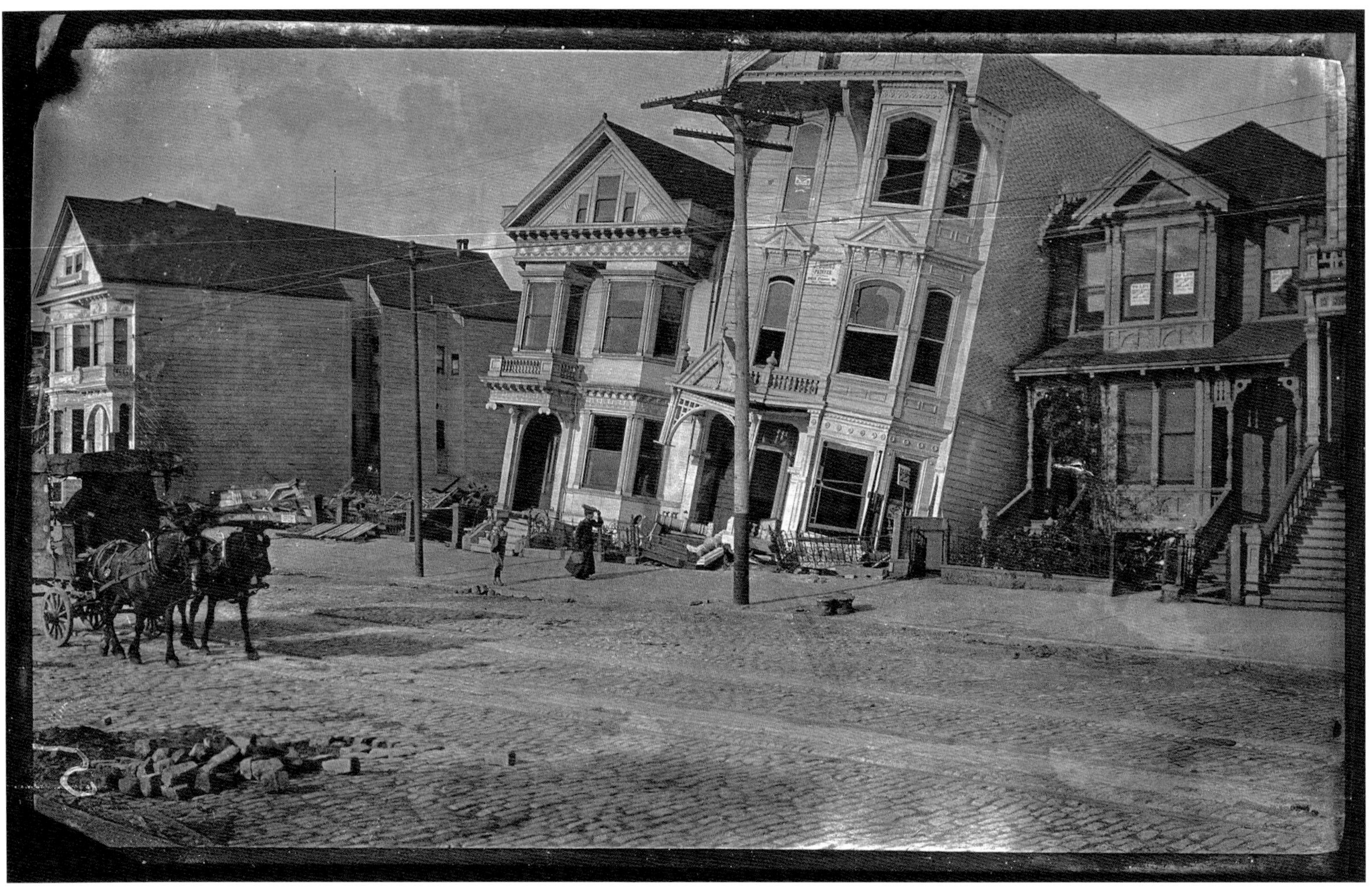

26.

Howard [now South Van Ness] near 18th Street, San Francisco
2018.21.6 (cat. 29)

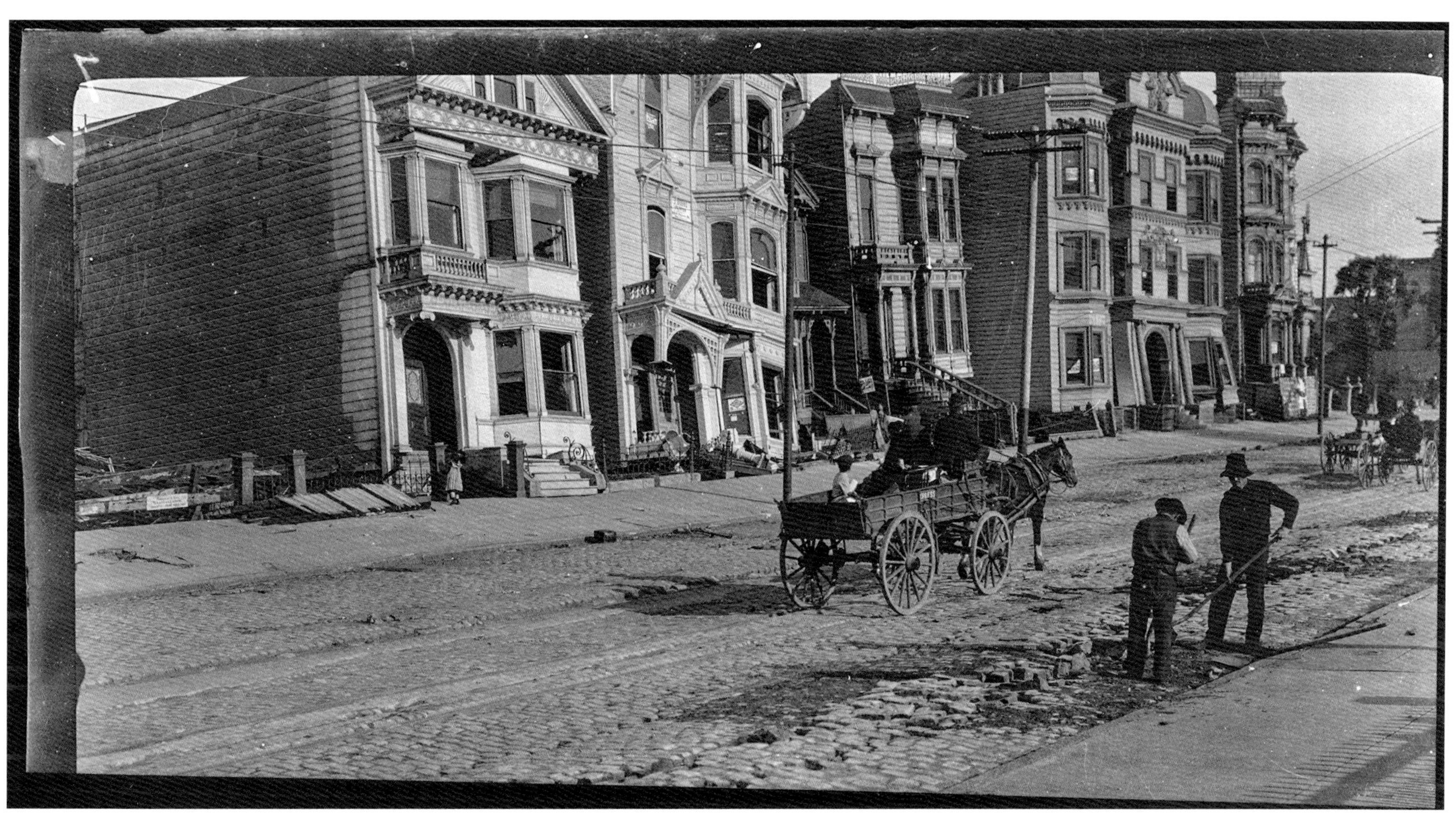

27.

Howard [now South Van Ness] near 18th Street, San Francisco
2018.21.7 (cat. 30)

FIRE

RUINS

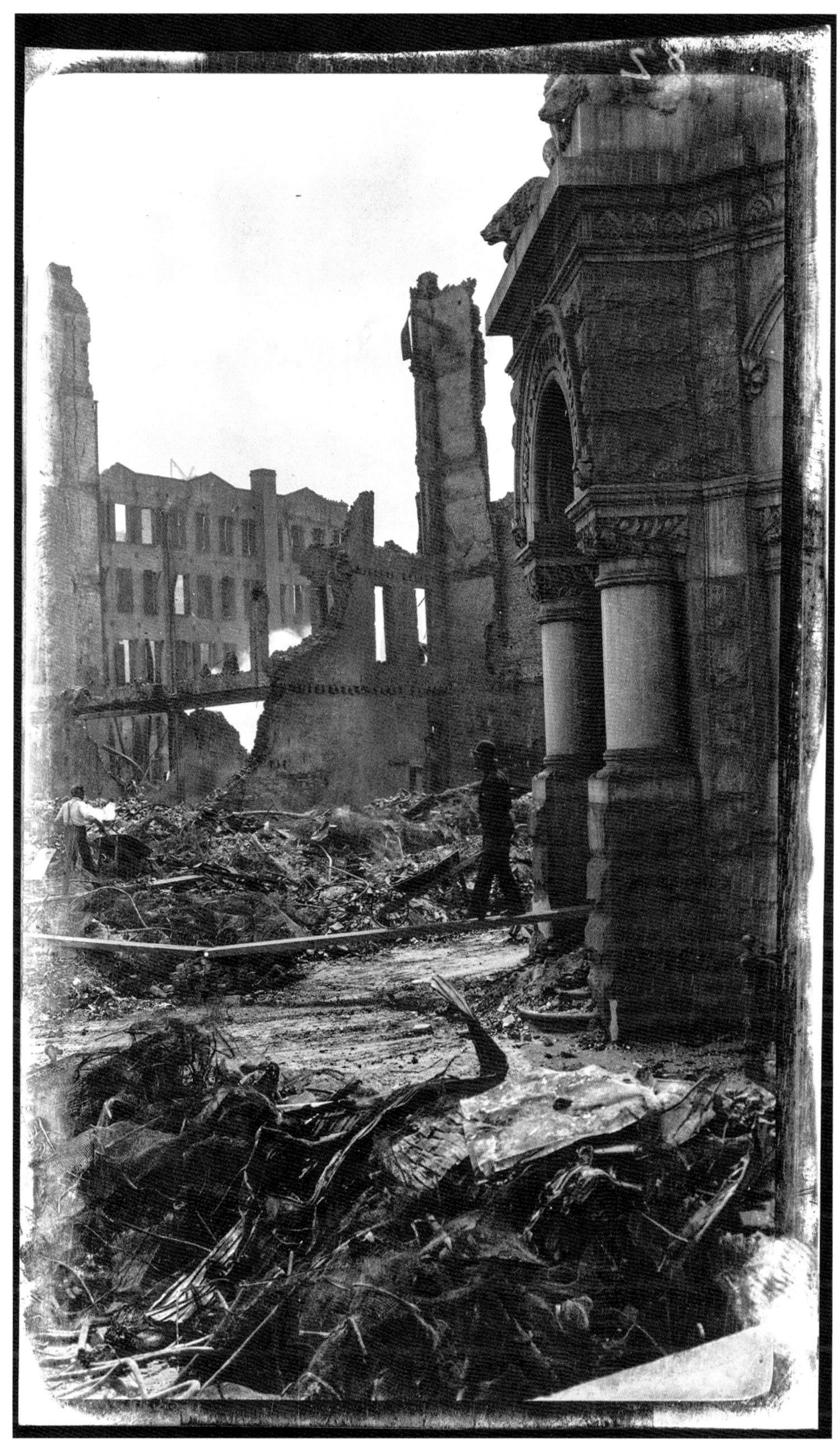

28.

First National Bank, Bush and Sansome, San Francisco
2018.21.76 (cat. 39)

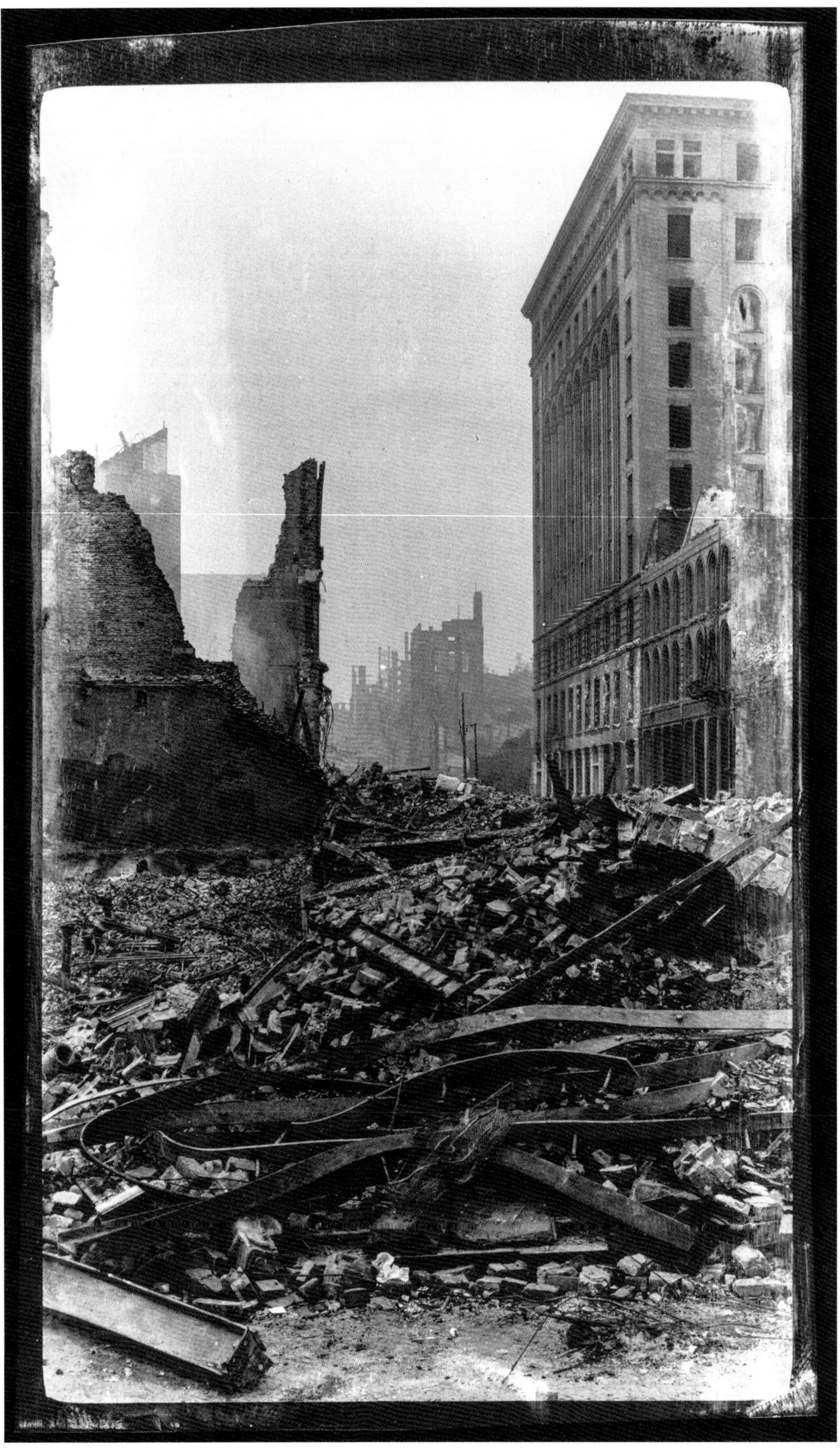

29.

Mills Building from Bush and Sansome, San Francisco
2018.21.30 (cat. 40)

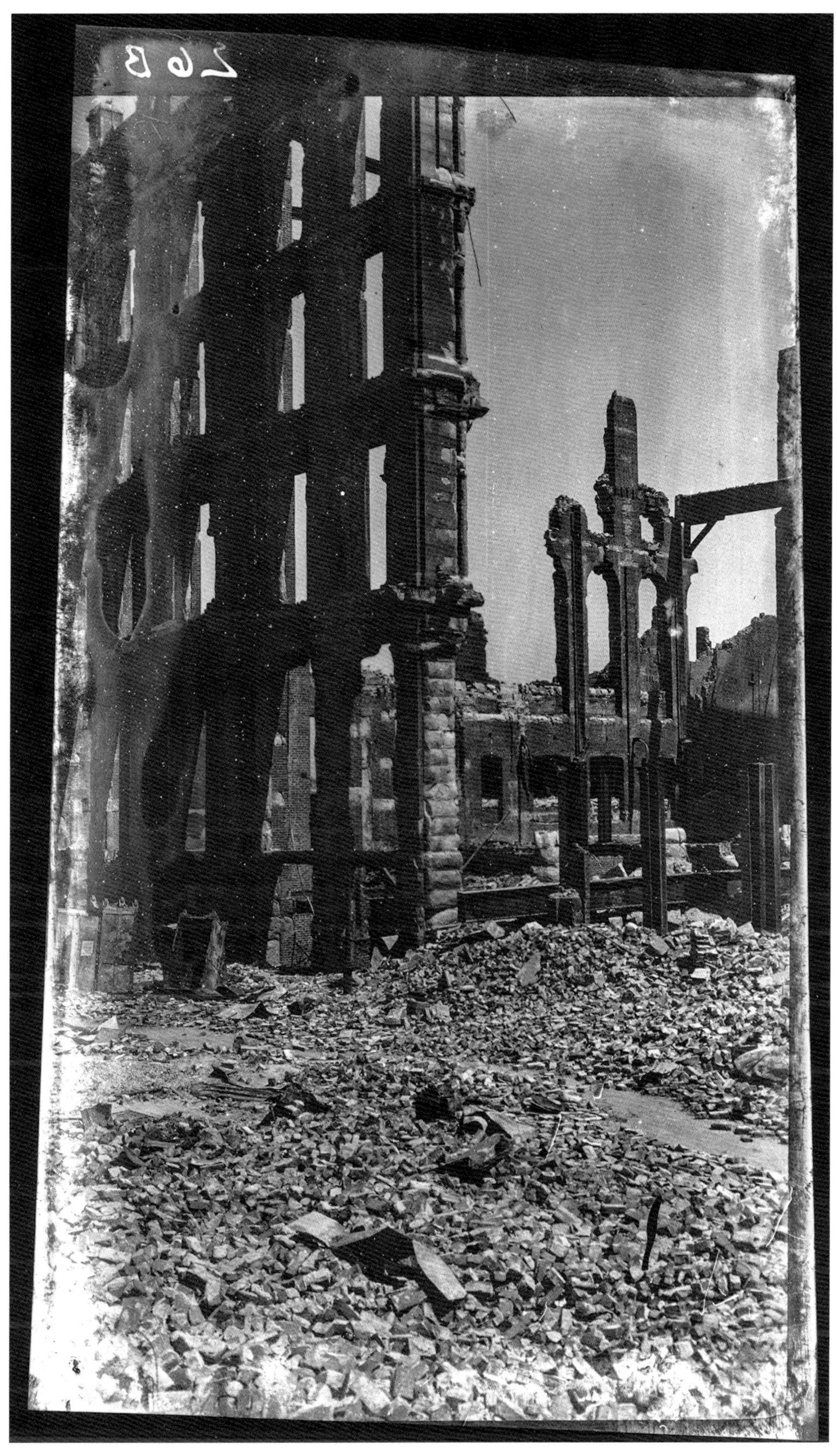

30.

The Stock and Bond Exchange, California and Sansome, San Francisco
2018.21.31 (cat. 41)

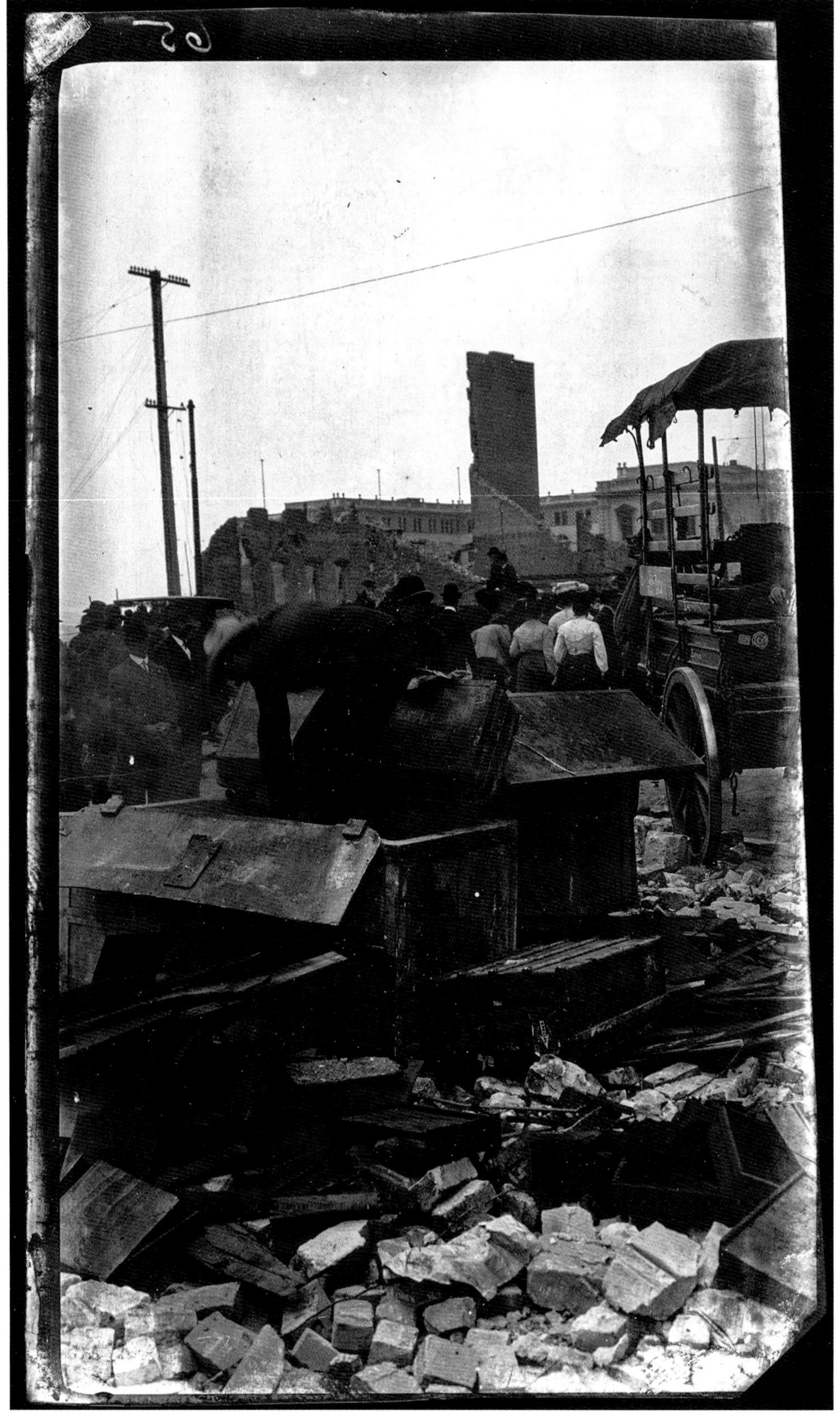

31.

Stevenson near 7th Street, San Francisco
2018.21.64 (cat. 42)

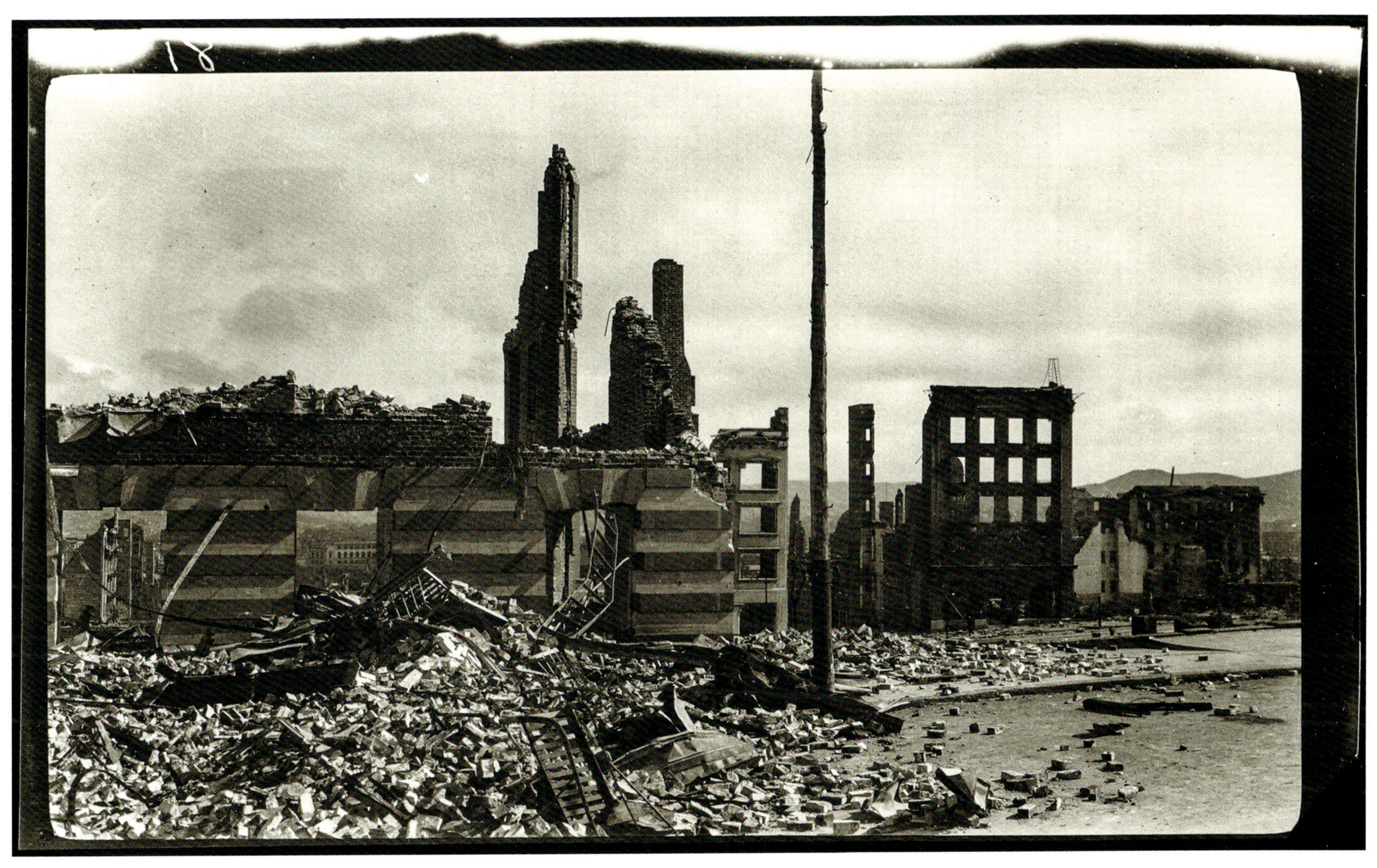

32.

Southwest corner Bush and Taylor, San Francisco
2018.21.74 (cat. 43)

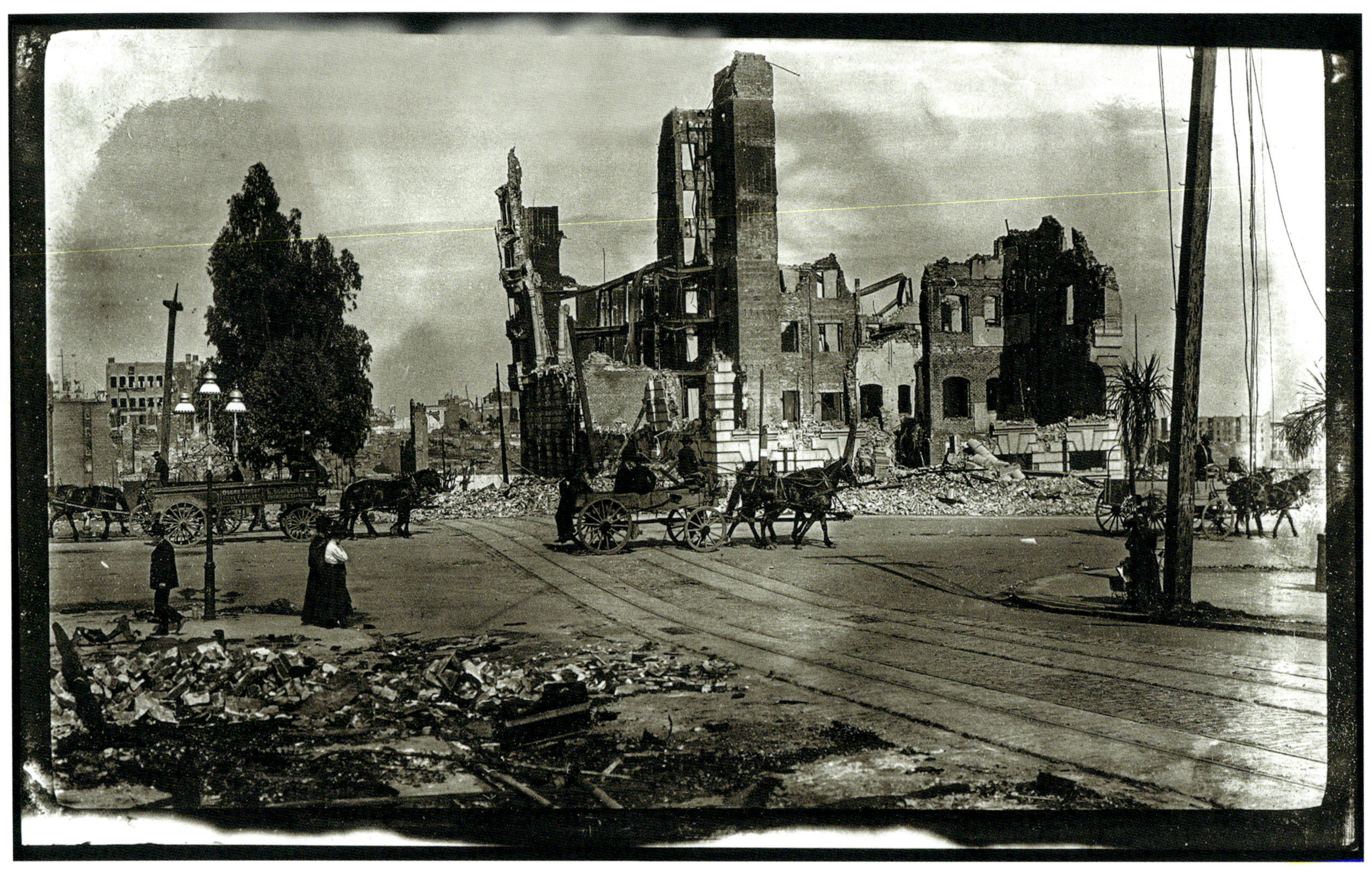

33.
St. Dunstan Hotel, Van Ness and Sutter, San Francisco
2018.21.70 (cat. 44)

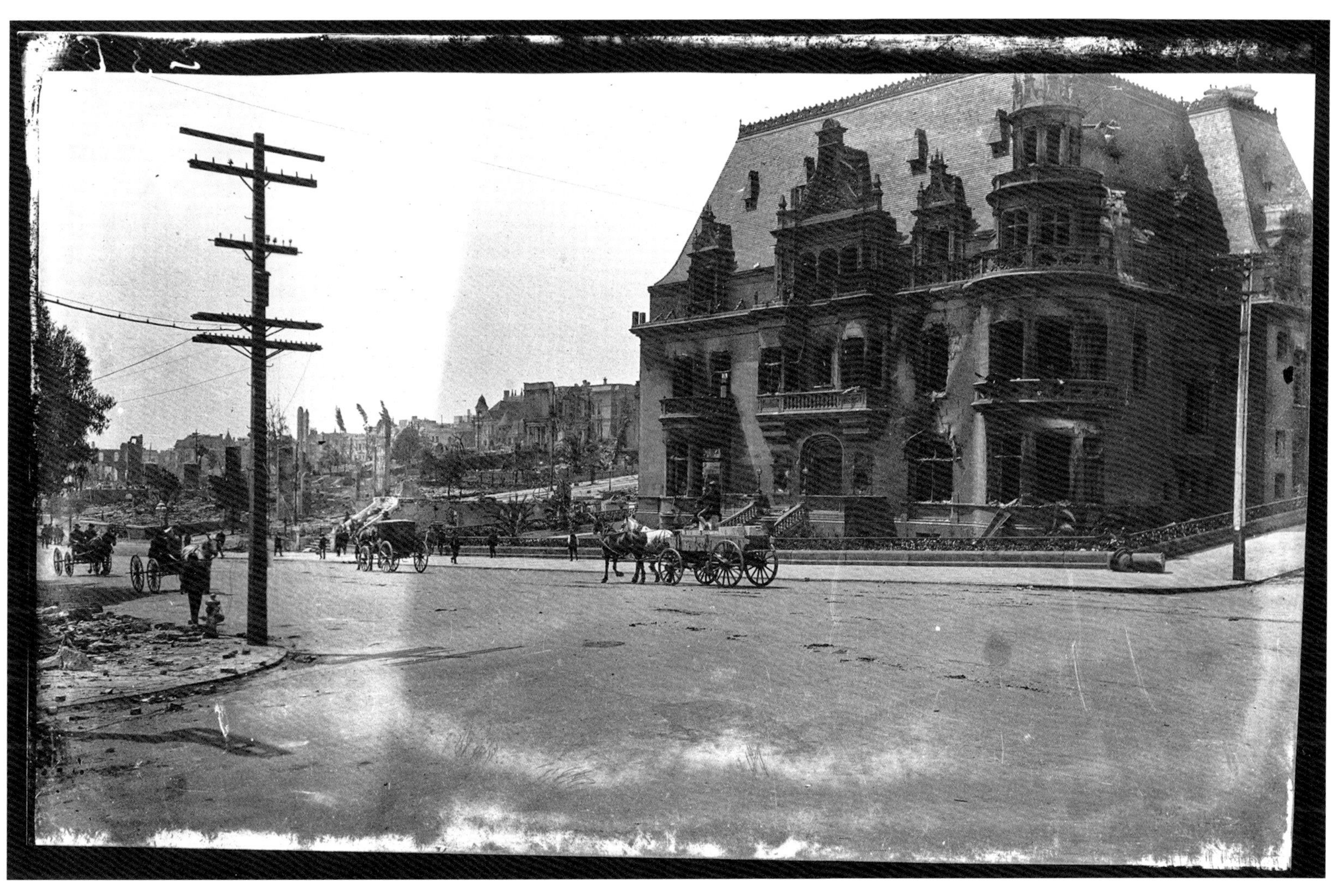

34.
Spreckels mansion, Van Ness and Clay, San Francisco
2018.21.27 (cat. 46)

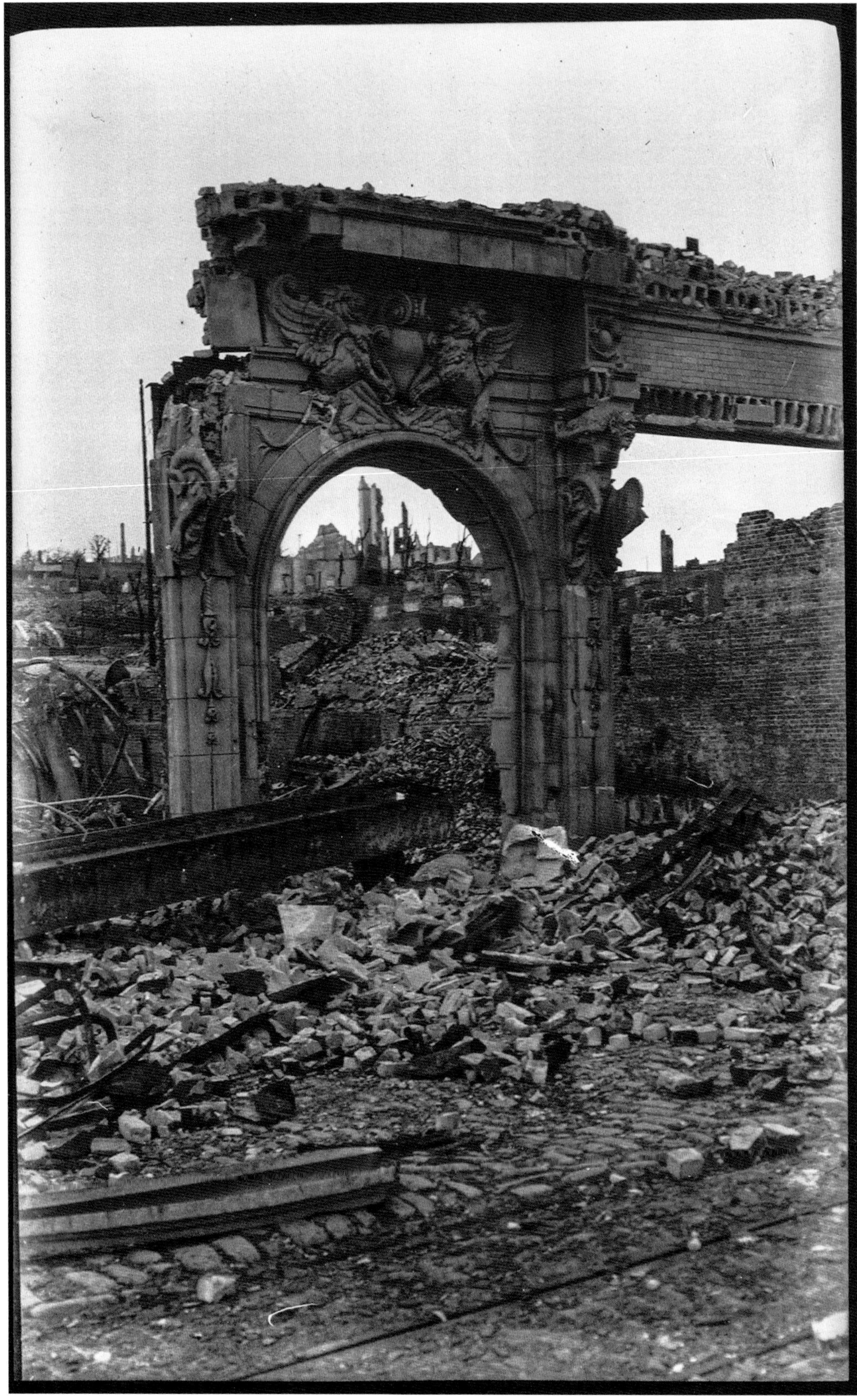

35.
Sequoia Hotel, Geary and Hyde, San Francisco
2018.21.40 (cat. 50)

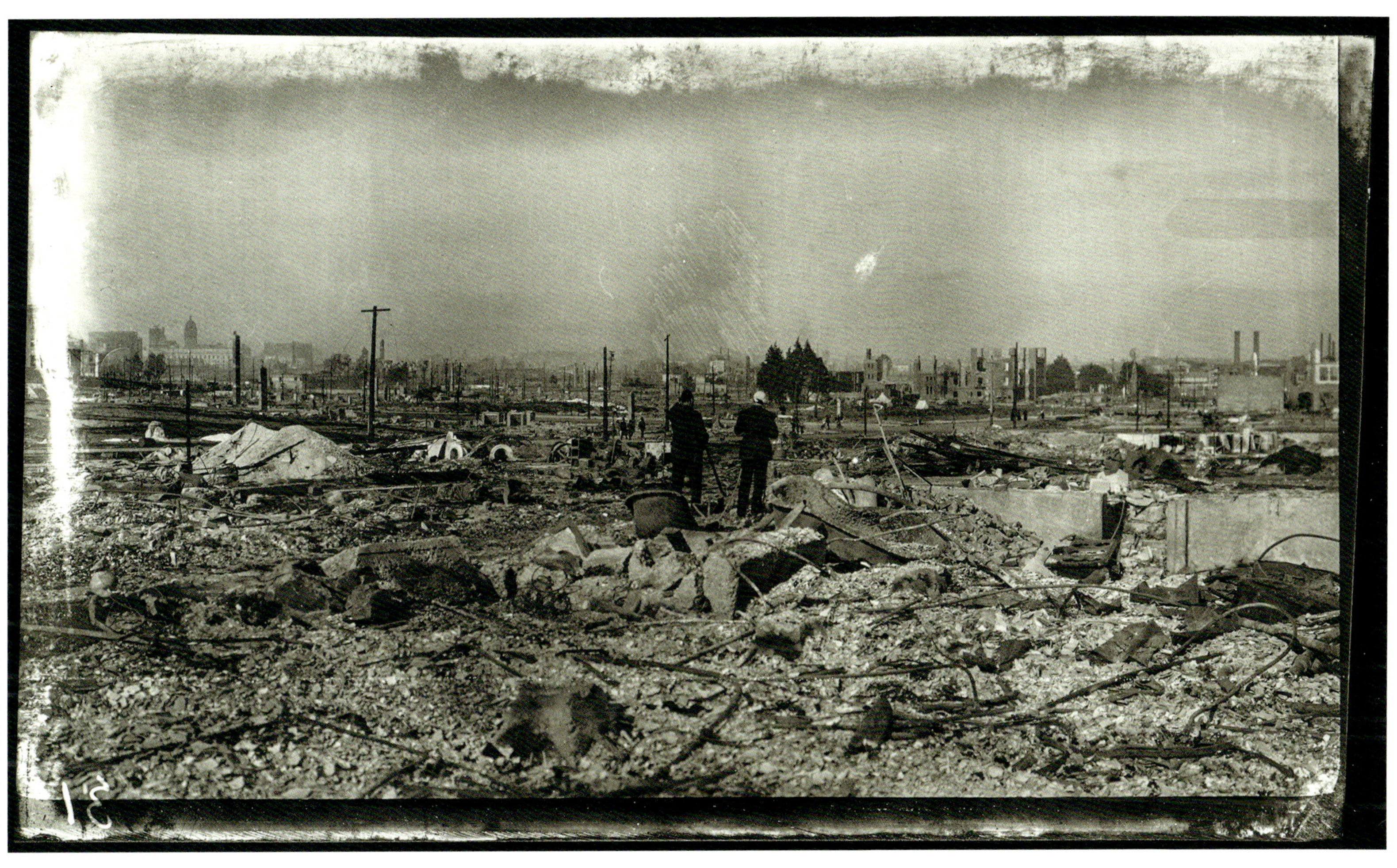

36.
Two men pose while looking at the general scene of ruin after the earthquake and fire, South of Market, San Francisco
2018.21.35 (cat. 51)

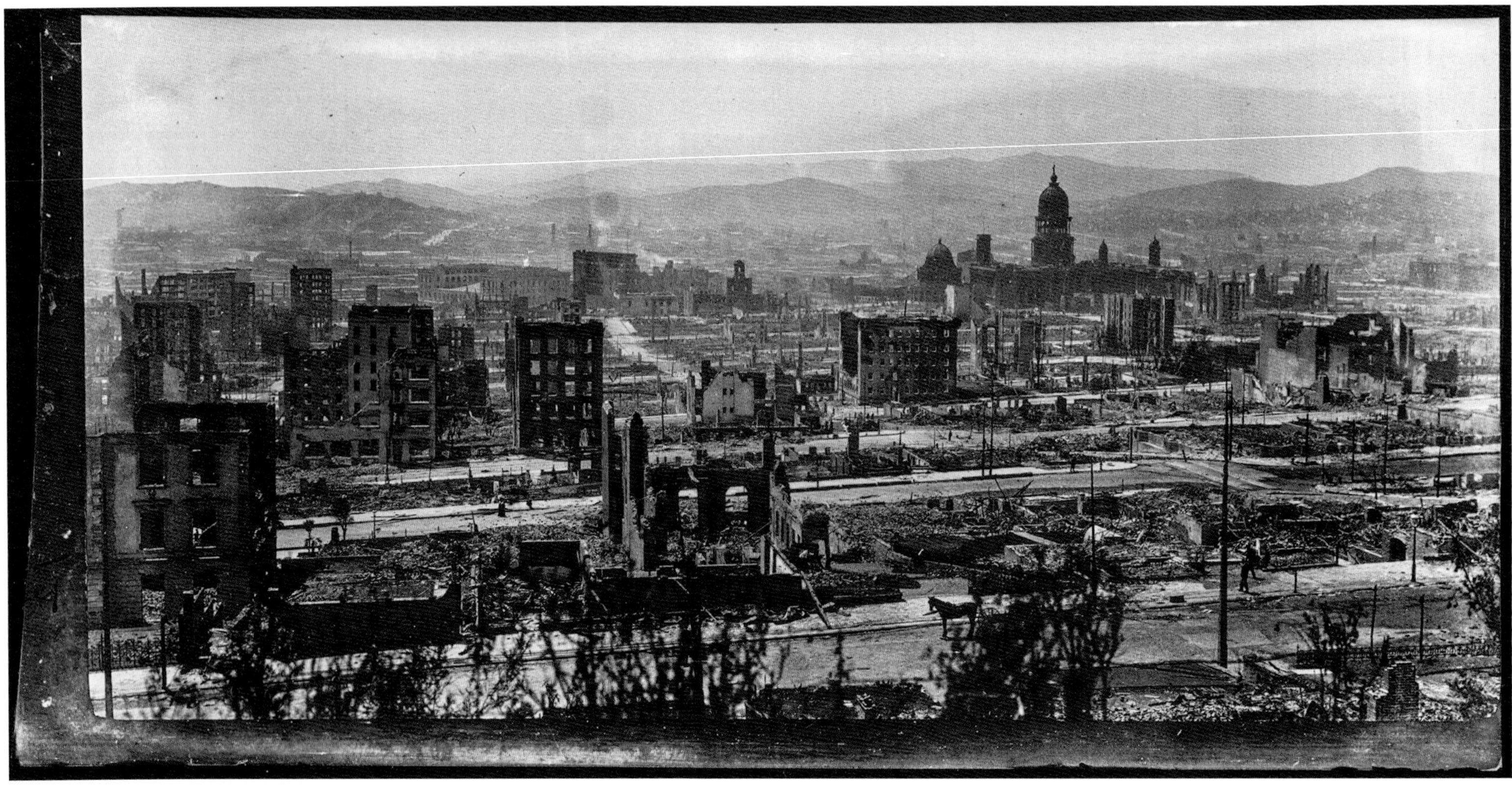

37.
City Hall from California between Jones and Taylor, San Francisco
2018.21.69 (cat. 52)

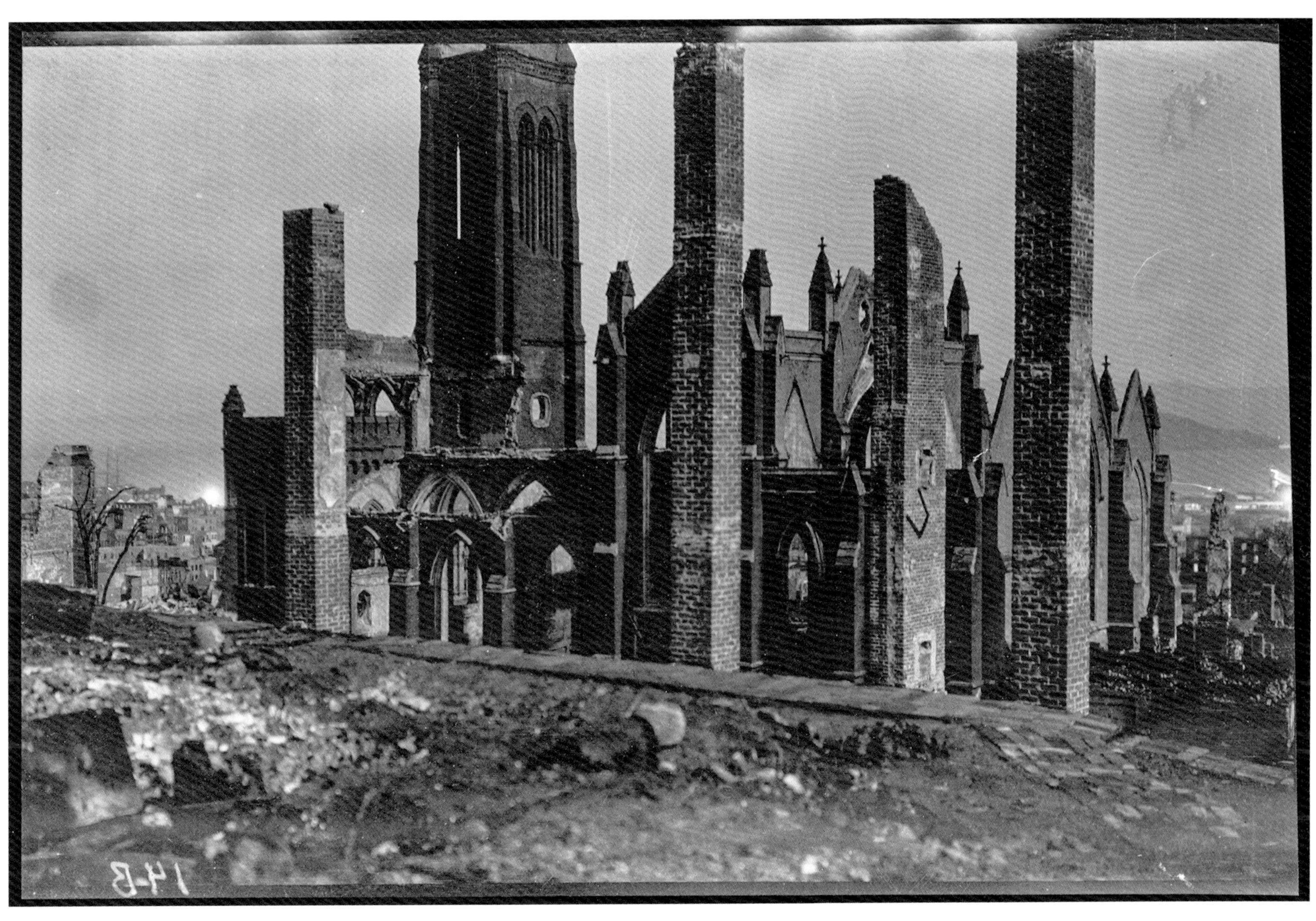

38.
Grace Church, California and Stockton, San Francisco
2018.21.14 (cat. 54)

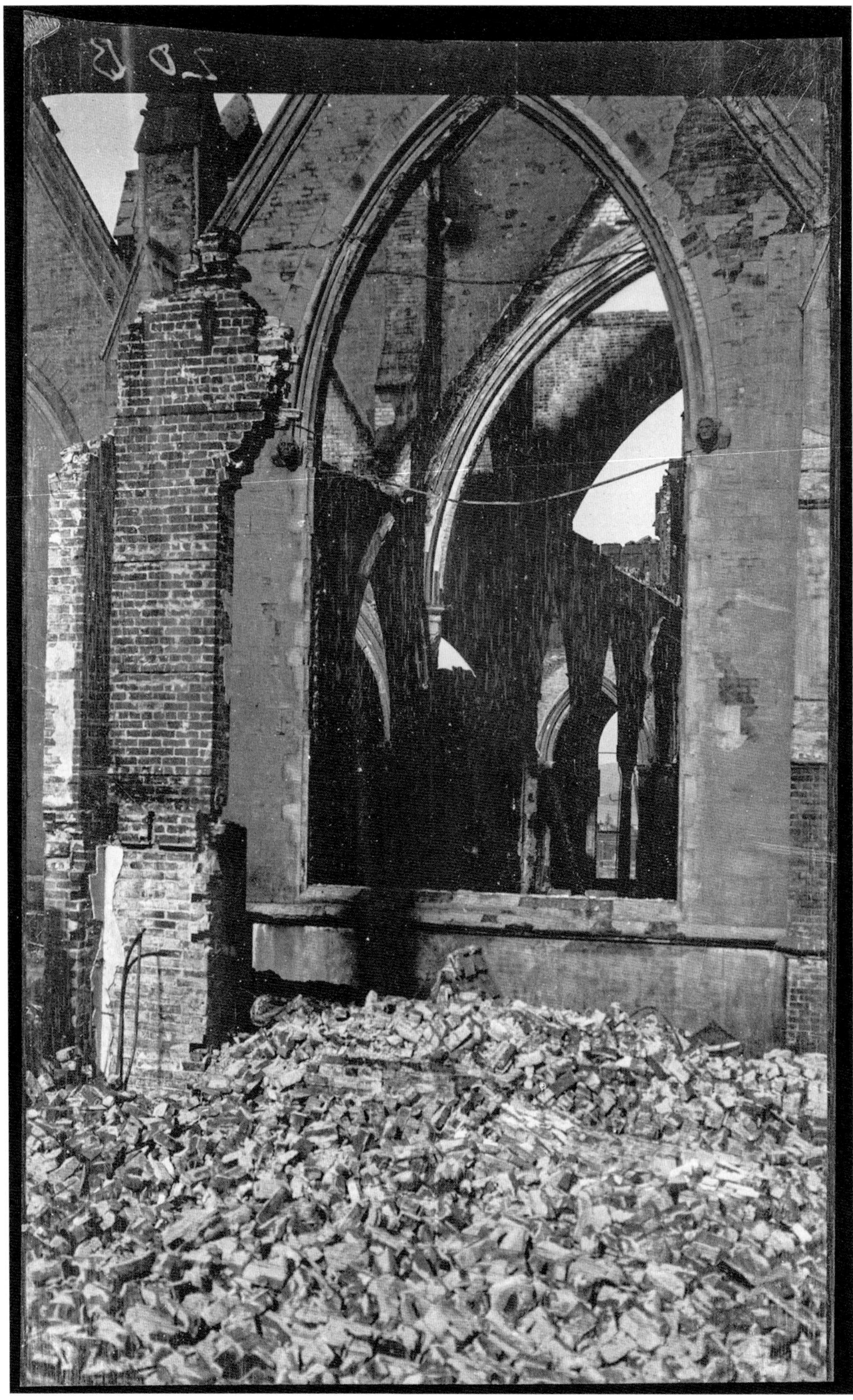

39.
Grace Church, California and Stockton, San Francisco
2018.21.21 (cat. 55)

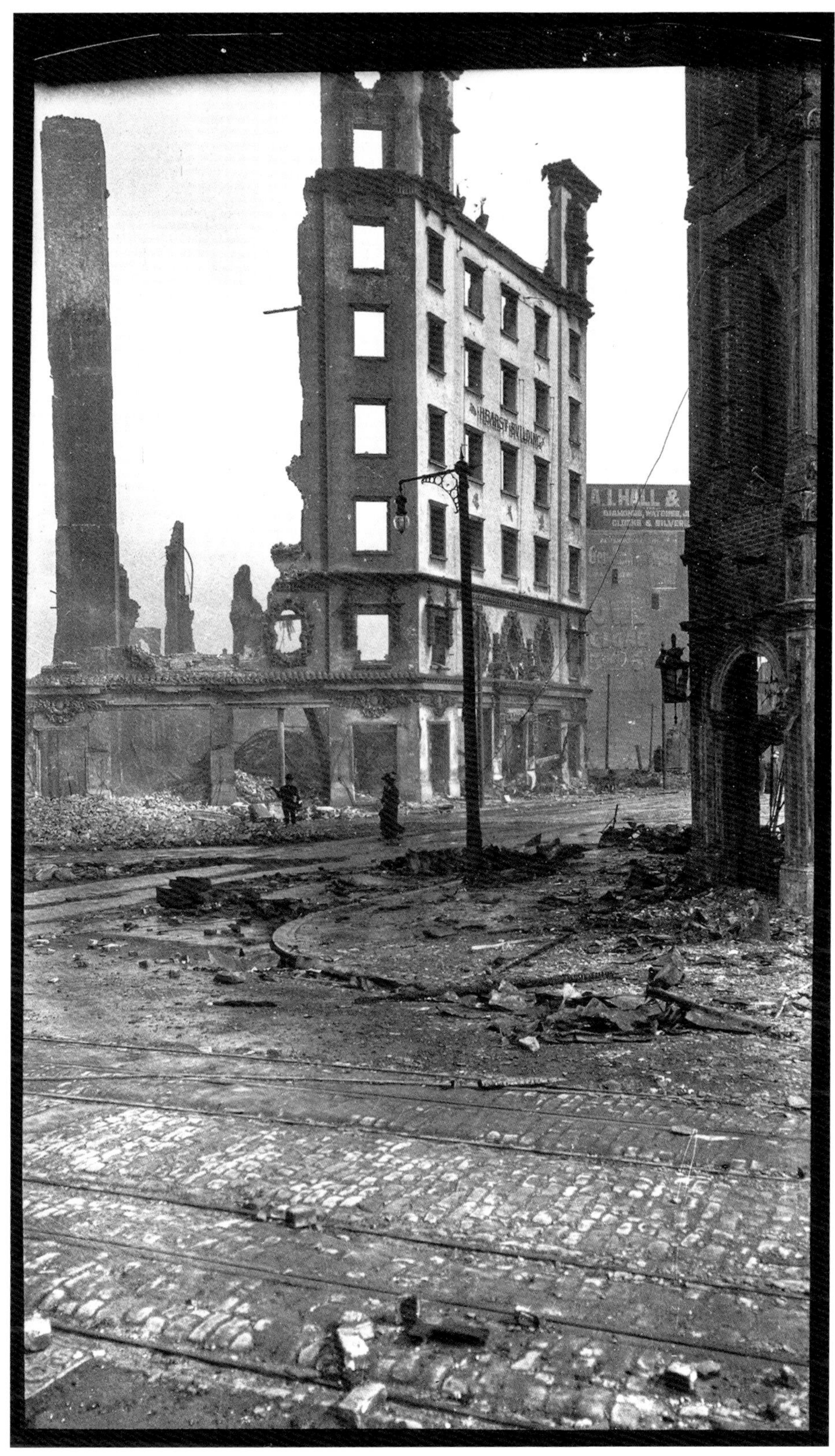

40.
Hearst Building, Market and Third Streets, San Francisco
2018.21.87 (cat. 60)

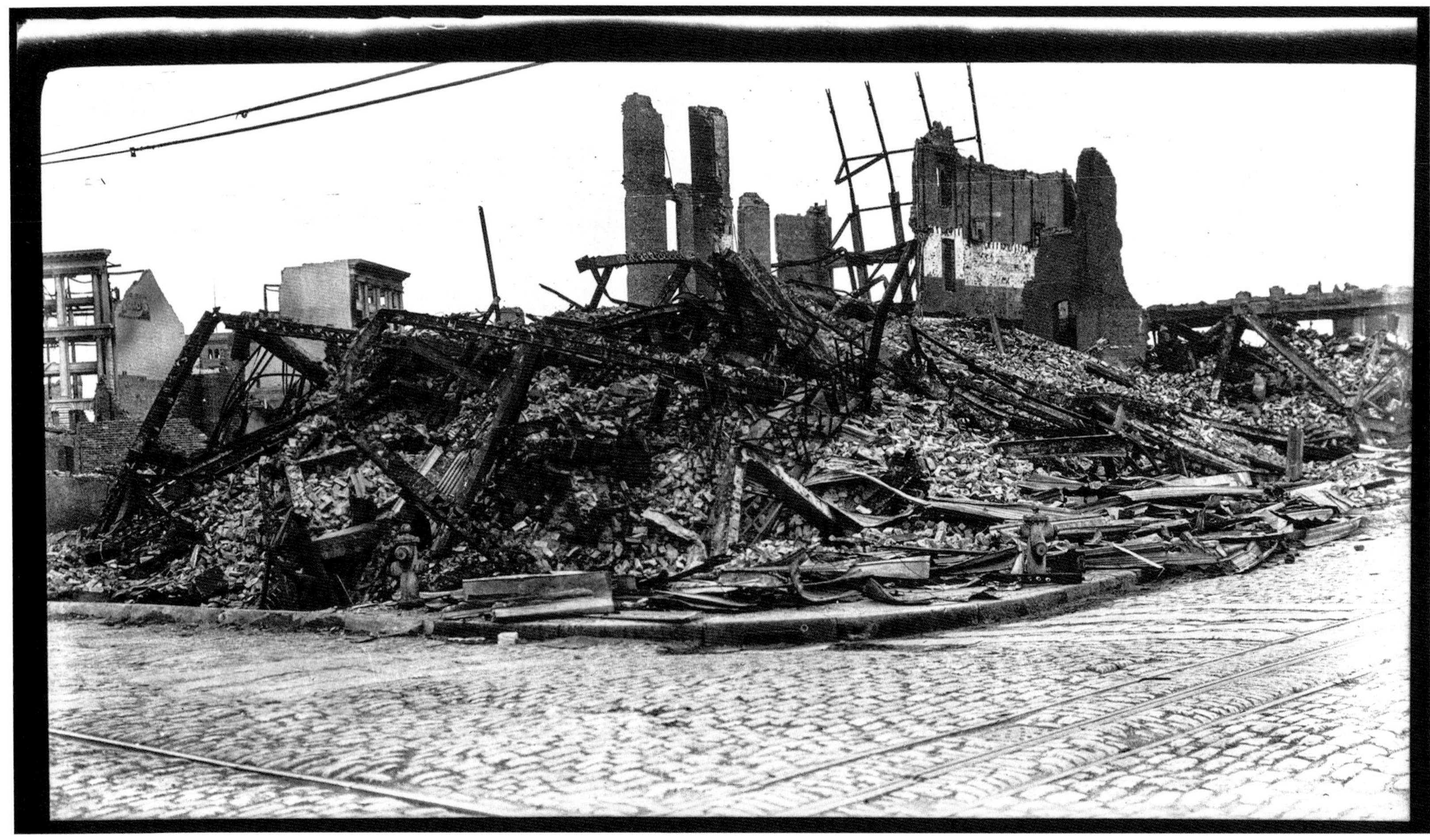

41.

Linda Vista Apartments, Turk and Jones, San Francisco
2018.21.88 (cat. 61)

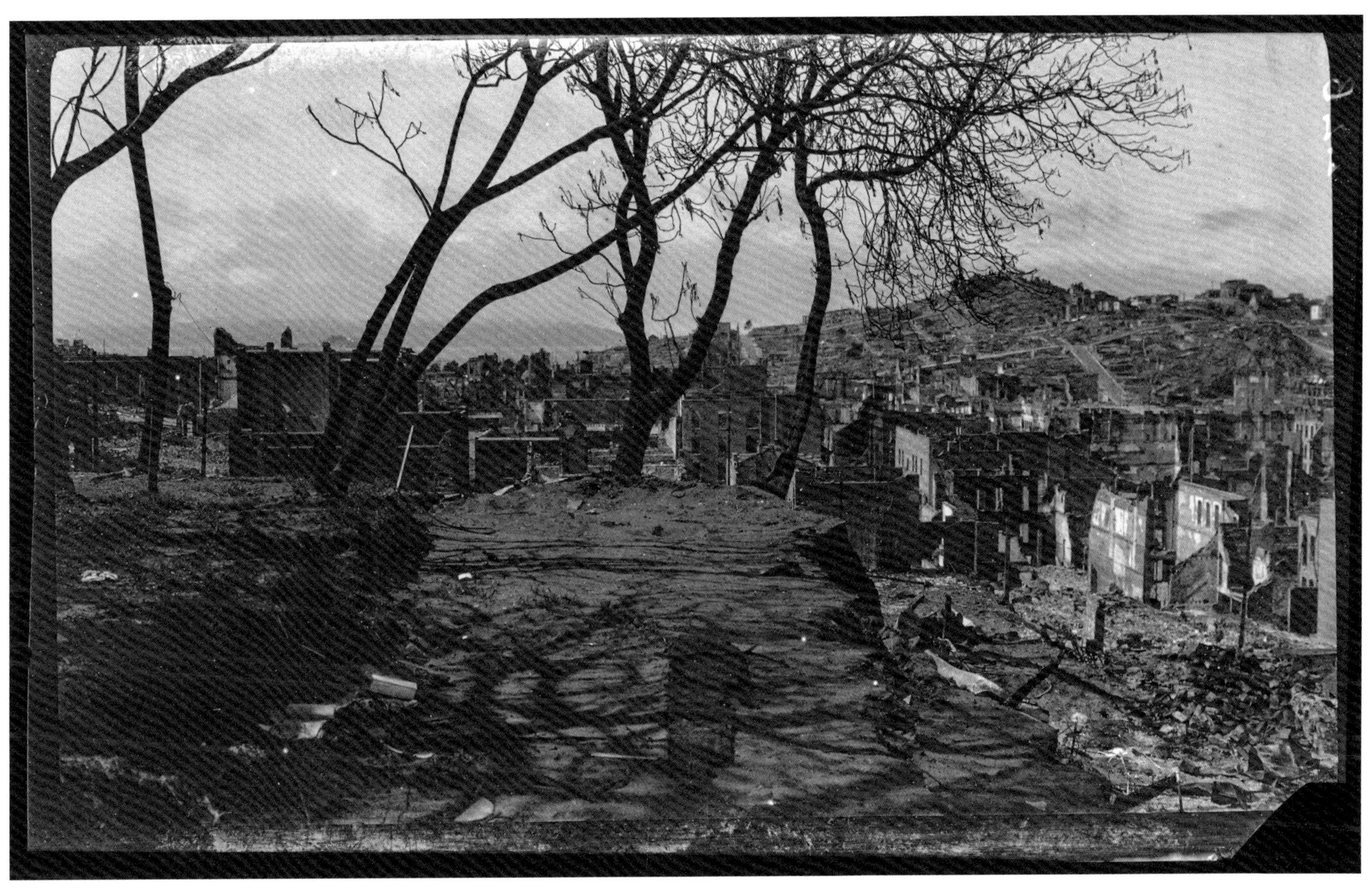

42.

Telegraph Hill from Nob Hill, San Francisco
2018.21.24 (cat. 63)

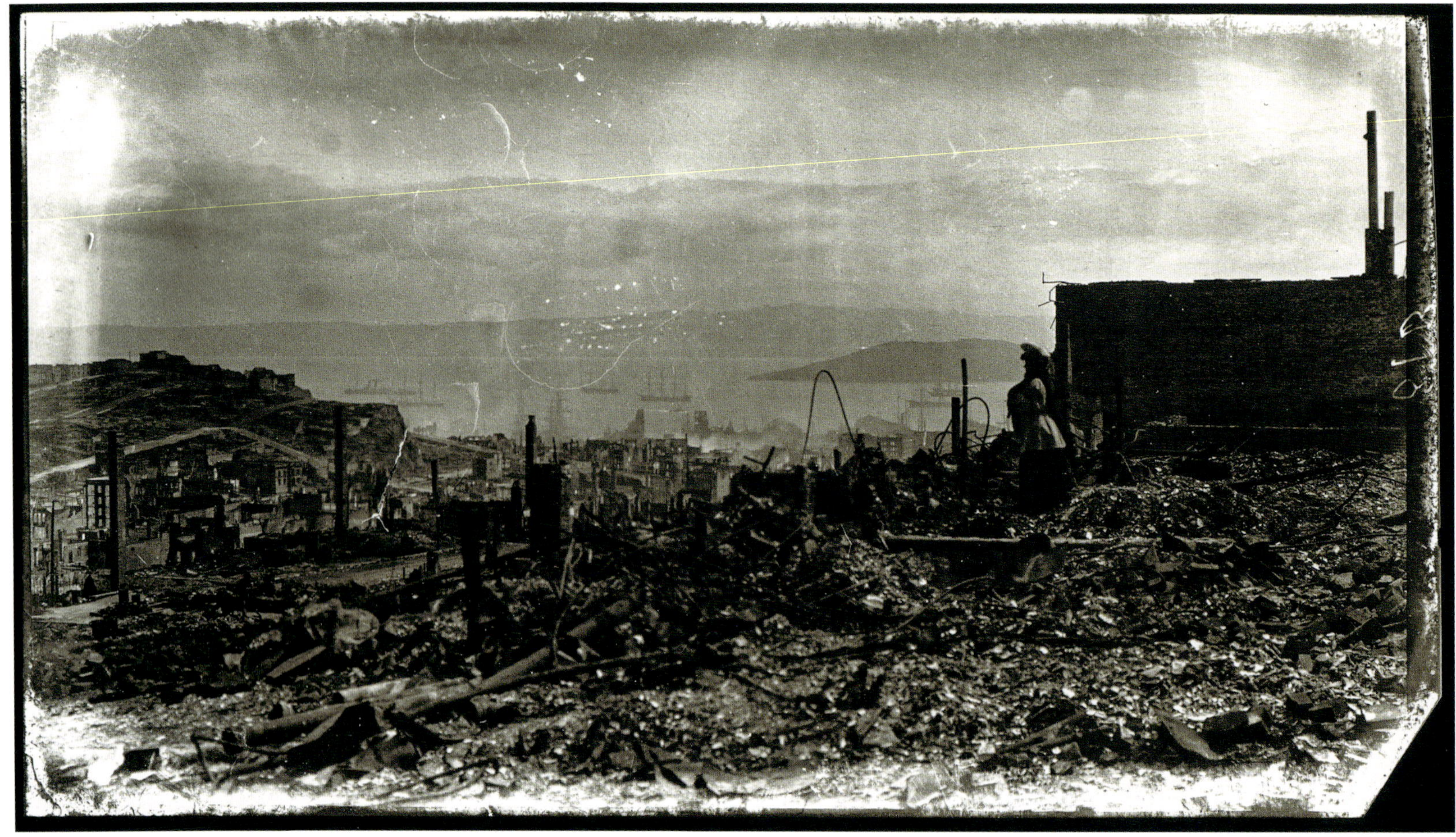

43·
Woman views devastated city from Nob Hill, San Francisco
2018.21.75 (cat. 64)

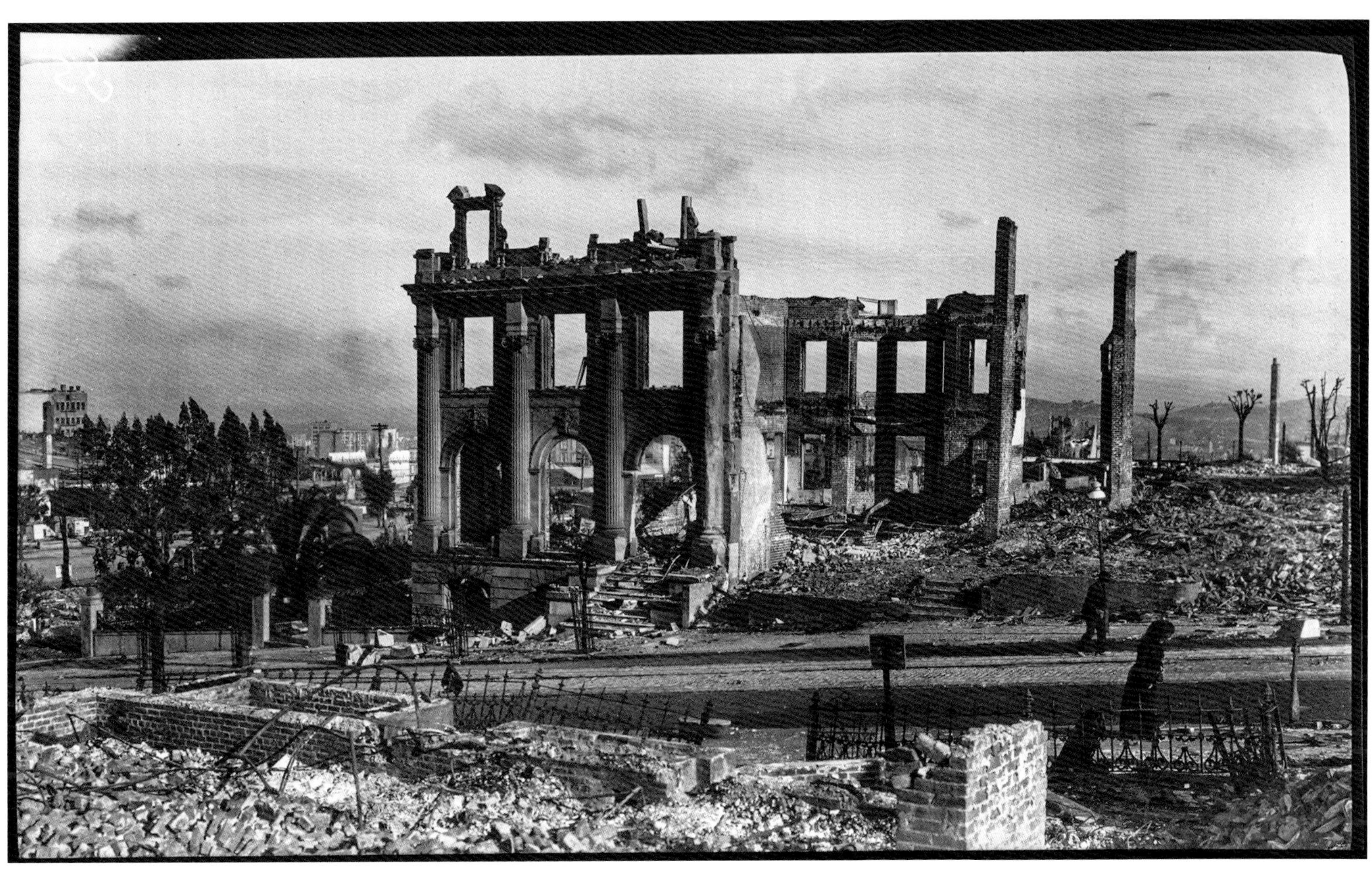

44.

J. Zenón Posadas mansion, Sacramento between Van Ness and Franklin, San Francisco
2018.21.38 (cat. 67)

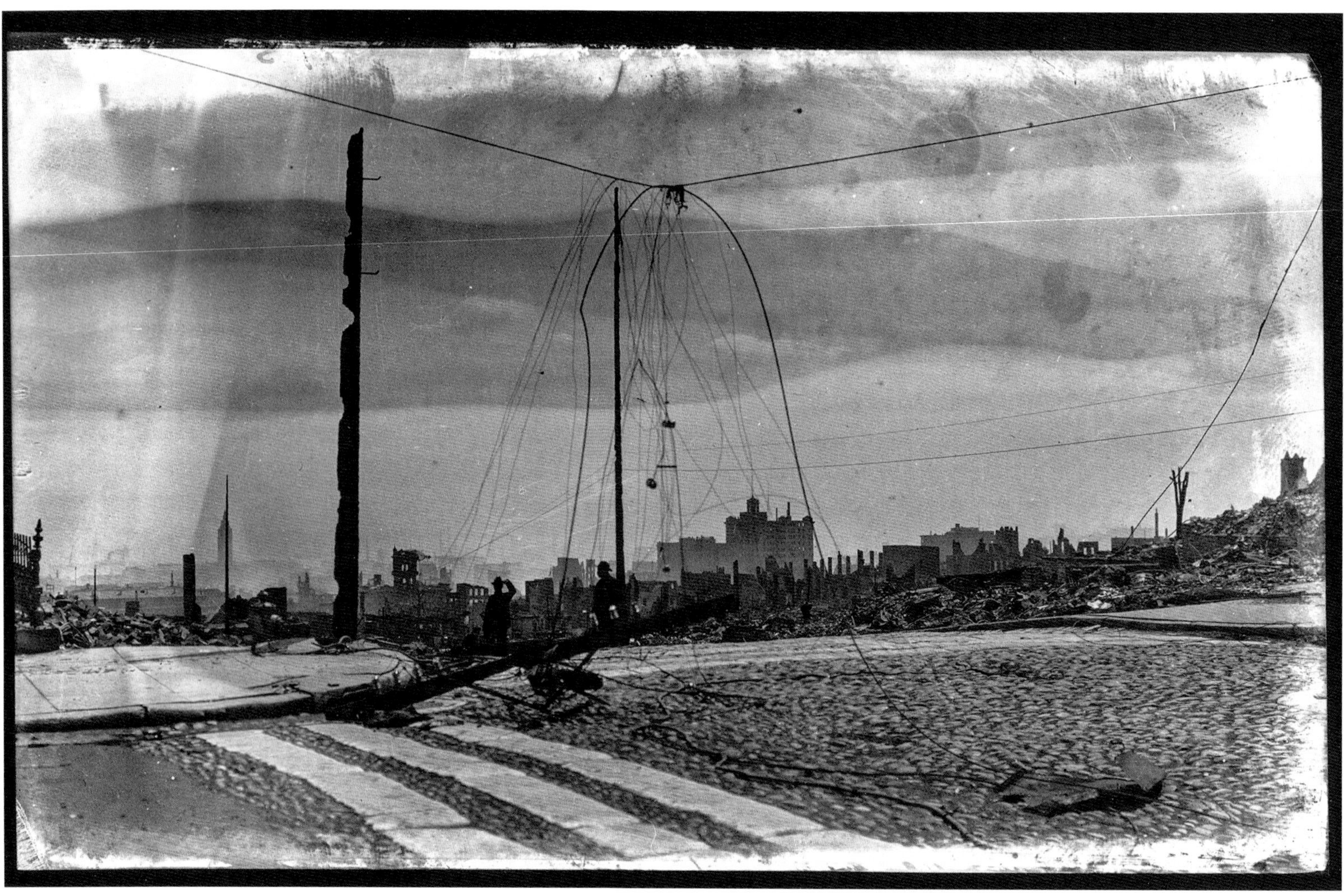

45.
Jackson looking east from Nob Hill, San Francisco
2018.21.71 (cat. 70)

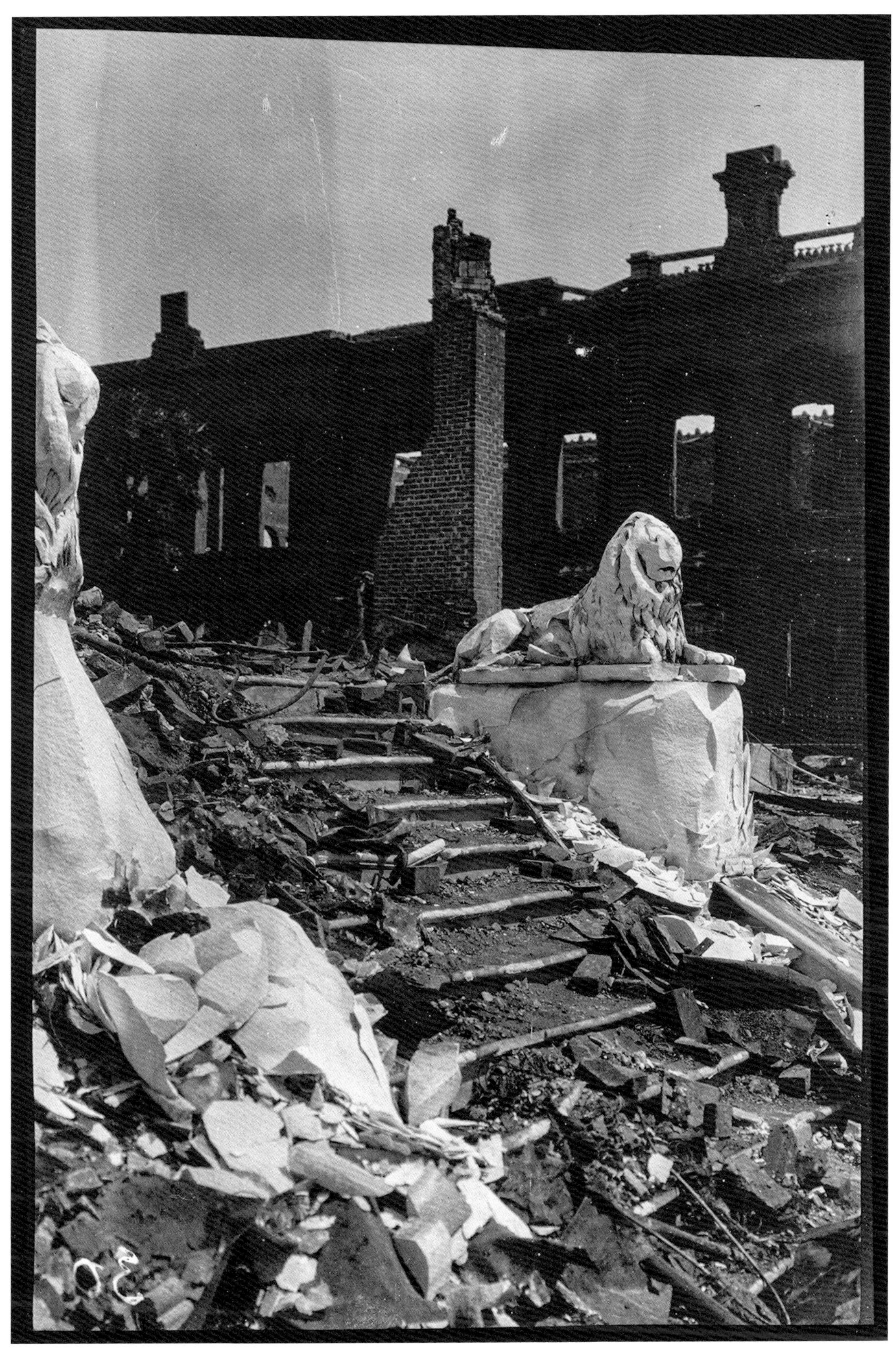

46.
Huntington mansion, California and Taylor, San Francisco
2018.21.34 (cat. 73)

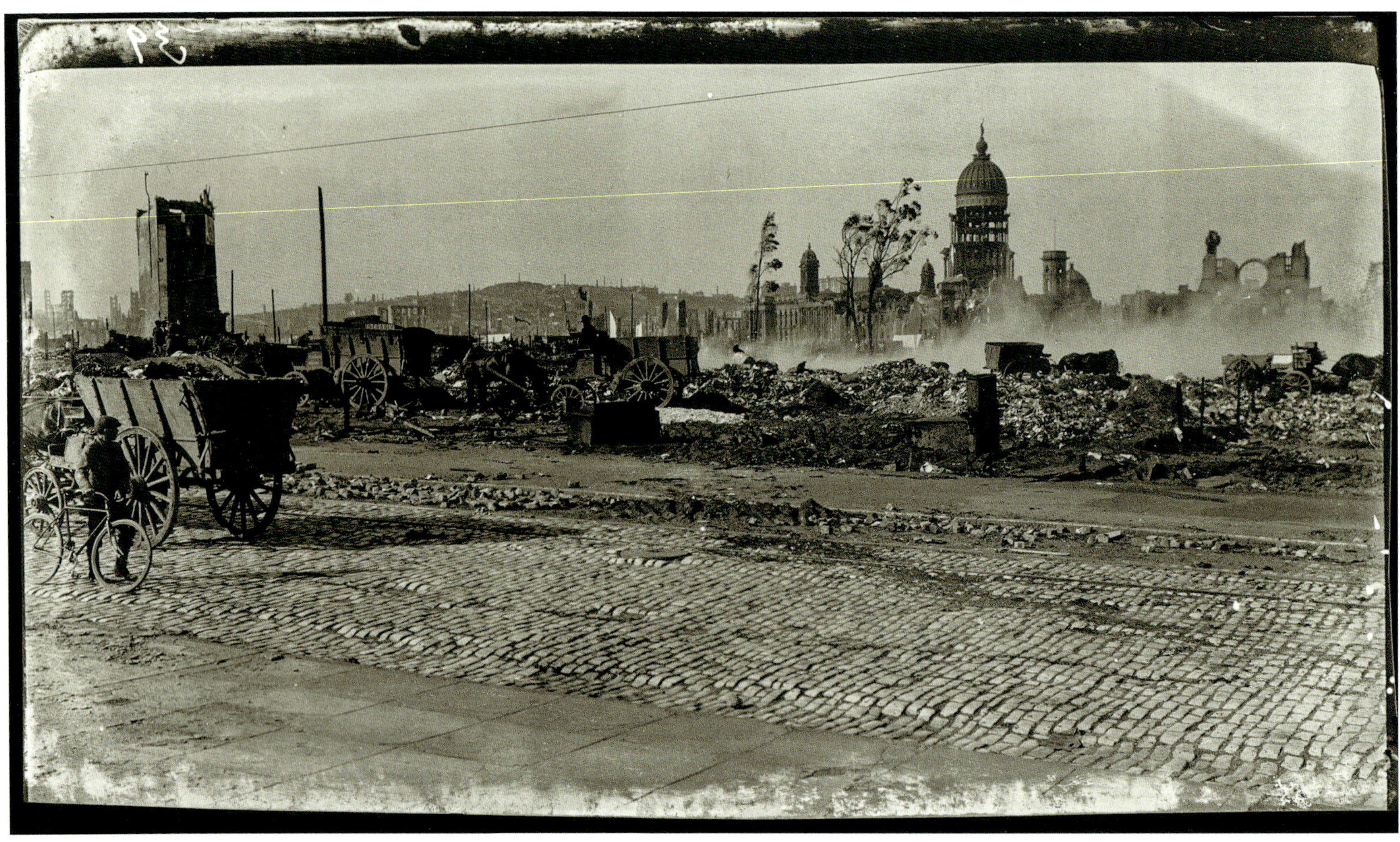

47.
City Hall from 12th Street near Market, San Francisco
2018.21.42 (cat. 76)

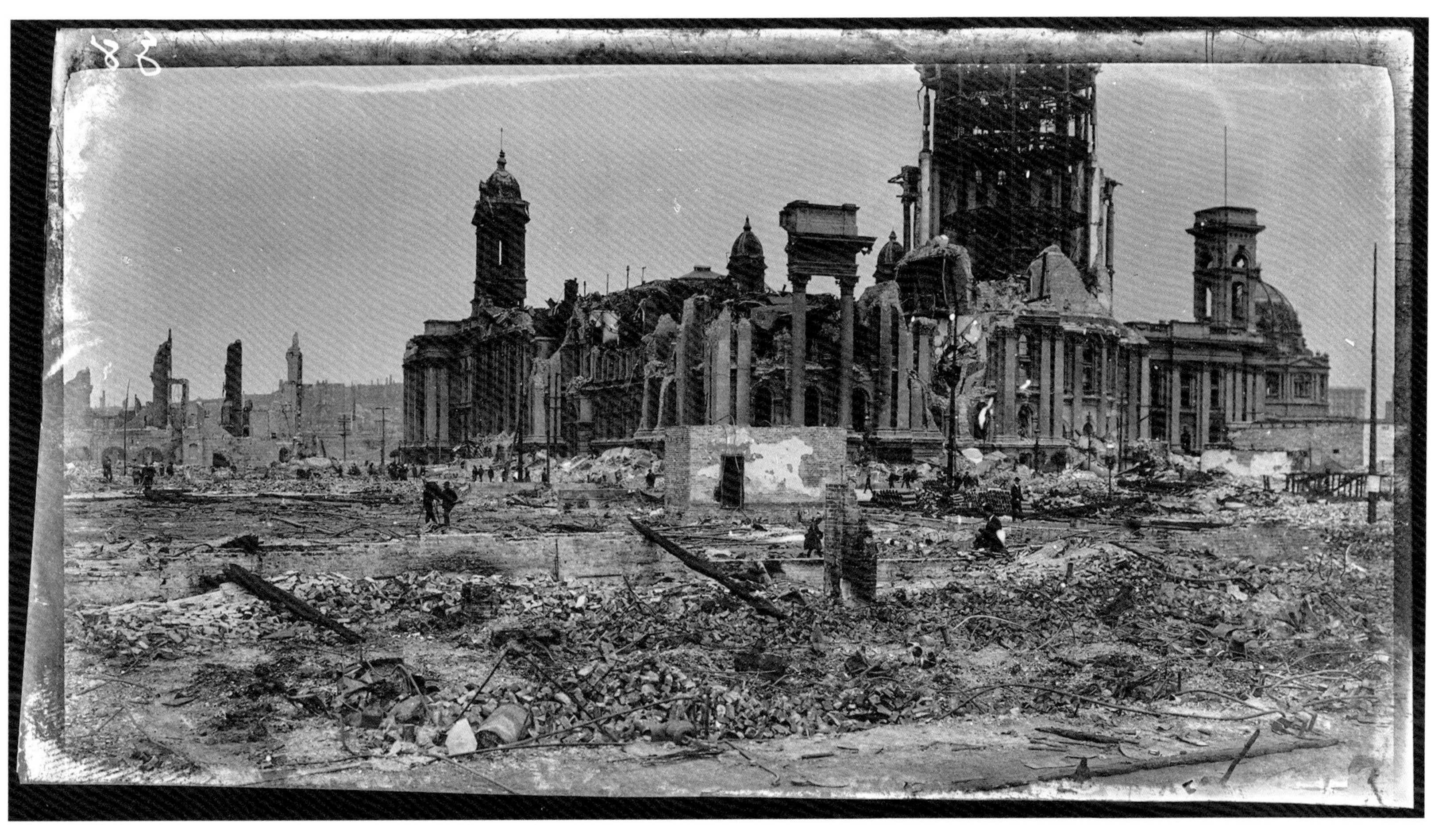

48.

City Hall from Hayes west of Larkin, San Francisco
2018.21.41 (cat. 79)

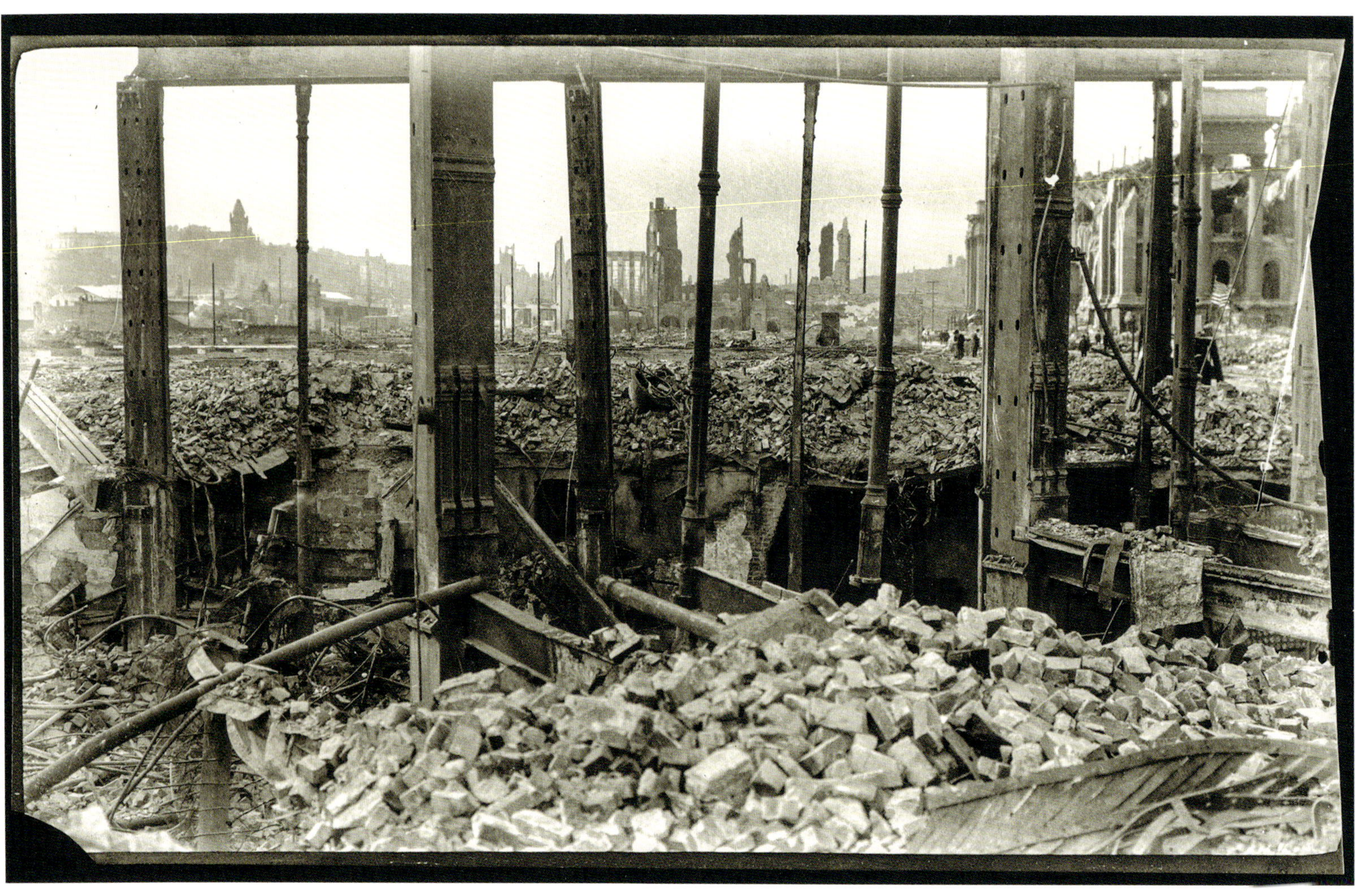

49.
City Hall through the ruins of the St. Nicholas Hotel, Market and Larkin, San Francisco
2018.21.2 (cat. 80)

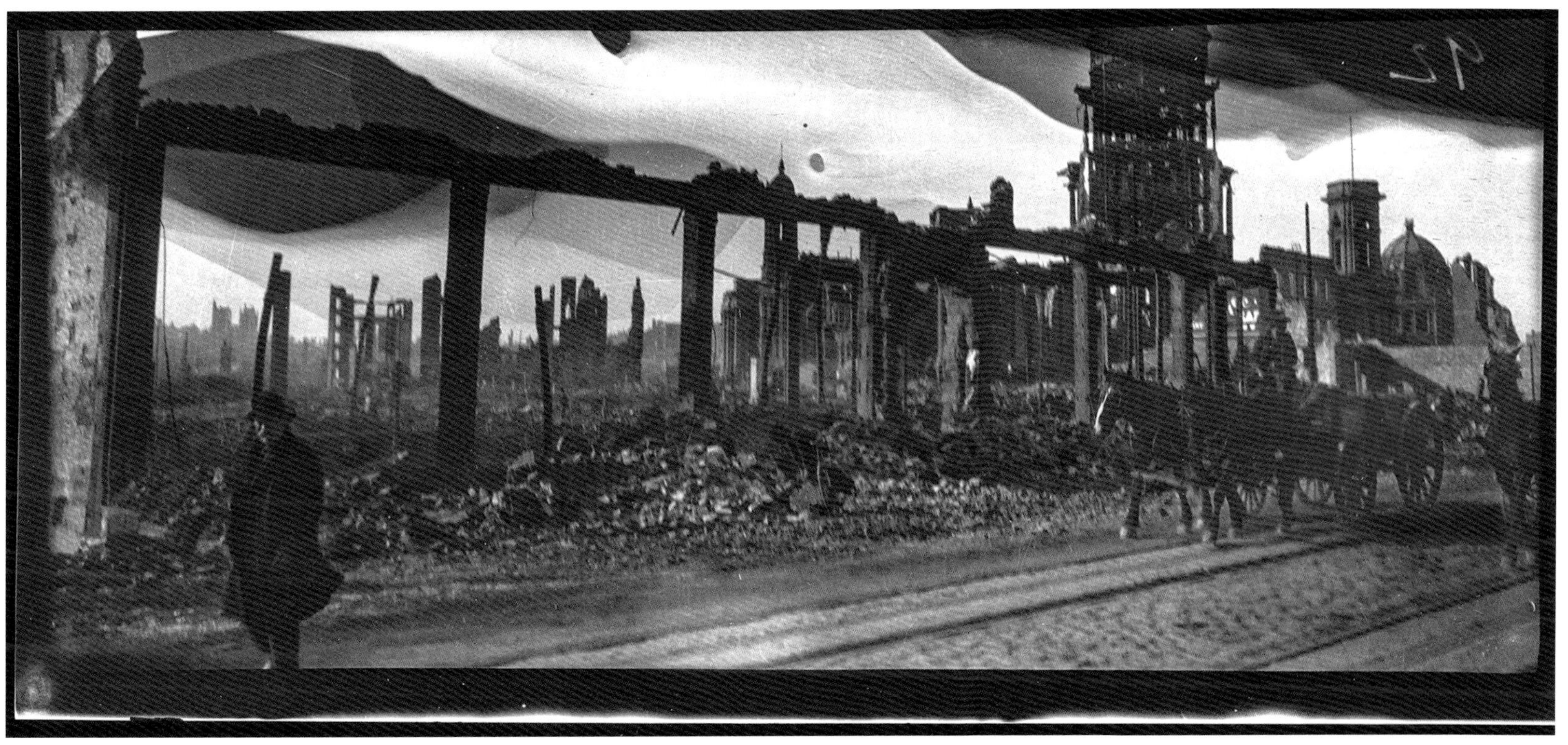

50.

City Hall through the ruins of the St. Nicholas Hotel, Market and Larkin, San Francisco
2018.21.82 (cat. 81)

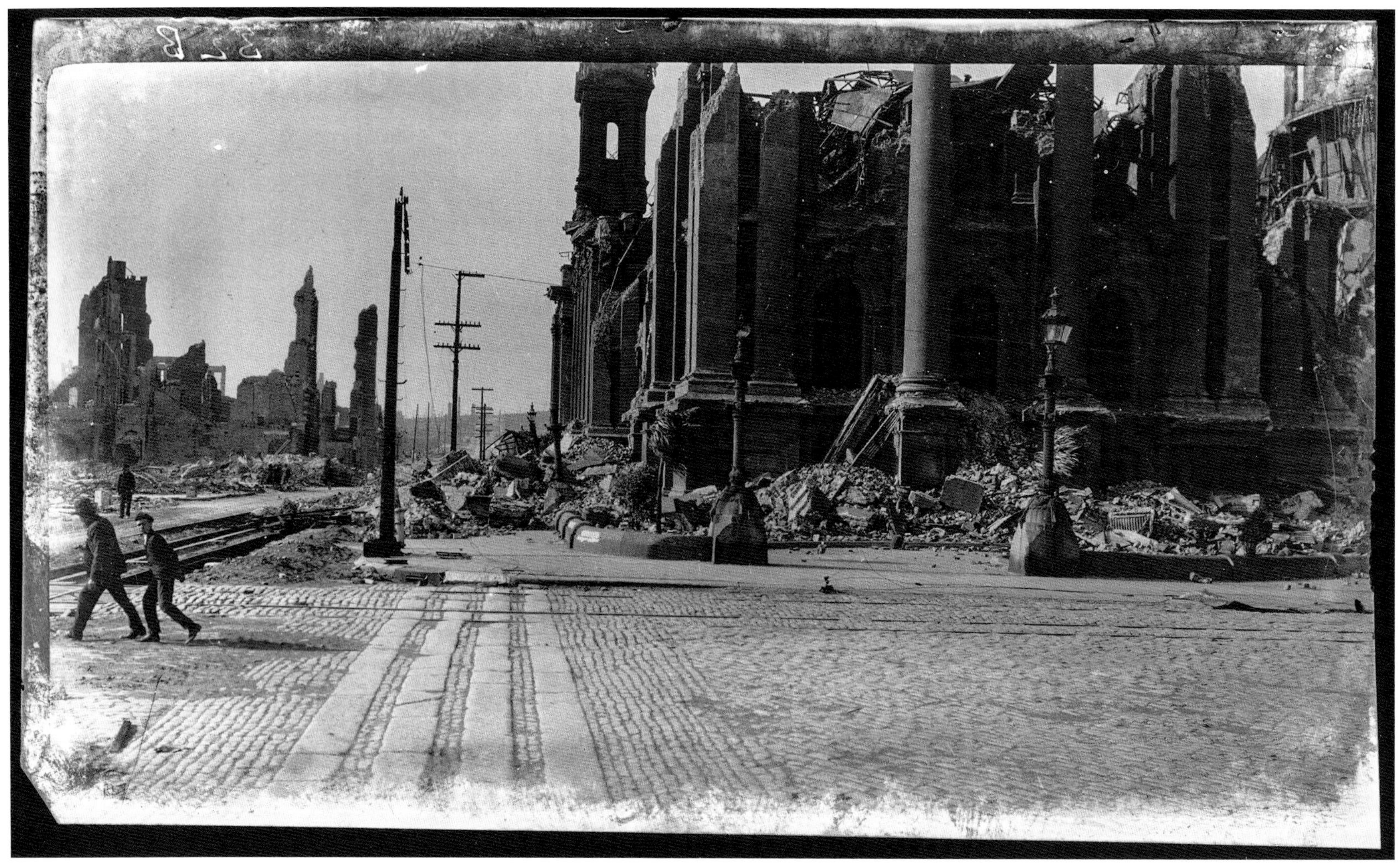

51.
City Hall, Larkin and Grove, San Francisco
2018.21.36 (cat. 84)

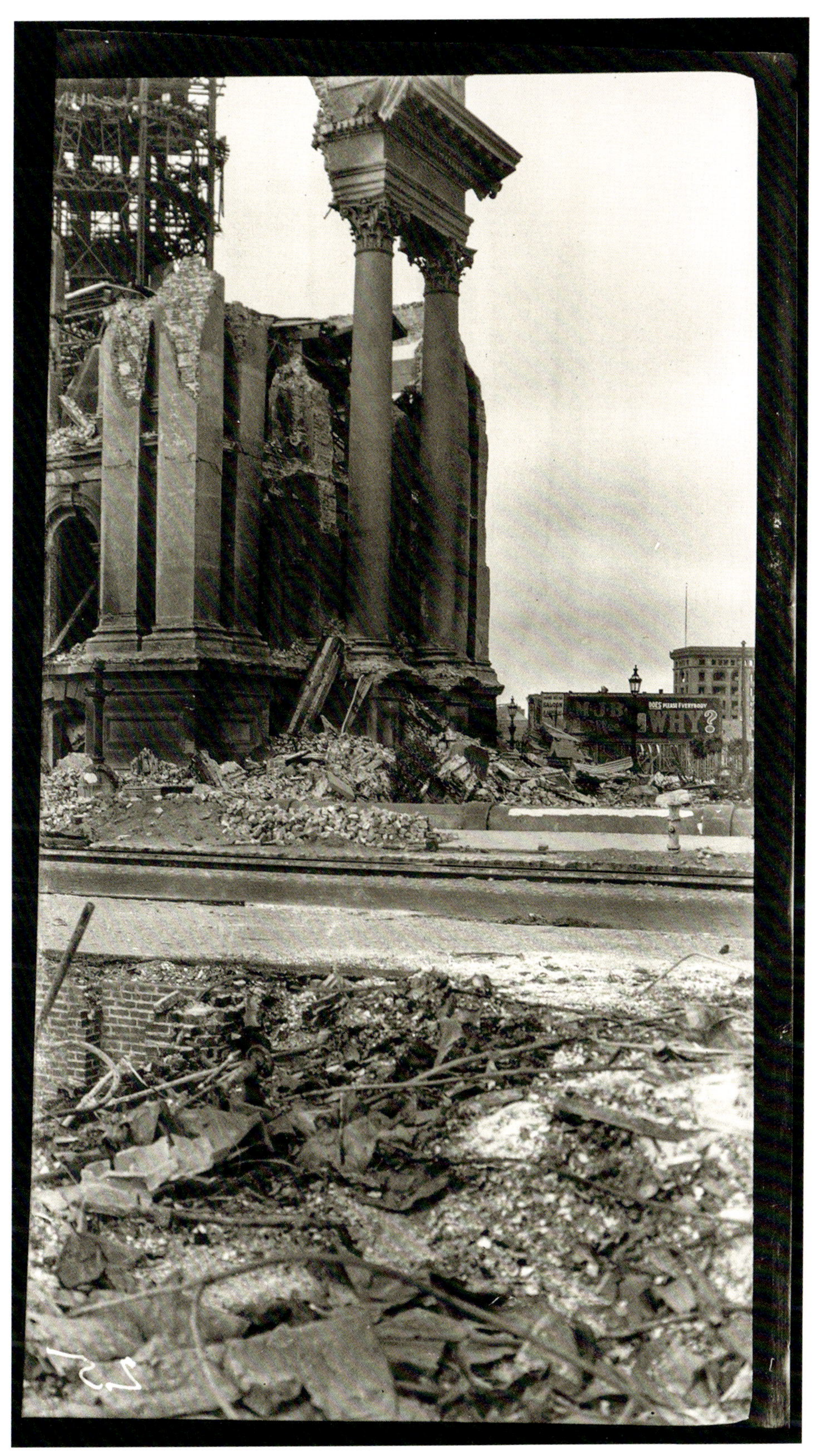

52.

City Hall from Larkin near Grove, San Francisco
2018.21.28 (cat. 85)

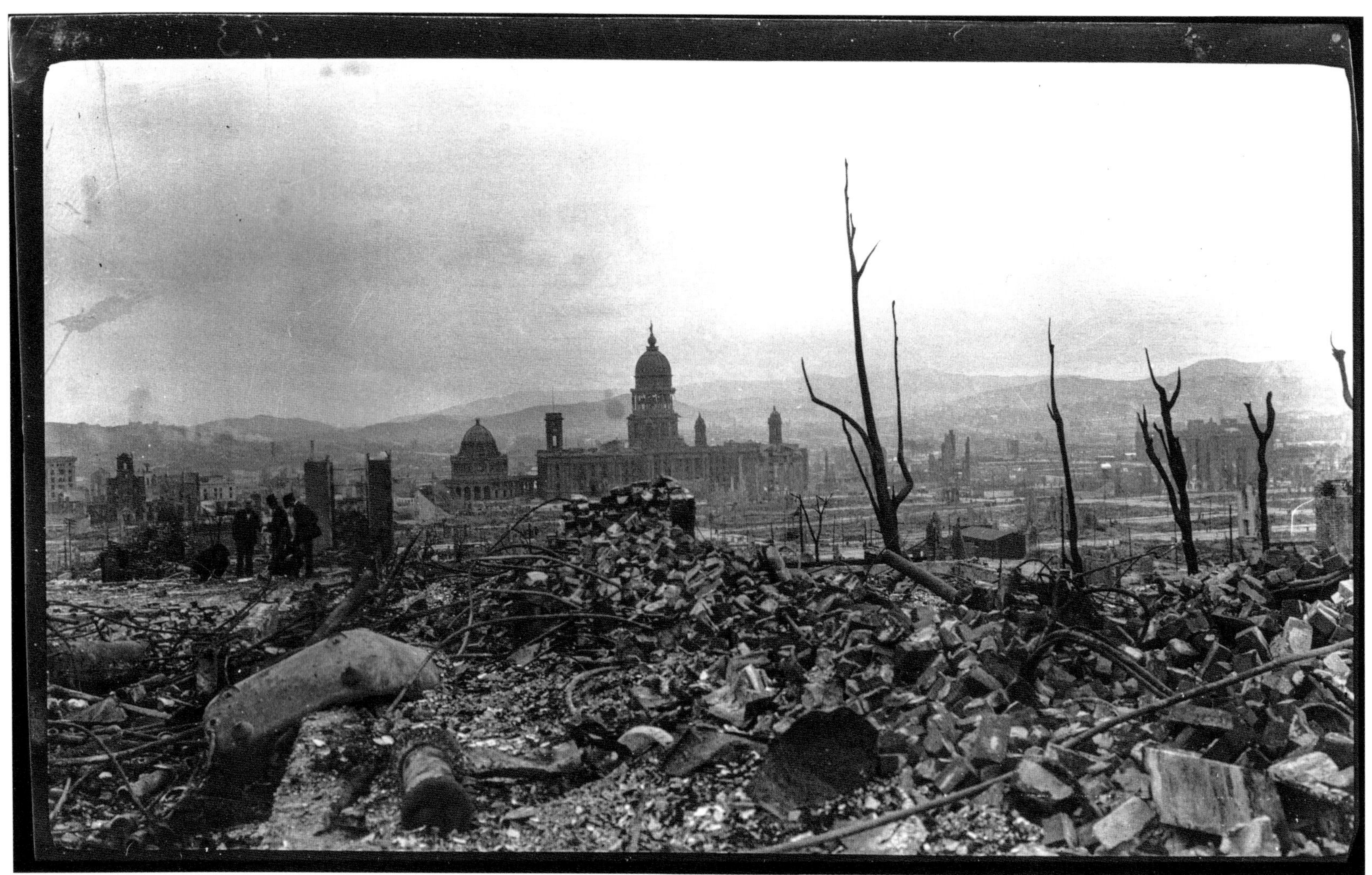

53.
City Hall from Sutter between Hyde and Leavenworth, San Francisco
2018.21.83 (cat. 86)

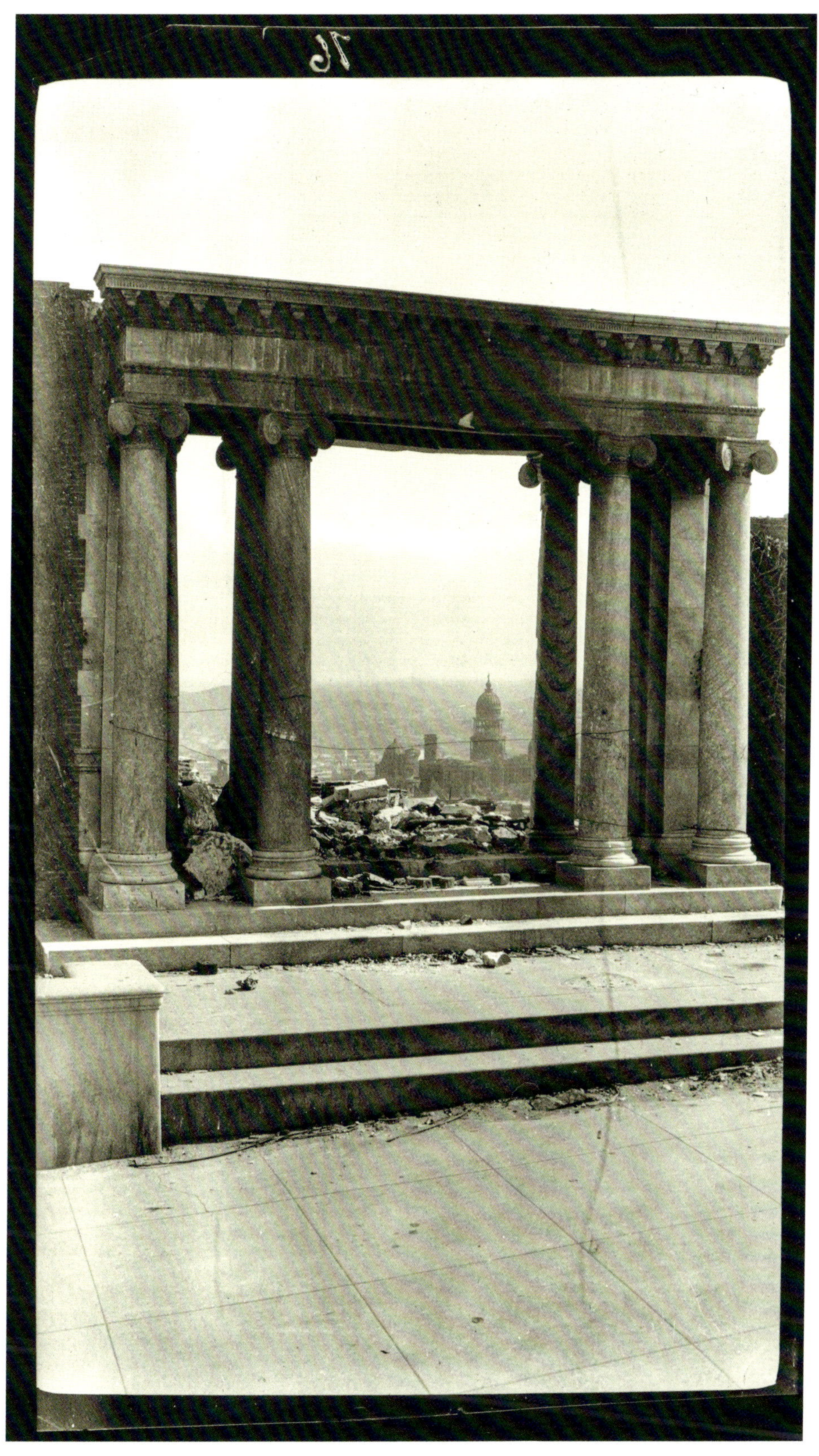

54.
Towne mansion, California and Taylor, San Francisco
2018.21.72 (cat. 88)

LIFE

ON THE STREETS

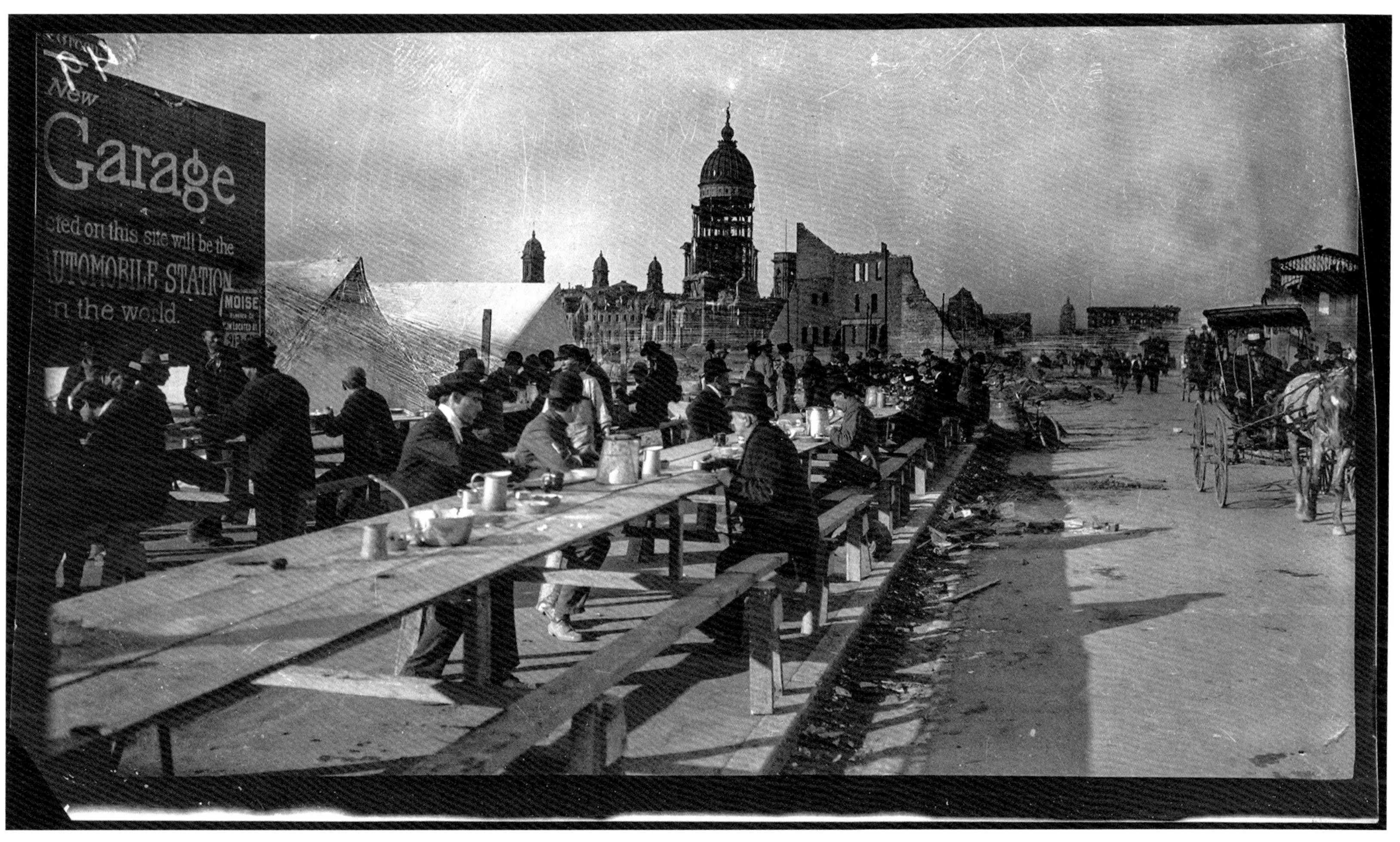

55.
Hot meal kitchen on Market near 10th Street, San Francisco
2018.21.52 (cat. 92)

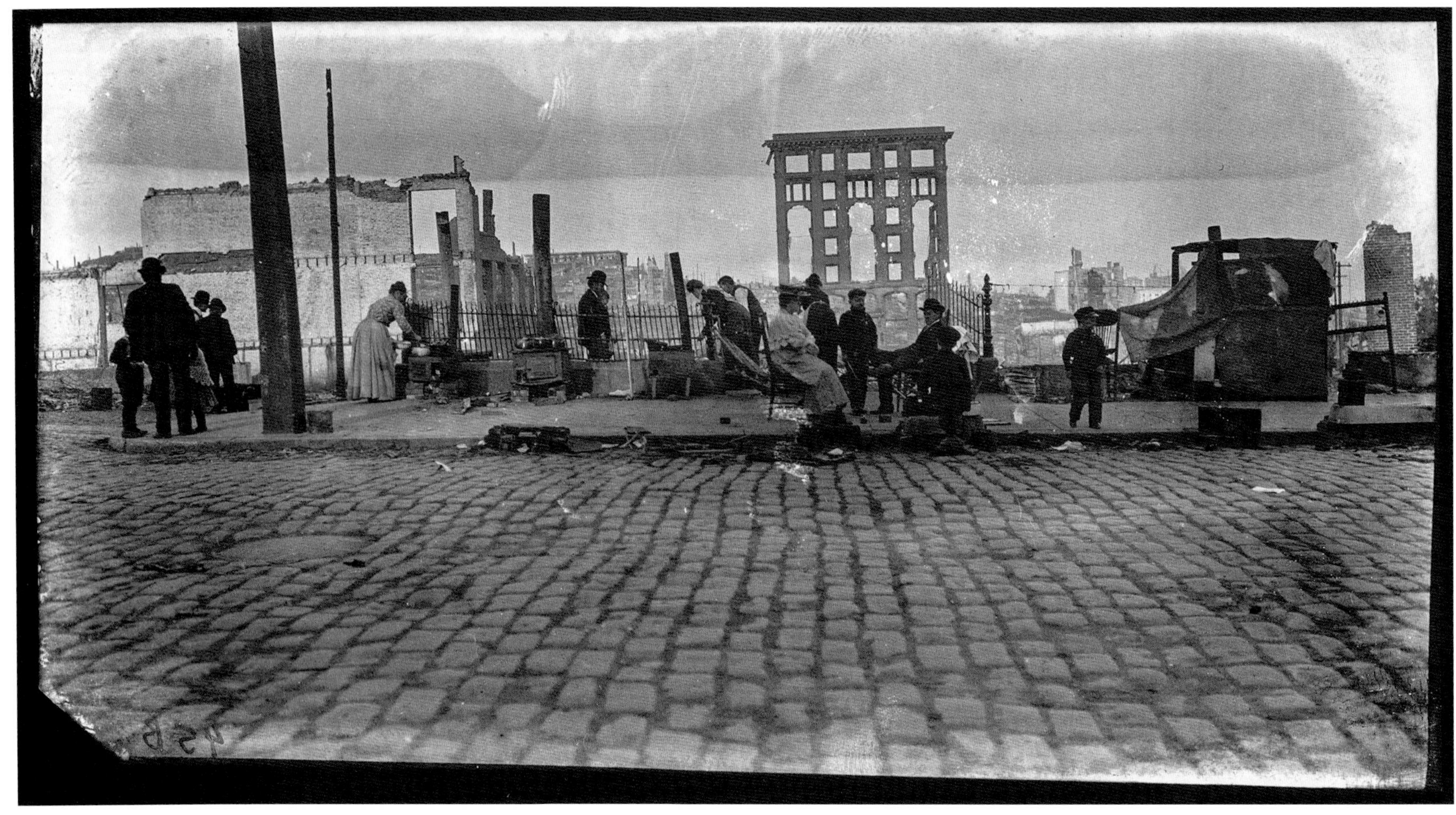

56.

Franklin between Bush and Pine, San Francisco
2018.21.48 (cat. 98)

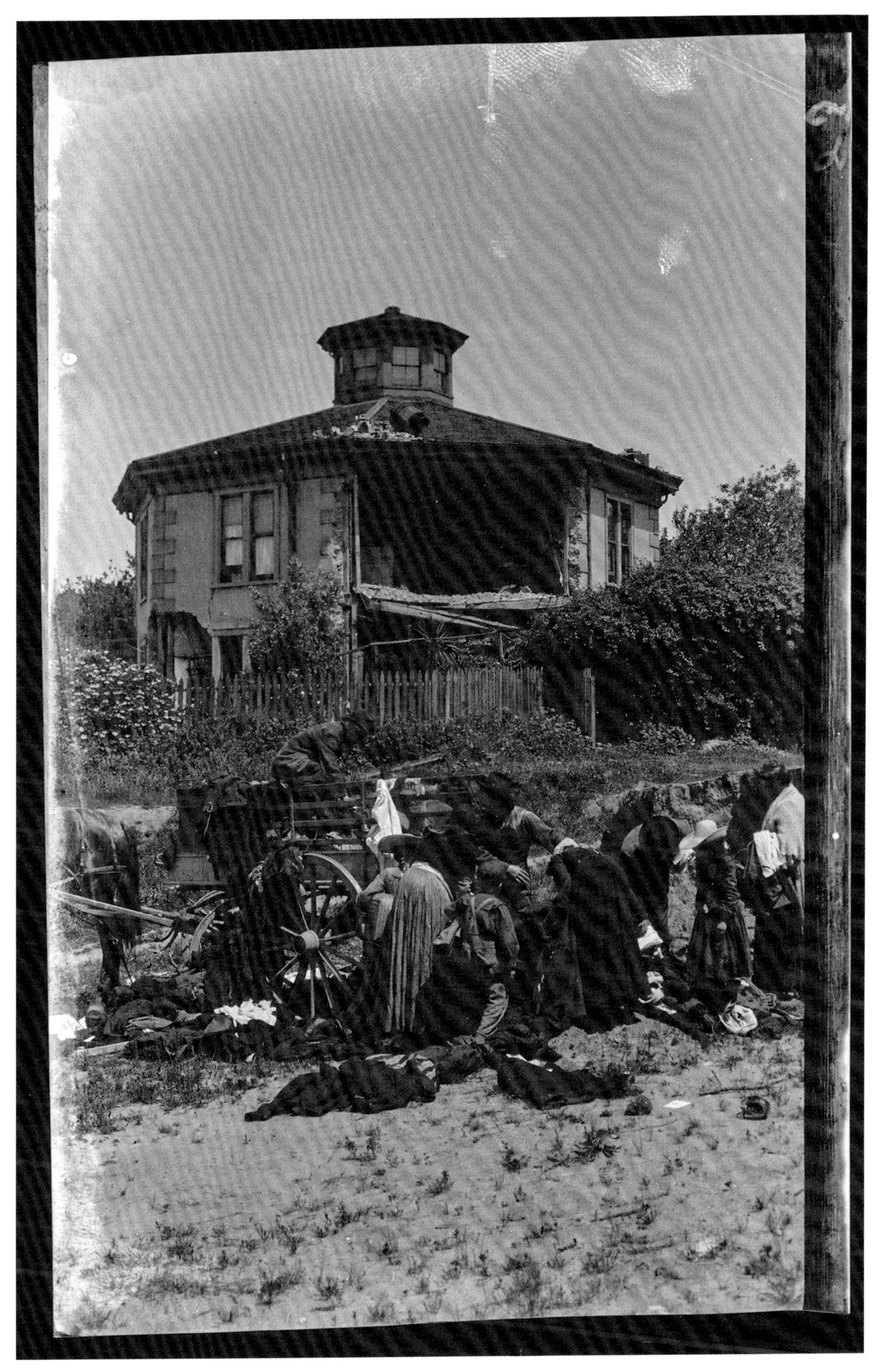

57.
Cavagnaro House, Gough near Union, San Francisco
2018.21.77 (cat. 100)

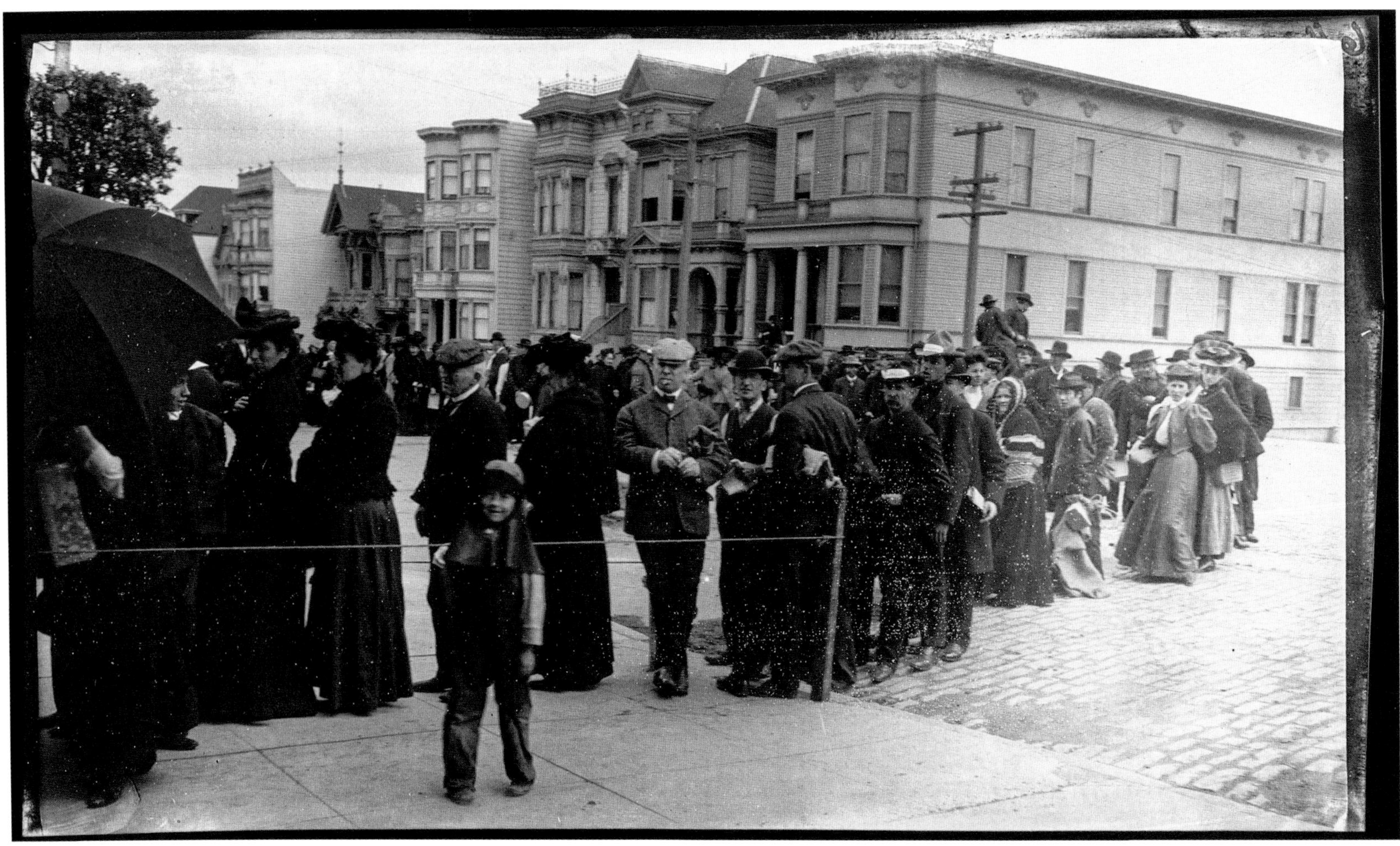

58.

People waiting for rations following the earthquake and fire (probably April 22, 1906), San Francisco
2018.21.63 (cat. 101)

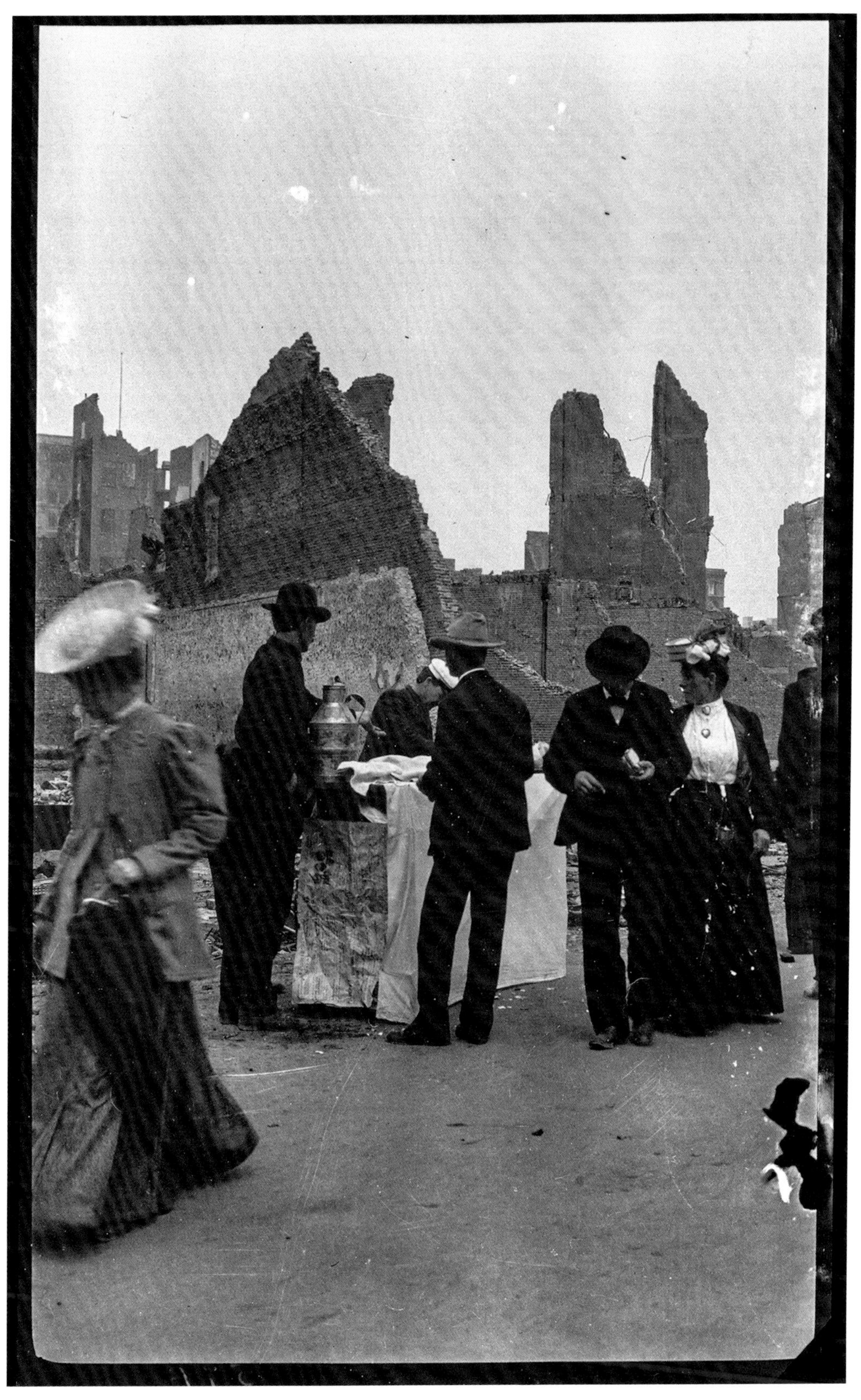

59.
Food vendor post–earthquake and fire, San Francisco
2018.21.57 (cat. 102)

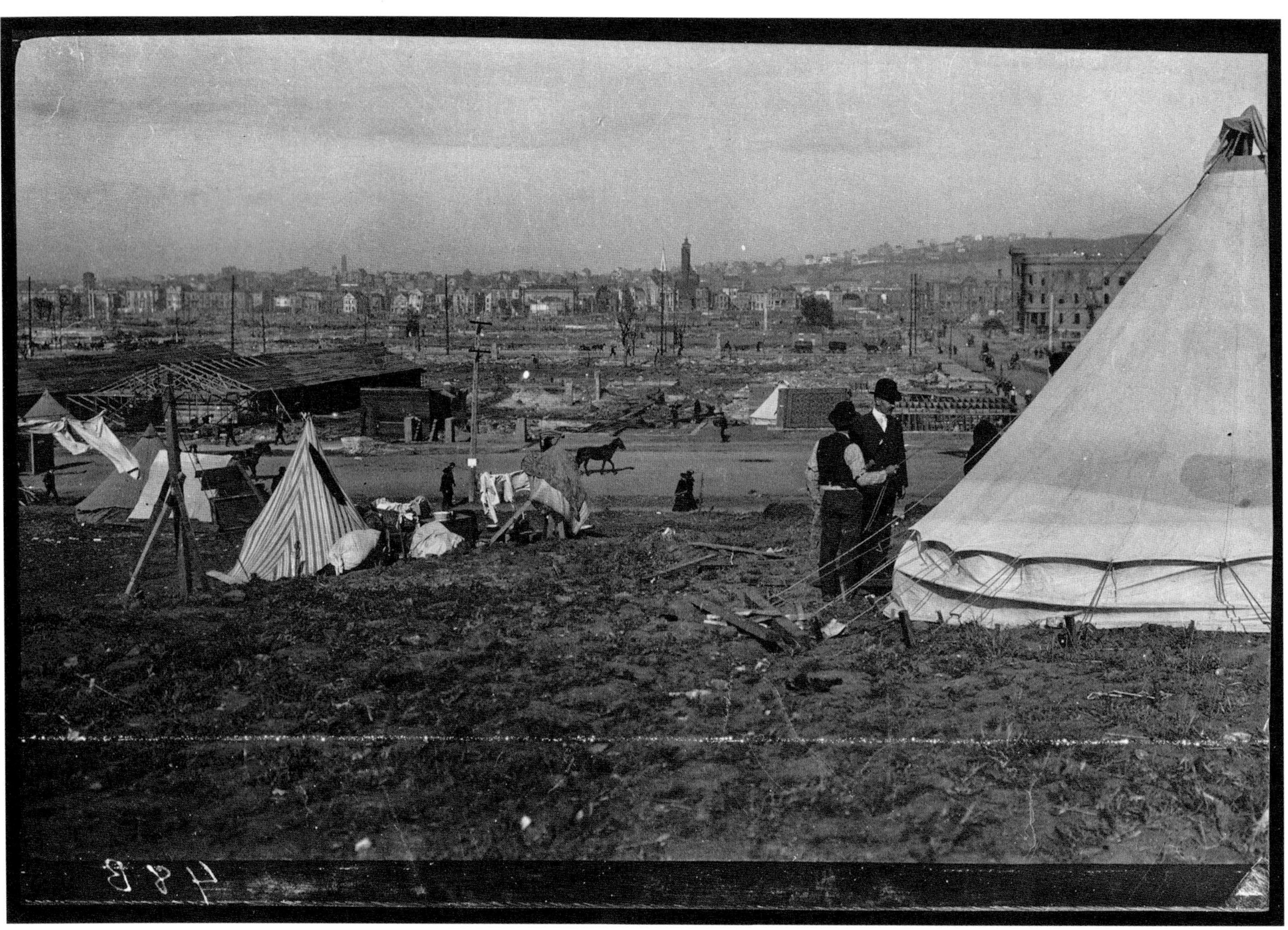

60.

Dolores Park near 19th Street, looking east, San Francisco
2018.21.50 (cat. 105)

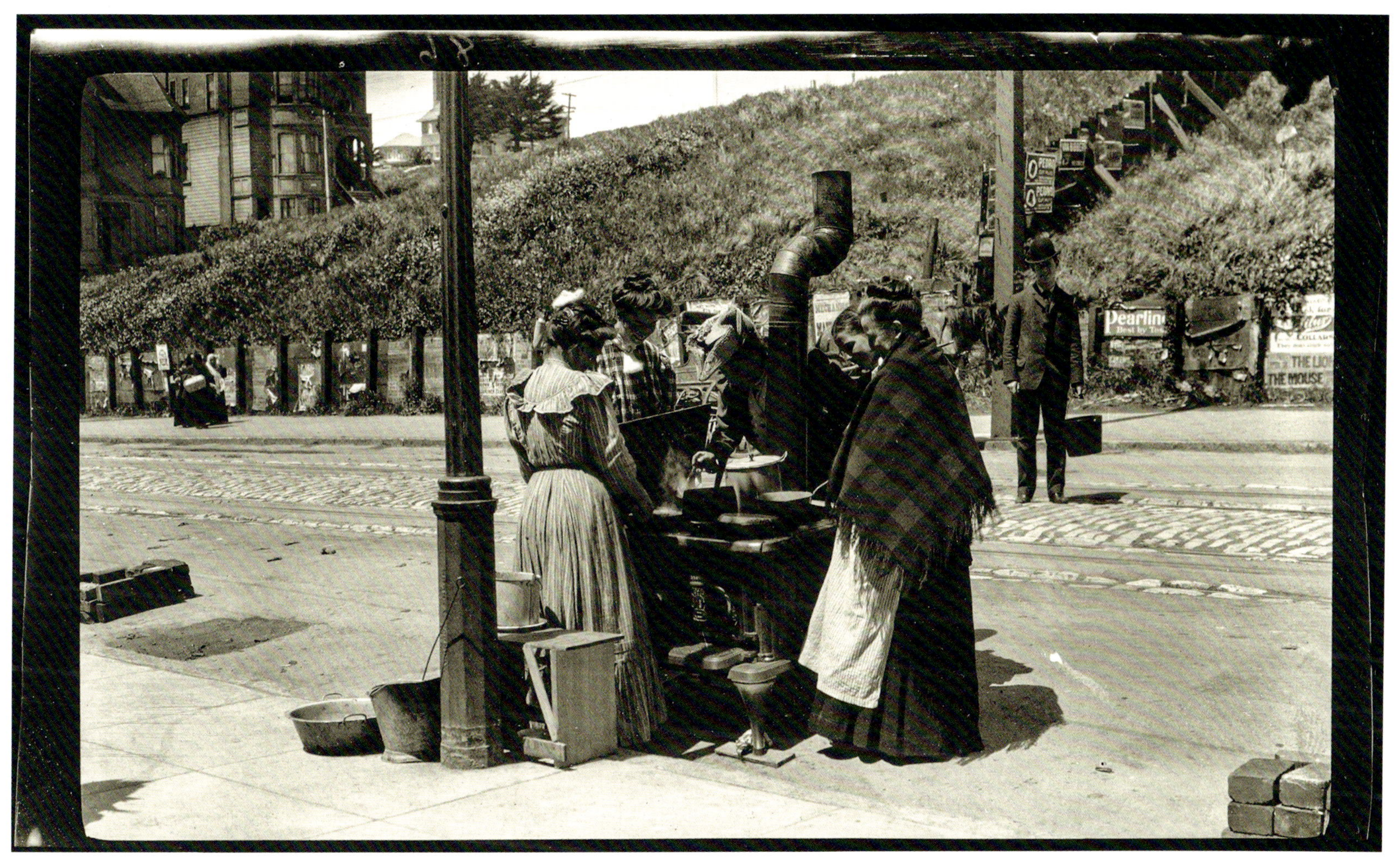

61.

A sidewalk kitchen, San Francisco
2018.21.79 (cat. 106)

THE MILITARY

PRESENCE

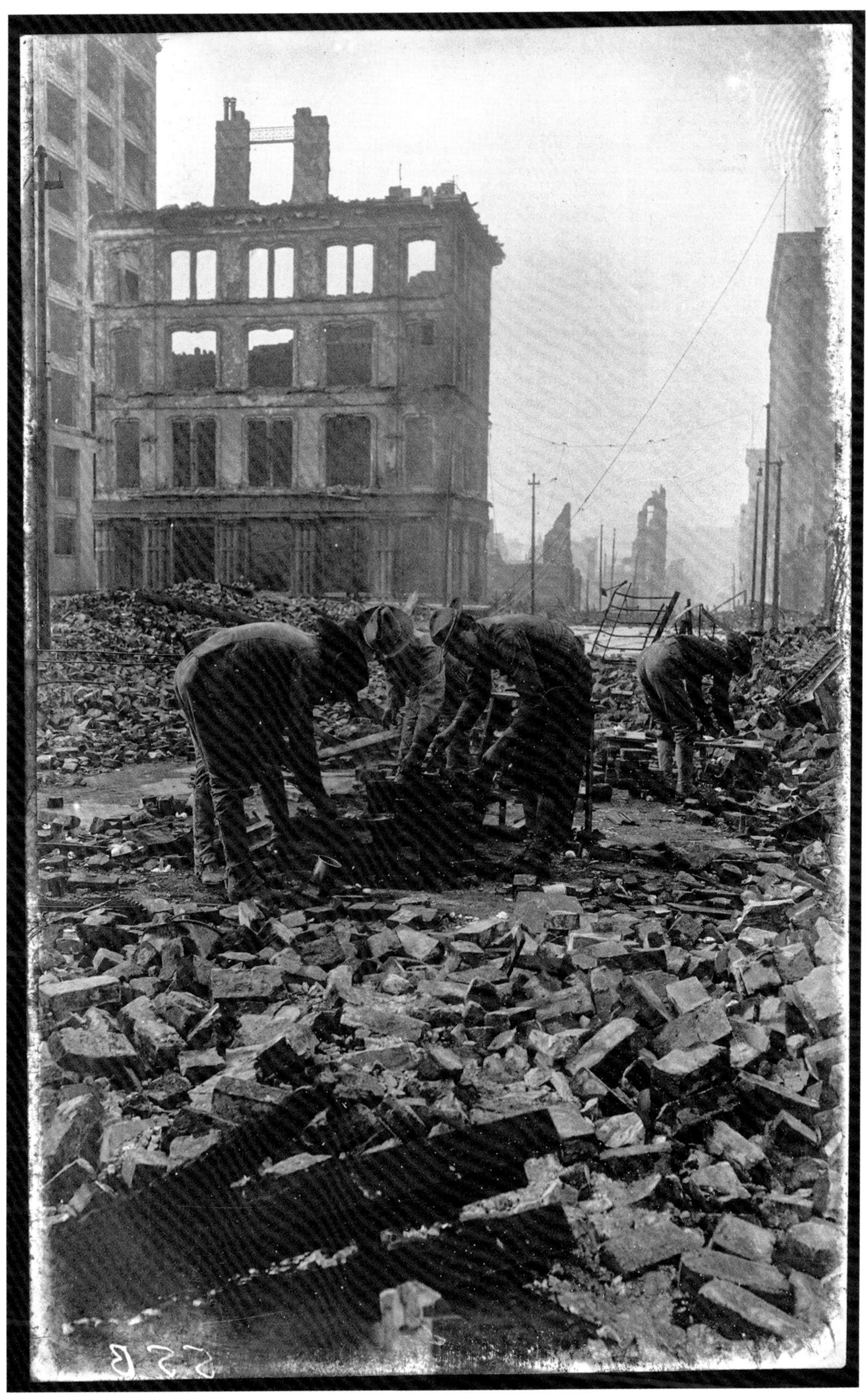

62.

Montgomery between Post and Sutter, San Francisco
2018.21.25 (cat. 109)

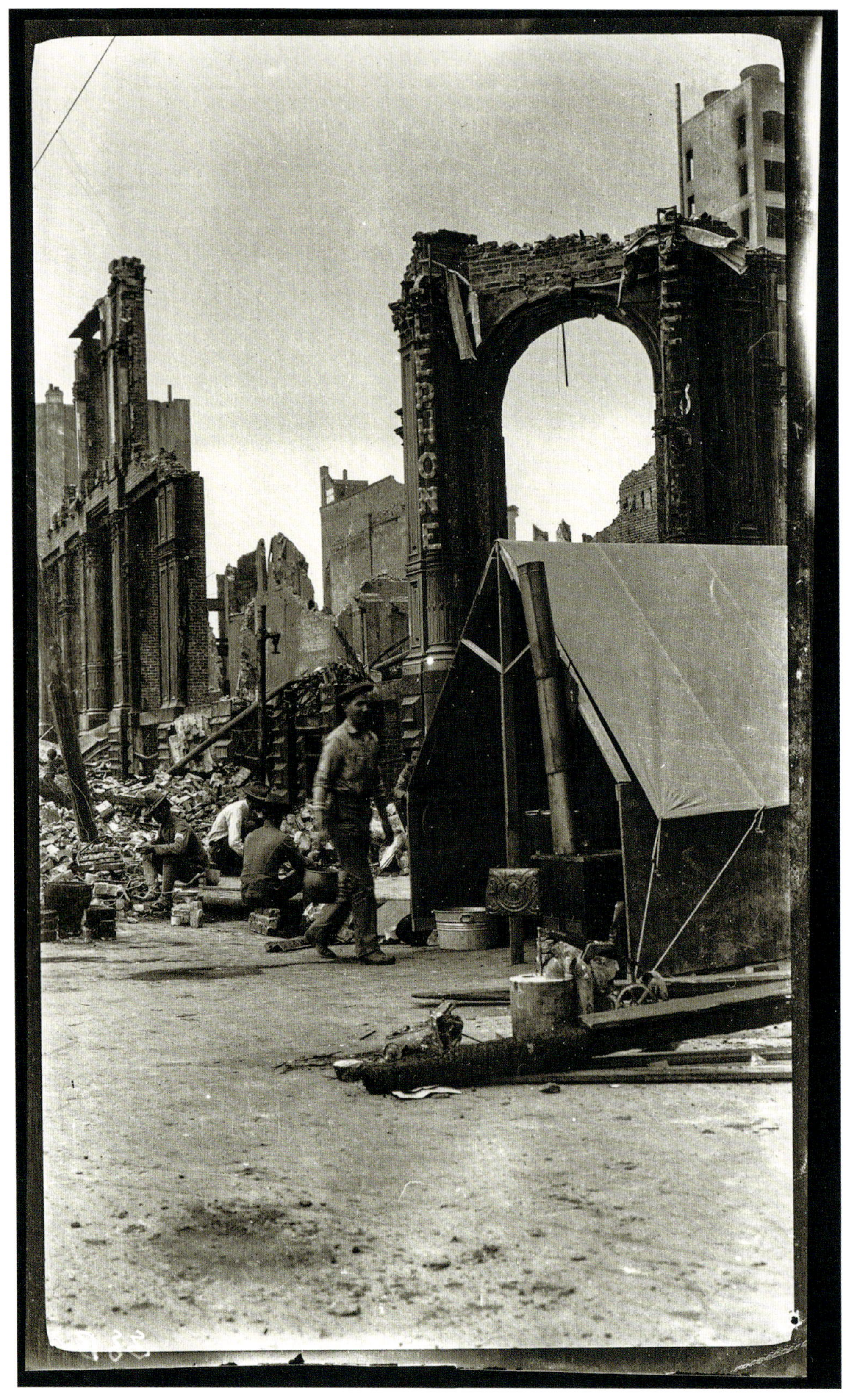

63.

St. Ann's Building, Powell and Eddy, San Francisco
2018.21.37 (cat. 110)

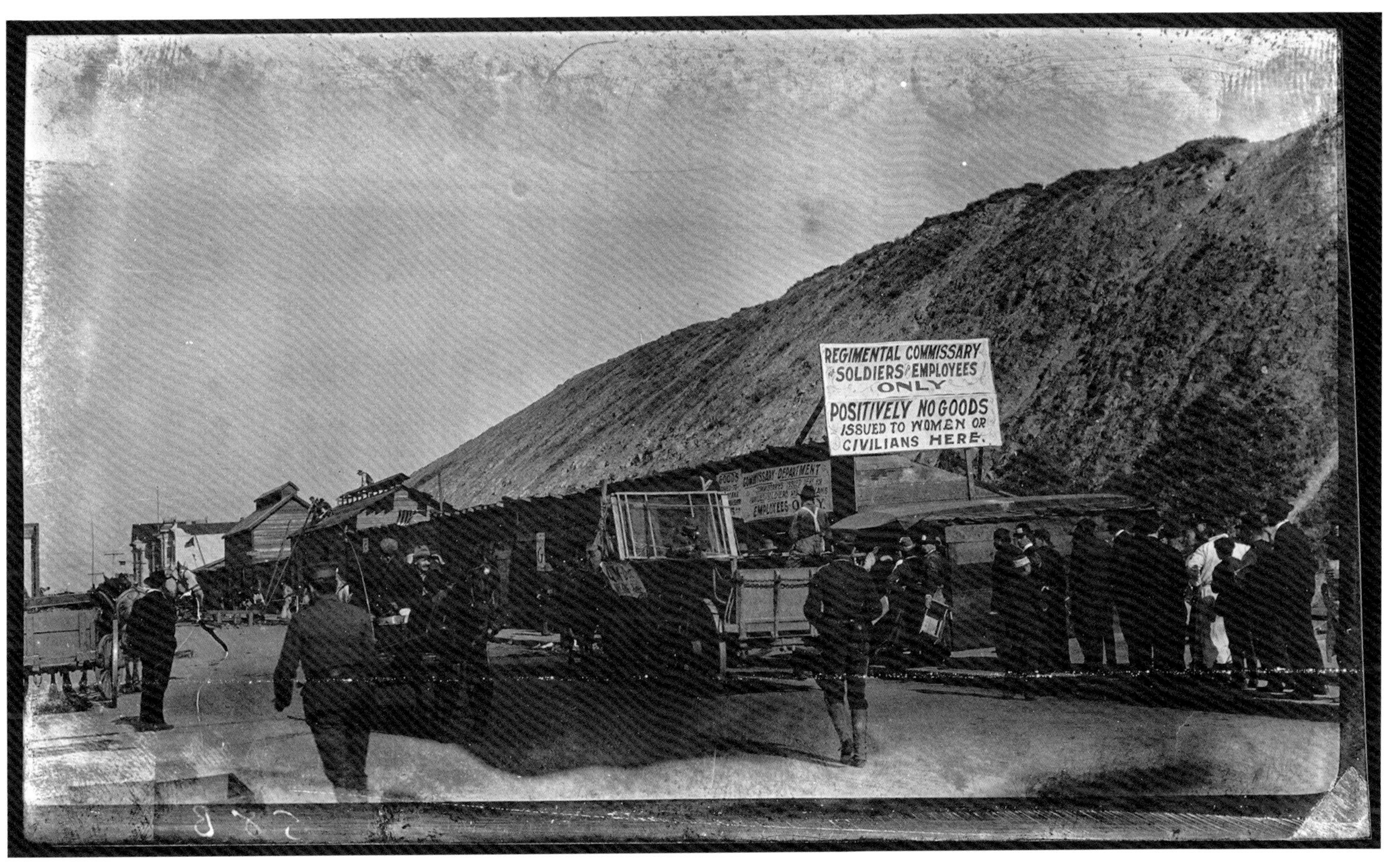

64.

Regimental commissary on Duboce between Market and Church, San Francisco
2018.21.59 (cat. 112)

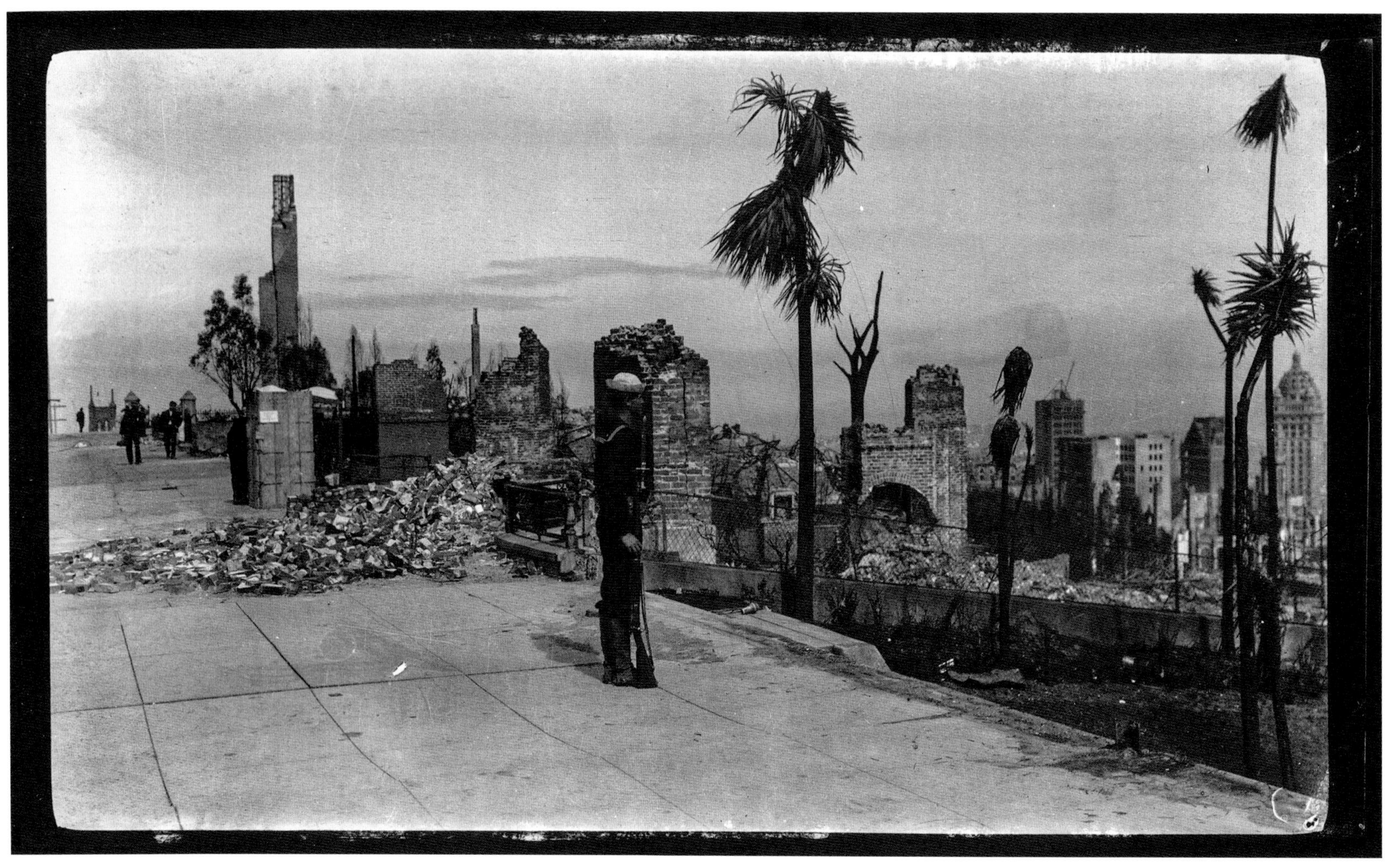

65.
California between Mason and Taylor, San Francisco
2018.21.29 (cat. 114)

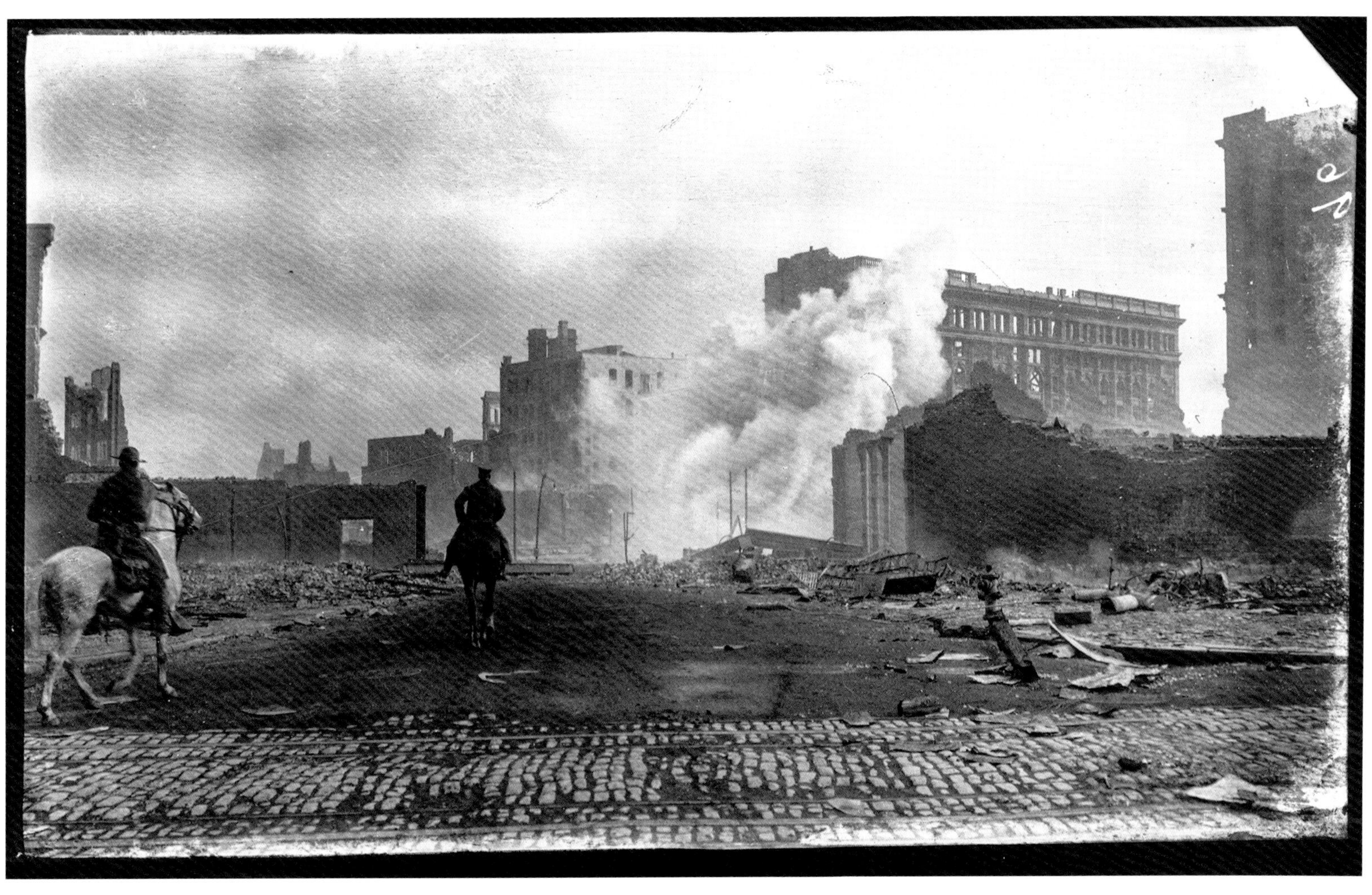

66.

The Emporium from Stockton and O'Farrell, San Francisco
2018.21.84 (cat. 115)

RELIEF

CAMPS

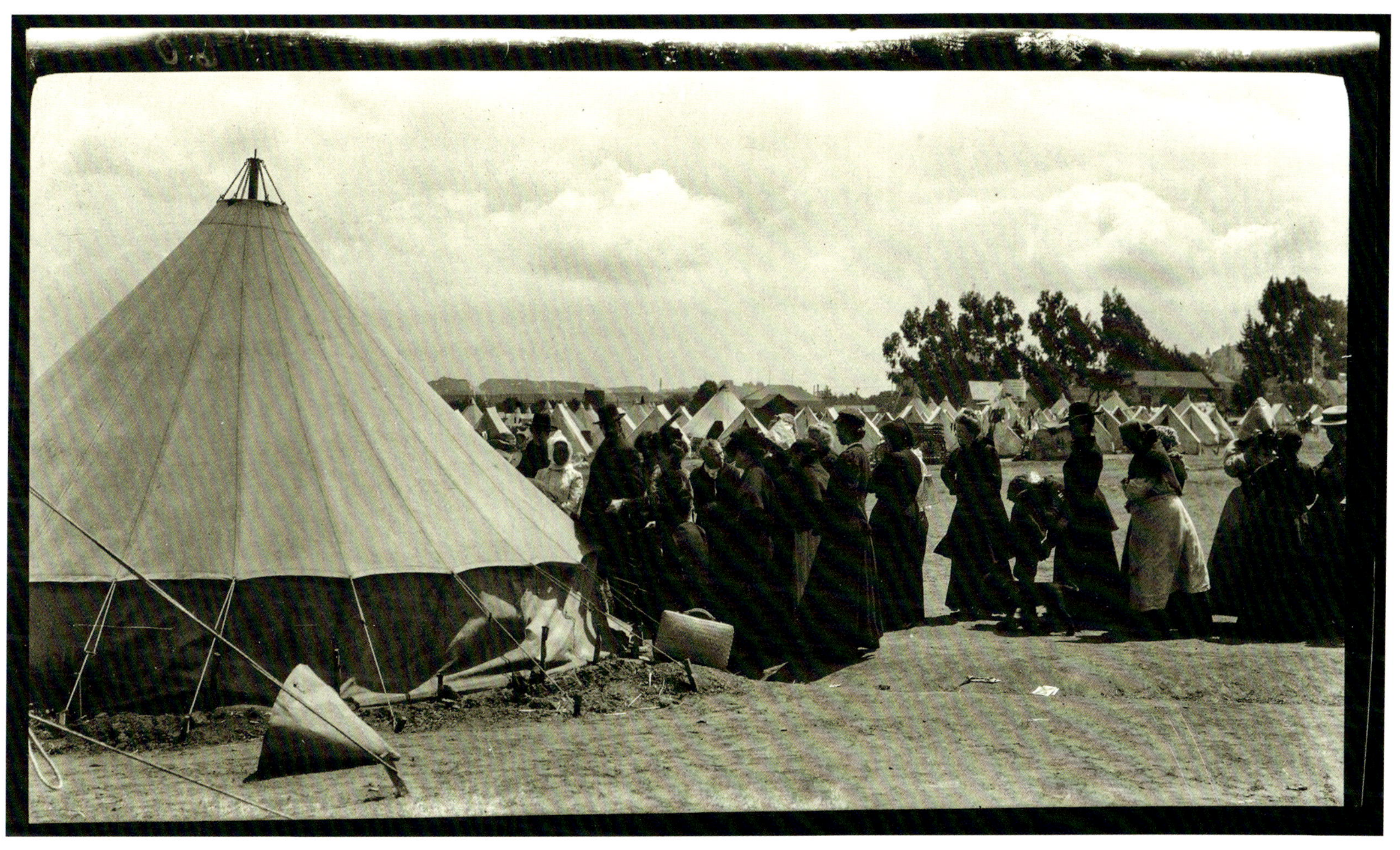

67.

Families in line for aid in an army relief camp, San Francisco
2018.21.60 (cat. 118)

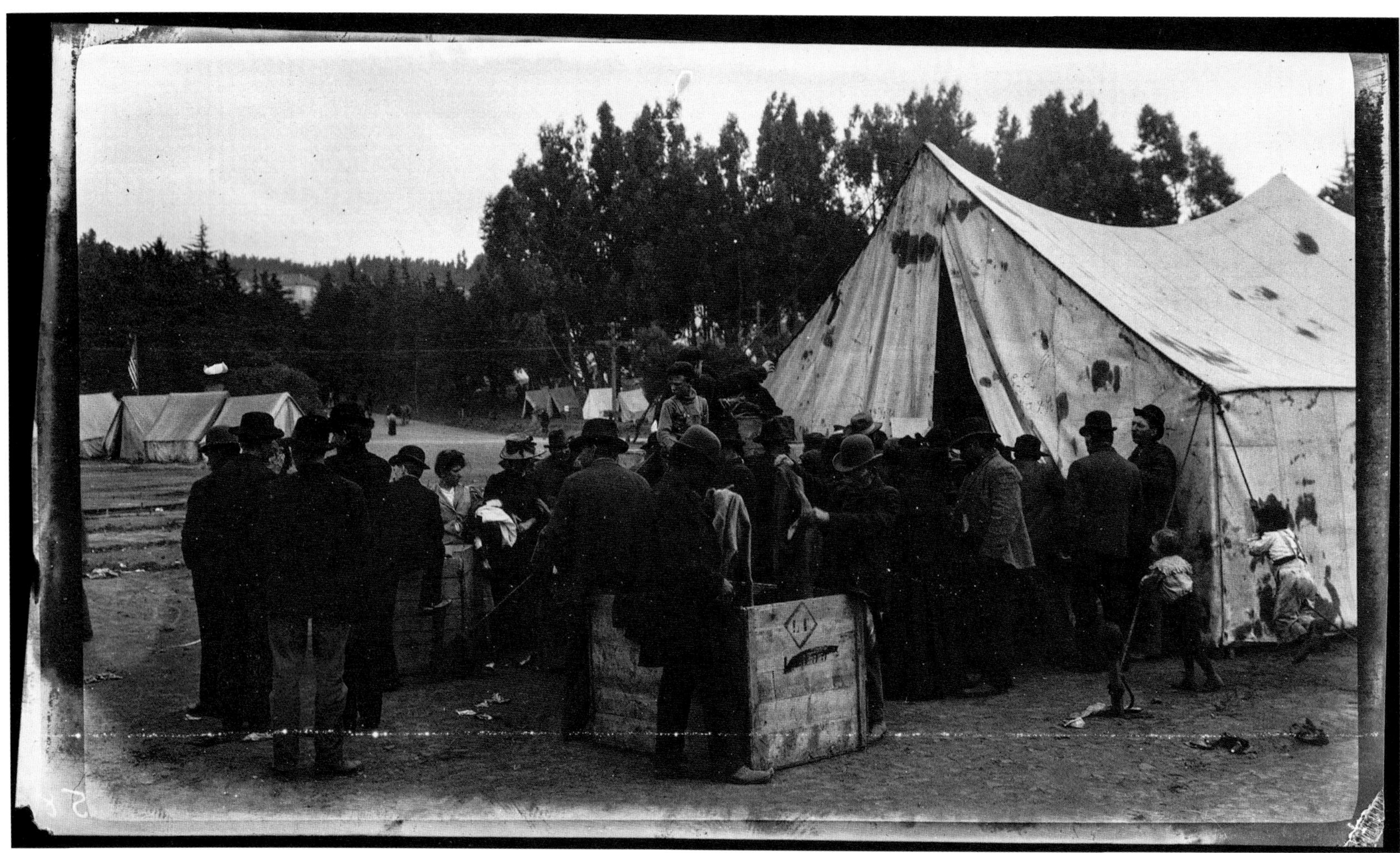

68.

Post–earthquake and fire clothing rations tent, San Francisco
2018.21.58 (cat. 120)

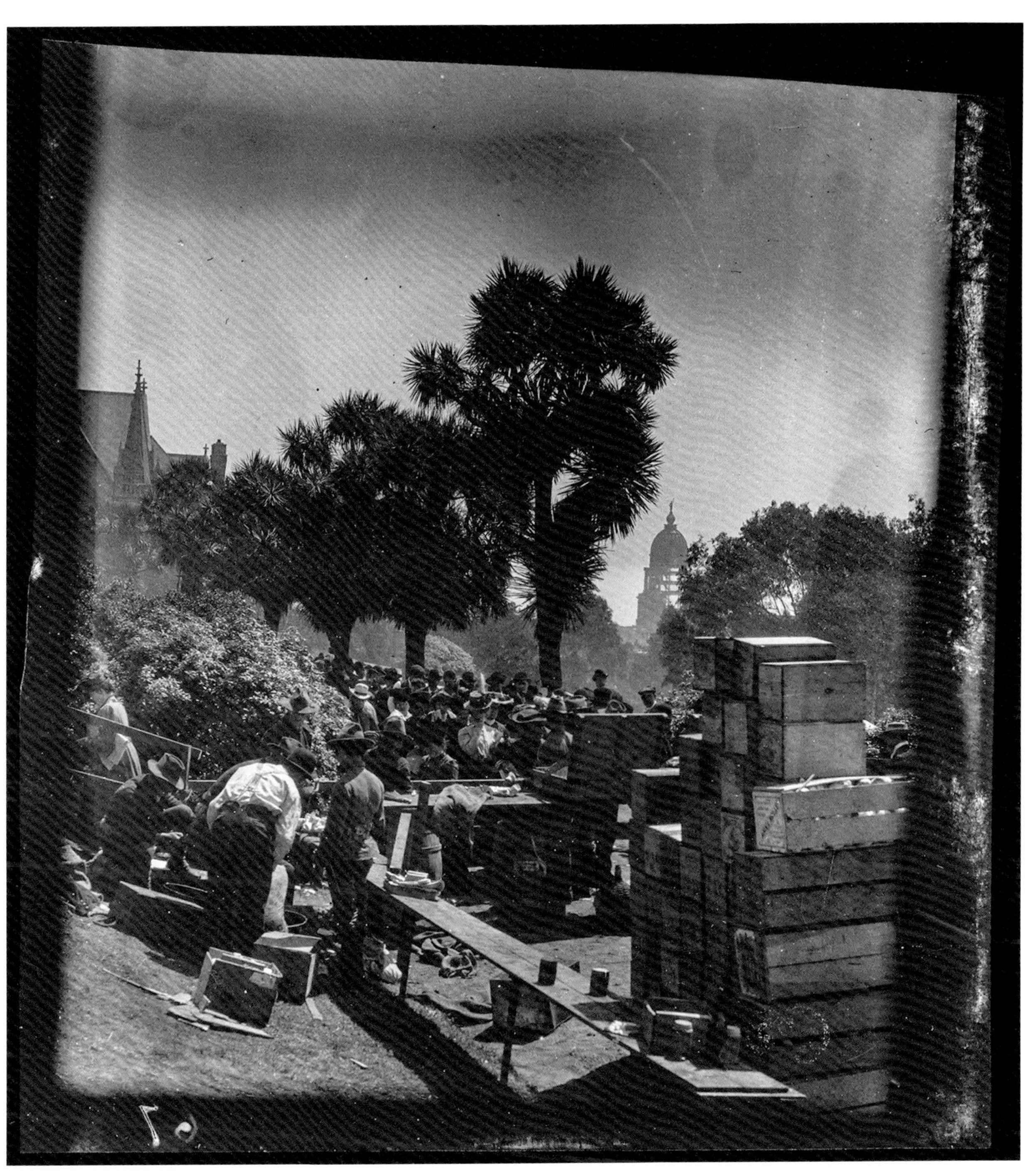

69.

Jefferson Square, Eddy near Laguna, San Francisco
2018.21.66 (cat. 124)

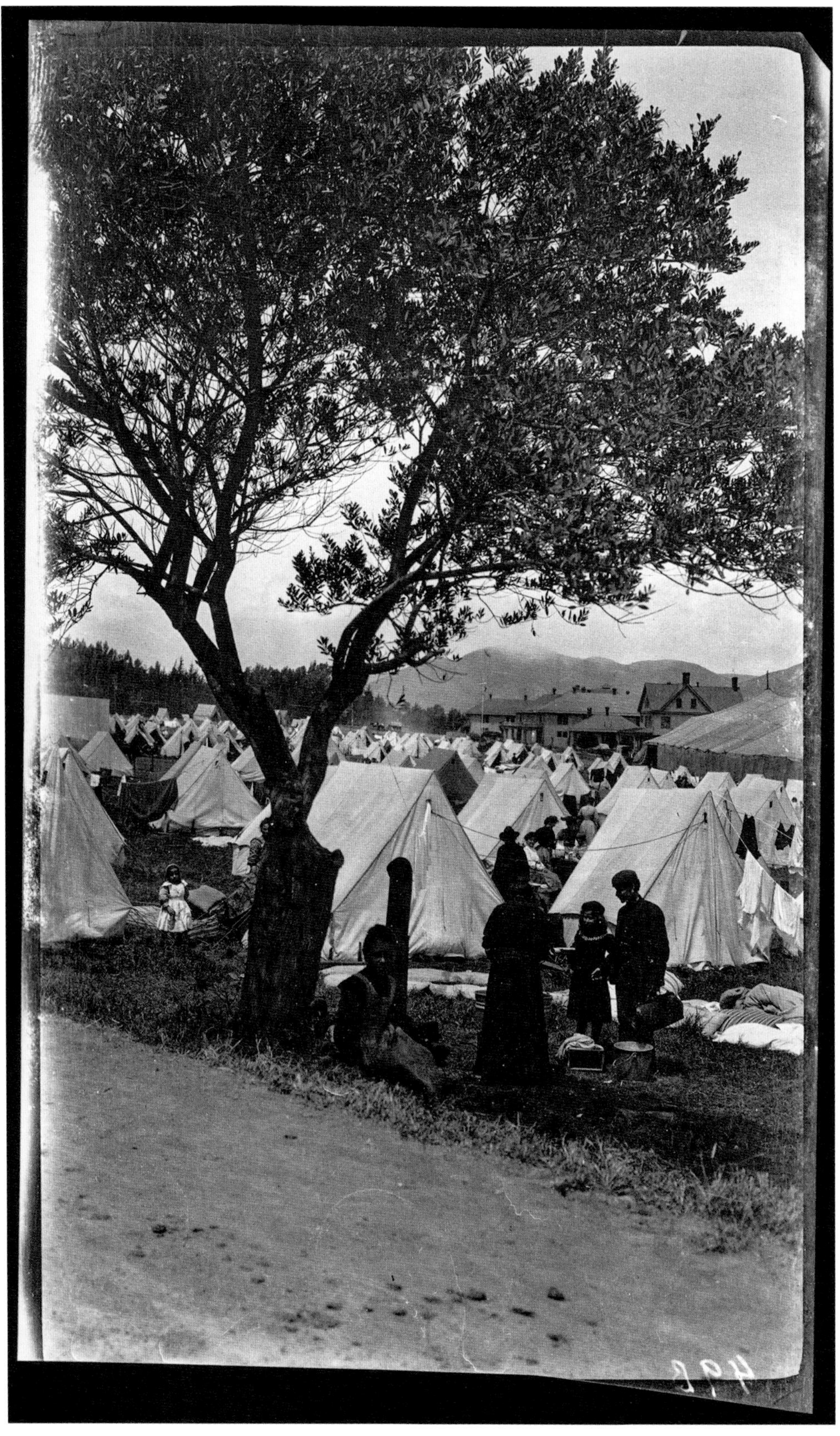

70.
The Presidio near the hospital, San Francisco
2018.21.51 (cat. 126)

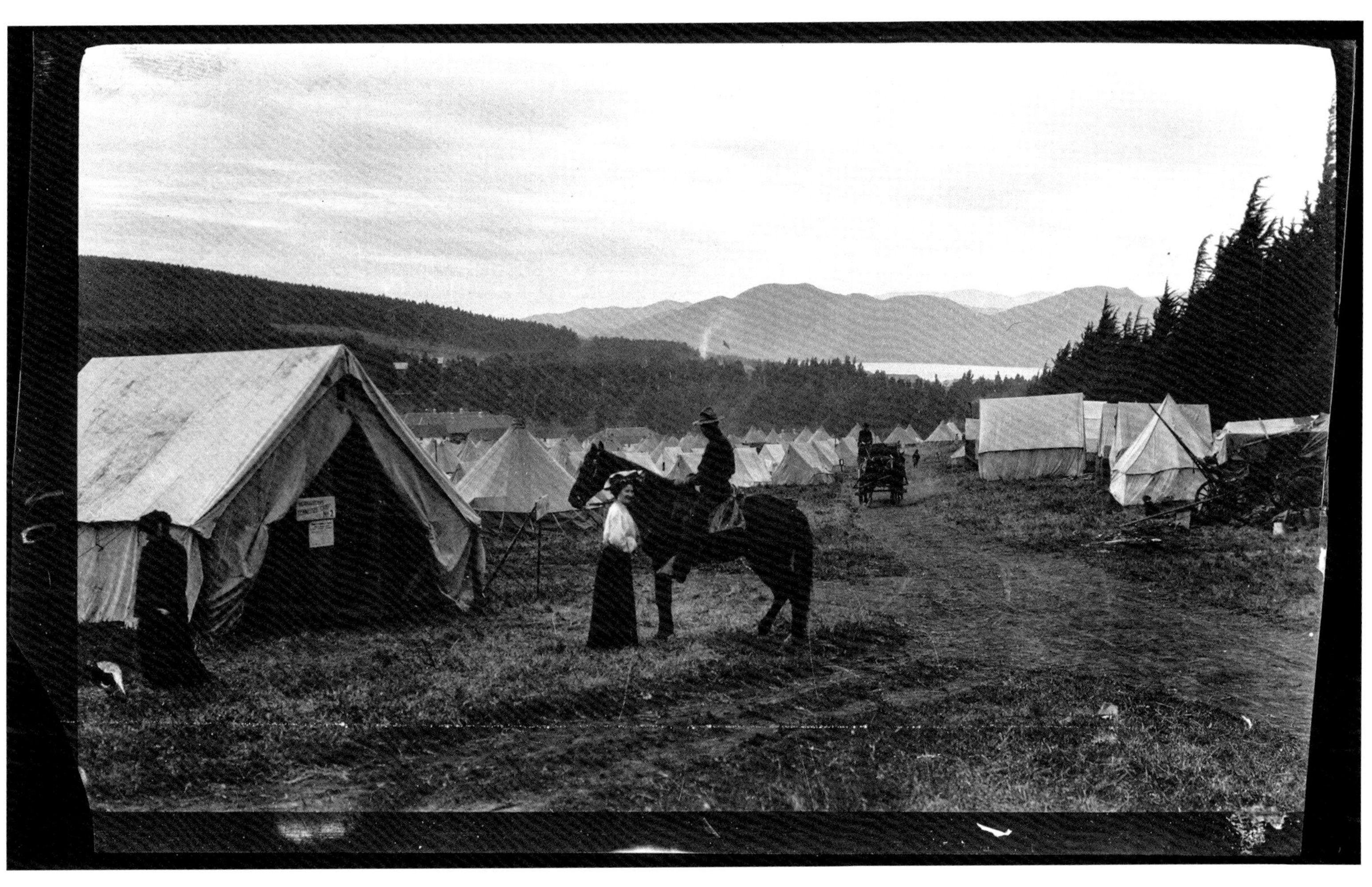

71.

Tennessee Hollow in the Presidio, San Francisco
2018.21.81 (cat. 129)

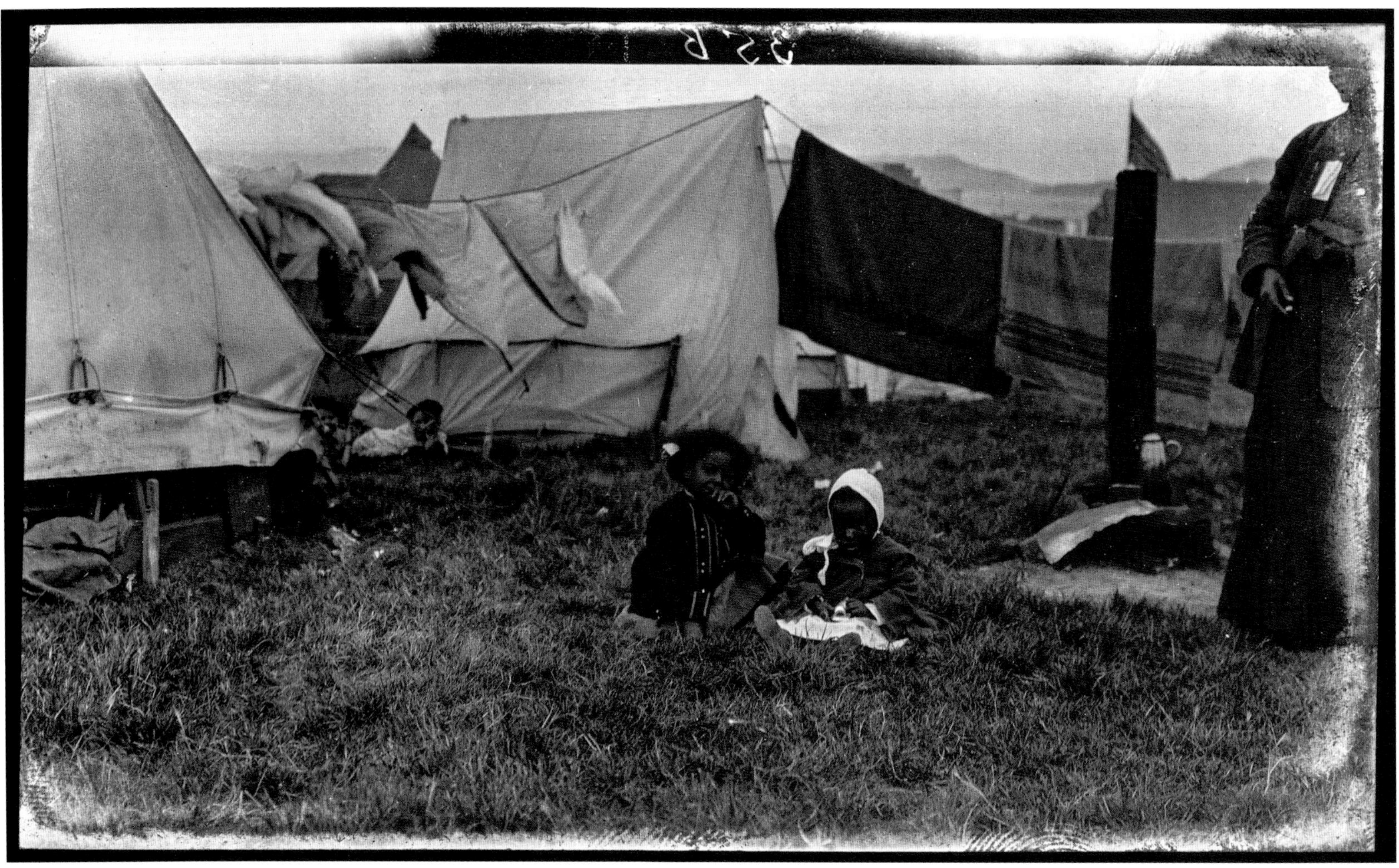

72.
Two children sit on grass in front of tents in the Presidio in the days following the earthquake and fire, San Francisco
2018.21.39 (cat. 130)

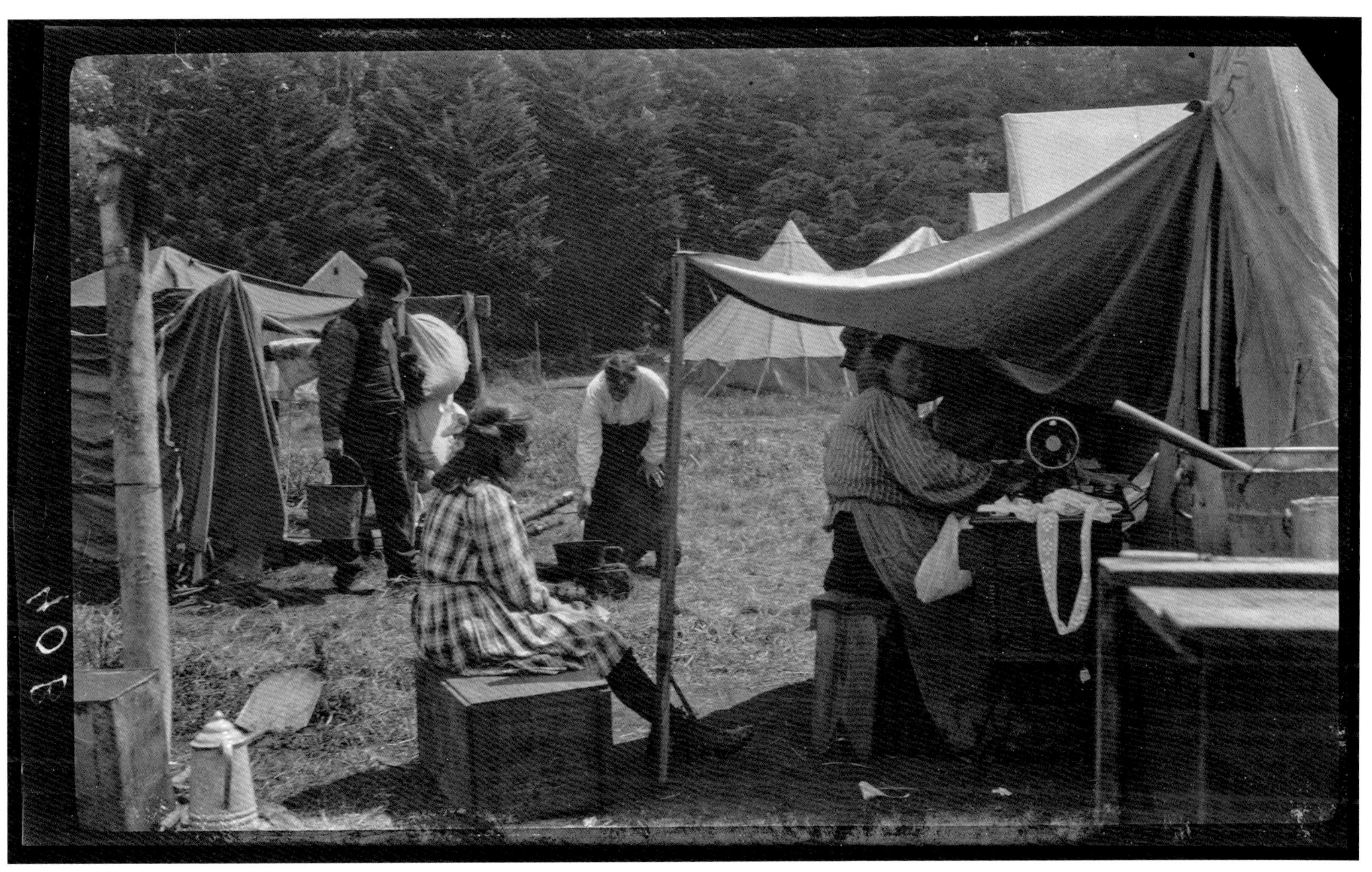

73.
Domestic scene in days following earthquake and fire. A family's activities in a relief camp, San Francisco
2018.21.44 (cat. 133)

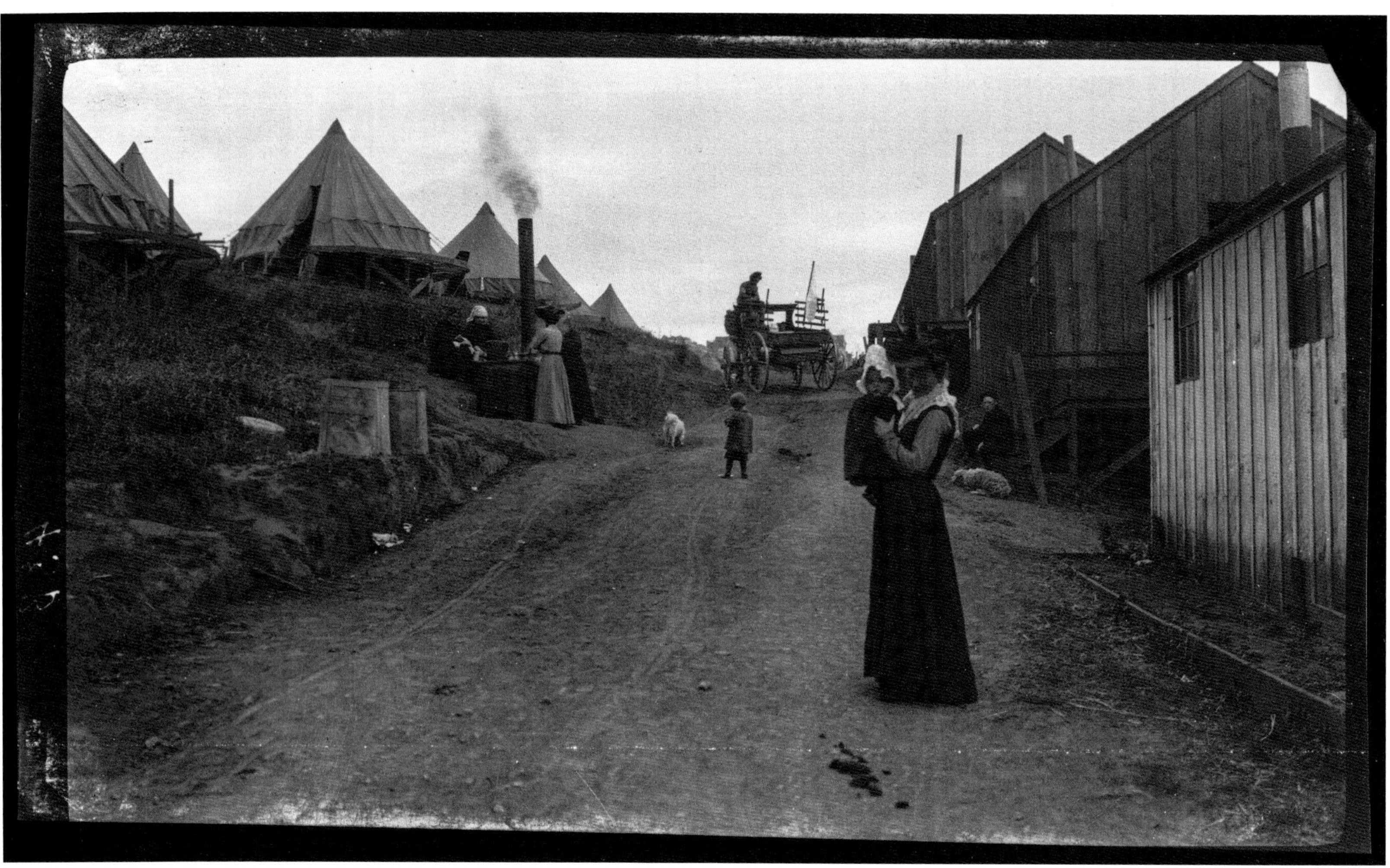

74.
Tennessee Hollow in the Presidio, San Francisco
2018.21.47 (cat. 139)

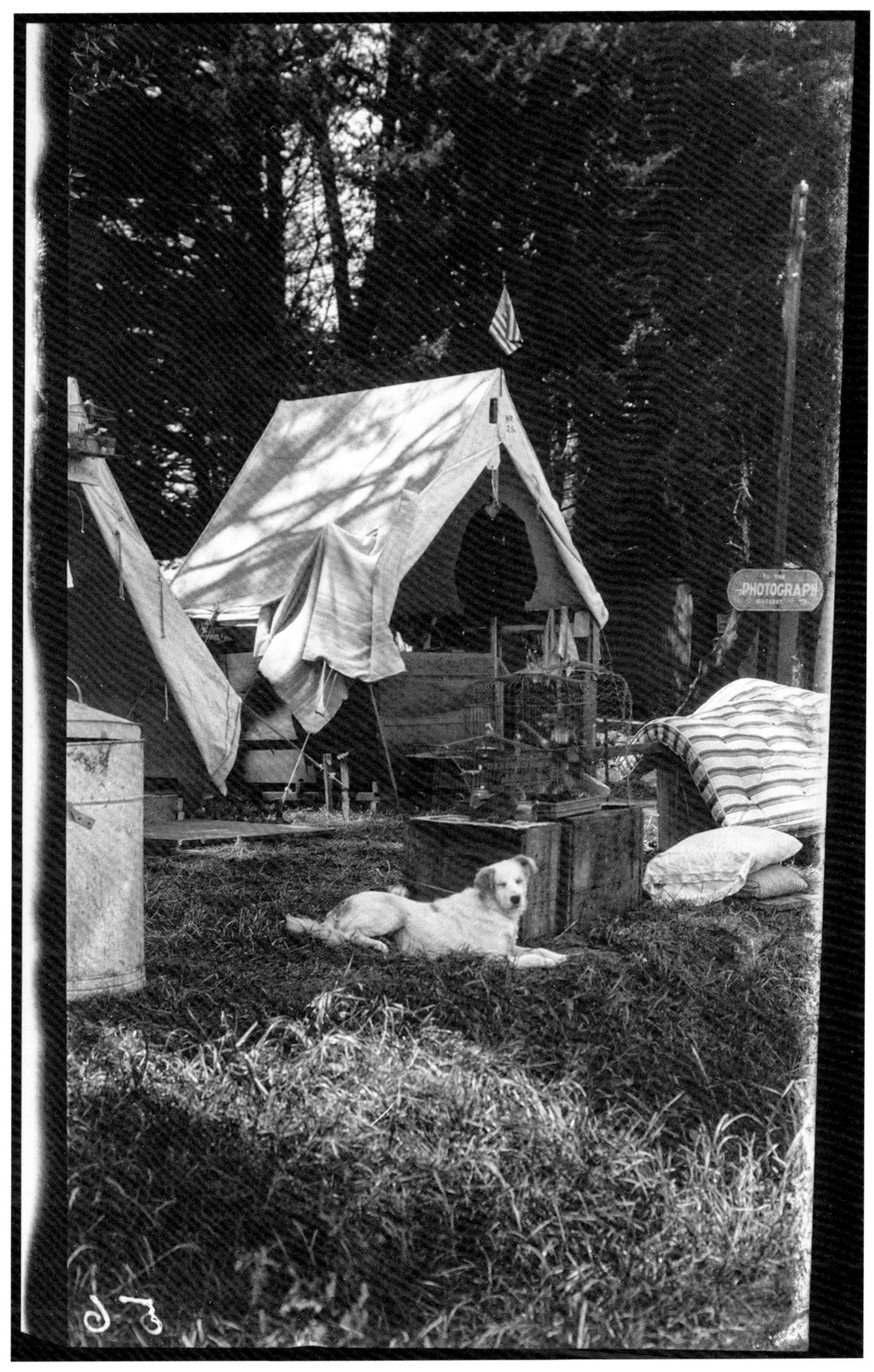

75.
Life in a relief camp. A large reclining dog in the foreground, San Francisco
2018.21.55 (cat. 140)

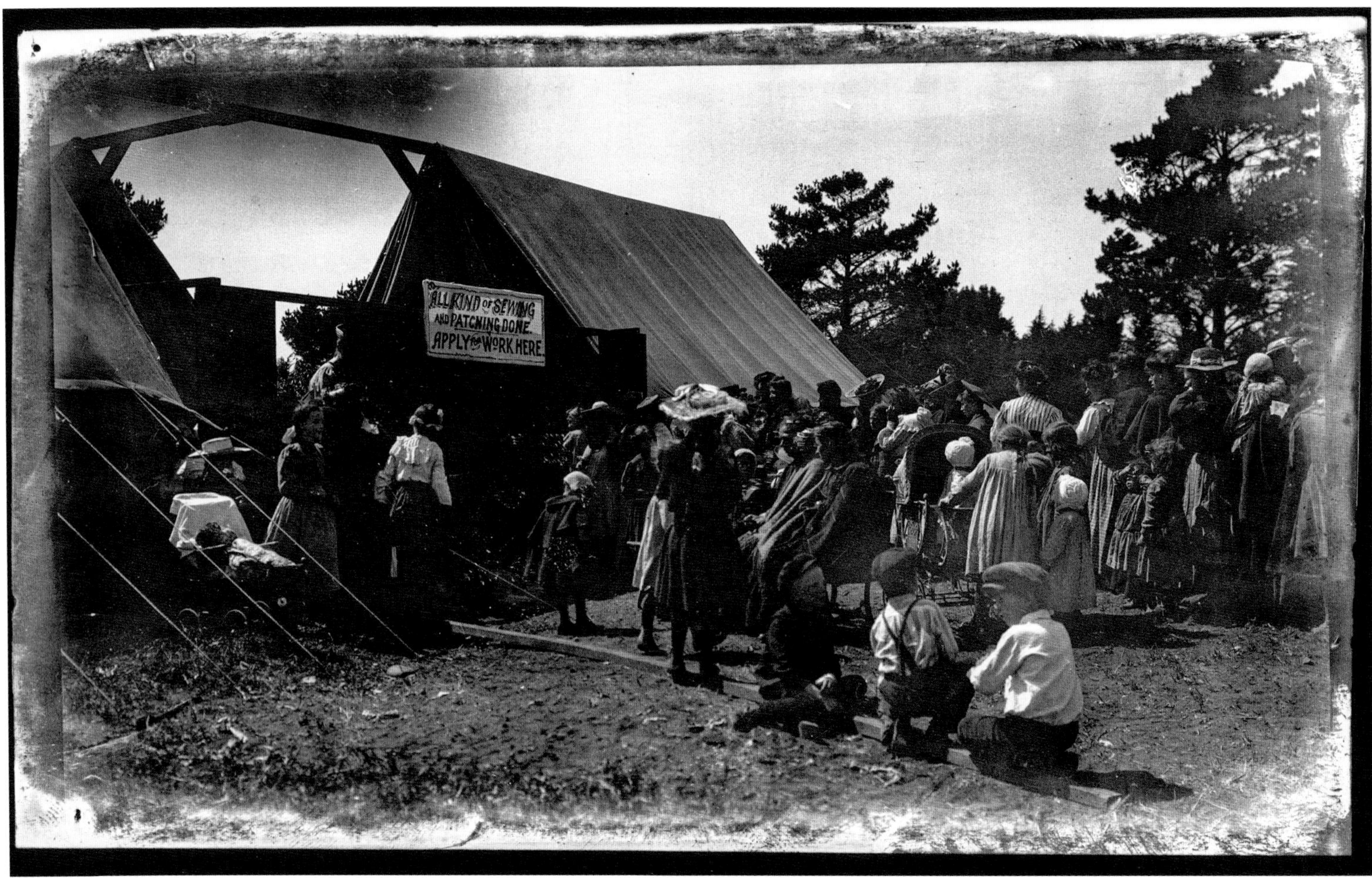

76.
Women and children standing in line outside sewing tent, San Francisco
2018.21.80 (cat. 141)

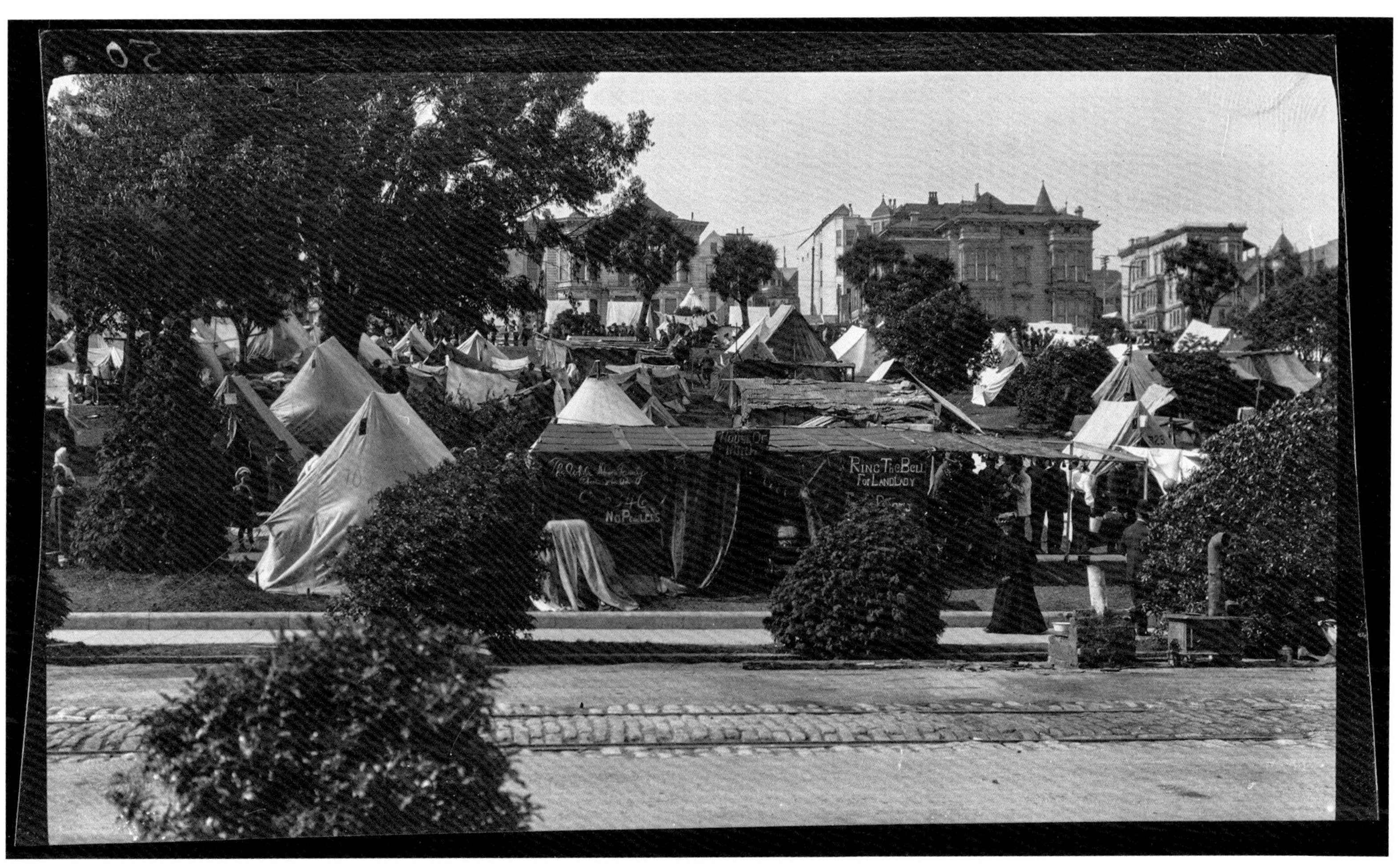

77.
Jefferson Square, San Francisco
2018.21.53 (cat. 142)

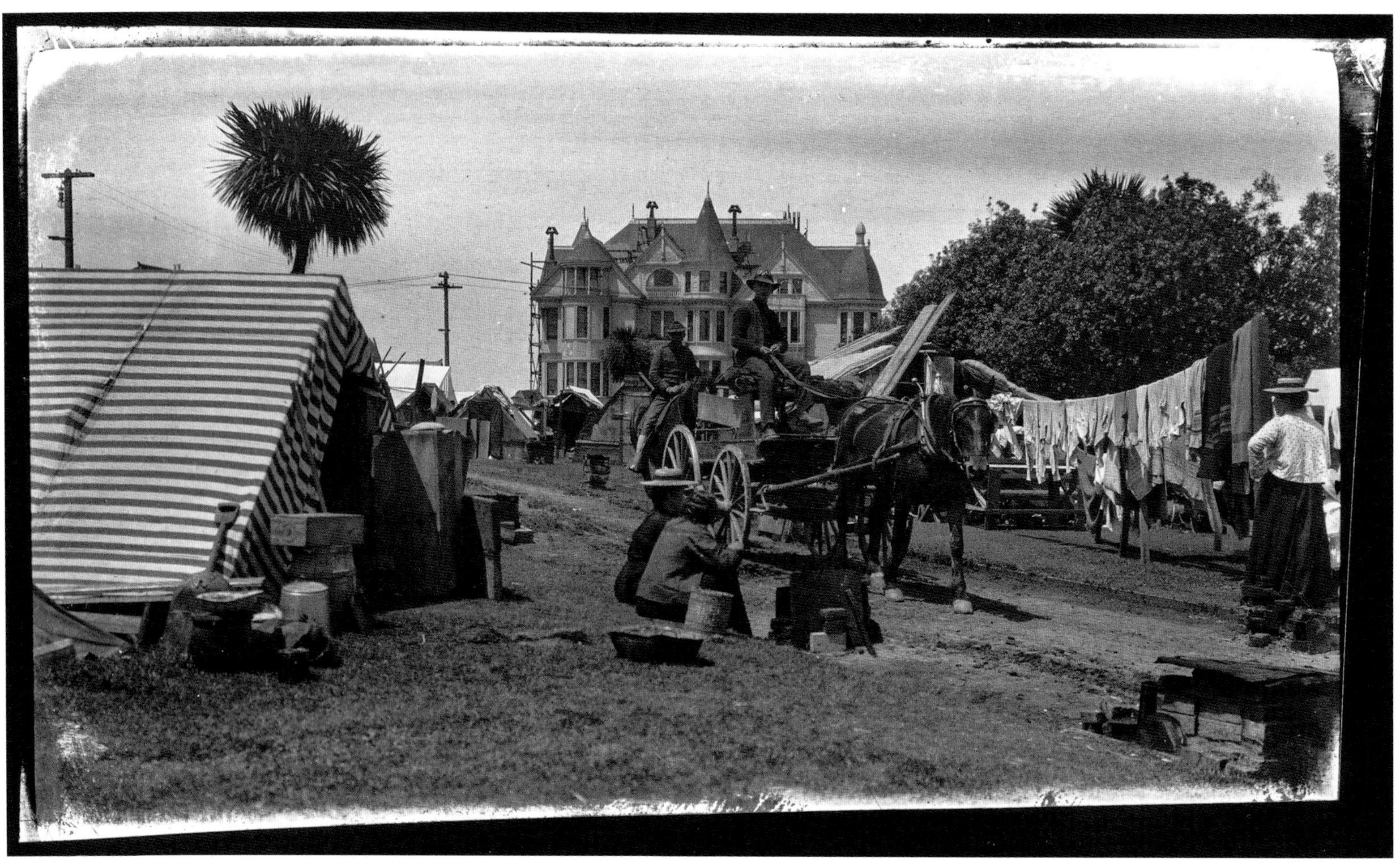

78.
Lafayette Park, San Francisco
2018.21.46 (cat. 147)

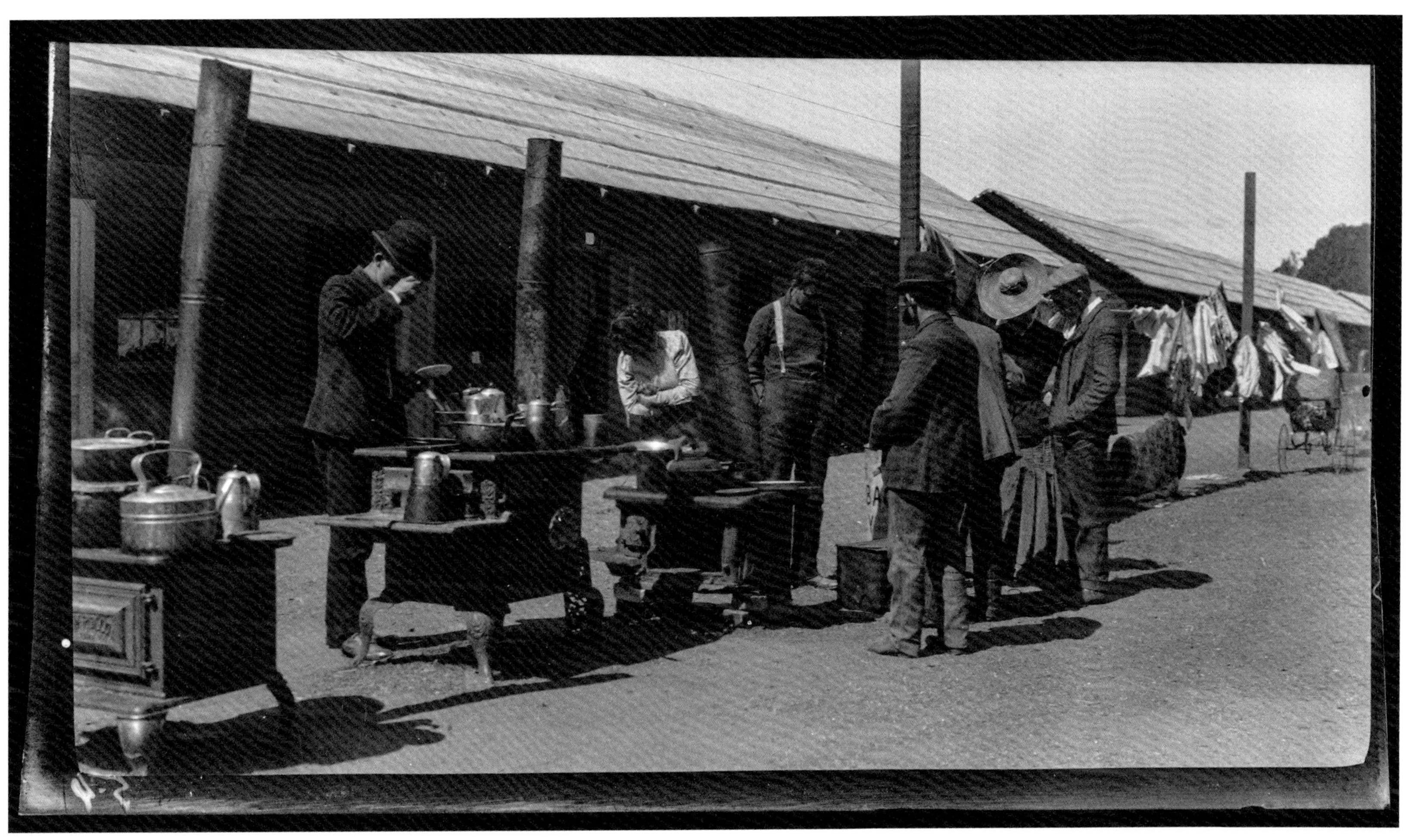

79.
Speedway Meadow, Golden Gate Park, San Francisco
2018.21.54 (cat. 148)

REBUILDING

THE CITY

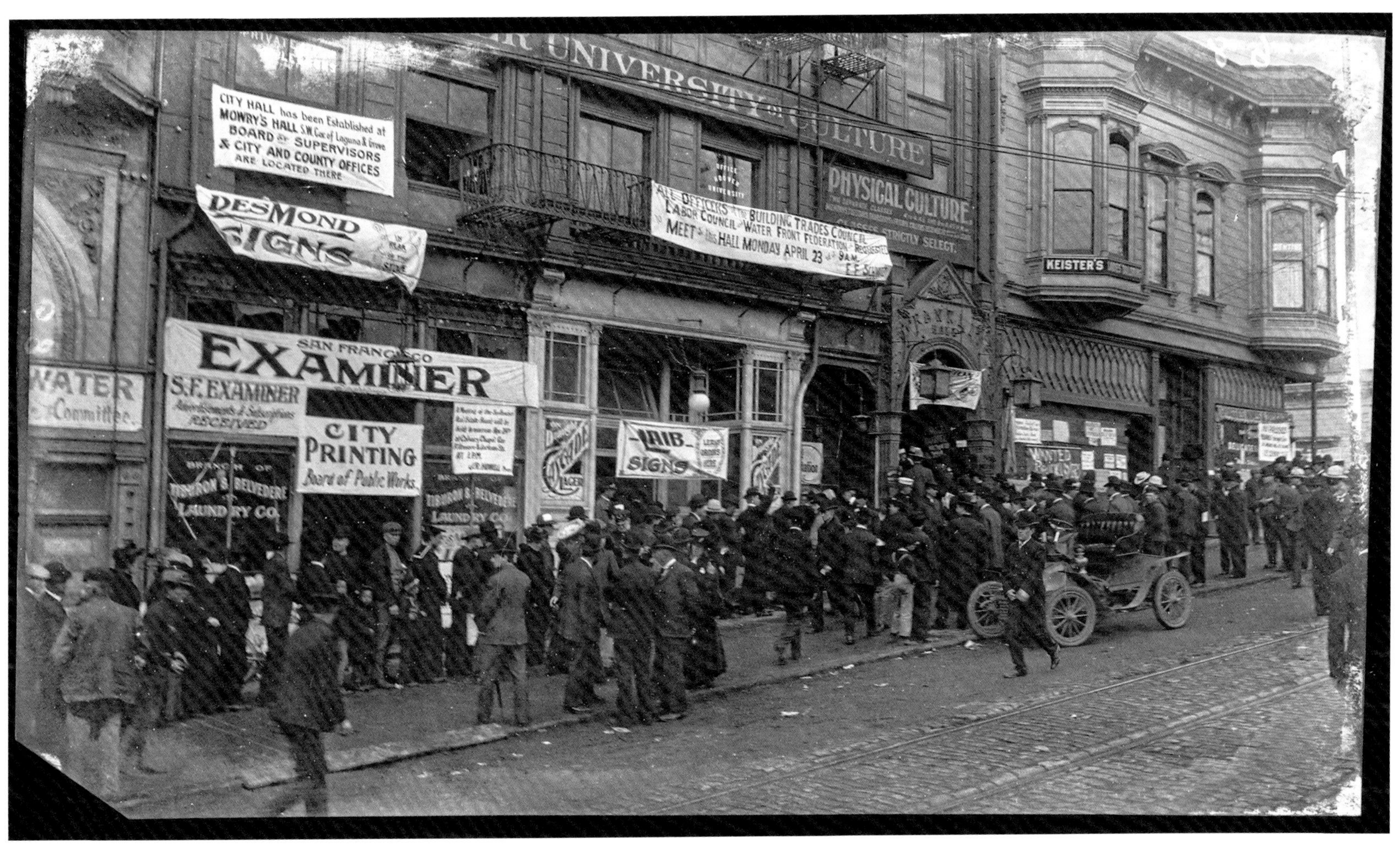

80.

Franklin Hall, Fillmore and Bush, San Francisco
2018.21.67 (cat. 149)

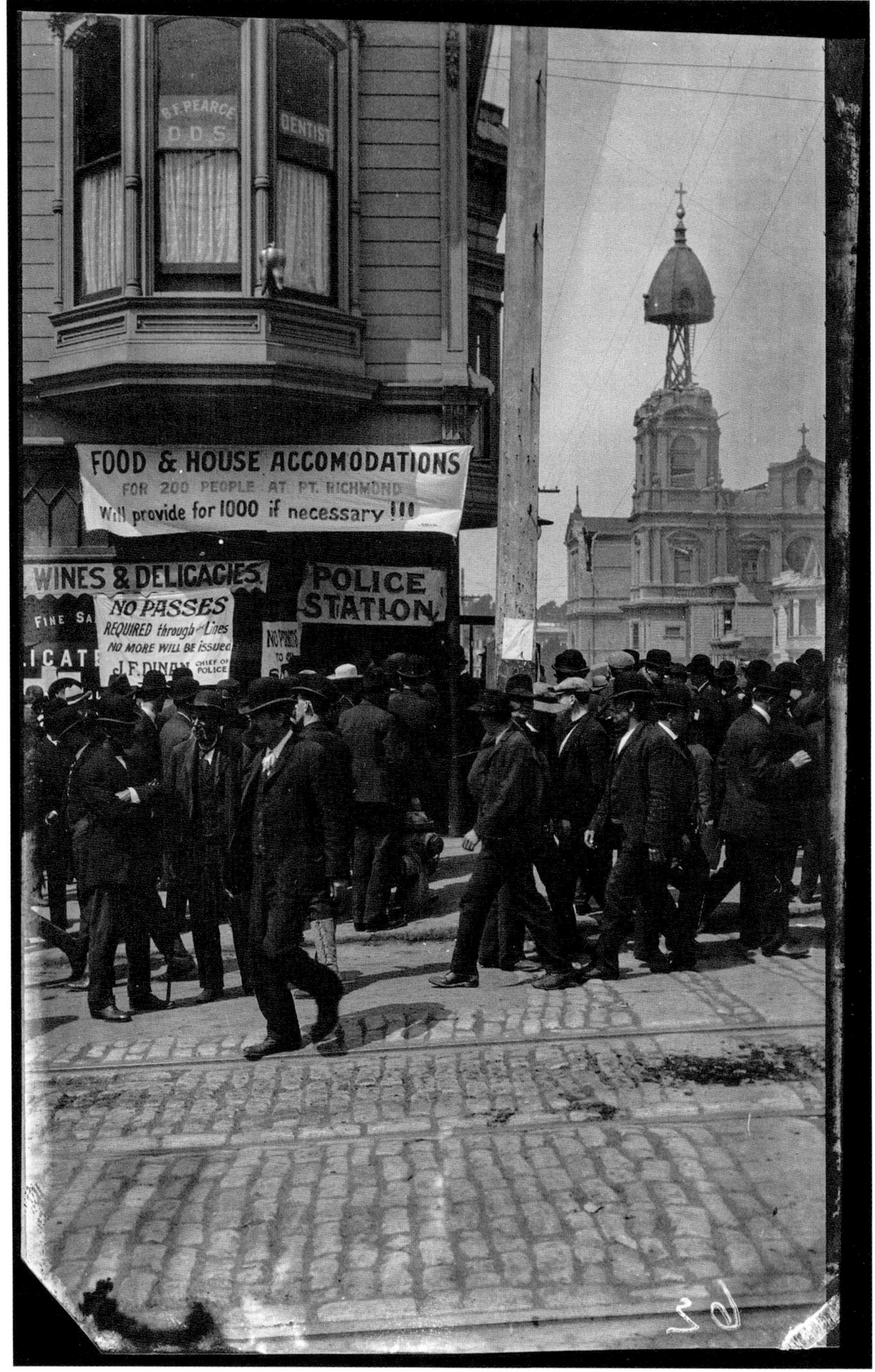

81.

Bush and Fillmore, San Francisco
2018.21.61 (cat. 150)

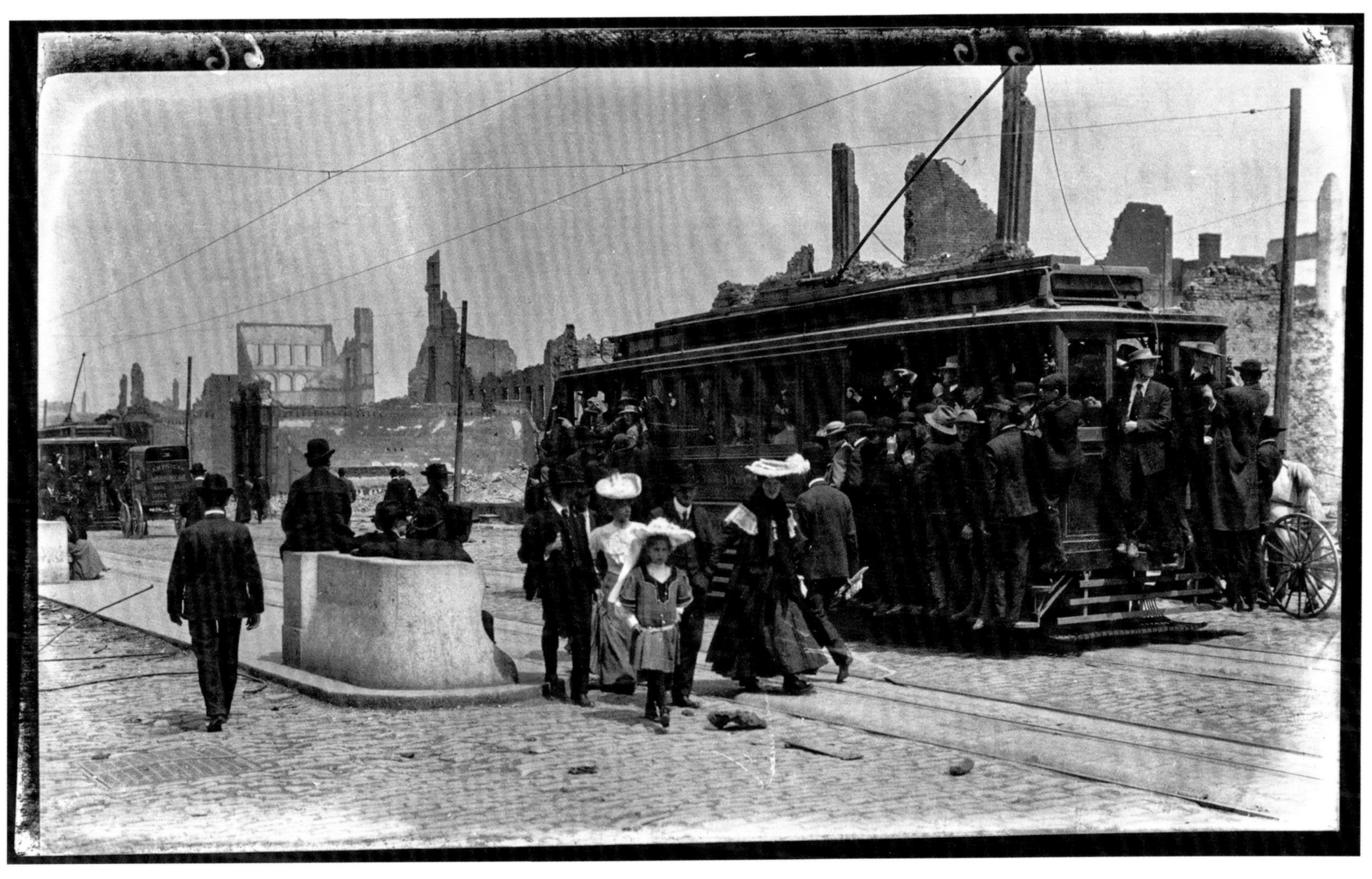

82.

Lower Market, San Francisco
2018.21.65 (cat. 152)

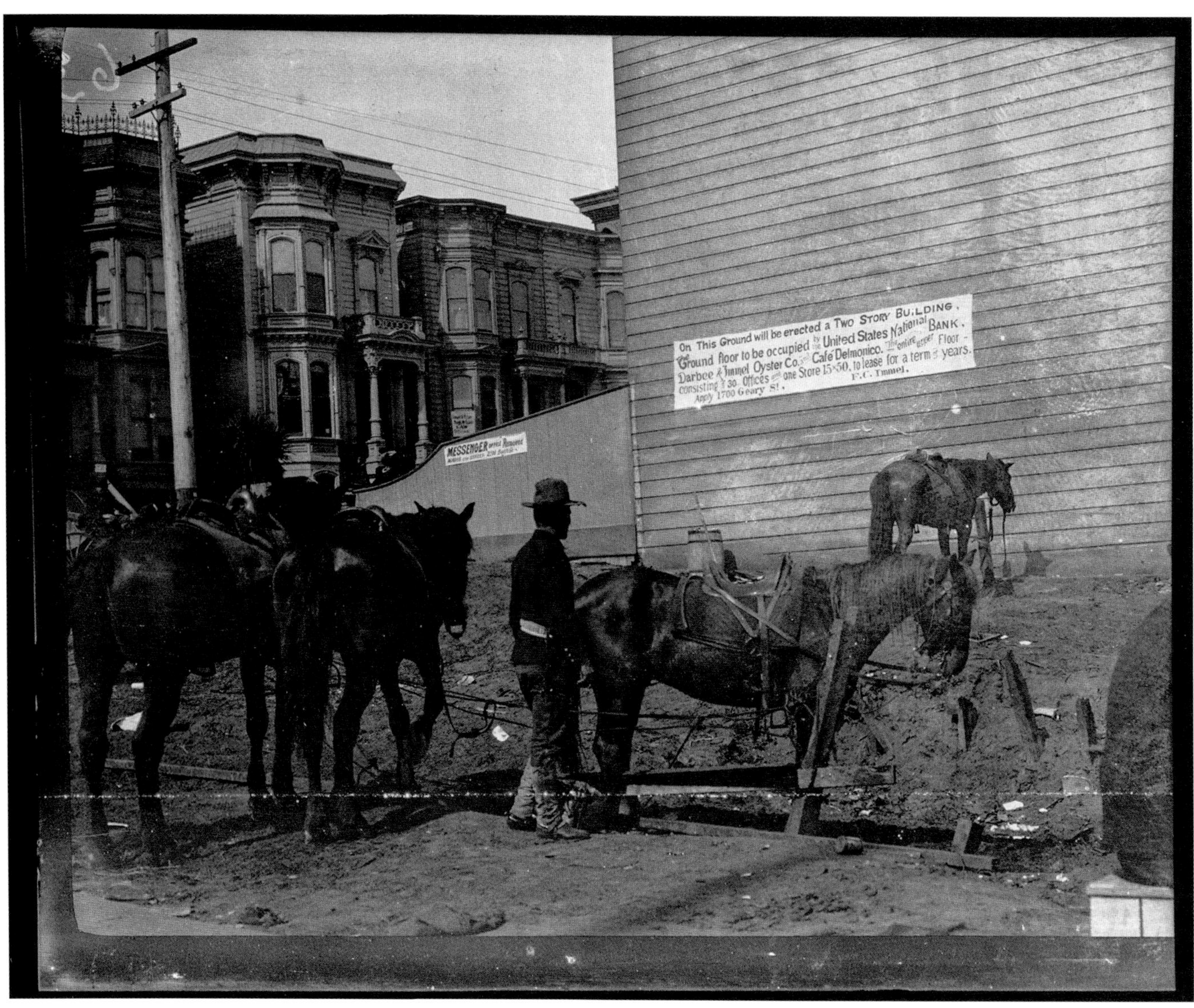

83.

Fillmore and Bush, San Francisco
2018.21.62 (cat. 154)

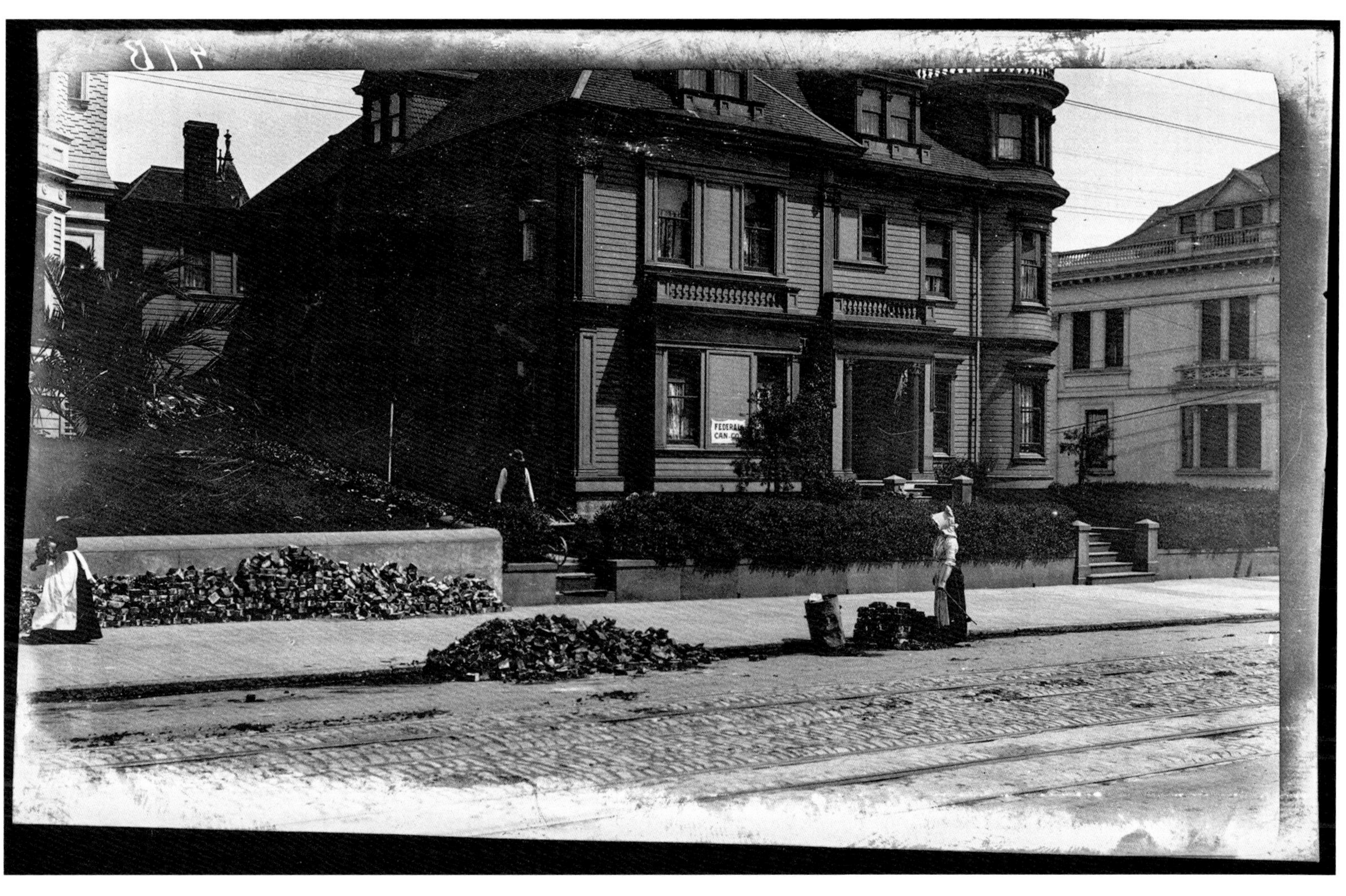

84.

Pacific and Buchanan, San Francisco
2018.21.49 (cat. 155)

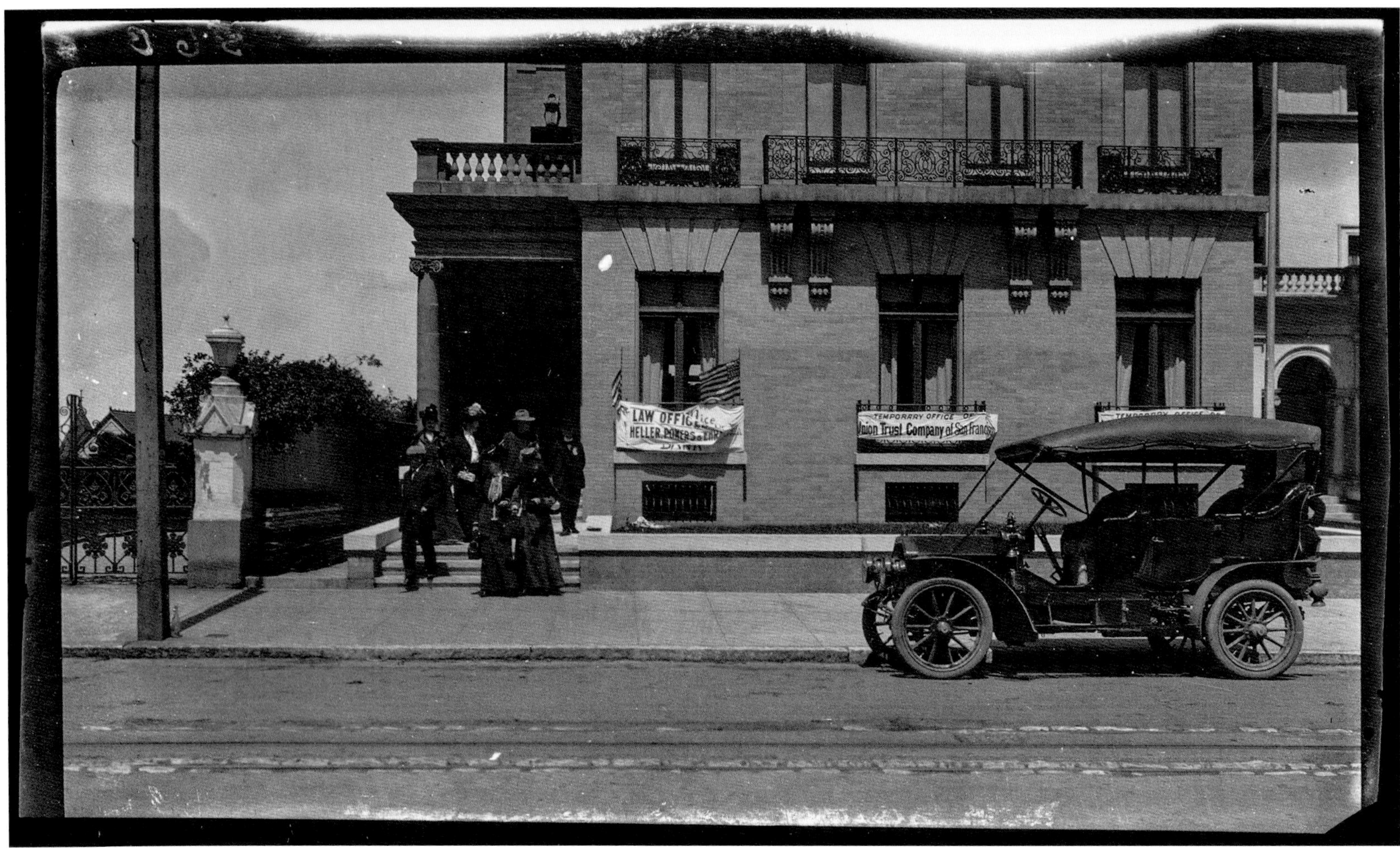

85.
E.S. Heller home, Jackson between Laguna and Octavia, San Francisco
2018.21.56 (cat. 156)

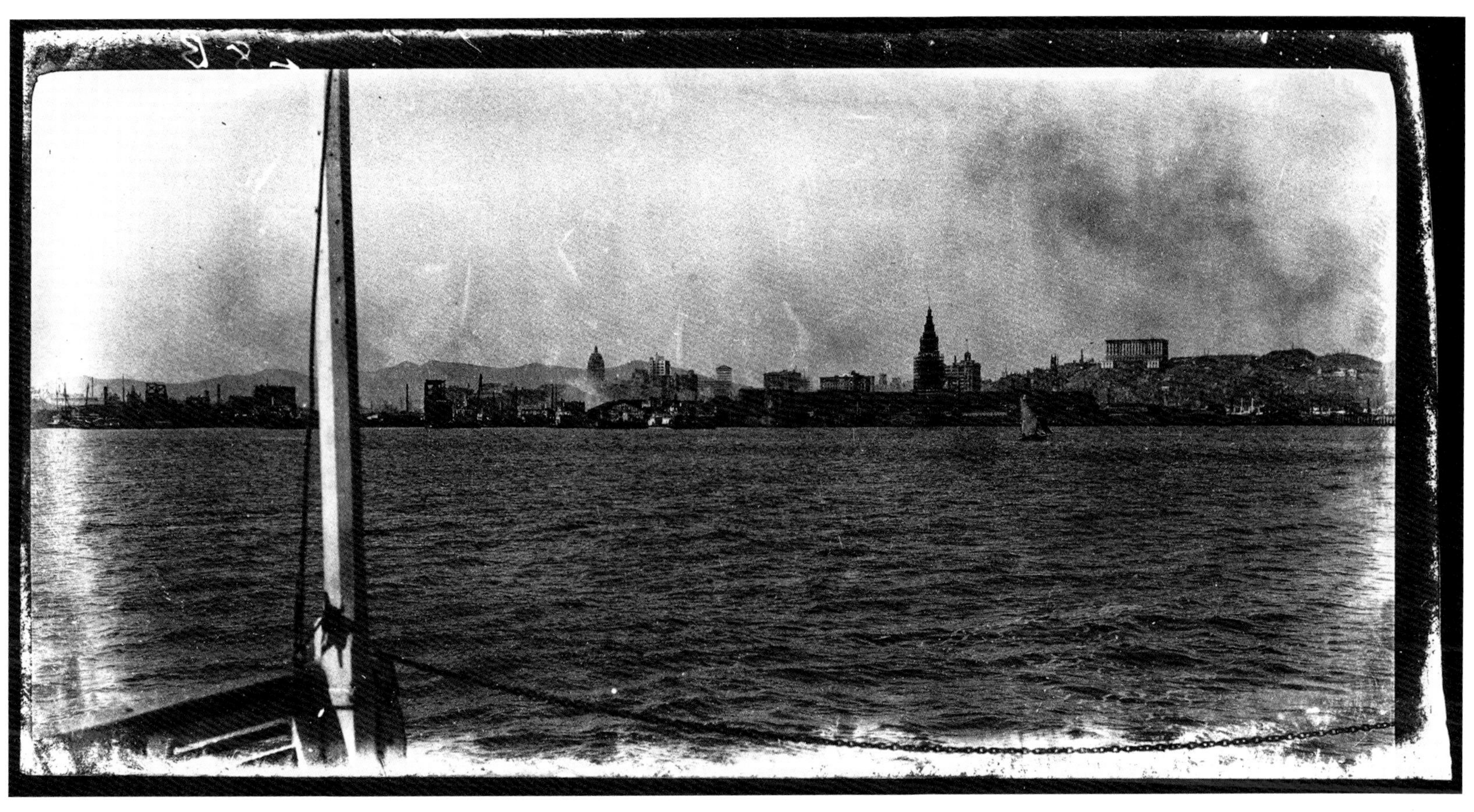

86.

View of San Francisco from the San Francisco Bay
2018.21.33 (cat. 157)

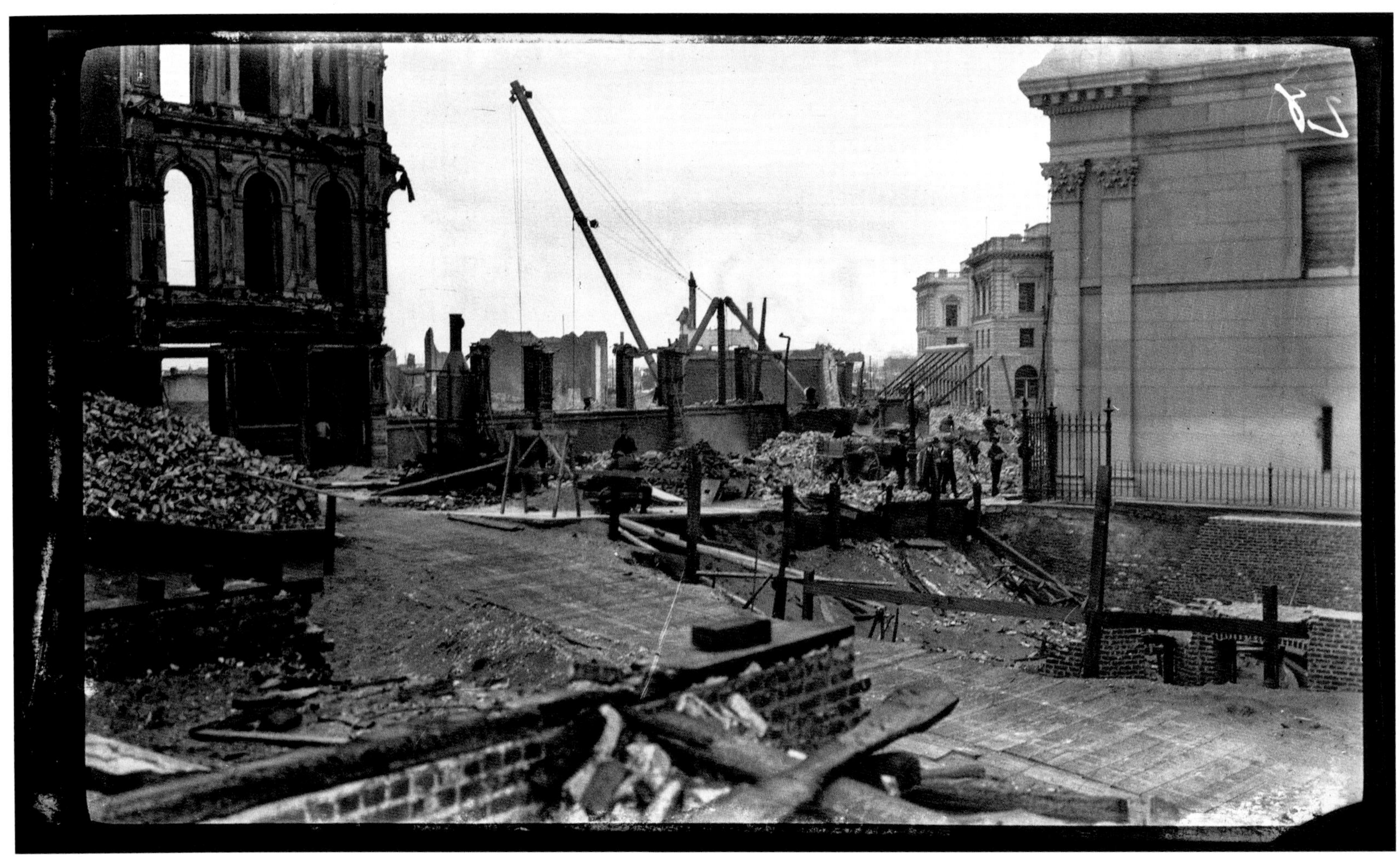

87.

Jones near Golden Gate, San Francisco
2018.21.32 (cat. 158)

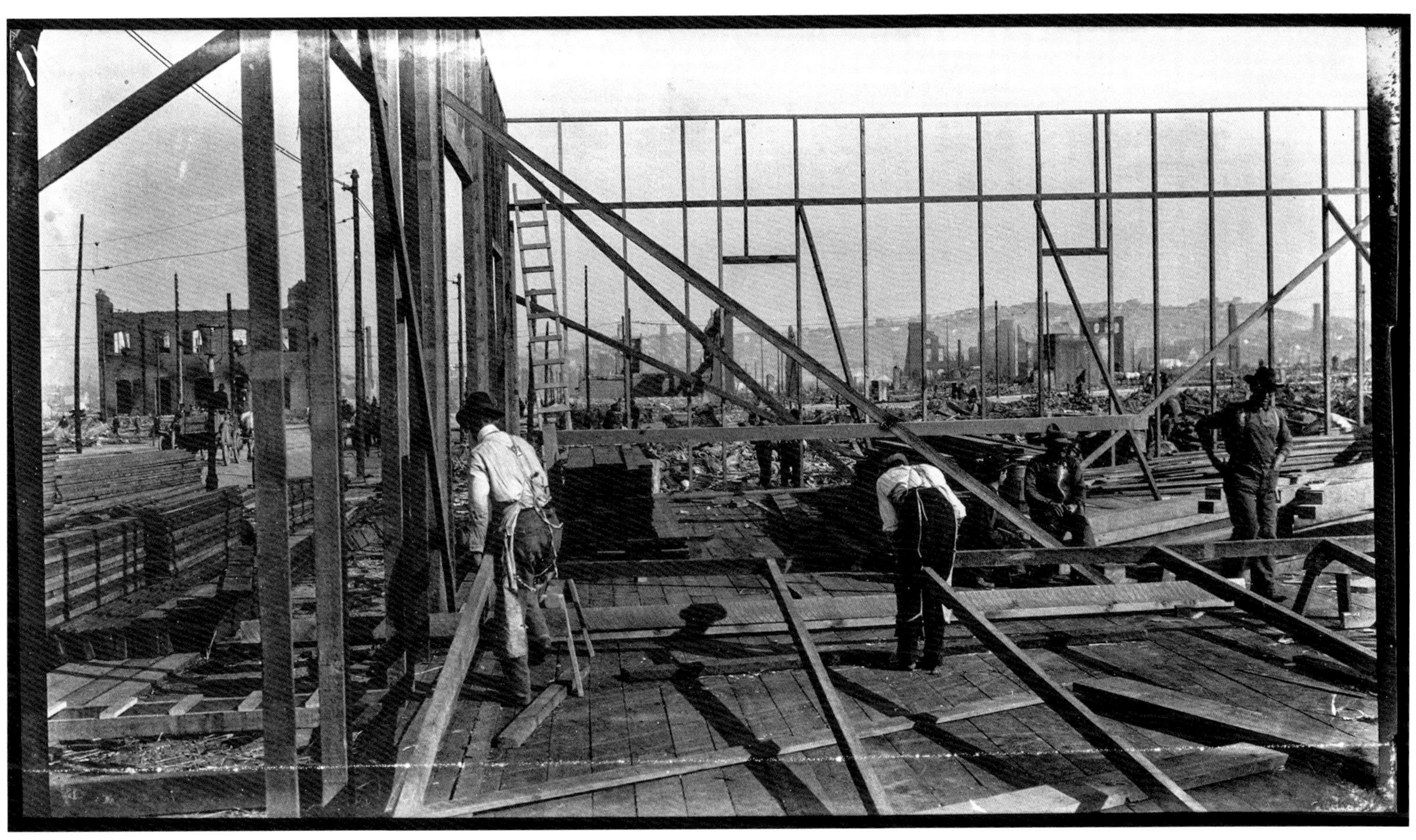

88.

Men work to rebuild the city surrounded by the ruins left by the earthquake and fire, San Francisco
2018.21.45 (cat. 159)

APPENDICES

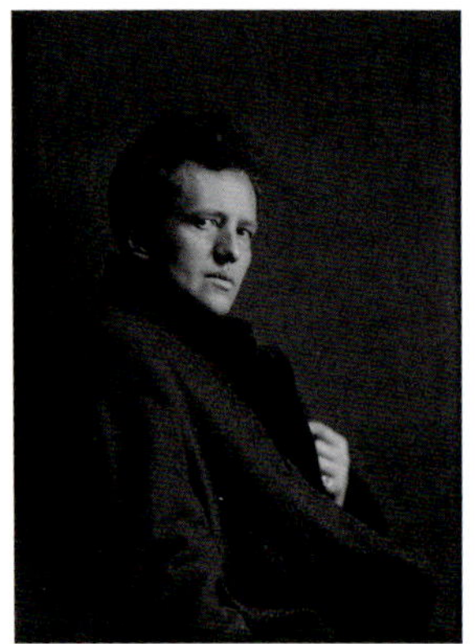

A BIOGRAPHICAL TIMELINE OF ARNOLD GENTHE

COMPILED BY

Lawrence Banka, Timothy Brown, James A. Ganz, and Natalie Pellolio

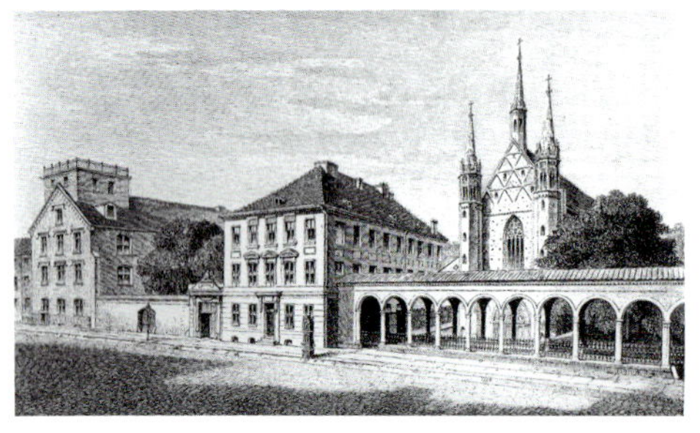

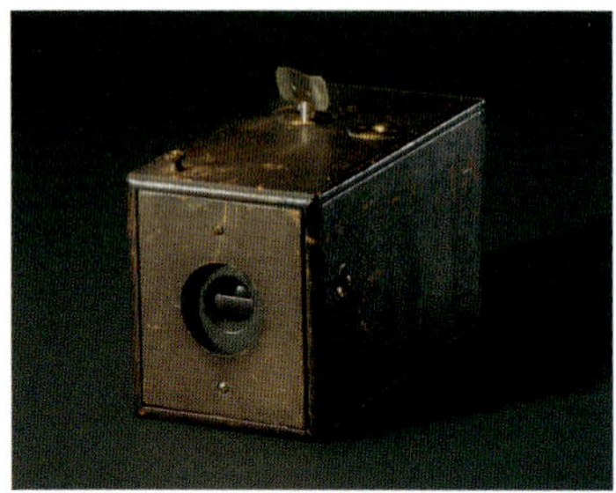

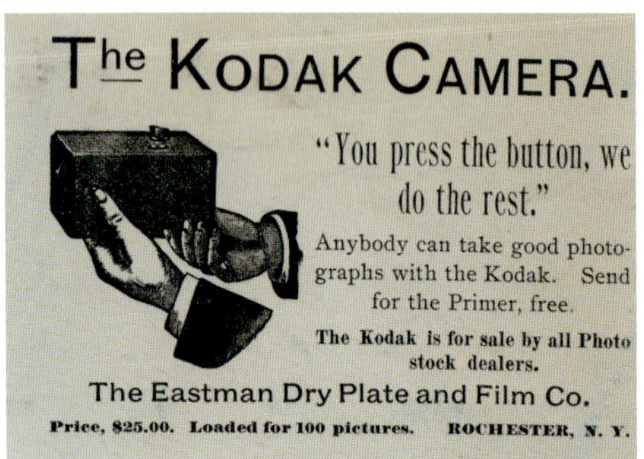

The Kodak Camera.

"You press the button, we do the rest."

Anybody can take good photographs with the Kodak. Send for the Primer, free.

The Kodak is for sale by all Photo stock dealers.

The Eastman Dry Plate and Film Co.

Price, $25.00. Loaded for 100 pictures. ROCHESTER, N. Y.

Arnold Genthe, Untitled (Self-portrait), 1900. Interpositive from glass plate negative, 7 × 5 in. (178 × 127 mm) (approx.). Arnold Genthe Collection, Prints and Photographs Division, Library of Congress, Washington, D.C.

Graues Kloster, Berlin

Kodak No. 1 box camera

Advertisement for the Kodak No. 1 box camera, 1888

1869
Arnold Genthe is born on January 8 in Berlin, Prussia (now Germany), to Hermann Genthe and Louise Zober Genthe. His father is a Latin and Greek teacher at the Graues Kloster, one of the oldest preparatory schools in Berlin.

1884
George Eastman, owner and co-founder of the Eastman Dry Plate and Film Company (later known as Kodak), files his patent for the first roll of film suited for mass production. This early prototype consists of a roll of paper coated in a light-sensitive gelatin emulsion and wound around a wooden spool. Eastman's roll film makes photography available to amateur photographers for the first time.

1886
Genthe's father dies in Hamburg, Prussia.

1888
Kodak introduces the No. 1 box camera, the first easy-to-use roll film camera commercially available to the public. The camera costs $25, or nearly $650 in today's dollars, and comes preloaded with a one-hundred-exposure roll of film mounted on a paper base. The company markets it using its soon-to-be famous slogan: "You press the button, we do the rest."

1889
Kodak introduces cellulose nitrate roll film, which soon replaces paper as the most popular commercial film base.

1890
The California Camera Club is founded in San Francisco, providing its members with access to darkroom facilities, a portrait studio, and exhibition galleries.

1893
The Brotherhood of the Linked Ring, a British photography club dedicated to defending the then-radical idea that photography could be art, holds its first annual photography show, which it models after the French concept of the salon—an annual juried exhibition of painting and sculpture. Its goal, in the words of the organizers, is to "exhibit only that description of pictorial photography in which there is distinct evidence of personal feeling and execution." The Linked Ring Photographic Salon inspires photography clubs worldwide to organize similar exhibitions with the goal of establishing photography's status as a fine art form.

1894
Genthe receives his doctorate with a thesis on philology from the University of Jena (Germany). He studies art history and French literature at the Sorbonne (France) before returning to Germany in 1895.

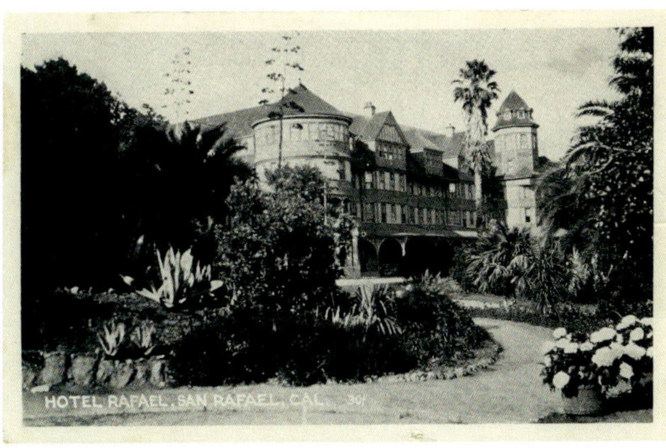

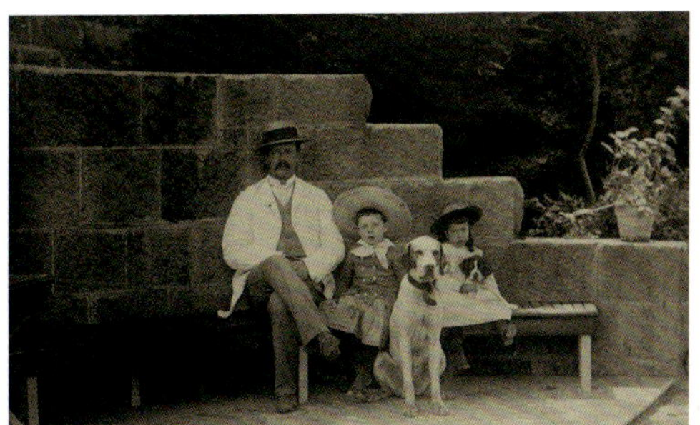

1895
Genthe first meets Baron Johann Heinrich von Schroeder, who hires him for a one-year contract as his son's tutor in San Francisco.

On June 14 Genthe arrives in New York Harbor on the steamship SS *Normannia* accompanied by the von Schroeder family, including Baron Johann Heinrich von Schroeder; his wife, the Baroness Mary Ellen Donahue von Schroeder, a wealthy San Francisco heiress; and their children, Johann Heinrich "Heini" von Schroeder, Marion Janet Isabella von Schroeder, and Editha Helene von Schroeder.

On June 26 Genthe arrives in San Francisco with the von Schroeder family. The *San Francisco Chronicle* reports: "Baron and Baroness von Schroder [*sic*] will arrive this morning from Europe and the East after an absence of two years. They are accompanied by their children. Upon their arrival they will go direct to the Hotel Rafael, where they will spend the entire summer. Quite a number of intimate friends will cross the bay to meet them."

Genthe begins visiting San Francisco's Chinatown and Telegraph Hill on his days off. He buys several books on photography and expresses a desire to photograph the city. As he writes in his autobiography, this is the point at which he begins to "look at things from a photographic view, although I had not yet bought a camera." He buys his first camera at a shop in San Rafael sometime between July and October.

On October 1 the Hotel Rafael closes for the winter. Genthe moves with the von Schroeder family to Eagle Ranch in Atascadero, California, just outside of San Luis Obispo.

On October 14 Genthe moves with the von Schroeder family to the Zimmerman residence at 1321 Sutter Street in San Francisco, where he has access to a small darkroom already installed in a closet on the top floor of the house.

1896
Genthe takes his first photographs of San Francisco's Chinatown, prompted in part by the fact that the only photographs of Chinatown that he can find to send to his family abroad are "crudely colored postal cards." As he will later describe in his autobiography: "For my first experiment I could scarcely have chosen a more difficult subject. The alleys and courtyards were so narrow that the light found its way through them for only an hour or two at midday. In order to get any pictures at all I had to hide in doorways or peer out from an angle of a building at some street corner." Despite these challenges, Genthe will eventually take more than two hundred photographs of Chinatown while living in San Francisco.

Genthe joins the California Camera Club and begins using the club's portrait studio and darkroom.

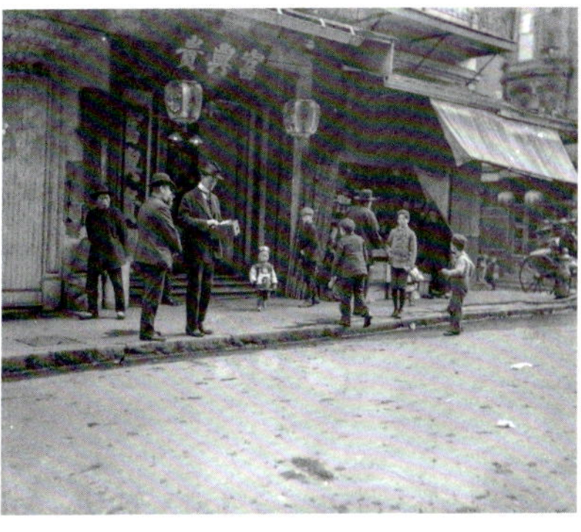

Postcard of the Hotel Rafael, San Rafael, California, ca. 1900

Baron von Schroeder and two of his children at Eagle Ranch, 1895

Arnold Genthe, *An Unsuspecting Victim, Chinatown, San Francisco* (Arnold Genthe with camera), ca. 1896. Interpositive from cellulose nitrate negative, 4 x 5 in. (102 × 127 mm) (approx.). Arnold Genthe Collection, Prints and Photographs Division, Library of Congress, Washington, D.C.

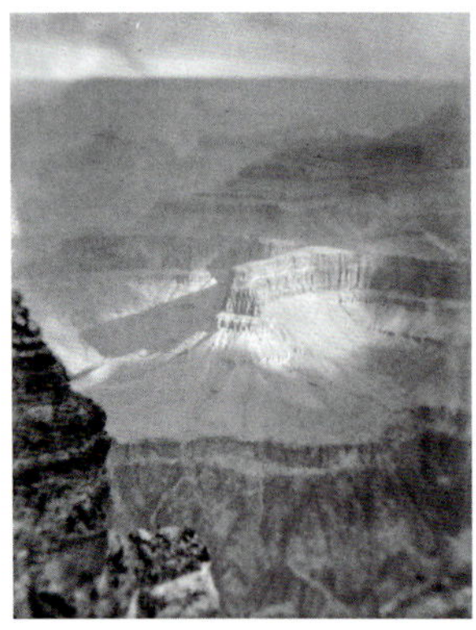

Genthe's mother, Louise, dies. Shortly thereafter his brother Hugo dies after being trampled by an elephant in British Central Africa (now the Republic of Malawi) while he was on an ivory hunt.

1897

On May 15 Genthe's photographs of Telegraph Hill appear in *The Wave*, the San Francisco weekly magazine edited by John O'Hara Cosgrave, accompanying an article written by Frank Norris.

Genthe's pupil Heinrich von Schroeder returns to Germany. Genthe decides to remain in San Francisco and pursue photography.

Genthe begins renting the photographer George H. Knight's studio space at 737 Sutter Street, sharing the space with the artist Oscar Maurer. He will continue to rent the studio until at least 1900.

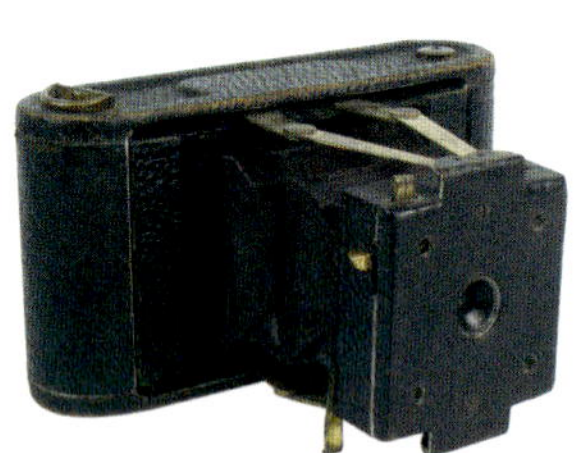

Genthe makes his first attempts at portrait photography. His early subjects are primarily men, who sit for his portraits in the California Camera Club portrait studio. As he will later recall: "Count Artsimovitch, the Imperial Russian Consul General, Baron Alexander von Schroeder, my pupil's uncle, and Fred Hall, the Turkish Consul, offered themselves as my first subjects." Ethel Crocker, the wife of the banker William Henry Crocker, brings in her three children to sit for a portrait and helps establish Genthe's reputation by recommending his services to friends and family. Genthe photographs the miniature painter Mira Edgerly, who brings the fifteen-year-old Alma de Bretteville to have her portrait taken.

On December 18 the San Francisco weekly *The Wave* publishes three photographic spreads by Genthe: "A Chinese Fishing Village," "Vistas in Little Mexico," and "Street Life in Chinatown."

1898

Kodak introduces the first Folding Pocket Kodak, replacing its earlier box models with a sleek design that can fit in one's pocket.

Arnold Genthe, Untitled (Grand Canyon, Arizona), 1899. Interpositive from cellulose nitrate negative, 5 × 4 in. (127 × 102 mm) (approx.). Arnold Genthe Collection, Prints and Photographs Division, Library of Congress, Washington, D.C.

Folding Pocket Kodak

In February Genthe exhibits his photographs of San Francisco's Chinatown at the California Camera Club's Second Annual Exhibition in San Francisco.

From March to April, Genthe exhibits his photographs at the Sketch Club at 723 Sutter Street as part of a charity exhibition sponsored by the Young Ladies' Social League of the First Presbyterian Church. The *San Francisco Chronicle* reports on April 1 that "Dr. A. Genthe of San Rafael" has won an honorable mention in portraiture and first prize for the best snapshot.

1899

During the summer Genthe spends six weeks traveling throughout Arizona and New Mexico with the anthropologist and photographer Frederick I. Monsen. Genthe produces forty-five glass negatives that include photographs of Acoma Pueblo, Canyon de Chelly, and the Grand Canyon.

Genthe's brother Siegfried, correspondent for the *Cologne Gazette*, visits San Francisco on his way from Samoa to Washington, D.C., and gives a lecture at the Palace Hotel on the political situation in Samoa.

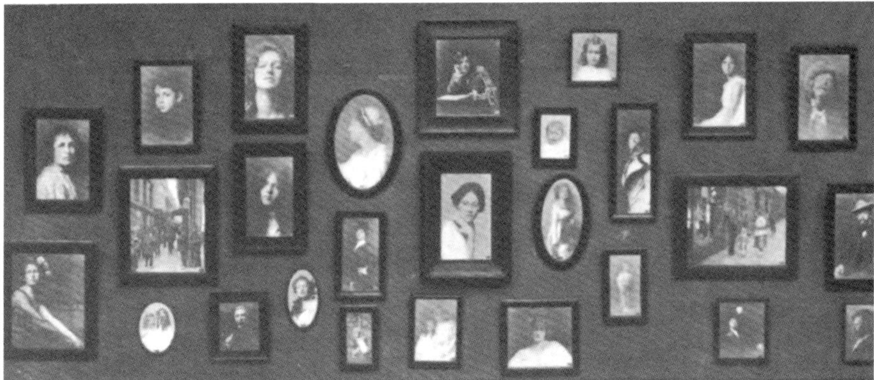

Genthe's portrait business begins to t hrive. By the end of 1899, he has recorded nearly nine hundred sittings.

1900
Genthe's residence is listed in the *Crocker-Langley San Francisco Directory* as 1532 Taylor Street, San Francisco.

Genthe begins renovations on a residence and studio at 790 Sutter Street. In his autobiography, he describes taking "a long lease on a three-story house on the corner of Sutter and Jones streets, where I added a fourth story with skylight for my studio." His architect, Newton J. Tharp, who designed the Dewey Monument in Union Square and the Grant Building on Market Street, will be appointed San Francisco's City Architect following the 1906 earthquake.

In December Genthe exhibits several bromide photographs at 139 Stockton Street. The Christmas issue of *Camera Craft* magazine includes his illustrated article entitled "The Children of Chinatown."

1901
Genthe joins the Bohemian Club (established in 1872), an elite men's social club founded by a group of Bay Area–based artists, actors, writers, and journalists. Early members include Jack London, Ambrose Bierce, Bret Harte, and Mark Twain.

In January Genthe shows twenty-seven photographs at the First San Francisco Photographic Salon at the Mark Hopkins Institute of Art (organized by the California Camera Club), winning the grand prize for best individual display and the first prize for portraiture.

From September to November, Genthe exhibits four portraits in the Ninth Annual Exhibition of the Photographic Salon in London, including *Portrait of Nance O'Neill*, *A San Francisco Girl*, *Study: Head and Hand*, and *Portrait of Miss May M.*

In October Genthe exhibits work in the Second Chicago Photographic Salon.

His photographs of Chinatown appear in *Overland Monthly* as illustrations to the essay "The Chinese Question," by Ho Yow, Imperial Chinese Consul-General to the Port of San Francisco.

Camera Craft magazine reports a fire in Genthe's studio: "A fire in the rear of Arnold Genthe's studio on October 30th inflicted considerable damage. Fortunately, Dr. Genthe

CAMERA CRAFT

A PHOTOGRAPHIC MONTHLY

VOL. II. SAN FRANCISCO, CALIFORNIA, DECEMBER, 1900. NO. 2.

THE CHILDREN OF CHINATOWN.

BY ARNOLD GENTHE.
WITH ILLUSTRATIONS BY THE WRITER.

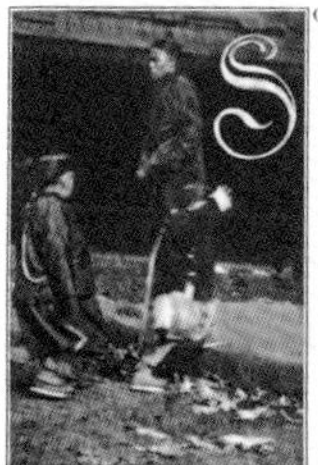

"NO PICTURE."

SOME one has said that the chief difficulty in obtaining good photographs in Chinatown, that most picturesque quarter of San Francisco, undoubtedly lies in the fact that the Chinamen have a very pronounced aversion to the camera. They believe that to be photographed by a white man means bad luck for them, and as soon as they see the ominous black box of the "White Devil" they run, protecting their faces with upheld arms. It might comfort them to know that the bad luck is mostly on the side of the enthusiastic camera fiend, who bravely and indiscriminately snaps his camera as they run angrily away, and who does his part of the swearing later on in the dark-room. But evidently they consider the man with the camera always a dangerous enemy, who has to be carefully avoided, a rather flattering tribute to the photographic ability of the many amateurs who make Chinatown their hunting grounds for scenes picturesque and novel.

Even the children are taught to run away from the black box, and it is indeed amusing to see the youngsters disappear with almost supernatural rapidity at the approach of a camera, be it a pocket kodak or an instrument of larger proportions. Even the very little children soon learn to know the camera, and let themselves willingly be carried to a place of safety by their big sisters and brothers.

The superstitious fear and, on the other hand, the bad light—the bright sunlight with the impenetrable shadows in the narrow alleys giving hard, contrary effects—make the photographing of "Young China" a rather difficult

Only known interior view of the First San Francisco Photographic Salon at the Mark Hopkins Institute of Art, January 1901. The photograph illustrated Oscar Maurer's review of the Salon in the May 1901 issue of *Camera Craft*. Genthe's photographs are discernible on the right.

"The Children of Chinatown," by Arnold Genthe, in *Camera Craft*, December 1900

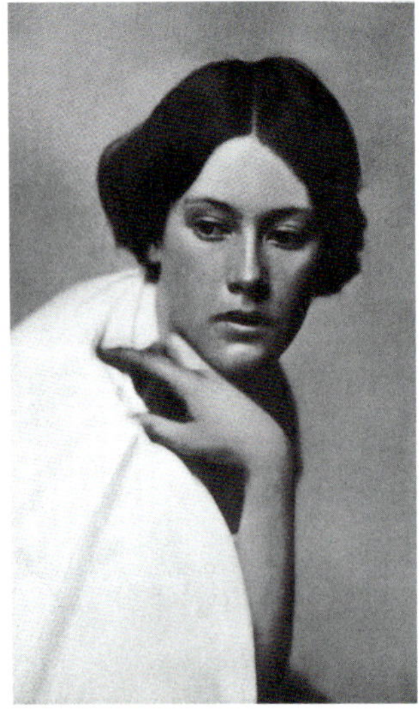

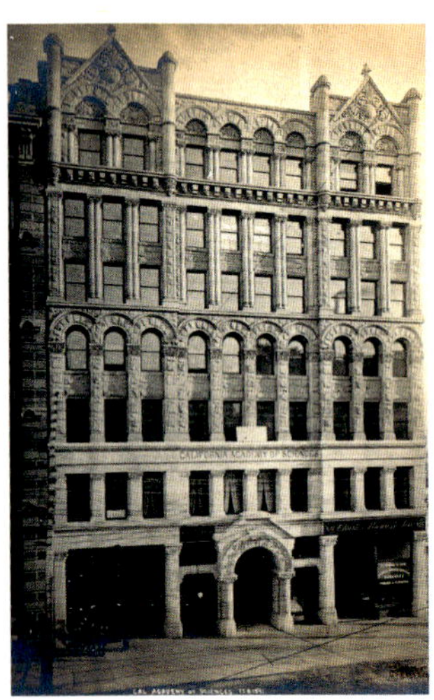

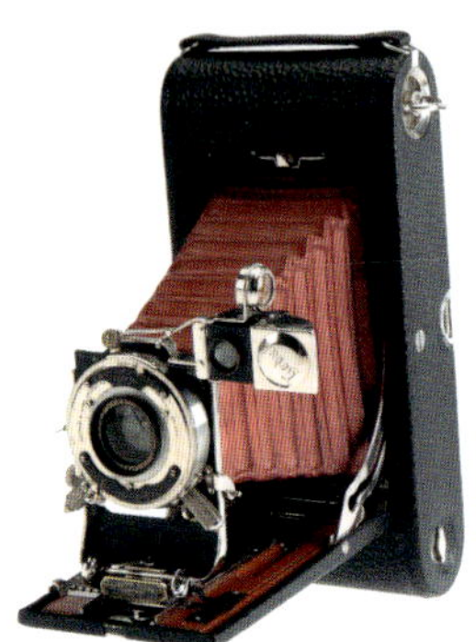

Arnold Genthe, *Study: Head and Hand*, from the catalogue for the Fourth Philadelphia Photographic Salon at the Pennsylvania Academy of the Fine Arts, 1901

California Academy of Sciences Building, Market Street, San Francisco, 1891

No. 3A, B2, Folding Pocket Kodak

was in the neighborhood and personally directed the removal of most of his negatives, only a few of which were damaged. The loss is fully covered by insurance."

From November to December, Genthe exhibits *Study: Head and Hand* in the Fourth Philadelphia Photographic Salon at the Pennsylvania Academy of the Fine Arts.

In December Elizabeth Gerberding publishes her children's book *The Golden Chimney: A Boy's Mine*, featuring photographs by Genthe.

1902

Genthe's studio and residence address are listed in the *San Francisco Blue Book* address directory as 737 Sutter Street, San Francisco.

In January Genthe exhibits twelve photographs in the Second San Francisco Photographic Salon at the Mark Hopkins Institute of Art. The works include *David Bispham as Wotan*, *Walter Damrosch*, *Man with Cigarette*, *A Profile Study*, *A Study for a Poster*, *A Challenge*, *Child with Cat*, *Prince Casimir P.*, *Margaret Anglin*, *A Poultry Stand in Chinatown*, *Portrait of Master L.S.*, and *An Ophelia Study*.

In May Genthe exhibits eleven photographs in the First Los Angeles Photographic Salon organized by the Los Angeles Camera Club. They are *Paderewski*, *Henry Miller as Sidney Carter (in "The Only Way")*, *Mme. Melba*, *A Challenge*, *An Ophelia Study*, *Study: Head and Hand*, *Mother and Child*, *Study for a Portrait*, *A Funny Story*, *Miss May M.*, and *Child with Cat*. He wins first prize for best collection and second and third prize in portraiture. As Oliver Lippincott remarks in *Camera Craft*, "[T]his well-known worker captured the judges completely, his exhibit being fairly plastered with multi-colored ribbons."

In August Genthe travels throughout Mexico.

In October he exhibits his photographs of Mexico in the California Camera Club galleries at the Academy of Sciences in San Francisco.

In November Genthe's article "Photographic Possibilities in Mexico," accompanied by a series of photographs from his travels to Mexico, is published in *Camera Craft* magazine.

1903

Kodak releases the No. 3A Folding Pocket Kodak, which is the model that Genthe will later use to photograph the 1906 earthquake. The camera uses 3 ¼-by-5 ½-inch postcard format roll film (No. 122), which allows its user to print their photographs as mailable postcards.

Brothers Auguste and Louis Lumière file a French patent for the autochrome process, which will become the first commercially viable color photography process in history. The brothers will begin marketing and selling the technology in 1907.

Genthe attends the first meeting of the Photographers' Association of California, a society of professional photographers established in 1903.

During the summer Genthe travels throughout New Mexico and Arizona.

In October he serves as chairman of the five-member Jury of Selection for the Third San Francisco Photographic Salon at the Mark Hopkins Institute of Art.

1904

Genthe travels to Mexico to attend Carnaval, an annual festival celebrated internationally to mark the beginning of the Catholic season of Lent.

In March Genthe's brother Siegfried is killed by robbers in Fez, Morocco.

On March 27 Genthe returns to San Francisco from Mexico. As the *San Francisco Call* reports on March 28: "The Pacific Coast Steamship Company's Curacao arrived yesterday from Guaymas . . . Dr. Genthe brought back a coat of tan which will gain him much envy. During his stay at Mazatlan Dr. Genthe spent some time hunting alligators and so successful a hunter did he prove that in addition to providing his friends with handsome dress suit cases he proposes to upholster his studio in alligator leather. The alligators found the doctor a relentless enemy. He hunted with rifle and camera. He became so expert that he took shots with the camera before using the rifle and after planting the fatal bullet dropped the firearm and with his Kodak recorded on faithful films the spasmodic struggles of the monsters in dissolution."

In May he is listed as a founding member of the Sequoia Club, a San Francisco–based social club established in 1892 with a focus on art appreciation.

Over the summer Genthe travels to Morocco and Germany via New York to settle his brother Siegfried's affairs and arrange for his brother's possessions to be shipped to San Francisco. He visits Belgium, Spain, and Paris and attends the Paris International Exhibition.

On October 15 Genthe arrives in New York before traveling to Washington, D.C., and Saint Louis, Missouri, en route to San Francisco. He arrives in San Francisco on October 24 and begins construction on an addition to his home and studio.

In December Genthe exhibits photographs in New York's First American Photographic Salon at the Clausen Galleries, with photographs selected by a jury of painters including William Merritt Chase, Robert Henri, and Childe Hassam. The exhibition is hosted by the Salon Club, a rival of Alfred Stieglitz's Photo-Secession group.

1905

In February Genthe exhibits photographs of Spain and Morocco at the Vickery, Atkins & Torrey Gallery in San Francisco.

In April Genthe has photographs exhibited in San Francisco's First American Photographic Salon in the Maple Room of the Palace Hotel.

During the fall Genthe visits Carmel-by-the-Sea, California, as a guest of fellow Bohemian Club member George Sterling. He decides to buy a plot of land in the budding town.

1905–1906

Genthe begins construction of his bungalow in Carmel-by-the-Sea. It is located on Camino Real Street and Eleventh Avenue.

1906

On January 28 the *San Francisco Call* reports that "Dr. Arnold Genthe is planning a bungalow for himself at Carmel-by-the-Sea, which will be ready for occupancy in the early summer. I understand the Doctor has purchased a number of rare rugs and odd bits of antique furniture to be used in its decoration."

On April 12 Genthe returns from a weeklong trip to Carmel-by-the-Sea with the writer and critic Barnett Franklin.

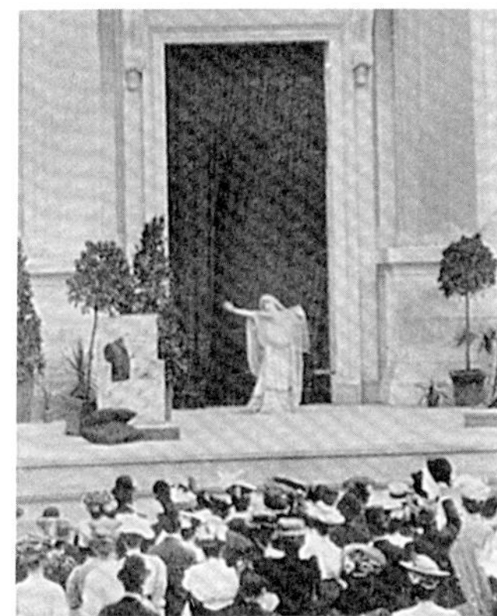

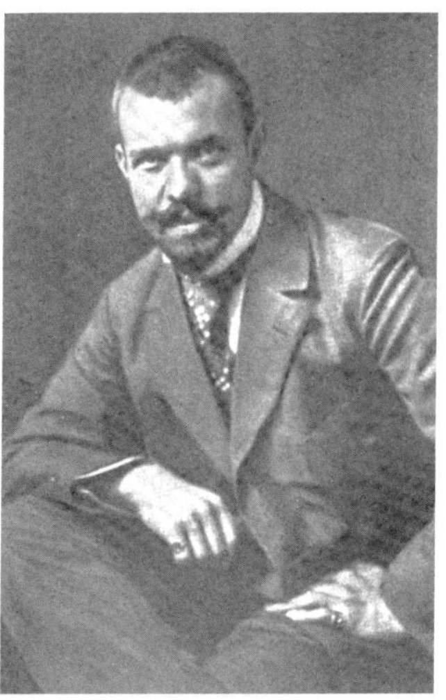

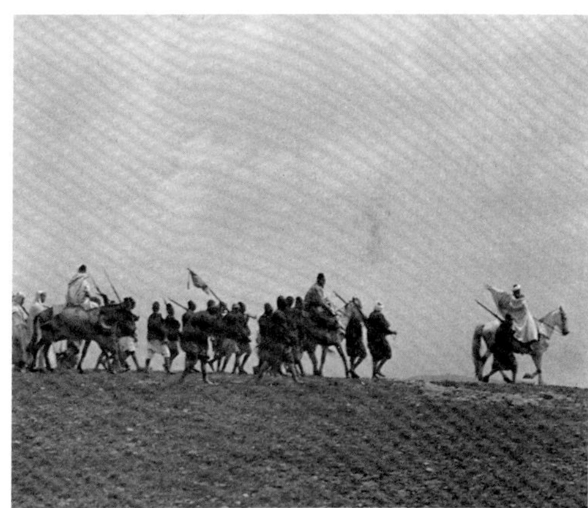

Arnold Genthe, Untitled (Sarah Bernhardt at Greek Theatre), 1906. Lantern slide, 5 × 4 in. (127 × 102 mm) (approx.). Arnold Genthe Collection, Prints and Photographs Division, Library of Congress, Washington, D.C.

Dr. Siegfried Genthe

Arnold Genthe, Untitled (Travel views of Morocco), 1904. Interpositive from cellulose nitrate negative, 4 × 5 in. (102 × 127 mm) (approx.). Arnold Genthe Collection, Prints and Photographs Division, Library of Congress, Washington, D.C.

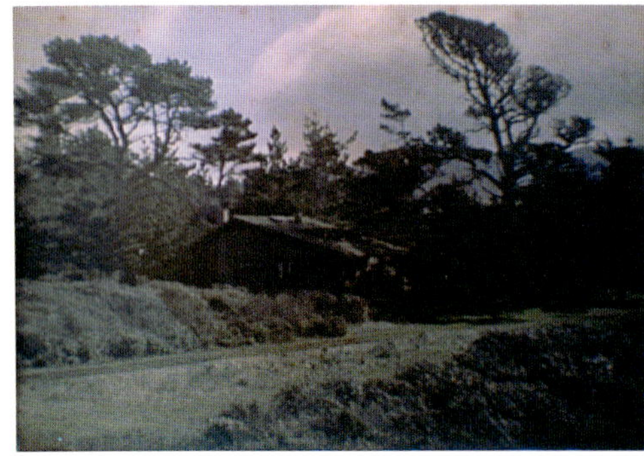

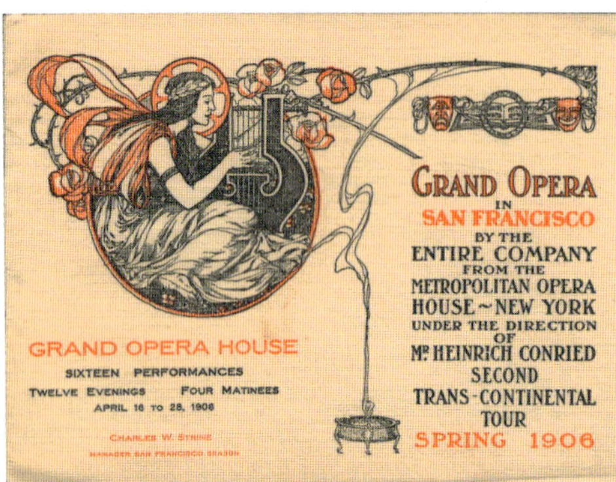

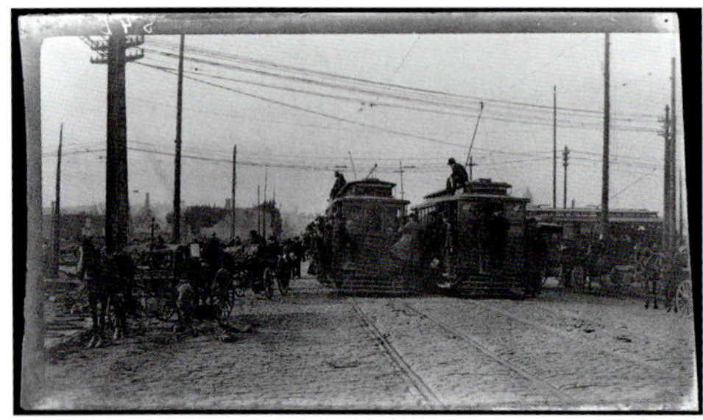

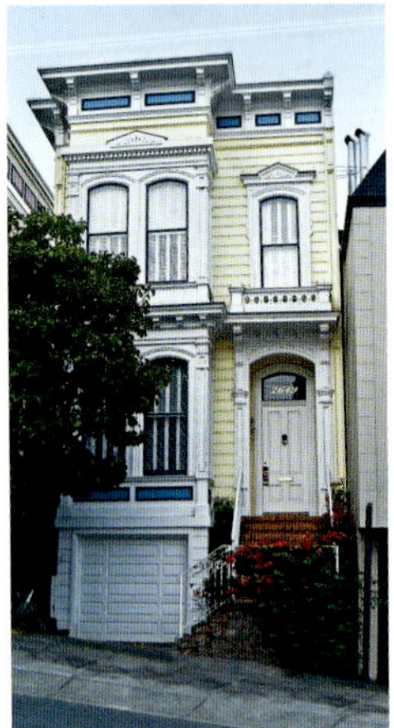

Arnold Genthe, Untitled (Arnold Genthe's bungalow in Carmel-by-the-Sea, California), ca. 1907–1911. Autochrome, 5 × 7 in. (127 × 178 mm). Arnold Genthe Collection, Prints and Photographs Division, Library of Congress, Washington, D.C.

San Francisco Grand Opera program. The opening night of the season was on April 17, 1906, the day before the 1906 earthquake.

Arnold Genthe, Untitled (Streetcars at Mission and 16th Streets), 1906. Interpositive from cellulose nitrate negative, 3 ⅛ × 5 ½ in. (79 × 140 mm). Fine Arts Museums of San Francisco, Museum purchase, James D. Phelan Bequest Fund, 1943.407.107

Joseph Greco, 2619 Octavia Street, 2012

On April 17 he attends the opening night performance of *Carmen* at the Grand Opera House in San Francisco.

April 18. Earthquake! At 5:12 a.m., a 7.9 magnitude earthquake strikes the San Francisco Bay Area. Genthe awakens to the sound of Chinese porcelain falling around him. He walks to visit his friends Milton and Mabel Bremer on Van Ness Avenue. The three decide to walk to the St. Francis Hotel for breakfast. The hotel remained open in the quake's immediate aftermath to serve breakfast to those displaced by the earthquake. Genthe returns to his studio to find that all of his hand cameras are damaged; he subsequently walks to George Kahn's camera shop on Montgomery Street where he borrows a Kodak folding pocket camera and multiple rolls of film. After spending the day photographing the city, he sleeps in Golden Gate Park. Fire destroys his home and studio at 790 Sutter Street.

On April 23 Genthe continues to photograph San Francisco, including Fillmore Street and Bush Street, in the aftermath of the earthquake.

On April 24 he places a personal ad in the *San Francisco Call* that reads: "ARNOLD GENTHE (790 Sutter st.) is at cor. Jackson and Maple" (otherwise known as the Cowdery residence). As he will later recall in his autobiography: "In the Frank Cowderys' home on Maple Street and later on in the Octavia Street home of Dr. Millicent Cosgrave (whose friendship throughout these years has meant so much to me) I had found a haven of rest. For several weeks I did not concern myself with any thought of the future. I blithely continued to take photographs."

On April 27 Genthe photographs the streetcars on Mission and Sixteenth Streets and Market Street. The streetcars would not start running again until several weeks later.

The April 30 edition of the *San Francisco Examiner* reports: "Dr. Arnold Genthe has taken some excellent photographs of our poor distracted-looking city. I met him the other day and he, cheerful under the circumstances, said that he had lost all of his plates, his films, his library—in fact, every treasure that he possessed in the world. He, too, like many other splendid men, is prepared to commence all over again. Dr. Genthe is at present at the home of the Cowderys, corner of Maple and Jackson streets."

On May 14 Genthe photographs the French actress Sarah Bernhardt playing the eponymous lead in Jean Racine's *Phèdre* in a benefit performance for earthquake relief at the Greek Theatre in Berkeley to a crowd of five thousand people. The Associated Press reports: "Madam Sarah Bernhardt, the actress, today visited the devastated sections of [San Francisco], making the trip in an automobile. The city, in its former aspect, had been well known to her, and when she saw the result of the conflagration she wept."

From May 23 to 27, Genthe stays in Carmel. In a letter to Jack London dated May 25, 1906, the poet George Sterling writes: "Genthe is in Carmel now. He lost everything he had, in the fire, and was pretty blue at first, but he has done lots of scene-photography since. His cottage here is about finished, and is a very pretty one." Shortly thereafter, the *San Francisco Call* reports: "Dr. Arnold Genthe is residing on Laurel Street when in town, though much of his time is being spent at Carmel-by-the-Sea where, in his artistic bungalow, he has established a studio."

From June to July, Genthe travels to Yosemite and takes photographs using the same Kodak camera that he used to photograph the aftermath of the earthquake.

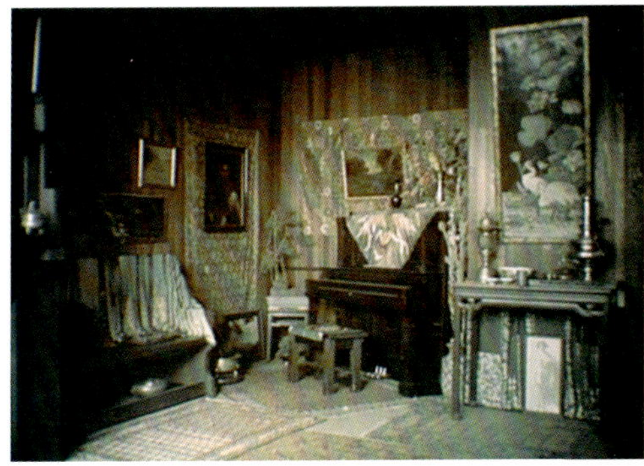

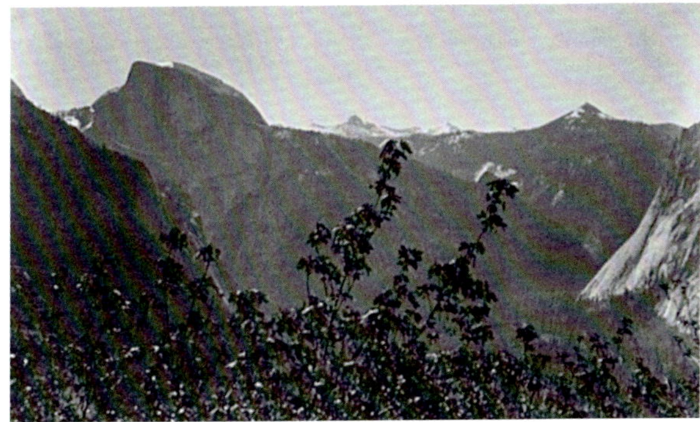

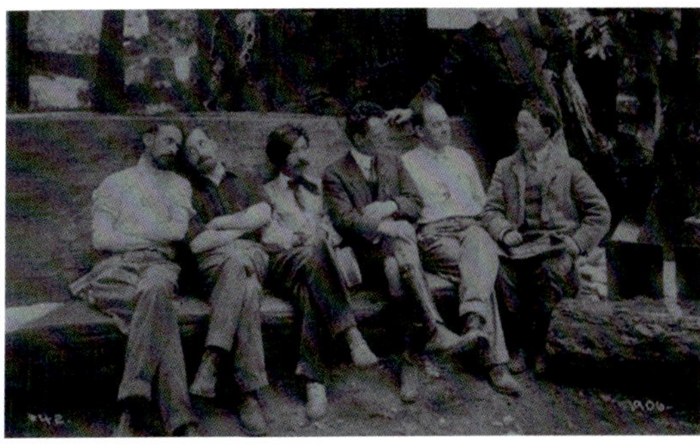

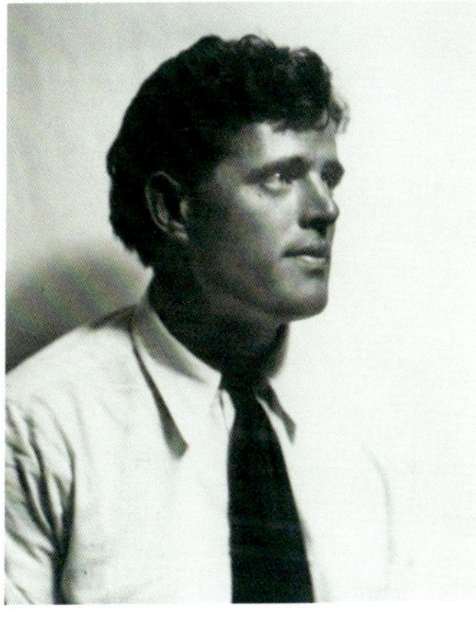

Arnold Genthe, Untitled (Interior of Arnold Genthe's Clay Street studio), ca. 1906–1911. Autochrome, 5 × 7 in. (127 × 178 mm) (approx.). Arnold Genthe Collection, Prints and Photographs Division, Library of Congress, Washington, D.C.

Arnold Genthe, Untitled (Travel views of Yosemite National Park), 1903–1906. Interpositive from cellulose nitrate negative, 5 × 7 in. (127 × 178 mm) (approx.). Arnold Genthe Collection, Prints and Photographs Division, Library of Congress, Washington, D.C.

Arnold Genthe (third from the right) and friends at the Bohemian Grove annual campout, 1906

Arnold Genthe, Untitled (Portrait of Jack London), 1906. Lantern slide, 5 × 4 in. (127 × 102 mm) (approx.). Arnold Genthe Collection, Prints and Photographs Division, Library of Congress, Washington, D.C.

On July 16 the *San Francisco Call* reports: "Notwithstanding the persistent rumor that Dr. Arnold Genthe was going to make New York his home, the talented clubman is to remain right in San Francisco. He has purchased a little Dutch cottage away out on Clay Street near Presidio Avenue and workmen are rapidly putting it in shape for the genial doctor's residence studio. Miss Julia Marlowe and E[dward] H[ugh] Sothern used every persuasion to coax Dr. Genthe to New York, offering either of their own apartments for a studio, but it is definitely settled now that he will remain in California. He has just returned from Yosemite with a fine collection of photographs, and as the valley is unusually magnificent this year it adds to the interest of the views secured."

As Genthe will later describe in his autobiography: "On Clay Street, not far from the gates of the Presidio, I discovered a picturesque one-story cottage. In its small garden was a fine old scrub-oak, and I believe it was this and not so much the house that made me decide to take a five-year lease. . . . And so I started to make a few structural changes and to get together the necessary equipment that would enable me to continue my work as a portrait photographer."

On July 17 the *San Francisco Call* reports: "Arnold Genthe, the photographer whose valuable cameras and negatives were destroyed by the great fire, has suffered further calamity. Genthe, with the aid of workmen, has been fitting up a studio at 3209 Clay Street, near Lyon. Last Sunday when he arrived to view the alterations he was informed by one of the men that his cameras had been smashed, his lenses taken and his negatives destroyed by some unknown enemy. Genthe reported the vandalism at police headquarters and O'Dea and Hicks worked on the case. The lenses were later found and the cameras can be repaired. Genthe has no clew to the perpetrator of the outrage."

In late July and early August, Genthe attends the Bohemian Grove campout in Monte Rio, California, which begins on July 23 and culminates in the annual High Jinks celebration on August 4.

In November Genthe's new studio is operational. The writer Jack London sits for a portrait.

1907
Genthe spends time in Carmel. There he photographs Jack London with fellow writers George Sterling, Mary Austin, and James "Jimmy" Hopper.

On April 20 Genthe joins the board of directors of the Hotel Del Monte Art Gallery in Monterey, California, and chairs the jury of the opening exhibition. He is the only photographer on the seven-member jury and shows his work in the opening exhibition mounted in the ballroom and in adjacent spaces at the hotel.

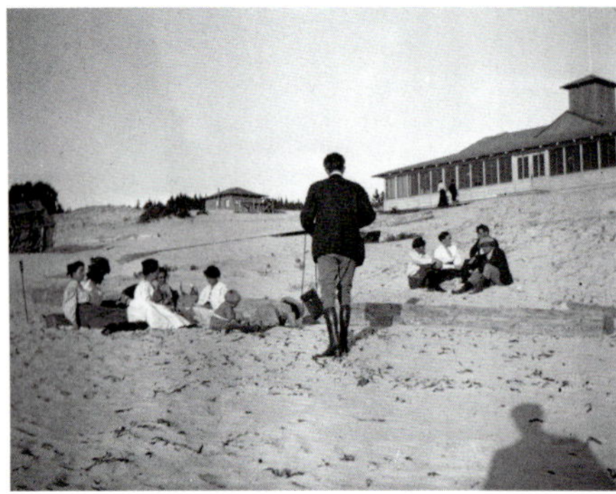

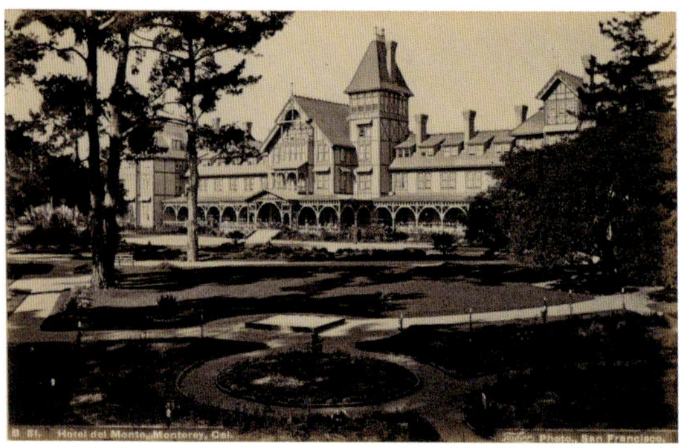

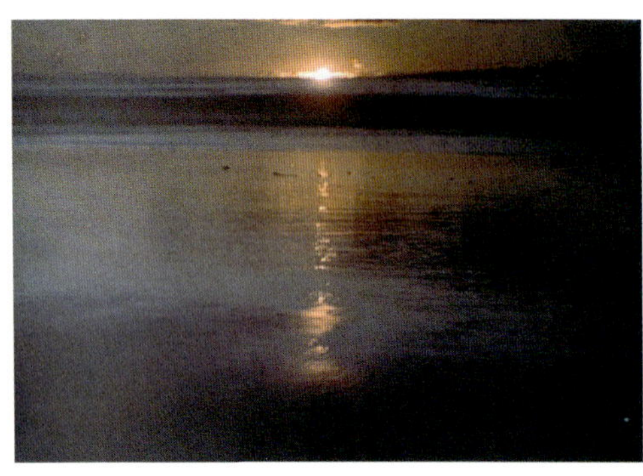

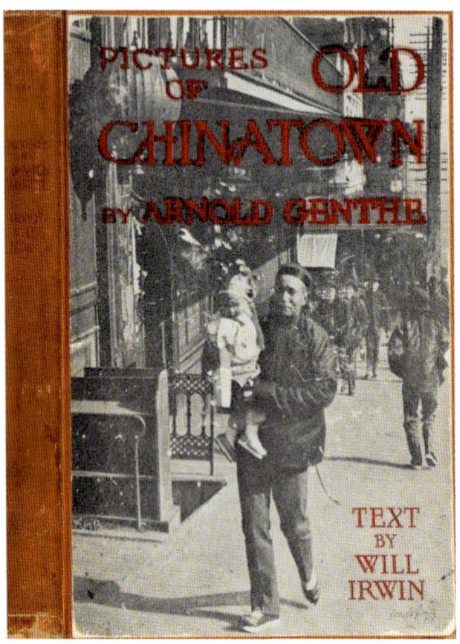

Hotel del Monte, Monterey, California

Arnold Genthe photographing George Sterling, Mary Austin, Jack London, and James "Jimmy" Hopper on the beach in Carmel-by-the-Sea, California, ca. 1910. Interpositive from cellulose nitrate negative, 4 × 5 in. (102 × 127 mm) (approx.). Arnold Genthe Collection, Prints and Photographs Division, Library of Congress, Washington, D.C.

Arnold Genthe, Untitled (Sunset, Carmel Bay, California), ca. 1906–1911. Autochrome, 5 × 7 in. (127 × 178 mm) (approx.). Arnold Genthe Collection, Prints and Photographs Division, Library of Congress, Washington, D.C.

Cover of Arnold Genthe's book *Pictures of Old Chinatown* (1908)

In July Genthe shows photographs in the monthly California Camera Club exhibition at 2206 Steiner Street, in San Francisco. *Camera Craft* reports: "The Print Committee has not been idle, as witnessed by the very fine exhibit of the work of Dr. Arnold Genthe, which adorned the walls of the main room and the director's room above, during July."

1907–1908

Genthe begins experimenting with the autochrome color photography process, primarily from his home in Carmel. He undertakes a series of autochrome photographs of sunsets, as well as portraits and other landscapes.

1908

From April to October, Genthe travels throughout Japan with a permit from the Ministry of War. He visits Kyoto, Mount Fuji—where he is trapped for two days by a snowstorm—the southern island of Shikoku, and the northern island of Hokkaido where he photographs the Ainu people. He takes more than seven hundred photographs.

On November 21 he publishes the book *Pictures of Old Chinatown*, which features reproductions of his photographs of San Francisco's Chinatown from ca. 1896 printed alongside text written by the journalist Will Irwin.

1909

In January *Overland Monthly* publishes a selection of his photographs of American stage actresses, including Ethel Barrymore and Julia Marlowe, to accompany the article "A Few First Aids to Disillusion in the Theatre," by Barnett Franklin.

1910

Genthe exhibits his photographs of Japan at the Vickery, Atkins & Torrey Gallery.

From November to December, he exhibits his photographs *After the Earthquake—San Francisco (Sacramento Street)* and *The First Light—San Francisco,* alternatively titled *Steps That Lead to Nowhere (After the Fire),* in the Open Section of the International Exhibition of Pictorial Photography at the Albright Art Gallery, Buffalo, New York. Alfred Stieglitz purchases ten of his photographs.

1911

In June Genthe leaves San Francisco for New York City after his lease on the Clay Street property expires. As the *San Francisco Chronicle* reports: "Dr. Arnold Genthe, another member of the jury [for the midsummer exhibition at the Hotel del Monte Art Gallery in Monterey], will soon leave for New York, where he will reside permanently." Shortly thereafter, he establishes a portrait studio on the top floor of the Thorley Building at Fifth Avenue and Forty-Sixth Street.

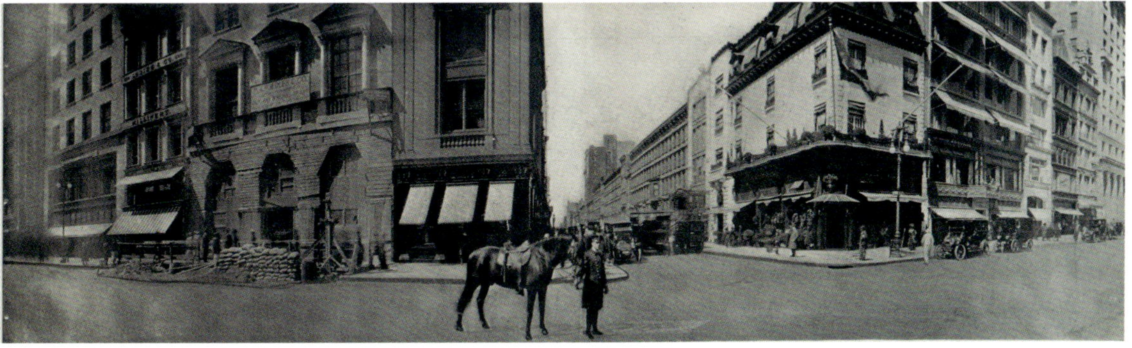

1913
On January 15 Genthe writes a feature article for the *New York Times* in which he offers advice to women who are interested in taking up photography. The article is printed alongside four of his photographs.

He publishes a revision of his 1908 book *Pictures of Old Chinatown*, with additional photographs and a revised text by Will Irwin.

At the invitation of Mrs. Woodrow Wilson, Genthe photographs the wedding of her daughter Jessie Woodrow Wilson to Francis Bowes Sayre at the White House.

1914
Genthe meets the dancer and choreographer Isadora Duncan, who had recently returned to New York City from France. He photographs Duncan and her dance troupe the "Isadorables," whom he would continue to photograph for the next few years.

1916
Genthe publishes *The Book of the Dance*, which features more than one hundred photographic plates depicting contemporary dancers including Isadora Duncan, as well as an essay by the poet and critic Shaemas O'Sheel.

Genthe photographs President Woodrow Wilson in his study at the White House.

On September 16 he photographs President Theodore Roosevelt in Oyster Bay, New York.

1917
In January Genthe sells his collection of four hundred Japanese prints at the Anderson Galleries, Inc., in New York to finance his new interest in Chinese painting, sculpture, and jade.

He photographs John D. Rockefeller and his estate in Pocantico Hills, New York, at the recommendation of the architect and landscape designer William Welles Bosworth.

Genthe exhibits his portraits of Isadora Duncan and Mrs. Henry Blossom at the First Annual Exhibition of the Society of Independent Artists at the Grand Central Palace in New York City.

1918
Genthe becomes a US citizen.

His portrait of Isadora Duncan is reproduced on a poster advertising *The Roll Call: A Masque of the Red Cross*, a play written by the poet and dramatist Percy MacKaye to promote donations to the American Red Cross in the aftermath of World War I.

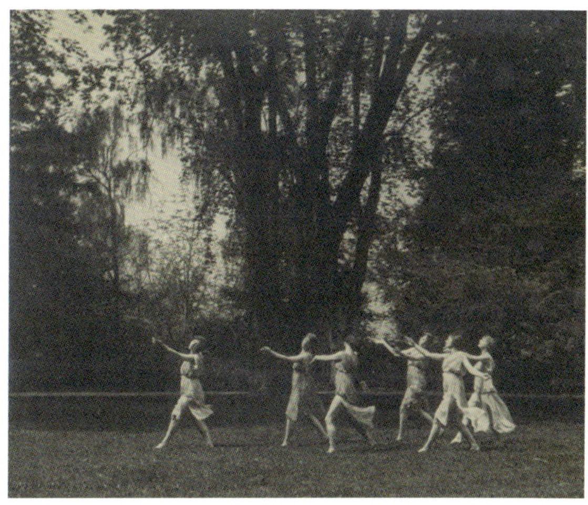

Thorley Building, New York, ca. 1911

Arnold Genthe, Untitled (The Isadorables), ca. 1914. Gelatin silver print, 10 3⁄8 × 12 5⁄8 in. (26.4 × 32.1 cm). Genthe Collection, New-York Historical Society Museum and Library

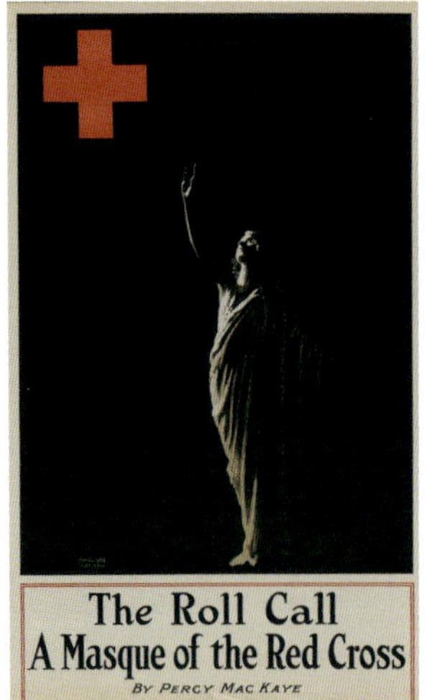

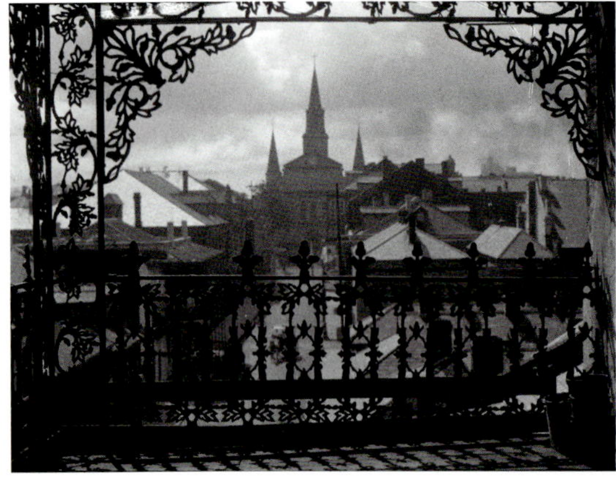

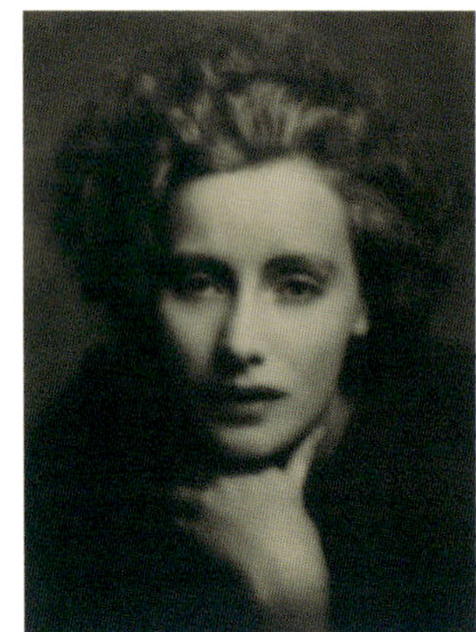

Poster for *The Roll Call: A Masque of the Red Cross,* by Percy MacKaye, 1918

Arnold Genthe, *A Vista Through Iron Lace, New Orleans,* 1920–1926. Interpositive from cellulose nitrate negative, 4 × 5 in. (102 × 127 mm) (approx.). Arnold Genthe Collection, Prints and Photographs Division, Library of Congress, Washington, D.C. This photograph appeared in Genthe's book *Impressions of Old New Orleans.*

Arnold Genthe, Untitled (Portrait of Greta Garbo), 1925. Gelatin silver print, 13 × 9⅞ in. (33 × 25 cm). Art Institute of Chicago, Reciprocal gift of the Library of Congress, 1952.491

1919
His photographs of John D. Rockefeller's gardens are featured in a privately printed book entitled *The Gardens of Kijkuit,* with text by William Welles Bosworth.

1920
In August Genthe serves as a judge for the "Perfect Foot" beauty contest, sponsored by the *Evening World* and held in the Grand Central Palace exhibition hall in New York City.

1923
In February Genthe advocates for teaching photography in public schools at the fifty-fifth meeting of the Pictorial Photographers of America.

1924
On November 26 Genthe photographs Andrew W. Mellon.

1925
Genthe photographs the actress Greta Garbo soon after her arrival to the United States from Sweden.

Genthe travels to New Orleans to photograph the French Quarter.

1926
Genthe publishes his book *Impressions of Old New Orleans: A Book of Pictures,* which includes a foreword by the novelist Grace King.

1926–1927
Travels to New Mexico, Mexico, Guatemala, and Cuba.

1927
From May 11 to June 13, Genthe exhibits his photographs of New Orleans at the California Palace of the Legion of Honor in San Francisco.

1929
Genthe publishes the book *Isadora Duncan,* with a foreword by the writer Max Eastman.

During the summer Genthe travels to Greece, including Crete and other islands, where he photographs the landscape and ancient architecture.

1930
An exhibition of his photographs from his trip to Greece, entitled *Fifty Recent Photographs of Greece and Rhodes,* opens at the Anderson Galleries in New York.

1931
From August to September, Genthe's photographs of Greece and its ancient monuments are exhibited at the M.H. de Young Memorial Museum in San Francisco.

1932
From October to November, Genthe exhibits work in the group show *Exhibition of Portrait Photography, Old and New* at the Julien Levy Gallery in New York.

1934
In June he exhibits a series of photographs at the Marjorie Woodhouse Leidy Memorial Gallery of Guild Hall in East Hampton, New York.

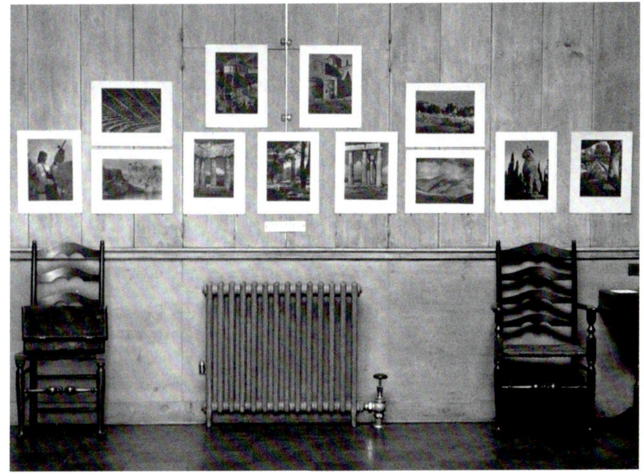

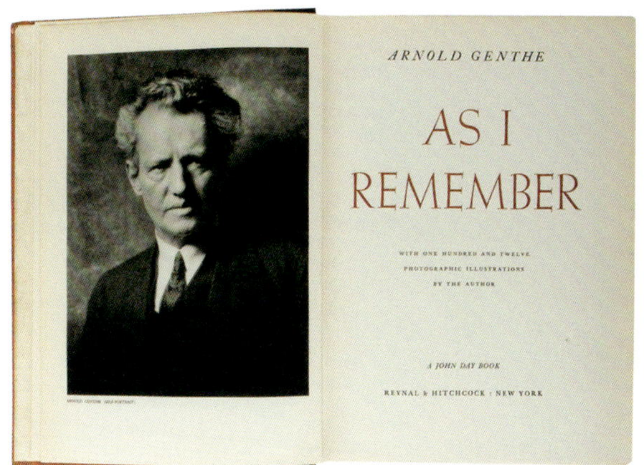

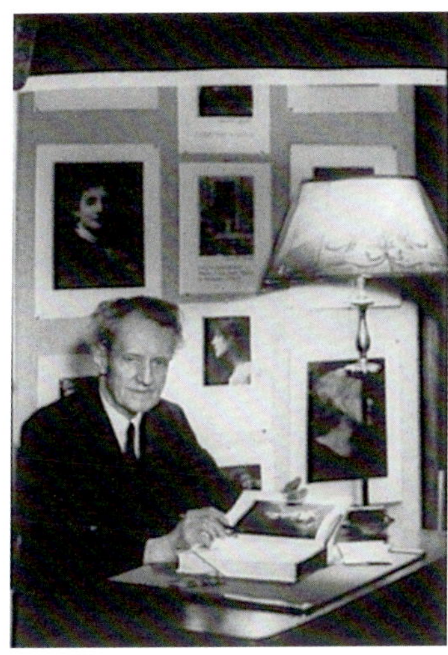

Installation view of the 1934 exhibition of photography at Guild Hall, East Hampton, New York

Arnold Genthe, *As I Remember* (1936), title page to the first edition

Arnold Genthe posing with his autobiography, 1936. Interpositive from negative, 7 × 5 in. (178 × 127 mm) (approx.). Arnold Genthe Collection, Prints and Photographs Division, Library of Congress, Washington, D.C.

1936
Genthe publishes his autobiography, *As I Remember*, which is illustrated with 112 of his photographs.

1937
In January he visits his friends Mr. and Mrs. Bertram Alanson in San Francisco and is interviewed by Carolyn Anspacher, who was photographed by Genthe as a child, for the *San Francisco Chronicle*.

In June Genthe is hospitalized with a serious illness in New York. He cancels a planned trip to Greece.

In September he visits his friends the Alansons in San Francisco and stays with them as he recuperates from his illness.

1938
Genthe travels to Italy.

1941
He exhibits his photographs of Isadora Duncan at the Museum of Modern Art in New York. In a review of the exhibition published in the *Bulletin of the Museum of Modern Art*, the renowned critic Lincoln Kirstein refers to “the great photographs of Genthe.”

An exhibition of his work entitled *Theatrical Portraits* opens at the Museum of the City of New York.

1942
On August 9 he passes away from a coronary occlusion while visiting friends in New Milford, Connecticut.

Following his death, the Library of Congress—at the direction of the poet and then-Librarian of Congress Archibald MacLeish—acquires all of the prints and negatives found in his studio for $750 and transfers them to Washington, D.C. Shortly thereafter, the California Palace of the Legion of Honor purchases approximately 170 of the negatives depicting California subjects and transfers them to San Francisco.

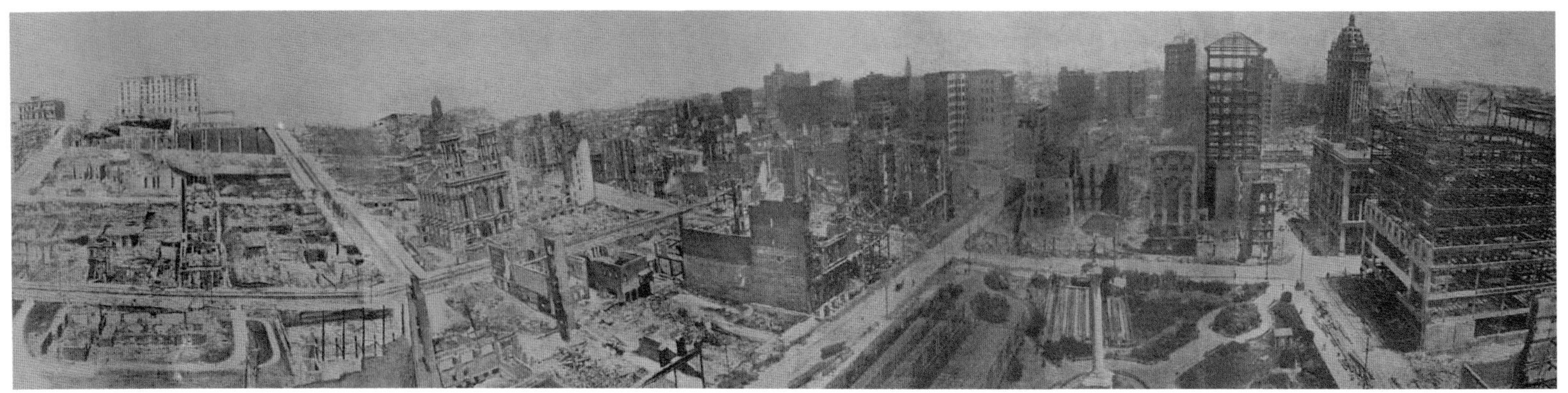

A HISTORICAL CHRONOLOGY OF SAN FRANCISCO

Compiled by Natalie Pellolio

4000–3000 BCE The peninsula occupied by present-day San Francisco emerges as a result of declining sea levels, which in turn create the San Francisco, San Pablo, and Suisun Bays. Indigenous settlements begin to emerge on the newly formed bay shores.

500 CE The direct ancestors of the Yelamu tribelet of the Ramaytush Ohlone people first settle on the land occupied by present-day San Francisco. The Yelamu thrive for centuries in coastal and bay-shore villages.

1768 Prior to the arrival of the Spanish in 1769, the Yelamu live in five villages on the land occupied by present-day San Francisco. They are Amuctac (near present-day Visitacion Valley), Chutchui (near present-day Mission Dolores), Petlenuc (near the present-day Presidio), Sitlintac (near present-day Mission Bay), and Tubsinte (also near present-day Visitacion Valley). The Yelamu migrate seasonally between villages, living in Sitlintac, Tubsinte, and Petlenuc in the winter and in Amuctac and Chutchui during the summer. As the smallest of the eleven Ohlone tribelets, the Yelamu population numbers roughly two hundred at the time of Spanish arrival and colonization.

1769 Captain Don Gaspar de Portolá leads an overland expedition north from New Spain (present-day Mexico) as part of the first European land survey of the coast of the territory known as Alta California, with the goal of securing the Spanish Empire's occupation of the region. In November, Portolá and his party become the first-known Europeans to see the San Francisco Bay. Portolá claims the area for the Viceroyalty of New Spain, a territory of the Spanish Empire, but does not establish a settlement.

1776 Colonel Juan Bautista de Anza leads an expedition to the San Francisco peninsula with the goal of establishing a Spanish military fort and church. Anza assigns his second-in-command, Officer José Joaquín Moraga, to oversee the construction of the Presidio of San Francisco adjacent to Petlenuc village and the Mission San Francisco de Asís at Chutchui village. On June 29, the colonists mark the official founding of their settlement. They name it Yerba Buena, after the *Clinopodium douglasii* plant found in the region.

1791 The colonists build a second adobe church at a nearby site, replacing the original Mission with a larger church that still stands today.

1810–1820 The population of indigenous people living at Mission San Francisco de Asís reaches its peak of roughly 1,100. Many live at the Mission as indentured servants who oversee ranching, farming, and wool production and are forced to endure impoverished living and working conditions. Once they are baptized, indigenous residents are forced to give up their native language, diet, and cultural practices and are forbidden from leaving the Mission. By 1850, ninety percent of Ohlone people will have perished as a result of colonial violence, disruption of tribal life, and exposure to European disease.

1821 Mexico wins independence from Spain and gains control of Alta California. The Mexican government begins to gradually secularize the mission system and divide its land into private land grants. Yerba Buena is left relatively neglected by Mexico, though a military post at the Presidio is retained.

1835 William Richardson, a Mexican citizen of English descent who settled in Yerba Buena in 1822, builds a homestead near present-day Portsmouth Square. Soon after, he is granted the land title by Governor Figueroa and draws up plans for a pueblo. He moves with his family to his ranch in Sausalito in 1841 but is considered by many to be the founder of modern San Francisco.

1846 **In May**, Congress declares war on Mexico at the urging of Democratic President James K. Polk, who had run for president in 1844 on a platform of western territorial expansion. Critics of the war, including army lieutenant and future president Ulysses S. Grant, attack it as a conquest for the expansion of slavery to the western territories—a view widely held among soldiers in the rank and file army.

In July, the US Navy claims victory in the Battle of Yerba Buena, taking Alta California by force under the command of Commodore John D. Sloat.

In August, Lieutenant Washington A. Bartlett is named Alcalde of Yerba Buena. He submits a petition to change the name of the settlement to San Francisco, which takes effect the following year.

1848 **In January**, James Marshall, a carpenter hired by John Sutter to aid in the construction of his sawmill in the Sierra Nevada mountains, discovers flakes of gold in the riverbed beneath the partially built mill. Though rumors circulate nationally about Marshall's discovery, the news is not formally announced until December 5, 1848, when President Polk confirms the discovery of gold in California in an address to Congress.

In February, San Francisco becomes a US military territory by the terms of the Treaty of Guadalupe Hidalgo, which marks the end of the Mexican–American War.

1849 The California Gold Rush begins in the wake of President Polk's announcement of the discovery of gold at Sutter's Mill. Thousands of people begin traveling to California in search of opportunity. Between 1848 and 1849, San Francisco grows from a small settlement of 1,000 people to a large city with a population of more than 25,000. By the end of the Gold Rush, around 1855, more than 300,000 people will have migrated to California.

Although records of earthquakes in California before 1850 are scarce, the Gold Rush, and the attendant circulation of newspapers in the Sierra foothills, contributed to an increase in written accounts of seismic events.

1850 **In April**, San Francisco is officially incorporated as a city.

In September, California is granted statehood as the thirty-first state, entering the Union as a free (non-slavery) state under President Millard Fillmore.

1851 On May 3–4, a fire destroys almost three-quarters of the city, which at the time comprises many wooden buildings and sidewalks. It is the most destructive of seven large fires in the city between December 1849 and June 1851.

1854 The San Francisco Mint is established, producing more than $4 million in gold coins in its first year.

1859 Silver is discovered at the Comstock Lode in Virginia City, Nevada, constituting the first major discovery of silver in the United States. The fortunes generated from silver mining at the Comstock Lode catapult San Francisco from a growing city to a major metropolis.

1868 An earthquake of magnitude 7.0 occurs on October 21 and causes significant damage to buildings in San Francisco. Although its epicenter is in Hayward, California, located twenty miles east of the city, the earthquake becomes known as the Great San Francisco Earthquake.

1869 In May, Leland Stanford, the president of the Central Pacific Railroad, drives the final spike uniting the eastern and western branches of the first American transcontinental railroad in Promontory, Utah. The event marks the end of a nearly ten-year-long process of funding and building the railroad's infrastructure, which provides the first-ever rail access into California—a state that was previously reachable only by ship or on foot. Owned by Stanford and fellow San Francisco–based financiers Collis P. Huntington, Charles Crocker, and Mark Hopkins, who were together known as "The Big Four," the rail line is built primarily by Chinese immigrant laborers. Recruited by Crocker, the Chinese laborers are forced to endure xenophobia and perilous working conditions while being paid a fraction of the wages paid to white laborers.

1870 Surveyor and landscape designer William Hammond Hall is assigned by the city to develop Golden Gate Park on a 1,013-acre plot of land consisting primarily of sand dunes. The decision to build a park on the plot is controversial; the *Sonoma Democrat* describes the plot as having "wind continually sweeping over it that would take the hair off a polar bear and a fog resting on it heavy enough to give asthma to a sea lion." Today, the park thrives with 680 acres of forests, 130 acres of meadows, and ten lakes.

1872 Construction begins on a new city hall at a site bounded by Market, McAllister, and Larkin Streets. The building, projected to cost $1.5 million, is expected to take three years to complete. Finished twenty-seven years later, in 1899, at a cost of $6 million, the new building will be destroyed in the 1906 earthquake.

1882 In May, President Chester A. Arthur signs the Chinese Exclusion Act prohibiting all Chinese immigration to the United States for ten years (it will be extended in 1892 with the signing of the Geary Act, made permanent in 1902, and finally repealed in 1943). It is the first federal act prohibiting all members of a specific ethnic group from immigrating to the United States, and is written largely as a reaction against the influx of Chinese immigration to San Francisco coinciding with the Gold Rush and the construction of the railroads.

1887 The first seismographs in the United States are installed at two sites in the Bay Area: Lick Observatory, on Mount Hamilton, and the University of California, Berkeley.

1894 The California Midwinter International Exposition of 1894 takes place in the newly completed Golden Gate Park. It is the first world's fair to be hosted in the western United States, and more than two million people attend. President Benjamin Harrison appoints businessman Michael H. de Young as the fair's commissioner. The following year, the fair's Fine Arts Building will be made into a public museum called the M.H. de Young Memorial Museum.

1898 The Ferry Building, a reinforced Beaux Arts–style building with arched arcades and a distinctive clock tower, replaces an older wooden structure along the city's eastern waterfront. It is the connection for travelers to and from the East Bay and San Francisco's connection to the transcontinental railroads that terminated in Oakland.

April 18, 1906 **5:12 a.m.**: An earthquake with an estimated magnitude of 7.9 hits the San Andreas Fault in the Pacific Ocean just west of San Francisco, lasting forty-five to sixty seconds. The earthquake is felt as far north as Coos Bay, Oregon, and as far south as Los Angeles. Fires ignited by ruptured gas lines destroy 28,188 structures in San Francisco alone, causing as much as from $350 million to $500 million worth of damage in 1906 dollars. More than three thousand people perish in the disaster.

6:30 a.m.: General Frederick Funston sends a message to Colonel Charles Morris at the Presidio and to Captain M.L. Walker at Fort Mason ordering all available army troops to report for duty at the Hall of Justice at Portsmouth Square, preempting a declaration of martial law. Four officers and 126 troops of the First Engineer Battalion arrive with rifles and twenty rounds of ammunition each, followed by the California National Guard and federal troops. The troops will patrol the city for the next twenty-four hours without rest.

8:14 a.m.: A major aftershock hits San Francisco, causing more structures to collapse. Nearly all of the city's water lines are now damaged, making it extremely difficult for firefighters to combat the growing fires. Firefighters and army troops begin dynamiting compromised structures in an attempt to control the spread of the fires, though many of the resulting explosions have the adverse effect of igniting new ones.

9:30 a.m.: A fire starts at 395 Hayes Street due to residents attempting to cook breakfast in a fireplace with a broken flue. The fire, later named the "Ham and Eggs Fire," ravages much of the neighborhood known as Western Addition and eventually destroys the Mechanics' Pavilion and City Hall.

10:00 a.m.: A military telegraph is established between the Presidio and the military's headquarters at Haight and Market Streets, serving as a critical communication line as the city works to repair its damaged telegraph and telephone lines.

10:05 a.m.: The U.S.S. *Chicago* receives a report of the disaster from the DeForest Wireless Telegraph Station in San Diego while en route from San Diego to Long Beach, California. The ship immediately changes course for San Francisco, where it arrives the following evening and docks at Fort Mason. The ship will provide essential telegraph communication for the city while local telegraph lines continue to be repaired, and will help bring more than twenty thousand displaced residents to safety across the San Francisco Bay in Marin County.

10:30 a.m.: The U.S.S. *Preble* arrives from the navy base at Mare Island to aid in the firefighting effort along the waterline and to provide support for the nearby Harbor Emergency Hospital.

1:00 p.m.: St. Mary's Hospital is evacuated. Patients are taken to the river steamer *Modoc*, which has just arrived from Sacramento, and are relocated to Oakland. The fire begins to overtake the downtown San Francisco area.

3:00 p.m.: Mayor Eugene Schmitz forms the Committee of Fifty to address safety concerns and make decisions in real time about how best to protect the city. The controversial committee includes politicians, newspapermen, military officials, and entrepreneurs but not a single member of the city's Board of Supervisors. At the same time, the mayor issues an unconstitutional proclamation authorizing federal troops and police officers to kill any person found looting or committing a crime.

4:00–6:30 p.m.: The neighborhood known as the Chinese quarter, or Chinatown, catches fire in large part due to the improper use of dynamite for demolition in adjacent neighborhoods. The fire completely destroys the neighborhood and displaces its Chinese population, forcing many residents to relocate to Berkeley and Oakland in the aftermath.

8:00 p.m.: The fires have now burned roughly three square miles of the city, and continue to grow.

8:40 p.m.: General Funston telegraphs the War Department in Washington, D.C., to request tents and rations, reporting a death toll of one thousand. At 4:55 a.m. the next day, Secretary of War William Howard Taft sends a telegraph message to General Funston to notify him that 200,000 rations and tents from eight army bases are being sent directly to San Francisco.

9:00 p.m.: The fire overtakes Nob Hill. General Funston, working with the mayor and his Committee of Fifty, announces that firefighters no longer have access to water and that dynamite is the only way to control the fires. By the next morning, the city will be unrecognizable. The more than fifty fires caused by the earthquake will burn for four days before being extinguished by rainfall. Eighty percent of the city's structures will be destroyed, leaving roughly 325,000 San Francisco residents homeless. The city immediately begins its effort to rebuild.

FIRST DAYS OF THE 1906 EARTHQUAKE AND FIRESTORM

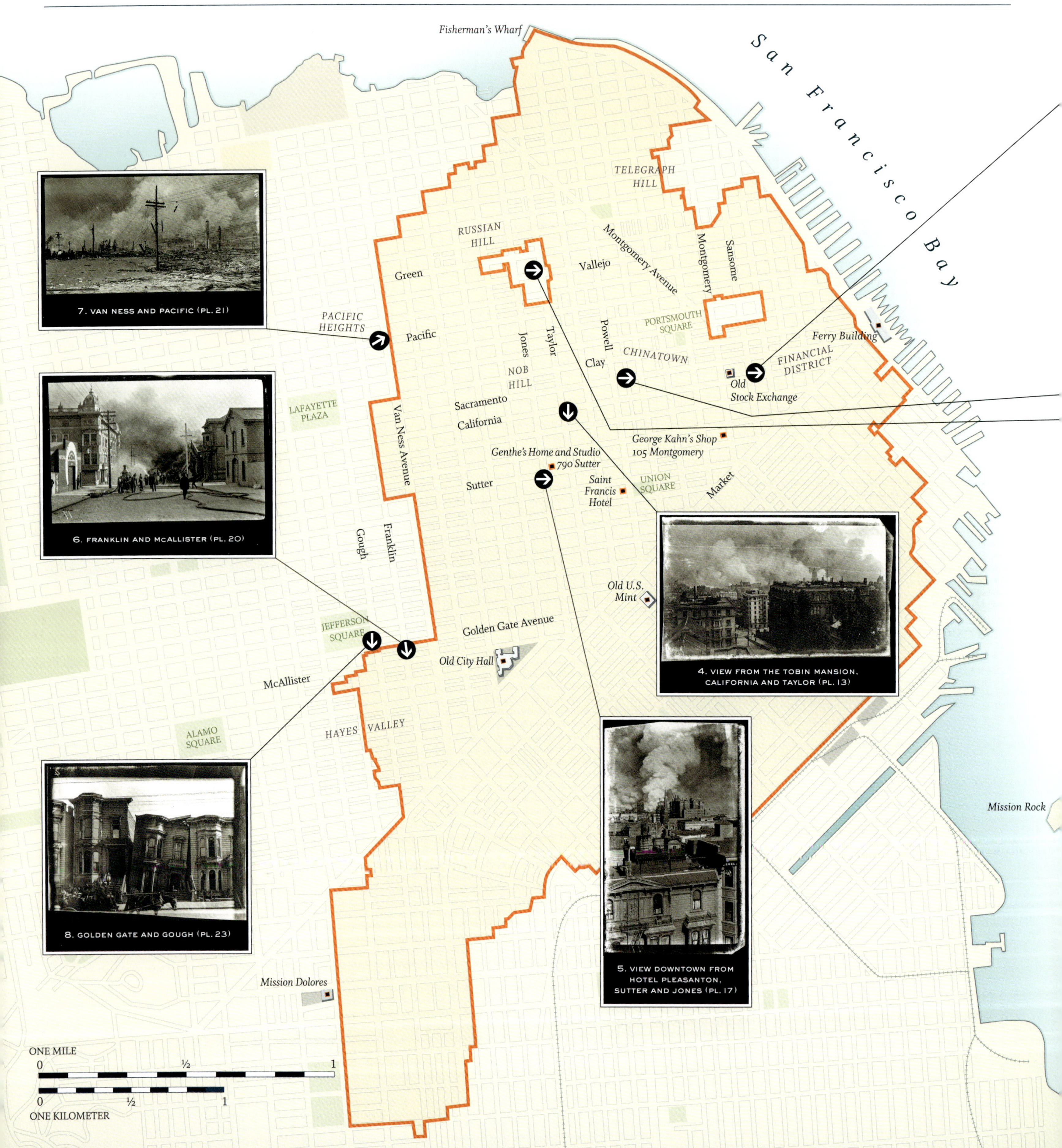

7. VAN NESS AND PACIFIC (PL. 21)

6. FRANKLIN AND McALLISTER (PL. 20)

8. GOLDEN GATE AND GOUGH (PL. 23)

4. VIEW FROM THE TOBIN MANSION, CALIFORNIA AND TAYLOR (PL. 13)

5. VIEW DOWNTOWN FROM HOTEL PLEASANTON, SUTTER AND JONES (PL. 17)

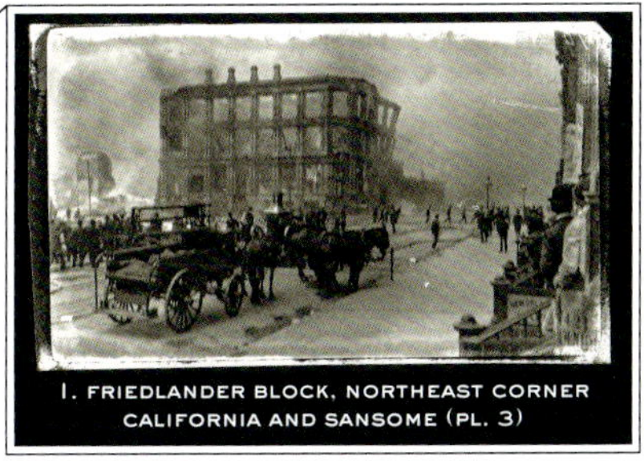

1. FRIEDLANDER BLOCK, NORTHEAST CORNER CALIFORNIA AND SANSOME (PL. 3)

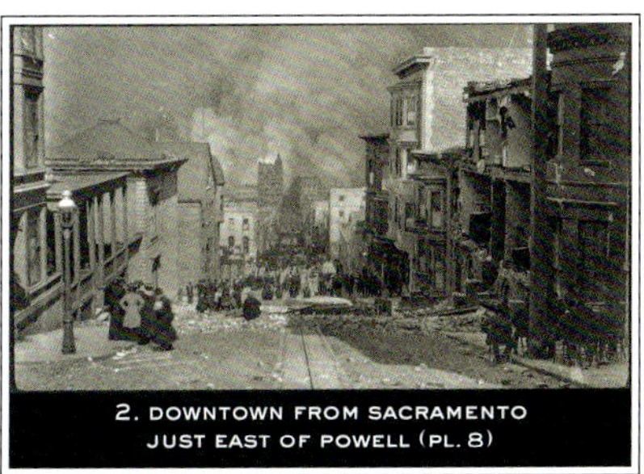

2. DOWNTOWN FROM SACRAMENTO JUST EAST OF POWELL (PL. 8)

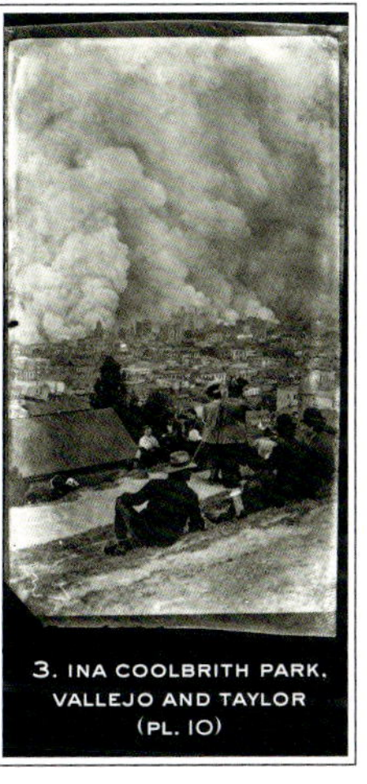

3. INA COOLBRITH PARK, VALLEJO AND TAYLOR (PL. 10)

THIS MAP SHOWS the northeastern section of San Francisco, the most densely populated and heavily developed area of the city. The tinted area outlined in orange designates the parts of the city ravaged by the fires that burned for three days following the April 18, 1906, earthquake. This area encompasses the financial district downtown, the manufacturing areas south of Market, and many residential neighborhoods. Selected photographs, among the first by Arnold Genthe on April 18 and in the days immediately after, are numbered in the order he took them. Arrows indicate the direction his camera was facing.

Map compiled by Victoria Binder, Karin Breuer, and James A. Ganz

CARTOGRAPHY: ADRIAN KITZINGER

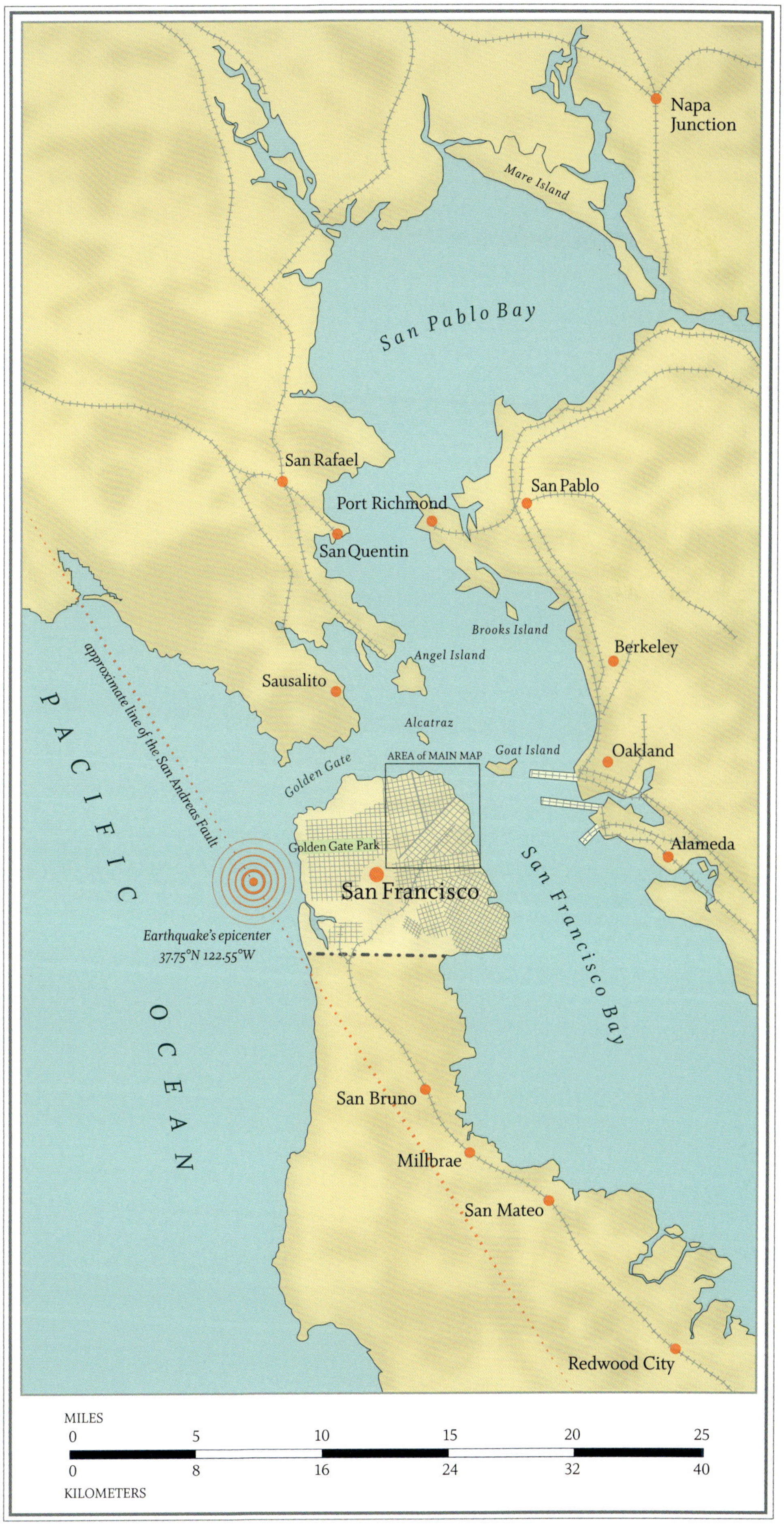

Napa Junction
Mare Island
San Pablo Bay
San Rafael
San Pablo
Port Richmond
San Quentin
Brooks Island
Angel Island
Berkeley
Sausalito
Alcatraz
Goat Island
AREA of MAIN MAP
Oakland
Golden Gate
approximate line of the San Andreas Fault
PACIFIC OCEAN
Golden Gate Park
Alameda
San Francisco
San Francisco Bay
Earthquake's epicenter 37.75°N 122.55°W
San Bruno
Millbrae
San Mateo
Redwood City

MILES 0 5 10 15 20 25
0 8 16 24 32 40 KILOMETERS

"EARTHQUAKE AND FIRE"

from Arnold Genthe's *As I Remember* (1936)
with an introduction and commentary
by James A. Ganz

Upon the 1936 publication of Arnold Genthe's autobiography, As I Remember, *literary critics reserved special praise for the dramatic chapter devoted to the San Francisco earthquake and fire. George Currie, reviewing the book for the November 23, 1936, issue of the* Brooklyn Daily Eagle, *wrote: "One dwells upon the San Francisco fire because Mr. Genthe contrives to make it vivid and simple to one who at the time was dismayed, frightened, and prayerful, more than three thousand miles away but not three thousand miles from black hysterical headlines in the daily press of the more settled East."*

Elsewhere in the book, Genthe chides his friend Sarah Bernhardt for embellishing her own reminiscences of the disaster, but it is important to acknowledge that the author's own physical and temporal distance from the events he describes may account for minor inconsistencies with both the historical record as well as the visual evidence of his own photographs. Readers today may also be disturbed by Genthe's stereotyped references to his Japanese valet, Hamada, which are a reminder of the pervasive racism of the era in which the book was published. The remarks highlight the fact that Genthe's narrative is told from the point of view of a relatively privileged member of San Francisco society. Nevertheless, it serves as one of the most notable first-person accounts of the events of April 18, 1906.

EARTHQUAKE AND FIRE

One of the great social events of the opera season in the spring of 1906 was the joint appearance of Enrico Caruso and Olive Fremstad in *Carmen*. A large and enthusiastic audience filled the house for this gala occasion. It was the night of April 17th. After a quiet supper party with some friends, I walked home and went to bed with the music of *Carmen* still singing in my ears. It seemed as if I had scarcely been asleep when I was awakened by a terrifying sound—the Chinese porcelains that I had been collecting in the last years had crashed to the floor. (My interest in Chinese porcelains ever since then has been purely platonic.) The whole house was creaking and shaking, the chandelier was swinging like a pendulum, and I felt as if I were on a ship tossed about by a rough sea. "This can't go on much longer," I said to myself. "When a house shakes like this, the ceiling is bound to collapse. As soon as the plaster begins to fall, I'll cover my head and accept what comes."

An ominous quiet followed. I was about to get up when I found Hamada, my Japanese servant, standing beside me. An earthquake was, of course, no new experience for him, but now he looked thoroughly frightened and was as pale as a Japanese can be. "Master," he said, "very bad earthquake—many days nothing to eat—I go, yes." Before I could say anything he was on his way downstairs. I looked at the clock; the time was a quarter past five. I looked out of the window and saw a number of men and women, half-dressed, rushing to the middle of the street for safety. Pushing his way through them, with a sack of flour over his shoulder and carrying a basket of provisions, was Hamada.

I went to the top floor to see what had happened to my studio. The chimney had fallen through the roof, most of the book shelves had collapsed and the books were buried under mounds of plaster from the wall and ceiling. A sixteenth-century wood sculpture of Buddha had landed right side up and stood unharmed and inscrutable in the midst of the debris—"serene, indifferent of fate."

The earth continued to indulge in periodic tremors, though less violently. I started to get dressed and decided that the most suitable "earthquake attire" would be my khaki riding things—I was to live in them for weeks.

The streets presented a weird appearance, mother and children in their nightgowns, men in pajamas and dinner coat, women scantily dressed with evening wraps hastily thrown over them. Many ludicrous sights met the eye: an old lady carrying a large bird cage with four kittens inside, while the original occupant, the parrot, perched on her hand; a man tenderly holding a pot of calla lilies, muttering to himself; a scrub woman, in one hand a new broom and in the other a large black hat with ostrich plumes; a man in an old-fashioned nightshirt and swallow tails, being startled when a friendly policeman spoke to him, "Say, Mister, I guess you better put on some pants.". . . But there was no hysteria, no signs of real terror or despair. Nor did buildings show an alarming evidence of destruction; here and there parts of damaged walls had fallen into the streets, and most chimneys had collapsed. At Delmonico's,[1] the front of one of the rooms on the third floor had fallen into the street. A chair with some clothes had been carried with it. The distressed owner called out to a passing workman, "Do you want to make $20?" "Sure," he replied, "what is it?" "See that suit there? I want you to bring it up to me here." Just then another shock occurred. "Ah, you better come and get it yourself."

After wandering about for a while, I went to the house of some dear friends of mine, Milton and Mabel Bremer (she is now married to my old friend Bertram Alanson). I found them calmly sitting on the front steps. The one thing that Mabel was apparently most anxious to save was a pair of evening slippers—a purchase of the day before—which she thrust into my large coat pockets. But it did not save them. I left them at my studio when I returned there later and they were burned with all my possessions.

We decided that it would be a good idea to have some breakfast and went to the St. Francis Hotel which had not been damaged. When we arrived we saw that we were not the only ones who had had the brilliant idea of breakfasting there. The lobby and the dining room were crowded. Near the entrance we saw Enrico Caruso with a fur coat over his pajamas, smoking a cigarette and muttering, " 'Ell of a place! 'Ell of a place!" He had been through many earthquakes in his native Italy but this one was too much for him. It appeared that when he was awakened by the shock, he had tried his vocal cords without success. " 'Ell of a place! I never come back here." And he never did.

Inside the hotel, people in all kinds of attire from evening clothes to nightgowns went milling about. There was no gas or electricity, but somehow hot coffee was available which, with bread and butter and fruit, made a satisfying breakfast. When I asked the waiter for a check he announced with a wave of his hand, "No charge today, sir. Everyone is welcome as long as things hold out."

After seeing my friends home, I went back to my studio to get a camera. The one thought uppermost in my mind was not to bring some of my possessions to a place of safety but to make photographs of the scenes I had been witnessing, the effects of the earthquake and the beginning of the conflagration that had started in various parts of the city. I found that my hand cameras had been so damaged by the falling plaster as to be rendered useless. I went to Montgomery Street to the shop of George Kahn, my dealer, and asked him to lend me a camera. "Take anything you want. This place is going to burn up anyway." I selected the best small camera, a 3A Kodak Special. I stuffed my pockets with films and started out. It was only then that I began to realize the extent of the disaster which had befallen the city. The fire had started simultaneously in many different places when the housewives had attempted to get breakfast for their families, not realizing what a menace the ruined chimneys were. All along the skyline as far as eye could see, clouds of smoke and flames were bursting forth. The work of the fire department was badly hampered, as the water mains had burst.

By this time the city had been put under martial law with General [Frederick] Funston in supreme command. He decided to check the progress of the conflagration by dynamiting a block in advance of the fire in order to create a breach over which the flames could not leap. All day and night the detonations resounded in one's ears and yet the fire continued to make headway. By noon the whole town was in flight. Thousands were moving toward the ferry hoping to get across the bay to Oakland or Alameda. On all streets leading to Golden Gate Park, there was a steady stream of men, women and children. Since all wagons or automobiles had been commandeered by the military authorities, only makeshift vehicles were available. Baby carriages and toy wagons, carts constructed out of boxes and wheels, were used to transport groceries, kitchen utensils, clothes and blankets; trunks mounted on roller skates or even without them were being dragged along by ropes. No one who witnessed these scenes can ever forget the rumbling noise of the trunks drawn along the sidewalks—a sound to which the detonations of the blasting furnished a fitting contrapuntal accompaniment.

Farther out on Geary and Sutter Streets, men and women cooked on improvised stoves on the sidewalks and as the crowds passed they called out invitations to stop for a rest and a cup of coffee. Up on the hill the wealthy were taking strangers into their homes, regardless of any risk they were running. I recall the picture of Henry J. Crocker laughing heartily as he carried the pails of water from the faucet in his garden to a little iron stove, probably one of his children's toys, set up by the curb in front of his red stone mansion [at 1100 California Street].

I have often wondered, thinking back, what it is in the mind of the individual that so often makes him feel himself immune to the disaster that may be going on all around him. So many whom I met during the day seemed completely unconscious that the fire which was spreading through the city was bound to overtake their own homes and possessions. I know that this was so with me. All morning and through the early afternoon I wandered from one end of the city to the other, taking pictures without a thought that my studio was in danger.

As I was passing the home of some friends on Van Ness Avenue, they were on the porch and called out, "Come in and have a drink." While we were raising our glasses, there occurred another shock. Everyone but my hostess and I ran outside. "Let us finish anyway," she said.

"Sure," I said, giving her as a toast the line from Horace, "And even if the whole world should collapse, he will stand fearless among the falling ruins."

On my way to the Bohemian Club[2] I met Charles K. Field. "You dummy," he said. "What are you doing here? Don't you know that your house is going to be blown up?" This was the first time I had thought of such a possibility. Turning back I hurried up Sutter Street to find a militiaman guarding the entrance of my studio.

"You can't get in here," he said, handling his rifle in an unpleasant manner.

"But it's my home," I said.

"I don't care whether it is or not. Orders are to clear all houses in the block. If you don't do as I say, I shoot, see?"

There were rumors that some of the militia, drunk with liquor and power, had been shooting people. I did not want to argue with him, but I did want to get inside, with the hope that I might save a few of my things.

"How about a little drink?" I asked.

"Well, all right," he replied eagerly.

In my cellar I had been keeping a precious bottle—Johannisberger Schloss 1868, which I had brought from the Bremer Rathskeller in 1904—reserving it for a special occasion worthy of it. There had been several gay events that might have justified its consumption, but now there was no doubt about it. The special occasion had arrived. I knew that to my unwelcome guest it would mean nothing, so I brought out for him a bottle of whiskey and while he poured himself drink after drink, I sipped the wine, if not with the leisurely enjoyment that it called for, at last getting some of its exquisite flavor without having to gulp it down with barbarous haste. When my militia friend had absorbed enough of his bottle, he pushed me through the door saying, "Now you have got to get out of here or I'll have to shoot you, see?"

From a safe distance I watched with others the dynamiting of the block of our homes. There was no expression of despair. ("Well, there it goes!" "That's that!" being the only comments heard.) That night I slept in Golden Gate Park together with thousands of others who were in the same plight. The crowd there suggested more a camping out than refugees from a disaster in which they had lost their homes and all their material possessions. A cheerful spirit seemed to prevail throughout and whatever one had was gladly shared.

The fire raged all the next day and well into the morning after, when it was stopped at Van Ness Avenue, which was wide enough to break the spread of the flames. Ten square miles lay devastated with hardly a building intact. In some parts of the city dynamiting continued and the crash of toppling walls could still be heard.

The day of the earthquake, a committee of outstanding citizens met with the mayor and the military authorities and it was unanimously voted that the mayor be empowered to draw checks for any amount for the relief of the sufferers—the committee guaranteeing the payment. The relief measures were carried out with remarkable efficiency. All vehicles and foodstuffs were commandeered for the public good. No food was sold in the shops. Rich and poor had to stand in line at the relief stations to receive their daily rations. On Market Street, rough tables and benches had been put up for the length of several blocks to accommodate the hundreds of people for whom food was being provided. In the military reservation, the Presidio, a city of tents had sprung up affording a shelter for thousands of homeless. In the public squares likewise, tents and shelter of a more substantial form were put up, the occupants readily adapting themselves to this new mode of housekeeping. Some of these shacks were marked "Excelsior Hotel," "The Ritz," "The Little St. Francis," "New Palace Hotel," etc.

In the houses no cooking was permitted; it had to be done

on stoves put up on the sidewalks. Water was rationed to be used only for drinking and cooking purposes. Not more than one lamp or candle was permitted in each home. It had to be out by eight o'clock and those who had no business to attend to were obliged to stay indoors. Military patrols on all streets saw that these rules were carried out, and over a period of many weeks of this mode of improvised living, there was not a complaint of neglect or an instance of wrongdoing.[3]

During the day, piling bricks became the enforced pastime of pedestrians. Any man walking through the burned district was likely to be stopped by a soldier or marine and ordered to do his share. Several times while I was out taking pictures, I was put to work.

Rebuilding started while the ruins were still smoking. On top of a heap of collapsed walls, a sign would announce, "On this site will be erected a six-story office building to be ready for occupancy in the Fall." An entertaining illustration of the indomitable spirit of San Francisco was furnished by Mattias [*sic*] (whose restaurant was almost as popular as Coppa's).[4] Having been very prosperous he had decided to take a long vacation and visit his relatives in Spain. He closed his establishment, placing a sign on the door: "Gone to Spain. Will be back in six months." He had been gone only a few weeks when he received a cable from his brother: "Everything lost. Come back at once." When he returned, he found not a house standing in the district where his restaurant had been. Undismayed, he put up a large sign: "Gone to Hell. Will be back in three months." And he was. His was the first building completed in that neighborhood. I recall that Professor [Henry] Morse Stephens of the University of California made a delightful dedication speech at the opening of the restaurant.

In the Frank Cowderys' home on Maple Street and later on in the Octavia Street home of Dr. Millicent Cosgrave (whose friendship throughout these years has meant so much to me) I had found a haven of rest. For several weeks I did not concern myself with any thought of the future. I blithely continued to take photographs. Of the pictures I had made during the fire, there are several, I believe, that will be of lasting interest. There is particularly the one scene that I recorded the morning of the first day of the fire (on Sacramento Street, looking toward the Bay) which shows, in a pictorially effective composition, the results of the earthquake, the beginning of the fire and the attitude of the people [Genthe reproduces this photo in the book; see pl. 8].[5] On the right is a house, the front of which had collapsed into the street. The occupants are sitting on chairs calmly watching the approach of the fire.[6] Groups of people are standing in the street, motionless, gazing at the clouds of smoke. When the fire crept up close, they would just move up a block. It is hard to believe that such a scene actually occurred in the way the photograph represents it. Several people upon seeing it have exclaimed, "Oh, is that a still from a Cecil De Mille [*sic*] picture?" To which the answer has been, "No, the director of this scene was the Lord himself." A few months ago an interview about my work—I had told the story of that fire picture—appeared in a New York paper with the headline, "His pictures posed by the Lord, says photographer."

The ruins of Nob Hill became a rich field for my camera. All that remained standing of the Towne residence on California Street was the marble columned entrance. The picture I made of it by moonlight brought out its classic beauty. Charles K. Field found the title for it, "Portals of the Past," by which the portico is known today. It has been removed to Golden Gate Park where in a setting of cypresses it remains a noble monument to a noble past. Charles Rollo Peters made a large painting of it, using my photograph, for the Bohemian Club, and for once the photographer was given credit by a painter. Over his signature on the canvas he inscribed, "With thanks to Arnold Genthe."[7]

On the other side of California Street, in front of the Huntington home, were two marble lions, the traditional commonplace guardians of a home of wealth. The terrific heat of the flames had broken off parts of the stone here and there, simplifying and ennobling their form, as a great sculptor might have done. Of another house all that remained were some chimneys and a foreground of steps. Beyond them was devastation with only the lights of the Mission District visible in the distance. It was another scene that had to be taken by moonlight so as to bring out its full significance. I called the picture "Steps That Lead to Nowhere" [Genthe reproduces this photo in the book; see fig. 51].

The attitude of calmness of which I have spoken, the apparent indifference of the people who had lost everything, was perhaps not so much a proof of stoic philosophy that accepts whatever fate brings. I rather believe that the shock of the disaster had completely numbed our sensibilities. I know from my own experience that it was many weeks before I could feel sure that my mind reacted and functioned in a normal manner. If I had shown any sense, I might easily have saved some of the things I valued most—family papers, letters and photographs of my parents and brothers, books written by my closest relatives, and of course my more important negatives, which I could have carried away in a suitcase. As it was, practically everything I possessed had gone up in smoke.

To make my loss more complete, it happened that less than two years before, all my family possessions, including my brother Siegfried's, had been brought to San Francisco from Hamburg: the library of over three thousand volumes, some two hundred of which had been written by members of my family in the last century, several pieces of furniture designed by my architect grandfather, family portraits painted by [Johann David] Gruson in the eighteenth century.

Since the death of my brother Siegfried, no family ties had remained to hold me in Germany. As a correspondent for the *Cologne Gazette* he had traveled all over the world, his last assignment being Morocco, where he had been sent during the Buhamara rebellion at the beginning of 1903. He had lived in Fez for a year and was ready to return to Germany, where I had planned to join him. We were to start out together on a several months' expedition to Persia. His trunks were all packed and he was to leave Fez the next day. That afternoon he went out for his daily ride, though he had frequently been warned against these solitary excursions on account of the unrest of the tribes. Not far from the outskirts of the city, he was killed by bandits, who were merely after his fine Arab stallion.

I went to Germany in the summer of 1904—I have never been back since—and had all his belongings shipped to my house in San Francisco. As I needed more space, I had added to my studio the top floor of the adjoining house which was on the level with the studio floor, and there in rooms filled with furniture, books and paintings that I treasured, I had created for myself a background and an atmosphere which gave me peace and happiness. Now all this had gone up in smoke and with it all evidence of the work I had done since the beginning of my career. The thousands of negatives which I had made during that time were now but chunks of molten, iridescent glass, fused together in fantastic forms. Everything I possessed was destroyed except my enthusiasm for work. However, I still had my bungalow at Carmel and, more important, my old negatives of Chinatown. The latter were saved in a curious manner. Before returning to New York, Will Irwin had come to my studio, and looking through my Chinatown pictures remarked, "You really ought not to keep these plates and films here. Some day the whole city will burn up. There'll never be another Chinatown like this one, and you have its only picture record." I heeded his warning, giving all the negatives into the keeping of a friend who had put them into his vault. They were not damaged in the fire.

Among the many telegrams I received was one from Edward Sothern and Julia Marlowe. "Now that you have lost everything," it read, "you should come to New York. We will see that you find a fully equipped studio waiting for you, so that you can start work without delay." It was heartening and consoling to have this fine proof of real friendship. The temptation was great, but I was not willing to leave San Francisco then. I wanted to stay, to see the new city which would rise out of the ruins. I felt that my place was there. I had something to contribute, even if only in a small measure, to the rebuilding of the city. I started my search for a new studio. It would take years before the business section would be rebuilt. No one knew exactly just where the new center of the city was to be. Location was unimportant. On Clay Street, not far from the gates of the Presidio, I discovered a picturesque one-story cottage. In its small garden was a fine old scrub-oak, and I believe it was this and not so much the house that made me decide to take a five-year lease. My friends encouraged me. "Don't worry about being so far out. We'll come anyway, no matter where you are. The chief thing is for you to have a place that you like and where you feel you can work." And so I started to make a few structural changes and to get together the necessary equipment that would enable me to continue my work as a portrait photographer.

ARNOLD GENTHE'S 1906 EARTHQUAKE AND FIRE NEGATIVES

Considerations and Decisions in the Production of Exhibition Prints

VICTORIA BINDER AND BARRET OLIVER

Making prints from historical photographic negatives brings with it myriad technical and conceptual challenges, and the process of producing new exhibition-quality prints from Arnold Genthe's cellulose nitrate earthquake and fire negatives at the Fine Arts Museums was no exception. The final exhibition-quality prints are the result of numerous carefully determined technical decisions arrived at through a collaborative effort by the Museums' works-on-paper curatorial and conservation team and the photographic printmaker.[1]

INTERPRETING THE NEGATIVES

Genthe's earthquake and fire negatives display numerous technical elements, defects, and damages that complicate both our interpretation of them and our understanding of the photographer's intentions. When looking at Genthe's negatives, it is often difficult to distinguish between the types of photographic artifacts present and determine at what point in the negative's life-span they occurred. Some technical artifacts, like the frames of the negatives, are relatively straightforward.[2] The light leaks and wavy edges potentially came about when Genthe was taking pictures in the field, while the negatives' unevenly cut edges likely occurred during processing. However, artifacts like stains, scratches, and punctures fall into more ambiguous territory; they may be the result of Genthe's processing the negatives in less than ideal circumstances or of chemical aging and the physical handling of the negatives over time.

Another factor affecting our interpretation of the negatives is the varying range of exposures found in them.[3] Although Genthe was a practiced photographer with substantial experience using a hand camera and roll film, he (and other photographers of his time) faced many challenges when it came to exposure. In 1906 flexible gelatin roll film was still relatively new, and there was no guarantee that the products one purchased had been manufactured consistently. Adding to this, in the early twentieth century, there was no reliable system to calculate exposures; exposure times were usually arrived at through experience or trial and error. Unlike the "wet" plate process of previous decades and today's digital capturing of images, the technology during Genthe's time did not allow him to check whether the exposures were adequate upon capture.[4] Although it was possible to adjust and bring out some details in the darkroom, exposure in that environment was less than ideal.

GENTHE'S ARCHIVES AND EXISTING PRINTS

Sifting through a photographer's archives or consulting their original prints can introduce new variables to the process of interpreting their work. Genthe's photographs and negatives are found at art institutions across the United States, with the largest collection residing at the Library of Congress, in Washington, D.C., which acquired the majority of its works from Genthe's New York studio upon his death in 1942.[5] Although Genthe predominantly printed gelatin silver prints, his archives reveal that he used vastly different materials and techniques with this media, evidenced in his prints' range of textures, sheens, tones, and sizes. Genthe was also known to make serious alterations to his images. This is particularly apparent in his Chinatown photographs, in which he dramatically cropped the images, intentionally obscured details such as people and signs, and darkened parts of the overall image for dramatic effect.

Perhaps the factor that most complicates the process of interpretation is Genthe's stylistically diverse range of prints. This diversity reflects the fact that he was in fact several different types of photographer at once: he was a consummate professional producing high-quality portraits of celebrities and socialites, an artist creating works that reflect the Pictorialist aesthetics of the time, and a documentary street photographer. Genthe printed very few of his earthquake photographs close to the time of the 1906 event. The earliest known finished prints made by Genthe are a set of twenty-four gelatin silver photographs housed at the Bancroft Library, at the University of California, Berkeley. Although Genthe printed a small number of gelatin silver prints from his earthquake and fire negatives in varying sizes, tones, and sheens throughout his career, it is difficult to determine whether those prints were made soon after the earthquake or at a later date in his life.

Technical Choices

With these many variables in mind, the curatorial and conservation team at the Fine Arts Museums began the process of determining the parameters for the new exhibition prints, including choosing the type of media, size, tone, sheen, and degree of alteration, as well as which negatives to reproduce. The team's main objective was to produce exhibition prints that reflected Genthe's existing body of work while bringing out details and making as few alterations as possible.

In 2016 high-resolution scans were made of the negatives with minimal alterations and slight adjustments in tone.[6] These scans performed several functions: they provided a record of the negatives' condition at that current point in time, captured never-before-seen details, and served as a template from which the exhibition prints could be made.

Media

One of the team's primary decisions involved choosing which media on which to print the images from the high-resolution scans. The team considered both the relatively new media of digital inkjet prints and the traditional format of gelatin silver prints. Although recent advancements in inkjet technology and substrates make it possible to produce prints that resemble traditional photography, such prints often possess an element of crispness and regularity not found in traditionally printed photographs. This distinction reflects the fact that inkjet prints are produced through a more or less direct process in which data from the digital image file is sent to the printer. In contrast, gelatin silver prints are made through a multistep physical process that involves numerous variables, including paper, exposure, and development, which combine to produce qualities unique to the technique. For this reason the team decided to create gelatin silver prints, recruiting the expertise of master photographic printer Barret Oliver. The subsequent deliberations were made through a dynamic collaboration between the museum team and Oliver.

When determining the size, tone, and sheen of the new prints, the team consulted both the early set of Genthe's earthquake and fire prints at the Bancroft Library and the Chinatown prints in the collection of the Fine Arts Museums. The prints at the Bancroft are relatively small in size (averaging nine by six inches) and exhibit matte surfaces and subtle warm tones. The Museums' Chinatown prints are larger in format (averaging thirteen by nine inches). The tones in the Chinatown prints range from cool blacks to warm sepias, while the sheens range from low to high gloss.

Size

When deciding on the size of the new prints, a priority was ensuring that the details and textures of everyday life in turn-of-the-century San Francisco, especially after this major disaster, were as legible as possible. During Genthe's time, photographs were often printed rather small (as with the Bancroft's prints), and as a result, images' finer details were often obscured. For this reason, the team chose to emulate the approximate size of the Chinatown prints. To exploit the size of the 16-by-20-inch photographic paper, they chose a maximum dimension of 15½ inches. The decision to produce larger prints for this exhibition meant that more detailed information about the lives and surroundings of the earthquake survivors, including Genthe, would be discernible.

Tone and Sheen

To determine the tone and sheen of the photographic paper, the curatorial and conservation team once again looked to the prints housed at the Bancroft Library and to the Chinatown prints in the Museums' collection. They settled on a warm tone that resembled the Bancroft's prints but also reflected some of the cooler tones exhibited in the Chinatown prints. For the sheen, the team opted for a low-gloss surface, again striking a balance between the Bancroft's prints and the Museums' Chinatown prints.

Preserving Technical Artifacts and Defects

The numerous technical artifacts and defects in Genthe's prints, as well as the photographer's tendency to manipulate images during the darkroom and printing process, make it impossible to predict his final vision. For this reason, the team decided to keep alterations to a minimum, with only slight adjustments made to gray values. The team also opted to preserve the artifacts found in the negatives, which offer clues to their life-spans and to Genthe's process.[7]

Choosing Images to Print

Of the 155 negatives, the curators decided to reproduce 88 exhibition prints. The selection was based on the small number of earthquake and fire negatives that Genthe had chosen to print during his lifetime. The curators also selected images that were visually striking and best represented Genthe's aesthetic choices. Other images were selected for their success in depicting the full experience of the earthquake and its aftermath—the fires and rubble, the tent encampments and relief stations, the rhythms of daily life, and the eventual reconstruction.

Making the Exhibition Prints

Producing the exhibition gelatin silver prints involved several steps: selecting a photographic paper, creating digital negatives, and contact printing in the darkroom. Each element was interdependent on the others, with the printer making adjustments throughout and testing materials and procedure to bring out the most detail from individual images.

Gelatin silver photographic papers are composed of three layers: paper, baryta, and an emulsion of gelatin and light-sensitive silver compounds.[8] When the photographic paper is exposed to light through the negative, using either an enlarger or by contact printing, the light-sensitive silver compounds form a latent, or invisible, image. It is through the process of development that the exposed silver compounds are transformed into metallic silver particles forming a visible image. Subsequent fixing of the photographic paper removes the remaining unformed silver compounds. A final bath in water removes the fixing agent.

Photo Paper

Finding the perfect photographic paper for the new prints was one of the most challenging parts of the process. The specific material used to make photographic prints, in particular the silver compounds, has a decided, though almost imperceptible, effect on the way we read them. The term "black-and-white," when referring to photographs, is actually a misnomer. Real chemically produced photographs almost never have black shadows and white highlights. Rather, the image is often slightly colored due to the nature of the silver compounds. This can be difficult to detect, but it affects the mood of the picture. At the beginning of the twentieth century, the tone of the printing papers in common use was what is now described as a "warm" tone, tending toward brown. These types of papers are now all but gone from commercial production. Luckily Oliver was able to find one gelatin silver photographic paper manufactured in the Czech Republic that was close in tone to the early twentieth-century papers.[9]

Creating a Digital Negative

The negative is essentially a template from which multiple prints can be made. The prints can vary greatly from the original negative through manipulation in the darkroom. As Genthe's cellulose nitrate negatives of the 1906 earthquake and fire are part of the Museums' collection, important carriers of information, and artifacts of the earthquake themselves, it was not appropriate to make prints directly from the negatives. For this reason, Oliver produced digital negatives from the high-resolution scans. Negatives from the early twentieth-century exhibit denser gray values, particularly in the shadows. Using Photoshop, Oliver made slight adjustments to the images' density to bring out details in the mid-tones and shadows. The negatives were printed full size on a transparent polyester film using an Epson inkjet printer.[10]

Darkroom Techniques

Oliver tailored the darkroom process to the photographic paper, making adjustments in exposure and chemical formulas to achieve the most detail and desired tone. The photographic paper was exposed by means of contact printing, which involves the digital negative being placed in direct contact with the paper. Using standard, off-the-shelf chemistry for development did not give the desired rich tones and details. Using historic technical literature, Oliver created his own formulas for the developer, with the primary chemical being hydroquinone, which yields warm tones but is slow to develop. For this reason, he made adjustments to the entire system to achieve the desired results.

Conclusion

The question remains: Why make real chemical prints when digital printers are capable of such amazing detail and fidelity? Every technical system produces artifacts that are unique to it. Those artifacts are often invisible to us, especially when we are familiar with these systems, or when we might think they are better ("closer to the truth") than those that came before. Digital printing produces a print with an entirely different feel because the materials are different.[11] Chemical printing resulted in a reasonable approximation of what Genthe might have produced, allowing viewers to imagine how it might have felt to see these photographs in Genthe's own studio.

CATALOGUE CHECKLIST

NOTE TO THE READER

Unless otherwise noted, all works are untitled cellulose nitrate negatives made by Arnold Genthe (American, b. Germany, 1869–1942) in 1906 and are in the collection of the Fine Arts Museums of San Francisco, Museum purchase, James D. Phelan Bequest Fund.

FIRE AND SMOKE

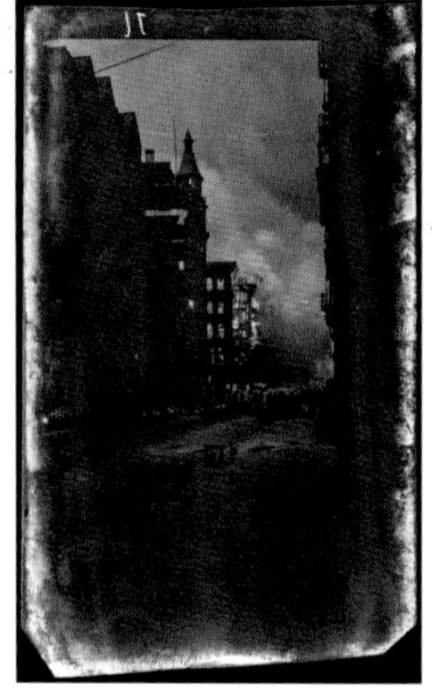

1. Bush near Montgomery looking east toward Sansome, San Francisco, 5 ¾ × 3 7/16 in. (146 × 87 mm), irreg. Digital preservation of the negative sponsored by Daniel Woodhead III, 1943.407.125 (pl. 1)

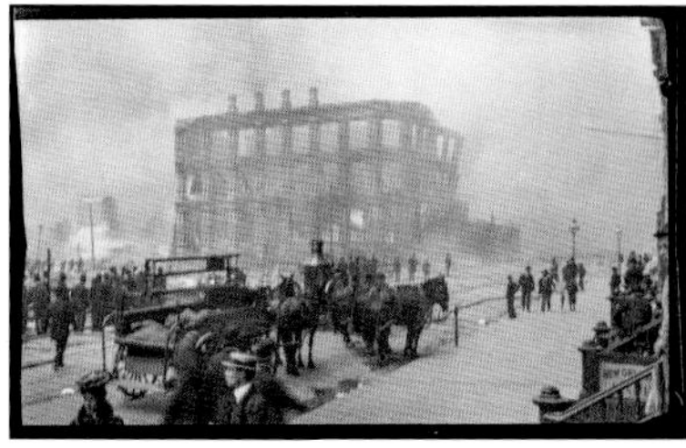

2. Friedlander Block, northeast corner California and Sansome, San Francisco, 3 ⅜ × 5 7/16 in. (86 × 138 mm), irreg. Digital preservation of the negative sponsored by Irene M. Dobbins, 1943.407.157 (pl. 2)

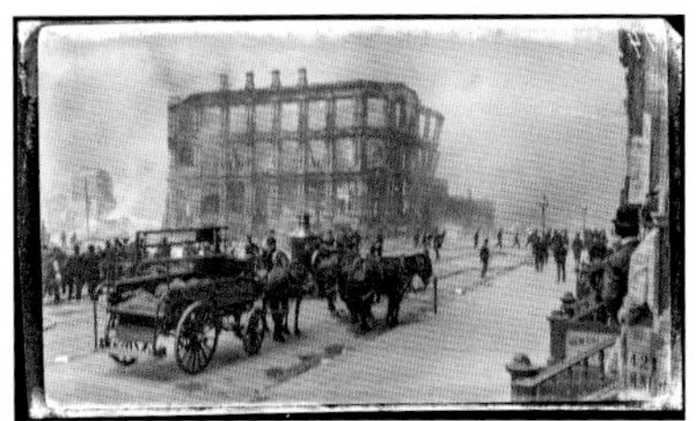

3. Friedlander Block, northeast corner California and Sansome, San Francisco, 3 5/16 × 5 ¾ in. (84 × 146 mm), irreg. Digital preservation of the negative sponsored by Karen and Malcolm Whyte, 1943.407.28 (pl. 3)

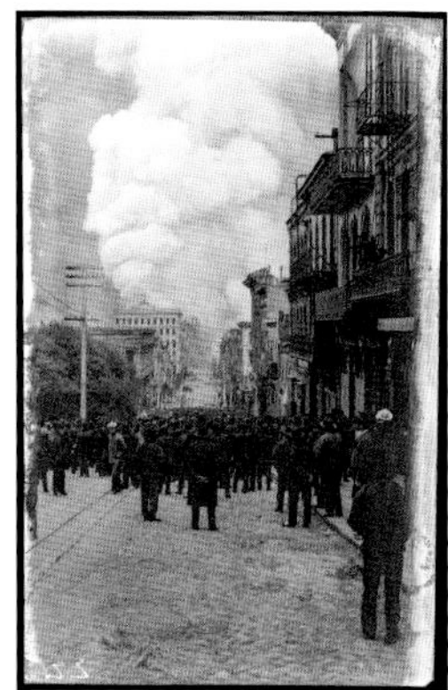

4. Clay east of Dupont (Grant), San Francisco, 5 ¼ × 3 7/16 in. (133 × 87 mm), irreg. Digital preservation of the negative sponsored by Alan Selsor, 1943.407.44 (pl. 4)

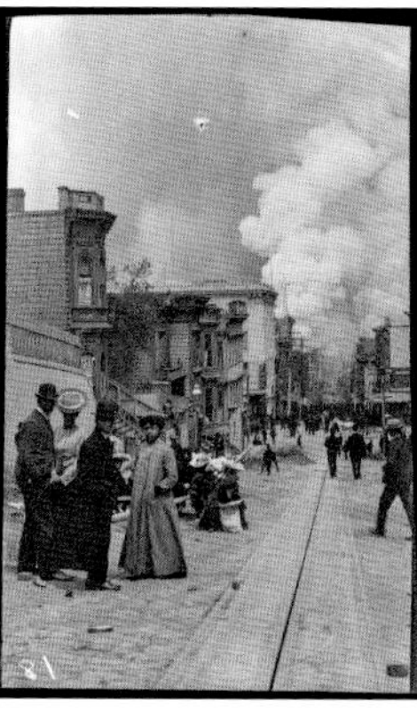

5. Clay west of Stockton, San Francisco, 5 3/16 × 3 5/16 in. (132 × 84 mm), irreg. Digital preservation of the negative sponsored by Mary Jo Gordon and Patrick Dowd, 1943.407.36 (pl. 5)

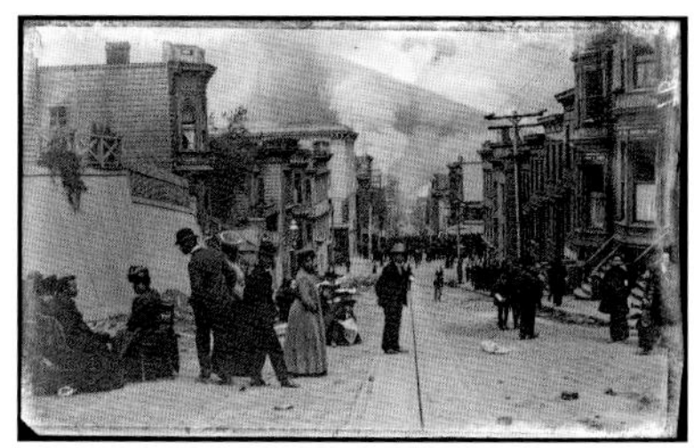

6. Clay west of Stockton, San Francisco, 3 ⅜ × 5 7/16 in. (86 × 138 mm), irreg. Digital preservation of the negative sponsored by Michael and Joyce Axelrod, 1943.407.19 (pl. 6)

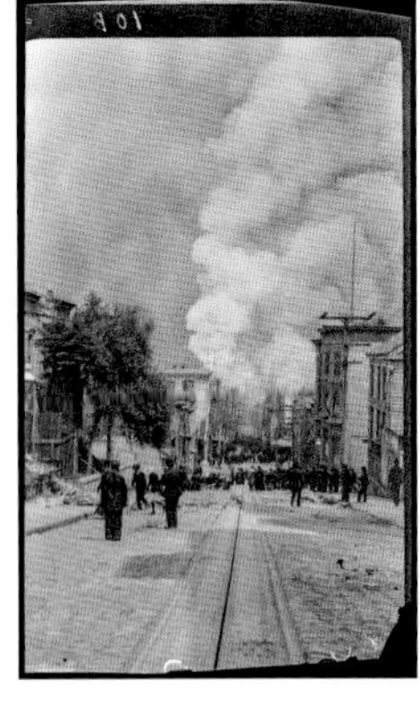

7. Clay west of Stockton, San Francisco, 5 9/16 × 3 5/16 in. (141 × 84 mm), irreg. Digital preservation of the negative sponsored by Elizabeth D. Moyer, PhD and Michael C. Powanda, PhD, 1943.407.22.1 (pl. 7)

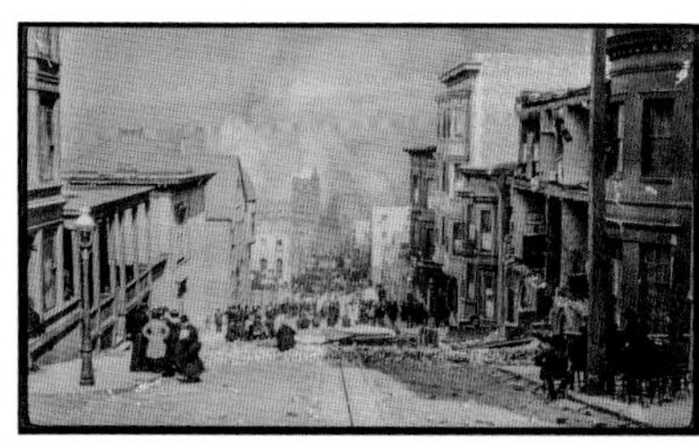

8. Downtown from Sacramento just east of Powell, San Francisco, 3 ⅛ × 5 9/16 in. (79 × 141 mm), irreg. Digital preservation of the negative sponsored by Lucy Young Hamilton, 1943.407.3 (pl. 8)

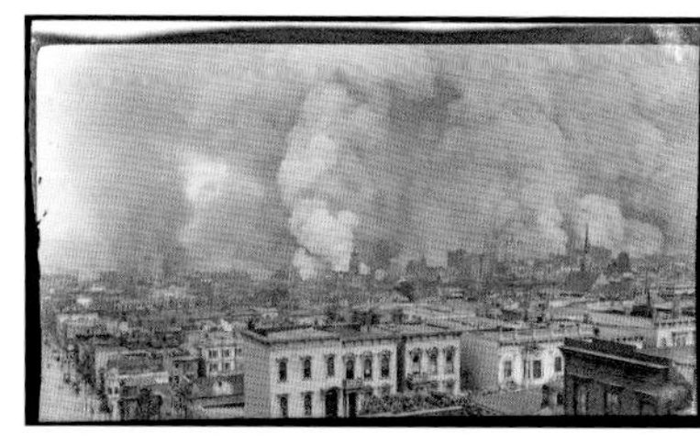

9. View of the burning city from Broadway west of Taylor, San Francisco, 3 ⅛ × 5 7/16 in. (79 × 138 mm), irreg. Digital preservation of the negative sponsored by Guillermo Rettally and John Garvin, 1943.407.42 (pl. 9)

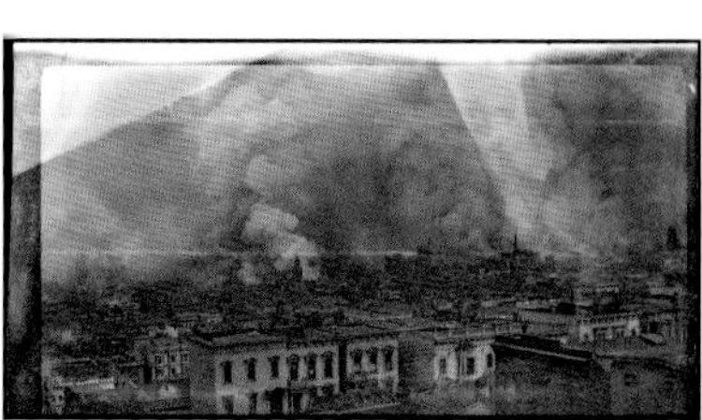

10. View of the burning city from Broadway west of Taylor, San Francisco, 3 1/16 × 5 13/16 in. (78 × 148 mm), irreg. Digital preservation of the negative sponsored by Morten Steen Hansen, 1943.407.163

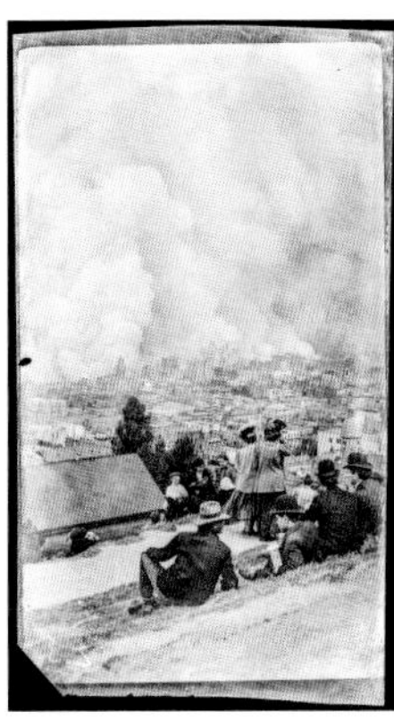

11. Ina Coolbrith Park, Vallejo and Taylor, San Francisco, 5 3/4 × 3 3/8 in. (146 × 86 mm), irreg. Digital preservation of the negative sponsored by Jim and Elaine Kohn, 1943.407.47 (pl. 10)

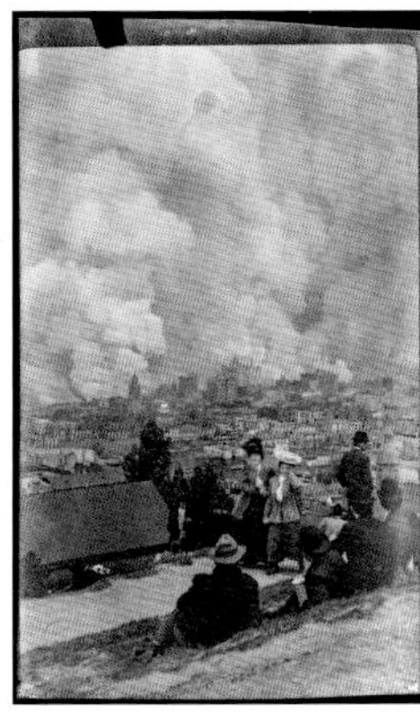

12. Ina Coolbrith Park, Vallejo and Taylor, San Francisco, 5 1/4 × 3 1/4 in. (133 × 83 mm), irreg. Digital preservation of the negative sponsored by Rayna Bernard, 1943.407.23.1 (pl. 11)

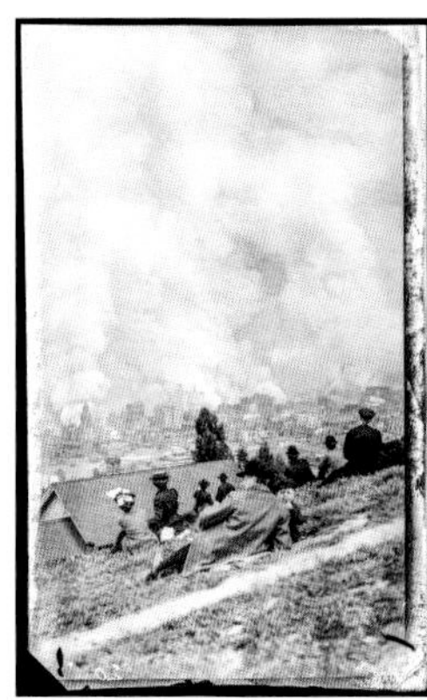

13. Ina Coolbrith Park, Vallejo and Taylor, San Francisco, 5 1/2 × 3 7/16 in. (140 × 87 mm), irreg. Digital preservation of the negative sponsored by Jack and Margrit Vanderryn, 1943.407.40 (pl. 12)

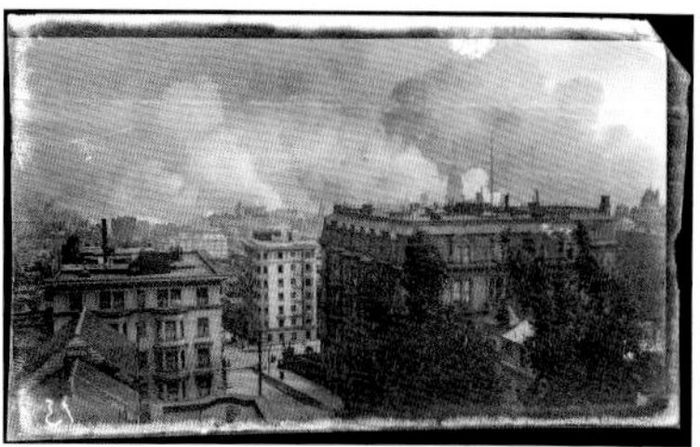

14. View from the Tobin mansion, California and Taylor, San Francisco, 3 5/16 × 5 7/16 in. (84 × 138 mm), irreg. Digital preservation of the negative sponsored by Michelle L. Wilson, 1943.407.26 (pl. 13)

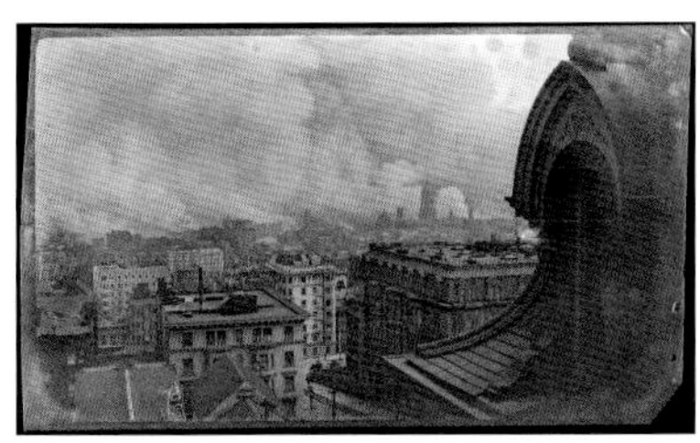

15. View from the Tobin mansion, California and Taylor, San Francisco, 3 3/8 × 5 3/4 in. (86 × 146 mm), irreg. Digital preservation of the negative sponsored by Charles and Norma Schlossman, 1943.407.30 (pl. 14)

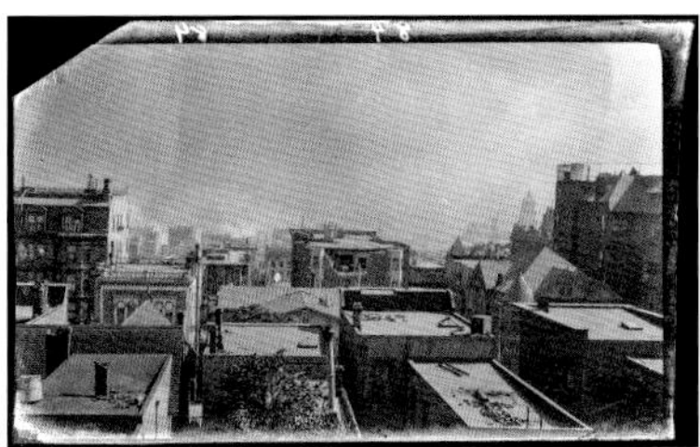

16. View south from the Sherwood mansion, California between Taylor and Jones, San Francisco, 3 7/16 × 5 5/8 in. (87 × 143 mm), irreg. Digital preservation of the negative sponsored by Janet King and Stephen Yeatman, 1943.407.139 (pl. 15)

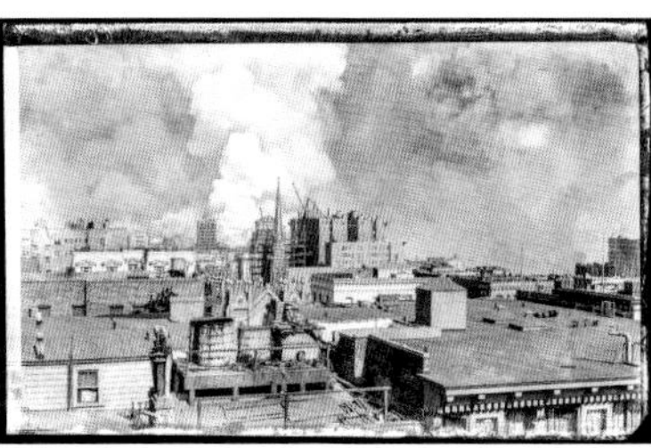

17. View downtown from Hotel Pleasanton, Sutter and Jones, San Francisco, 3 3/8 × 5 1/2 in. (86 × 140 mm), irreg. Digital preservation of the negative sponsored by Daniel Woodhead III, 1943.407.21.1 (pl. 16)

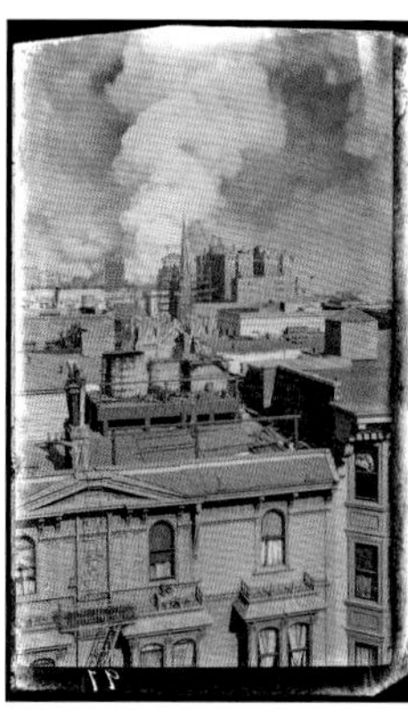

18. View downtown from Hotel Pleasanton, Sutter and Jones, San Francisco, 5 1/2 × 3 7/16 in. (140 × 87 mm), irreg. Digital preservation of the negative sponsored by Karen and Malcolm Whyte, 1943.407.153 (pl. 17)

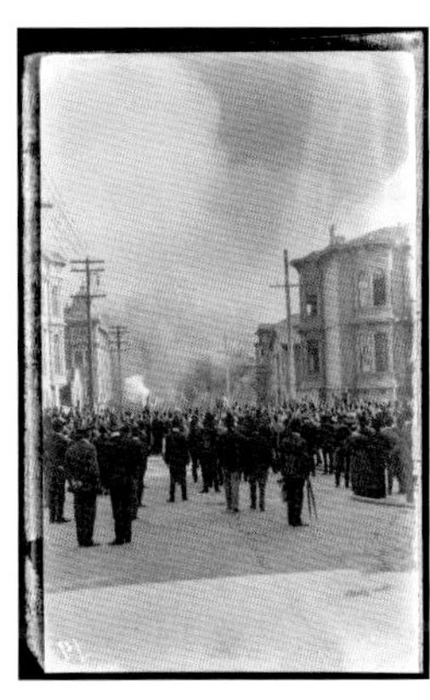

19. Franklin and McAllister, San Francisco, 5 5/16 × 3 7/16 in. (135 × 87 mm), irreg. Digital preservation of the negative sponsored by Elizabeth D. Moyer, PhD and Michael C. Powanda, PhD, 1943.407.38 (pl. 18)

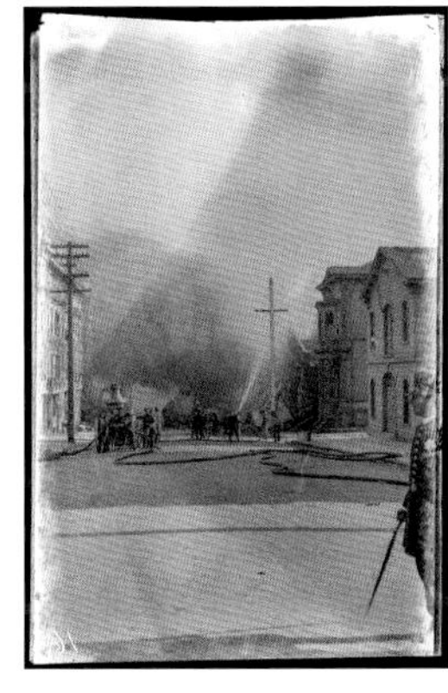

20. Franklin and McAllister, San Francisco, 5 1/8 × 3 5/16 in. (130 × 84 mm), irreg. Digital preservation of the negative sponsored by Karin and David Chamberlain, 1943.407.32 (pl. 19)

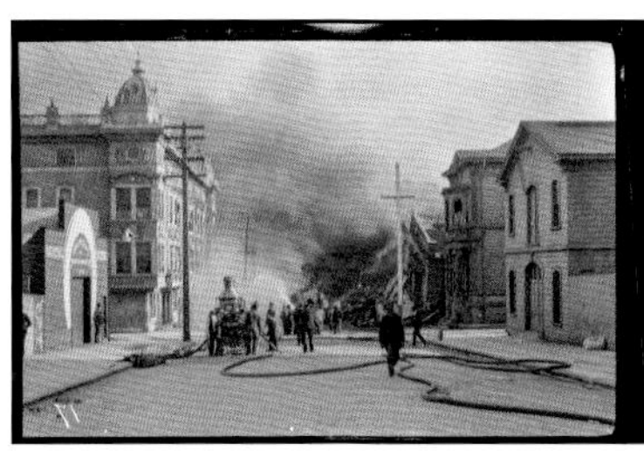

21. Franklin and McAllister, San Francisco, 3 3/8 × 5 5/16 in. (86 × 135 mm), irreg. Digital preservation of the negative sponsored by the San Francisco Auxiliary of the Fine Arts Museums of San Francisco, 1943.407.34.1 (pl. 20)

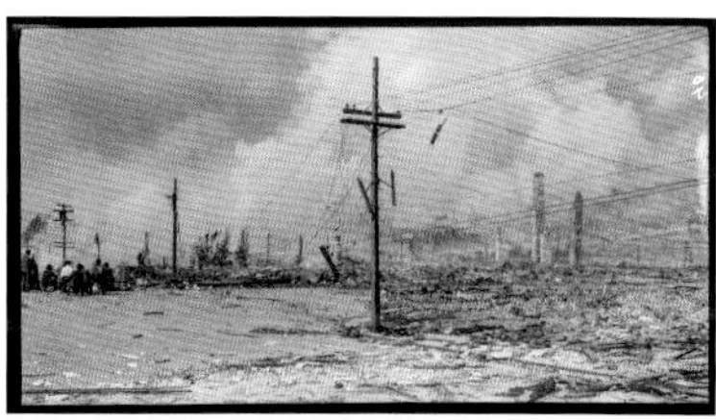

22. Van Ness and Pacific, San Francisco, 2 15/16 × 5 5/8 in. (75 × 143 mm), irreg. Digital preservation of the negative sponsored by the Schauble Family, 1943.407.76.1 (pl. 21)

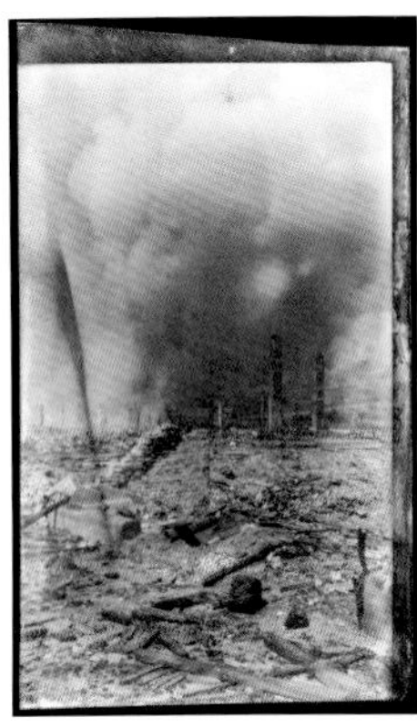

23. Van Ness and Pacific, San Francisco, $5\frac{9}{16} \times 3\frac{1}{4}$ in. (141 × 83 mm), irreg.
Digital preservation of the negative sponsored by Leslie and Diane Lynch, 1943.407.131 (pl. 22)

EARTHQUAKE DAMAGE

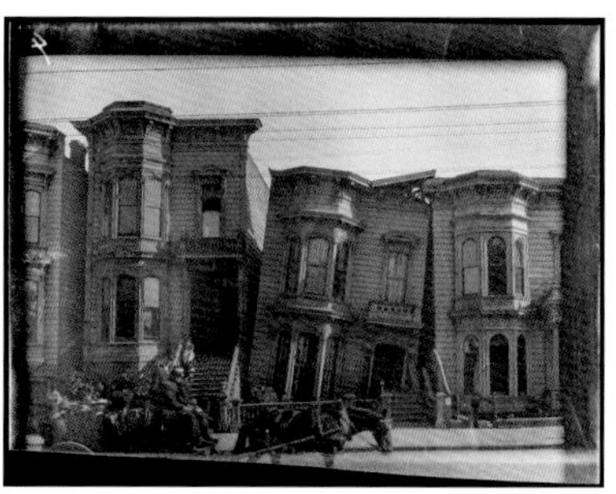

24. Golden Gate and Gough, San Francisco, $3\frac{1}{4} \times 4\frac{5}{16}$ in. (83 × 110 mm), irreg.
Digital preservation of the negative sponsored by Ann Jennings and Robert Polacchi, 1943.407.12 (pl. 23)

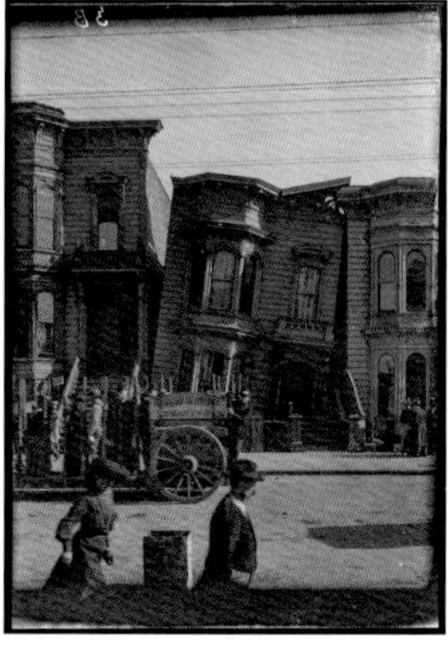

25. Golden Gate and Gough, San Francisco, $4\frac{5}{16} \times 3\frac{1}{16}$ in. (110 × 78 mm), irreg.
Digital preservation of the negative sponsored by Michael and Joyce Axelrod, 1943.407.11.1 (pl. 24)

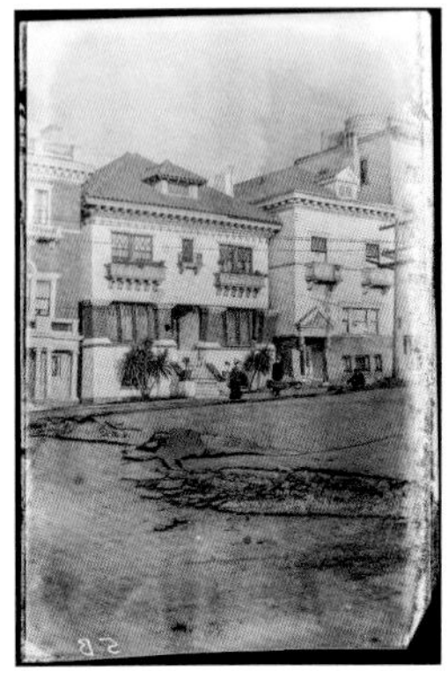

26. Musto house, Van Ness Avenue, San Francisco, $5 \times 3\frac{5}{16}$ in. (127 × 84 mm), irreg.
Digital preservation of the negative sponsored by Jane R. Lurie, 1943.407.15

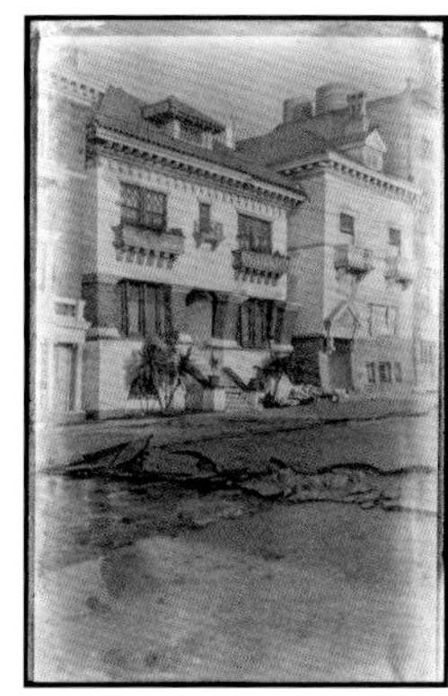

27. Musto house, Van Ness Avenue, San Francisco, $5\frac{1}{16} \times 3\frac{5}{16}$ in. (129 × 84 mm), irreg.
Digital preservation of the negative sponsored by an anonymous donor, 1943.407.10

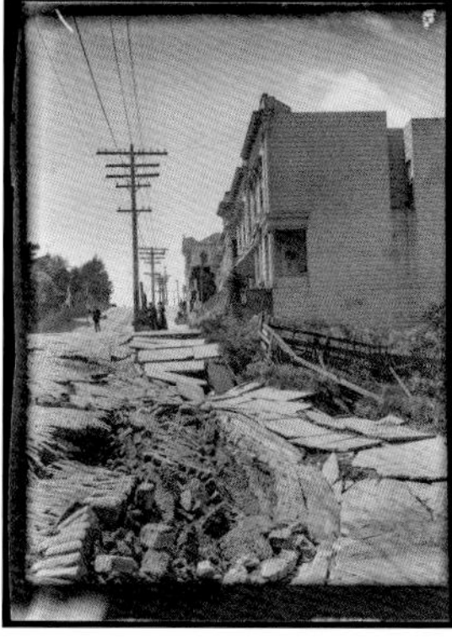

28. Union west of Steiner, San Francisco, $4\frac{5}{16} \times 3\frac{1}{8}$ in. (110 × 79 mm), irreg.
Digital preservation of the negative sponsored by Peggy and Tim Brown, 1943.407.6.1 (pl. 25)

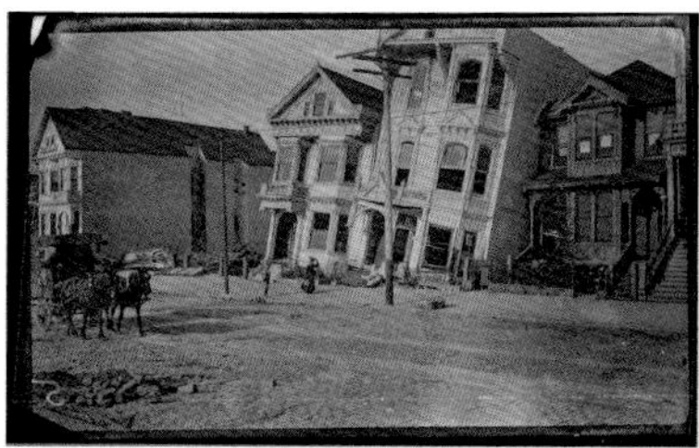

29. Howard [now South Van Ness] near 18th Street, San Francisco, $3\frac{7}{16} \times 5\frac{5}{8}$ in. (87 × 143 mm), irreg.
Digital preservation of the negative sponsored by Lucy Young Hamilton, 1943.407.14 (pl. 26)

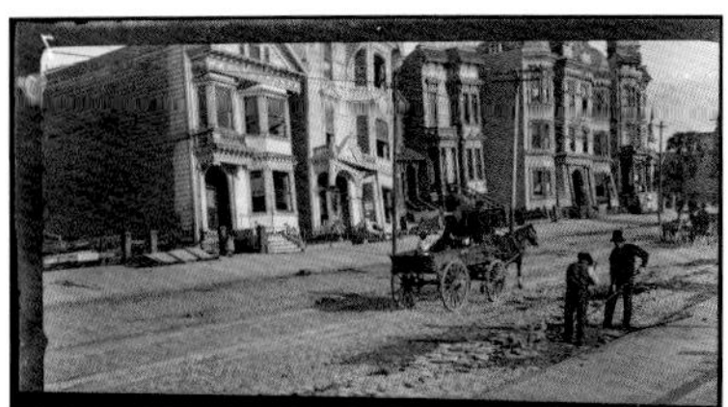

30. Howard [now South Van Ness] near 18th Street, San Francisco, $3 \times 5\frac{5}{8}$ in. (76 × 143 mm), irreg.
Digital preservation of the negative sponsored by Andrew C. McLaughlin III and Carrick C. McLaughlin, 1943.407.18 (pl. 27)

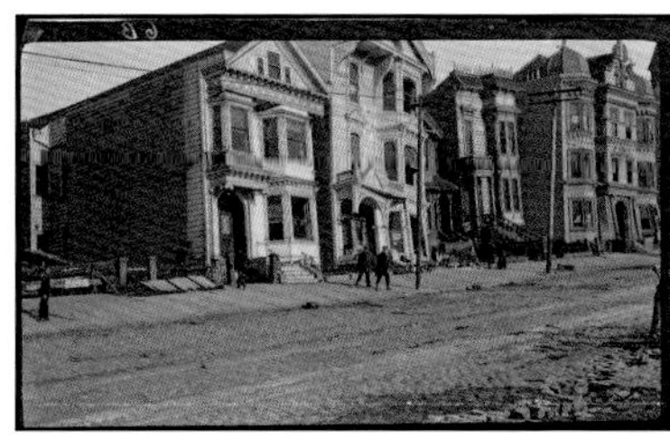

31. Howard [now South Van Ness] near 18th Street, San Francisco, $3\frac{5}{16} \times 5\frac{5}{8}$ in. (84 × 143 mm), irreg.
Digital preservation of the negative sponsored by John A. Musante, 1943.407.17

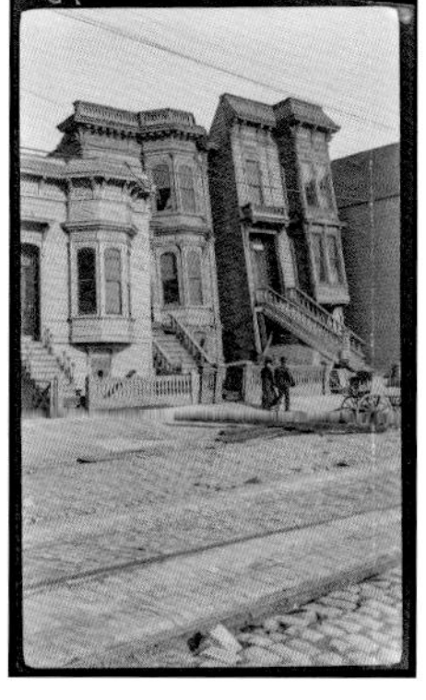

32. Howard between 17th and 18th Streets, San Francisco, $5\frac{3}{4} \times 3\frac{3}{8}$ in. (146 × 86 mm), irreg.
Digital preservation of the negative sponsored by Charles S. Pyle, 1943.407.13

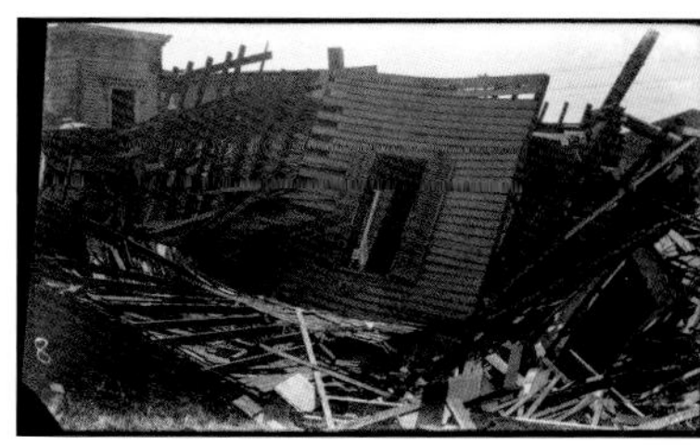

33. Collapsed wooden plank houses, San Francisco, $3\frac{1}{4} \times 5\frac{1}{2}$ in. (83 × 140 mm), irreg.
1943.407.20

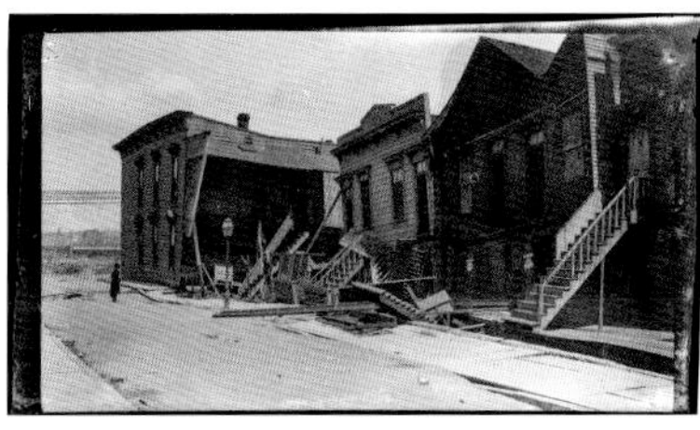

34. Dore between Bryant and Brannan, San Francisco, 3 5/16 × 5 13/16 in. (84 × 148 mm), irreg. 1943.407.8

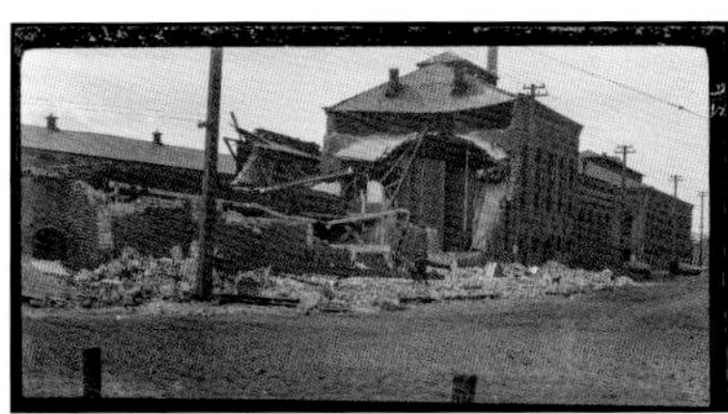

35. San Francisco Gas and Electric Company, North Beach Station, Bay and Fillmore, San Francisco, 2 5/16 × 5 5/8 in. (59 × 143 mm), irreg. Digital preservation of the negative sponsored by Margaret and Tom Vinson, 1943.407.9

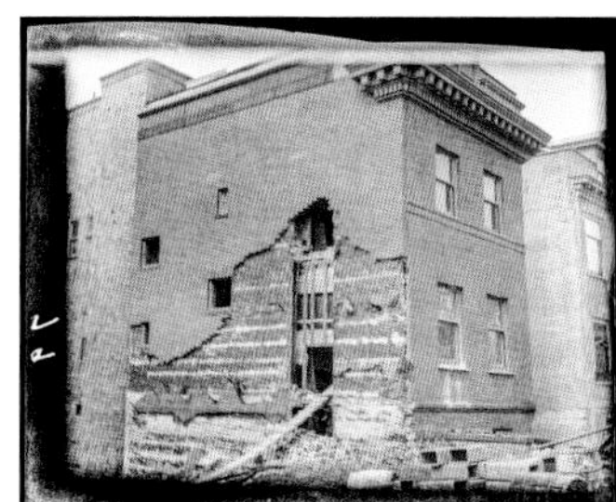

36. Collapsed exterior wall on the side of a large brick building, San Francisco, 3 5/16 × 4 3/16 in. (84 × 106 mm), irreg. 1943.407.133

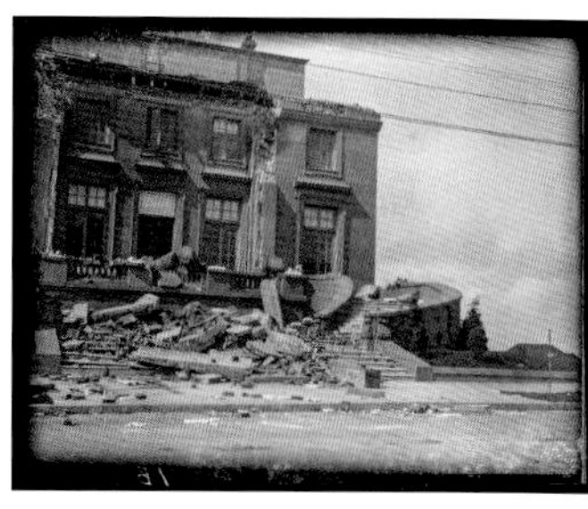

37. Koshland House, Washington and Maple, San Francisco, 3 3/16 × 4 in. (81 × 102 mm), irreg. 1943.407.7

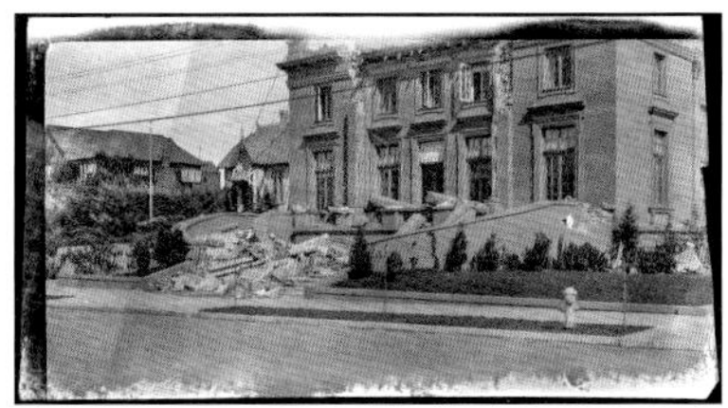

38. Koshland House, Washington and Maple, San Francisco, 3 × 5 9/16 in. (76 × 141 mm), irreg. Digital preservation of the negative sponsored by Karin and David Chamberlain, 1943.407.16

FIRE RUINS

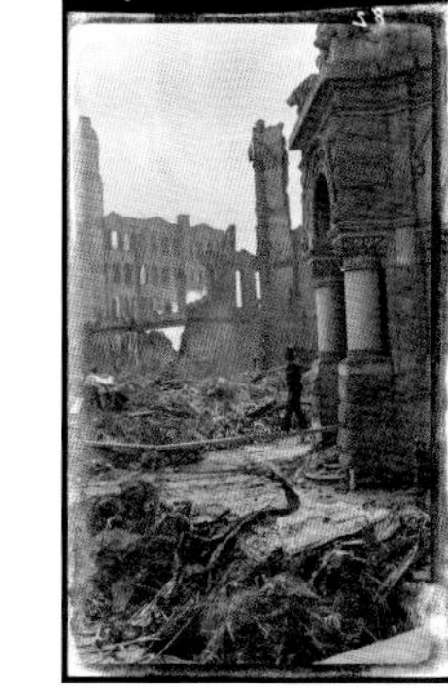

39. First National Bank, Bush and Sansome, San Francisco, 5 3/4 × 3 7/16 in. (146 × 87 mm), irreg. Digital preservation of the negative sponsored by the San Francisco Auxiliary of the Fine Arts Museums of San Francisco, 1943.407.137 (pl. 28)

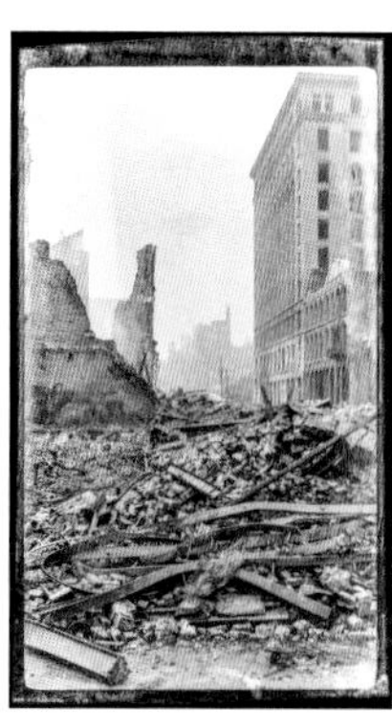

40. Mills Building from Bush and Sansome, San Francisco, 5 3/4 × 3 7/16 in. (146 × 87 mm), irreg. Digital preservation of the negative sponsored by Matthew Silverberg, 1943.407.53 (pl. 29)

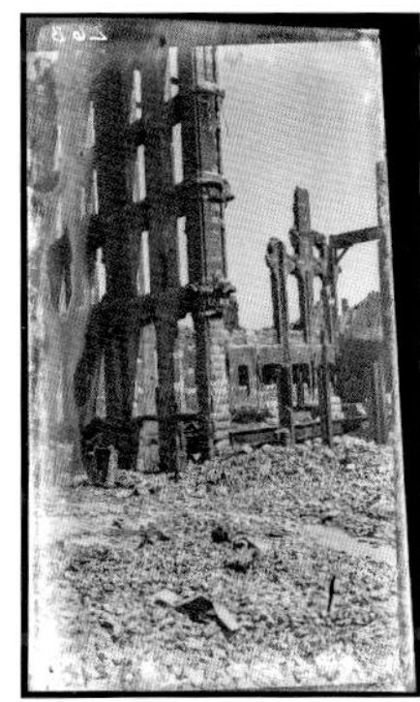

41. The Stock and Bond Exchange, California and Sansome, San Francisco, 5 11/16 × 3 3/8 in. (144 × 86 mm), irreg. Digital preservation of the negative sponsored by A. Crawford Cooley, 1943.407.54 (pl. 30)

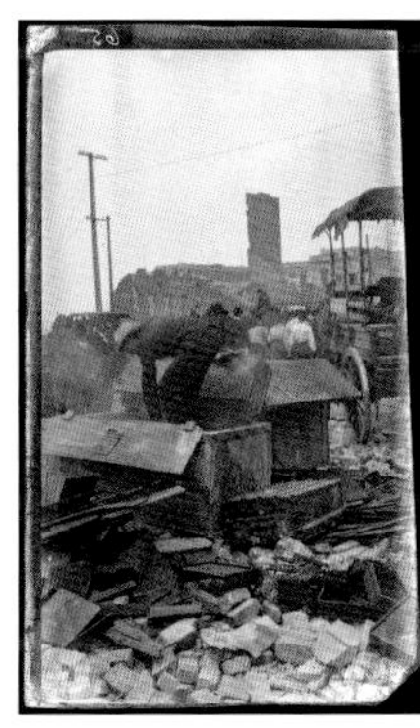

42. Stevenson near 7th Street, San Francisco, 5 11/16 × 3 3/8 in. (144 × 86 mm), irreg. Digital preservation of the negative sponsored in memory of Cynthia Kelly, 1943.407.121 (pl. 31)

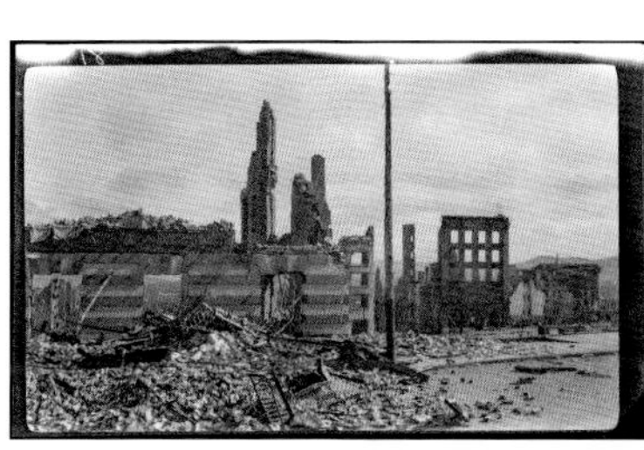

43. Southwest corner Bush and Taylor, San Francisco, 3 7/16 × 5 13/16 in. (87 × 148 mm), irreg. Digital preservation of the negative sponsored by Sandra and Paul Bessières, 1943.407.135 (pl. 32)

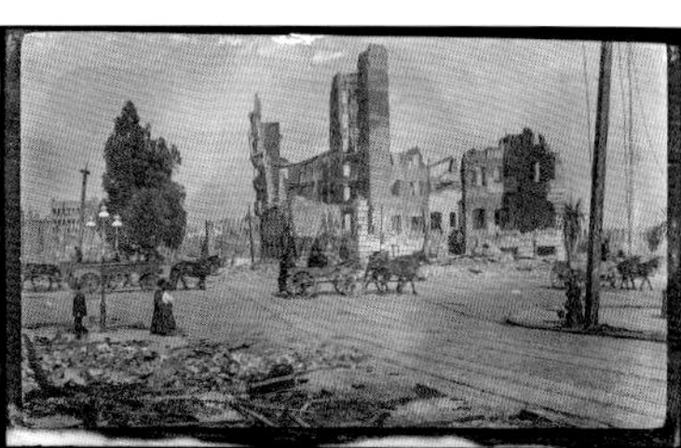

44. St. Dunstan Hotel, Van Ness and Sutter, San Francisco, 3 3/8 × 5 3/4 in. (86 × 146 mm), irreg. Digital preservation of the negative sponsored by Anne M. Zucchi, 1943.407.128.1 (pl. 33)

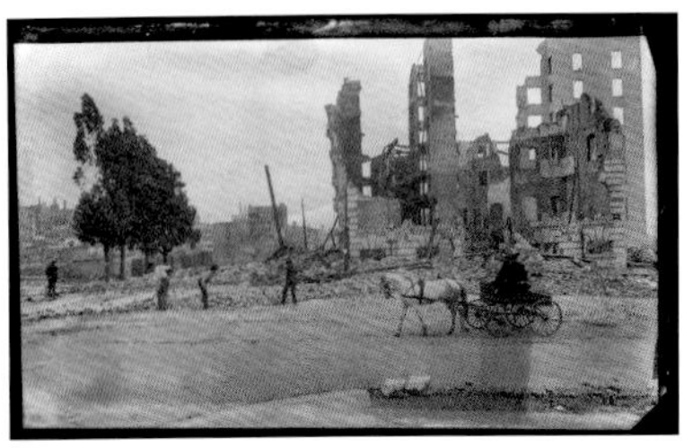

45. St. Dunstan Hotel, Van Ness and Sutter, San Francisco, 3 ⅜ × 5 ½ in. (86 × 140 mm), irreg. Digital preservation of the negative sponsored by Karen A. Levine and Mark Nigara, 1943.407.1

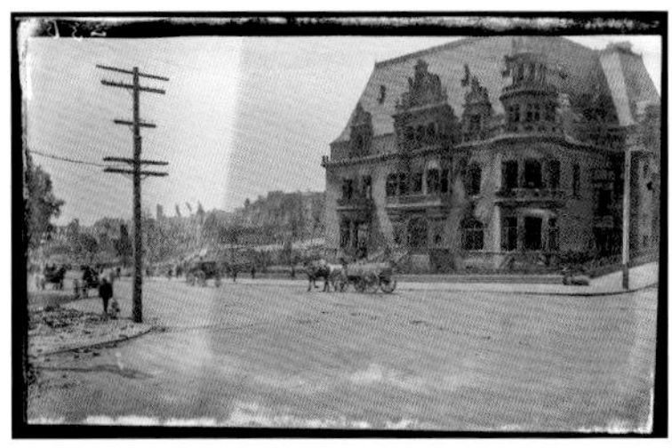

46. Spreckels mansion, Van Ness and Clay, San Francisco, 3 7⁄16 × 5 ½ in. (87 × 140 mm), irreg. Digital preservation of the negative sponsored by Edith H. Bergstrom, 1943.407.48 (pl. 34)

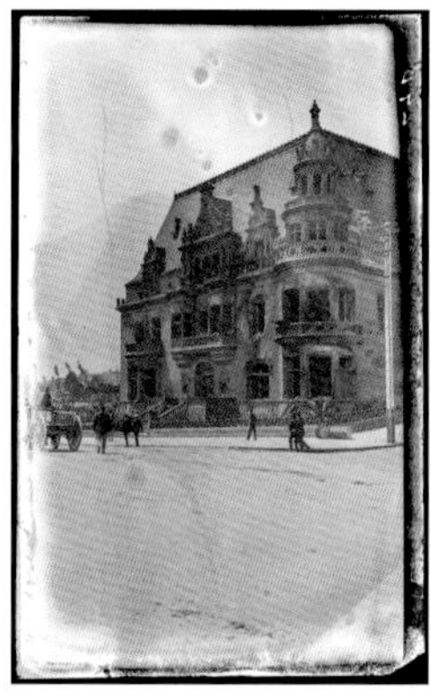

47. Spreckels mansion, Van Ness and Clay, San Francisco, 5 7⁄16 × 3 7⁄16 in. (138 × 87 mm), irreg. Digital preservation of the negative sponsored by Lynda Tunney, 1943.407.50

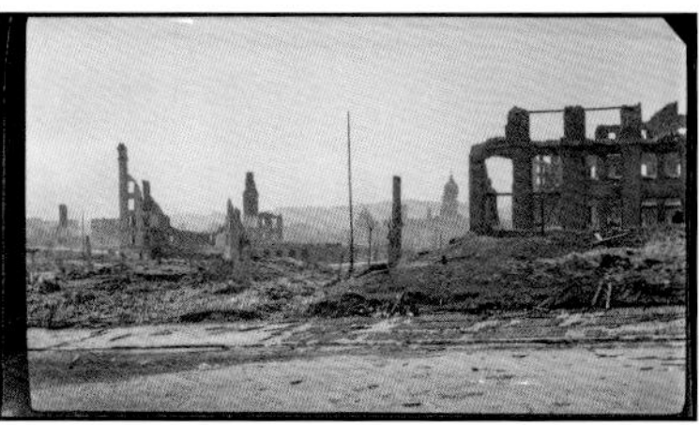

48. City Hall from Pine east of Van Ness, San Francisco, 3 3⁄16 × 5 11⁄16 in. (81 × 144 mm), irreg. Digital preservation of the negative sponsored by Cathie Hehman, 1943.407.161

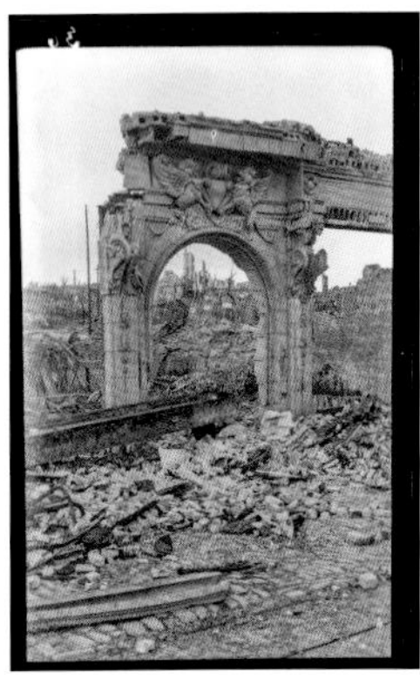

49. Sequoia Hotel, Geary and Hyde, San Francisco, 5 5⁄16 × 3 ⅜ in. (135 × 86 mm), irreg. Digital preservation of the negative sponsored by Constance Yu, 1943.407.71.1

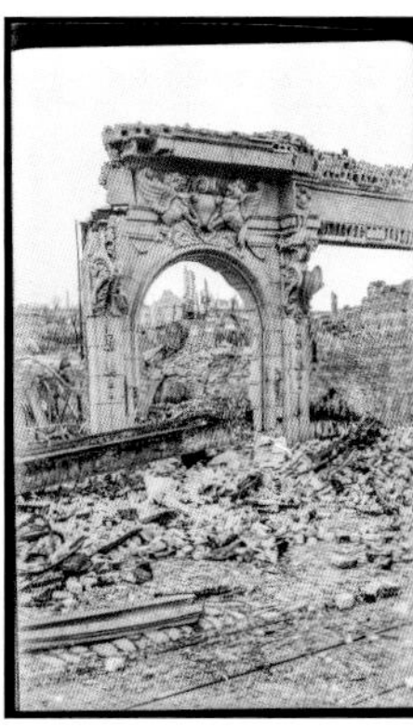

50. Sequoia Hotel, Geary and Hyde, San Francisco, 5 ¼ × 3 3⁄16 in. (133 × 81 mm), irreg. Digital preservation of the negative sponsored by Lawrence Banka and Judith Gordon, 1943.407.72 (pl. 35)

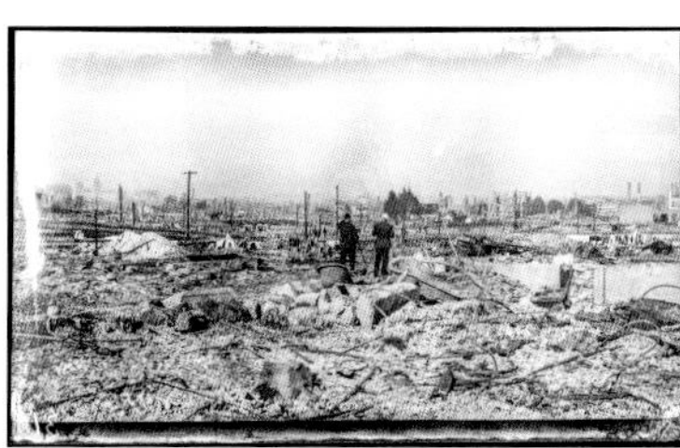

51. Two men pose while looking at the general scene of ruin after the earthquake and fire, South of Market, San Francisco, 3 ¼ × 5 ½ in. (83 × 140 mm), irreg. Digital preservation of the negative sponsored by Ann M. Dawson, 1943.407.63 (pl. 36)

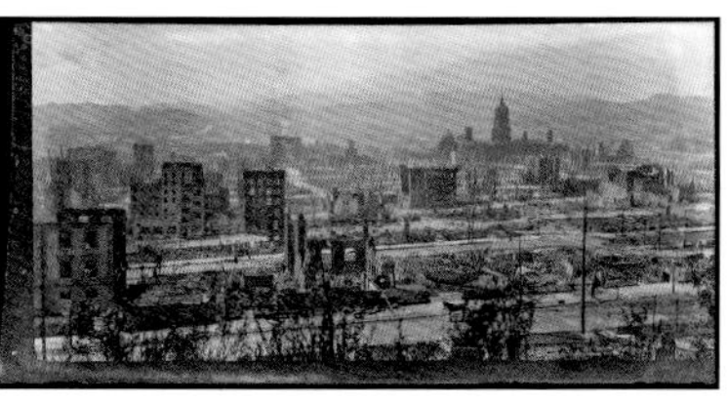

52. City Hall from California between Jones and Taylor, San Francisco, 2 13⁄16 × 5 ¾ in. (71 × 146 mm), irreg. Digital preservation of the negative sponsored by Jane R. Lurie, 1943.407.126.1 (pl. 37)

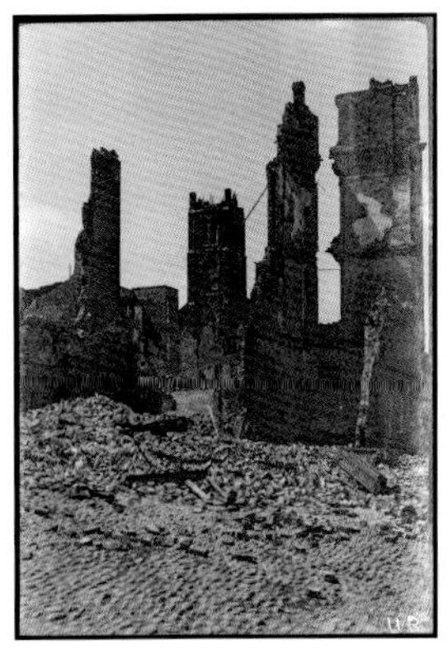

53. St. Mary's Church, Grant and California, San Francisco, 4 ⅝ × 3 ¼ in. (117 × 83 mm), irreg. Digital preservation of the negative sponsored by Jane R. Lurie, 1943.407.24

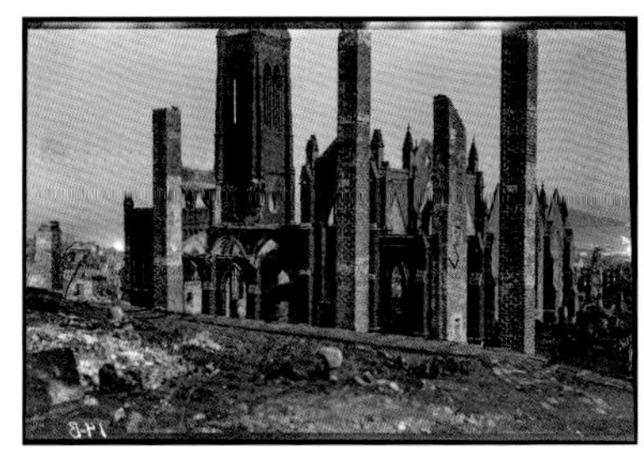

54. Grace Church, California and Stockton, San Francisco, 3 5⁄16 × 5 1⁄16 in. (84 × 129 mm), irreg. Digital preservation of the negative sponsored by Heather Marx and Steve Zavattero, 1943.407.29.1 (pl. 38)

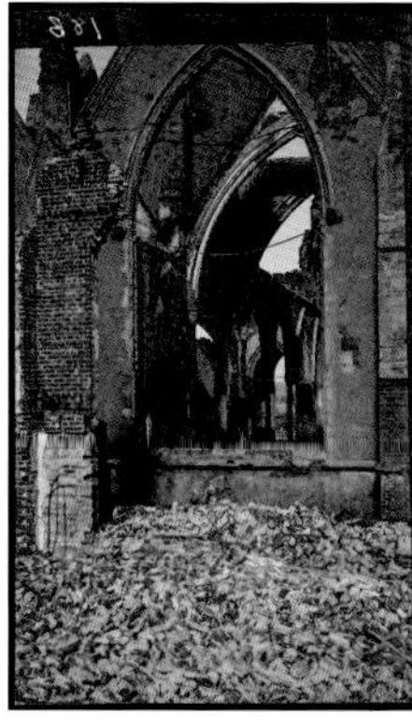

55. Grace Church, California and Stockton, San Francisco, 5 5⁄16 × 3 ¼ in. (135 × 83 mm), irreg. Digital preservation of the negative sponsored by Elizabeth D. Moyer, PhD and Michael C. Powanda, PhD, 1943.407.41.1 (pl. 39)

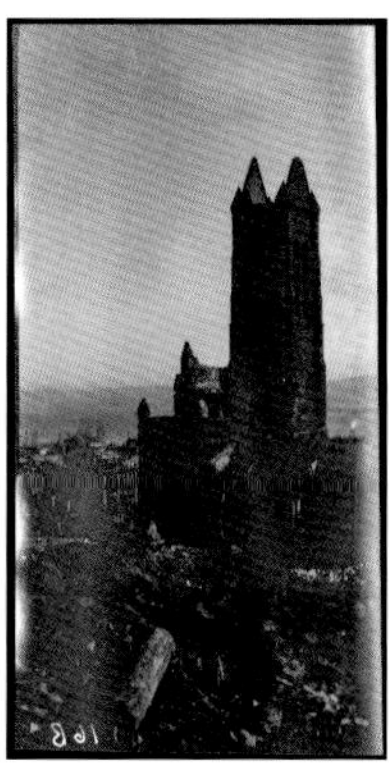

56. Grace Church, California and Stockton, San Francisco, 4 15⁄16 × 2 9⁄16 in. (125 × 65 mm), irreg. 1943.407.33

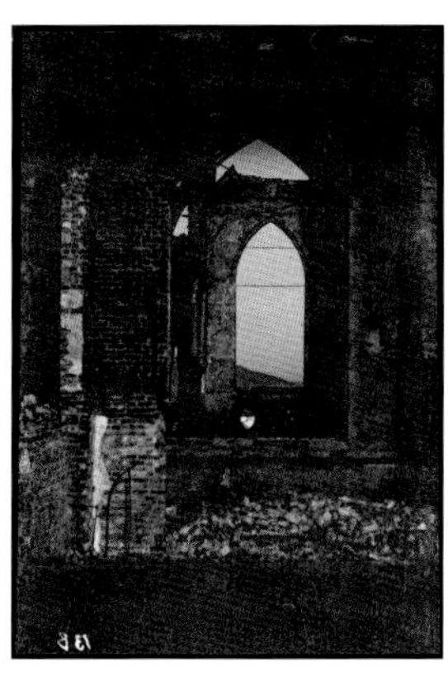

57. Grace Church, California and Stockton, San Francisco, 4 15/16 × 3 7/16 in. (125 × 87 mm), irreg. 1943.407.27

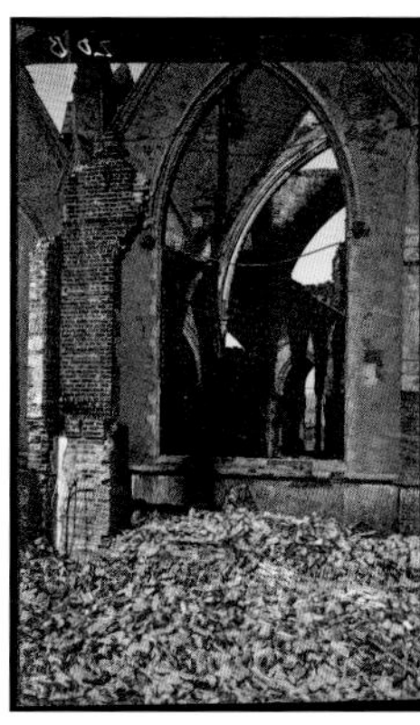

58. Grace Church, California and Stockton, San Francisco, 5 3/8 × 3 1/4 in. (137 × 83 mm), irreg. 1943.407.37

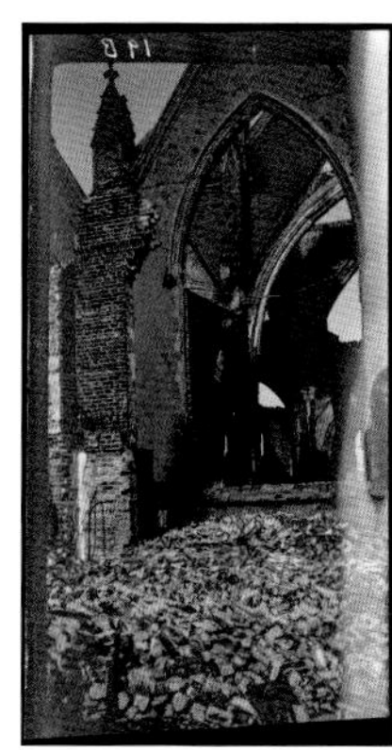

59. Grace Church, California and Stockton, San Francisco, 5 5/16 × 2 7/8 in. (135 × 73 mm), irreg. 1943.407.39

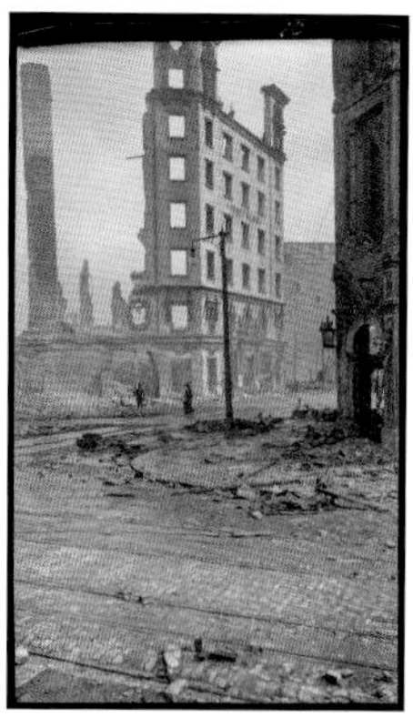

60. Hearst Building, Market and Third Streets, San Francisco, 5 5/16 × 3 1/16 in. (135 × 78 mm), irreg. Digital preservation of the negative sponsored by Julia Dolby-Frist, 1943.407.158.1 (pl. 40)

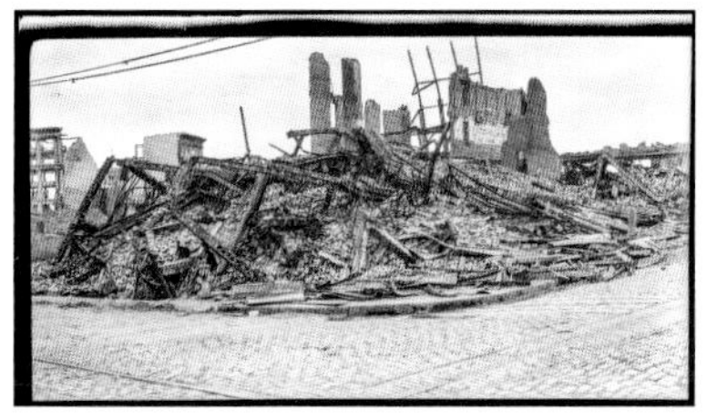

61. Linda Vista Apartments, Turk and Jones, San Francisco, 3 1/16 × 5 1/2 in. (78 × 140 mm), irreg. Digital preservation of the negative sponsored by Mary N. Lannin, 1943.407.162 (pl. 41)

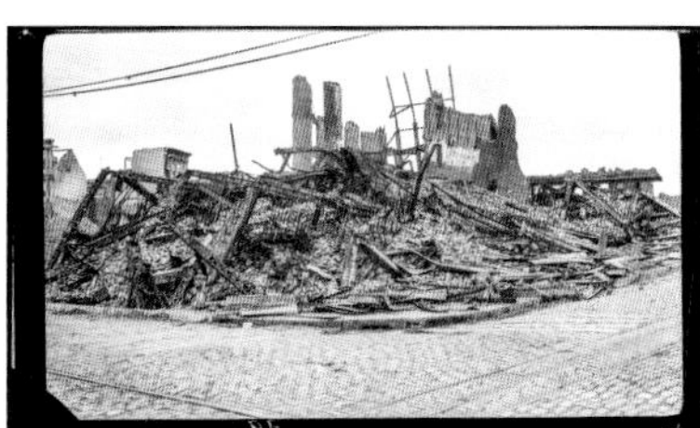

62. Linda Vista Apartments, Turk and Jones, San Francisco, 3 7/16 × 5 7/8 in. (87 × 149 mm), irreg. Digital preservation of the negative sponsored by an anonymous donor, 1943.407.155

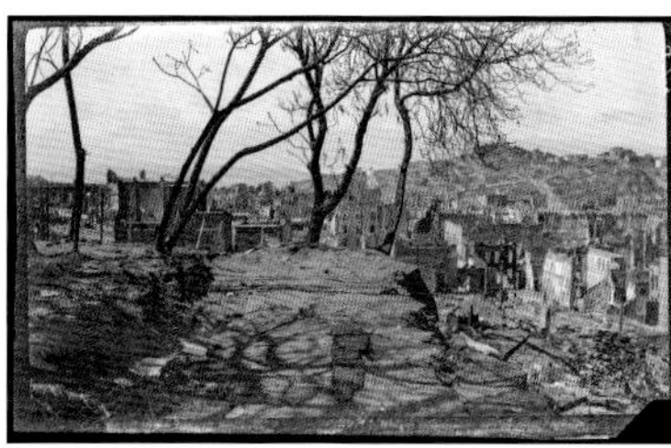

63. Telegraph Hill from Nob Hill, San Francisco, 3 3/8 × 5 11/16 in. (86 × 144 mm), irreg. Digital preservation of the negative sponsored by Elizabeth D. Moyer, PhD and Michael C. Powanda, PhD, 1943.407.45.1 (pl. 42)

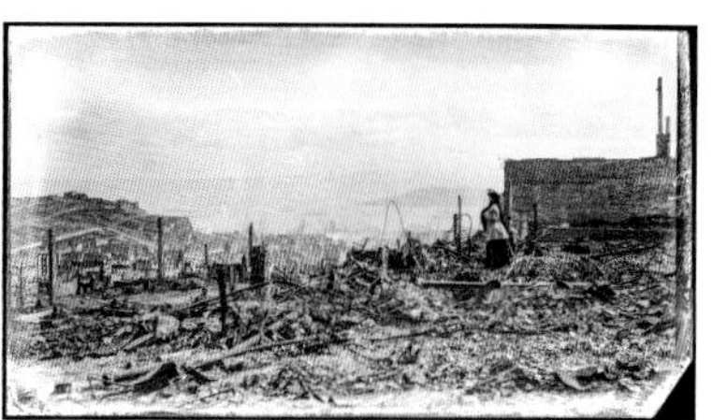

64. Woman views devastated city from Nob Hill, San Francisco, 3 1/16 × 5 5/8 in. (78 × 143 mm), irreg. Digital preservation of the negative sponsored by Daniel F. Donovan and Giacinto A. Jondonovan, 1943.407.136 (pl. 43)

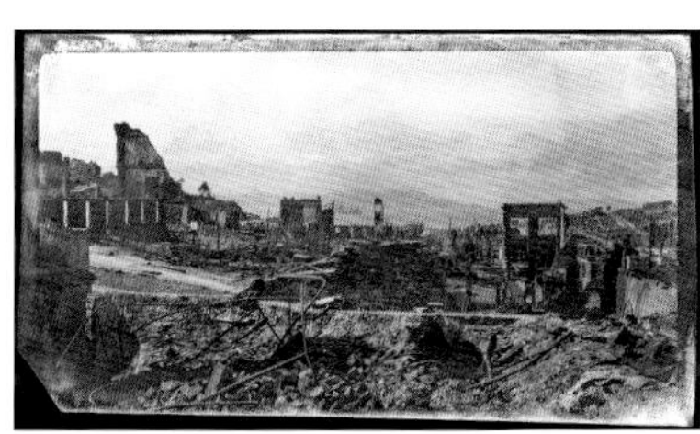

65. View north from California between Powell and Stockton, San Francisco, 3 1/4 × 5 13/16 in. (83 × 148 mm), irreg. Digital preservation of the negative sponsored by Dave Himmelblau, 1943.407.59

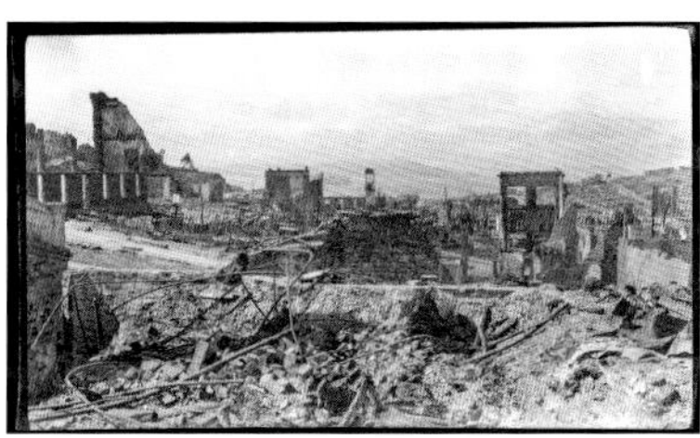

66. View north from California between Powell and Stockton, San Francisco, 3 1/4 × 5 5/8 in. (83 × 143 mm), irreg. Digital preservation of the negative sponsored by Judy and Bob Leet, 1943.407.67

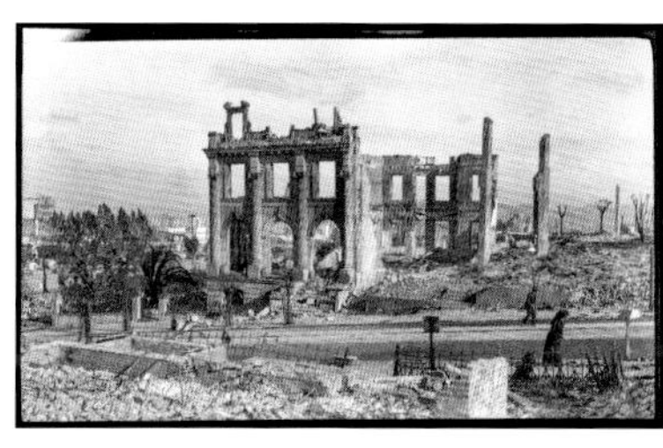

67. J. Zenón Posadas mansion, Sacramento between Van Ness and Franklin, San Francisco, 3 1/4 × 5 1/2 in. (83 × 140 mm), irreg. Digital preservation of the negative sponsored by Sylvia G. Ross, 1943.407.69.1 (pl. 44)

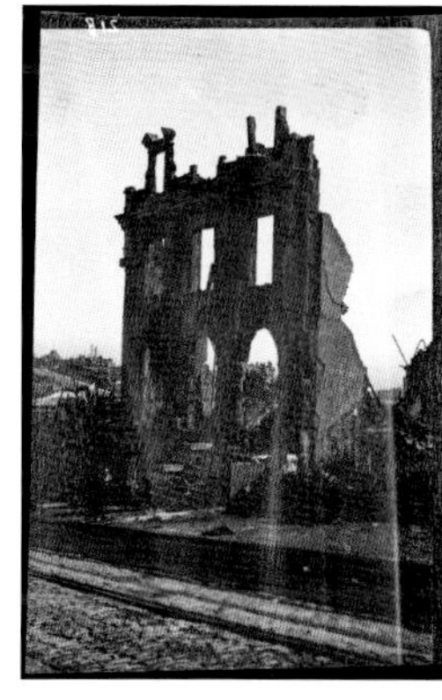

68. J. Zenón Posadas mansion, Sacramento between Van Ness and Franklin, San Francisco, 4 7/8 × 3 3/16 in. (124 × 81 mm), irreg. 1943.407.43

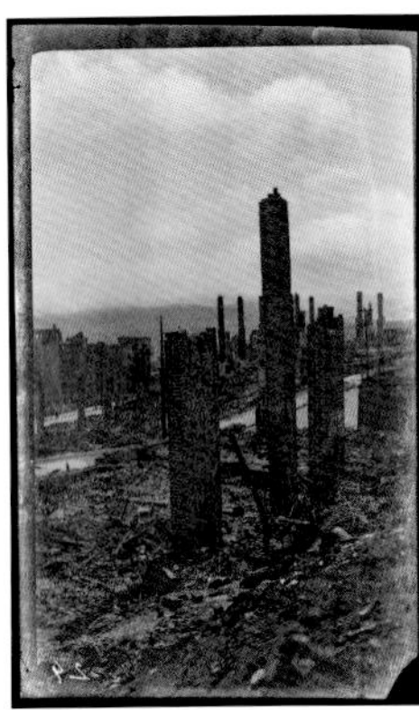

69. Northeast corner of Powell and Pine, San Francisco, 5 9/16 × 3 7/16 in. (141 × 87 mm), irreg. Digital preservation of the negative sponsored by Karin and David Chamberlain, 1943.407.49

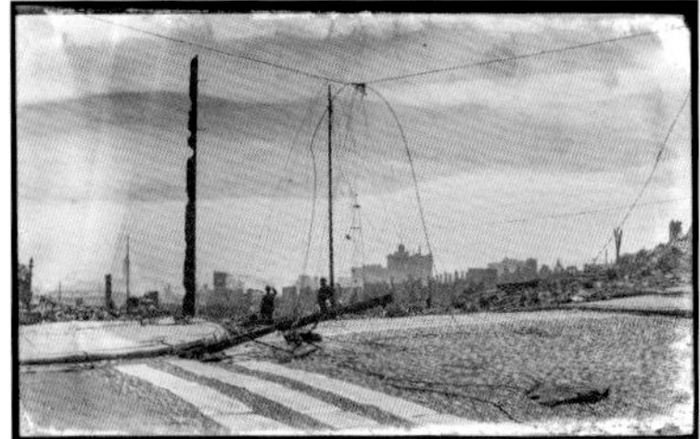

70. Jackson looking east from Nob Hill, San Francisco, 3 5/16 × 5 5/16 in. (84 × 135 mm), irreg. Digital preservation of the negative sponsored in memory of Cynthia Kelly, 1943.407.129 (pl. 45)

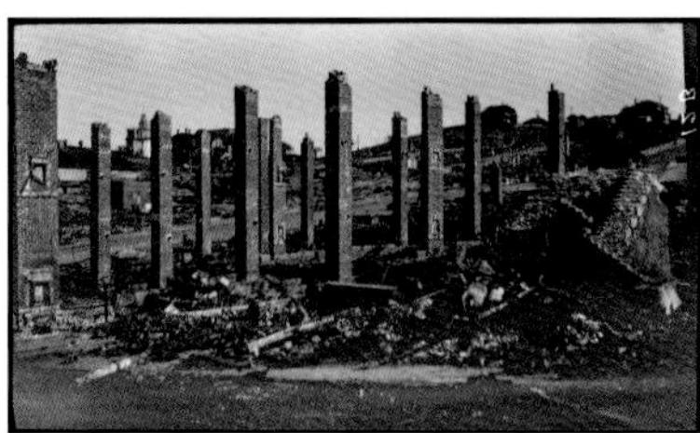

71. Broadway and Leavenworth, San Francisco, 3 3/16 × 5 1/2 in. (81 × 140 mm), irreg. 1943.407.25.1

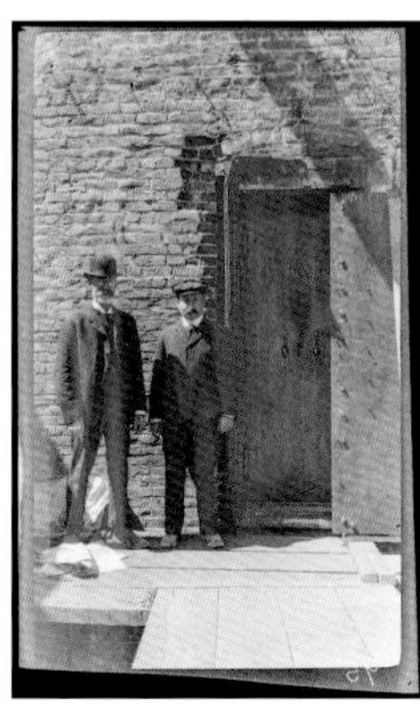

72. Wells Fargo Nevada National Bank vault, Pine and Montgomery, San Francisco, 5 11/16 × 3 1/2 in. (144 × 89 mm), irreg. 1943.407.151

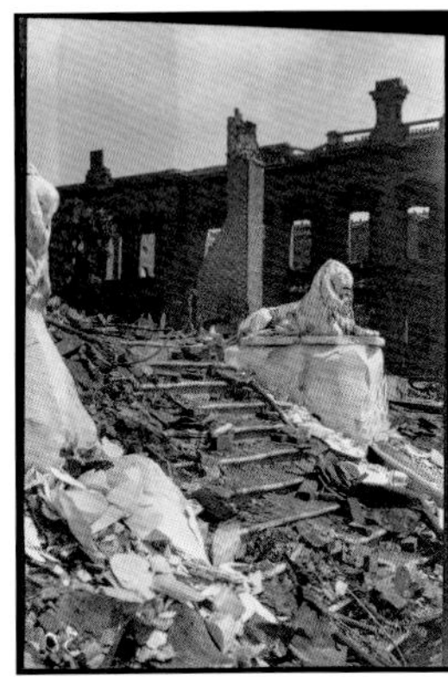

73. Huntington mansion, California and Taylor, San Francisco, 4 7/8 × 3 5/16 in. (124 × 84 mm), irreg. Digital preservation of the negative sponsored by Ken Becker and Nancy Luter, 1943.407.61 (pl. 46)

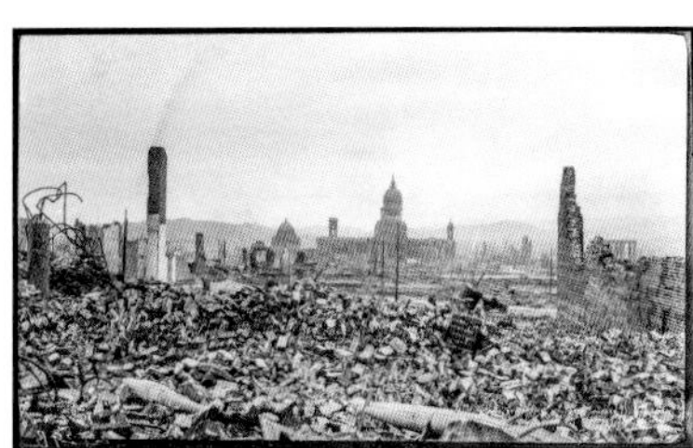

74. O'Farrell between Larkin and Hyde, San Francisco, 3 1/4 × 5 9/16 in. (83 × 141 mm), irreg. Digital preservation of the negative sponsored by Jack and Margrit Vanderryn, 1943.407.60

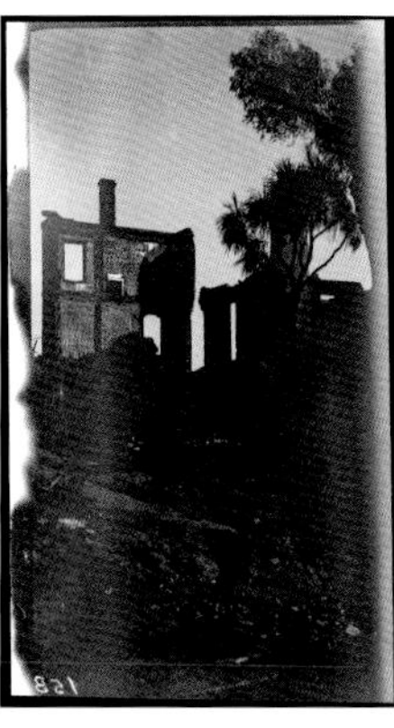

75. Ruins on a hill, San Francisco, 4 15/16 × 2 7/8 in. (125 × 73 mm), irreg. 1943.407.31

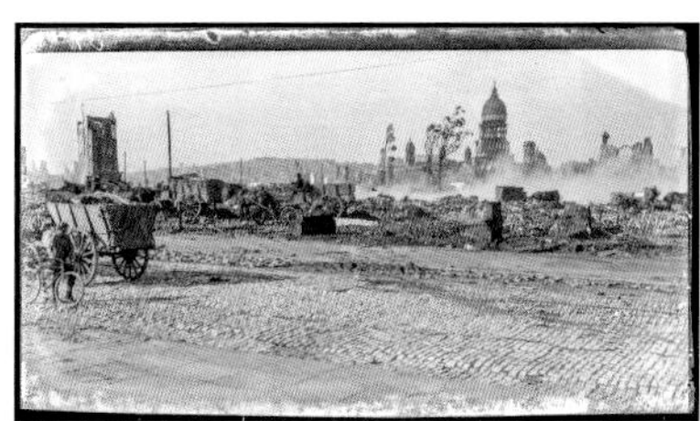

76. City Hall from 12th Street near Market, San Francisco, 3 1/8 × 5 1/2 in. (79 × 140 mm), irreg. Digital preservation of the negative sponsored by Ayako Onoda, 1943.407.75 (pl. 47)

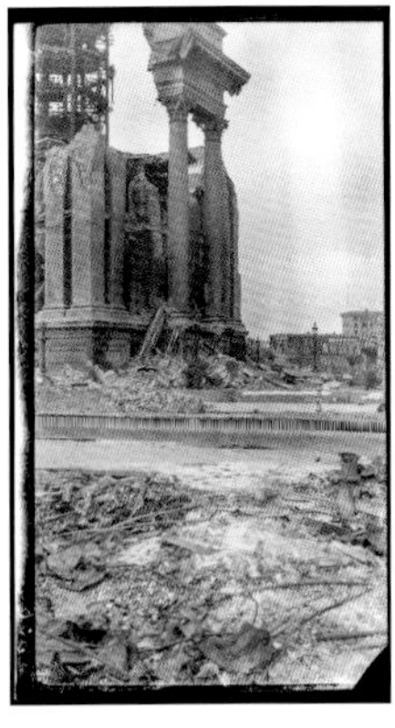

77. City Hall from Grove and Larkin, San Francisco, 5 5/8 × 3 3/16 in. (143 × 81 mm), irreg. 1943.407.62

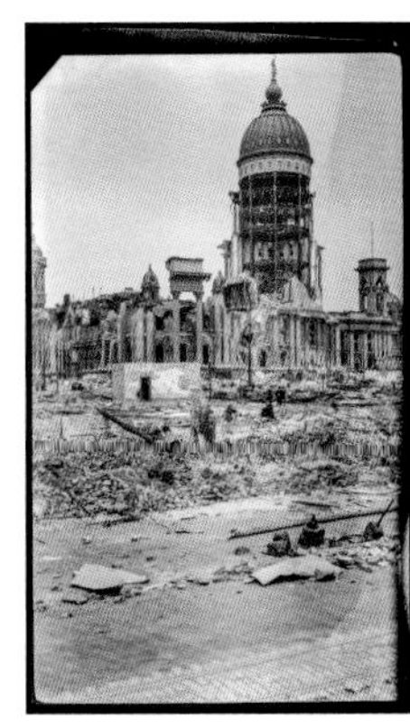

78. City Hall from Hayes and Larkin, San Francisco, 5 11/16 × 3 5/16 in. (144 × 84 mm), irreg. Digital preservation of the negative sponsored by Deborah Doyle and Eric Hall, 1943.407.160

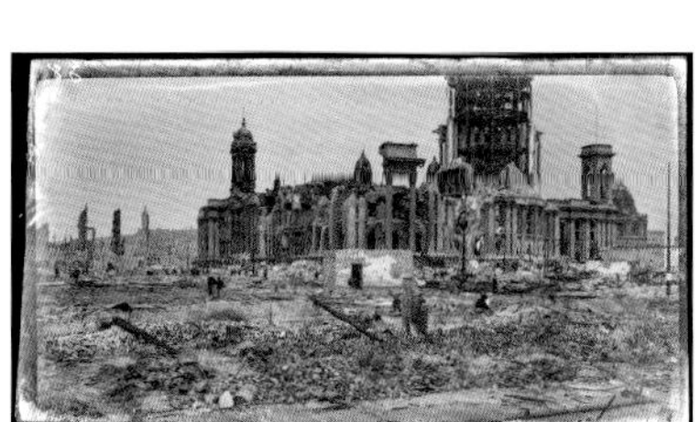

79. City Hall from Hayes west of Larkin, San Francisco, 3 1/16 × 5 11/16 in. (78 × 144 mm), irreg. Digital preservation of the negative sponsored by Catherine E. Burns, 1943.407.74 (pl. 48)

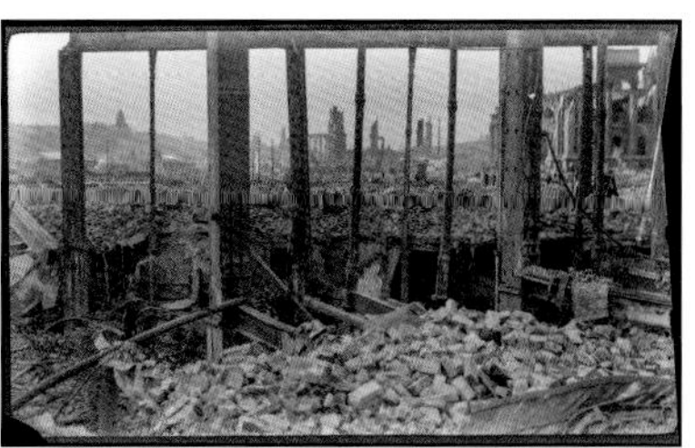

80. City Hall through the ruins of the St. Nicholas Hotel, Market and Larkin, San Francisco, 3 5/16 × 5 1/2 in. (84 × 140 mm), irreg. Digital preservation of the negative sponsored by Anne M. Zucchi, 1943.407.5.1 (pl. 49)

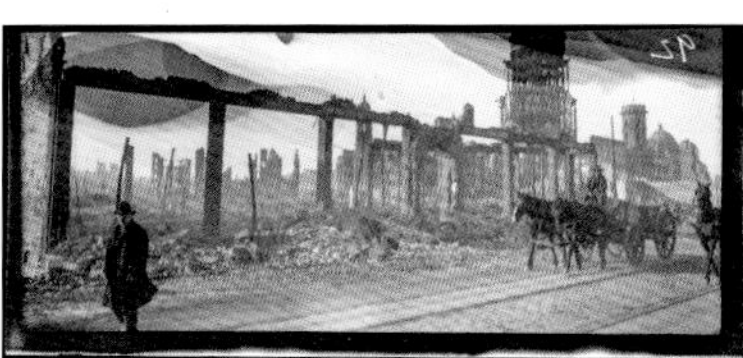

81. City Hall through the ruins of the St. Nicholas Hotel, Market and Larkin, San Francisco, 2 ½ × 5 ¹³⁄₁₆ in. (64 × 148 mm), irreg.
Digital preservation of the negative sponsored by Lourdes Livingston, 1943.407.148.1 (pl. 50)

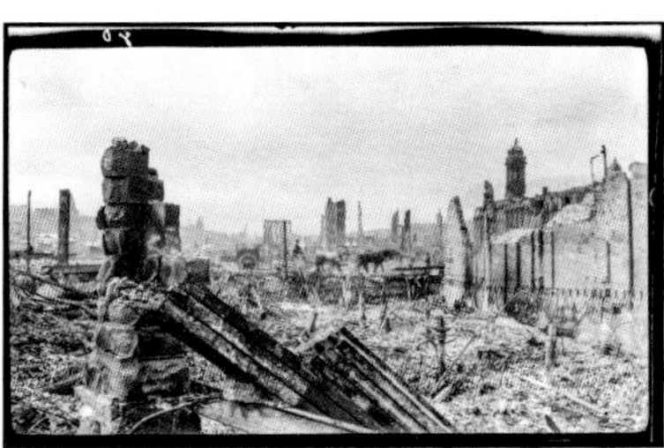

82. City Hall through the ruins of the St. Nicholas Hotel, Market and Larkin, San Francisco, 3 ½ × 5 ⅝ in. (89 × 143 mm), irreg.
Digital preservation of the negative sponsored by Deborah Doyle and Eric Hall, 1943.407.134

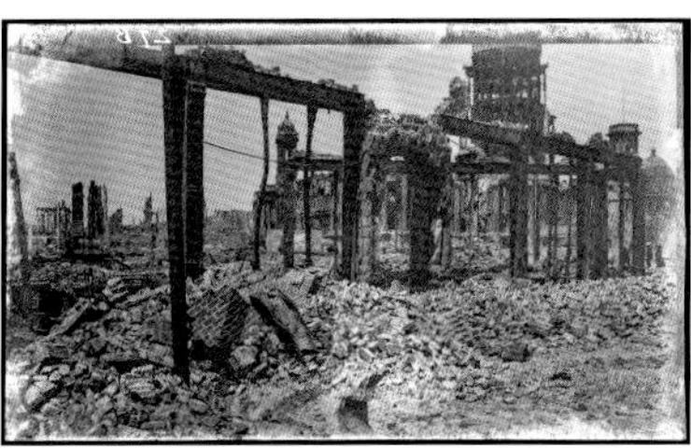

83. City Hall through the ruins of the St. Nicholas Hotel, Market and Larkin, San Francisco, 3 ¼ × 5 ½ in. (83 × 140 mm), irreg.
Digital preservation of the negative sponsored by Ellen and Howard Brown, 1943.407.56

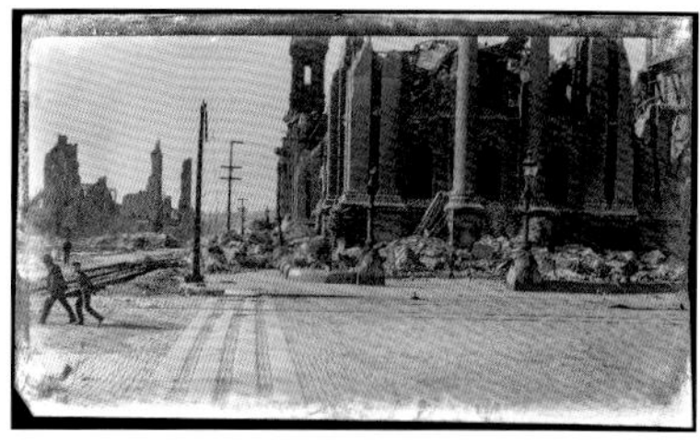

84. City Hall, Larkin and Grove, San Francisco, 3 ¼ × 5 ⁹⁄₁₆ in. (83 × 141 mm), irreg.
Digital preservation of the negative sponsored by Dan and Boo DeWitt, 1943.407.65 (pl. 51)

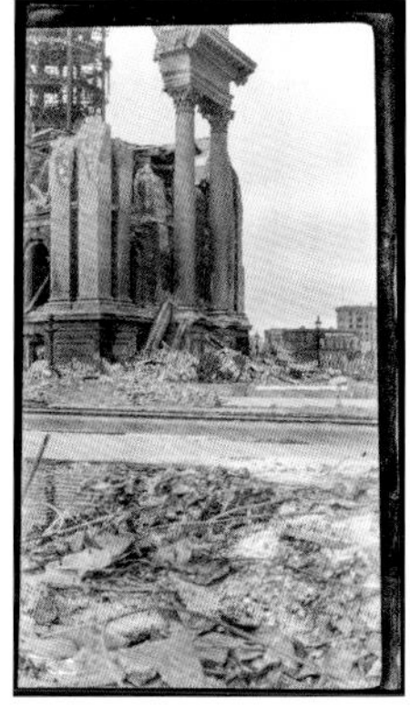

85. City Hall from Larkin near Grove, San Francisco, 5 ⅝ × 3 ³⁄₁₆ in. (143 × 81 mm), irreg.
Digital preservation of the negative sponsored by Daniel Woodhead III, 1943.407.51 (pl. 52)

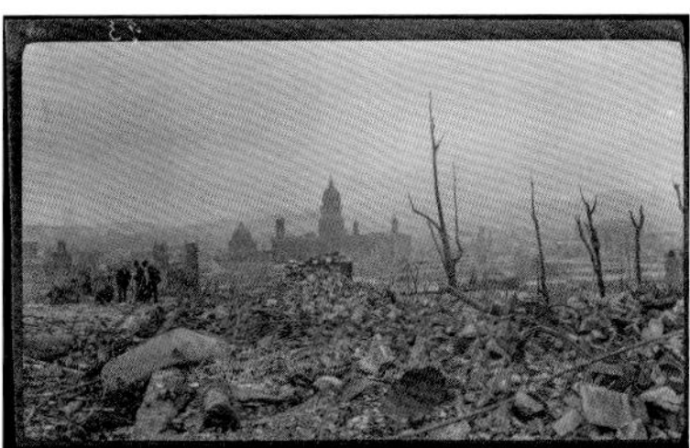

86. City Hall from Sutter between Hyde and Leavenworth, San Francisco, 3 ⁷⁄₁₆ × 5 ⅝ in. (87 × 143 mm), irreg.
Digital preservation of the negative sponsored by Lucy Young Hamilton, 1943.407.149.1 (pl. 53)

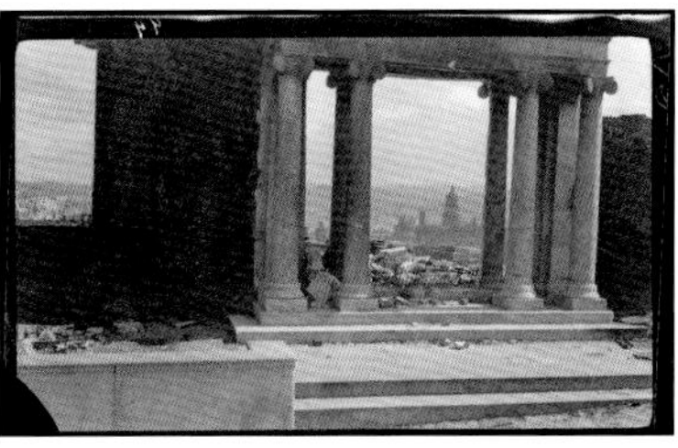

87. Towne mansion, California and Taylor, San Francisco, 3 ⁷⁄₁₆ × 5 ⅝ in. (87 × 143 mm), irreg.
Digital preservation of the negative sponsored in memory of Justice John B. Molinari, 1943.407.150

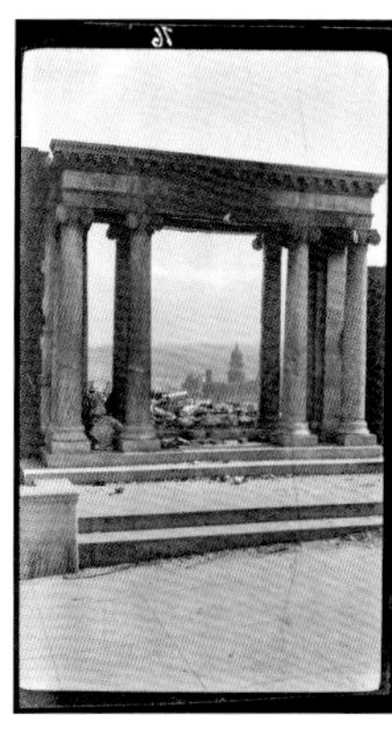

88. Towne mansion, California and Taylor, San Francisco, 5 ⅞ × 3 ⁵⁄₁₆ in. (149 × 84 mm), irreg.
Digital preservation of the negative sponsored by Pam Martori and Bob McCaskill, 1943.407.130.1 (pl. 54)

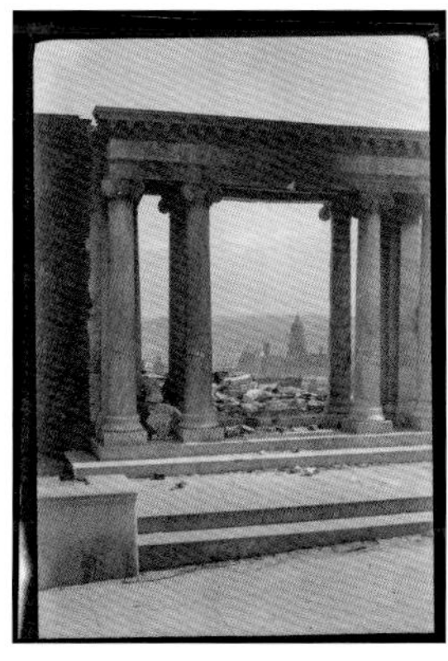

89. Towne mansion, California and Taylor, San Francisco, 5 × 3 ⁷⁄₁₆ in. (127 × 87 mm), irreg.
1943.407.164

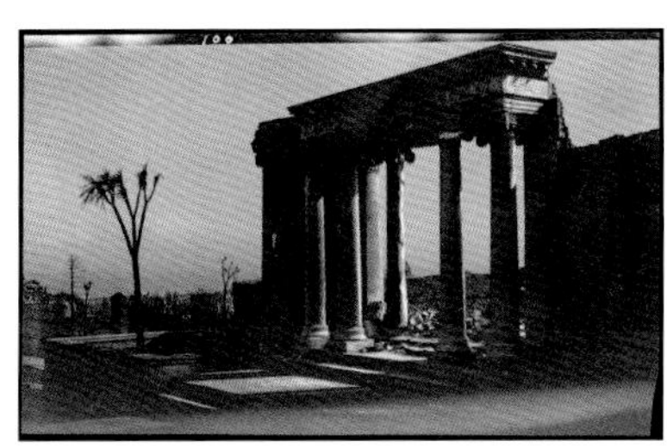

90. Towne mansion, California and Taylor, San Francisco, 3 ⅛ × 5 in. (79 × 127 mm), irreg.
Digital preservation of the negative sponsored by Robert C. and Susan L. Hill, 1943.407.156.1

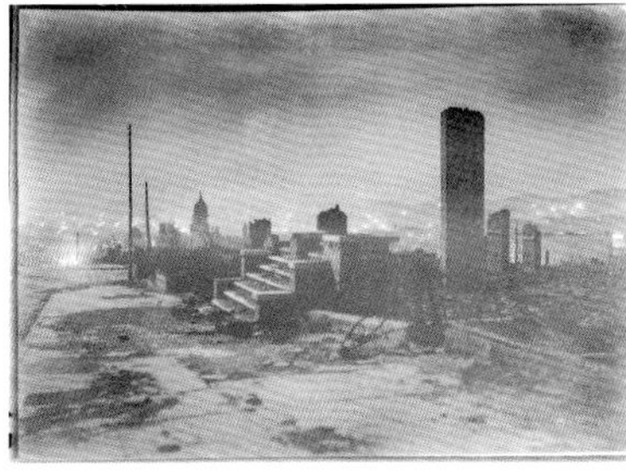

91. *Steps That Lead to Nowhere (After the Fire)*, San Francisco. Cellulose acetate negative, 4 ¾ × 6 ⅝ in. (121 × 168 mm)
Support for the negative preservation project provided by Peter Lewis and Emiko Kaji, 1943.407.4.1

LIFE ON THE STREETS

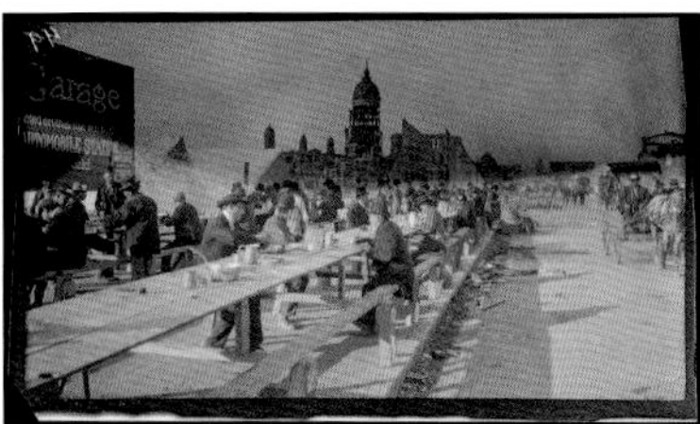

92. Hot meal kitchen on Market near 10th Street, San Francisco, 3 3/16 × 5 3/4 in. (81 × 146 mm), irreg. Digital preservation of the negative sponsored by Ann Jennings and Robert Polacchi, 1943.407.96.1 (pl. 55)

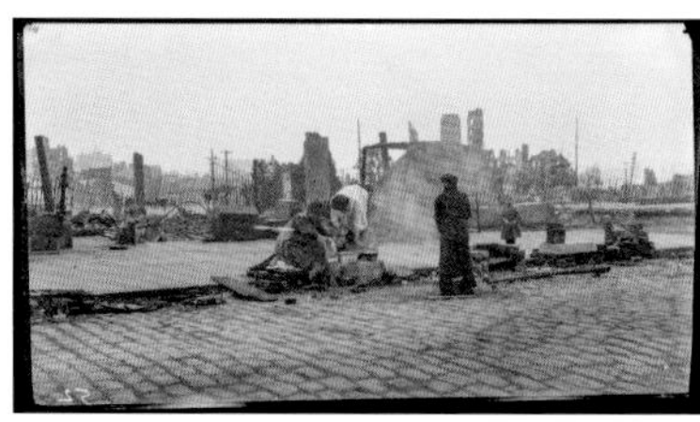

93. Franklin near Bush, San Francisco, 3 1/16 × 5 11/16 in. (78 × 144 mm), irreg. Digital preservation of the negative sponsored by Jane R. Lurie, 1943.407.102

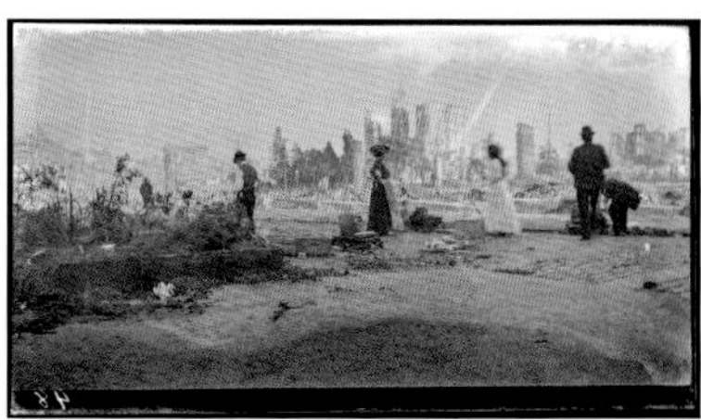

94. Bush and Franklin, San Francisco, 2 7/8 × 5 3/16 in. (73 × 132 mm), irreg. Digital preservation of the negative sponsored by Robert C. and Susan L. Hill, 1943.407.93

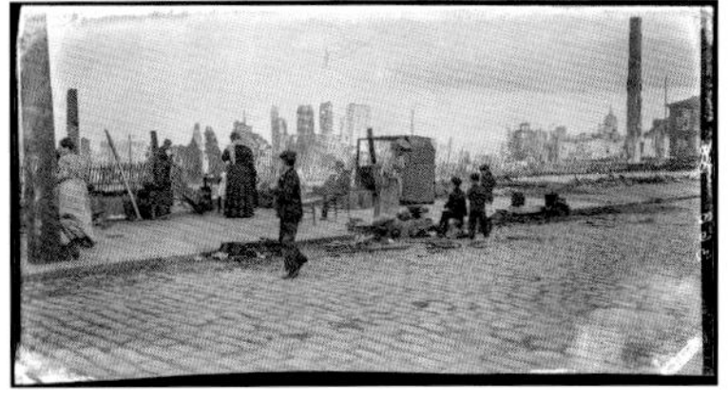

95. Franklin north of Sutter, San Francisco, 2 15/16 × 5 5/8 in. (75 × 143 mm), irreg. Digital preservation of the negative sponsored by Constance Yu, 1943.407.73

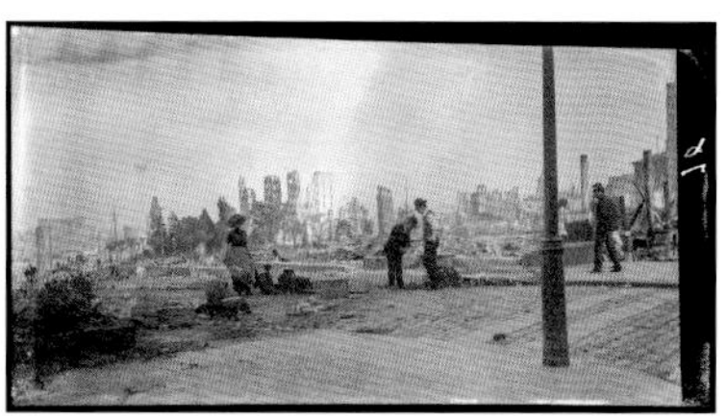

96. Bush and Franklin, San Francisco, 3 × 5 3/4 in. (76 × 146 mm), irreg. Digital preservation of the negative sponsored by Elena Sheehan, 1943.407.132

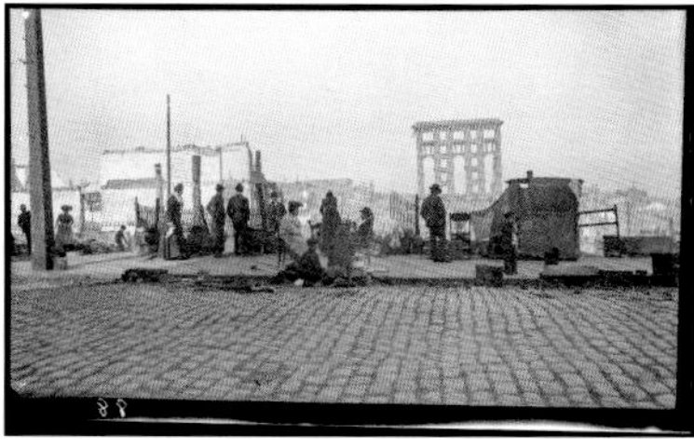

97. Franklin between Bush and Pine, San Francisco, 3 5/16 × 5 9/16 in. (84 × 141 mm), irreg. Digital preservation of the negative sponsored by Jennifer and Gordon Hull, 1943.407.143.1

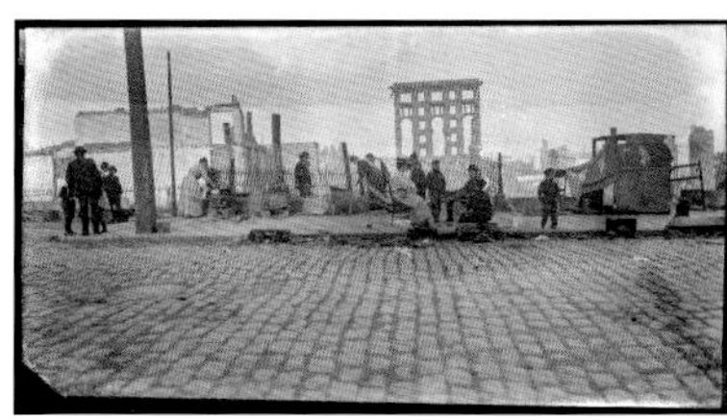

98. Franklin between Bush and Pine, San Francisco, 2 15/16 × 5 9/16 in. (75 × 141 mm), irreg. Digital preservation of the negative sponsored by Hannah Dolby, 1943.407.88 (pl. 56)

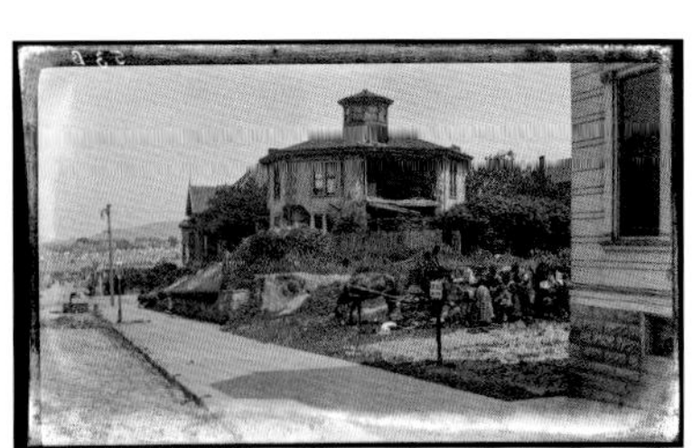

99. Cavagnaro House, Gough near Union, San Francisco, 3 5/16 × 5 5/8 in. (84 × 143 mm), irreg. Digital preservation of the negative sponsored by Shirley and Farrel Schell, 1943.407.105

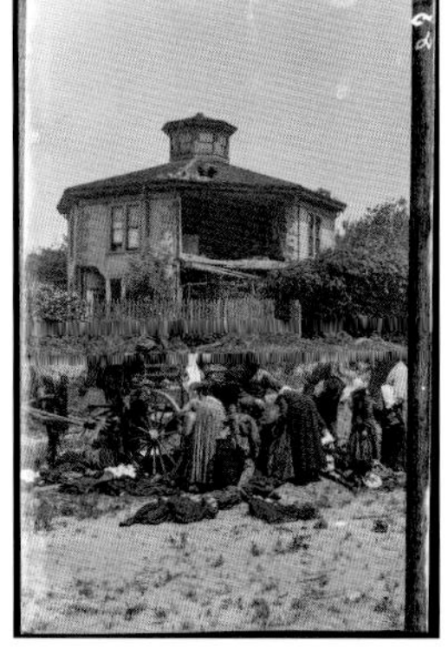

100. Cavagnaro House, Gough near Union, San Francisco, 5 1/4 × 3 1/2 in. (133 × 89 mm), irreg. Digital preservation of the negative sponsored by Anne M. Zucchi, 1943.407.138.1 (pl. 57)

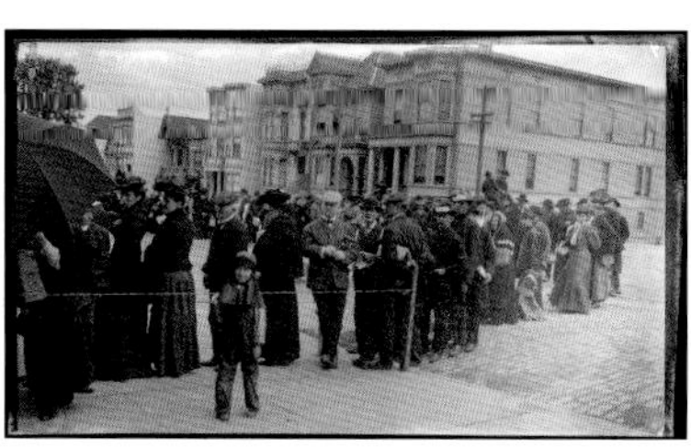

101. People waiting for rations following the earthquake and fire (probably April 22, 1906), San Francisco, 3 5/16 × 5 11/16 in. (84 × 144 mm), irreg. Digital preservation of the negative sponsored by Lawrence Banka and Judith Gordon, 1943.407.120 (pl. 58)

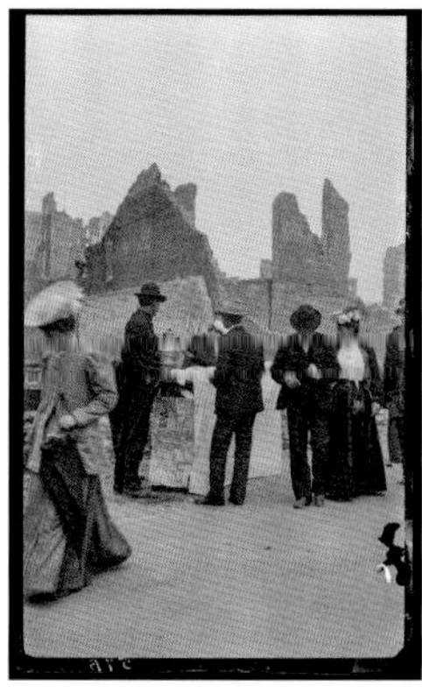

102. Food vendor post–earthquake and fire, San Francisco, 5 7/16 × 3 3/8 in. (138 × 86 mm), irreg. Digital preservation of the negative sponsored by the Schauble Family, 1943.407.112 (pl. 59)

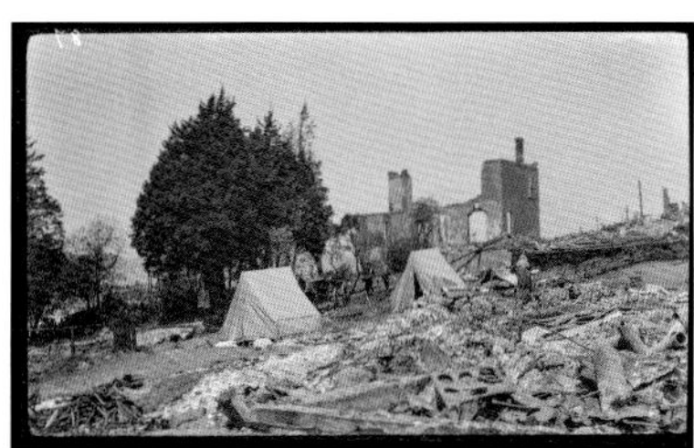

103. Two tents stand among debris and ruins on a sloped hillside, San Francisco, 3 5/16 × 5 1/2 in. (84 × 140 mm), irreg. Digital preservation of the negative sponsored by Mark Liao, 1943.407.142

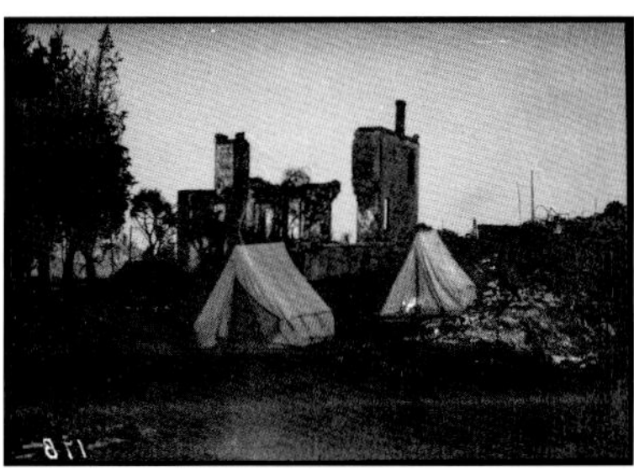

104. Two tents stand among debris and ruins on a sloped hillside, San Francisco, 3 1/16 × 4 7/16 in. (78 × 113 mm), irreg. 1943.407.35

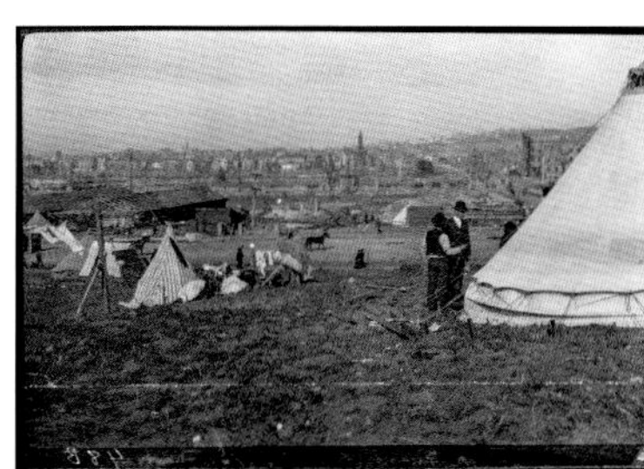

105. Dolores Park near 19th Street, looking east, San Francisco, 3 7/16 × 5 1/16 in. (87 × 129 mm), irreg. Digital preservation of the negative sponsored by Carla and Robert Kennis, 1943.407.94.1 (pl. 60)

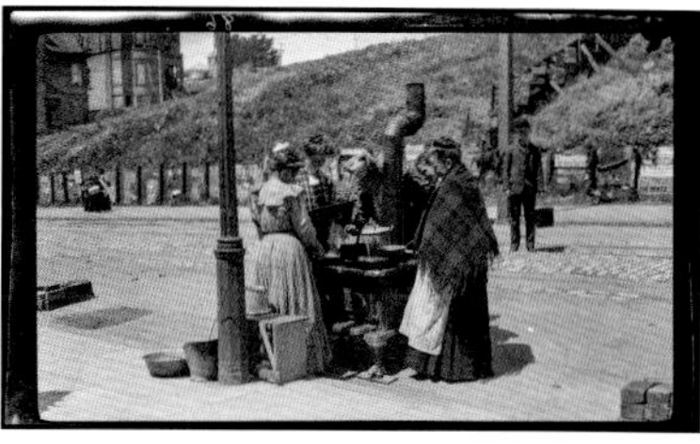

106. A sidewalk kitchen, San Francisco, 3 7/16 × 5 7/8 in. (87 × 149 mm), irreg. Digital preservation of the negative sponsored by the San Francisco Auxiliary of the Fine Arts Museums of San Francisco, 1943.407.141.1 (pl. 61)

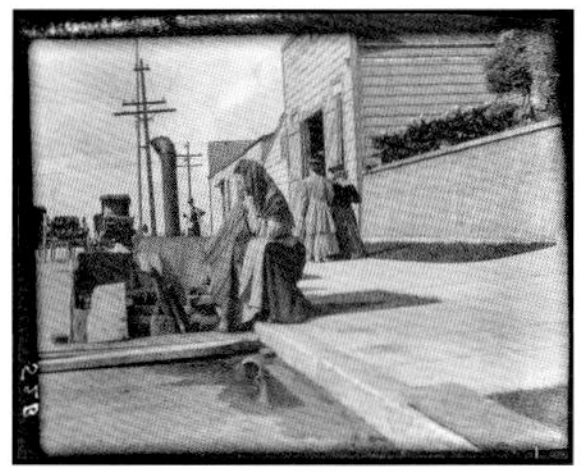

107. A sidewalk kitchen, San Francisco, 3 3/16 × 4 in. (81 × 102 mm), irreg. 1943.407.103

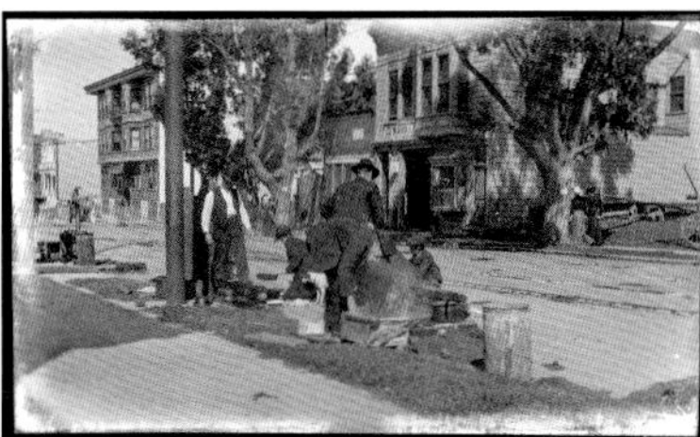

108. Sacramento between Locust and Laurel, San Francisco, 3 3/16 × 5 3/8 in. (81 × 137 mm), irreg. Digital preservation of the negative sponsored by Guillermo Rettally and John Garvin, 1943.407.89

THE MILITARY PRESENCE

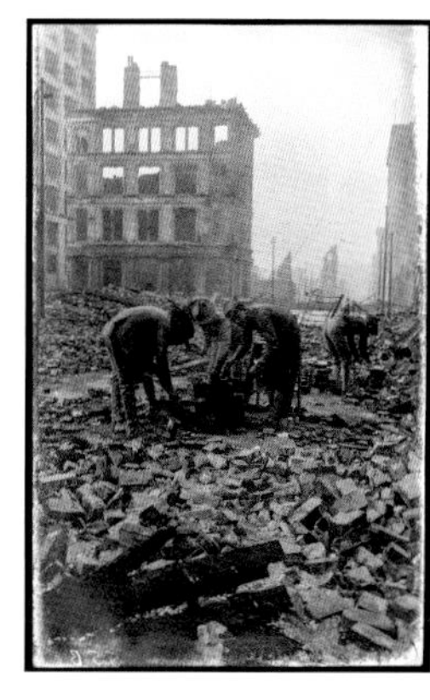

109. Montgomery between Post and Sutter, San Francisco, 5 1/16 × 3 1/4 in. (129 × 83 mm), irreg. Digital preservation of the negative sponsored by Jerold B. Rosenberg, 1943.407.46 (pl. 62)

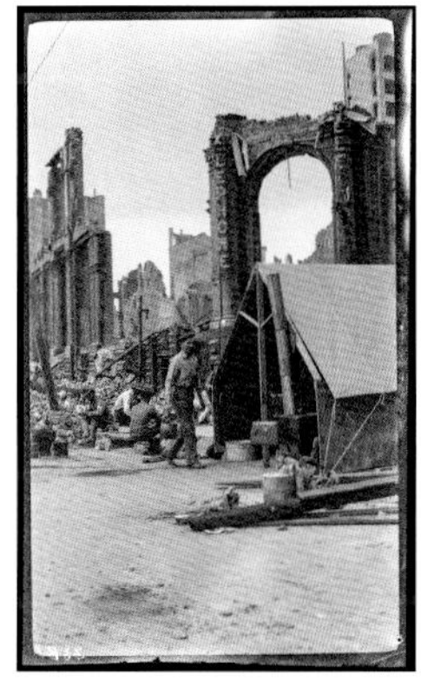

110. St. Ann's Building, Powell and Eddy, San Francisco, 5 5/8 × 3 3/8 in. (143 × 86 mm), irreg. Digital preservation of the negative sponsored by Lisa Dolby Chadwick, 1943.407.66 (pl. 63)

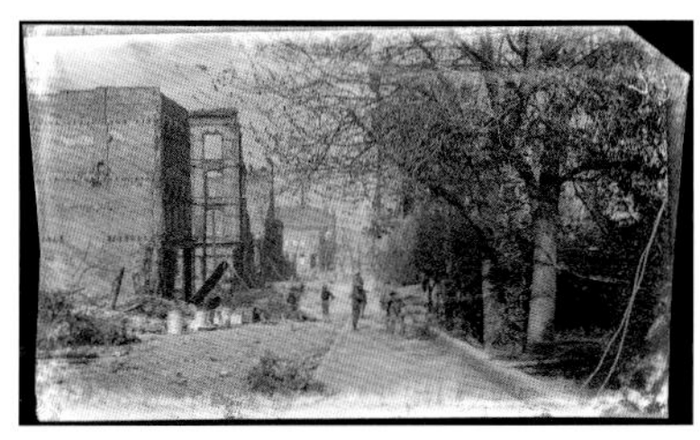

111. Washington Street at Portsmouth Square, San Francisco, 3 3/16 × 5 1/2 in. (81 × 140 mm), irreg. 1943.407.64

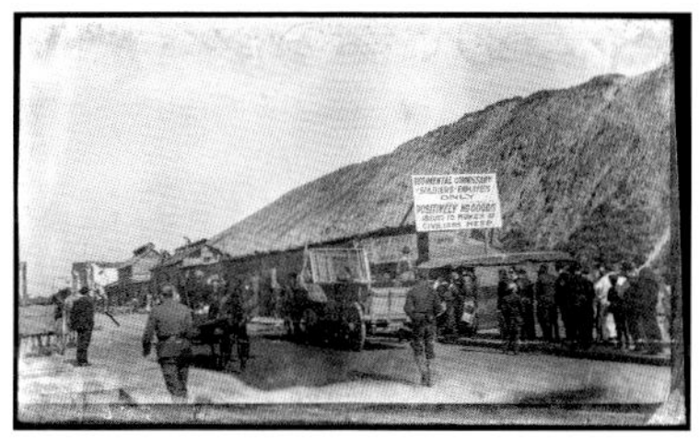

112. Regimental commissary on Duboce between Market and Church, San Francisco, 3 3/16 × 5 7/16 in. (81 × 138 mm), irreg. Digital preservation of the negative sponsored by Peter Lewis and Emiko Kaji, 1943.407.114.1 (pl. 64)

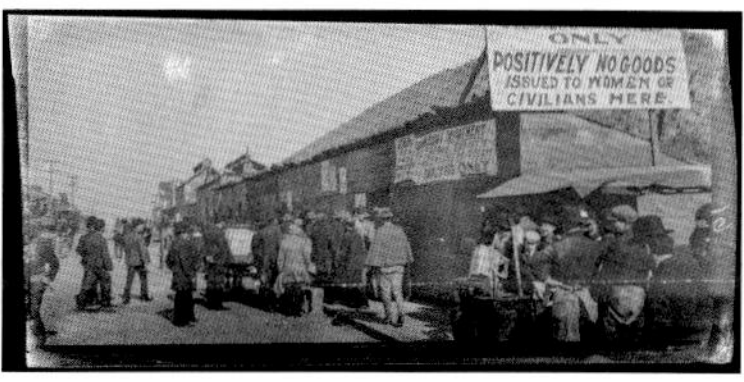

113. Regimental commissary on Duboce between Market and Church, San Francisco, 2 3/4 × 5 3/4 in. (70 × 146 mm), irreg. Digital preservation of the negative sponsored by Lourdes Livingston, 1943.407.117

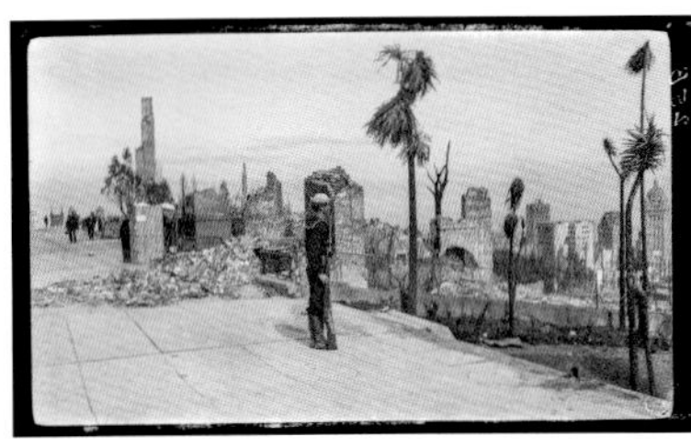

114. California between Mason and Taylor, San Francisco, (86 × 148 mm) $3\frac{3}{8} \times 5\frac{13}{16}$ in., irreg. Digital preservation of the negative sponsored by Daniel F. Donovan and Pia D. Jondonovan, 1943.407.52.1 (pl. 65)

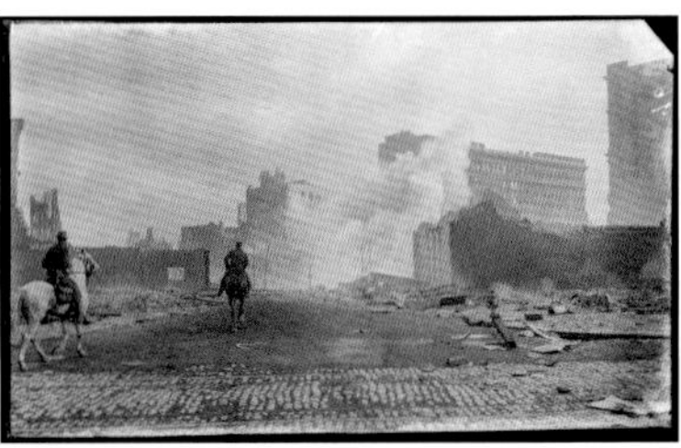

115. The Emporium from Stockton and O'Farrell, San Francisco, $3\frac{1}{4} \times 5\frac{7}{16}$ in. (83 × 138 mm), irreg. Digital preservation of the negative sponsored by Michelle L. Wilson, 1943.407.152 (pl. 66)

RELIEF CAMPS

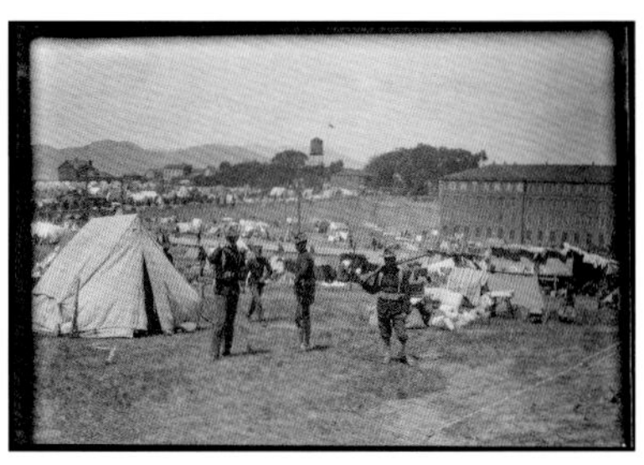

116. Van Ness and North Point, San Francisco, $2\frac{3}{4} \times 4\frac{1}{4}$ in. (70 × 108 mm), irreg. Digital preservation of the negative sponsored by an anonymous donor, 1943.407.159

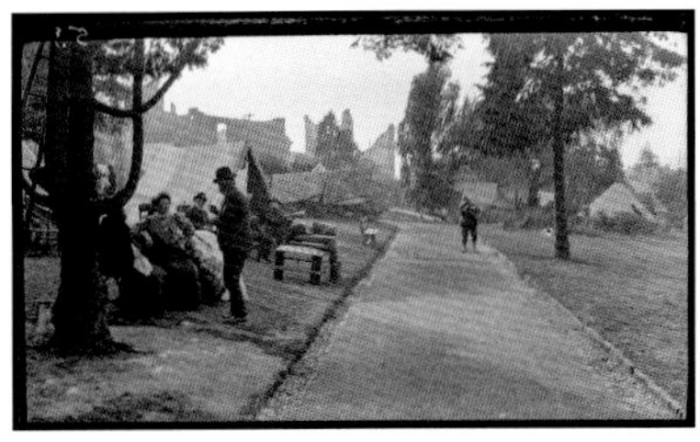

117. Northwest from Kearny through Portsmouth Square, San Francisco, $3\frac{3}{16} \times 5\frac{1}{2}$ in. (81 × 140 mm), irreg. Digital preservation of the negative sponsored by the San Francisco Auxiliary of the Fine Arts Museums of San Francisco, 1943.407.104.1

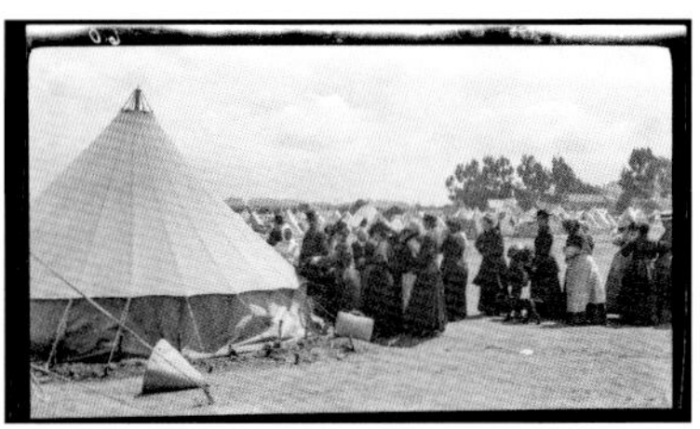

118. Families in line for aid in an army relief camp, San Francisco, $3\frac{3}{16} \times 5\frac{11}{16}$ in. (81 × 144 mm), irreg. Digital preservation of the negative sponsored by Karin and David Chamberlain, 1943.407.116 (pl. 67)

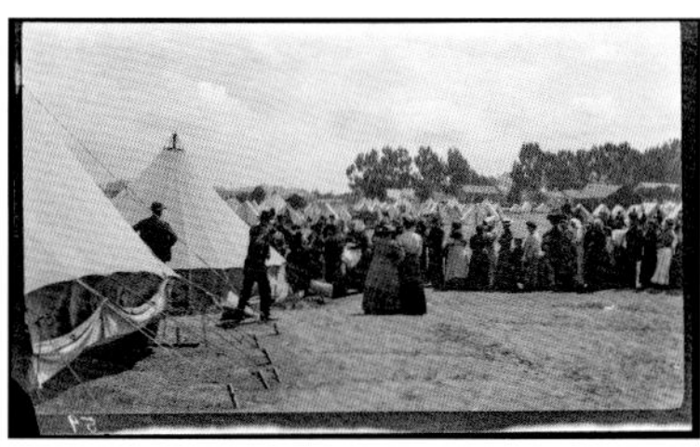

119. Families in line for aid in an army relief camp, San Francisco, $3\frac{5}{8} \times 5\frac{11}{16}$ in. (92 × 144 mm), irreg. Digital preservation of the negative sponsored by Phyllis Brooks Schafer, 1943.407.115

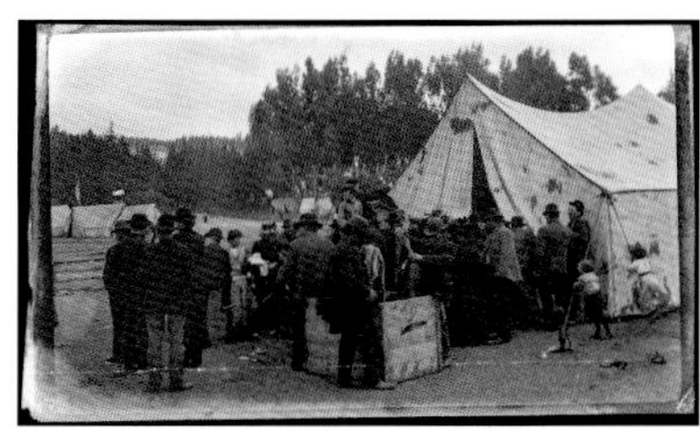

120. Post–earthquake and fire clothing rations tent, San Francisco, $3\frac{3}{8} \times 5\frac{13}{16}$ in. (86 × 148 mm), irreg. Digital preservation of the negative sponsored by the Wummer Family, 1943.407.113 (pl. 68)

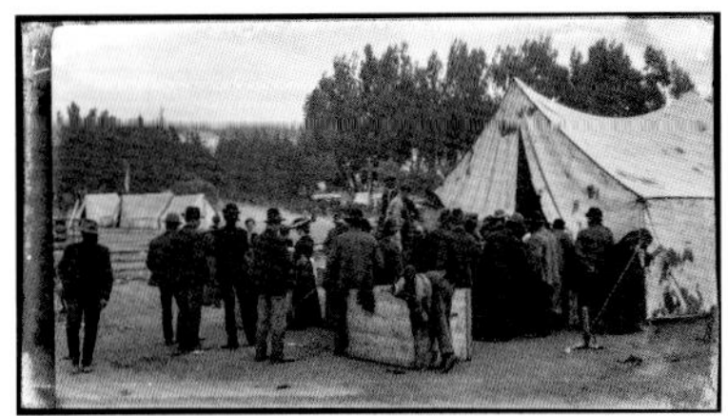

121. Post–earthquake and fire clothing rations tent, San Francisco, $3\frac{1}{8} \times 5\frac{3}{4}$ in. (79 × 146 mm), irreg. Digital preservation of the negative sponsored by Linda Kraft Jesmok, 1943.407.100

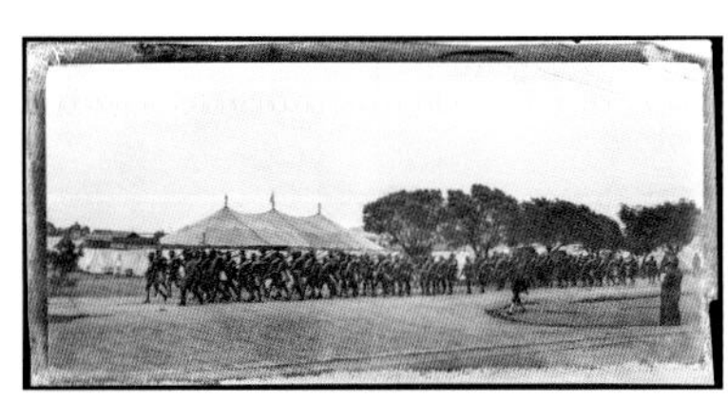

122. The Presidio near the hospital, San Francisco, $2\frac{3}{4} \times 5\frac{11}{16}$ in. (70 × 144 mm), irreg. 1943.407.87

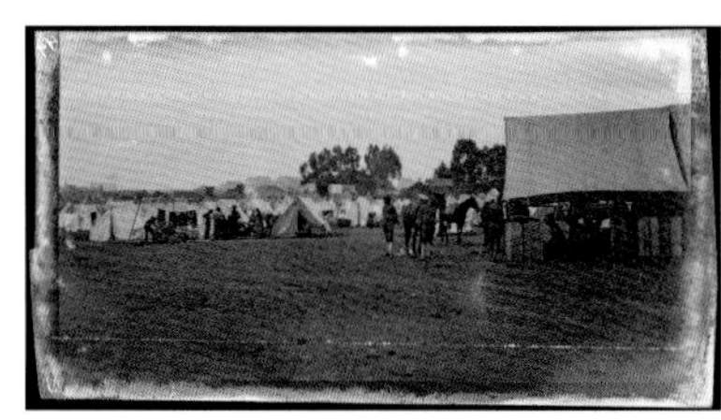

123. Soldiers and horses stand near tent in the Presidio following the earthquake and fire, San Francisco, $3\frac{3}{16} \times 5\frac{13}{16}$ in. (81 × 148 mm), irreg. 1943.407.85

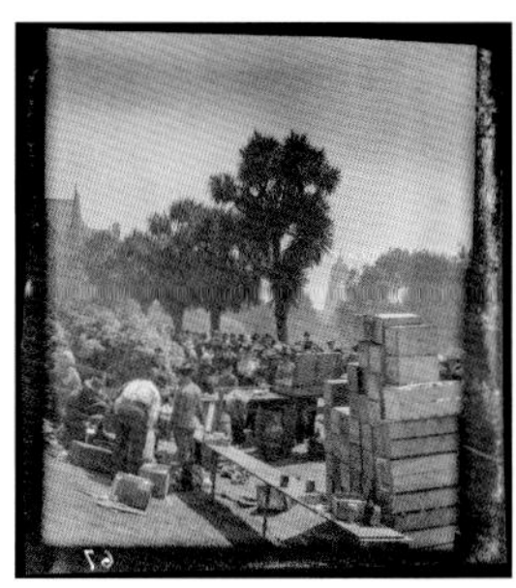

124. Jefferson Square, Eddy near Laguna, San Francisco, $3\frac{3}{4} \times 3\frac{7}{16}$ in. (95 × 87 mm), irreg. Digital preservation of the negative sponsored by Sandra and Paul Bessières, 1943.407.123 (pl. 69)

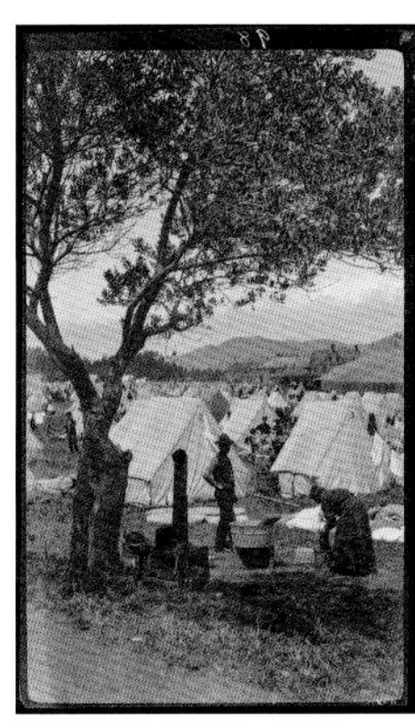

125. The Presidio near the hospital, San Francisco, 5 ⅝ × 3 ⅜ in. (143 × 86 mm), irreg. Digital preservation of the negative sponsored by Holly Hitchcock, 1943.407.154

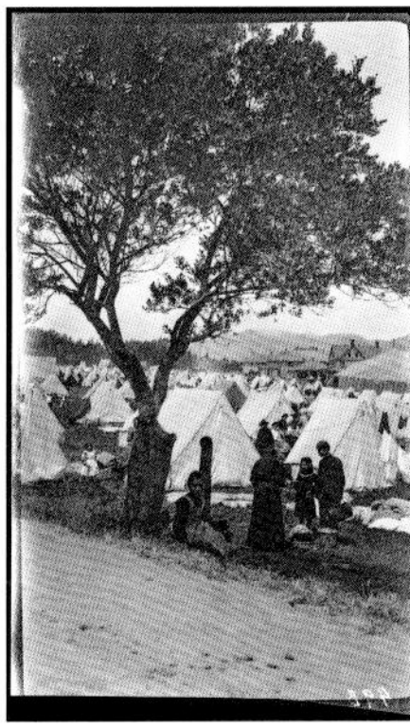

126. The Presidio near the hospital, San Francisco, 5 ⅝ × 3 ⅜ in. (143 × 86 mm), irreg. Digital preservation of the negative sponsored by Mary N. Lannin, 1943.407.95 (pl. 70)

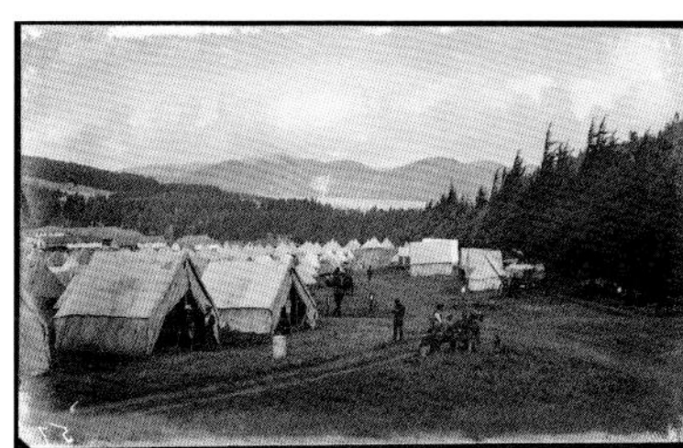

127. Tennessee Hollow in the Presidio, San Francisco, 3 ¼ × 5 5/16 in. (83 × 135 mm), irreg. Digital preservation of the negative sponsored by Joanne Murray, 1943.407.111

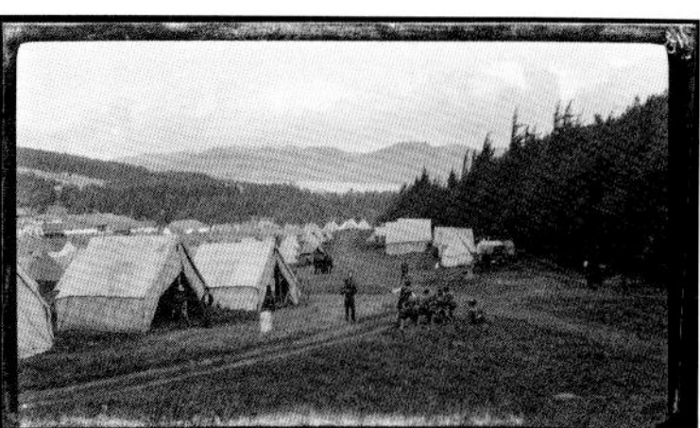

128. Tennessee Hollow in the Presidio, San Francisco, 3 5/16 × 5 13/16 in. (84 × 148 mm), irreg. Digital preservation of the negative sponsored by the John Nerness Family, 1943.407.83

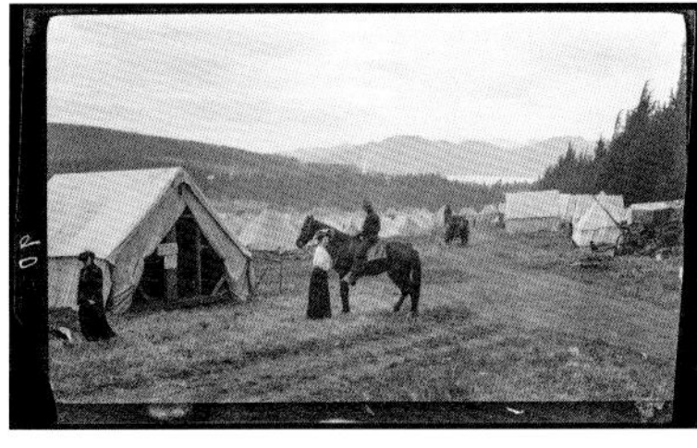

129. Tennessee Hollow in the Presidio, San Francisco, 3 7/16 × 5 ¾ in. (87 × 146 mm), irreg. Digital preservation of the negative sponsored by Edith H. Bergstrom, 1943.407.146 (pl. 71)

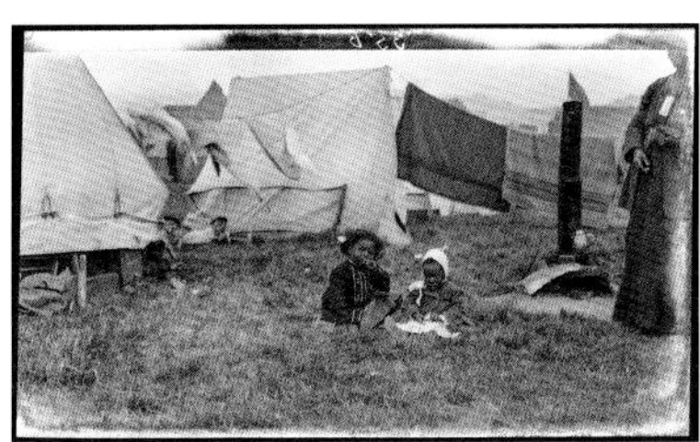

130. Two children sit on grass in front of tents in the Presidio in the days following the earthquake and fire, San Francisco, 3 ⅛ × 5 ¼ in. (79 × 133 mm), irreg. Digital preservation of the negative sponsored by Michelle L. Wilson, 1943.407.70 (pl. 72)

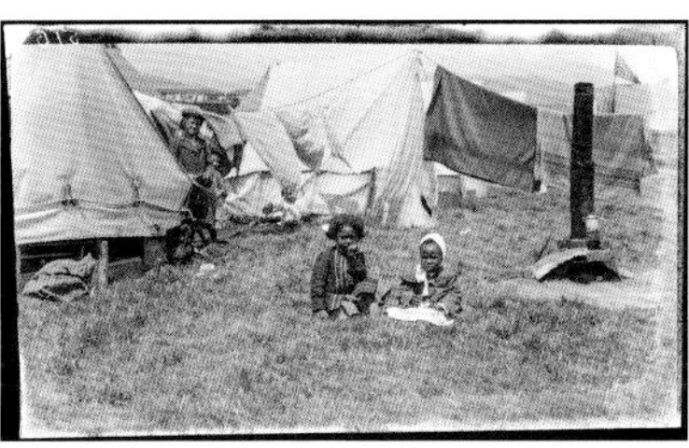

131. Two children sit on grass in front of tents in the Presidio in the days following the earthquake and fire, San Francisco, 3 ¼ × 5 9/16 in. (83 × 141 mm), irreg. 1943.407.101

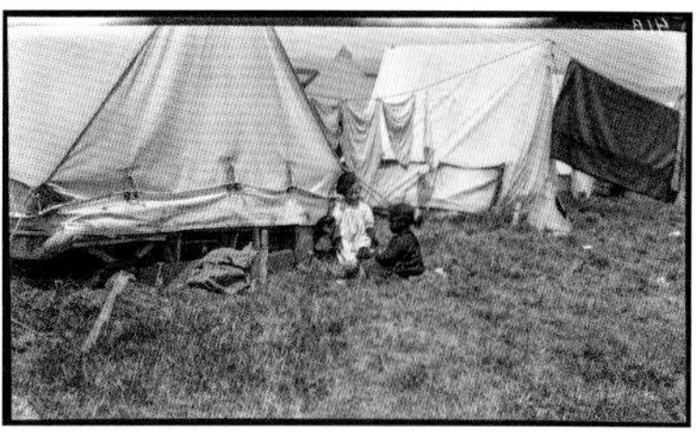

132. Two children sit on grass in front of tents in the Presidio in the days following the earthquake and fire, San Francisco, 3 ⅛ × 5 5/16 in. (79 × 135 mm), irreg. Digital preservation of the negative sponsored by William and Polly Clark, 1943.407.80

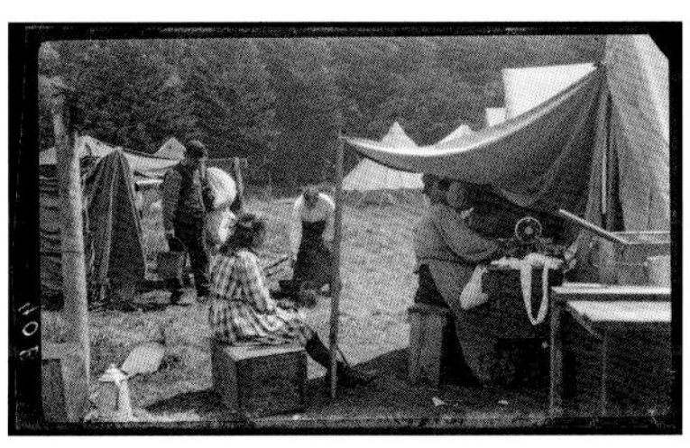

133. Domestic scene in days following earthquake and fire. A family's activities in a relief camp, San Francisco, 3 ⅜ × 5 ¾ in. (86 × 146 mm), irreg. Digital preservation of the negative sponsored by Stella Dolby, 1943.407.78.1 (pl. 73)

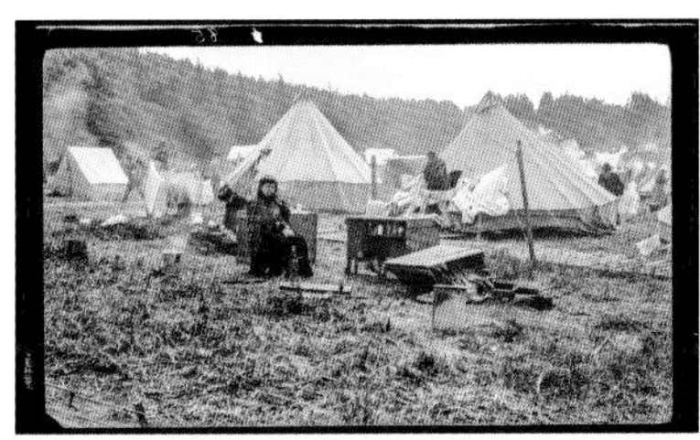

134. Relief camp scene, San Francisco, 3 7/16 × 5 ¾ in. (87 × 146 mm), irreg. Digital preservation of the negative sponsored by Leslie and Diane Lynch, 1943.407.140

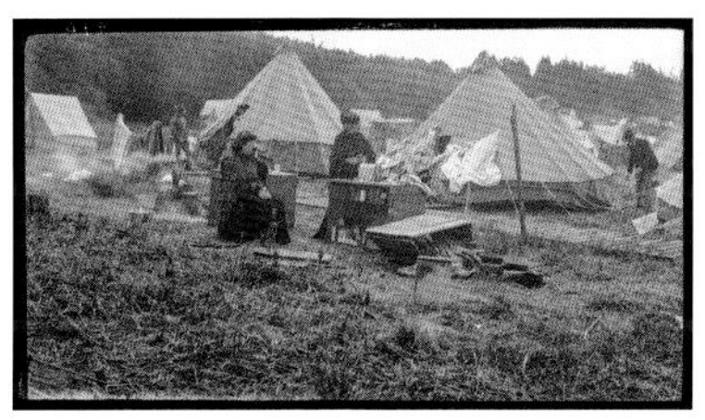

135. Two women sit in an outdoor kitchen in a relief camp, San Francisco, 3 × 5 7/16 in. (76 × 138 mm), irreg. 1943.407.86

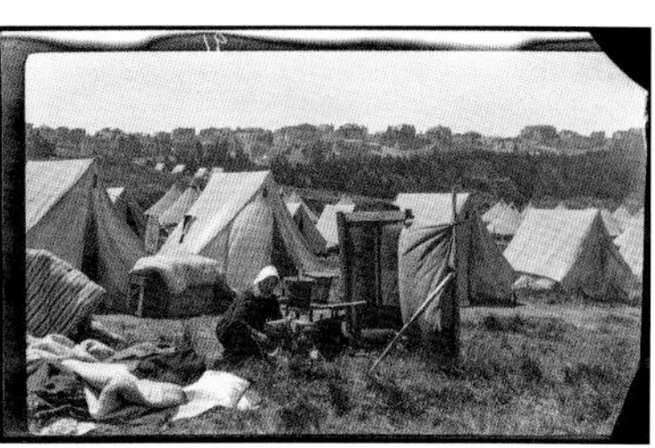

136. Relief camp, woman with birdcage, San Francisco, 3 7/16 × 4 ⅝ in. (87 × 117 mm), irreg. Digital preservation of the negative sponsored by Irene M. Dobbins, 1943.407.147

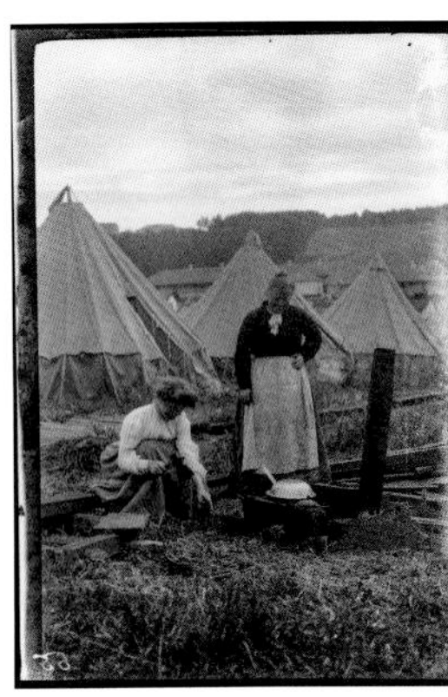

137. Two women working at their temporary stove in a relief camp, San Francisco, 4 ⅞ × 3 ⅜ in. (124 × 86 mm), irreg. Digital preservation of the negative sponsored by Daniel Woodhead III, 1943.407.108

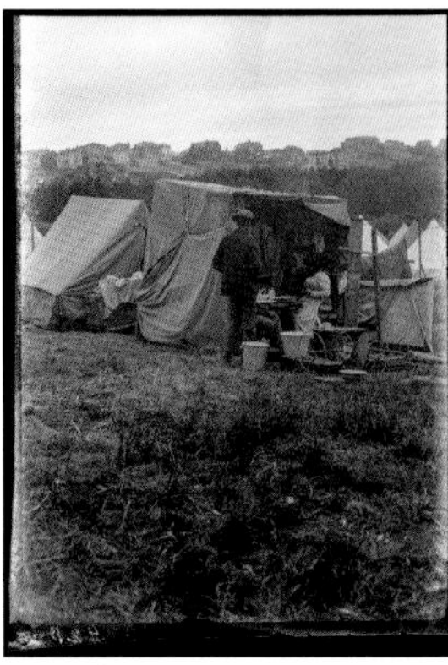

138. Domestic meal scene in a relief camp after the earthquake and fire, San Francisco, 4 ⅝ × 3 ⅜ in. (117 × 86 mm), irreg. Digital preservation of the negative sponsored by Pat and Penny Barrett, 1943.407.82

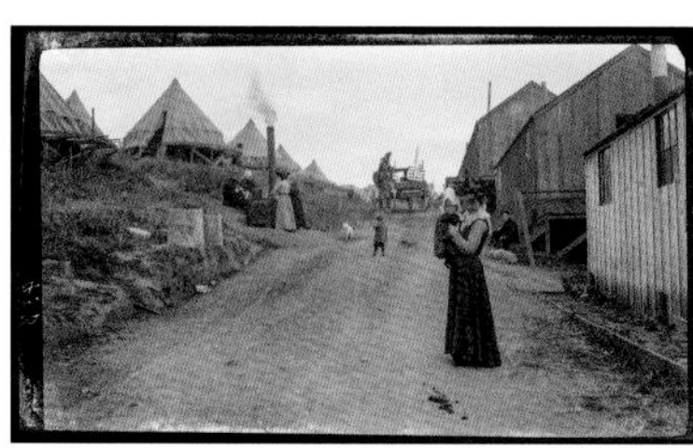

139. Tennessee Hollow in the Presidio, San Francisco, 3 5/16 × 5 ¾ in. (84 × 146 mm), irreg. Digital preservation of the negative sponsored by the Handlery Foundation, 1943.407.84 (pl. 74)

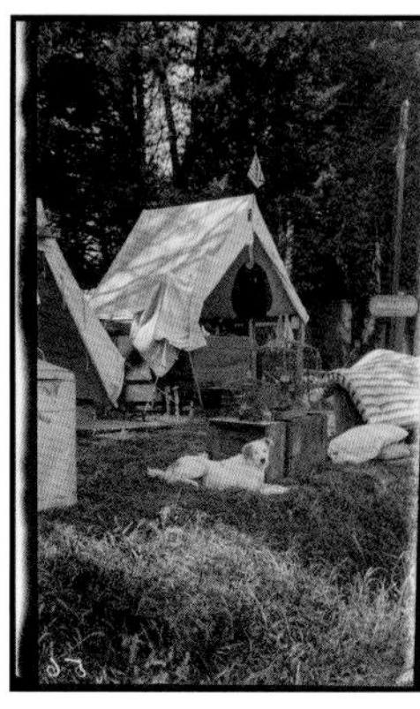

140. Life in a relief camp. A large reclining dog in the foreground, San Francisco, 5 × 3 ¼ in. (127 × 83 mm), irreg. Digital preservation of the negative sponsored by the San Francisco Auxiliary of the Fine Arts Museums of San Francisco, 1943.407.109 (pl. 75)

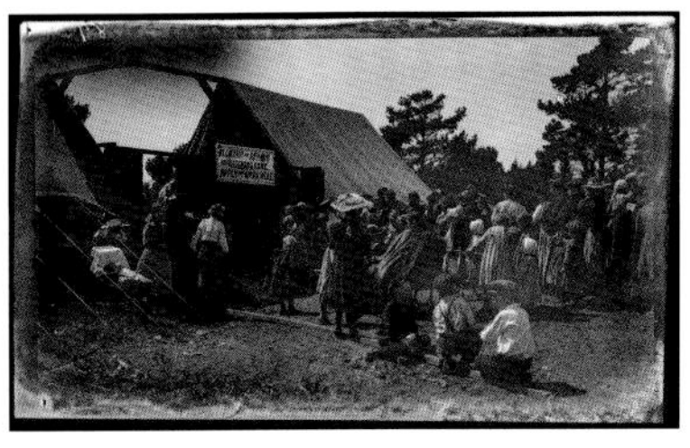

141. Women and children standing in line outside sewing tent, San Francisco, 3 ½ × 5 13/16 in. (89 × 148 mm), irreg. Digital preservation of the negative sponsored by Elena Sheehan, 1943.407.145 (pl. 76)

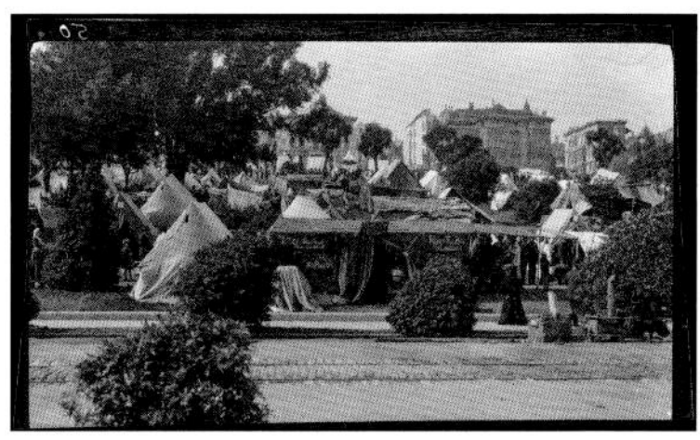

142. Jefferson Square, San Francisco, 3 5/16 × 5 ¾ in. (84 × 146 mm), irreg. Digital preservation of the negative sponsored by Karla Gibson, 1943.407.98 (pl. 77)

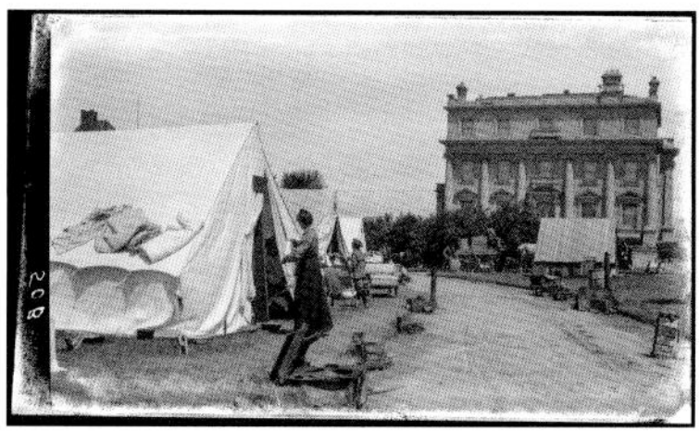

143. Lafayette Park, San Francisco, 3 5/16 × 5 ¾ in. (84 × 146 mm), irreg. 1943.407.99

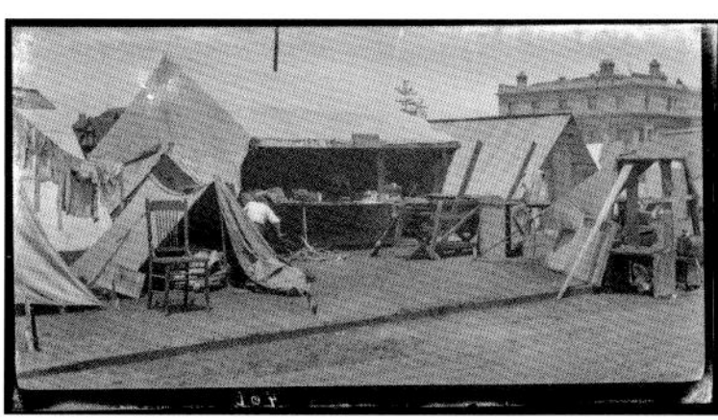

144. Lafayette Park, San Francisco, 2 13/16 × 5 ⅝ in. (71 × 143 mm), irreg. Digital preservation of the negative sponsored by William and Polly Clark, 1943.407.90

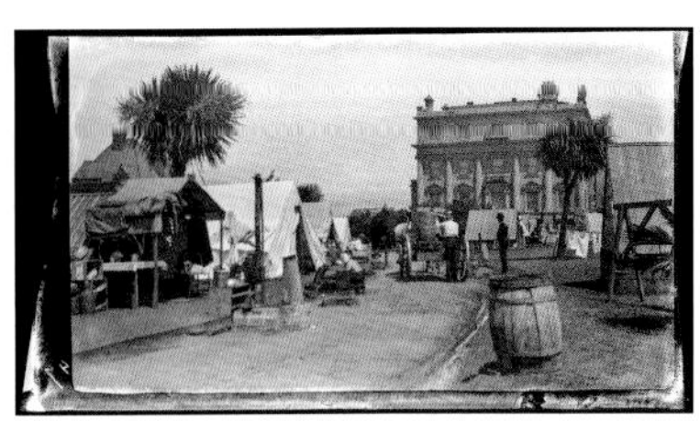

145. Lafayette Park, San Francisco, 3 5/16 × 6 in. (84 × 152 mm), irreg. 1943.407.91

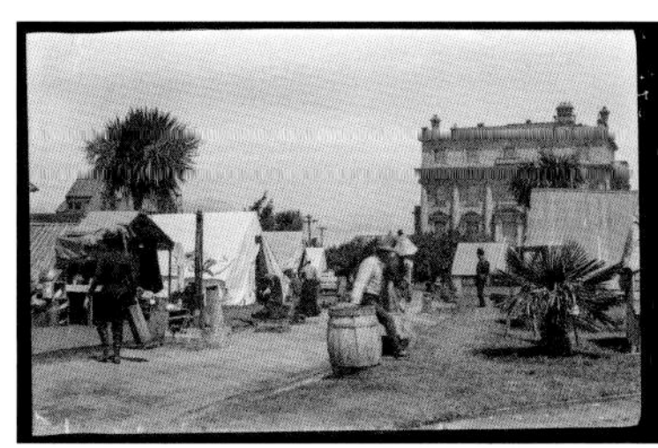

146. Lafayette Park, San Francisco, 3 ¼ × 5 5/16 in. (83 × 135 mm), irreg. Digital preservation of the negative sponsored by an anonymous donor, 1943.407.68

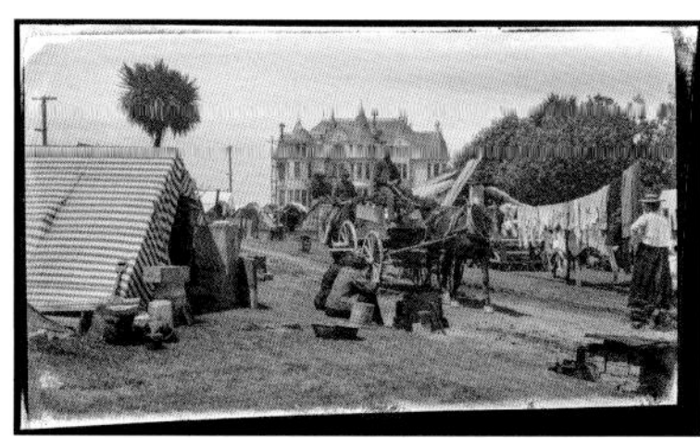

147. Lafayette Park, San Francisco, 3 ¼ × 5 11/16 in. (83 × 144 mm), irreg. 1943.407.81 (pl. 78)

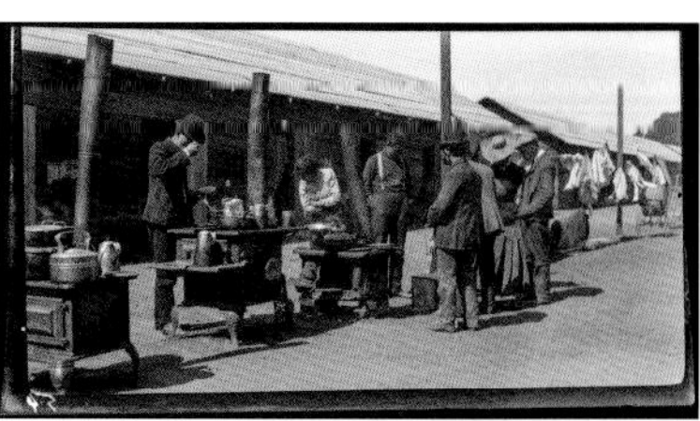

148. Speedway Meadow, Golden Gate Park, San Francisco, 3 ⅛ × 5 ¾ in. (79 × 146 mm), irreg. Digital preservation of the negative sponsored by Joyce and Al Zavattero, 1943.407.106.1 (pl. 79)

REBUILDING THE CITY

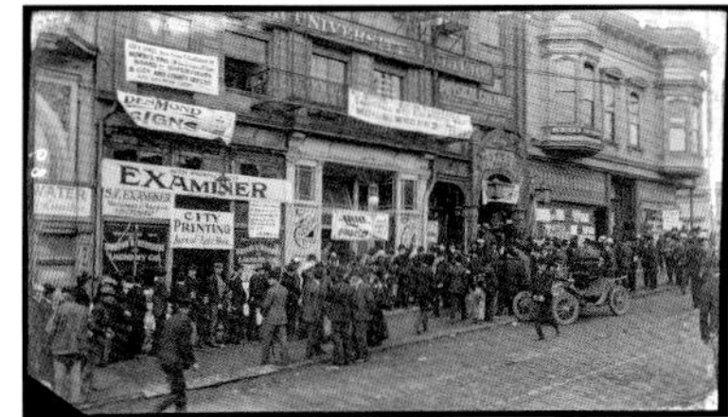

149. Franklin Hall, Fillmore and Bush, San Francisco, 3 1/16 × 5 1/2 in. (78 × 140 mm), irreg. Digital preservation of the negative sponsored by the San Francisco Auxiliary of the Fine Arts Museums of San Francisco, 1943.407.124 (pl. 80)

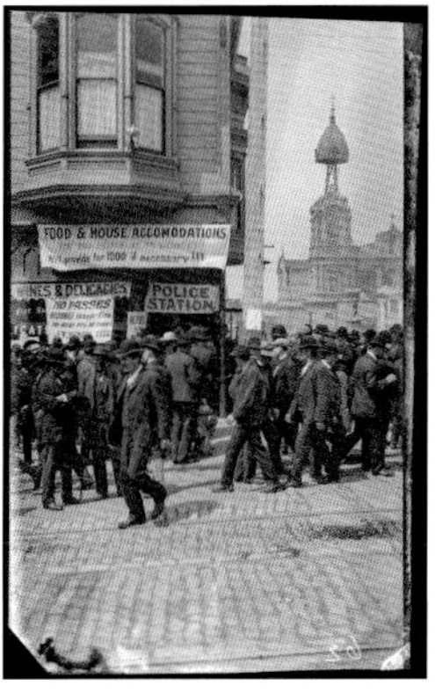

150. Bush and Fillmore, San Francisco, 5 1/4 × 3 3/8 in. (133 × 86 mm), irreg. Digital preservation of the negative sponsored by Anne M. Zucchi, 1943.407.118.1 (pl. 81)

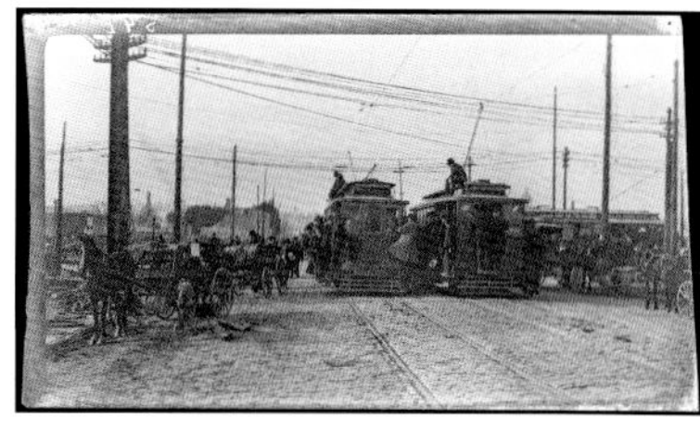

151. Cable cars begin running 4/27 (16th Street and Mission, San Francisco), 3 1/8 × 5 1/2 in. (79 × 140 mm), irreg. Digital preservation of the negative sponsored by Bob Spivock, 1943.407.107

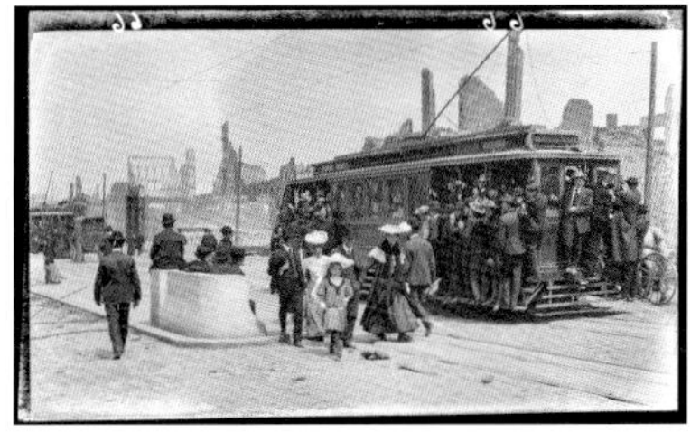

152. Lower Market, San Francisco, 3 1/8 × 5 1/8 in. (79 × 130 mm), irreg. Digital preservation of the negative sponsored by Violet Dolby-Frist, 1943.407.122 (pl. 82)

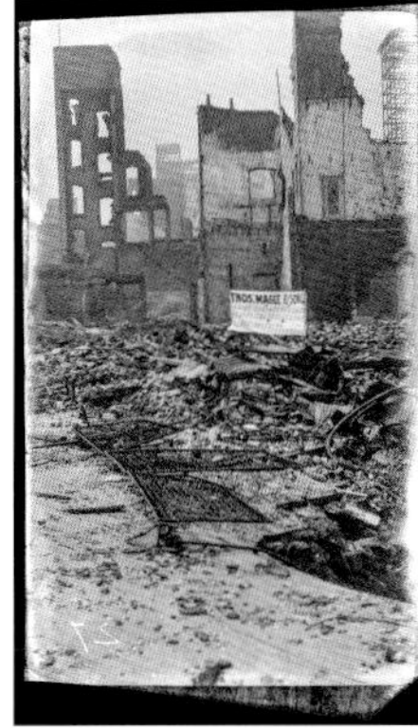

153. Market and Kearny, San Francisco, 5 3/4 × 3 5/16 in. (146 × 84 mm), irreg. Digital preservation of the negative sponsored by Anne Turner, 1943.407.55

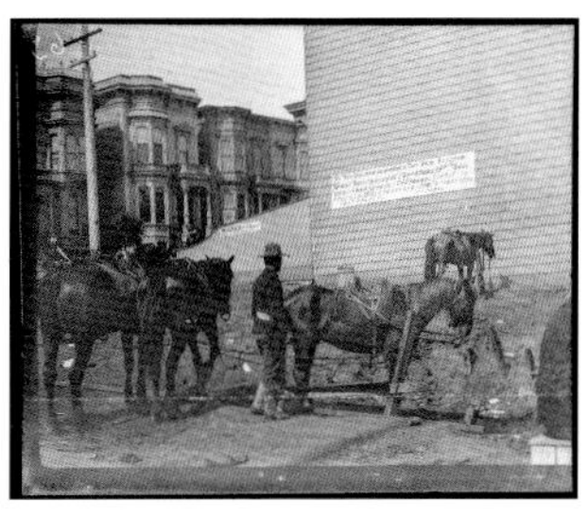

154. Fillmore and Bush, San Francisco, 3 3/8 × 4 3/16 in. (86 × 106 mm), irreg. Digital preservation of the negative sponsored by A. Crawford Cooley, 1943.407.119 (pl. 83)

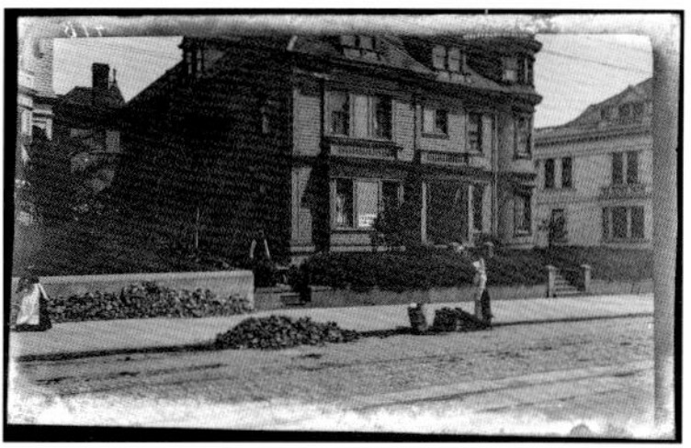

155. Pacific and Buchanan, San Francisco, 3 7/16 × 5 1/2 in. (87 × 140 mm), irreg. Digital preservation of the negative sponsored by Michelle L. Wilson, 1943.407.92 (pl. 84)

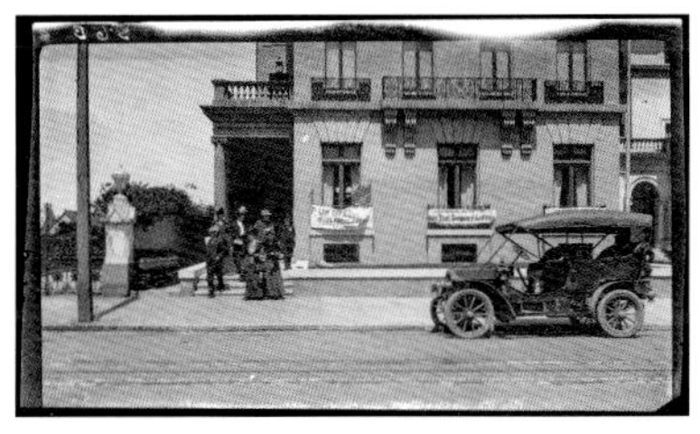

156. E.S. Heller home, Jackson between Laguna and Octavia, San Francisco, 3 5/16 × 5 11/16 in. (84 × 144 mm), irreg. Digital preservation of the negative sponsored by James Wesley and Elizabeth Kinnear, 1943.407.110.1 (pl. 85)

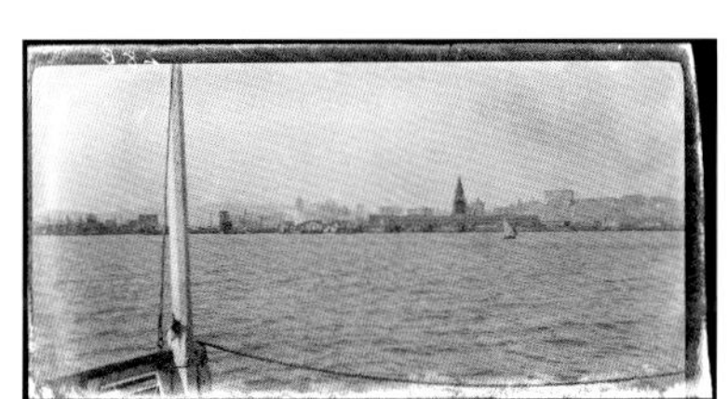

157. View of San Francisco from the San Francisco Bay, 2 15/16 × 5 3/4 in. (75 × 146 mm), irreg. 1943.407.58 (pl. 86)

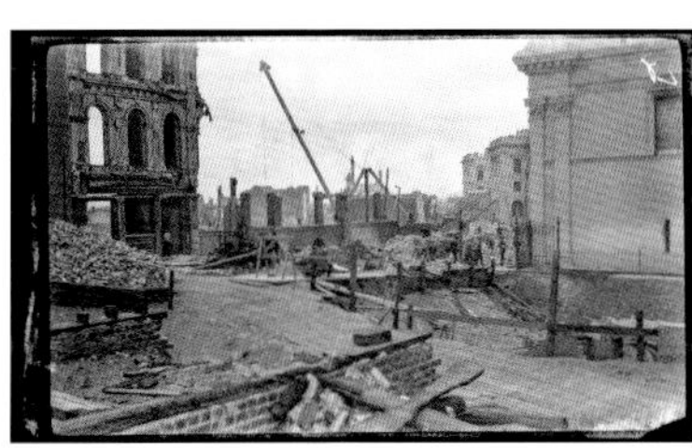

158. Jones near Golden Gate, San Francisco, 3 5/16 × 5 7/16 in. (84 × 138 mm), irreg. Digital preservation of the negative sponsored by Eloice and John Helms, 1943.407.57 (pl. 87)

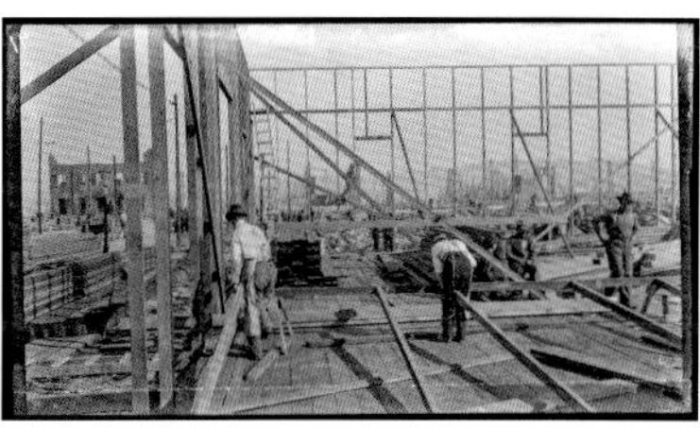

159. Men work to rebuild the city surrounded by the ruins left by the earthquake and fire, San Francisco, 3 1/8 × 5 11/16 in. (79 × 144 mm), irreg. Digital preservation of the negative sponsored by Michael Zimmer, 1943.407.79 (pl. 88)

NOTES

BINDER

1. In 1881 George Eastman founded the Eastman Dry Plate Company with the financial support of Henry Strong. In 1884 the business was reregistered as the Eastman Dry Plate and Film Company, and again in 1892 as the Eastman Kodak Company.
2. Philip L. Fradkin, *The Great Earthquake and Firestorms of 1906: How San Francisco Nearly Destroyed Itself* (Berkeley: University of California Press, 2006), 282.
3. Robert L. Shanebrook, *Making Kodak Film* (Rochester, New York: Robert L. Shanebrook, 2016); and "Nitrocellulose," Encyclopædia Britannica, accessed March 1, 2018, britannica.com/science/nitrocellulose. Cellulose nitrate, also generally known as nitrocellulose, is essentially made by reacting a cellulosic material, typically wood pulp, with nitric acid. The degree of nitrogen content determines the potential flammability. Nitration above 12.5 percent is considered highly flammable and potentially explosive. Names associated with highly nitrated cellulose include pyrocellulose and guncotton. A content below 12.5 percent is considered moderately flammable. Names associated with moderately nitrated cellulose include pyroxylin, xyloidin, collodion, and celluloid.
4. Kat Eschner, "Once Upon a Time, Exploding Billiard Balls Were an Everyday Thing," *Smithsonian Magazine*, April 6, 2017, smithsonianmag.com/smart-news/once-upon-time-exploding-billiard-balls-were-everyday-thing-180962751.
5. In 1883 G. Frank E. Pearsall was actually the first one to introduce the new design of a self-casing folding camera with his Pearsall Compact Camera. Unfortunately the design did not catch on until the introduction of the Kodak No. 4 in 1890. Rob Niederman, "Pearsall Compact," Antique and 19th Century Cameras (website), accessed January 5, 2020, antiquewoodcameras.com/Pearsall-Camera.html. "Unbeknownst to Pearsall at the time, the 'DNA' of his 1883 Compact Camera would eventually be rediscovered in 1890 by George Eastman, adopted by all major builders, and appear in every one of the smaller, refined self-casing cameras made through the mid 1900s!"
6. Arnold Genthe, *As I Remember* (Rahway, New Jersey: Quinn & Boden Company, Inc., 1936), 35.
7. Rob Niederman, camera historian and photographer, has identified the camera Genthe is holding in the photograph as potentially a Newman & Guardia No. 2 camera, manufactured in England approximately 1893–1902.
8. "Curacao Arrives," *San Francisco Call*, March 29, 1904, 10. Genthe earned a doctorate in philology from the University of Jena in 1894.
9. Genthe, *As I Remember*, 89.
10. Ibid.
11. *No. 3A Folding Pocket Kodak*, product manual (Kiswick, California: Smith and Enke, 1904).
12. Todd Gustavson, curator of technology, George Eastman Museum, Rochester, New York, email to author, January 28, 2020. Lens openings on Kodak cameras from the early 1900s are marked in U.S. (Uniform Scale) stops, not f-stops.
13. Arnold Genthe, "The Children of Chinatown," *Camera Craft* 2, no. 2 (December 1900): 101.
14. George Sterling to Jack London, May 25, 1906, George Sterling Papers, Henry E. Huntington Library, San Marino, California.
15. "The Majority Will Return," *San Francisco Call*, August 19, 1906, 24.
16. "What Society Is Doing," *San Francisco Examiner*, April 30, 1906, 16.
17. "Je vous remercie de vos si jolies et si douloureuses photographies. Vous aussi vous avez tout perdu dans l'horrible catastrophe." Genthe, *As I Remember*, 100, 103. English translation from Toby Gersten Quitslund, "Arnold Genthe: A Pictorial Photographer in San Francisco, 1895–1911" (PhD diss., George Washington University, Washington, D.C., 1988).
18. "Madame Sarah Bernhardt, Farewell Performance, Venice, May 18th and 19th," *Los Angeles Express*, May 18, 1906, 7.
19. Arnold Genthe, San Francisco, California, 1906, Album (164 proofs), LOT 3445, Library of Congress, Prints and Photographs Division, Washington, D.C.; Arnold Genthe, The San Francisco Earthquake and Fire of 1906 [graphic], 2004.004:1-24-PIC, University of California, Berkeley, Bancroft Library.
20. Christine Hult-Lewis, Reva and David Logan Curatorial Assistant, Bancroft Library Pictorial Collection, email to author, April 26, 2019.
21. Genthe, "The Children of Chinatown," 102.
22. Barret Oliver printed exhibition-quality gelatin silver photographs in 2017, using high-resolution scans made by Chicago Albumen Works in 2015 from Genthe's cellulose nitrate negatives. The overall tone of the prints is a result of curatorial decisions based on a selection of Genthe's Chinatown prints in the collection at the Fine Arts Museums of San Francisco and the Bancroft prints.
23. A thorough survey of the artifacts found in the negatives would likely reveal more information and possibly provide further insight into the sequence in which they were taken.
24. The No. 3A Folding Pocket Kodak manual gives a basic description of two general methods of developing negatives: daylight or darkroom. Daylight developing was performed by placing the negative roll in a light-sealed Kodak Tank Developer or Kodak Developing Machine. Darkroom development was done by either continuously passing the entire roll (without the black protective paper) through a tray of developer for several minutes, or by cutting the roll along with the black paper into individual exposures and immersing the negatives (without the black paper) in the tray. For the latter it was recommended to submerge no more than three or four negatives at a time. *Picture Taking with the No. 3A Folding Pocket Kodak* (Rochester, New York: Eastman Kodak Co., ca. 1904–1906), 34–43.
25. Plate 7 (FAMSF 2018.21.10) shows an example where Genthe trimmed the negative, revealing the beginning of another exposure at the top.
26. Curling of nitrate film was a big problem. However, by 1906 manufacturers were applying non-curling layers of gelatin to the back of the negatives. That being said, the Genthe nitrate negatives in the collection at the Fine Arts Museums of San Francisco are highly sensitive to the slightest change in temperature and humidity and will slowly bow and relax when first coming out of their vaporproof packaging. One can imagine that full immersion in a solution would have a more dramatic effect.
27. The negative cat. 10 (FAMSF 1943.407.163) shows graphite pencil retouch around the boundaries, filling in cloud shapes.

BINDER AND OLIVER

1. The team working on the project at the Fine Arts Museums of San Francisco included Victoria Binder, Karin Breuer, Julian Cox, Debra Evans, and James A. Ganz.
2. The frame, or outer edges, of an image is the result of the exposure of the negative while it is in contact with an actual metal frame inside the camera.
3. Exposure is the amount of light that reaches the film when a photograph is being taken. A "good" exposure is one in which the film receives enough light to give a proportional reading of all the tones in the original scene. The exposure that occurs during the taking of a photograph is primarily determined by the photographer's choice of film and their adjustment of the camera's various controls.
4. Prior to the introduction of gelatin photographic materials, the vast majority of negatives were made using the "wet" process. Although this process had many drawbacks, it also had its advantages, as it allowed the photographer to see the resulting negative in the moment. This meant that if the exposure was inadequate, the photographer could make another exposure on the spot. Gelatin film was "dry," which meant that it was developed—sometimes minutes, sometimes days—after the exposure. In either case, it was too late for the photographer to make another exposure of the same scene if their original exposure proved unsatisfactory.
5. Both the Library of Congress and the California Palace of the Legion of Honor purchased works from Arnold Genthe's estate upon his death in 1942. The Library of Congress acquired the bulk of the materials. The Legion of Honor acquired the 1906 earthquake and fire negatives and a set of Chinatown prints.
6. Arnold Genthe's earthquake and fire negatives were scanned at high resolution by Chicago Albumen Works, Housatonic, Massachusetts.
7. In 2011 paper and photograph conservator Tim Vitale undertook a pilot project with the Achenbach Foundation for Graphic Arts, scanning a small selection of negatives and producing digital ink-jet prints. During this pilot project, the curators and conservators considered retouching Genthe's images. Vitale created several ink-jet prints with retouching, removing flaws and image artifacts. Ultimately, it was decided that the images would not be retouched.
8. The baryta layer of a gelatin silver photograph is a thin coating composed of primarily barium sulfate and gelatin that separates the paper base from the gelatin silver emulsion. Its function is to obscure the fibers of the paper base and impart a smooth surface for the gelatin silver emulsion.
9. The photographic paper that Barret Oliver used was Foma Fomatone 131 VC FB Warmtone Glossy 16×20.
10. The negative substrate that Barret Oliver used was Pictorico Over Head Projector Transparency.
11. For a great explanation of the ways that printing techniques can affect the psychological perception of images, see William M. Ivins Jr., *Prints and Visual Communication* (Cambridge, Massachusetts: MIT Press, 1969); and Estelle Jussim, *Visual Communication and the Graphic Arts* (New York: R.R. Bowker, 1974).

BIRT

1. Rodger C. Birt and Karin Breuer, "Fact(s) or Fictions: Arnold Genthe's *Fin de Siècle* Photographs of Chinatown," *The Argonaut* 10, no. 2 (fall 1999): 24–39; Maxine Hong Kingston and Emmet Condon, "San Francisco's Chinatown: A View from the Other Side of Arnold Genthe's Camera," *American Heritage* 30, no. 1 (December 1978); Anthony W. Lee, *Picturing Chinatown: Art and Orientalism in San Francisco* (Berkeley and Los Angeles: University of California Press, 2001); John Kuo Wei Tchen, *Genthe's Photographs of San Francisco's Old Chinatown* (New York: Dover Publications, 1984).
2. Arnold Genthe, *As I Remember* (New York: Reynal & Hitchcock, 1936), 32. Genthe exhibited the photographs and sold them to journal editors in the late 1890s and early 1900s, printing them directly from the negatives free of any alterations. However, after 1906, in the three publications featuring the same photographs, they are dramatically retouched.
3. Among the better scholarly studies of African American history in the Bay Area, two stand out: Douglas Henry Daniels, *Pioneer Urbanites: A Social and Cultural History of Black San Francisco* (Philadelphia: Temple University Press, 1980); and Albert S. Broussard, *Black San Francisco: The Struggle for Black Equality in the West, 1900–1954* (Lawrence: University Press of Kansas, 1933).
4. Jack D. Forbes, "Black Pioneers: The Spanish-Speaking Afroamericans of the Southwest," *Phylon* 27, no. 3 (1966): 241–244.
5. On early Anglo–African American settlers in California, see Kenneth G. Goode, *California's Black Pioneers: A Brief Historical Survey* (Santa Barbara, California: McNally & Loftin, 1974); and Rudolph Lapp, *Blacks in Gold Rush California* (New Haven, Connecticut: Yale University Press, 1977).
6. Daniels, *Pioneer Urbanites*, 18.
7. Philip P. Ethington, *The Public City: The Political Construction of Urban Life in San Francisco, 1850–1900* (Berkeley: University of California Press, 2001), 188. Contestation with Chinese residents for domestic positions and menial work that most white San Franciscans rejected likely helped fuel anti-Chinese racism among Black residents.
8. Yong Chen, *Chinese San Francisco, 1850–1943: A Trans-Pacific Community* (Stanford, California: Stanford University Press, 2000), 199.
9. It would take another half century before the Black and Asian American communities united to fight the ugly racism that afflicted them both. See ibid., 200.
10. Wikipedia, s.v. "*Flâneur*," last modified April 23, 2021, 16:09, en.wikipedia.org/wiki/Fl%C3%A2neur#cite_note-6. For full text, see Charles Baudelaire, *The Painter of Modern Life* (New York: Da Capo Press, 1964). Originally published, in French, in *Le Figaro*, 1863.
11. Broussard, *Black San Francisco*, 73.
12. Ho Yow, "The Chinese Question," *Overland Monthly* 38, no. 4 (October 1901): 253.
13. Genthe, *As I Remember*, 49; Frank Norris, "Among Cliff Dwellers," *The Wave* 16 (May 15, 1897).
14. How nonwhite San Franciscans used photographic media for personal and communal advantage is discussed in Daniels, *Pioneer Urbanites*; Tchen, *San Francisco's Old Chinatown*; and Amy DeFalco Lippert, *Consuming Identities: Visual Culture in Nineteenth-Century San Francisco* (Oxford: Oxford University Press, 2018), 204.
15. Genthe narrates his first hours of the earthquake's aftermath in his *As I Remember*, 87–89.
16. For a discussion of photographers other than Genthe working in the immediate aftermath and beyond, see Rodger C. Birt and Marvin R. Nathan, *History's Anteroom: Photography in San Francisco 1906–1909* (Richmond, California: William Stout Publishers, 2011), 24–39.
17. Genthe, *As I Remember*, 94.
18. Regarding the course of the fire over its three-day life, see Gladys Hansen, *Denial of Disaster: The Untold Story and Photographs of the*

San Francisco Earthquake of 1906* (San Francisco: Cameron and Company, 1989); and William Bronson, *The Earth Shook, The Sky Burned: A Moving Record of America's Great Earthquake and Fire: San Francisco, April 18, 1906* (Garden City, New York: Doubleday, 1959).

19. Broussard, *Black San Francisco*, 22–23.
20. Goode, *California's Black Pioneers*, 110.

BREUER

1. An unattributed periodical article on the website for the Museum of the City of San Francisco, sfmuseum.org/hist11/notedphotographer.html.
2. Last will and testament of Arnold Genthe, July 2, 1930, 7740–7741. In her dissertation Toby Gersten Quitslund surmised that Genthe feared someone might print from his negatives or release his work prints as finished photographs. Toby Gersten Quitslund, "Arnold Genthe: A Pictorial Photographer in San Francisco, 1895–1911" (PhD diss., George Washington University, Washington, D.C., 1988), 286.
3. The letter, on stationery from the studio of Arnold Genthe, is one of many documents regarding the San Francisco photographs in Genthe's estate archived in the Arnold Genthe Papers, San Francisco Fire and Earthquake & San Francisco Chinatown Collection, Achenbach Foundation for Graphic Arts, Fine Arts Museums of San Francisco. Alanson was Genthe's longtime friend; the photographer stayed at Alanson's Russian Hill home when he visited San Francisco in 1937.
4. Arnold Genthe Papers.
5. The exhibition was on view from April 1 to 30, 1943.
6. Hirsh was the official photographer for the Legion of Honor and the de Young from circa 1937 to 1954. He was likely the same photographer Howe consulted about the quality of the material received from the estate and referred to in one of Howe's letters to Nancy Lee in January 1943. I am indebted to Paul Hertzmann of San Francisco for not only alerting me to the existence of a set of copy prints of Genthe's negatives in Hirsh's estate but also donating them to the Fine Arts Museums of San Francisco in 2019.
7. Undated clipping from an unknown San Francisco newspaper, found in Arnold Genthe Papers.
8. These prints were labeled "Print from duplicate of original negative." For many years the inventory of copy prints and negatives was kept in general curatorial files at the Achenbach Foundation for Graphic Arts, and later in the Fine Arts Museums of San Francisco Photo Services Department files, until digitization eliminated the need for such distribution. A booklet with numbered descriptions of the so-called "Seutter" negatives remains on file at the Achenbach.
9. Arnold Genthe Papers.
10. Ibid. Twenty-two of Adams's prints from Genthe's negatives reside in the collection of the Art Institute of Chicago, and a similar number is held by the George Eastman House, Rochester, New York.
11. Ibid.
12. The exhibition was on view from December 17, 2005, to June 4, 2006, and was accompanied by the catalogue *After the Ruins, 1906 and 2006: Rephotographing the San Francisco Earthquake and Fire* (Berkeley and San Francisco: University of California Press and Fine Arts Museums of San Francisco, 2005).
13. Mark Klett, "Mark Klett, Rephotography, and the Story of Two San Franciscos: An Interview with Karin Breuer," in *After the Ruins, 1906 and 2006: Rephotographing the San Francisco Earthquake and Fire*, 10. The catalogue reproduced twelve of the fourteen Genthe exhibition prints. All fourteen of Klett's exhibition prints were acquired by the Fine Arts Museums in 2005, shortly before the exhibition opened.
14. Arnold Genthe Papers.
15. Carl Nolte, "Tragic History Fading / $40,000 Needed to Preserve Photographer's Peerless Images of the '06 Quake," *San Francisco Chronicle*, April 17, 2015, sfgate.com/bayarea/article/Without-40-000-priceless-1906-S-F-quake-photos-6205223.php.

GANZ

1. Jack London, "The Story of an Eye-Witness," *Collier's* 37 (May 5, 1906), reprinted in *The Portable Jack London*, ed. Earle Labor (New York: Penguin, 1994), 486–491. See also Jeanne Campbell Reesman, Sara S. Hodson, and Philip Adam, *Jack London, Photographer* (Athens: University of Georgia Press, 2010), 115–148.
2. Arnold Genthe, *As I Remember* (New York: John Day, 1936), 89.
3. Ibid. In an advertisement in the May 20, 1906, edition of the *San Francisco Chronicle*, Kahn listed his new address as 2026 Steiner Street near Pine, and assured customers: "Record books saved."
4. Edith Irvine did not print any of her gelatin dry plate negatives, which are now kept in the collection of the Brigham Young University Library Special Collections, Provo, Utah.
5. Lawrence J. Kennedy, "The Progress of the Fire in San Francisco April 18th–21st, 1906: As Shown by an Analysis of Original Documents" (master's thesis, University of California, Berkeley, 1908), sfmuseum.org/1906/kennedy.html.
6. George W. Brooks, *The Spirit of 1906* (San Francisco: The California Insurance Company of San Francisco, 1921), 15. Brooks was the founder of the California Insurance Company of San Francisco, whose office was at 230 California Street.
7. Ibid., 12–13.
8. Ibid., 13–14.
9. See Anthony W. Lee, *Picturing Chinatown: Art and Orientalism in San Francisco* (Berkeley and Los Angeles: University of California Press, 2001).
10. Genthe, *As I Remember*, 94.
11. The inscribed Genthe photograph of Sacramento Street is held at the Museum of Fine Arts, Houston (accession number 82.9). The Clay Street photograph illustrated in figure 12, also exhibited in Adams's 1940 exhibition and now held in the collection of the Amon Carter Museum of American Art, Fort Worth, Texas, is inscribed "10 a.m.," which is also incorrect.
12. Douglas Henry Daniels, *Pioneer Urbanites: A Social and Cultural History of Black San Francisco* (Berkeley and Los Angeles: University of California Press, 1990), 97–99.
13. "They All Say No. Powell-Street Residents Protest. No Chinese School Wanted," *San Francisco Call*, March 11, 1894, 7; "Angry Citizens. Removal of the Chinese Public School. Objections to Extending the Limits of Chinatown—Further Action Contemplated," *San Francisco Call*, March 13, 1894, 3.
14. Carol Green Wilson, *Chinatown Quest: One Hundred Years of Donaldina Cameron House, 1874–1974* (San Francisco: California Historical Society, 1974), 76.
15. H.D. Miller, "The Great Sushi Craze of 1905, Part 2," An Eccentric Culinary History (website), accessed April 4, 2020, eccentricculinary.com/the-great-sushi-craze-of-1905-part-2.
16. *San Francisco Sanborn Fire Insurance Map* (New York: Sanborn–Perris Map Company, Ltd., 1905), vol. 1, 39.

17. "San Francisco Bay Area Writers and Artists: Oral History Transcript / Elsie Martinez, 1962–1969," 72–73, Calisphere, accessed April 4, 2020, calisphere.org/item/ark:/13030/hb6j49p1b8.
18. Tómas F. Summers Sandoval Jr., *Latinos at the Golden Gate: Creating Community & Identity in San Francisco* (Chapel Hill: University of North Carolina Press, 2013), 77.
19. Henry Lafler, "My Sixty Sleepless Hours: A Story of the San Francisco Earthquake," *McClure's Magazine* 27, no. 3 (July 1906): 277.
20. Andrea Rees Davies, "Points of Origin: The Social Impact of the 1906 San Francisco Earthquake and Fire," in *Flammable Cities: Urban Conflagration and the Making of the Modern World*, ed. George Bankoff, Uwe Lübken, and Jordan Sand (Madison: University of Wisconsin Press, 2012), 283.
21. Genthe, *As I Remember*, 90.
22. Sitter Register 1 (1898 to 1906), Arnold Genthe collection, Supplementary archives, Library of Congress, Washington, D.C.
23. Louise Herrick Wall described the burning of the Bella Vista in "Heroic San Francisco: A Woman's Story of the Pluck and Heroism of the People of the Stricken City," *Century Magazine*, August 1906.
24. Genthe, *As I Remember*, 92.
25. William Bronson, *The Earth Shook, The Sky Burned: A Moving Record of America's Great Earthquake and Fire: San Francisco, April 18, 1906* (Garden City, New York: Doubleday, 1959), 61; and Toby Gersten Quitslund, "Arnold Genthe: A Pictorial Photographer in San Francisco, 1895–1911" (PhD diss., George Washington University, Washington, D.C., 1988), 266.
26. Charles G. Norris, *Brass: A Novel of Marriage* (New York: E.P. Dutton & Company, 1921), 169–170. The Hotel Pleasanton also served as a setting for Norris's novel *Hands* (New York: Farrar & Rinehart, 1935). Other Genthe clients who lived in the Pleasanton included Miss Eleanor Blake, Miss A.R. Callaway, Judge J.A. Cooper, and Mr. M.A. Potter.
27. Letter dated April 29, 1906, excerpted in *Pacific Commercial Advertiser*, May 14, 1906, 2.
28. Frank Hittell, "Holding Back the Volunteers," originally published in *The Argonaut*, March 19 and 26, 1927, reprinted in Malcolm E. Barker, *Three Fearful Days: San Francisco Memoirs of the 1906 Earthquake and Fire* (San Francisco: Londonborn, 1998), 247–248.
29. Ibid.
30. William Carew, "Captain Truck Co. 7. Station 3050–17th St.," website for the Museum of the City of San Francisco, accessed April 4, 2020, sfmuseum.net/conflag/t7.html.
31. Stephen D. Russell, "Experiences of Captain Stephen D. Russell, Engine No. 27," website for the Museum of the City of San Francisco, accessed April 4, 2020, sfmuseum.net/conflag/e27.html.
32. The Kronenberg Building was announced in the *San Francisco Chronicle*, April 2, 1899, 32. For more on Frederick Kronenberg, see Bill Yenne, *San Francisco Beer: A History of Brewing by the Bay* (Charleston, South Carolina: American Palate, 2016), 40.
33. Dennis Smith, *San Francisco Is Burning: The Untold Story of the 1906 Earthquake and Fire* (New York: Viking, 2005), 226.
34. San Francisco police and municipal archives, 1910, quoted in Gladys Hansen, Richard Hansen, and Dr. William Blaisdell, *Earthquake, Fire and Epidemic: Personal Accounts of the 1906 Disaster* (San Francisco: Untreed Reads, 2013), 117.
35. Bronson, *The Earth Shook*, 64.
36. "What Society Is Doing," *San Francisco Examiner*, April 30, 1906.
37. Genthe, *As I Remember*, 99–100.
38. "Mais votre jeunesse, votre courage sont des biens qui vous restent. . . . La vie s'ouvre devant vous, la fortune vous tire le bras. Allez, courage, mon jeune ami. Je sens, je devine, que tout va être beau pour vous." Ibid., 103. Translation from the French is my own.

GENTHE

1. Delmonico's was a hotel with a popular French restaurant located at 110–112 O'Farrell Street.
2. An elite men's social club founded in 1872, San Francisco's Bohemian Club became, in Genthe's words, "the rendezvous of wits, bon vivants and celebrities—writers, painters, sculptors, musicians, men of the theater, and those who occupied high places in government and finance." Arnold Genthe, *As I Remember* (New York: John Day, 1936), 59. Genthe joined in 1901 and enjoyed close friendships with many of the club's members, including Charles K. Field, Porter Garnett, Jack London, and George Sterling.
3. Genthe's rosy picture of life in San Francisco under martial law is contradicted by numerous documented reports of robberies and looting by members of the public as well as by army personnel in the aftermath of the earthquake.
4. Genthe refers to the Mexican restaurant run by Matias Mortigia, originally located at 525 Broadway Street, and reopened at 726 Broadway Street after the earthquake. Coppa's refers to the Italian restaurant owned by Giuseppe Coppa at 628 Montgomery Street in the Montgomery Block. Both establishments were popular with the artists and writers who belonged to the Bohemian Club.
5. Genthe was at this location in the early afternoon; see Ganz, "Retracing Genthe's Journey Step-by-Step," this volume.
6. Genthe was mistaken that the Asian men sitting on the street were residents of the collapsed boardinghouse, which was occupied exclusively by Black tenants; see Ganz, "Retracing Genthe's Journey Step-by-Step," this volume.
7. The painting in the collection of the Bohemian Club does not bear the inscription described by Genthe.

GÖRGEN

This research was generously supported by the Terra Foundation for American Art, the Peter E. Palmquist Memorial Fund, and the Laboratoire de Recherches sur les Cultures Anglophones (LARCA) at the University of Paris. The author wishes to thank James A. Ganz, Karin Breuer, and Dennis Reed.

1. "With the Camera," *San Francisco Chronicle*, June 24, 1893, 9.
2. *Constitution and By-Laws of the California Camera Club* (San Francisco: [no publisher identified], 1896), 10.
3. Membership numbers are in "Editorial," *Camera Craft* 1, no. 1 (1900): 26; "Editorial," *Camera Craft* 1, no. 4 (1900): 192–193. Publications mentioning the California Camera Club include Margery Mann, ed., *California Pictorialism* (San Francisco: San Francisco Museum of Modern Art, 1977), 15–26; Michael G. Wilson, "Northern California: The Heart of the Storm," in *Pictorialism in California: Photographs 1900–1940*, ed. Dennis Reed and Michael G. Wilson (Los Angeles and San Marino, California: J. Paul Getty Museum and Huntington Library, 1994), 1–19; and Stacey McCarroll, *California Dreamin': Camera Clubs and the Pictorial Photography Tradition* (Seattle: University of Washington Press, 2004), 16–28. For an extensive discussion of the California Camera Club, see Carolin Görgen, "'Out Here It Is Different': The California Camera Club and Community Imagination through Collective Photographic Practices. Toward a Critical

Historiography, 1890–1915" (PhD diss., Université Paris VII Denis Diderot and École du Louvre, 2018).

4. Paul Spencer Sternberger, *Between Amateur and Aesthete: The Legitimization of Photography as Art in America, 1880–1900* (Albuquerque: University of New Mexico Press, 2001), xv–xvi. In 1893 women represented only 7.6 percent of American camera club members; see Margaret Denny, "Catherine Weed Barnes Ward: Advocate for Victorian Women Photographers," *History of Photography* 36, no. 2 (2012): 160. Numbers are derived from Walter Sprange, *The Blue Book of Amateur Photographers Being a Directory of the Various Amateur Photographic Societies in the United States of America* (Beach Bluff, Massachusetts: Walter Sprange, 1893).
5. Pictorialism generally refers to a loose movement of photographers striving for the recognition of the medium amid the fine arts, most active between 1880 and 1920, although the chronology extends to the mid-twentieth century. See Keith Davis, *An American Century of Photography: From Dry-Plate to Digital*, 2nd ed. (Kansas City, Missouri, and New York: Hallmark Cards Inc. and Harry N. Abrams, Inc., 1999), 46–51; Sarah Greenough, "'Of Charming Glens, Graceful Glades, and Frowning Cliffs': The Economic Incentives, Social Inducements, and Aesthetic Issues of American Pictorial Photography," in *Photography in Nineteenth-Century America*, ed. Martha A. Sandweiss (New York and Fort Worth: Harry N. Abrams, Inc., Publishers with the Amon Carter Museum, 1991), 258–281; Thomas Padon, ed., *TruthBeauty: Pictorialism and the Photograph as Art, 1845–1945* (Vancouver, British Columbia: Vancouver Art Gallery and Douglas & McIntyre, 2008); and Christian A. Peterson, *After the Photo-Secession: American Pictorial Photography, 1910–1955* (New York: W.W. Norton, 1997).
6. On the ambiguous role of commercial photography, see Ulrich Keller, "The Myth of Art Photography: A Sociological Analysis," *History of Photography* 8, no. 4 (1984): 249–275; and Anne McCauley, "The Photo-Secession and the Paradox of Pictorialist Commercial Photography, 1904–1912," in *Clarence H. White and His World: The Art & Craft of Photography, 1895–1925*, ed. Anne McCauley (Princeton, New Jersey, and New Haven, Connecticut: Princeton University Art Museum and Yale University Press, 2017), 89–125.
7. Toby Gersten Quitslund, "Arnold Genthe: A Pictorial Photographer in San Francisco, 1895–1911" (PhD diss., George Washington University, Washington, D.C., 1988), 90–92.
8. See Rodger C. Birt, "The San Francisco Album and Its Historical Moment: Photography, Vigilantism, and Western Urbanization," in George Robinson Fardon, *San Francisco Album: Photographs 1854–1856*, ed. Jeffrey Fraenkel and Hans P. Kraus Jr. (San Francisco: Chronicle Books, 1999), 99–122; and Martha A. Sandweiss, *Print the Legend: Photography and the American West* (New Haven, Connecticut: Yale University Press, 2004).
9. See Peter E. Palmquist, "The Pioneers: Landscape and Studio," in *Capturing Light: Masterpieces of California Photography, 1850 to the Present*, ed. Drew Heath Johnson (Oakland and New York: Oakland Museum of California and W.W. Norton, 2001), 3–20; and Jennifer A. Watts, "Picture Taking in Paradise: Los Angeles and the Creation of Regional Identity, 1880–1920," *History of Photography* 24, no. 3 (2000): 243–251.
10. Sheri Bernstein, "Selling California, 1900–1920," in *Made in California: Art, Image, and Identity, 1900–2000*, ed. Stephanie Barron, Sheri Bernstein, and Ilene Susan Fort (Berkeley: University of California Press, 2000), 65–98. Also see Susan Landauer, *California Impressionists* (Athens, Georgia, and Irvine, California: Georgia Museum of Art and Irvine Museum, 1996), 14–18.
11. Archibald J. Treat, "Speech at Annual Dinner of the PCAPA, March 8, 1889," Archibald J. Treat Papers, California Historical Society, San Francisco.
12. Anita Ventura Mozley, "The Stanfords and Photography," in *Museum Builders in the West: The Stanfords as Collectors and Patrons of Art, 1870–1906*, ed. Carol M. Osborne (Stanford, California: Stanford University Museum of Art, 1986), 107.
13. See Wilson, "Northern California: The Heart of the Storm," 4–5; and "George W. Reed," *Pacific Coast Photographer* 1, no. 2 (1892): 24–25.
14. Information on photographers from Carl Mautz, *Biographies of Western Photographers: A Reference Guide to Photographers Working in the 19th Century American West* (Nevada City, California: Carl Mautz Publishing, 1997).
15. "The Yosemite Valley by the California Camera Club," *San Francisco Chronicle*, February 27, 1891, 5.
16. "California Camera Club News," *Pacific Coast Photographer* 1, no. 3 (1892): 51.
17. John Kuo Wei Tchen, *Genthe's Photographs of San Francisco's Old Chinatown* (New York: Dover Publications, 1984).
18. Quitslund, "Arnold Genthe: A Pictorial Photographer in San Francisco, 1895–1911," 61, 83–84.
19. Arnold Genthe, *As I Remember* (New York: Reynal & Hitchcock, 1936), 205; and Charles F. Lummis, *Some Strange Corners of Our Country: The Wonderland of the Southwest* (New York: Century Co., 1898).
20. Mildred Abronda, *The Magic Lantern Man: Theophilus Hope D'Estrella* (Fremont, California: California School for the Deaf, 1985), 47–50.
21. "Pacific Coast Salon a Fact," *Camera Craft* 1, no. 5 (1900): 264–267; "Editorial," *Camera Craft* 1, no. 5 (1900): 272–273. See also Wilson, "Northern California: The Heart of the Storm," 5–6.
22. Arnold Genthe, "Rebellion in Photography," *Overland Monthly* 43 (1901): 93–96. See also Katrina Miottel, "'Rebellion in Photography': Northern California Photographers at the Turn of the Century" (unpublished MA thesis, Stanford University, California, 1985), 6–9; and Wilson, "Northern California: The Heart of the Storm," 6–7.
23. Other artists who trained at the Hopkins Institute—including Laura Adams, Anne Brigman, and Adelaide Hanscom—also participated in salons, where they gained increasing recognition. Based in Berkeley, this female circle played with mystical themes. Brigman staged dramatic outdoor photographs of female nudes and would go on to become one of the household names of California Pictorialism. *Catalogue of the First Los Angeles Photographic Salon* (Los Angeles: A.S.C. Forbes, 1902). See also Susan Ehrens, *A Poetic Vision: The Photographs of Anne Brigman* (Santa Barbara, California: Santa Barbara Museum of Art, 1995); and Ann M. Wolfe et al., *Anne Brigman: A Visionary in Modern Photography* (New York: Rizzoli Electa, 2018).
24. Arnold Genthe, "What Various Prominent Critics Have to Say of the Second San Francisco Salon Just Passed," *Camera Craft* 4, no. 4 (1902): 171.
25. A.L. Coombs to Alfred Stieglitz, January 15, 1902 (The Alfred Stieglitz / Georgia O'Keeffe Archive, Yale Collection of American Literature, Beinecke Rare Book and Manuscript Library, Yale University, New Haven, Connecticut).
26. "Editorial," *Camera Craft* 7, no. 6 (1903): 255.
27. Peter E. Palmquist, "William E. Dassonville: An Appreciation," in *William E. Dassonville, California Photographer, 1879–1957*, ed. Susan

Herzig and Paul Hertzmann (Nevada City, California: Carl Mautz Publishing, 1999), 23–30. Palmquist cites Dassonville as Ansel Adams's first contact at the California Camera Club. Adams was a fan of Charcoal Black and used the paper until the 1930s.

28. "The California Camera Club," *Camera Craft* 10, no. 4 (1905): 245.
29. Fayette J. Clute, "With Earthquake and Fire," *Camera Craft* 12, no. 4 (1906): 149–151.
30. The San Francisco Fire Department used dynamite to strategically destroy buildings in an effort to control the extent of the fires, a measure whose efficiency is still contested today. See "1906 Earthquake: Fire Fighting," National Park Service, nps.gov/prsf/learn/historyculture/1906-earthquake-fire-fighting.htm.
31. Henry D'Arcy Power, "Earthquake and Fire: From a Photographer's Viewpoint," *Camera Craft* 12, no. 4 (1906): 155–160.
32. Archibald J. Treat to his sister Eleanor Treat, April 27, 1906, 3, Archibald J. Treat Papers, California Historical Society, San Francisco.
33. Linda and Wayne Bonnett, *Taber: A Photographic Legacy* (Sausalito, California: Windgate Press, 2004), 142.
34. "Priceless Negatives Destroyed by the Fire," *San Francisco Call*, May 5, 1906, 11.
35. "Editorial," *American Amateur Photographer* 18 (1906): 255; "The Relief Fund for California Photographers," *Camera Craft* 13, no. 1 (1906): 255–256.
36. Louis J. Stellmann, "Through the Ruins with a Premoette," *Camera Craft* 14, no. 1 (1907): 3–7.
37. Louis J. Stellmann, *The Vanished Ruin Era: San Francisco's Classic Artistry of Ruin Depicted in Picture and Song* (San Francisco: Paul Elder and Company, 1910), vii–viii.
38. Genthe, *As I Remember*, 96–97.
39. Arnold Genthe and Will Irwin, *Pictures of Old Chinatown* (New York: Moffat, Yard and Company, 1908). The book underwent three editions between 1908 and 1913 (after 1908 as *Old Chinatown: A Book of Pictures*). For a critical discussion, see Anthony W. Lee, *Picturing Chinatown: Art and Orientalism in San Francisco* (Berkeley and Los Angeles: University of California Press, 2001), 152–181.
40. Rodger C. Birt and Marvin R. Nathan, *History's Anteroom: Photography in San Francisco 1906–1909* (Richmond, California: William Stout Publishers, 2011), 18. See also Susanne Leikam, *Framing Spaces in Motion: Tracing Visualizations of Earthquakes into Twentieth-Century San Francisco* (Heidelberg, Germany: Universitätsverlag Winter, 2015), 234–239.
41. "The California Camera Club," *Camera Craft* 16, no. 1 (1909): 28.
42. Quoted from newspaper clippings in "Scrapbook of clippings relating to photographer Arnold Genthe, 1902–1916," Bancroft Library, University of California, Berkeley.
43. Suzanne Riess, "Dorothea Lange: The Making of a Documentary Photographer" (Berkeley, California: Regional Oral History Office, Bancroft Library, University of California, Berkeley, 1968), 87. On further connections between the club and well-known twentieth-century photographers, see Görgen, "'Out Here It Is Different,'" 507–531. For the earthquake's semi-centennial in 1956, Adams was commissioned by the Legion of Honor, San Francisco, to reprint some of Genthe's negatives. See James A. Ganz, *Artistic San Francisco* (San Francisco and Petaluma, California: Fine Arts Museums of San Francisco and Pomegranate Communications Inc., 2011), 42.

TERRY

1. Nick Yablon, *Untimely Ruins: An Archaeology of American Urban Modernity, 1819–1919* (Chicago: University of Chicago Press, 2009), chap. 5. In this chapter, titled "'Plagued by Their Own Inventions': Reframing the Technological Ruins of San Francisco, 1906–1909," the author presents a deeply researched, multidisciplinary investigation of the varied uses to which ruins were deployed in the aftermath of the 1906 earthquake.
2. Arthur Inkersley, "An Amateur's Experience of Earthquake and Fire," *Camera Craft* 12, no. 5 (June 1906): 200.
3. *San Francisco Examiner*, April 20, 1906, 3.
4. *Collier's* 37, no. 6, May 5, 1906, 21.
5. Yablon, *Untimely Ruins*, 192–193; and Susanne Leikam, "Visualizing Hunger in a 'City of Plenty': Bread Line Iconographies in the Aftermath of the 1906 San Francisco Earthquake and Fire," *Amerikastudien / American Studies* 58, no. 4 (2013): 589.
6. For more on the changes in photographic technology, see Binder, "Freezing Fire: Arnold Genthe and His Camera," this volume.
7. See *Crocker-Langley San Francisco Directory* (San Francisco: H.S. Crocker Company, 1905), esp. 2225–2226. These numbers do not include the numerous photoengraving operations that mass-produced photographic negatives for commercial print jobs.
8. Toby Gersten Quitslund, "Arnold Genthe: A Pictorial Photographer in San Francisco, 1895–1911" (PhD diss., George Washington University, Washington, D.C., 1988), 249–254.
9. In the nineteenth century, commercial photographers and those employed by the United States Geological Survey were primarily responsible for those images of destruction that were widely transmitted. For more information, see Leikam, "Visualizing Hunger in a 'City of Plenty,'" 585.
10. Edgar A. Cohen, "With a Camera in San Francisco," *Camera Craft* 12, no. 5 (June 1906): 183.
11. Ibid.
12. See Yablon, *Untimely Ruins*, 216; and Genthe, *As I Remember* (New York: Reynal & Hitchcock, 1936), 93. Some scholars have even suggested that there was a more nefarious motivation behind limiting photographers' access. San Francisco archivist Gladys Hansen spent many years studying the immediate aftermath of the earthquake, and in *Denial of Disaster: The Untold Story and Photographs of the San Francisco Earthquake and Fire of 1906* (San Francisco: Cameron and Company, 1989) she and her coauthor, former San Francisco fire chief Emmet Condon, present retouched photographs that they say were intended to both mislead the public in terms of the scale of the devastation and to blame fires for collapsed buildings that could not withstand the earth's shake.
13. Henry D'Arcy Power, "Earthquake and Fire: From a Photographer's Viewpoint," *Camera Craft* 12, no. 4 (May 1906): 156–158. Charles Derleth Jr., professor of structural engineering at the University of California, Berkeley, and others used these sorts of photographs to form image collections that could be consulted when the time came to reconstruct the city. Also see Yablon, *Untimely Ruins*, 209.
14. Cohen, "With a Camera in San Francisco," 185.
15. Ibid., 186.
16. Ibid., 189.
17. Genthe, *As I Remember*, 94.
18. Ibid., 262–263.
19. For more on Genthe's route through the city on April 18, see Ganz,

"Retracing Genthe's Journey Step-by-Step," this volume.

20. Sixty images taken by Irvine of the 1906 earthquake are in the archive held by the Brigham Young University, Provo, Utah, Harold B. Lee Library Archives. These have all been digitized and are available at contentdm.lib.byu.edu/digital/collection/EdithIrvine/search/searchterm/1906-04!Irvine%2C%20Edith/field/date!creato/mode/exact!exact/conn/and!and/order/nosort/ad/asc.
21. Wilma Marie Plunkett, "Edith Irvine: Her Life and Photography" (master's thesis, Brigham Young University, Provo, Utah, 1990), 31.

BIBLIOGRAPHY

Abronda, Mildred. *The Magic Lantern Man: Theophilus Hope D'Estrella.* Fremont, California: California School for the Deaf, 1985.

After the Ruins, 1906 and 2006: Rephotographing the San Francisco Earthquake and Fire. Berkeley and San Francisco: University of California Press and Fine Arts Museums of San Francisco, 2005.

American Amateur Photographer 18. Editorial. (1906): 255.

"Angry Citizens. Removal of the Chinese Public School. Objections to Extending the Limits of Chinatown—Further Action Contemplated." *San Francisco Call*, March 13, 1894, 3.

Bernstein, Sheri. "Selling California, 1900–1920." In *Made in California: Art, Image, and Identity, 1900–2000.* Edited by Stephanie Barron, Sheri Bernstein, and Ilene Susan Fort. Berkeley: University of California Press, 2000, 65–98.

Birt, Rodger C. "The San Francisco Album and Its Historical Moment: Photography, Vigilantism, and Western Urbanization." In George Robinson Fardon, *San Francisco Album: Photographs 1854–1856.* Edited by Jeffrey Fraenkel and Hans P. Kraus Jr. San Francisco: Chronicle Books, 1999, 99–122.

Birt, Rodger C., and Karin Breuer. "Fact(s) or Fictions: Arnold Genthe's *Fin de Siècle* Photographs of Chinatown." *The Argonaut* 10, no. 2 (fall 1999): 24–39.

Birt, Rodger C., and Marvin R. Nathan. *History's Anteroom: Photography in San Francisco 1906–1909.* Richmond, California: William Stout Publishers, 2011.

Bonnett, Linda, and Wayne Bonnett. *Taber: A Photographic Legacy.* Sausalito, California: Windgate Press, 2004.

Bronson, William. *The Earth Shook, The Sky Burned: A Moving Record of America's Great Earthquake and Fire, San Francisco, April 18, 1906.* Garden City, New York: Doubleday, 1959.

Brooks, George W. *The Spirit of 1906.* San Francisco: The California Insurance Company of San Francisco, 1921.

Broussard, Albert S. *Black San Francisco: The Struggle for Black Equality in the West, 1900–1954.* Lawrence: University Press of Kansas, 1933.

"The California Camera Club." *Camera Craft* 10, no. 4 (1905): 245.

"The California Camera Club." *Camera Craft* 16, no. 1 (1909): 28.

"California Camera Club News." *Pacific Coast Photographer* 1, no. 3 (1892): 51.

Camera Craft 1, no. 1. Editorial. (1900): 26.

Camera Craft 1, no. 4. Editorial. (1900): 192–193.

Camera Craft 1, no. 5. Editorial. (1900): 272–273.

Camera Craft 7, no. 6. Editorial. (1903): 255.

Carew, William. "Captain Truck Co. 7. Station 3050–17th St." Museum of the City of San Francisco (website). Accessed April 4, 2020. sfmuseum.net/conflag/t7.html.

Catalogue of the First Los Angeles Photographic Salon. Los Angeles: A.S.C. Forbes, 1902.

Chen, Yong. *Chinese San Francisco, 1850–1943: A Trans-Pacific Community.* Stanford, California: Stanford University Press, 2000.

Clute, Fayette J. "With Earthquake and Fire." *Camera Craft* 12, no. 4 (1906): 149–151.

Cohen, Edgar A. "With a Camera in San Francisco." *Camera Craft* 12, no. 5 (June 1906): 183.

Constitution and By-Laws of the California Camera Club. San Francisco: [no publisher identified], 1896, 10.

Coombs, A.L. A.L. Coombs to Alfred Stieglitz, January 15, 1902. The Alfred Stieglitz / Georgia O'Keeffe Archive, Yale Collection of American Literature, Beinecke Rare Book and Manuscript Library, Yale University, New Haven, Connecticut.

Crocker-Langley San Francisco Directory. San Francisco: H.S. Crocker Company, 1905, esp. 2225–2226.

"Curacao Arrives." *San Francisco Call*, March 29, 1904, 10.

Daniels, Douglas Henry. *Pioneer Urbanites: A Social and Cultural History of Black San Francisco.* Berkeley and Los Angeles: University of California Press, 1990. First published 1980 by Temple University Press (Philadelphia).

Davies, Andrea Rees. "Points of Origin: The Social Impact of the 1906 San Francisco Earthquake and Fire." In *Flammable Cities: Urban Conflagration and the Making of the Modern World.* Edited by George Bankoff, Uwe Lübken, and Jordan Sand. Madison: University of Wisconsin Press, 2012, 273–292.

Davis, Keith. *An American Century of Photography: From Dry-Plate to Digital.* 2nd ed. Kansas City, Missouri, and New York: Hallmark Cards Inc. and Harry N. Abrams, Inc., 1999.

Denny, Margaret. "Catherine Weed Barnes Ward: Advocate for Victorian Women Photographers." *History of Photography* 36, no. 2 (2012): 156–171.

Ehrens, Susan. *A Poetic Vision: The Photographs of Anne Brigman.* Santa Barbara, California: Santa Barbara Museum of Art, 1995.

Encyclopædia Britannica. "Nitrocellulose." Accessed March 1, 2018. britannica.com/science/nitrocellulose.

Eschner, Kat. "Once Upon a Time, Exploding Billiard Balls Were an Everyday Thing." *Smithsonian Magazine*, April 6, 2017. smithsonianmag.com/smart-news/once-upon-time-exploding-billiard-balls-were-everyday-thing-180962751.

Ethington, Philip P. *The Public City: The Political Construction of Urban Life in San Francisco, 1850–1900.* Berkeley: University of California Press, 2001.

Fradkin, Philip L. *The Great Earthquake and Firestorms of 1906: How San Francisco Nearly Destroyed Itself.* Berkeley: University of California Press, 2006.

Ganz, James A. *Artistic San Francisco.* San Francisco and Petaluma, California: Fine Arts Museums of San Francisco and Pomegranate Communications Inc., 2011.

Genthe, Arnold. *As I Remember.* New York: Reynal & Hitchcock, 1936.

———. *As I Remember.* Rahway, New Jersey: Quinn & Boden Company, Inc., 1936.

———. "The Children of Chinatown." *Camera Craft* 2, no. 2 (December 1900): 99–104.

———. Papers. San Francisco Fire and Earthquake & San Francisco Chinatown Collection. Achenbach Foundation for Graphic Arts, Fine Arts Museums of San Francisco.

———. "Rebellion in Photography." *Overland Monthly* 43 (1901): 92–96.

———. San Francisco, California, 1906. Album. Library of Congress, Prints and Photographs Division, Washington, D.C.

———. "Scrapbook of clippings relating to photographer Arnold Genthe,

1902–1916." Bancroft Library, University of California, Berkeley.
———. "What Various Prominent Critics Have to Say of the Second San Francisco Salon Just Passed." *Camera Craft* 4, no. 4 (1902): 165–171.
Genthe, Arnold, and Will Irwin. *Pictures of Old Chinatown*. New York: Moffat, Yard and Company, 1908.
"George W. Reed." *Pacific Coast Photographer* 1, no. 2 (1892): 24–25.
Goode, Kenneth G. *California's Black Pioneers: A Brief Historical Survey*. Santa Barbara, California: McNally & Loftin, 1974.
Görgen, Carolin. "'Out Here It Is Different': The California Camera Club and Community Imagination through Collective Photographic Practices. Toward a Critical Historiography, 1890–1915." PhD diss., Université Paris VII Denis Diderot and École du Louvre, 2018.
Greenough, Sarah. "'Of Charming Glens, Graceful Glades, and Frowning Cliffs': The Economic Incentives, Social Inducements, and Aesthetic Issues of American Pictorial Photography." In *Photography in Nineteenth-Century America*. Edited by Martha A. Sandweiss. New York and Fort Worth, Texas: Harry N. Abrams, Inc., Publishers with the Amon Carter Museum, 1991, 258–281.

Hansen, Gladys, and Emmet Condon. *Denial of Disaster: The Untold Story and Photographs of the San Francisco Earthquake and Fire of 1906*. San Francisco: Cameron and Company, 1989.
Hansen, Gladys, Richard Hansen, and Dr. William Blaisdell. *Earthquake, Fire and Epidemic: Personal Accounts of the 1906 Disaster.* San Francisco: Untreed Reads, 2013.
Hittell, Frank. "Holding Back the Volunteers," originally published in *The Argonaut*, March 19 and 26, 1927. Reprinted in Malcolm E. Barker, *Three Fearful Days: San Francisco Memoirs of the 1906 Earthquake and Fire*. San Francisco: Londonborn Publications, 1998, 247–248.
Ho Yow. "The Chinese Question." *Overland Monthly* 38, no. 4 (October 1901).

Inkersley, Arthur. "An Amateur's Experience of Earthquake and Fire." *Camera Craft* 12, no. 5 (June 1906): 200.
Ivins, William M., Jr. *Prints and Visual Communication*. Cambridge, Massachusetts: MIT Press, 1969.

Jussim, Estelle. *Visual Communication and the Graphic Arts*. New York: R.R. Bowker, 1974.

Keller, Ulrich. "The Myth of Art Photography: A Sociological Analysis." *History of Photography* 8, no. 4 (1984): 249–275.
Kennedy, Lawrence J. "The Progress of the Fire in San Francisco April 18th–21st, 1906: As Shown by an Analysis of Original Documents." Master's thesis, University of California, Berkeley, 1908. sfmuseum .org/1906/kennedy.html.
Kingston, Maxine Hong. "San Francisco's Chinatown: A View from the Other Side of Arnold Genthe's Camera." *American Heritage* 30, no. 1 (December 1978).
Klett, Mark. "Mark Klett, Rephotography, and the Story of Two San Franciscos: An Interview with Karin Breuer." In *After the Ruins, 1906 and 2006: Rephotographing the San Francisco Earthquake and Fire*. Berkeley and San Francisco: University of California Press and Fine Arts Museums of San Francisco, 2005.

Lafler, Henry. "My Sixty Sleepless Hours: A Story of the San Francisco Earthquake." *McClure's Magazine* 27, no. 3 (July 1906).
Landauer, Susan. *California Impressionists*. Athens, Georgia, and Irvine, California: Georgia Museum of Art and Irvine Museum, 1996.
Lapp, Rudolph. *Blacks in Gold Rush California*. New Haven, Connecticut: Yale University Press, 1977.
Lee, Anthony W. *Picturing Chinatown: Art and Orientalism in San Francisco*. Berkeley and Los Angeles: University of California Press, 2001.
Leikam, Susanne. *Framing Spaces in Motion: Tracing Visualizations of Earthquakes into Twentieth-Century San Francisco*. Heidelberg, Germany: Universitätsverlag Winter, 2015.
———. "Visualizing Hunger in a 'City of Plenty': Bread Line Iconographies in the Aftermath of the 1906 San Francisco Earthquake and Fire." *Amerikastudien / American Studies* 58, no. 4 (2013): 583–606.
Lippert, Amy DeFalco. *Consuming Identities: Visual Culture in Nineteenth-Century San Francisco*. Oxford: Oxford University Press, 2018.
London, Jack. "The Story of an Eye-Witness." *Collier's* 37, May 5, 1906. Reprinted in *The Portable Jack London*. Edited by Earle Labor. New York: Penguin, 1994.
Lummis, Charles F. *Some Strange Corners of Our Country: The Wonderland of the Southwest*. New York: Century Co., 1898.

"Madame Sarah Bernhardt, Farewell Performance, Venice, May 18th and 19th." *Los Angeles Express*, May 18, 1906, 7.
"The Majority Will Return." *San Francisco Call*, August 19, 1906, 24.
Mann, Margery, ed. *California Pictorialism*. San Francisco: San Francisco Museum of Modern Art, 1977.
Martinez, Elsie. "San Francisco Bay Area Writers and Artists: Oral History Transcript / Elsie Martinez, 1962–1969." Calisphere. Accessed April 4, 2020. calisphere.org/item/ark:/13030/hb6j49p1b8.
Mautz, Carl. *Biographies of Western Photographers: A Reference Guide to Photographers Working in the 19th Century American West*. Nevada City, California: Carl Mautz Publishing, 1997.
McCarroll, Stacey. *California Dreamin': Camera Clubs and the Pictorial Photography Tradition*. Seattle: University of Washington Press, 2004.
McCauley, Anne. "The Photo-Secession and the Paradox of Pictorialist Commercial Photography, 1904–1912." In *Clarence H. White and His World: The Art & Craft of Photography, 1895–1925*. Edited by Anne McCauley. Princeton, New Jersey, and New Haven, Connecticut: Princeton University Art Museum and Yale University Press, 2017, 89–125.
Miller, H.D. "The Great Sushi Craze of 1905, Part 2." An Eccentric Culinary History (website). Accessed April 4, 2020. eccentricculinary .com/the-great-sushi-craze-of-1905-part-2.
Miottel, Katrina. "'Rebellion in Photography': Northern California Photographers at the Turn of the Century." Unpublished master's thesis, Stanford University, California, 1985.
Mozley, Anita Ventura. "The Stanfords and Photography." In *Museum Builders in the West: The Stanfords as Collectors and Patrons of Art, 1870–1906*. Edited by Carol M. Osborne. Stanford, California: Stanford University Museum of Art, 1986.

Niederman, Rob. "Pearsall Compact." Antique and 19th Century Cameras (website). Accessed January 5, 2020. antiquewoodcameras.com /Pearsall-Camera.html.
"1906 Earthquake: Fire Fighting." National Park Service. nps.gov/prsf /learn/historyculture/1906-earthquake-fire-fighting.htm.

No. 3A Folding Pocket Kodak. Product manual. Kiswick, California: Smith and Enke, 1904.

Nolte, Carl. "Tragic History Fading / $40,000 Needed to Preserve Photographer's Peerless Images of the '06 Quake." *San Francisco Chronicle*, April 17, 2015. sfgate.com/bayarea/article/Without-40-000-priceless-1906-S-F-quake-photos-6205223.php.

Norris, Charles G. *Brass: A Novel of Marriage*. New York: E.P. Dutton & Company, 1921.

———. *Hands*. New York: Farrar & Rinehart, 1935.

Norris, Frank. "Among Cliff Dwellers." *Wave* (May 15, 1897).

"Pacific Coast Salon a Fact." *Camera Craft* 1, no. 5 (1900): 264–267.

Pacific Commercial Advertiser. May 14, 1906, 2. Excerpted letter dated April 29, 1906.

Padon, Thomas, ed. *TruthBeauty: Pictorialism and the Photograph as Art, 1845–1945*. Vancouver, British Columbia: Vancouver Art Gallery and Douglas & McIntyre, 2008.

Palmquist, Peter E. "The Pioneers: Landscape and Studio." In *Capturing Light: Masterpieces of California Photography, 1850 to the Present*. Edited by Drew Heath Johnson. Oakland and New York: Oakland Museum of California and W.W. Norton, 2001, 3–20.

———. "William E. Dassonville: An Appreciation." In *William E. Dassonville, California Photographer, 1879–1957*. Edited by Susan Herzig and Paul Hertzmann. Nevada City, California: Carl Mautz Publishing, 1999, 23–30.

Peterson, Christian A. *After the Photo-Secession: American Pictorial Photography, 1910–1955*. New York: W.W. Norton, 1997.

Picture Taking with the No. 3A Folding Pocket Kodak. Rochester, New York: Eastman Kodak Co., ca. 1904–1906.

Plunkett, Wilma Marie. "Edith Irvine: Her Life and Photography." Master's thesis, Brigham Young University, Provo, Utah, 1990.

Power, Henry D'Arcy. "Earthquake and Fire: From a Photographer's Viewpoint." *Camera Craft* 12, no. 4 (1906): 155–160.

"Priceless Negatives Destroyed by the Fire." *San Francisco Call*, May 5, 1906, 11.

Quitslund, Toby Gersten. "Arnold Genthe: A Pictorial Photographer in San Francisco, 1895–1911." PhD diss., George Washington University, Washington, D.C., 1988.

Reesman, Jeanne Campbell, Sara S. Hodson, and Philip Adam. *Jack London, Photographer*. Athens: University of Georgia Press, 2010.

"The Relief Fund for California Photographers." *Camera Craft* 13, no. 1 (1906): 255–256.

Riess, Suzanne. "Dorothea Lange: The Making of a Documentary Photographer." Berkeley, California: Regional Oral History Office, Bancroft Library, University of California, Berkeley, 1968.

Russell, Stephen D. "Experiences of Captain Stephen D. Russell, Engine No. 27." Museum of the City of San Francisco (website). Accessed April 4, 2020. sfmuseum.net/conflag/e27.html.

San Francisco Sanborn Fire Insurance Map. New York: Sanborn–Perris Map Company, Ltd., 1905, vol. 1, 39.

Sandoval, Tómas F. Summers, Jr. *Latinos at the Golden Gate: Creating Community & Identity in San Francisco*. Chapel Hill: University of North Carolina Press, 2013.

Sandweiss, Martha A. *Print the Legend: Photography and the American West*. New Haven, Connecticut: Yale University Press, 2002.

Shanebrook, Robert L. *Making Kodak Film*. Rochester, New York: Robert L. Shanebrook, 2016.

Smith, Dennis. *San Francisco Is Burning: The Untold Story of the 1906 Earthquake and Fire*. New York: Viking, 2005.

Sprange, Walter. *The Blue Book of Amateur Photographers Being a Directory of the Various Amateur Photographic Societies in the United States of America*. Beach Bluff, Massachusetts: Walter Sprange, 1893.

Stellmann, Louis J. "Through the Ruins with a Premoette." *Camera Craft* 14, no. 1 (1907): 3–7.

———. *The Vanished Ruin Era: San Francisco's Classic Artistry of Ruin Depicted in Picture and Song*. San Francisco: Paul Elder and Company, 1910.

Sterling, George. George Sterling to Jack London, May 25, 1906. George Sterling Papers, Henry E. Huntington Library, San Marino, California.

Sternberger, Paul Spencer. *Between Amateur and Aesthete: The Legitimization of Photography as Art in America, 1880–1900*. Albuquerque: University of New Mexico Press, 2001.

Tchen, John Kuo Wei. *Genthe's Photographs of San Francisco's Old Chinatown*. New York: Dover Publications, 1984.

"They All Say No. Powell-Street Residents Protest. No Chinese School Wanted." *San Francisco Call*, March 11, 1894, 7.

Treat, Archibald J. "Speech at Annual Dinner of the PCAPA, March 8, 1889." Archibald J. Treat Papers, California Historical Society, San Francisco.

Wall, Louise Herrick. "Heroic San Francisco: A Woman's Story of the Pluck and Heroism of the People of the Stricken City." *Century Magazine* (August 1906).

Watts, Jennifer A. "Picture Taking in Paradise: Los Angeles and the Creation of Regional Identity, 1880–1920." *History of Photography* 24, no. 3 (2000): 243–251.

"What Society Is Doing." *San Francisco Examiner*, April 30, 1906, 16.

Wilson, Carol Green. *Chinatown Quest: One Hundred Years of Donaldina Cameron House, 1874–1974*. San Francisco: California Historical Society, 1974.

Wilson, Michael G. "Northern California: The Heart of the Storm." In *Pictorialism in California: Photographs 1900–1940*. Edited by Dennis Reed and Michael G. Wilson. Los Angeles and San Marino, California: J. Paul Getty Museum and Huntington Library, 1994, 1–19.

"With the Camera." *San Francisco Chronicle*, June 24, 1893, 9.

Wolfe, Ann M., Susan Ehrens, Alexander Nemerov, Kathleen Pyne, and Heather Waldroup. *Anne Brigman: A Visionary in Modern Photography*. New York: Rizzoli Electa, 2018.

Yablon, Nick. *Untimely Ruins: An Archaeology of American Urban Modernity, 1819–1919*. Chicago: University of Chicago Press, 2009. See esp. chap. 5, "'Plagued by Their Own Inventions': Reframing the Technological Ruins of San Francisco, 1906–1909."

Yenne, Bill. *San Francisco Beer: A History of Brewing by the Bay*. Charleston, South Carolina: American Palate, 2016.

"The Yosemite Valley by the California Camera Club." *San Francisco Chronicle*, February 27, 1891.

INDEX

Page numbers in *italics* refer to illustrations.

ACKNOWLEDGMENTS

KARIN BREUER, CURATOR IN CHARGE,
ACHENBACH FOUNDATION FOR GRAPHIC ARTS

This catalogue originated through the exceptional efforts of the staff at the Fine Arts Museums of San Francisco and the many contributors to its pages. We particularly acknowledge the efforts of Victoria Binder, head of paper conservation; James A. Ganz, former curator; and Colleen Terry, former associate curator, Achenbach Foundation for Graphic Arts. We are grateful for the expertise and support of the many artists and scholars who contributed their words and thoughts to this book: Victoria Binder, Rodger C. Birt, James A. Ganz, Carolin Görgen, Richard Misrach, and Colleen Terry. The authors recognize Lawrence Banka for his extensive and valuable research of Arnold Genthe's photographs of the 1906 San Francisco earthquake and firestorm, as well as Natalie Pellolio, former assistant curator, Achenbach Foundation for Graphic Arts, for the concise and informative chronologies included in this work. We thank Barret Oliver for his technical contributions to this project. This catalogue was brought to completion under the leadership of Thomas P. Campbell, director and CEO, and was earlier championed by Max Hollein, former director and CEO, and Colin B. Bailey, former director.

Special gratitude is given to other staff, present and past, throughout the Museums who have directly supported this project in myriad ways over the years. We thank Melissa E. Buron, director of the Art Division, and Julian Cox, former chief curator and founding curator of photography. We extend our appreciation to Abigail Dansiger, head of library and archives, whose meticulous research supported this project; Susan Grinols, director of photo services and imaging, and Robert Carswell, digital assets and rights manager, for their valuable assistance throughout the process of documenting Genthe's imagery; and Randy Dodson, head photographer, for creating the beautiful photography that we have added to our archives and illustrates so much of this publication. We are indebted to the conservation staff who analyzed and tested the works and prepared them for publication: Jane Williams, director of conservation and head of objects conservation; Allison Brewer, paper conservator; Debra Evans, former head of paper conservation; and Anisha Gupta, Andrew W. Mellon fellow in paper conservation, 2016–2018.

Outside of the Museums, we thank Timothy Brown, Bruce Chinn, Emiliano Echeverria, Jack von Euw, John Freeman, Kristen Gaylord, Douglas Gist, Todd Gustavson, Bob Holloway, Christine Hult-Lewis, John Martini, Micah Messenheimer, Christina Moretta, Doug Munson, Toddy Munson, Linda Murray, Rob Niederman, Carl Nolte, Jon Quitslund, Andrew Robb, Wendy Welker, and Nick Wright. Additional thanks to the Achenbach Graphic Arts Council, San Francisco Auxiliary, and the Belvedere-Tiburon Auxiliary for their interest in and support of the project.

This catalogue was produced by the Publications Department at the Fine Arts Museums, and was expertly overseen by Leslie Dutcher, director of publications; Nikki Bazar, former editor; and Victoria Gannon, editor. We also acknowledge the supporting efforts of Trina Enriquez, editor; José Jovel, publications associate; and Barbara Morucci, editorial assistant. This book has been supported by the Andrew W. Mellon Foundation Endowment for Publications. We are grateful to Catherine Mills for her innovative design and typesetting, Adrian Kitzinger for his mapmaking work, Klaus Prokop and his colleagues at Cantz for the fine prepress work and printing, and Chris Gruener and Jan Hughes at Cameron and Company for their wonderful partnership and their help to distribute this volume in the trade. We also thank David Plant, general partner of Plant Construction, for his support of this project and his continued support of book publishing over the years.

Furthermore, we thank the many other individuals and their teams at the Museums whose work behind the scenes enabled the realization of this project, including Jason Seifer, chief financial officer; Megan Bourne, chief of staff; Patty Lacson, director of facilities and operations; Amanda Riley, director of development; Linda Butler, director of marketing, communications, and visitor experience; Miriam Newcomer, director of communications; Skot Jonz, former manager of board relations; Jenny Sonnenschein, executive assistant to the director and CEO and board administrator; and Lexi Paulson, administrative coordinator for the Art Division. We also extend our gratitude to Stuart Hata, director of retail operations; Rose Burke, merchandise manager; and Tim Niedert, book and media manager.

We recognize and thank the major donors to the Genthe Negatives Preservation Fund: Dagmar Dolby in honor of Hannah Dolby, Stella Dolby, Julia Dolby-Frist and Violet Dolby-Frist; Lucy Young Hamilton; Anne M. Zucchi; and the San Francisco Auxiliary of the Fine Arts Museums of San Francisco.

Finally, we wish to acknowledge and remember Toby Gersten Quitslund (1939–2017), whose 1988 doctoral dissertation, "Arnold Genthe: A Pictorial Photographer in San Francisco, 1895–1911," was a valuable source of information and inspiration for the authors of this book.

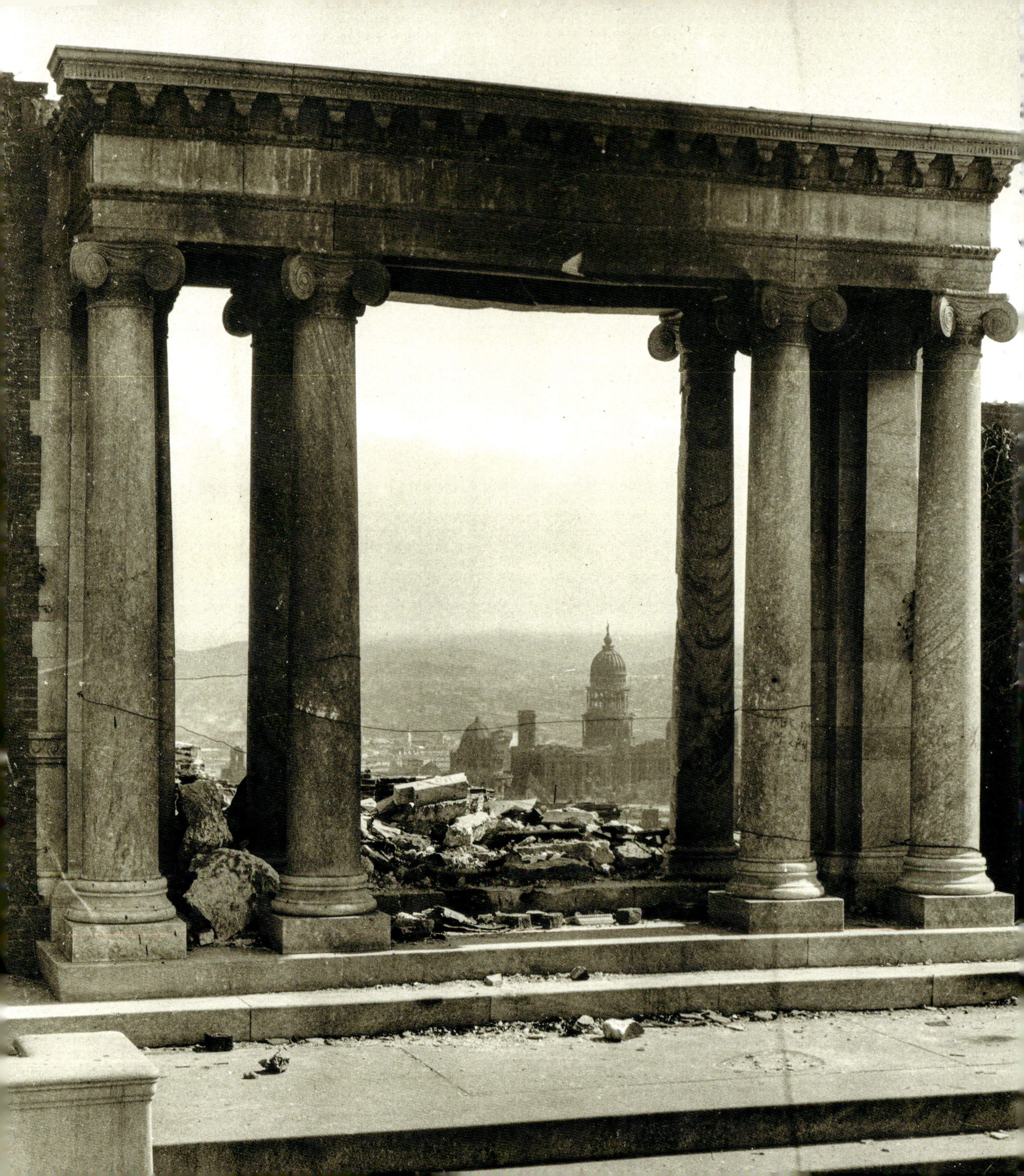

CREDITS

All plate illustrations are copyright © Fine Arts Museums of San Francisco, photograph by Randy Dodson. All negatives in the catalogue checklist are copyright © Fine Arts Museums of San Francisco, scanned by Cinetech. The map is by Adrian Kitzinger and designed by Catherine Mills. All decorative details are drawn from plate and figure artworks featured in this volume: p. 2: pl. 53; p. 4: pl. 25; p. 14: pl. 33; p. 70: pl. 26; and p. 228: pl. 54.

Essay illustrations: 1, 22, 23: Genthe Collection, Prints and Photographs Division, Library of Congress, Washington, D.C. 2, 11, 14, 21, 24, 25, 30, 45, 47, 52: Copyright © Fine Arts Museums of San Francisco, photograph by Randy Dodson. 3: Photograph by Mark Klett and Michael Lundgren. Courtesy of the Fine Arts Museums of San Francisco. 4: Dennis Reed Collection. Photo © Museum Associates / Los Angeles County Museum of Art. 5, 41: *Camera Craft* magazine, courtesy of the San Francisco Public Library. 6: Courtesy of the J. Paul Getty Museum, Los Angeles. © Estate of William E. Dassonville. 7: *Camera Craft* magazine, courtesy of the Art History / Classics Library, University of California, Berkeley. 8, 29: Courtesy of The Bancroft Library, University of California, Berkeley. 9, 10, 19, 42: Courtesy of L. Tom Perry Special Collections, Harold B. Lee Library, Brigham Young University, Provo, Utah. 12: Courtesy of the Amon Carter Museum of American Art, Fort Worth, Texas. 13: Courtesy of the California Historical Society, San Francisco (FN-33644). 15: Courtesy of the California History Room, California State Library, Sacramento. 16: Courtesy of Linden Publishing. 17: Artotype no. 11, "S.F. News Letter," May 28, 1887, Bancroft Library. Courtesy of The Bancroft Library, University of California, Berkeley (BANC PIC 1905.02960:07–PIC). 18: Courtesy of the California Historical Society, San Francisco (FN-33769). 20, 27, 28, 49, 51: Copyright © Fine Arts Museums of San Francisco, scanned by Cinetech. 26: *The Wave* magazine, May 15, 1897. Courtesy of the Internet Archive, San Francisco. 31, 34, 36: Courtesy of the Fine Arts Museums of San Francisco, photograph by Randy Dodson. 32: Jack London Papers, The Huntington Library, San Marino, California (JLP 485 Alb. 47 #05808). 33, 35: Copyright © Fine Arts Museums of San Francisco, photograph by Allison Brewer. 37: Reprinted with the permission of the *San Francisco Examiner*, Clint Reilly Communications. Image produced by ProQuest LLC as part of ProQuest® Historical Newspapers, www.proquest.com. 38, 40: *Collier's* magazine, May 5, 1906. Courtesy of Rory Phillips. 43, 44, 46, 48, 50: Courtesy of Pace Gallery, New York; Fraenkel Gallery, San Francisco; and Marc Selwyn Fine Art, Los Angeles. © Richard Misrach 2021.

Timeline and chronology illustrations: p. 170 (top), p. 171 (bottom), p. 172 (top), p. 174 (top), p. 175 (top and bottom), p. 176 (top), p. 177 (top left, top right, and bottom), p. 178 (top left and center), p. 179 (bottom), p. 180 (center), p. 181 (top left and bottom): Genthe Collection, Prints and Photographs Division, Library of Congress, Washington, D.C. p. 170 (second from top): Copyright akg-images. p. 170 (second from bottom): Photograph by Mary I. Stroud. National Museum of American History, Smithsonian Institution, Washington, D.C. (PG.000169). p. 170 (bottom): Courtesy of the George Eastman Museum, Rochester, New York. p. 171 (top left): Courtesy of the Anne T. Kent California Room, Marin County Free Library. p. 171 (top right): Courtesy of the California Historical Society (PC-PA0242, Album #2). p. 172 (bottom): Reproduced with permission of the owner of Redbellows (www.redbellows.co.uk). p. 173 (left and right): Photographers' Association of California, published by Fayette J. Clute, 1900. Courtesy of the University of California. p. 174 (center): Courtesy of the San Francisco History Center, San Francisco Public Library. p. 174 (bottom), p. 180 (top): Copyright © Fine Arts Museums of San Francisco, photograph by Randy Dodson. p. 175 (center): Allgemeiner Verein für Deutsche Literatur, 1905. Courtesy of the New York Public Library. Scanned by Google Books. p. 176 (second from top): Courtesy of the Museum of Performance and Design, Performing Arts Library, San Francisco. p. 176 (second from bottom): Copyright © Fine Arts Museums of San Francisco, scanned by Cinetech. p. 176 (bottom): Photograph by Joseph Greco. p. 177 (center): From *Berkeley Bohemia: Artists and Visionaries of the Early Twentieth Century* by Shelley Rideout (Layton, Utah: Gibbs Smith, 2008). Courtesy of the Oakland Museum of California. p. 178 (top right), p. 182: Courtesy of The Bancroft Library, University of California, Berkeley. p. 178 (bottom): Courtesy of Ohio State University, Columbus. Scanned by Google Books. p. 179 (top): Courtesy of the New York Public Library (https://digitalcollections.nypl.org/items/510d47dc-9b5d-a3d9-e040-e00a18064a99). p. 180 (bottom): Courtesy of the Art Institute of Chicago and the Library of Congress, Washington, D.C. Image provided by Art Resource, New York. p. 181 (top right): Courtesy of Heritage Auctions (www.ha.com).

AMONG THE RUINS

ARNOLD GENTHE'S PHOTOGRAPHS OF THE 1906 SAN FRANCISCO EARTHQUAKE AND FIRESTORM

Among the Ruins: Arnold Genthe's Photographs of the 1906 San Francisco Earthquake and Firestorm is published by the Fine Arts Museums of San Francisco and Cameron + Company to honor the works of Arnold Genthe in the collection of the Museums and the donor campaign that made the conservation of the original photographic negatives possible.

This book is published with the assistance of the Andrew W. Mellon Foundation Endowment for Publications and generous donors listed on pp. 8–9 of this volume.

**de Young **
\ Legion of Honor
fine arts museums
of san francisco

Fine Arts Museums of San Francisco
Golden Gate Park
50 Hagiwara Tea Garden Drive
San Francisco, CA 94118-4502
www.famsf.org

Leslie Dutcher, director of publications
Trina Enriquez, editor
Victoria Gannon, editor
José Jovel, publications associate
Barbara Morucci, editorial assistant

Cameron + Company
a division of ABRAMS
149 Kentucky Street, Suite 7
Petaluma, CA 94952
www.cameronbooks.com

Project management by Victoria Gannon
Edited by Nikki Bazar with Victoria Gannon
Picture research by José Jovel
Proofread by Susan Richmond
Index by Jane Friedman
Map by Adrian Kitzinger
Designed and typeset by Catherine Mills
Color separations, printing, and binding by Cantz, a brand of Raff & Wurzel Druck GmbH, Germany

Library of Congress Control Number: 2021935642

ISBN: 978-1-951836-15-3

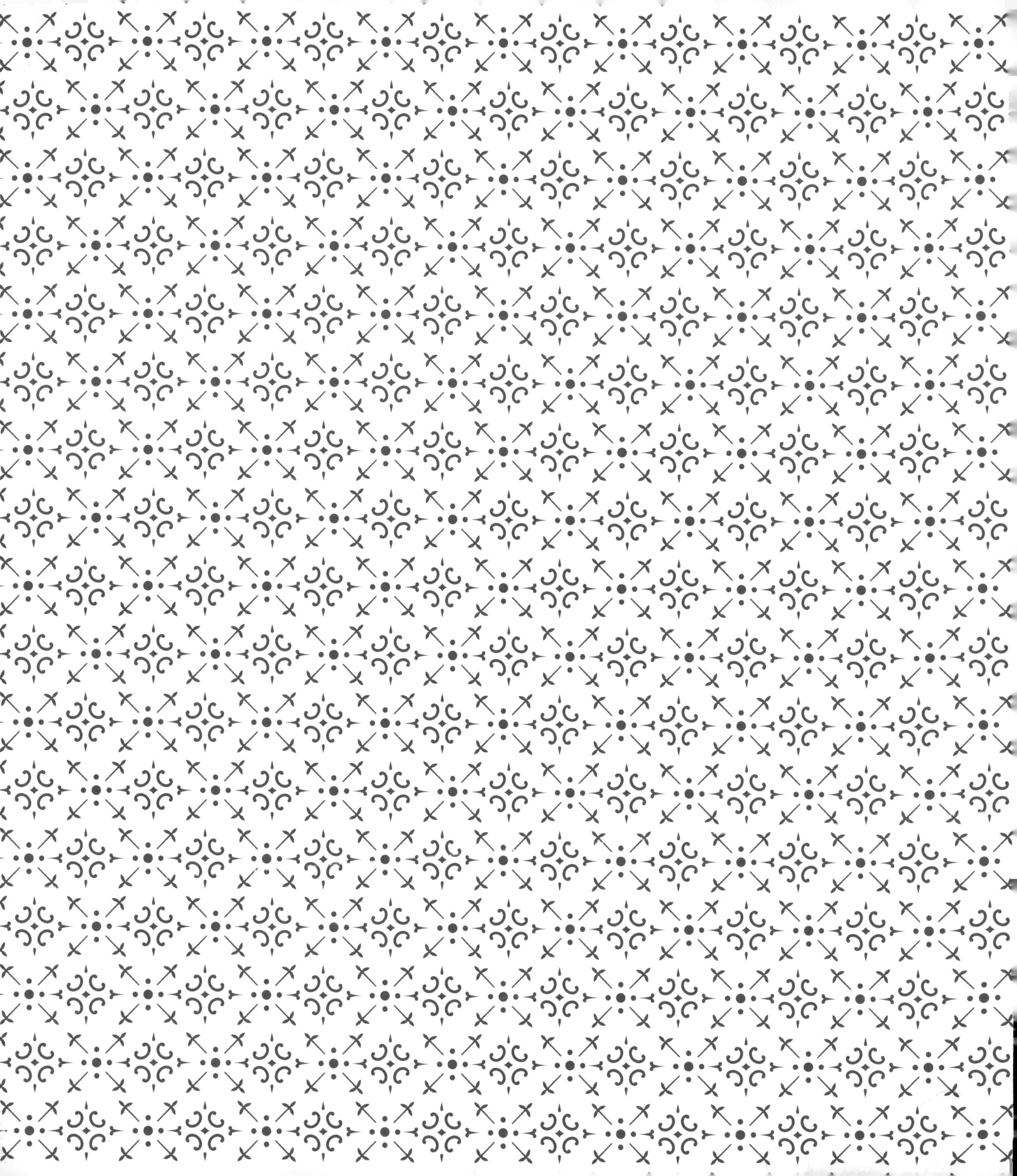